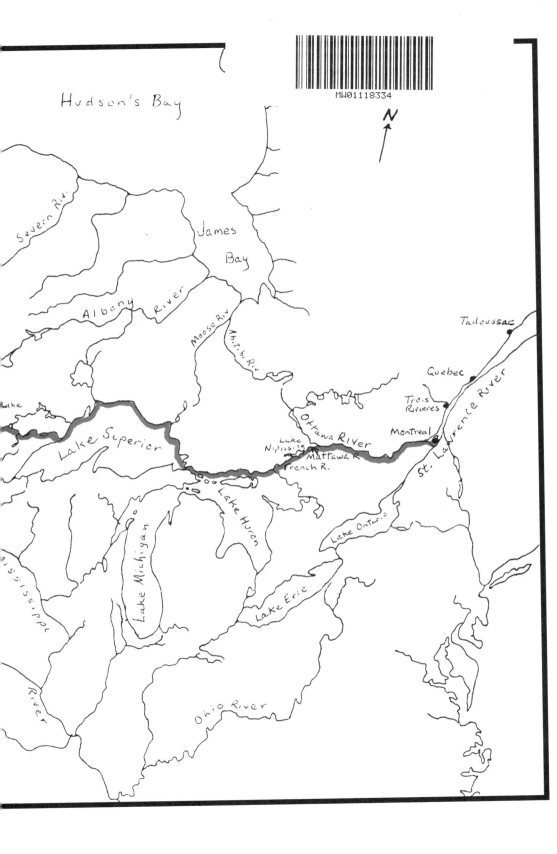

A Modern-Day Voyageur Family

Paddling the 3,000 Mile Fur Trade Canoe Route Across the U.S. and Canada

Timothy J. Kent

With essays by Dorothy J. Kent,
Kevin S. Kent, and Benjamin T. Kent

For Bruce,
with my Best wishes
T. Kent
Doree Kent
5/25/17

Silver Fox Enterprises
Ossineke, Michigan
2009

Published by Silver Fox Enterprises
P.O. Box 176
11504 U.S. 23 South
Ossineke, MI 49766

All drawings by the author
All photographs by Timothy, Dorothy, Kevin, and Benjamin Kent
Typeset by Model Printing, Alpena, Michigan
Printed by Thomson-Shore, Inc., Dexter, Michigan

Publishers Cataloging-in-Publication Data
Kent, Timothy J.
A Modern-Day Voyageur Family, Paddling the 3,000 Mile Fur Trade Canoe Route Across the U.S. and Canada
760 pp., 6.125 by 9.25 inches
Includes index.

Contents:
1. Canoeing and Canoe Camping. 2. Watercraft. 3. Transportation.
4. Indians/Native Americans, U.S and Canada. 5. Exploration, U.S. and Canada.
6. Fur Trade, U.S. and Canada. 7. Commerce, U.S. and Canada. 8. North American History. 9. U.S. History. 10. Canadian History.

Library of Congress Catalog Card Number 2009902806
International Standard Book Number 978-0-96572-306-0

Front Cover: Kevin and Ben Kent on the Mattawa River in Ontario, at ages seven and five, just after each boy had earned his voyageur sash.

Other Books by Timothy J. Kent:

Birchbark Canoes of the Fur Trade, Volumes I and II

Tahquamenon Tales, Experiences of an Early French Trader and His Native Family

Ft. Pontchartrain at Detroit, A Guide to the Daily Lives of Fur Trade and Military Personnel, Settlers, and Missionaries at French Posts, Volumes I and II

Paddling Across the Peninsula, An Important Cross-Michigan Canoe Route During the French Regime

Rendezvous at the Straits, Fur Trade and Military Activities at Fort De Buade and Fort Michilimackinac, 1669-1781, Volumes I and II

Within the Sphere of the Master, My Recollections as a Student and Long Time Colleague of Adolph Herseth, Trumpeter Supreme of the Chicago Symphony Orchestra

Acknowledgements

Numerous individuals from the previous four centuries were of assistance in the successful execution of our paddling project. First, credit must be given to innumerable explorers, traders, missionaries, military officers, and administrators from the fur trade era, whose records of daily life in that period have educated and inspired us. In addition, I am grateful to the many archivists, librarians, and scholars who have worked to both preserve that early documentation and make it available.

I must also express my appreciation to those individuals who provided physical assistance for our adventures. These include producers and suppliers of the canoe, various items of equipment, clothing, and maps, as well as our various shuttle drivers across Canada, and our seaplane pilot during our journey into the Athabasca country.

In addition, my thanks are extended to the many conservationists in the U.S. and Canada who have labored to preserve huge portions of the wilderness, which is absolutely crucial for all of us on this planet.

Finally, I must wholeheartedly thank my wife Doree and our sons Kevin and Ben, who joined me in pursuing a very ambitious goal over the course of sixteen summers. Without their great enthusiasm, all-out effort, patience, and endurance, this family project could not have been accomplished. I would not wish to trust my life and safety on a wilderness canoe voyage to anyone else but them.

Timothy J. Kent

Dedicated to the memory of Verlen Kruger

*And to all the other paddlers whose
adventures have inspired us*

We do not receive wisdom.

We must discover it for ourselves,
after a journey that no one
can take for us or spare us.

French novelist Marcel Proust (1871-1922)

Table of Contents

List of Illustrations

I
Introduction

Life is a great big canvas.
Throw all the paint you can at it.
Danny Kaye

There is only one success:
. To be able to spend your life in your way.
Christopher Morley

You are never too old to be what you might have been.
George Eliot

See your life as a gift from the great unknown,
And your job is to receive it.
Mary Chapin Carpenter

Our family project of paddling the mainline fur trade canoe route across the United States and Canada from end to end was inspired by genealogy and history. For nearly a decade before the paddling project began, I had been deeply involved in researching, in great detail, about 725 of my French and French Canadian direct ancestors, who had come from over 120 communities in France. At the same time, I was also avidly studying the fur trade era, and especially its French period, which extended from the latter 1500s to 1760. (The following British and American administration of the trade extended from 1760 to about 1850, and to an even later date in many remote regions.)

From a wide variety of sources, I was able to glean many details about numerous ancestors who had worked in various capacities in the North American fur trade, from about 1618 to at least 1758. Some of them had been employed in the occupations of fur trade company manager, clerk, interpreter, and trader, as well as outfitter, investor, fur buyer, and trans-Atlantic shipping merchant. Others had worked as voyageurs (the French term for canoe paddlers), and as guides of entire brigades of canoes. Finally, some of them had been employed as laborers, and in such trades as birchbark canoe builder, cutler, gunsmith, and fort carpenter.

In addition, other ancestors had served as soldiers in New France, in the Carignan-Salières Regiment in the 1660s and the Troupes de la Marine during the 1680s and 1690s. Besides all of these individuals, a great many of my ancestors who had lived in the St. Lawrence Valley had been farmer-settlers, or they had worked at a wide variety of other trades, such as a tailor or a wooden shoe maker. One had become a fencing master and taught the fine art of handling a sword.

The knowledge that many of these forebears had been involved in various aspects of the fur trade, as well as in the early life of the St. Lawrence Valley, where the greatest portion of the trade had been based, really enlivened the history of the period for me. In the course of my research, I made numerous genealogical and historical study trips to various locales in the St. Lawrence and Saguenay Valleys of Quebec. Many exciting weeks were also spent in various archives in Toronto, Ottawa, Cornwall, St. Regis, Curran, and other places in Ontario. In the process, I located the original notary documents pertaining to each ancestor who had been associated with the fur trade, transcribed the scrawled handwriting of these documents, and translated them with my wife Doree's help. Having gathered an immense amount of data, I decided to eventually produce a book of detailed biographies of these various individuals.

Visiting all of the specific locales in Quebec and Ontario where the French ancestors had lived, worked, and died, often locating the specific pieces of property that they had owned, gave me a good sense of the geography and history of the areas of eastern Canada where they had tread, plowed, paddled, and raised their broods. However, in the course of devouring period journals, maps, and other documents of the fur trade era, I longed to experience first-hand the full extent of the interior regions where much of the trade had been carried out, far to the west of the St. Lawrence Valley. I loved poring over old journals, which described in minute detail canoe travel to and from the interior, as well as daily life at the forts, posts, and camps. I was eager to see and experience for myself the exact terrain of the mainline route that had been traveled by most of the fur trade and military personnel, settlers, and missionaries who had ventured westward from the St. Lawrence settlements. I longed to absorb the drama of the vast water route and to hike the portage paths that were many centuries old. I also dreamed of experiencing both the joys and the extreme challenges of the ancient canoe trail. Knowing that numerous generations of my French ancestors working in the fur trade had covered this exact route, over the course of 140 years beginning in about 1618, increased my yearning to travel the route in the original way. So, I began to develop the idea of our little "voyageur" family paddling the mainline canoe route across the U.S. and Canada from end to end, in a series of annual segments. This challenging family project, which we ultimately tackled over a series of fifteen consecutive summers, would involve my wife Doree, our sons Kevin and Ben, and our faithful dog Toby.

In carrying out this extensive project, I intended to gain insights into the physical, mental, and emotional lives of the men and women, both French and native, who had worked in the fur trade. By physically experiencing much of what they had done on a daily basis, and doing it in the very same landscapes in which they had operated, I hoped to at least partially comprehend what the lives of these people had been like. I was driven by curiosity and a passion for the kind of detailed information that was not to be found in books or ancient documents. It had to be lived to be learned.

The liquid highway that I have termed the mainline canoe route of the fur trade era stretched from Montreal to the Great Lakes to Ft. Chipewyan on Lake Athabasca, in northern Alberta. This route, some 3,000 miles long, consisted of a series of watercourses ranging from small rivers to lakes the size of seas, which sometimes required portages or land carries between them. A great many rapids, waterfalls, and other obstructions in the rivers also required such portages. Many primary and secondary branches, again composed of rivers and lakes, extended outward from the mainline route; these branches reached myriad destinations all across North America. This vast system of interconnected watercourses provided the highways that were navigated by native, and later European, travelers. There also existed a huge network of land paths across all areas of the continent, which had been developed by the native populations over the course of thousands of years. However, for carrying considerable amounts of cargo over long distances, watercraft were the most efficient mode of transport, rather than any methods of land transportation. Thus, the canoe routes of North America comprised the main highways on which the vast majority of fur trade, military, and religious personnel had traveled and hauled cargo for hundreds of years.

The mainline route extended across three watershed systems, which were separated from each other by various heights of land. The easternmost watershed of the route extended from Montreal to a little west of Lake Superior. These waters drained eastward into the Atlantic Ocean, via the St. Lawrence River; the latter river was the only waterway on the Atlantic seaboard that offered easy access into the far western interior. The second watershed, extending from the height of land west of Lake Superior to the La Loche (Methye) Portage, flowed to Hudson's Bay, through both the Nelson and Churchill Rivers. The third and final watershed, which drained northward to the Arctic Ocean via the Mackenzie River, began on the north side of the La Loche Portage. This portion of the route included the Clearwater and Athabasca Rivers and Lake Athabasca.

The most common inbound cargoes, which were transported along the mainline waterway into the regions which lay to the southwest, west, and northwest of the St. Lawrence Valley, consisted of European merchandise and provisions. The usual outbound cargoes were composed of furs and hides, which were hauled from those interior regions out to the St. Lawrence settlements. These furs and hides were used, to a certain degree, by the population that was settled there. However, the bulk of them were destined for trans-Atlantic shipment to European markets.

Our family project of paddling the mainline route from end to end was not undertaken with the ultimate goal of writing a book. We did it because it was an extremely enriching, educational, and exciting activity that we could share together over many years while the boys were growing up. In order to help us later remember, savor, and relive the adventures that we experienced along the water highway, I kept a very detailed daily journal, updating it every few hours. In addition, I marked the specific route that we covered on detailed topographical maps, and we kept a good photographic record of the scenery along the way. Wanting to savor our family adventures privately, I did not arrange any media events during the course of the trips. These voyages were private affairs that we were doing for ourselves.

The decision that we later made, to share with others the experiences that we had while traveling the route, by means of a book and a DVD of photos, involved two main points. First of all, we wanted to encourage other families, couples, and individuals to take on either the same or similar adventures, even if these activities were carried out on a reduced scale; this called for a how-to guidebook. Second, we wished to allow those interested individuals who would probably never take part in such adventures in person, for various reasons, to vicariously share in our experiences. This latter aspect would reach out to those people who have a deep interest in history, nature, geography, and travel.

These two primary reasons for writing the book explain its degree of detail, concerning our equipment, clothing, and foods, as well as our day-to-day experiences. The various chapters could have each presented a thumbnail synopsis, or a broad overview, of the experiences of that given section of the route, as is typically found in magazine articles and many canoe trip books. However, this approach would not have served either of our main purposes in sharing our adventures. Thus, a full-length book, filled with myriad details of our daily life en route, was decided upon.

Those readers who are familiar with my historical works are aware of my passion for documenting the smallest details of daily life in the past, focusing primarily on the French and native populations. For those who have not yet read my book *Tahquamenon Tales*, I would explain that one aspect of this documentation involved recreating in great detail the lives of a French trader of the 1600s and his native or Métis (mixed native and French) family. I first spent sixteen years studying and replicating the various items of daily life of the native populations of the midwest region, as well as the primary items that the French traders brought into the area. Then our family carried out our own private living-history research for a decade, by spending a week or more each year in an isolated wilderness setting, living with just these ancient articles, without modern items to interfere with our learning. Every year, we would paddle in our birchbark canoe to a remote site on a lake or river, and there we would focus on a couple different aspects of wilderness living, such as hunting and trapping, woodworking, cooking, hide tanning, sewing, recreation, etc. First, we would learn by the hands-on approach how to do each of the tasks that were related to that particular subject area, by using traditional native materials and techniques. Then, we would repeat each of those tasks using imported French implements and materials. We did this to determine if the new imported items brought improvements over the traditional native methods, and if so, specifically why the improvements took place. In the process, we also became familiar with many of the native customs that the French adopted, such as methods of hunting and trapping, and traveling by snowshoes and toboggan in winter and by canoe during the unfrozen months. French colonists also adopted many native garments, learned to harvest a wide array of wild foods, and took up native methods of warfare. We came to realize that the myriad exchanges that took place between the two cultures went in both directions during much of the French period. Carrying out this living-history research was very thought-provoking for us, and an excellent learning experience for the entire family.

Usually in early June of each year, we would spend a week or more doing our living-history research from a base camp, utilizing our birchbark canoe and 1600s-era gear and materials. Each August, when my four-week vacation was usually scheduled, we would do our long-distance paddling trip, using our fiberglass canoe and modern equipment and supplies.

The principle of documenting our experiences in full, realistic detail applies to this paddling book just as it did in *Tahquamenon Tales*, the book about our recreations of seventeenth century lifeways. While carrying out our canoeing adventures, we experienced and learned both intensely and in great detail, and that is how the present book reads. It is a continuation of the long tradition of accounts penned by both ancient and modern travelers, whose detailed reports are of interest to enthusiasts of early fur trade, military, missionary, and canoeing history.

For this volume, I chose not to include any footnotes, even when quoting passages directly from early sources. Nearly all of my other works are replete with bibliographical footnotes, sometimes involving as many as 1,300 of them per chapter. However, to allow the text of this travel account to flow freely, the decision was made to omit all footnotes.

I must confess that I appear to have a genetic propensity for producing books. This suspicion is based on the fact that I am descended from a long line of master printers and book sellers in Paris. Gutenberg pioneered the concept of the moveable-type press in Germany, and began printing the Bible in about 1450. About ninety years later, my ancestor Louis Sevestre began his forty-one year career as a master printer in Paris, which spanned the years from 1543 to 1584. He was followed by his son Thomas, who was a printer and book seller at the University of Paris from 1586 to 1605. His son Etienne likewise carried on the same tradition during his lifetime, working until about 1625. Finally, Charles Sevestre, the fourth generation of my printer-and-book seller ancestors in Paris, left the Old World in 1636, and emigrated with his family to Quebec. There, he became the clerk of the fur trading company for all of New France, running the warehouse. So my genetic code seems to be rather heavily imprinted with producing books!

Personal Background

The following capsules of personal background information are provided as a hearty encouragement to families, couples, and individuals to tackle wilderness canoe travel, whatever their level of experience. From the information that follows, it is obvious that we were extremely inexperienced as paddlers when we began the mainline project. However, I had grown up with waterways rooted in my psyche, in a region that is surrounded by the Great Lakes and which lay at the very heart of the action during the fur trade era.

I grew up in the tiny crossroads community of Ossineke, in the northeastern Lower Peninsula of Michigan, a mile-and-a-half west of the shore of Lake Huron. This area of sandy lowland, only fifty feet above the present lake level, had previously been the bottom of the lake during various glacial and early post-glacial periods. Just to the west of our property, separated by only a fallow field, the Devil River flows past in a deep wooded ravine, en route to the lake. Beginning as early as six or seven thousand years ago, a prehistoric native village had flourished for many generations on a portion of the land that later became the field, at the edge of the ravine. From the far side of the river, the land rises quickly to the west, ascending ninety feet over the span of a half-mile; the western edge of this slope represents the location of the shoreline of the lake fifteen thousand years ago. Thus, I grew up on an ancient sandy lake bottom. During my youth, I often fished and swam in the Devil River and along the shores of Lake Huron. On those occasions when I traveled even a few miles inland to higher ground, to commercially pick strawberries or to visit friends and relatives, I felt like a land-locked farm boy. As an ingrained aquatic creature (but lacking fins or gills), I was always glad to return to my lowland shoreline area, adjacent to the river.

In spite of this considerable exposure to present and former waterways, my background included almost no experience in handling watercraft. The only exception had been a week at Boy Scout camp when I was age eleven, when I had earned the canoeing and rowing merit badges on a small and placid inland lake. Through Scouting, I had been steeped in native crafts and lore, and in camping during all seasons of the year with rather minimal equipment (including one particular weekend outing in which the nighttime temperature plunged to minus 27 degrees Fahrenheit). However, I had been raised with almost no experience in water travel.

Doree, growing up in the town of Alpena, ten miles to the north of Ossineke where the Thunder Bay River flows into Lake Huron, had likewise acquired almost no experience in handling watercraft. Her entire time logged in a canoe consisted of two afternoons that she had once spent on the river with her boyfriend at the time. However, she had been athletic all of her life, and had played serious volleyball and tennis during all of her adult years.

No expertise in wilderness canoeing had resulted from my long training as a trumpet player, or my subsequent two years as a member of an opera orchestra in Germany, or the three years I spent as a free-lance player in Chicago (doing long-running musicals and Las Vegas-style shows, and recording film scores as well as radio and television commercials), or my eighteen years as a member of the Chicago Symphony Orchestra. Nor did my second career as a historian of the colonial period and the fur trade entail any watercraft experiences. By the same token, Doree's education and employment as a family and individual therapist and an adoption counselor did not provide her with any watercraft skills, either.

However, odd as it may seem, our respective training and occupations did aid us considerably in the course of our paddling adventures. From our early years as young students onward, we had learned to set goals and then do whatever was necessary to achieve those goals. In the process, we had accrued many layers of solid confidence, and we had also learned how to live and thrive with moderate risks. In addition, Doree's extensive experience as a therapist undoubtedly helped both her and our boys cope with a man who was hell-bent on re-enacting many aspects of the lives of his French ancestors.

Years before the boys were born, Doree and I had begun tent camping in a modest fashion, based from an automobile. After the two youngsters arrived, we had continued these camping vacations, exposing the boys to moderate outdoor experiences. The seeds of the canoeing adventures were planted in 1982, when we were looking for further physical activities that we all could share together as a family. At that time, Kevin and Ben were ages six and four, we parents were 33 years old, and I had been a member of the Chicago Symphony for three years. Doree suggested that we take up tennis, while I thought that puttering with a canoe during our car-based campouts would be fun. The canoeing idea won out.

As a crash course in canoes and paddling, I checked out all fourteen of the books on the subject that were in the public library of our community, Oak Park, Illinois. Poring over these various works, I was exposed to a wealth of experience and knowledge that had been gained by a variety of individuals. From these authors, I learned about canoes, paddles, equipment, clothing, and foods, as well as many tips on canoe handling and the skills of reading and running watercourses.

I also took advantage of the great store of knowledge that was available from Ralph Frese at his Chicagoland Canoe Base in northwestern Chicago. From Ralph, I purchased an Old Town fiberglass canoe, the top-of-the-line Canadienne model, which he had designed for the company. The design traits of this craft made it an outstanding vehicle for long-distance tripping, which included a wide variety of waterways ranging from fast white water to giant lakes. At Ralph's shop, I also acquired a roof rack, canoe repair materials, paddles, life preservers (PFDs), neoprene wet suits for springtime white water jaunts, Duluth packs, a waterproof military ammo box for the camera, and various other items of gear, plus a great deal of accurate and practical information.

Based on the time-tested suggestions in the various paddling books, we then gathered and adapted the rest of the necessary gear and clothing, and learned to dry and assemble the most appropriate and practical food supplies to augment some purchased dehydrated meals. Finally, it was time to put all of the reading, thinking, planning, and preparation into action on the water.

II

The Preliminary Year: Getting Ready

*The purpose of life is to live it, to taste experience to the utmost, to
reach out eagerly and without fear for newer and richer experiences.*
Eleanor Roosevelt

All things are difficult before they are easy.
Thomas Fuller

*Twenty years from now, you'll be more disappointed with the things
you didn't do than with the things you did.*
Mark Twain

They can do all because they think they can.
Virgil

At this point, in the early summer of 1983, I had not yet thought
of paddling along the mainline fur trade route that extended
across the U.S. and Canada. We were still envisioning rather modest
to moderate canoe trips within the midwest region. However, over
the course of three voyages that were spaced out over eleven weeks
of the summer, we would advance from a family of absolute novices
on the water into paddlers who were moderately equipped to handle
certain waterways. The sequence of these three trips eased us into
canoe tripping very gradually and pleasantly.

The first venture took place in the comfortable June climate
of southwestern Kentucky, where we took jaunts from a tent base
camp every other day during a week-long vacation in civilization.
The second trip, paddling for 11/2 days down a very gentle river
in northeastern Illinois, only slightly removed from civilization,
involved our first overnight camp as paddlers. This meant our first
experiences with hauling all of the sleeping and cooking gear, and
setting up and dismantling a riverside campsite. The final voyage of
the summer entailed six days of paddling in the Boundary Waters

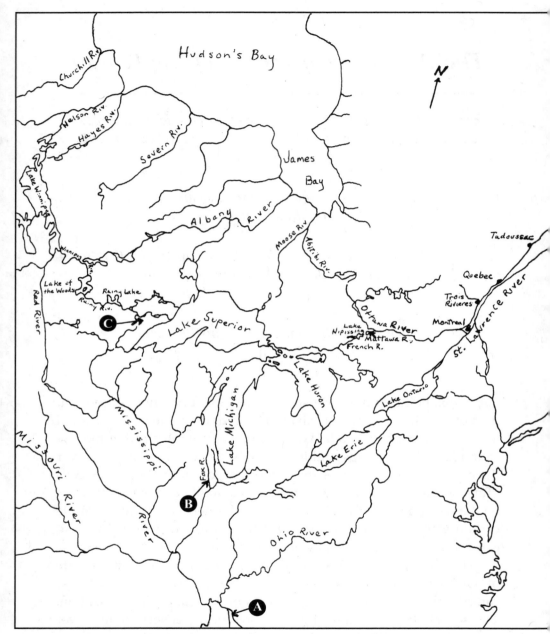

Figure 3: The Three Voyages of The Preliminary Year
A. Land Between The Lakes, B. Fox River, C. Boundry Waters Canoe Area Wilderness.

Canoe Area Wilderness in northern Minnesota, including rather long days covering moderate mileages, a number of portages (our first experience with this necessary aspect of long-distance tripping), and overnight camps.

Land Between the Lakes Trip, June 6-12, 1983

Kevin was age 6 3/4 and Ben was 4 11/12, and both were ripe for expanding their horizons beyond the car-based camping that they had enjoyed since birth. To make their first canoe camping experience as pleasant as possible, Doree and I chose the warm climate of the Land Between the Lakes outdoor recreational area in southwestern Kentucky. This long peninsula of preserved nature had been created when the Tennessee Valley Authority dammed the parallel courses of the Cumberland and Tennessee Rivers, a few miles above where they each flowed into the Ohio River. The resulting peninsula, some 45 miles long and from six to nine miles wide, lay between Lake Barkley (the dammed Cumberland River) and Kentucky Lake (the dammed Tennessee River).

Arriving at the campsite on the shores of Kentucky Lake after an eight-hour drive from home in Oak Park, we set up our moderately large wall tent. We had brought this overly spacious tan-and-brown shelter, instead of our standard-sized green tent, so we would have plenty of room for romping in case rainy weather kept us inside for long periods. During the entire first night at our new base camp, the bullfrogs in the nearby wetlands croaked incessantly, sounding like an entire orchestra of cellos without a conductor.

Day Two dawned clear, sunny, and balmy, with no wind, perfect weather conditions for our first time on the water as family paddlers. The boys, outfitted in their red and blue ball caps and orange life preservers, first waded in the still water of the cove beside the campsite, while we parents admired our brand new canoe on the tan sand of the shoreline. At this stage, we could not imagine the great adventures that we would experience in this craft over the many years ahead; but the canoe was intuitively aware of what lay before it. The dark green fiberglass hull, designed by my friend Ralph Frese as the top-of-the-line Canadienne model for the Old Town Canoe Company, had graceful, modest lines. Its form would help us glide along very easily, and it would hold a straight track while traveling on wind-swept open water; it would also allow us to make quick maneuvers when running fast, turbulent rapids. Over time, the underside of that pristine green hull would take on an entire network of scrapes and scratches, gifts from many a boulder and rock ledge in wild and dangerous situations (Ralph used to say there was a story for every scratch). But the craft would never once fail us. At this point, none of us in the family could have known what exhilarating paddling activities loomed in our future.

The boys learned on that first launch that the canoe was always to be first placed empty on the water; and only then were the gear and eventually the people to be loaded into the floating craft from the shallows. There would be no loading in while the stern was solidly ashore, and then pushing off with a grinding of the hull. Likewise, there would be no driving of the bow up onto the shoreline at landings, but instead an offshore unloading in the shallows. Although both shoreline launches and landings are very commonly portrayed in supposedly authentic historical films, no birchbark craft could have endured that kind of treatment for long, and it was not healthy for a fiberglass hull, either. Only a dugout canoe, carved from a single log, could endure such rough handling.

Kevin and Ben were lifted into their positions in the center two areas of the floating craft, between the thwarts, seated on the little wooden seat boards that I had made for them. These boards would keep their bottoms high and dry, above the water that would collect on the floor, brought in by our feet and sometimes rain and waves. With Doree in the bow seat, I launched us from the stern for our first-ever paddling jaunt. As we easily glided over the still water of the cove, our hearts soared like hawks!

During the morning, we traveled south along the wooded shoreline of the lake to a swimming area for an extended break, and then paddled back to camp for lunch. After a little fishing in the lagoon of the base camp, both from the shore and in the canoe, we paddled north along the shore and then halfway through the canal connecting Kentucky Lake and Lake Barkley. Along the canal, Ben particularly delighted in watching black swallows swoop in and out of their nests of mud high on the bridge pillars.

Back out on the lake, bathed by the warm rays of the sun, we wanted to intentionally capsize the craft, to both get accustomed to the sensations and practice how to handle the situation. But Kevin, our usually fearless and independent son, would have nothing to do with this, and he insisted that we leave him on shore during the practice session. So we three purposely capsized in relatively deep water (being quite surprised at the considerable effort it took to make the craft actually overturn), swam it to the shallows, bailed it out, and loaded up again with Kevin. After completing a total of eight miles of leisurely paddling for the day, we treated ourselves to a meal at a restaurant that served country home style dinners cooked on old wood-burning ranges, and then enjoyed a fine evening swinging on the restaurant porch. Before bed, Kevin and I lay on an air mattress in the clearing near the camp and gazed at the array of huge, bright constellations that filled the sky.

Day Three consisted of on-land activities, including a visit to the Woodland Nature Center, a woods hike to Honker Bay to observe the wild geese, a stop at the Golden Pond Visitor Center to absorb a planetarium show and many exhibits, and a fascinating visit to Homeplace 1850. Here, sixteen early farm buildings from the peninsula had been assembled to recreate a two-generation farm of the nineteenth century, where the antics of the goats provided considerable entertainment. Although we thought seeing fifty bison quietly grazing in a secluded meadow would be the finale of the day, we still had in store a sighting after dark of the very bright planet Venus, low on the western horizon above the waters of the lagoon. In addition, a skunk sauntered through the area next to our tent site just before we turned in, leaving a hint of a scent as its calling card.

We spent most of Day Four on the water, much of it at a secluded and thickly wooded sandy cove on Kentucky Lake. The boys, beginning to grasp the beauty of canoe travel, were intrigued that they were inhabiting this secretive place that could only be reached by water. While we were at the cove, I relished my first practice session of solo paddling; due to the locations of the two seats in the craft, I paddled while sitting on the bow seat, facing toward the stern.

During the course of our nine miles of paddling during the day, we crossed the mouths of several wide bays, getting accustomed to being relatively far from shore; we also enjoyed the adventure of paddling deep into the Duncan Bay Eagle Sanctuary. We were already discovering two of the most valuable aspects of canoeing: being able to watch nature slowly unfold before us at the speed of arm-driven paddles, and having opportunities for long, detailed conversations interspersed with periods of comfortable silence.

To keep the paddling experiences fresh, we spent Day Five engrossed in activities on land, starting with observing a coal barge passing through the locks at Kentucky Dam. After purchasing bows and arrows in the village, the boys had their first archery lessons from old Dad, followed by swimming at a beach and then their first horseback ride, along a trail that meandered through the woods and along the shore of Kentucky Lake. Those docile brown-and-white steeds seemed mighty large for our two miniature riders!

Our seven miles of paddling on Day Six would introduce us to traveling on moderate waves in somewhat windy conditions. We soon grew accustomed to the slight flexing of the hull as it rode the waves, and the soft creaking sounds that the thwarts made with each flex. With the canoe completely empty of cargo, this would be the least amount of stability that we would experience in the many years of tripping that lay ahead. During all other voyages from then on, we would be loaded with food for the entire journey plus the gear. While spending the day exploring, and also swimming at various spots along the wooded shoreline, we were intrigued to paddle from the lake (the flooded dammed river) into an old limestone quarry that was now also flooded by the backwaters of the dam; the sheer walls of light tan rock, rising fifty feet above the surface of the water, were a little daunting. During the final hour of paddling back to our base camp, Ben slept deeply; this was the first of a great many naps he would enjoy in the passenger spot during the years ahead. After an evening smorgasbord dinner to celebrate the completion of a fine canoeing vacation, we drove along the canopied woods road to the Nature Center, looking for wildlife. The boys were delighted to spot a deer, a skunk, and a raccoon along the way.

During the long drive home on Day Seven, we reviewed the great times that we had all enjoyed on this trip, including perfect weather (sunny and in the 80s every day), fine paddling experiences, numerous wildlife sightings (six deer, two skunks, one coon, one squirrel, one great blue heron, and many toads, frogs, and turtles), excellent meals, and a great many interesting attractions and activities. Kevin summed it up with the exclamation, "I really like this canoeing!"

Lower Fox River Trip, early July, 1983

The lowest section of the Fox River was to be the scene of our first overnight canoe adventure. This watercourse flows south and then southwest, ranging from twenty to eighty miles west of Lake Michigan, until it joins the Illinois River about ninety miles southwest of downtown Chicago. Just a few weeks after our introduction to paddling, Kevin was now 6 10/12 years old, and Ben had celebrated his fifth birthday the week before.

For the sixty-mile drive from Oak Park, we awakened early, dressed in our paddling clothes, and loaded the canoe atop the car and the gear inside its trunk. By noon, we had driven southwestward to the Fox River at Millington, where we left our car by the river bridge, and put in at 1:00. The sky was brooding and threatening rain, but the air temperature was comfortably warm, about 80 degrees, and the river water was warm as well.

After advancing about five miles on the gentle current, we stopped to explore at the mouth of Rood Creek. For another three miles, down to about the community of Sheridan, the riverbanks continued to be dark, rich soil, covered by a thick wall of lush green deciduous trees, while the river water was a muddy dark brown. At one point, we watched a muskrat scamper along the right bank and then dive into its riverbank den. Below Sheridan, the shorelines became more often high cliffs of tan sandstone, covered on their upper reaches with thick deciduous forest. Many swallows darted to and from their nests in holes partway up the face of several of the cliffs.

While spending four pleasurable hours on the water, five or six bouts of rain, in some cases heavy downpours, cooled us down and kept us comfortable. After each spell of rain, the boys cheerfully sponged out the puddle that accumulated on the canoe floor. To add to our comfort, there were no biting insects on the rampage.

At 5:00, having covered about fifteen miles of easy cruising, we decided to halt for the night, a little southwest of the community of Norway. After locating a campsite on an inviting gravel-and-sand bar, on the left bank under a steep limestone cliff, we set up the small green wedge tent and arranged all of the gear and bedding. As evening approached, many rather large fish began jumping and feeding in the shallows, with their tail and back fins projecting well above the water's surface.

Soon, almost continuous rain began to fall, ranging from medium to very hard downpours. Within minutes, a huge torrent began to flow down the steep forest slope and cliff above our campsite, right onto the gravel bar where we had pitched the tent! Apparently, an unseen ravine high above us gathered and funneled rainwater down to this spot on a regular basis, forming the substantial bar of sand and gravel that projected well out into the river from the bank. To divert the heavy flow away from the tent, Kevin and I dug a small trench with the folding shovel, but this only worked for about half an hour. Then the torrent began to wash gravel right out from beneath the tent. So Doree and I, ankle-deep in water, hustled to unstake the shelter and lifted it, with all of its bedding, gear -- and Ben -- still inside, onto the adjacent bank of higher solid ground, where we had earlier tied the canoe to a tree for the night. After making this alteration to our campsite, we munched on some gorp and soon turned in for the night, with the rain still coming down. But we were cozy, safe, secure, and dry all night, lulled by the patter of raindrops on the overlay of the tent. This turned out to be an excellent test for the first-time use of this brand new shelter, as well as a test of our abilities to handle a small crisis as a team.

We awakened to find the river level quite high, well above the gravel bar where we had originally pitched the tent. When Kevin raised the nylon tarp that covered the pile of gathered firewood, six or seven mice scurried away from the dry haven they had found during the rainstorms. For our breakfast, we cooked for the first time the French treat called galette. The boys hovered expectantly over the little fire as the thick patties made of flour, salt, water, raisins, cinnamon, and brown sugar simmered in butter in the stainless steel frying pan. While eating the treat and washing it down with hot chocolate, we watched a muskrat swim leisurely by, along the far side of the river. Before putting the canoe in the water, I practiced portaging it while wearing a loaded Duluth pack, as I would possibly need to do in certain emergency situations. This was my first experience with the sensations of portage pads (mounted on the center thwart of the overturned canoe) pressing down on the tops of my shoulders: definitely not a pleasant feeling, and not an acquired taste, either!

The weather was sunny and balmy, and again there were no blood-sucking insects on the attack. From our campsite down to about the community of Wedron, we glided beneath the high, forest-covered sandstone cliffs that flanked the river. We absolutely delighted in our downstream pace: with a good breeze at our backs, we covered seven miles in two hours. Feeling so good, I forgot to pay attention to the map, and misread it. Instead of taking out at the canoe livery on the left shore below Wedron as planned, we continued to proceed south in the backwater of the Dayton Dam for another two miles, almost to the dam itself, which is located seven miles above the junction of the Fox River with the Illinois River. As a result, after our lunch break, it took an hour of considerable effort, paddling against the moderate head wind, to work our way back upstream to the take-out place. Including the extra distance that we had overshot and then back-tracked to reach the take-out spot, the mileage of the trip totaled about 26 miles on the river.

At the tavern adjacent to the canoe livery, I arranged with a customer to drive me the fifteen miles by road to Millington, for a fee of $10.00, to retrieve the car. While driving back to the family, it felt strange to be zooming along at such speed, with absolutely no effort on my part. During the short trip back to Oak Park, we stopped to enjoy a restaurant meal, as our reward for having completed this brief but pleasurable and educational voyage.

Boundary Waters Trip, August 19-24, 1983

We now felt ready to up the stakes considerably, by canoeing in a true wilderness environment. So we set our sights on a week-long paddle in the Boundary Waters Canoe Area Wilderness of northern Minnesota. Our particular route would run parallel to and about eight to ten miles south of the mainline fur trade route, which extended along the Minnesota-Ontario border.

Before beginning the paddling adventure, we spent five days on the road pumping ourselves up, by studying the history of the fur trade era in Wisconsin, Minnesota, and adjacent Ontario. We pored over the recently-excavated materials from Ft. Folle Avoine at the office of the archaeologist and in the museum at Webster, Wisconsin; ingested Minnesota history amid the original buildings of Ft. Snelling near Minneapolis, the reconstructed Northwest Company (N.W.C.) post near Pine City, the reconstructed fort at Grand Portage, and the Voyageur Center at Ely; and spent a full day at the reconstructed Ft.

William of the N.W.C. near Thunder Bay, Ontario. The night before our put-in, we camped at the national forest campground about seven miles east of Ely, Minnesota.

Day One

In the morning, I was in great pain and could barely walk. I walked stooped over, since I had seriously pulled some muscles in my back the day before, while reaching into the shower to wash Ben's hair. How inopportune the timing! Tim helped me hobble around the campground to loosen my muscles a little, then he packed the gear into the car and drove us to the put-in location at the Lake One landing. This was at the terminus of Fernberg Road, twenty miles east-northeast of Ely and about three miles southeast of the lower end of Moose Lake. Although my injured back did not make for an auspicious beginning, we unloaded everything beside the lake, parked the car in the lot in the woods, and prepared for our first wilderness launch, thankful for the sunny warm weather and the cloudless skies. (Doree)

Kevin, age 6 11/12, and Ben, age 5 2/12, were absolutely primed to go. I had earlier shown them on the detailed paddling map where our round-trip journey would take us over the following days, in a shallow arc from west to east and then back over generally the same route to the beginning point. We would travel generally eastward through Lakes One, Two, Three, and Four, the Kawishiwi River, and Hudson, Insula, and Alice Lakes, before turning back westward to repeat the series in reverse.

At 10:30, we shoved off with great anticipation, finally on our first real wilderness jaunt. Almost immediately, I was struck by the difficulty of relating shore and water features to those on an airplane-view map. At first, all I could make out were numerous gradations of green hues in the distance. Self-doubt attempted to rear its ugly head. But we kept paddling in the various directions that I hoped matched the course that I had chosen on the chart; and each time when I felt we had gotten lost, we came out just where I had intended. I was learning to recognize, through gradual experience, the myriad gradations of green as measures of distance and as representations of land forms, and I was also getting accustomed to our canoe-level view in relation to the bird's-eye view of the map. In addition, the very gradual unfolding of the openings in the route ahead took time to understand. It was abundantly clear that I was as green as the forest that was passing slowly by. The elongated horseshoe shape of the narrow upper half of Lake One, with its various dead-end bays, projecting peninsulas, and turns, and the maze of small islands scattered throughout the oval lower half of the same lake, offered a quick three-mile school in reading land and water features and relating them to elements on a chart.

The passageway that would take us from Lake One to Lake Two consisted of a 165 yard portage, a miniature lake to paddle, and then another carry of 250 yards. When we arrived at the first portage, a large party of about fifteen canoes was just coming out. So we paddled into the cove at the end of the lake to wait, and were pleased to find there an old offshore beaver lodge. Watching from a distance the action at the portage (and at each portage thereafter), we saw a full repertoire of the poor behaviors that the canoeing books had mentioned: paddling the loaded craft right onto the rocks and sand of the landing, instead of stepping into the shallows, unloading offshore, and lifting the empty canoe onto the landing; grinding the bottom of the craft on rocks; using paddles as pushing poles; a family of four all joining in to carry a single canoe; banging the craft down hard on the ground at the end of a portage, instead of wading into the shallows and placing it on the water, etc. It was entertaining for us to watch all of this unfold, offering us a cram course in the antithesis of proper canoeing etiquette.

Although we had some apprehensions about making our first portage, it went just fine. Each of the boys, while wearing his life preserver, carried his sleeping bag in a backpack, his paddle in one hand, and his seat board in the other hand. Noting the roughness of the rocky path, I decided to first take the Duluth pack (weighing 65 pounds) plus some miscellaneous items, and then return for the canoe by a casual and unloaded walk back. During my second loaded trip over (with the canoe), due to the short length of the portage, the pain in the upper surface of my shoulders, where the two portage pads mounted on the center thwart bore down, did not last long. (During all of my future years of carrying the canoe, even after switching to softer pads, I never did learn to appreciate those sensations in my shoulders beneath the pads, and the longer the portage, the more they hurt!) Doree had wondered if she could manage the carry at all, with her badly pulled back muscles. But that day, although she did not sing, whistle, or chat too much, she paddled, portaged her heavy Duluth pack and other gear, helped set up camp, cooked, and cleaned right along with the rest of the family, in spite of her stooped posture. Like an experienced voyageur, my good-natured mate pushed through her pain!

When we traversed the small lake between the first and second portages, the boys did all the paddling from their midsection positions, using the two short paddles that we had bought for them in Ely (I just kept us on course for the 1/8 mile from my stern position). Bursting with pride, they belted out a little French ditty along the way.

At the far side of the pond-sized lake, we met a man who had misplaced his canteen. Since we had seen it back across the lake at the landing, I unloaded the canoe, took him back over the miniature watercourse to retrieve it, and returned with him. After our second portage, we took in a delicious lunch, while sprawled out on a massive granite ledge that had been warmed by the sun. A thick peanut butter-and-honey mixture spread on crackers, accompanied by koolaid, never tasted better!

Admiring the scenery around us, we noted how clean and sparkling this entire region appeared, compared to the Kentucky and Illinois settings where we had previously paddled, with their rich dark soils, mostly deciduous forest cover, and brown silty waters. Here in the Canadian Shield country, the land was dominated by dramatic granite ledges and boulders, with a rather thin layer of sandy soil supporting mainly a coniferous forest, and clear, shining water that varied from bluish to greenish hues depending on the light in a given setting. Our route during this trip would take us through forests of mainly pine and spruce, with some scattered patches of birch.

On Lake Two, as we explored a beckoning side detour up the long, slender arm on the north side of the lake, we roused a mother mallard with nine ducklings in tow. Later, while we headed from the base of the arm toward the entrance of Lake Three, a considerable wind and moderately large waves picked up. With all four of us digging in hard with our paddles, we were soon sheltered from the breeze behind a line of three small islands. From there, we watched a party of five canoes traveling straight into the wind and barely inching forward. After resting in the welcome lee of the islands, we passed onto Lake Three, and shortly located a beautiful campsite for an early halt at 2:30, having covered seven miles and two portages since the late-morning launch.

On a bed of reddish brown pine needles beneath the canopy of pines, Ben and I set up the tent, inflated the air mattresses, and spread out the sleeping bags, while Doree and Kevin cooked a well-deserved meal of commercially freeze-dried pea soup, plus sweet and sour pork with rice, washed down with koolaid and followed by M & Ms and tea.

While we parents cleaned and stowed away the dishes, the boys enjoyed exploring the rocky shoreline, where they discovered a tiny sand beach. Later, we all watched a loon diving for fish just offshore from our site, and laughed at the antics of two chipmunks skittering around the camp. Except for a couple of biting flies, there were no other insects out to prey on us! This had been a wonderful first day of wilderness tripping, and we looked forward to many more of the same.

Day Two

Before loading the canoe for the day's travel, we let the boys practice paddling alone, with Kevin in the stern, Ben in the bow, and Dad riding along as cargo (and occasional steersman) in one of the midsection compartments. We were all amazed that they really could do it by themselves! As the craft zipped along on the glassy surface, Kevin crowed with glee, "I'm so proud!"

We decided to aim for a campsite somewhere on Lake Insula by the end of the day, so we could then use it as a base camp for several day trips. Setting off at 10:00, we leisurely paddled four miles in the warm sunlight through Lakes Three and Four. In the narrow, winding passage of two miles that led from Lake Four to Hudson Lake, we made three short portages of 110, 140, and 55 yards, to circumvent a number of spirited rapids and falls. On these relatively short portages, it was time-consuming for me to untie and unload all of the gear for the carry, and then reload and retie it all again at the end, especially since I was using a single long rope to secure all of the packs to the thwarts. But I wanted to ensure the safety of our gear in case our lack of experience led to a capsize, even under these ideal paddling conditions; so I doggedly stuck with the program. However, I quietly vowed to work out a better system of pack fasteners in the future.

Near the end of the first carry, I absorbed for my memory-bank the sun-dappled scene ahead of me: Tim, loaded with a bulging Duluth pack on his back as well as some items in his left hand, was casually walking hand-in-

hand with little Ben, who was wearing his life preserver and doing his part by carrying the yellow-and-white koolaid jug. They were descending a slope that overlooked a lovely scene of placid blue water and matching blue sky. After the second portage, we took a relaxed lunch break before continuing on our way. (Doree)

We easily proceeded over the 11/2 mile length of Hudson Lake, to reach the rather major portage that led to a narrow half-mile section of the Kawishiwi River and then to Lake Insula. The length of the carry, 1/3 of a mile, was easily manageable; the difficulty lay in the ascent and descent of a 35-foot-high hill, with very rough and rocky footing. In addition, the descent into Insula was very steep. This obstacle seemed to have served as somewhat of a filter, keeping most other paddling parties to the west; we saw virtually no other canoeists during our next two days on the eastern side of the portage.

By 3:30, we had finished the carry and had reloaded, and within an hour we had progressed three miles on Lake Insula, wending our way around two huge mid-lake islands. Along the way, we passed a group of four loons, who dived when we came near. We also spotted an otter several canoe lengths away, swimming toward the nearby island with no apparent concern.

Deciding that eleven miles was sufficient progress for the day, Doree spied a beautiful campsite location on the eastern tip of a rather small, pine-clad island, a good place to settle in for two nights. As we slid into the shallows and glided to a halt, she turned toward me in her seat, pointed to the area in front of me, and whispered "Look." Both boys were fast asleep, shoulder to shoulder in their compartment, with their little paddles draped over themselves, exhausted from their contributions to our progress.

After setting up camp, we feasted on cream of asparagus soup, beef bourguignon with noodles, galette with raisins, koolaid, and milk. The fire crackled and danced into the evening as we undertook our tasks, included hanging the food pack by a rope far out on a high limb in a large, isolated pine, as protection against bears. Then we eavesdropped on the conversation that several loons were having out on the water. A few scattered raindrops fell during both our dinner and the evening, but not enough to require any rain gear.

Day Three

Intent upon exploring more of Lake Insula and another section of the Kiwishiwi River as far as Alice Lake, we left the base camp at 9:00 under solid grey skies and occasional raindrops. First Kevin, then Ben, took his turn paddling for a while in the bow position, while Doree rode as passenger in the middle, squeezed in beside the non-paddling son and providing some motherly cuddling. Watching each boy during his turn in the bow seat, swathed in a hooded sweatshirt, windbreaker, raincoat, cap, and life preserver, I was delighted to see the miniature paddle of blond wood flash as it was worked by a little pair of arms and a narrow set of shoulders. In the tripping years that lay ahead, we parents would revel in observing those arms enlarge, those shoulders widen, and those paddle strokes strengthen with each passing year.

After making our way for about four miles in a zigzag course around a number of islands, we spent a pleasant 1 1/2 hours on a high rocky island with steep sides of barren granite, crowned by about twenty tall pines. There, we enjoyed the scenery, picked our fill of ripe blueberries, and ate lunch. At noon, we departed on the trek to Lake Alice. Because of this year's particularly low water levels, there was not enough depth to paddle in the narrow rocky passage between the easternmost big island and the mainland at the exit of Lake Insula. After we had all clambered out and lightened the craft, and had pulled it through the very shallow passageway, Ben spotted a grouse on the mainland; the bird looked much like a mottled brown-and-white chicken.

Along the scenic three-mile section of the Kawishiwi River that led into Lake Alice, our green hull glided past various secluded inlets that were nearly filled with floating lily pads, many of them decorated with a single large white or yellow blossom. In one very narrow and shallow area of the watercourse, we made an easy hundred-yard portage. Just before entering Alice Lake, we discovered a large beaver lodge, a large conical mound of dry peeled saplings adjacent to the shoreline. A number of freshly peeled sticks in the topmost layer, not yet dried, indicated that this home was currently occupied by some flat-tailed residents. After cruising around in a portion of the lake for a time, we returned to our base camp, arriving at 5:15. Kevin had paddled half of the entire day's trip in the bow, contributing considerably to our fourteen miles of travel. During the jaunt, we had watched one turtle sunning on a log, as well as six loons afloat and fishing.

Our night's feast consisted of vegetable soup, macaroni and cheese, banana pudding, and koolaid, followed by an early bedtime. The weather this day had been overcast, reaching a high in the mid 60s, with intermittent sprinkles from our awakening until our sleeping, with one fifteen-minute period of heavy rain in the afternoon.

Day Four

After giving the boys an early-morning compass and map lesson, it was time to pack up and begin to retrace our route, under blue skies hung with a few stationary, fluffy white clouds. After heading west through Lake Insula and back over the big portage into Hudson Lake, we decided to take a slightly different route out, by paddling up the 21/2 mile length of the long, slender northern arm of the lake. Along the route, we stopped to study a rather large but low beaver lodge adjacent to the shore, made mostly from an accumulation of cut and peeled food sticks. We collected a few samples to bring home, to show friends how the beavers chewed off the bark at mealtimes. At the northernmost tip of Hudson Lake, near the portage into Fire Lake, we observed a female mallard with her nine little ones following close behind, as well as two loons, a single turtle, and another pair of turtles sunning themselves on a low rock. After a short portage of 55 yards, we found a welcoming campsite on a granite ledge overlooking Fire Lake, bringing to a close six miles of travel. Except for some moderate head wind, today's weather had been perfect.

As we feasted on chicken à la king, cream of celery soup, and koolaid, Doree spotted two moose, apparently a cow and her spring-born calf, entering the smooth-surfaced lake about a quarter-mile away and intending to swim to an island. These gangly-looking animals, spending much of their time in the water eating plants and seeking refuge from biting insects and heat, can swim up to six miles an hour for long periods. Besides water plants, they also consume grasses, twigs, and buds, taking in up to 45 pounds of vegetation a day. Although they have excellent hearing, they also have poor vision, so we were able to observe these two because we had been eating silently when they came out of the woods. During our evening at the site, after taking a brisk swim while wearing our life preservers, we enjoyed a popcorn party and the boys had a lesson in hatchet safety. Afterward, when we peeked under the rock slab where we had eaten our dinner, to our surprise we discovered twelve frogs lined up looking at us!

This voyage, our first as paddlers in a true wilderness setting, was turning out to be vastly different from our highway-and-car-camping trips of previous years. Imbued with both excitement and mild uncertainties, we were now totally immersed in the natural world, not observing it as a visual image from a comfortable distance. Because we had to look closely at many details around us for our own health and survival, we were sensitized to taking in information from various of our senses. We now had a deep engagement with and a close connection to the natural world, with active involvement instead of passive observation. Interacting with the wilds, we found ourselves filled with many sensations, including elation, awe, and a certain degree of fear of the unknown. We were beginning to grasp the fact that the wild world must be appreciated not only as a series of pleasant images, but also as an entire complex ecosystem, embracing both its lovely and its unlovely aspects. During the course of the trip, we were observing and coming to better understand how Mother Earth conserved and recycled all elements and all energies, and we soon realized that even the tiniest aspects of nature were important, contributing their respective parts to the total picture.

We were asleep inside the cozy tent by 9:00, but I was awakened after a couple of hours with a dizzying sugar-low episode (these would plague me throughout my adult life). My ever-helpful wife had put a packet of hot chocolate mix in the sealed cooking kit outside the shelter, so I consumed that food to stabilize me. Doree came out of the tent and, as we held one another close, we savored the impressive sight of the full moon reflecting brightly on the placid surface of the lake.

Day Five

So that Kevin and Ben could practice paddling together without parents or a load of cargo in the canoe, I tied together both of the painter ropes and the tie-down rope for the packs, forming a long tether; this 75 foot safety line was then fastened to the eyebolt projecting above the bow deck of the craft. While I held the opposite end of the line on shore, the boys happily maneuvered around on the glassy surface, thoroughly enjoying themselves and feeling very adventurous.

After a 9:00 launch, we paddled the 11/2 mile length of Fire Lake to its very narrow outlet passage, which required two short portages of 110 and 165 yards around a pair of rapids. At the first carry, we found a beaver lodge with air bubbles rising from its submerged area, apparently indicating that a resident was at home. The nearby dam, about fifteen feet long and extending a foot or more above the surface of the water, had been fashioned by beavers from cut sticks, some logs of six-inch diameter or more, and a considerable amount of hauled soil. This water-control barrier had been in position for a number of years, as indicated by the grass and small bushes that had grown along its top. Just after the second portage, the narrow, heavily shadowed passage was flanked by sheer granite cliffs that rose ten to fifteen feet straight up from the water.

Paddling into the long northern arm of Lake Four, we stopped for a lunch break, where the boys, envisioning a delicious chowder in the evening, gathered a supply of 39 live clams from the bottom in the shallows. Then we advanced through Lake Four, Lake Three (with a long looping detour to nearly its southern end), and most of Lake Two. At 3:30, having covered ten miles for the day, we found a campsite on the north shore of the lake, near the exit portages.

For our evening meal, we feasted on beef bourguignon and koolaid, but after trying the elaborate clam chowder that we had fussed over, we found that it had a dark and unappealing flavor, and the clams were awfully tough. Twice during the night, I was up to take care of sugar lows. I was apparently letting my fuel supply drop too low during the exerting portion of the day, and then eating an overly large evening meal to compensate for the hunger. I concluded that it would be better to keep feeding my furnace steadily at intervals all day while paddling, to keep my system on a more even keel.

Day Six

By good fortune, Mother Nature reserved the majority of the dirty weather for the final day of paddling. For several hours before we got up, it rained heavily, and the downpour continued during the entire packing-up operation. During the two portages out to Lake One and the final three miles of paddling on that lake, we had moderately heavy winds and light rainfall.

As we approached the Lake One landing and the completion of our journey, a number of other parties were also converging on the same destination. These various groups of Boy Scouts and burly fishermen were in decent paddling shape at the end of their respective trips, and they apparently wanted to show their stuff. But Tim and I delighted in easily sprinting ahead of all of them, and made it to the landing first. We were able to carry this off partly because my back had now returned to normal. (Doree)

After loading the canoe atop the car and the gear into the trunk,· we were off by 12:30, all marveling at the strange sensations of having a motorized vehicle propel us along so quickly. In Ely, we downed huge, succulent hamburgers at a restaurant, to celebrate our successful introductory wilderness voyage, during which we had covered over fifty miles and had made fourteen portages. Afterward, we began our reluctant transition back to "civilization."

En route home, when we learned that a party of native people were departing to gather wild rice on Grouse Bay of Bowstring Lake, on the Leech Lake Reservation in Minnesota, we threw our canoe on the water and accompanied the group. That night, during a heavy storm, a large tree was felled by a bolt of lightning directly onto our rented cottage; oddly enough, we had been safer in a nylon tent on a wilderness riverbank! We also thoroughly enjoyed our visit with the famous birchbark canoe builder Bill Hafeman near Big Fork, as well as a fur trade study trip to Madeleine Island and Chequamegon Bay of Lake Superior, where our trader ancestor Claude David had lived and worked with the Ottawas and Hurons between 1660 and 1663.

Some of the quiet conversations that we had shared during long hours of easy cruising during the canoe trip had focused on Claude David and his many adventures. During those long days together on the water, we had also sung French songs, as well as leading the boys in fun practice sessions of mental addition and subtraction, plus forming simple sentences using names of things, adjectives, and verbs, all in French.

This introductory year of paddling had brought us plenty of fun, lots of growth, and myriad experiences, and we were looking forward to many more such adventures in the future. Our original intention had not been that long-distance canoeing would become a major activity for our little family. However, by the end of this summer's growth process, I was thoroughly hooked on it. Doree was not yet entirely sure, wanting to leave the options open.

III

First Voyage
Mattawa River, June 19-22, 1984

Go confidently in the direction of your dreams!
Live the life you've imagined. As you simplify your life,
the laws of the universe will be simpler.
Henry David Thoreau

Do not go where the path may lead,
Go instead where there is no path and leave a trace.
Ralph Waldo Emerson

Commit yourself to a dream.
Nobody who tries to do something great but fails is a total failure.
Why?
Because he can always rest assured that he succeeded in life's
most important battle -- He defeated the fear of trying.
Robert H. Schuller

The greatest danger for most of us lies not in setting our aim
too high and falling short, but in setting our aim too low
and achieving our mark.
Michelangelo

My inspiration to paddle the mainline fur trade route from end to end came on a bright, shining day during the early winter of 1984. This was the day I learned that about three-quarters of the Mattawa River in southern Ontario, a significant and well-documented portion of the mainline route, had been preserved in nearly pristine condition. About eighty percent of the roughly twenty-five miles of protected waterway lay within Mattawa River Provincial Park, while the other twenty percent was located in Samuel de Champlain Provincial Park (both had been established in 1970). In addition, the

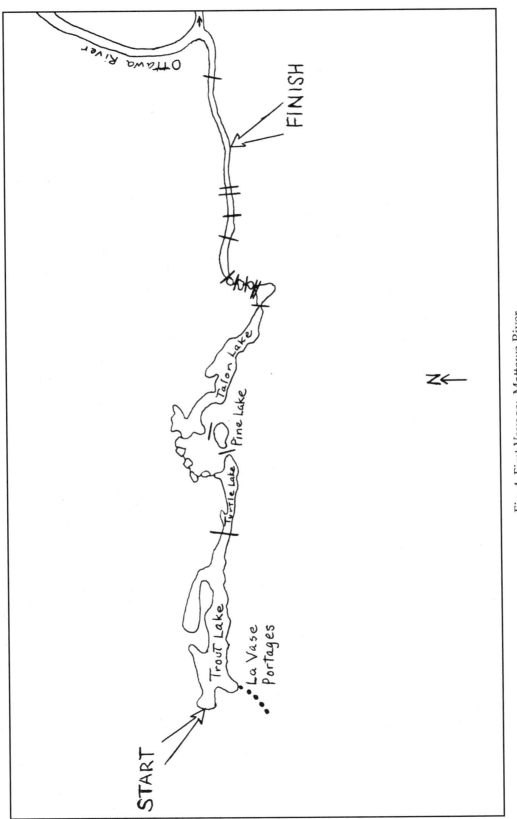

Fig. 4, First Voyage: Mattawa River

upriver half of the remaining eight miles down to its mouth was also virtually untouched and uninhabited. The only structures within the latter wild section were those of L'Auberge des Pionniers (The Pioneers' Inn), a modest nature camp for children with a few cabins and a lodge. After ordering and studying the printed materials from the two provincial parks, and contacting the L'Auberge owner-manager for assistance, my plans for canoeing this river, as well as many other waterways in the future, began to fall into place.

When the concept of paddling the mainline route from end to end came to me, I knew that our family would not cover the distance of roughly 3,000 miles in one, two, or three voyages. A friend and fur-trade-historian colleague of mine had paddled very lengthy segments of the mainline route on several different occasions. He admitted that he could only remember those trips in a blurry, hazy overview. Learning from his experiences, I wanted to divide the entire route into a considerable number of manageable annual segments, for several reasons. First of all, our boys were only five and seven years old at the outset, certainly not ready to handle journeys that would run for months at a time. But Doree and I were not gluttons for punishment, either; we wanted to relish each day of every trip with enthusiasm. In addition, we wished to remain keenly aware of the natural world that we would be paddling through, and appreciate it fully.

So we decided to tackle the mainline route in a number of reasonable voyages, the total number of which we could not determine at the time. The length of each annual segment would be based partly on the physical capabilities of Kevin and Ben as they grew up (and on us parents as well), plus the locations of the roads that intersected with the mainline water route. These roads would be necessary to facilitate the work of our shuttle driver each year, since we would be operating with a single vehicle. The project eventually took a total of fifteen consecutive summers to complete. The trips began with a modest thirty-five miles on the Mattawa River, and gradually grew to more than three hundred miles on the jaunts in the far northwestern areas, where there are very few roads intersecting the water highway.

When it was time to canoe the Mattawa in June of 1984, Kevin was age 7 3/4 and Ben was 5 11/12. To reach the watercourse which they were so eager to paddle, we put in twelve long hours on the road the first day. The following day, we were inspired by early French and native history at Ste. Marie-Among-the-Hurons, near Midland, Ontario. At this excavated and reconstructed Jesuit fortress and mission center, which had operated in the heart of Huron country from 1639 to 1649, our ancestor Etienne Racine had served as a carpenter during the years 1644 to 1646. It was fascinating for us to consider that he might have fashioned with his own hands some of the preserved wooden elements of the buildings that had been excavated. For the boys, one of the particular highlights of the day was chatting at length with two native women in their bark-covered long house.

On the day before putting in, we explored the Mattawa River route by car, including Champlain Provincial Park, with its displayed reproduction of a 36 foot *canot du Maître*, the largest size of cargo canoe, and various other fur trade exhibits. We also visited Explorers' Point at Mattawa, at the junction of the Mattawa and Ottawa Rivers. At this latter location, a N.W.C. post had been established as early as 1810, followed by a H.B.C. facility which was operated from the 1820s until 1909. Of the seven areas of concentration of French speakers now living in Ontario, one is here at Mattawa, while two more lie a little to the northwest; in addition, one concentration is located a little to the west of Mattawa, and another is at Sault Ste. Marie. The remaining two areas of concentration lie south and east of the city of Ottawa, in the area from which my maternal grandmother had immigrated to Michigan with her parents and siblings in 1887. My maternal grandfather had immigrated to Michigan three years earlier, from the area of Lac St. Jean, 125 miles north of Quebec City.

In Mattawa, we bought topographical maps for the paddling trip, and then drove westward to the little nature resort called L'Auberge on the Mattawa River, for an evening of swimming in the river and a night in a cabin. Since I was so keyed up, poised to launch the huge family project, I slept mighty fitfully that night, if it could even be termed sleeping. The persistent thumping sounds coming from beneath the cabin during part of the night did not help my dozing situation much, either. In the morning, the owner explained that one of the local beavers had developed a taste for the upright support posts of that particular building, and had been visiting nightly to gnaw on them.

Day One

Arising at 5:00 to dress the boys and ourselves in our paddling clothes, we downed a quick breakfast of gorp and instant breakfast drink, and were soon on our way. Danny Neault, the owner of L'Auberge, drove westward with us to the town of North Bay; he would bring the car back to L'Auberge, and keep it there until we would arrive back via the water after our easterly voyage. During the drive, he related the story of two little boys who had been mauled and killed by a black bear in the area of the river a couple weeks earlier. The kids had been fishing, and unfortunately, they had stowed their catch in their pants pockets before encountering the bear. The smell of fish had apparently instigated the attack, but when the boys had run in panic, they had become the bear's target, rather than the fish. This was a sobering tale for all of us, but we were convinced that our chances of a dangerous bear encounter would be much reduced: we would not be fishing, and we planned to stow our edibles out of reach at night, by hoisting them up with a rope thrown over a high limb of a tree, well out from the trunk. However, this story would return to haunt Doree and me on the very next day.

At 9:30, we launched from the Ministry of Natural Resources Work Center east of the town of North Bay; this facility was located at the western end of Trout Lake, the headwaters of the Mattawa River. Only a slight breeze ruffled the water, and in the dome above, numerous pale blue openings were scattered throughout the white fluffy cloud cover, allowing rays of sunlight to peek through and warm us. Our first three miles of paddling, around Pilot Point and down to the bottom of Dugas Bay, were not part of the actual mainline route. At the place of our first break, on the grass-covered sandy shoreline at the bottom of the bay, we finally joined the legendary route.

There, I explained to the boys that, if we had been headed southward over the height of land to Lake Nipissing on the mainline passage (where we would travel the next year), we would now make the arduous seven-mile trek from Trout Lake that involved a short carry and the three La Vase (Mud) Portages, plus about five miles of paddling. First, there would be a short carry, then a pond 2/10 of a mile long to be paddled, followed by an 8/10 mile portage over a low ridge to a tiny tributary stream of the La Vase River. This stretch of 11/2 miles of muddy little creek was navigable only because beavers had dammed it, producing two elongated ponds with a portage of about 725 paces between them, before the water flowed into the main branch of the La Vase River. This somewhat larger waterway also required a thousand-yard portage around a pair of rapids, at about the midpoint of the run of four miles down to Lake Nipissing. To begin our trip the following year, in 1985, we would paddle only the lower reaches of the La Vase River, and then continue across Lake Nipissing.

When we embarked from the foot of Dugas Bay on Lac de la Truite (Trout Lake), we were elated to be finally paddling, for the very first time, on the long-anticipated mainline fur trade route! From now on, each area of the waterways and each step on the portage paths would be in the track of our forefathers.

Advancing three miles in an hour through the island-studded lake, which was surrounded by low, evergreen-covered hills, we paused for another short break. Then our paddles took us over the remainder of Trout Lake, to a one-hour lunch stop on Camp Island, at the outlet of the lake. Just before our landing, a lone gull made about ten very low passes over the canoe, like a dive-bomber; but the swooping bird did not spatter us with any white offerings. During our exploration of this high sandy island covered with pine and birch, we located some patches of my favorite flower, orange and red Indian paint brushes, sunning themselves on an exposed ledge next to the shoreline.

When we left the lake and began traveling down the Mattawa River itself, I realized what an excellent choice this had been for our first excursion on the mainline route. Besides its wild and scenic beauty, it was narrow, not at all massive in scope, giving us the impression that it was certainly within our capabilities at the time. It was no coincidence that the French had dubbed this waterway La Petite Rivière. That said, however, its rough and rocky course did drop a total of 160 feet over the 33 miles from the outlet of Trout Lake to the mouth at the Ottawa River. This degree of drop made considerable amounts of water rush down the narrow channel, often only a few yards wide, and also froth and tumble down various rapids and waterfalls.

While progressing 4 1/2 miles along a slender stretch of the rock-bound river, we passed a tiny island with a strange, spooky feature that is seldom seen in canoe country: the ruins of a tall brick chimney, with no remains of the former house visible among the spruce and birch trees that had reclaimed the piece of ground. We also slid easily over the area where the Rapides de la Tortue (Turtle Rapids) had once required a portage, before the rocky obstructions had been blasted away and flooded out during the logging era. Later, as we were traveling the two mile length of Lac de la Tortue (Turtle Lake), Kevin was thrilled to paddle in the bow seat, now using his mother's full size paddle instead of his own miniature one from the previous year.

The outlet passage of Turtle Lake, located on its northern shore, consists of a row of five slender ponds separated by five sets of rapids. This route would require five portages before the channel curves eastward to enter the upper end of Lac du Talon. I explained to the family that, to circumvent this labor-intensive section of the Mattawa, the voyageurs had instead traveled to the eastern end of Turtle Lake and up a small river into Robichaud Lake. Portaging overland then brought them to a spot further down on Lac du Talon, so that 11/2 miles was cut off the paddling distance, in addition to obviating the five rapids and their respective portages on the Turtle Lake outlet. We would likewise follow the customary route of the voyageurs, eliminating the series of five portages.

As Turtle Lake narrowed to its eastern tip, we encountered another first in our paddling experiences. To reach the portage path around a rapids at the mouth of the small river leading to Robichaud Lake, we had to drag the loaded craft over an old grass-covered beaver dam, beside its adjacent beaver lodge. This took us to Portage de la Mauvaise Musique (Bad Music Portage), the first actual voyageur carry that we had ever done. As we tramped over this 200 pace portage on the right shore, around the rapids and toward Robichaud or Pine Lake, we definitely felt that the spirits of our ancestors and thousands of other voyageurs, traders, missionaries, and soldiers were accompanying us. Kevin guessed that the French had probably named the rapids and portage "Bad Music" after the whine of hordes of mosquitoes that accompanied us up the muddy incline, and also along the path through the thick hemlock and maple forest. We were certainly grateful to have fine-mesh head nets to wear!

At 6:30, in about the middle of Robichaud Lake's 11/2 mile diameter, we located an excellent campsite on a small pine-clad island. Several of its domes and folds of granite were completely barren, too rounded and smooth to allow any soil to accumulate or any plants to gain a foothold. This day, while covering about fourteen miles, we had seen two great blue herons, as well as several loons and gulls. It had been a nearly perfect weather day, reaching a high of about 70 degrees, very comfortable for our first-ever paddling on the mainline voyageur route.

The commercially-made freeze-dried dinner tasted lousy and, as usual, it did not contain nearly enough protein to refuel us after the heavy work that we had been doing. This prompted Tim and me to decide that, after this voyage, we would produce all of our own dried dinner materials at home, instead of buying commercially-made meals. Up to this point, I had already been baking our supplies of gorp, assembling the peanut butter-honey mixture, and buying at the grocery store various other items for the breakfast and lunch meals and all of the snacks. Now, due to our latest decision, I would also dry considerable amounts of meat, vegetables, and fruit in an electric dehydrator. (Doree)

After supper, the boys discovered a stand of lady slippers in the woods above the camp. Then Kevin very considerately and patiently fanned away the mosquitoes from me while I practiced, since I could not play the trumpet with my head net covering my face. During this trip, I would have no respite from practicing, and would be obliged to put in several sessions each day; the Symphony's usual June vacation period was only ten or eleven days long, and I would be back at work as soon as the canoe trip was completed.

Once we were comfortably ensconced in the tent for the night, with maps in hand, we discussed the terrain that we were covering on this trip. Here we were once again in the Canadian Shield country, to which we had been introduced during the previous summer, on our Minnesota trip. The Shield is a huge expanse of metamorphic and igneous rock, either exposed or barely covered with a thin layer of soil, that makes up over two million square miles of the surface of North America. The area includes a large portion of Canada, stretching from the St. Lawrence Valley westward to the Plains and northward to the Arctic; it also includes northeastern Minnesota, an area of northern Wisconsin, the adjacent third of the Upper Peninsula of Michigan, and the Adirondack region of northern New York. In addition, the Shield lies beneath the accumulated sediments of all of the interior prairies and plains. This ancient rocky expanse, formed in the Precambrian Period between 2.5 and 3.6 billion years ago as the Earth's crust and oceans were developing, contains some of the oldest rocks on our planet. Metamorphic granite and greenstone, originally formed as sedimentary rocks, were altered under intense heat and pressure to form the surface crust, while igneous rocks, in molten form, erupted or oozed from cracks in the crust. The resulting Shield was the first large portion of North America that was permanently elevated above the level of the global sea.

Millions of years following its formation, after considerable amounts of soil had accumulated on the surface of the Shield, a series of at least four glacial periods occurred. In each instance, glaciers more than a mile thick covered and scoured the entire region, first advancing southward and westward from the Hudson's Bay region, and then retreating by melting at their southern edges. This forward and backward action of these immensely heavy ice sheets scraped and rearranged the accumulated soil, hauling much of it to the south and west in the region, and leaving the remainder as a thin scattered coating. The hard bedrock of the Canadian Shield resisted this erosion to a certain extent, but it was often gouged out and its hills were somewhat leveled. After the final retreat of the last glaciers, the Shield was left exposed in many areas, forming the characteristic gently rolling hills and low tablelands of this rugged and rocky country. To this day, smoothed, polished, and grooved exposed bedrock surfaces testify to the tremendous forces of the former glacial action.

The meltwaters of the retreating glaciers filled the largest of the gouged depressions, forming the present Great Lakes. In addition, more than a million smaller lakes were also formed in other depressions dotting the landscape, while myriad rivers of all sizes drained from higher to lower elevations. Over thousands of years, vegetation slowly returned, more soil was gradually created as the generations of plants lived and died, and forests eventually covered the region. A huge, conifer-dominated boreal forest grew in a massive arc across the entire southern half of the Shield, with a region of mixed coniferous and deciduous forest developing along its southernmost fringes, where the soil was more fertile.

Nearly all portions of the mainline fur trade canoe route lay within the Canadian Shield country, with only three exceptions. The eastern exception was a section along the lower reaches of the Ottawa River, extending from a little upriver from the present city of Ottawa down to Montreal; the bedrock of this area consists of older sedimentary rocks. The first western exception was the territory which lay immediately west of the lowest reaches of the Winnipeg River and all of Lake Winnipeg, plus the Saskatchewan River and the adjacent Cumberland Lake. The other western section that lay outside of Shield country included the uppermost section of the Churchill River plus the Clearwater and Athabasca Rivers. In these two western areas of prairies and plains, the Shield bedrock is overlain with later deposits of sedimentary soil.

After this discussion about millions and even billions of years of history, we were all ready for sleep, after an excellent day. We dozed off to the haunting calls of loons out on the water, and the deep croaking of bullfrogs at the shoreline.

Day Two

As would be our custom throughout all of our years of paddling, we began our day with a cold breakfast consisting of a high-powered gorp mixture plus a fortifying instant breakfast drink, which provided plenty of energy yet took very little time. Throughout the day on the water, we would ingest various snacks and a cold lunch while afloat or on shore, after which we would finally enjoy a piping hot meal in the evening, when the day's traveling was completed.

Leaving the campsite at 9:30 under clear blue skies, we paddled on perfectly calm water, right behind the delicate wake of a mink that was swimming across Robichaud Lake. After only half a mile, when we arrived at the landing of the Portage Pin de Musique, we realized that Kevin had left his assigned tie-down rope back at the site on the island. So he and I paddled the empty canoe back for it, giving the youngster his first chance to work in the *gouvernail* position from the rear seat and do the steering. Before departing on this jaunt in the empty craft, I had demonstrated for both boys how to do the J stroke in the stern, to offset the natural tendency of the bow of the canoe to turn toward the side opposite that of the stern paddle. However, after Kevin had traveled in a complete circle three times, instead of in his intended straight-line course, he claimed, "It's a lot harder than I thought!"

After retrieving the rope, we returned to Doree and Ben and made the portage of 450 paces through the pines into Lac du Talon. During this carry, Ben used his ears and his smattering of French to create his own translation for the name Pin de Musique (Music of the Pine) Portage: "The Wind in the Trees." This sound was especially obvious on this overland carry, since there was no sound of tumbling white water action nearby. At the end of the path, after its steep and challenging final fifty yards of decline, we took a delightful two-hour break. While I sat on an offshore boulder and practiced the trumpet, surrounded by shimmering blue water, the boys swam and then tried fishing for some of the pike, pickerel, bass, and trout that live in these waters. Off on her own, Doree paddled solo for the first time, making the empty craft glide and turn happily on the smooth surface.

Finally, we headed out on Lac du Talon at 12:30. A breeze had picked up during our long break, but it had calmed again by the time we pushed off. In some places along the shoreline, massive areas of completely barren granite rose at a gradual angle from the water, while extensive stands of pine, spruce, or hemlock lined most of the route. The panorama of the scenery seemed to float slowly by as we glided silently over the placid water. By 3:30, we had paddled southeast for six miles along the length of the lake, with a relaxing break in the middle on the sandy shores of Grasswell Point. We now entered the narrow half of the Mattawa River, where jagged and jumbled cliffs often rose directly from the water's edge.

Downriver 3/4 of a mile, we arrived at the Chute du Talon. As we approached the landing on the right shore, Doree kept a sharp eye out for any submerged boulders or logs in our path, as one of her duties as the *avant*. After unloading, we sought the vantage point of the little concrete dam that had been constructed at some point across the top of the falls, to maintain the level of Talon Lake. The long downhill run with several ledges, dropping a total of about forty feet in elevation, presented a boiling white froth along the entire left half of the channel; the right half had numerous gatherings of exposed boulders and ledges standing above the rampaging whiteness. A short distance below, the quieted water rested, as it flowed as smooth and black as lava through a picturesque gorge that was flanked with broken vertical cliffs topped with evergreen forest.

At about 4:30, beside the head of the portage trail, we loaded the boys with their backpacks, seat boards, and paddles, and sent them off to start the carry ahead of us, while we put on our own burdens. Loaded with our packs, Doree and I made the difficult trek of 330 paces with a great deal of effort. In 1789, Alexander Mackenzie had described this portage as the toughest one for its length on the entire mainline route. We could hardly believe that the boys had managed the path alone ahead of us, especially the challenging six-foot vertical ledge of rock that extended across the trail at one point. We tried to picture one boy boosting his brother up to the top of the ledge, and then the upper boy reaching down to help pull up the other brother. It was hard imagining them doing that, particularly while hauling their loads. When we finally reached the river below the falls at the end of the trail, after the final thirty yards of extremely steep decline, we saw that they had not arrived!

Backtracking, with our hearts and minds racing, we searched twice over the entire portage, and, with ever-growing panic, also examined every possible side route that they might have taken away from the portage path. We tried using our signal whistles (we each wore a neck lanyard that held a whistle, Swiss Army knife, and waterproof case of matches) and also bellowed their names repeatedly; but the roar of the falls completely covered our whistles and our shouts. We were getting frantic by this point, as we recalled the very recent bear-killing-two-boys incident that our shuttle driver had related.

After having spent about half an hour searching, as a last resort, we decided to check an unlikely grass-covered two-track service road that led southward for two miles, away from the dam, to a locked gate at Highway 17. After about a quarter-mile, to our immense relief, we found Kev's pack, abandoned in the middle of the trail. They had taken **this** route! (At the very beginning of the carry, only about ten steps from the canoe, the boys had turned right, onto the two-track lane that led south, away from the river.) Shortly after coming upon Kevin's pack, we found Ben's hat, and then his pack as well. Soon we met Kev, retracing his steps. They had walked 1 1/2 miles, almost the entire length of the service road, before reaching a split in the trail. Not knowing which route to take, Kevin had started back to look for us, soon followed by Ben. When we finally met Kevin, we had been separated from the boys for about 45 minutes. Shortly, Ben also arrived, and we had a tearful but very joyous family reunion. Together we walked forward to the split in the two-track lane, about a mile away, to pick up the remaining gear that they had left behind. Then it took a half-hour to return from there to the canoe, at the beginning of the portage path. With the retracing of their steps, the boys had already hiked a total of five miles, none of it on the correct route. What a wild and frightening experience this had been for Doree and me!

With the canoe on my shoulders, and Doree and the boys bringing the remaining gear, we once again made the portage around the falls.

After this last trip over, I revealed to the family what Alexander Mackenzie had written: "Here many voyageurs have been crushed to death by the canoes or received irrecoverable injuries." His comment reflected the fact that the largest birchbark cargo canoes, measuring 36 feet in length, had weighed up to six hundred pounds when empty. Wrestling them over this difficult portage had required a massive effort, and had sometimes resulted in damage to both the carriers and the craft. The number of people who carried a canoe was not standardized, but was based on such factors as the size and weight of the specific craft, the length of the portage and the degree of difficulty of its terrain, the wind and weather at the time, the number of people in the party, and their physical condition, which was related to illness, injuries, exhaustion, and food intake. In 1799, when John Robertson noted that six men were often used to carry the largest cargo canoes, he commented, "From the rugged unevenness of some of the paths across the carrying places, the whole weight of the canoe will often rest on one or two men who (if they are not able to support it) often are crushed dreadfully, & sometimes are killed by it." We often reminded ourselves of the torments that many thousands of individuals, both native and French and both men and women, had endured on the very same portage trails that we also trod.

After finally returning to the water at 7:00, with the rumble of the Talon Falls in the background, we proceeded a mile before landing for the night on the north shore of little Pimisi Lake. We had covered nine miles today, with ideal sunny weather reaching a high of about 75 degrees. During the night, I was up twice for a couple scoops of peanut butter, to stave off the dizziness of sugar lows. But I felt deeply relieved and thankful that the boys and their mother were safely nestled in their warm sleeping bags, as I crawled back in and settled next to them.

Day Three

Deserving a good rest after two productive travel days, and knowing that much of this day would be spent making portages around five obstacles, we slept in. Then, while lounging in the tent, I described an important sight that we had missed back at the Talon Falls, while we had been so distracted about getting separated from each other. A number of potholes are to be seen in certain horizontal areas of exposed rock there. These circular depressions were formed by the grinding action of sand and stones being whirled around in a depression in the rock, driven by a tremendous force of water. They harken back to an ancient time when the Mattawa had been a mighty torrent, part of the main outlet of the upper three Great Lakes and Georgian Bay. About 10,000 years ago, the glaciers had retreated northward for a considerable distance, and their huge amounts of meltwater had created the Great Lakes to the south. The weight of the massive ice sheets was so great that the Earth's crust, beneath the regions where the glaciers had been and where they still were, was depressed a great deal. As a result, the main outflow of the upper three Great Lakes and Georgian Bay at this time was eastward, in a downward direction toward the depressed land. The waters flowed in a giant channel that now comprises, from west to east, the French River, Lake Nipissing, Trout Lake, the Mattawa River, and the Ottawa River, flowing out to join the St. Lawrence.

Ever since the retreat of the glaciers, the depressed land beneath their former locations north and northeast of the Great Lakes has been rebounding upward in elevation, causing the Shield to tilt upward toward the northeast and downward toward the southwest. In early times, the northern region rose at a rate of about a foot per decade. Eventually, the land along the northern shores of the upper Great Lakes and Georgian Bay had risen enough that, by about 4,000 years ago, the outlet flow changed from eastward to southward; it has been located there ever since, at the foot of Lake Huron. This rebounding action of the Earth's crust is still continuing to this day, since the last of the glaciers receded from North America only about 6,000 years ago. The land along the eastern side of Hudson's Bay has risen five feet in the last century, while the land in the area of the Mattawa River has risen about seventeen to twenty inches during the same period.

After my mini-lecture on the ancient waterways, we were all glad that the Mattawa had eventually become a small rushing river whose flow we could handle. We slowly packed up the gear, and then I practiced the trumpet while the boys enjoyed swinging from a high limb of a tall red pine, with the rope that had suspended the food pack there during the night.

Beneath a light blue sky, with puffy white clouds ambling off toward the east, we were finally under way at noon. After a quarter-mile, at the outlet of Pimisi Lake, the river makes a jog to the north for two miles, before resuming its usual easterly direction. It is in that two-mile span that we would face a series of five obstructions. When we reached the first rapids at the outlet of the lake, we discovered that Ben had left his assigned canoe bailer back at the campsite. During the trip that he and I made to retrieve it with the empty canoe, he relished his first opportunity to serve as the *gouvernail*.

This particular set of rapids begins with the ruins of a wooden logging dam visible beneath the surface. To make the portage, called Décharge des Perches, we unloaded on the right shore at 12:45, and carried over all of the gear. Then we easily ran our very first rapids, with the canoe empty, as the voyageurs had often done here when they were downbound and there was sufficient water depth (hence the name *décharge*, "unloaded"). When they were upbound, after poling up this rapids, the voyageurs would have traditionally thrown away their *perches* (pushing poles) with some joyful ceremony. They would no longer need these iron-shod poles, which they had sometimes used to advance against the powerful current and rapids of the Ottawa and Mattawa Rivers up to this point. In 1685, the French officer Lahontan noted the use of poles in certain instances when paddles did not suffice: "When they have occasion to run up against rapid currents, they make use of poles of pine wood; and the setting of the craft along with these is what they call *piquer le fond* [piercing the bottom]."

Over the next 13/4 miles, four more obstacles lay in the channel. Within sight of the Rapides des Perches, which we had just passed, was an unnamed rapids, a quarter-mile away; here, we portaged the gear on the right shore for two hundred paces, and then ran the canoe down empty, since there was enough water to carry us over the low stones. Another quarter-mile brought us to the Portage de la Cave, requiring a hundred-pace carry of everything on the left shore. Some areas of exposed horizontal rock here contained potholes or "caves," which had been gouged out by whirling stones and sand driven by the ancient torrential channel during the glacial era. A quarter-mile further, around a slight bend in the channel, lay Portage de la Prairie (Meadow Portage), where we made a 280 pace carry on the left shore over nearly flat ground.

The four rapids that we had encountered so far this morning had all been shimmering and sparkling downhill cascades, with only a slight, gradual drop. However, ten minutes paddling now brought us to a much different feature, the impressive Chute des Paresseux. This set of falls consists of a vertical curtain of thundering white water that plunges 20 to 25 feet to the new level of the riverbed. After making the difficult carry of 400 paces on the right, with its challenging boulder-strewn path along a dry streambed, we welcomed a lunch break below the falls. During our conversation, we marveled that the voyageurs had called this the "Falls of the Lazy Ones!" From our picnic spot, we could see surviving remnants of an old timber chute from 1930s logging operations skirting along the left edge of the drop. During springtime drives, the floating logs had been directed down this chute, rather than going over the falls and becoming jammed together in a giant mass below.

A short distance downstream, we glided silently past the Porte de l'Enfer, the cave opening in the side of a tall cliff that paddlers long ago had termed the Gate of Hell. The voyageurs had believed (or professed to believe) that a man-eating monster lived in this cave; however, by good fortune, the vicious people-eater did not choose to make an appearance during our short time coasting by.

Ben paddled as the *avant* in the bow seat for a mile, until we located a particularly beautiful place to camp. The site offered an extensive area of sandy beach along the north shore, where a small river cascaded down from the slope above; over the centuries, the little watercourse had deposited a large supply of clean tan sand at the edge of the Mattawa. When we landed at 6:00, we had covered only 3 1/2 miles since our morning departure, but we had made five portages. Even more importantly, we had been both successful and exhilarated by our very first experiences at running rapids. After dinner, the boys found a toad hopping near the shoreline, and created an extensive maze for him in the sand. As darkness was descending, signalling that it was time for them to hit the sack, they released the little fellow to continue his life of freedom.

Day Four

Before loading the canoe for the day, the boys and I embarked upstream on the barely-ruffled surface for a paddling practice session, after which we returned to the campsite to pick up Mom. Then, with Kevin as the *gouvernail*, Ben as the *avant*, and we parents as passengers in the midsection, the boys took their voyageur canoeing test, using our full size paddles. With no adult help, they traveled upriver for a quarter-mile around a curve, turned around, returned, and landed the canoe at the campsite. After having eagerly anticipated this event for nearly a year, the boys had finally passed the voyageur exam and had earned their sashes, at ages seven and five! With much ceremony, their father wrapped their tiny waists with new, brightly colored woven sashes, after which the beaming pair had their portrait taken together in front of the canoe, as proud as two peacocks.

At 10:30, we departed downstream, under a powder blue sky that was smeared with some wispy white streamers. Over the course of the next 31/2 miles, we handled three sets of rapids, first paddling down the fast current of Rapides Les Épingles (Straight Pin Rapids). Then, at both Portage des Grosses Roches and Décharge Campion, we portaged the gear and then zoomed happily down the rapids in the empty craft. The first of these two décharges was done on the left shore, where the 150 pace trail led us over knee-high boulders, hence the name Big Rocks Portage. The second décharge was carried out along the right shore, involving a carry of 180 paces. After taking a lunch break below the third set of rapids (in Champlain Provincial Park), we passed over the old Décharge des Roses, which can now be paddled, since the floodwaters behind the Hurdman Dam near Mattawa now extend upriver as far as this locale and cover the low rocks.

Warmed by the early-afternoon sun, we glided smoothly down the much wider, dam-flooded river for another 3 1/2 miles, beneath high, broadly rounded slopes that were thickly clad with evergreens. In this wide-open setting, with the many rapids and falls now behind us, it felt very relaxing to cruise quietly, passing entire battalions of tall trees marching from the white-smeared blue sky right down to the water's edge. When we reached L'Auberge, where our car had been kept during our voyage, we decided to end our trip here at 3:00, rather than paddling the remaining five miles of flooded Mattawa River down to the town of Mattawa. We would cover that final stretch two years later, when we would paddle the upper Ottawa River.

This day, we had covered seven miles, bringing to 35 our total for the trip; we had also run five rapids and had made ten portages during the journey. During each of the four days on the water, we had been blessed with ideal weather, which we interpreted as a good omen for our long-term family project on the mainline route. On this river, which we apparently had all to ourselves, we had learned a great deal, and we had increased our canoe-trekking competency. The Kents were now determined to take on the next and more challenging segment in 1985.

After departing from L'Auberge (flying down the asphalt highway at 60 m.p.h., which seemed amazing after paddling for days at 3 m.p.h.) we visited Ft. St. Joseph, on St. Joseph Island in northern Lake Huron. This was the locale to which the British forces had moved in 1796 (staying until 1812), after being required to vacate the post on Mackinac Island and depart from American territory. During those sixteen years, the local native population had built a considerable number of birchbark canoes for the military and fur trade personnel on the island. En route home, we also attended, as observing visitors, a rendezvous of reenactors of French and native lifeways at Ft. Michilimackinac at the Straits.

IV

Second Voyage
La Vase River, Lake Nipissing, French River, and Georgian Bay
June 16-26, 1985

Ce ne sont pas les mots qui comptent mais les actions.
(literally: It is not the words that count, but the actions.
figuratively: Actions speak louder than words.)
French proverb

*Life is like playing a violin in public
And learning the instrument as one goes on.*
Samuel Butler

*I am always doing that which I cannot do
In order that I may learn how to do it.*
Pablo Picasso

We knew in advance that this year's excursion would be much more demanding than the voyage on the Mattawa had been the previous year. First of all, it would be considerably longer, over 125 miles, and those particular miles would require greater lake and river paddling skills, including traveling for the first time on one of the Great Lakes. In addition, much of the trip would take place in settings that were considerably more remote. Even the arrangements with the shuttle driver were more complicated.

After my C.S.O. concert on Saturday evening, Doree and the boys picked me up outside of Orchestra Hall in downtown Chicago at 10:30 P.M., ready for the long drive that lay ahead. As we drove throughout the night and all of the next morning, up the center of Michigan and eastward from Sault Ste. Marie, I managed to get in two hours of sleep. Fifteen hours after departure, we connected at 1:30 P.M. with the shuttle driver in Wahnipitae, twelve miles east of

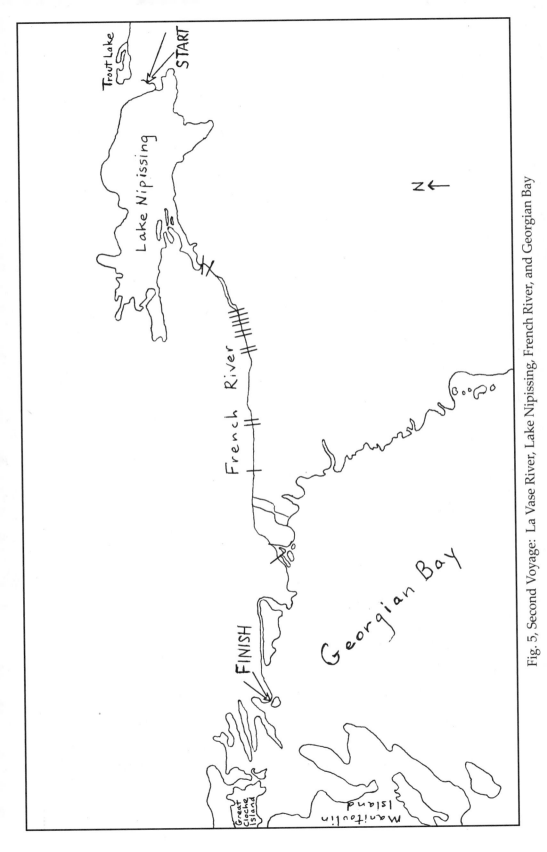

Fig. 5, Second Voyage: La Vase River, Lake Nipissing, French River, and Georgian Bay

Sudbury. The young man, an employee of a lodge on Georgian Bay in Killarney, had been driven by a colleague 65 miles north, to meet us and ride with us to North Bay. From our rendezvous point, it took only 1 1/2 hours to cover the seventy miles to our put-in location, on the La Vase River just south of the town of North Bay, after which the driver took our vehicle back to Killarney to await our eventual arrival there. Unbeknown to us, various of the other staff members of the lodge laid bets with him as to when (and even if!) we would eventually show up to retrieve our car.

Day One

By 4:45 P.M., we had loaded the canoe, tied down the packs, and were happily cruising down the Rivière La Vase (Mud River), traveling the two miles to its mouth at Lake Nipissing. This lowest stretch of the La Vase, the only portion of the waterway that is now wide enough and clear of obstructions for practical canoeing, represented two of the five paddling miles in the voyageur route that connected Trout Lake to Lake Nipissing (plus two miles of portaging). As we descended the river, we were pleased to see a great blue heron, a finch, and a number ducks.

At the mouth of the river, on the eastern shore of the lake, we halted to study the attractive monument that had been erected in Champlain Park, to honor the legions of canoe travelers who had passed this spot centuries earlier. The eight-foot-tall pyramid, built of mortar-laid stones, displays on each of its four faces a different bronze plaque depicting a historic scene, while its pinnacle bears a bronze sculpture of a beaver gnawing the bark from a tender sapling. I captured the scene on film, along with our own two young descendants of voyageurs and traders: Kevin, age 8 3/4, and Ben, age 6 11/12.

A wide peninsula juts deeply into the southeastern end of Lac Nipissing. As a result, the mainline canoe route, extending from the mouth of the La Vase to the southern shore of the lake and then westward toward its outlet (the French River), involved a southwesterly passage of eleven miles that was very dangerous when the weather was not cooperative. It first required a traverse across a wide bay, then a paddle of several miles along the end of the peninsula, and finally a second traverse across an even broader bay, all in an area that was often whipped by prevailing westerly winds.

Since the weather was very favorable on this occasion, with robin's egg blue skies, some hanging white clouds, and only a slight breeze out of the southeast, Doree and I easily made the first bay crossing, while singing voyageur songs. After traveling this first stretch of four miles in an hour and twenty minutes, we skirted along the shoreline of the end of the peninsula for another 3 1/2 miles. When we reached the second bay, and were floating amid a group of tiny offshore islets, we faced the decision of whether to make the traverse or not. It was 8:40 P.M., after an all-night drive from Chicago and a productive evening of paddling behind us. But this stretch was often a wind-swept and dangerous crossing, and at this moment it was glassy smooth; in addition, the sky had now entirely cleared, and the inviting orange orb low on the horizon in front of us offered plenty of encouragement. So I leaned on my crew to cross the bay, in spite of our fatigue, as a Father's Day gift to me from the family. During the 4 1/2 mile traverse, which we covered in an hour and twenty minutes, a spectacular orange and purple sunset lifted our spirits for much of the way.

When we reached the shoreline at 10:00, in complete darkness, we managed to find a campsite on a large barren rock ledge that sloped up gradually from the water's edge. After building a cheery fire, we spent two hours setting up camp with only the flickering light from the blaze, since the flashlight had given out almost immediately, in spite of having brand new batteries.

While crossing the second bay, as we had paddled just to the north of the group of ten Gull Islands in the dark, we had heard what sounded like a massive flock of gulls there. At our campsite nearly two miles away, we continued to hear their raucous activity on the islands during the entire setup procedure, and while we drifted off to a very welcome sleep. This day, between 4:45 and 10 P.M., we had advanced two miles on the La Vase River and twelve miles on Lake Nipissing, blessed with beautiful weather all the way.

Day Two

Today would be overcast and dreary, with occasional showers on and off all day and evening. At 11:00 we put in, eager for a chance to try out our newly rigged, provisional canoe sail. The sailing rig consisted of the rubber head from a toilet plunger, placed on the floor of the canoe with its slender hollow end facing upward to receive and hold the wooden mast; a radiator clamp to fasten the upright mast to the second thwart from the bow; two nylon cords running from the tip of the mast down to the center thwart, serving as guy lines to hold the mast securely upright; a square sail of blue nylon fabric (the floor of an old pup tent); a long nylon line passing through an iron staple driven into the top of the mast, to raise and lower the upper boom of the sail; and two long lines attached to the ends of the lower boom of the sail and extending back to the thwart in front of me at the stern, to control the angle of the sail to the wind. We had a medium breeze blowing from the southeast to assist us in traveling northwest, and, to our great delight, the sail pulled the canoe forcefully over the water!

Even a light-to-moderate assist from a sail was very helpful during a long-distance trip, as the voyageurs knew so well. At minimum, a following wind kept the canoe gliding steadily forward while the paddles were brought forward for each new stroke. And the stronger the wind blew, the more it increased the forward speed of the craft while requiring less effort from the paddlers. During the entire French period of the fur trade, virtually every canoe was equipped with an official sailing rig. Contrary to the depictions of many modern historians, sails were not usually cobbled together by using a tarp or a blanket, a rope, and a couple of poles when the wind was from a helpful direction. The square sail that was carried on each craft, made of tightly-woven linen cloth, ranged in size from four by six feet for the smallest canoes up to nine by ten feet for the largest 36 foot craft. Fr. Charlevoix noted in 1721 just how helpful these wind-harnessing devices were: "All of these canoes, the smallest not excepted, carry sail, and with a favorable wind, make twenty leagues [61 English miles] a day. Without sails, you must have able canoe men to make twelve [36 miles] in still water."

As we glided steadily along, about a quarter-mile out from the low shoreline covered with spruce, pines, and birches, we covered four miles in 1 1/3 hours, with just light paddling to supplement the sail power. Upon reaching Pointe de la Croix (Cross Point), we decided to pause for a lunch break. This was the location where the voyageurs had erected wooden crosses in honor of their colleagues who had drowned during Lake Nipissing crossings. Since this body of water lay in a generally east-west direction, and was very shallow for its size, prevailing westerly winds could easily arrive unannounced, roar down the fifty-mile length of the lake, and whip it very quickly into a maelstrom of raging waves. These dangerous seas would batter the eastern end of the lake, where the canoes were completely exposed during their passage of eleven miles from the La Vase River mouth to the minimal protection of the southern shore. Along this stretch of the mainline route, a disproportionate number of capsizes and drownings had occurred on a regular basis.

From Point de la Croix, six more miles of westward sailing and paddling brought us to the exit of Lake Nipissing and the beginning of the Rivière des Français (French River), marked by an array of islands of all sizes. Leaving the water at 3:30, having covered ten miles for the day, we camped on a small islet south of Brown Island. To celebrate our safe passage of 22 miles over the potentially dangerous lake, we feasted on a traditional voyageur meal of pea soup and galette, while loons floating on the bay nearby kept us company with their tremulous calls. Nestled in our sleeping bags by 7:30, we slept like logs for a full twelve hours.

Day Three

A chilly, grey day, one that would be entirely spent laboring against head winds, as we began our travels down the 72 mile length of the French River, headed southwestward toward Georgian Bay of Lake Huron. The cheering aspect of this situation was that, had we still been on the exposed shores of Lake Nipissing, we would have been windbound, not advancing at all against the domineering wind and waves. Doree and I packed up the gear in the tent while the boys entertained themselves outside in the light rain; but the rainfall stopped for a time to facilitate our loading and launching.

We began our forward progress at 10:45, paddling against a rather strong head wind and medium waves to advance five miles in two hours, before taking a lunch break for an hour on an islet south of Bragdon Island. Then we dug in against a more formidable head wind and larger waves for another 1 1/2 miles, followed by a second one-hour rest in a long, slender inlet on the south shore. Here, I practiced in the rain while sitting on a barren ledge at the water's edge, ending with a particular tune that was chosen to cheer the forces: "Raindrops keep falling on my head...Cryin's not for me..." Again on the move, we contended with strident waves and a persistent head wind to make another 3 1/2 miles.

We finally left the water at 5:45, after having worked very diligently to advance ten miles for the day. Doree (who is just 5 feet 2 inches and weighs 115 pounds) had paddled great during the entire trial of seven cold and rainy hours, steadily laboring from her position in the bow seat and leading us in such songs as *Vent Frais* and *En Roulant Ma Boule Roulant*. The exertion had kept our upper bodies relatively warm, swathed in polypropylene underwear, a shirt, hooded sweatshirt, and hooded raingear. But our hands, swollen from the long day of constant hard pulling against the oncoming wind, and exposed to the cold driving rain, felt like numb claws.

At our campsite on the sheltered east end of Wright Island, we reveled in finally finding ourselves out of the grip of the westerly winds. For the first time, we set up a shelter for cooking and eating, suspending the large tarp of brown nylon fabric from two trees and two upright paddles with a long, white nylon cord. After a restorative meal of whitefish stew with noodles and vegetables, plus a side dish of stewed apples, we absorbed the cheery warmth of the fire under the shelter. At the farthest reach of the yellow glow of the flames, darkness enveloped the trees. Finally shedding our wet shoes, socks, and trousers, we were stretched out on our air mattresses in the tent by 9:30, lulled to delicious dreams by the calling of loons on the bay.

When a sugar low haunted me during the night, I forced myself out of the tent for a hit on the peanut butter container, which was hanging from a tree.

Day Four

Spending two hours of the morning under the rain shelter beside a crackling fire, drying out the boy's clothes, seemed to make their day start easier. While basking in the warmth of the blaze, we chatted about the ancient history of the French River. The rebounding of the Earth's crust after the immensely heavy glaciers had retreated far to the north had caused a height of land to slowly rise just east of the present Lake Nipissing; this eventually halted the eastward outflow of water from the upper three Great Lakes and Georgian Bay, around 2,000 B.C. Over the following thousand years or so, further tilting of the land mass caused Georgian Bay to recede westward, leaving Lake Nipissing as a separate body of water, instead of as an arm of Georgian Bay. By about 800 B.C., after further rebounding action, Lake Nipissing had developed an outlet river flowing westward, the

French River. The course of the river followed a network of intersecting fault lines in the Canadian Shield bedrock, massive cracks that had formed before the glacial era. As a result, the overall waterway consists of a labyrinth of rockbound passageways that resembles more a collection of long and very slender lakes and channels than a typical river; its generally straight segments have very few bends and curves. From the outlet of Lake Nipissing to the westernmost outlet of the river at Georgian Bay, the waterway drops about 58 feet in elevation, over a southwestward and westward course of about 66 miles (our meandering course on the river would measure about six miles longer).

From our departure at 10:30 under lead-colored skies, Kevin paddled two miles in the bow, to reach the Portage Chaudière des Français. This portage path on the left shore entirely skirted the area of the Upper and Lower Chaudière Rapids, as well as the modern dam above them which controls the level of Lake Nipissing. The name Kettle (Chaudière) Rapids had been applied because of the several depressions that had been formed by whirling stones and sand in certain horizontal areas of the bedrock, when the torrents of the glacial lakes' outlet had flowed through here. The designation "of the French" was added to the name to distinguish these rapids on the French River from those with similar kettle-shaped depressions that were located on the Mattawa River. After making the 4/10 mile carry, which entailed a fifteen-minute walk each way over moderately rough terrain, we took a lunch break at the end of the trail. We had been pleased to find virtually no mosquitoes on this trip so far, after having endured so many hordes of them on the Mattawa the previous year. This was the one positive aspect of the windy conditions that had prevailed during the last two days.

After returning to the water at 1:00 and advancing half a mile, we came upon two beaver lodges in the same cove, as well as a mother mallard swimming quietly nearby with five babies in tow. A half-mile later, Kevin proudly ran his first rapids as a bow paddler, beside Keso Point. He then turned the *avant* position back to his mother, since she could handle the oncoming wind with much more strength and endurance. During the entire trek of nine miles from the portage lunch stop to our halt for the night, we faced a moderately strong head wind blowing from the southwest. Along certain sections of this route, which had the form of a long slender lake, we were able to hide behind various islands, to find some temporary shelter from *La Vieille*. Doree speculated that perhaps the voyageurs had given this name, "The Old Woman," to the wind because they found it to be an unpredictable nuisance, groaning and blustering, and because it also seemed vengeful at times. In response to *La Vieille*'s hindrances, we belted out the ancient ditty, "*L'autre jour sous un maronier...*" (The other day under a chestnut tree, I went there to sleep. The mosquitoes attacked, and I had to leave my chestnut tree.)

At about 5:30, we came ashore to camp beside Little Pine Rapids, the first of eleven rapids in a grueling sequence that had been dubbed the Five-Mile Rapids; we had covered 11 1/2 miles since the morning launch, tracing the full length of the Dokis First Nations Indian Reserve. The day had begun completely overcast and misting, and we had received some rain during the morning portage. But then the clouds had dispersed, and we had enjoyed beautiful sunny weather for the remainder of the day, although *La Vieille* had remained as our constant companion, blowing steadily into our faces.

The boys erected the tent, which was now their usual job, and gathered a good supply of dry wood for the fire. When the wind finally faded away in the evening, we encountered the first mosquitoes of the trip. After feasting on a stew of chicken and noodles, plus a treat of fried galette for dessert, we drifted off to sleep serenaded by the burbling of the gentle rapids that lay close at hand, whispering their ancient songs.

Day Five

Little did we know that this day would deliver a very big surprise. We started the morning by spreading all of the gear out on the rock ledges at the camp to dry in the sun, since everything had been dampened by several days of rain. Blessed with warm, beautiful weather for handling this extensive stretch of rapids, we finally set off at 10:30, and easily lined the loaded canoe down the right side of Petits Rapides des Pins (Little Pine Rapids), which was just a set of fast riffles. This was our very first experience with lining the canoe: Kevin hiked the bare shoreline ledges while holding the bow painter rope, while I followed with the stern painter, walking in the shallows. By lining instead of paddling, we could control the location of the canoe at all times as it slowly descended the rapids, by either bringing in or letting out the line at each end of the craft as needed. This strategy involved slow, cautious work, but it nearly always kept the canoe intact and the gear dry. Every French canoe was equipped with one or two towing lines, totaling about fifty feet in length, which were made of hempen linen cords twisted loosely together. In some cases, most of the crew members pulled a single line that was fastened to one or two of the thwarts near the bow, while the stern man, remaining in the craft, kept it away from the shore with a long pole.

After we had finished lining Petits Rapides des Pins, we proceeded a half-mile downriver to Grand Rapides des Pins (Big Pine Rapids), and also lined the loaded canoe there. In this instance, both Doree and I walked in thigh-deep water near the right shore, while handling the ropes. When we reached the final three-foot drop of these rapids, we decided that we would probably not be able to maintain control of the canoe while going down it. So we pulled the craft near shore, unloaded just the three big packs, and portaged them the few steps around the drop; then we carried the half-loaded canoe about fifteen feet, and reloaded it. A short distance downstream, we ran the Double Rapids (which actually had only a single drop) as well as the double set at the Ladder Rapids. In both of these cases, I did not scout the route first from the shoreline, but instead just stood up in the stern and determined the route that we would travel down the drop.

After taking a lunch break at noon just above the Petits Rapides Parisien, Doree and I easily sped down the upper set of Petits; a short distance ahead, the lower set awaited us in a narrow chute. At this point, I aimed the bow toward the left shore and pulled into a side bay, intending to rest a moment and read the rapids from the canoe. By doing this, I violated the "Number One Safety Rule" of river-runners: if a set of rapids is unfamiliar and is not entirely visible to you, you should get out on shore and scout its entire length. The section that we could see from the canoe looked manageable.

With full confidence, we started down the gentle slope, and quickly flashed through the various drops and obstacles. Then we entered the rather tall standing waves below, which had not been readable from above the drop. At the first haystack, we took in a little water, and at the second one some more. When the hull knifed through the third and tallest row of standing waves, we took in plenty of water, filling all of the spaces between and above the packs nearly up to the gunwales. At this point, the ungainly craft, wallowing deeply in the current but still pointed directly downstream, rolled over to the left in slow motion and dumped us out. Just at the moment we capsized, a heavy hailstorm suddenly pelted down on us! Shortly, it turned to rain, and an eerie mist began rising from the water.

At first, I was gasping for breath, since the water was so cold (even though I, like Tim, was wearing wet suit farmer-johns, without the long-sleeved wet suit top). With Ben holding fast at the bow beside me and Kevin and Tim doing the same at the stern, we kicked hard and maneuvered the overturned canoe through a number of whirlpools and big eddies over to the left shore. After turning the canoe back upright, Tim untied the pack that held our single change of clothes, and hoisted it onto the steaming rocks. The boys, who were perched on a ledge, shivering and shaking, stood like soldiers awaiting the next order. During a lull in the rain, I helped them locate and change into their dry outfits, while Tim bailed out the canoe. Although their teeth were chattering, the boys really maintained their dignity. At one point, the rain halted just long enough for them to don their dry clothes and their rain gear; then it poured hard again, and finally ended with hail for several minutes. Our first real capsize: we all survived. (Doree)

As soon as we were back on course, I informed the boys that a great assortment of items from capsized fur trade canoes had been discovered by divers in the pool below that very rapids, as well as half a mile upriver in the pool below the Ladder Rapids. The array of flintlock guns, gunflints, lead balls and shot, axes, knives, awls, scrapers, ice chisels, fire steels, brass kettles, brass thimbles, and thick brass wire that had been found on the bottom indicated that even highly experienced voyageurs had sometimes lost control of their craft, in the very same place as it had happened to us.

I wondered to myself: So why did we run these rapids if he knew there were some professional voyageurs who hadn't been able to pull it off? Then I glanced at Kevin and Ben, peering over the gunwales, studying the depths carefully, quickly forgetting how miserable they had been just a short time before. OK, I can be resilient, too! (Doree)

Soon the sky turned sunny and deep blue, with a few puffy clouds floating slowly by. That solitary rogue cloud, having unleashed its contents of rain and hail, had entirely disappeared. The mirror-like water reflected perfectly the shorelines of bare rock, scoured by ice and high water in the spring each year, as well as the spruce and pines standing tall behind, and the heavens above. As we paddled, we discussed one of the lessons that we had learned from our capsize adventure: when running a set of rapids that has very tall standing waves below a drop, we could avoid most of those waves by quickly turning off to the side and skirting the waves, after passing through the drop in its main tongue of deep water.

Very shortly downstream, we whisked down both the Devil's Chute and the Grand Parisien Rapids, after first checking each of them carefully from the shore. The Chute, in spite of bearing Lucifer's name, was an attractive narrow passage between a long slender island and the left shore. Finally, we easily shot down the double set of Rapides Croches (Crooked Rapids) in an S-shaped channel, after examining them from the canoe. Thus, we had completed eleven rapids in five miles, lining the first two and then running the remaining nine; this one stretch of the river had included the Devil's Chute plus seven named rapids, three of which had been double sets.

While we paddled four more miles, threatening dark grey and black clouds moved in menacingly low in the sky, but they resisted dropping any moisture on us. High on a huge, nearly barren rock incline, two white crosses stood solemnly, paying tribute to travelers who had died while en route along this stretch of the river. Just as we glided by this hill of rock, bright sunlight pierced the brooding sky and showered the incline with golden rays. The scene brought to mind the comment that Nicholas Garry, Deputy-Governor of the Hudson's Bay Company, had recorded during his westward voyage in 1821: "To every rapid is attached a melancholy history of canoes lost, and the crosses or burial places you meet with everywhere prove that they are but too true."

We stopped to closely examine an inlet where a beaver colony had once resided in an offshore lodge. When the water level had been high, the lower portion of the lodge, as well as the winter food supply of birch and poplar saplings stuck into the adjacent muddy bottom of the river, had been submerged. Now, with the water level three to four feet lower, the whole area was entirely dry and unusable. In addition to building the snug lodge, the flat-tailed rodents had also excavated a long curved canal in the shallows of the marshy shoreline area, to facilitate both traveling and hauling food and construction materials; this extensive shallow ditch skirted around the entire end of the inlet. It too, had all become dry land, due to the major drop in the water level.

Locating a campsite one mile east of Île Parisien at 6:30, we spread out all of the gear and clothing to dry, festooning each of the nearby rock ledges and bushes. Then we enjoyed a well-deserved feast, and repacked until midnight. We had covered nine miles today, including eleven rapids and our first unintentional capsize. We had no way of knowing that numerous other capsizes, more dramatic and dangerous than this initial one, lay in wait in our future.

Day Six

At breakfast, we ravenously devoured Doree's homemade gorp mixture: oatmeal, almonds, peanuts, various seeds, raisins, brown sugar, and chocolate chips, all mixed together and baked in the oven. When we parents had finished repacking the gear, and Kevin had completed his rather large sand sculpture depicting the Turtle Spirit, we put our paddles to the water at 11:30. By 3:00, we had covered ten miles under a gentle blue sky and cotton-ball clouds, and paused for a one-hour lunch break, just across the channel from the French River First Nations Indian Reserve. As we munched our meal of crackers loaded with a thick mixture of peanut butter and honey, we discussed a local tradition that extended back several centuries. This particular bend in the river's course was called Le Coude de l'Enfant Perdu (the Lost Child Bend). According to the ancient legend, a native woman had placed her little child on the shore here and had turned away for just a short time, but the baby vanished. A great search was made both along the riverbanks and in the water, but no clues to the child's demise could ever be found, even though its cries could be heard for six days. The only explanation that The People could imagine for this tragedy was that bad spirits had taken the little one away.

Proceeding two miles to the tiny community of French River, we stopped to buy flashlights. Shortly thereafter, the river narrowed to pass through an attractive section called the French River Gorge, flanked on both sides by vertical cliffs. This two-mile stretch brought us to the Sault du Recollet (Recollet Falls). As our bow approached the rim of the thundering precipice, I was concerned that the portage landing on the left shore, located just a few yards above the brink of the seven-foot drop, was dangerously close to the edge, considering the heavy amount of water that was flowing over the lip and the strength of the current. In fact, this had been a very real danger for the voyageurs in their heavily loaded craft, if they did not approach by closely hugging the left shore. Proof of this lies in the array of fur-trade-era artifacts that have been found by divers in the pool below.

An elevated wooden boardwalk for sliding power boats around the falls, built in about 1955 on the left shore over the original portage route of 50 yards, certainly made easy footing for our carry.

A mile below the falls, we ran the First Rapids, which was simply a ledge of rock extending across the river. Some 31/2 miles later, we landed to camp at 8:15, just east of the Second Rapids (which would be the penultimate rapids on the river; we would encounter one more set two days later, in the delta area). This day, we had covered twenty miles in 6 1/2 hours of paddling time, under mostly ideal canoeing conditions, and had spent an additional hour on our lunch break and another hour making the carry around the Recollet Falls.

<u>Day Seven</u>

Afloat at 10:30, we were appreciative of the beautiful sunny weather, with an air temperature of about 60 degrees and a medium breeze at our backs as we headed due west. It looked to be a perfect paddling day; however, those conditions were not to last for long. After running the small drop of the Second Rapids, we advanced five miles on the gleaming surface of the water, with each boy taking his turn in the bow seat. Every time Kevin and Ben paddled, it was obvious to us parents that they each felt more grown-up, and they actually became a little more mature. Along this five-mile stretch, we observed two great blue herons and a few pelicans; in addition, several eagles cruised high in the sky above us, circling with little effort on the rising air currents.

As we approached the open waters of Lac du Boeuf (Ox Bay), we could see in the distance whitecaps coming from the south, signalling the arrival of a new and much less benign weather front. At 11:45, when we arrowed out onto the open water of the bay, we suddenly found ourselves in three to four foot waves, and we quickly realized that we had no chance of making it safely across to the far shore. With some trepidation, we laid into our paddles to turn 90 degrees to the right, and plunged forward in the heavy surf to a narrow rocky inlet on the north shore. During all of this action, the boys were completely silent. Luckily for us, the cove had a sandy beach with a gradual rock ledge rising behind it; the place offered refuge to get off the water, but it also bore the direct, unbroken force of the southerly wind.

Using a couple of small driftwood logs, Doree and I quickly rolled the loaded craft out of the water to safety, and then we all threw together an improvised shelter against the gusting wind and the driving rain. Handy building materials included driftwood logs, broken pieces of a wooden boat, and even a section of a wooden dock, which had all been washed up previously. As we all huddled beneath the little makeshift structure, we were quite relieved to be safely on shore and under some sort of roof. After catching my breath, I brought out the trumpet and regaled the family with my usual practice routine, which was rather loud at the close range of two feet. Then we switched to a family sing-along with trumpet accompaniment, enjoying such appropriate tunes as *Michael Row Your Boat Ashore*. When it became clear that we were to be landlocked here for several hours while the storm raged, we built a fire under the shelter (which was a bit of a challenge with only wet materials at hand), and cooked pea soup as the main course and noodle soup as the side dish. After being windbound at this place of refuge for six hours, we eagerly departed in calm conditions at 5:45, and proceeded another seven miles.

It was a beautiful evening for paddling. Directly west of our emergency layover site lay the entrances of the three traditional paddling routes that each led out to Georgian Bay. One mile from our site, at the western end of Ox Bay, the Canoe Channel of the river headed due south; eight miles of paddling, including a jog to the west at about the middle of the passage, would take travelers out by way of the Eastern Outlet of the river. A second route began a mile west of Ox Bay. Here, the Main Channel extended southward over seven miles of paddling to Georgian Bay, again with a westward jog at about the midpoint, by way of the Main Outlet. These two routes would have been utilized by canoe travelers when they were headed for southern Georgian Bay, to the traditional lands of the Hurons and the Petuns about a hundred miles to the south. Our ancestor Etienne Racine would have taken one of these two passages when he traveled to the Jesuit mission center of Ste. Marie-Among-the-Hurons in 1644, and again when he departed from there in 1646, bound for Montreal.

Those travelers who were headed westward on Georgian Bay, destined for the upper Great Lakes region on the mainline route (like we were and like many of our other ancestors had been), did not usually take either of these channels. Instead, they continued due west at the place where the Main Channel turned south, paddling on the Western Channel of the river. Eight miles of westward and then southwestward travel along this route led to the three Western Outlets of the river, in its delta area.

From our layover site on Ox Bay, after cruising smoothly for about three miles along the Western Channel, Doree spotted two black bear cubs running on the top of the rock cliff that lined the north shore. We immediately stopped paddling, to quietly take in the scene. Almost immediately, the little ones snorted and then noisily scrambled up a tall pine. After we had watched and listened to them for a couple of minutes, floating at a safe distance offshore, the mother bear emerged from the tree line, looked us over casually, and then shuffled back into the woods. In our offshore location, we apparently offered little threat to her babies. It was difficult for us to imagine that these two little cubs, now only five or six months old, would eventually bulk up at maturity to as much as 500 pounds for females and a hulking 900 pounds for males. We wondered what they would encounter during their lives, which could stretch up to as long as thirty years.

While we glided over the placid surface of the evening calm, we discussed the history of the native people who had lived for thousands of years in the Canadian Shield country. I told the boys how humans had first entered the southern portions of the region around 11,000 years ago, after the retreat of the glaciers, and over the next several thousand years, they had gradually advanced further and further to the north. Living by hunting, trapping, fishing, and gathering, they migrated seasonally in an annual circuit that took full advantage of the various food sources that were available at different times of the year. Those groups farthest to the north followed the seasonal migrations of the caribou herds. The Shield people generally lived in small, extended family groups during the fall, winter, and spring, and in the summer gathered to live communally, often beside a river or a lake, where they fished and also carried out some trading. A network of exchange developed across the entire region, with such articles as furs, food items, woven mats, flint, pottery vessels, native copper, fishing nets, hematite or red ocher for paint, and shells being traded during summer gatherings and trading trips. The immense network of interconnected waterways served as the primary avenues for hauling considerable amounts of food supplies and trade items; these liquid highways were augmented by overland trails. About 1,500 to 2,000 years ago, those groups who lived on the southern fringes of the Shield country, where the soil was more fertile, adopted agriculture from their more southerly neighbors. As farming became more established over time for these people, they tended to remain in a permanent village location year round. Their surplus amounts of corn, beans, squash, pumpkins, sunflowers, gourds, and tobacco were added to the array of articles that were already being traded with those groups that lived further to the north.

As Tim talked, Kevin and Ben could comprehend most of this information, since many of their bedtime stories since birth had been about native people and ancient ways of life. But in this instance, after a long day of traveling, their heads sometimes drooped a little. Tim continued, as much for me and himself as for them. (Doree)

By about four hundred years ago, various tribal groups had become well established in different regions of the Shield country, where they were first encountered by the French when they arrived in North America during the late 1500s. Surveying from east to west, the Montagnais occupied the region to the north of the St. Lawrence that extended from the lower reaches of the river westward to about the St. Maurice River. Various groups of Algonkins and Northern Algonkins lived from the St. Maurice River westward to Georgian Bay and along the eastern portion of Lake Huron's northern shore, while Ojibwa groups resided in the western portion of Lake Huron's north shore and along Lake Superior's east coast. Ottawa groups occupied certain areas of the Georgian Bay coastline, as well as all of the Bruce Peninsula and Manitoulin Island. North of all of these nations lived various groups of Crees, while the Huron, Petun, and Neutral nations resided south of Georgian Bay. On the eastern section of the mainline canoe route, groups of Algonkins were found along the entire Ottawa River Valley, while various groups of northern Algonkins (such as the Nipissings) occupied the region of the Mattawa River, Lake Nipissing, the French River, and Georgian Bay. Ottawas also lived and traded on Georgian Bay.

Physical evidence of the early native people who once lived along the French River has survived in the form of pictographs. These ancient paintings, done on prominent faces of rock cliffs with a mixture of pulverized red ocher and animal fat or fish oil, were sometimes noted in the travel journals of fur trade personnel. For example, John Macdonnel wrote in 1793 of "various figures of animals etc. made by them on the face of the steep rocks in many places along the banks. Some leagues below Derreaud's Rapid is a figure of a man standing over an animal that lays under him...Two leagues from Lake Huron there is a figure of an ox, which gives name to a fine long view of the river called Lac du Boeuf [Ox Bay]." At these and other sacred sites, shamans over the centuries had drawn images of people, animals, canoes, and various objects that figured prominently in the spiritual beliefs of The People. When paddling past these locales, native travelers typically left an offering of some sort, often a small amount of tobacco. When Frenchmen began traveling these waterways of the interior, they very often adopted this native custom as well, leaving offerings of tobacco.

By now, I was paddling along in a very relaxed semi-trance, thinking about pictographs and searching the rock cliffs that we passed for traces of them, all the while considering how my life would have been as one of The People. (Doree)

Having finished for now our discussion of the original inhabitants of this region, and having logged twelve miles for the day, we halted at 8:30. Our site lay three miles northeast of the entrance to the Western Outlets, and seven miles from the open waters of Georgian Bay on our route. As had now become customary when arriving at a new campsite, Kevin set up the tent entirely by himself, needing adult help only for a couple of tall-person steps. The mosquitoes had become pretty fierce by this evening, calling for head nets, but we still had not encountered a single black fly, for which we were thankful.

Day Eight

When we emerged from the tent at 7:00, it was clear that the westerly wind and waves had picked up too much for us to travel; we were to be windbound in camp for a time. After the boys had played a few games with the miniature set of checkers and we had all enjoyed a leisurely breakfast, we slowly packed up, and at 11:00 decided to give it a try. After digging in against a strong head wind and big whitecaps for a half-hour, we had crawled forward only 3/4 mile. Then we were grounded for two hours in a sheltered cove, where further tournaments of checkers were played out between the two brothers on a bare rock ledge. At 1:00 we tried again, since the waves had reduced slightly. Slogging our way forward a couple more miles, we reached the entrance of the Western Outlets, where the waves flattened out but a moderate head wind still persisted. When our arrival alarmed a female mallard with seven ducklings, the mother floundered off to the left, acting as if she had a broken wing, to draw us away from her babies, who stayed along the right shore.

Of the three channels that fanned out like fingers in the Western Outlets, we took the center one, the Old Voyageur Channel. On the first detailed map that was produced of this specific area, created by the Geological Survey of Canada between 1847 and 1857, this central passage was labeled as the "Old Traveled Channel." As we approached its entryway, beneath completely overcast skies, the channel seemed to invite us to follow its narrow, island-studded passage. Once we were gliding down its waters, flanked on both sides by steep rock walls, we had the distinct and spooky sensation that the surface of the water was angling decidedly downhill, in the direction of the flow. After one mile, we reached the Petite Faucille (Little Sickle), a small rapids with a three-foot drop in the middle of a crescent-shaped, sharp bend in the river. We carried over the 25-pace portage on the left shore, crossing over the curved interior area of the "sickle."

A half-mile downstream, the channel narrowed to a very slender, straight passage about 100 yards long, with smooth cliff walls that sloped away from the water at a considerable angle. It was clear why the voyageurs had named this very distinctive feature La Dalle (the Eaves Trough). When John Bigsby traveled this way in 1819, he noted, "Our canoe flashed through it almost in a moment. Either of its sides I could have touched with a walking-stick." Two years later, Nicholas Garry described this particular place as "the banks of high rocks on each side so confined as scarcely to allow the canoe to pass; it had the appearance of a canal cut in the rock." Continuing down this channel, we made an abrupt turn to the west, and were immediately led to an extensive maze of channels and islands that filled the entrance to Georgian Bay, containing three major islands plus another three hundred or so smaller islands and individual shoals.

Skirting along the northernmost edge of the rocky maze for two miles, as far as we could go, I then turned our bow toward the southwest, again keeping to the outermost edge of the maze, parallel to the mainland. At 5:00, we were halted by a thunderstorm that dropped hail rather than raindrops, a half-mile from the final exposed entry into Georgian Bay; here we spent an hour eating and resting, and I practiced. This was the general location of La Grand Prairie (the Big Meadow), a broad and flat expanse of comfortable mainland that had offered a welcome campsite for all of the members of even a large brigade to gather. At this site, they had rested, repaired their canoes, and awaited favorable weather, before venturing out onto the open waters of Georgian Bay.

Like it or not, it was now our time to paddle onto those very waters. As we proceeded along the north shore of Georgian Bay for a mile-and-a-half, rocky shoals, some barely exposed above the surface and others slightly submerged, broke much of the force of the rough oncoming waves for a time. However, when we finally advanced beyond these helpful features, we were very soon forced ashore to camp, at 6:30. Our campsite, 2 3/4 miles northeast as the crow flies from Pointe Grondine, lay six miles west of the mouth of the Main Channel of the French River. Whenever westbound fur trade canoes had utilized the Western Outlets (as we had) rather than the Main Channel passage, they would have remained sheltered in the maze for these six miles, rather than traveling on the open lake. However, low water levels in the river may have sometimes forced brigades of the largest, heavily loaded craft to use the Main Channel, even if it did entail six extra miles on the open water.

After a long and arduous day, we had progressed just ten miles. Up to this point, we had completed 96 miles on our voyage, covering the La Vase River and Lake Nipissing in two days of paddling, and then the French River in 5 1/2 days on the water.

Day Nine

BRIIIIIIIIIIIING. I awakened to the alarm clock at 5 A.M., having set it with the hope of advancing westward on the exposed waters before the wind kicked up for the day. But when I heard the surf crashing against the bare rock shoreline not far from our tent, I knew that we were going nowhere, and returned to my dreams. We slept deliciously for a total of ten hours, resting well after our accomplishments of the previous week, and finally arose at 8:00. The westerly wind and the accompanying waves had not calmed at all during the night; they were just as vigorous as when we had been blown ashore the previous evening.

At midday, I made a feast of chicken stew with noodles. Afterward, Tim and the boys scarfed down the dessert of fried galette saturated in brown sugar syrup. (Doree)

By good fortune, our windbound time was to be spent under a

pale azure sky, tufts of lazy white clouds, and a beaming sun. As an added bonus, the wind had blown away all of the mosquitoes: this was pretty close to the Buddhist nirvana! To pass the time, we explored our landscape, which consisted mostly of pinkish granite bedrock interlaced with seams of milky white quartzite. For a considerable distance back from the water's edge, the rock was nearly barren, where raging storms and grinding cakes of lake ice had kept it well scoured century after century. In scattered locations, some short grasses and stunted bushes clung tenaciously to life, in places where a meager layer of soil had gathered in cracks and hollows in the rock. Further inland, where a thicker layer of sandy soil had accumulated, the sparse forest was made up of individual pines, widely spaced and often artistically distorted from a lifetime of buffeting westerly winds. We had set up our camp on the bed of reddish bronze pine needles beneath these trees, encircled and further sheltered by low bushes.

Lake waves had lapped and pounded this shoreline of solid rock for many thousands of years. From the viewpoint of the gulls that wheeled high above us, the scene extending westward for about fifteen miles looked as if many hundreds of whales and dolphins were frolicking in each of the deep bays and in the offshore waters. The bare backs of some were exposed to the sun, while others were visible only in the troughs between waves, and hundreds more were barely submerged. The surface of the water offered a strange sight, as the waves broke with white plumes of spray over considerable numbers of these rocky shoals that were otherwise mostly hidden from view. Whenever the wind and waves would subside in the following days, our paddling route would pass through this immense herd of whale-like shoals.

During the course of the relaxing day, we lounged in the warm sun, sitting with our backs against the overturned canoe, carried on long discussions, and did some woodcarving. Kevin's first masterpiece was a wooden knife, while Ben altered a naturally curved section of dried pine limb into a mythical creature that I immediately dubbed the Nipissing Nipple Nibbler.

The boys loved their Dad's change of character, as he chased them playfully amid the smooth undulations in the barren bedrock, growling, "I'm the Nipissing Nipple Nibbler, and I'm going to get you!" At times such as these, they and I learned about the lighter side of paddling trips, and of their Dad, who had such a serious side when it came to survival out here in the wilderness, and on stage at Orchestra Hall, where he performed for about 10,000 people each week in three or four concerts.

Just when I had begun to ache and brood just a little on this trip, Mother Nature had stepped in to hold us captive on this wind-swept, water-worn, granite bedrock for a day and a half. The kids and I would have probably enjoyed a full week, or at least several days, of kicking back in the sun here. Looking at my swollen hands, I vainly assessed how much damage the trip was inflicting; but after a day, I saw the swelling disappear. Like I regularly told my adolescent patients in the outpatient program of the psych hospital, "What doesn't kill you will make you strong." I would frequently tell them that a too-soft life would poorly prepare them for the big-time events of life, and that taking their fixes of drugs was but a respite, and would surely make life less endurable in the long run. Lying here in the warm sun upon thousands of years of Nature's creation, I closed my eyes, watched the reddish lining of my sun-drenched eyelids, and occasionally napped. (Doree)

Since we were on a canoe trip, it was only natural that many of my thoughts and some of our family discussions would focus on canoes. These vessels were one of the most ancient forms of watercraft, developed and refined by the native populations over thousands of years before the arrival of Europeans in North America. Among the two general types of native watercraft, the dugout canoe and the bark canoe, dugouts were the much more ancient invention. A dugout was a major advancement over a single floating log or two or more logs lashed together as a raft. One large log that was flattened somewhat on the bottom, tapered at one or both ends, and hollowed out on its interior was considerably more navigable, and also more efficient for hauling cargo and people, than one or more unaltered logs. In comparison, the much more complicated concept of a craft whose exterior was made of tree bark was not developed until thousands of years after the first dugouts. Dugout canoes, carved from a single log, were used by the native populations for a wide variety of tasks, not just for transportation. In fact, both dugouts and bark canoes were often owned and used by the same group of people at the same time, with the two different types of vessels being employed for different purposes. Both of these craft were utilized for both short trips and long-distance traveling, as well as for hunting, fishing, and gathering. Compared to bark canoes, dugouts were much more durable under rough usage, and required considerably less care in their upkeep and storage. This durability led to their being used more often for certain rough tasks, like near-shore fishing in very rocky areas, and for traveling on certain waterways, such as those that were shallow and strewn with boulders. It is absolutely false that nearly all dugout canoes were heavy, ungainly vessels that tipped at the slightest provocation, and could not be paddled easily or portaged readily from one waterway to another. From my detailed study of nearly five hundred specimens across the U.S. and Canada, I knew that many thin-walled examples were relatively light in weight, and considerable numbers of them had sleek hulls that would have handled well.

The birchbark canoe was the most efficient craft for long-distance cargo transport across the huge grid of interconnected waterways, since these watercourses varied from shallow rivers to churning rapids to huge lakes the size of seas. Hauling cargo on these liquid highways required a vessel with a number of specific traits. These traits included a great load capacity of up to several tons, yet shallow draft; much strength and durability, yet light weight for easy portaging; plus speed and ease of paddling and handling. The birchbark canoe, besides possessing all of these necessary traits, could also be built and repaired using materials that were often found in the forests along the routes, with minimal tools.

One of the earliest instances of Europeans grasping the value of canoes took place in 1603, during Champlain's very first voyage to New France. When he traveled up the St. Lawrence River as far as the present Montreal, he learned that it was of no use trying to travel further into the interior in heavy ship's boats. The only practical craft would be bark canoes, with skilled native paddlers and guides assisting the Frenchmen. For both the native and the French populations, the fur trade involved hauling merchandise and supplies from the St. Lawrence Valley westward into the interior regions, and also hauling furs and hides eastward out to the St. Lawrence settlements. So the bark canoes were constructed at canoe yards both along the St. Lawrence and at various locales in the interior. Even when particular building yards in both the east and the west were eventually operated by Europeans, they employed mostly native men, women, and children to do the work.

Besides white birch, certain other types of tree bark were sometimes used in the construction of bark canoes in the Great Lakes region, such as spruce and elm. However, most of these were temporary or emergency vessels, not built for long-term use. In my discussions with Kevin and Ben, I said, "Most people don't know that a birchbark canoe was not a wooden craft over which the bark was eventually installed on the exterior." It was not like a European-devised cedar-strip canoe, with its canvas added atop the exterior surface after the hull had been completed. A birchbark canoe was essentially a long envelope of bark, which was strengthened along its two upper edges with long strips of wood. These gunwale strips were lashed to the inside and outside of the bark, with the top edge of the bark sandwiched between them. The lashings were done with peeled and split roots from such trees as spruce and pine. The top area of these lashings was protected from abrasion by a gunwale cap of wood, which was pegged to the gunwale "sandwich." Each of the ends of the bark envelope was also strengthened and stiffened on the interior, with a wooden end frame unit. This unit, composed of a curved stempiece, a vertical headboard, and one or more horizontal braces, was lashed together, and was also lashed inside the bark at the end of the hull, with the same root material. A number of wooden thwarts were lashed across the open top between the gunwales, to add rigidity and strength to the vessel. Since canoe bark was usually only about 1/8 inch or less in thickness, an interior lining of wood was required, so that the people and cargo traveling in the canoe would not break through the bark. The lining consisted of many very thin strips of split cedar, which were laid in an overlapping pattern and then held in position by the pressure of the curved ribs.

The various seams were sealed and made waterproof with pine or spruce pitch. However, after this gum was removed from the tree and hardened, it was brittle and broke easily. So it was heated and mixed with a certain amount of animal fat before it was applied to the craft. As a result, the gum tended to flex or dent when it was bent or abraded, rather than breaking. The black color of the sealant was created by adding some pulverized charcoal to the melted mixture. The charcoal had no known function; it just created a hue that the native builders considered attractive.

Tim was not generally a talkative person. But when he landed on one of the topics that he had so thoroughly researched and thought about for a decade, he had plenty to say. So, with our encouragement, he continued his "sermon on the granite mount." (Doree)

The traditional high-ended style of canoe that was built and used by the Great Lakes native populations for many centuries had a relatively tall bow that tended to cut and deflect high waves in rapids and on lakes. On shore, when the craft was unloaded and overturned, the high ends created enough head room to make an instant shelter for paddlers and cargo. Among the many thousands of canoes that were utilized during the fur trade era, by both natives and Europeans, many were of this style, and the others were offshoots of this style. The offshoot versions had ends that were broadened outward considerably and raised higher, with a top that was usually very rounded. In addition, at each curved end of the craft, the undercut portion of the lowest cutwater edge curved downward and inboard over a considerably longer span before reaching the horizontal keel line.

I wanted the boys to be very clear about two widespread myths pertaining to the birchbark canoes that were used for commercial and military operations during the fur trade era. We often read that Europeans improved upon the native canoes, and that they also enlarged the native craft, until most of them were up to forty feet long, were paddled by fifteen or sixteen voyageurs, and hauled a bizillion pounds of cargo. Visit most of the fur trade sites in North America, and the tour guides will tell you these falsehoods, and also hand you a pamphlet that records them in print. First of all, Europeans did not improve in any way on the highly sophisticated birchbark canoe, which had been developed and refined by its native inventors over the course of many centuries. As for the assertion that Europeans enlarged the size of native canoes, period documentation from as early as 1670 recorded native birchbark canoes that measured up to 32 feet in length. This size continued to be the largest version that was utilized by both native and French paddlers until 1729. Then, the French builder Louis Le Maître increased this dimension by just four feet, so that the very longest craft were a maximum of 36 feet long. Vessels for hauling cargo and troops never expanded beyond the 33 to 36 foot range during the entire fur trade period, and these longest vessels were paddled by a crew of seven to ten voyageurs, no more.

These largest *canots du Maître* or Montreal canoes carried about 60 to 65 pieces of cargo, and about ten containers holding the provisions for the trip; also on board were the items of traveling equipment, the crewmen, and their personal baggage. The weight of the entire contents of this largest craft, including the weight of the bodies of the ten paddlers, totaled 31/2 to 41/2 tons. To be sure, this total weight of the contents of the vessel, 7,000 to 9,000 pounds, was a very large amount. However, it was not the claimed five or six tons of trade merchandise that is often mistakenly quoted, a figure that supposedly does not even include the weight of the provisions, the equipment, and the men themselves.

As for the exaggerated number of voyageurs per canoe that is typically depicted, this has a lot to do with the famous nineteenth century paintings of the artist Frances Anne Hopkins, as well as a very specialized model of oversize craft that was developed in the 1790s. During that particular decade, a very limited number of craft measuring 37 to 40 feet in length were created; these were typically manned by a crew of fourteen to sixteen paddlers. However, these vehicles were the stretch limousines of the period. They were used exclusively for swiftly transporting the executives of the major fur trade companies along the routes between Montreal and the far-flung interior posts. They were never utilized on runs that carried standard cargo or troops. Since Ms. Hopkins and certain other nineteenth century artists painted a number of dramatic scenes that included these extremely enlarged and impressive craft, with their crews of fourteen to sixteen paddlers hard at work, these images have become fixed in people's minds as the watercraft of the fur trade era.

In reality, the Montreal canoe, the bastard canoe, and the North canoe were the three standard sizes of cargo vessels, in descending order. The Montreal canoe measured a maximum of 36 feet, and it was handled by a total of seven to ten men. The smaller bastard canoe was 29 to 32 feet long, and it was crewed by six to eight paddlers. These two categories of vessels were most commonly used on the run between Montreal and the Great Lakes, and along the shores of those huge lakes. The North canoe, the craft that was normally used on the medium-sized and smaller waterways extending further into the interior from the Great Lakes, was a maximum of 28 feet long. It was worked by only four to six paddlers, and it carried a total capacity of about 11/2 tons, a total that included the weight of the cargo, the trip provisions, the equipment, and the crewmen.

Other common misconceptions about birchbark canoes relate to how delicate they were, and that they could only be utilized in the regions in which white birch trees grew large enough to produce good, thick canoe bark. For starters, bark craft were amazingly durable if they were treated properly, like so many other things in life. Before departing for the day, a bark canoe was soaked atop the water for a time. This softened to a degree the rather brittle dry bark of the bottom and lower walls, and made it more flexible. As a result, if the canoe were struck by submerged logs or rocks along the route, the bark exterior would tend to bend and flex, rather than break or be punctured. In addition, bark canoes were always loaded and unloaded while floating offshore, in water deep enough so that the fully loaded craft did not make contact with the bottom. They were never dragged onto or off of a shoreline, whether loaded or unloaded; and after being unloaded while afloat, they were carried onto shore. Traveling in a bark canoe entailed walking in the water at every departure and every arrival, no matter the water temperature, and also clambering over the gunwales and into the water whenever obstructions hindered forward progress en route.

Since the boys and I were accustomed to doing living-history research in the wilderness each year, using a birchbark canoe, we could easily relate to most of this information. However, we still had certain questions about these canoes, such as how long they would last. (Doree)

The life span of a cargo canoe, as it was used on the most demanding routes for about six months out of the year during the paddling season, typically ranged from three to eight years. This length of life was possible under heavy usage because of three aspects of care. These included proper usage; appropriate repairs done before, during, and after each journey; and good storage conditions between voyages and over the winters. Proper storage during the frozen months typically involved a roof structure of some sort, to limit the weight of the snow that could accumulate on the overturned craft, which was raised off the ground on a rack of some sort. In addition, in many cases the bottom area of each rib inside the canoe was tapped from its usual flat position into an angled position. This reduced the pressure that was exerted by the ribs onto the cedar sheathing strips that lined the interior, which in turn tended to reduce the likelihood of the bark splitting during extreme temperature fluctuations. A much different method was also sometimes employed for safely storing a birchbark canoe over the winter: this entailed burying it in a pit below the frost line.

While on a journey, a birchbark canoe could be readily repaired, when it sustained damage to either its bark exterior or the various wooden elements. The standard equipment that was carried on each trip included the simple tools that were needed for making such repairs: a hatchet, a crooked knife, and a robust awl for drilling holes. In addition, an ample supply of canoe bark, as well as peeled and split roots of spruce or pine for sewing, and a generous supply of sealant gum, were also carried on virtually every trip. Thus, it was not usually necessary to search for these materials on shore when repairs were required.

This is why the birchbark canoe was definitely not limited in its region of usage to only the areas where birch trees grew large. Numerous journeys that extended many hundreds of miles south of the white birch zone were undertaken for centuries, by simply taking along the needed repair materials. In Michigan, the birch zone extended south to about the foot of Saginaw Bay in Lake Huron, and in southwestern Wisconsin down to about the Illinois border. Bark canoe construction even flourished in certain area well to the south of this zone, such as at Detroit, since the builders could harvest bark from areas further to the north, or instead trade for it with groups that lived within the birch territory.

Besides repair materials and tools, the standard equipment of a fur trade canoe during the French period also included the following items: paddles, setting poles, a sailing rig, a fifty-foot towing rope, a sponge, a set of poles for the bottom of the canoe (to evenly distribute the weight of the cargo and paddlers), and a tarpaulin to cover the cargo, as well as supplies of powder and lead, some cooking containers, stocks of provisions, sometimes fishing hooks and line, and long strips of birchbark (or occasionally a tarp) that were laid over a framework of poles to make a traveling shelter. This framework often consisted of the set of poles from the bottom of the craft, laid at an angle from the raised side of the overturned canoe down to the ground. In various instances, the cargo of furs and hides that was transported out to the St. Lawrence Valley was covered while traveling with ten to fifteen loose bear hides, rather than with a canvas tarpaulin.

Although birchbark is quite durable and decay-resistant, not a single canoe that was made of it many centuries ago has been found, either under water or in a land excavation. Underwater excavations have only rarely unearthed a few elements from these vessels, such as a thwart, a rib, a segment of gunwale elements pegged together, or a portion of root-sewn bark. As a result, the complete specimens in museum collections date from the last 2 1/2 centuries. The oldest known surviving miniature models were built by native craftsmen in the mid-1700s, while the oldest surviving full size craft date from the very end of the 1700s and the early decades of the following century.

In my research, I had located and studied in great detail four full size cargo canoes of the fur trade, the largest measuring 29 feet in length, as well as four miniature models of cargo canoes, all dating from the 1800s. These eight craft were preserved in museum collections in the U.S., Canada, and England.

Later in the day, as the sun lost its intensity and the shadows gradually lengthened, the boys enjoyed hearing about their ancestor Etienne Tremblay, who was a well-respected builder of birchbark canoes and a carver of canoe paddles in the St. Lawrence Valley. Born on Christmas Day in 1690, he grew up with his large family of fifteen siblings at La Petite Rivière St. François Xavier, a small village on the north shore of the St. Lawrence about forty miles downriver (northeast) from Quebec. When Etienne was age twenty-five, he married a local fifteen-year old girl [Kevin and Ben's eyes widened at this news], and they settled at the little village of Les Eboulements, about eighteen miles downriver from La Petite Rivière. According to church records, the couple officially resided at Les Eboulements for the rest of their lives; it was at this community that their children were born, baptized, and married.

It is only because of an unusual series of circumstances that we know that Etienne and his younger brothers Louis (born in 1695) and Jean (born in 1701), all settled at Les Eboulements, were birchbark canoe builders and paddle carvers. During the 1740s and 1750s, Canadian-born Joseph Cadet held the office of *munitionnaire* (supply officer) of New France, supplying the provisions for the French troops in Canada. He was eventually convicted of embezzlement of public funds, and was sent to Paris to serve his sentence in the Bastille Prison. When he was released in 1766, he purchased land in France, where he planned to build a Canadian-style farm. On May 5, 1766, he wrote to a Monsieur Houdin of Quebec, who he knew was returning to France. (Britain had now taken over New France, after the Seven Years' War.) Cadet requested that Houdin bring back to France various Canadian items, such as a small *calèche* (carriage), horse collars, bearskins to decorate those collars, and a plow ("as they are made in Canada"). He even asked Houdin to hire a good plowman for nine years, to work on Cadet's farm in France.

The most significant items that he requested (since they are the proof of the special occupation of Etienne Tremblay and his brothers) were the following: "Two canoes or at least pre-cut bark to make a 4-place canoe and another of 5 places, and ready-to-assemble frames and ribs of cedar; 200 pounds of canoe gum, the resin to make the canoes and repair them whenever they should split; and 10 fathoms of bark to patch them. In other words, what I am asking you to acquire is pre-cut canoe parts and rolled bark for 2 canoes, ready to be assembled in France...Take care to request good quality bark with small grain...Call on Sieurs Etienne, Louis, or Jean Tremblay, three brothers at Eboulements near Baie St. Paul. Write to them in my name; one or the other will supply these items. Make sure to also ask them to supply 40 well-made and polished paddles of maple."

Obviously, Cadet knew canoe-building, including qualities of bark, as he was confident that he could assemble the pre-cut parts in France. He may have felt that unassembled canoe parts would survive a ship's journey to France better than two assembled craft. The four-place canoe that he ordered was probably fourteen to sixteen feet long if built in traditional native sizes, or up to nineteen to twenty feet long if built in fur trade sizes. It was divided into four spaces for paddlers, passengers, and cargo by five thwarts. A letter from New France in 1709 indicated that the four-place canoe was the size that was normally used when an entire native family traveled. The five-place canoe, which Cadet also ordered, was roughly a yard longer. The measurement of a *brasse* or fathom that was used by Cadet in reference to the repair bark was equivalent to 5.278 feet in France. Thus, he ordered about fifty linear feet of bark for making repairs. When Audet requested "frames and ribs of cedar," he presumably meant all of the wooden elements that would be required for the two craft. Thus, the only items that he did not include in his order were peeled and split roots for the lashings. He must have felt that he could acquire these roots, or appropriate substitutes, in France.

Further information may never be uncovered about the Tremblay brothers' canoe-building expertise. Certainly their canoes were held in high esteem, or Cadet would not have specifically ordered canoes or pre-cut parts made by them. Etienne's fourteen children were born with some regularity over a twenty-eight year period between

1717 and 1745, at Les Eboulements. All but two of these pregnancies would have begun approximately during the fall and winter months of September through March (the two exceptions beginning in about early June and early August). This appears to be probably evidence that Etienne was regularly away from home working during all of the spring and summer months each year, at least until he was age fifty-five (when his last child was born). These annual absences, plus his respected reputation as a canoe builder, leads to the speculation that he worked each spring and summer away from home in a canoe yard.

It is not known whether the canoe production yard of Etienne Tremblay and his two younger brothers was located in the area near their village of Les Eboulements, or instead at a considerable distance from the community. It is highly likely that they employed Montagnais craft workers in their yard, for at least some phases of production. This was certainly a well-established practice at numerous canoe yards during the entire fur trade era. In traditional native society, men cut the bark and fashioned the wooden elements of a canoe, while women and children installed the root lashings and applied the sealant gum. The Tremblays may have hired native individuals who lived a settled life at one of the mission stations, or instead those who lived in the traditional Montagnais lifestyle of hunting, trapping, and fishing in the interior, emerging on the St. Lawrence only during the summer months. Church records of the period indicate that the three Tremblay brothers and their wives were friends and associates of the native population of the region. From 1737 on, they appeared as godparents at a number of baptisms of native children and as witnesses at several weddings of native couples. The three French couples witnessed at least twelve baptisms and three weddings of native people at scattered intervals over a span of some thirty years. The records indicate that some of the native participants in these ceremonies were from the region, while others resided as far away as Tadoussac, Îles Jeremie, and Sept Îles, far down on the Gulf of St. Lawrence. In January of 1760, all three of the brothers appeared as witnesses at Les Eboulements for the marriage of a Montagnais man who resided at Tadoussac and a Micmac woman. These associations at important liturgical occasions between the three canoe craftsmen and the native population may be circumstantial evidence that the brothers employed native craft workers in their canoe and paddle production. This may have involved the gathering of bark, wood, roots, and pitch, as well as some or all phases of production. It may also reflect business associations that were established by the delivery of their canoes and paddles to widely dispersed posts in the region called the King's Domain, which extended far down the Gulf of St. Lawrence.

By the time the order from Cadet for canoes and paddles arrived in Canada, during the summer of 1766, all three of the canoe-builder brothers were still living with their families at Les Eboulements, presumably in semi-retirement: Etienne was 75, Louis was 71, and Jean was 65. We can speculate that when Etienne went to his grave the following year, on September 20, 1767, he had the satisfaction of knowing that two Tremblay canoes had brought many happy reminiscences of the Canadian homeland to an exiled Canadian in France.

On the fur trade routes, the birchbark canoe was replaced, for the most part, by canvas-covered, wood strip canoes during the 1870s and 1880s. These held sway until versions crafted from aluminum, Kevlar, and plastics gradually took over from the late 1940s on. Other craft that replaced the traditional birchbark canoes in the fur trade included wooden boats of various kinds, including York boats, scows, and bateaux.

During the course of our extensive windbound time, the wind and waves did not abate one bit, neither during the day nor the evening. However, as a result, we had shared plenty of the aforementioned canoe information (some of it remained in my head, to be discussed later), and we were deeply rested and healed from this Nature-imposed time spent on shore. The voyageurs had referred to such windbound intervals, when no forward progress was possible, as being *dégradé* (debased or ashamed). However, they labored under very real time constraints, hurrying to complete their voyage safely during the interval between the break-up of the ice in May and the return of the ice in November. Spending enforced time on shore posed no serious problems for us; it just hindered my usual urges to keep moving, see new territory, and have more enriching adventures.

Day Ten

When the alarm clock sounded at 4 A.M., I could hear from my bed quite a bit of wave action at the shoreline. But my ears registered that the action was much reduced from the previous day-and-a-half while we had been windbound, which was encouraging. After returning to my dreams for another half-hour, I crawled out of the tent, checked the water, and was very pleased to find that it was moderately flat and workable! Packing up quickly in the chilly near-dark, we were on our way at 6 A.M., just as the first golden rays of sunlight peeked over the tops of the pines off to the east. Within forty minutes, we had crossed the mouth of Three Mile Bay (naturally, three miles wide) in a southwesterly direction, to reach Pointe Grondine (Rumbling or Growling Point), the goal that we had been seeing in the distance from our windbound camp. Then we skirted for three miles the large peninsula that juts down from the Pointe Grondine First Nations Indian Reserve, all the while threading our way among innumerable whale-back shoals of bare rock that lay just below or just above the surface. Since the moderate head wind and medium waves would most likely grow in intensity as the day progressed, we decided at this point to take the alternate northern route, to which the voyageurs had often resorted when the open lake was menacing.

Turning northeast, we made our way partway up the six-mile length of Beaverstone Bay, to halt at Square Rock, the first island that we came to in the sheltered bay. We had covered eight miles in 2 3/4 hours of paddling, before eating any nourishment. Knowing how hard their parents had been laboring to reach sheltered waters, the boys registered no complaints about the meal schedule. During our breakfast stop of 45 minutes on the low, diminutive island of solid rock, we marveled at its many folds and domes, virtually barren of vegetation. This lump of granite remembered hundreds of paddlers who had rested on its bare back over the centuries. When we pushed off after the break, under a blue sky containing thin swipes of white clouds, it felt excellent to be off the big waters of the main body of the lake, sheltered from its boisterous wind and waves! However, a moderate breeze out of the north soon picked up, as *La Vieille* continued to assert herself. After four miles of slow going against this head wind, advancing toward the northeast and north, we exuberantly turned left at 11:00 to enter Collins Inlet.

Shortly after our arrival in this westward-reaching passage, which was flanked by rock cliffs that were capped with evergreen forest, an otter swam a couple of canoe lengths in front of us for a time, before leisurely crossing to the other side of the channel. Only its snout, eyes, and very low forehead, all in shades of dark brown, appeared slightly above the surface, creating a delicate wake. While making our way along the entire twelve-mile length of Collins Inlet, Ben put in a fine session as the *avant*. To break up the afternoon's labors, we made rest stops from 11:45 to 1:15, 3:15 to 3:45, and 5:15 to 5:30. When a bald eagle made several cruising passes high above us, it prompted a conversation about the various birds that we had spotted during this trip, and how they each made their living.

One wild creature that I hoped we would not encounter during this journey was the massasauga rattlesnake. I was aware that only along this particular segment of the mainline canoe route would we be traveling in rattlesnake territory. And even here, the rattlers are usually found only in the delta area of the French River and on the adjacent offshore islands in Georgian Bay, where they live amid rocks, brush, and downed trees, feed on frogs and mice, and are hunted by raccoons and red foxes. In 1830, Frances Simpson, wife of the Governor of the H.B.C. for all of North America, mentioned these serpents in her travel diary when her party of two canoes spent the night on the French River upstream from the Recollet Falls: "Encamped at 7 P.M. The evening was close, with appearance of rain, and I felt rather uncomfortable from an apprehension that we should be visited during the night by some of the snakes with which this place is infested." Not wanting to frighten Doree and the boys, I chose not to tell them about these reptiles until after our voyage, particularly since the snakes almost always retreat from an encounter with people, and if they are surprised, they usually give warning with their tail rattle. They rarely strike humans except in self-defense, and their bites are almost never fatal for people, particularly since 20 to 50 percent of strikes do not even inject venom. I respected the right of these serpents to live on this planet as much as me and my family; all of Earth's creatures, the crawlers, the runners, the swimmers, and the fliers, have an equal right to live here. I just preferred that we not encounter any rattlers during our trip through their beautiful homeland.

At 7:00, we landed at a spot on the north shore that lay directly across the channel from South Point, the westernmost tip of Collins Inlet and the end of our sheltered route that had taken us off the main waters of Georgian Bay for most of a day. The campsite was on the southern edge of Killarney Provincial Park, and five miles from the community of Killarney, our ultimate destination. Assessing our day, I announced that, between 6 A.M. and 7 P.M., we had put 25 miles behind us, mostly against head winds. Before we dozed off in the tent at 10:00, my final journal entry read, "Doree has been a <u>super-woman</u> throughout this entire ten days of paddling and camping." I could not imagine many women opting for this kind of arduous canoe trip.

In spite of my deep, fatigue-induced sleep during each of our paddling trips, it was not unusual for me to be awakened suddenly in the night by a sharp sound outside the tent, or occasionally by a soft snort. I would then lie wide awake, listening very intently for a while. The next thing I would know, it would be morning. In this case, my dreaming was disturbed by distinct scratching sounds on the heavy canvas of the Duluth pack, which was suspended by a long rope far out on a high limb of a nearby tree. Apparently, some tree-climbing creature had made its way out onto the long limb, to see if it could raid the food supplies that were stowed inside the buckle-closed pack. Judging from the volume of the sounds, I pictured a raccoon or some other nocturnal animal of similar size. Since the scratching continued for a considerable time, I assumed that we would discover at morning's light that all of our goodies had been devoured.

Day Eleven

Arising at 4:30 A.M. (to find the contents of the food pack entirely unscathed!), we were paddling by 6:00, with the hopes of avoiding the wind and waves that we expected to develop later on the open water. The surface of Georgian Bay was almost completely smooth when we departed, marred only by a slight breeze out of the northeast. As we headed toward the southwest, a beautiful sunrise over my left shoulder cast its rippling golden track across the water. After about fifteen or twenty minutes, the wind began to really pick up, and the waves grew bigger and brawnier. By the time we were about halfway across the bay, aiming for the lighthouse at Red Rock Point that marked the passageway through the rock-bound coastline to Killarney, we found ourselves in a heavy surf, with whitecaps that were traveling in exactly the same direction as our canoe. These were the largest waves that we had ever experienced as paddlers. With no choice but to continue, and with our hearts in our throats, we rode the surf across the bay. However, we could not keep pace with the ever-quickening speed of the waves. As the silvery foam of each roller approached from behind, passed beneath the canoe, and lifted it up, much of our control waned at the moment when only the center area of the hull was balanced on the crest of the wave. Then, as the ridge of frothing water moved forward and the craft settled into the trough preceding the next wave, we regained control of our direction. This pattern made for rather uncomfortable traveling, literally on a slippery slope. Paddling hard in the surf, I directed all of my fear-induced energy into the wood of the paddle and the water that it grabbed with each stroke.

At this point, Tim was working too hard in the stern to continuously sing with the boys and me, but for us three, the time to sing away our fears was now! We belted out many verses of various of the French songs that we knew: 'Vent frais, vent du matin,' and 'Entendez vous sur l'ormeau,' and 'En roulant ma boule roulant.' The voyageurs were very aware that, the way the human brain works, you can't be scared to death and sing at the same time. In this situation, the singing allowed us to take the mental focus off the waves swelling right up to the gunwales, and let us relax somewhat and function more efficiently. Just like the voyageurs, who often sang to drive away fear, and sometimes to alleviate boredom, we matched the songs to the rhythm of the paddle strokes and used those melodies to quell our misgivings. Even though Tim didn't always have enough extra breath to sing along with us on this frightening occasion, our singing helped him relax, too. (Doree)

Finally, after about thirty minutes of rough going, I reassured the boys that, if we capsized here at the finale, their life preservers would keep them afloat, and Mom and I would try to toss them up onto the rocks that lined the shore. However, with a collective sigh of relief, we zoomed past the turbulence beside the lighthouse and safely into the rock-bound entrance of Killarney Channel. We had streaked across the 5 1/2 miles of the traverse in an hour and ten minutes, with the full force of the waves and wind pushing us along. If we had raised the sail during the crossing, we probably would have capsized from an overabundance of wind power.

After my heartbeat had almost returned to normal, we arrived at the lodge at 7:15 A.M., where we unloaded the canoe, packed the car, paid for the shuttle driver service, and were ready to be on our way by 8:30. In talking to one of the staff members at the lodge, we learned that, when various bets had been laid as to our projected arrival date, even the most optimistic individuals had envisioned that the trip would take us at least a week longer than it actually did. The least optimistic ones had thought that we would not make it at all, and would need to be rescued.

As we drove west toward Sault Ste. Marie, we halted at a truck stop for a welcome and well-earned celebration meal of greasy burgers and fries, and a complete change of clothes. Finally, dry and warm shoes and socks! We were both older and wiser than when we had launched this memorable voyage of 127 miles. It seemed as if months of experiences had transpired, rather than just eleven days, since we had pushed off on the smooth surface of the La Vase River! All along the route, we had taken each of the challenges that had arisen as opportunities to learn and grow, and we had utilized French songs to help lighten our load on various trying occasions.

During our trip home, we spent three days at the Straits of Mackinac, absorbing the ancient history of the area and imagining the roles that our ancestors had played there in that history. On the third day, we visited a rendezvous of fur trade reenactors at Ft. Michilimackinac.

Our experiments with the use of a sail on this trip had been so successful that we decided to make the sailing rig a permanent part of our setup. Ralph Frese of the Chicagoland Canoe Base mounted a fiberglass-covered wooden mast step onto the floor of the craft, fastening it with strips of fiberglass. In addition, he replaced the standard second thwart from the bow, the one immediately behind the bow seat, with a more robust version, which swelled in width in the midsection to accommodate a hole to support the mast. For my part, I installed two separate loops of nylon cord around the center thwart, to which I would clip the ends of the two guy lines of the mast, and attached a metal fixture near the right end of the thwart in front of my stern seat, where I could easily lash the halyard in a figure-eight pattern when the sail was raised.

The year following our venture down the French River, in 1986, this waterway became the first one in all of Canada to be designated as a Canadian Heritage River. In addition, three years later, much of its corridor received further protection, with the creation of the French River Provincial Park.

V

Third Voyage
Upper Ottawa River
August 22-30, 1986

I always remember an epitaph which is in the cemetery at Tombstone,
Arizona. It says, "Here lies Jack Williams. He done his damnedest."
I think that is the greatest epitaph a man can have.

Harry Truman

A ship in harbor is safe,
But that is not what ships are built for.

John A. Shedd

The truth that many people never understand, until it is too late,
is that the more you try to avoid suffering the more you suffer,
Because smaller and more insignificant things begin to torture you
in proportion to your fear of being hurt.

Thomas Merton

No one ever gets far unless he accomplishes the impossible
at least once a day.

L. Ron Hubbard

Preceding the canoe trip, we spent four days on an excursion to Moose Fort, the second oldest post of the H.B.C. This facility, established in 1673 at the southern end of James Bay (the 300-mile-long, southern projection of Hudson's Bay), was built three years after the company had been formed in 1670. During our trip on the Polar Bear Express train, which covered the 186 miles between Cochrane and Moosonee, Ontario in four hours, we were fascinated to watch the changes in the Canadian Shield forest as we traveled northward. As the train paralleled the course of the Abitibi River, and finally the Moose River, the forest of spruce, birch, and poplar soon changed

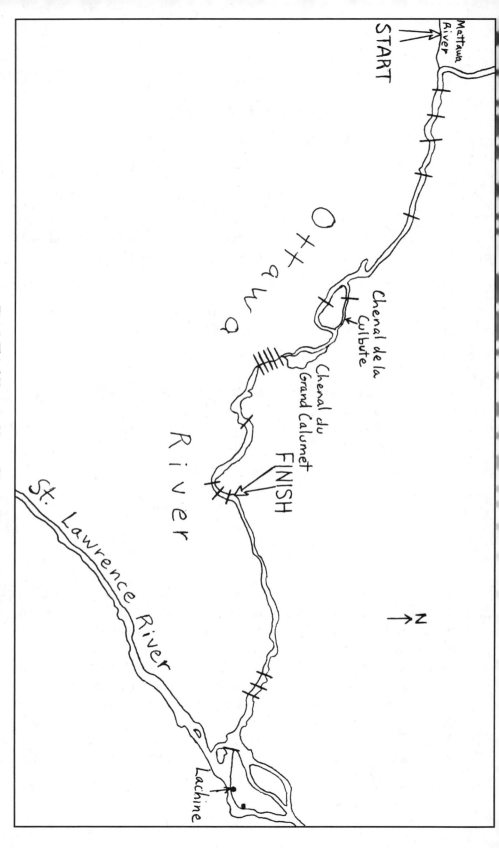

Fig. 6, Third Voyage: Upper Ottawa River

to spruce and fir. Then, as we entered the Hudson's Bay lowlands, a huge area of peat bogs bordering James Bay and Hudson's Bay that extends for hundreds of miles to the south, the forest cover withered before our very eyes. The stunted spruce and tamarack trees growing in the bogs were just slender, head-high stalks, with puny limbs extending out only a few inches from the trunk. The only time we saw regular forest cover in the region was when the train passed over one of the river valleys, where spruce and poplars of standard size grew in the well-drained soil. At the end of the line at Moosonee, we hired a native man and his motorized freight canoe to take our family the remaining thirteen miles down to the mouth of the Moose River, to see the open waters of James Bay under a perfect blue sky. Back upriver, it was time to visit the site of the H.B.C. post itself, on the big island in the middle of the river. Various buildings dating from the 1840s to the 1860s have survived, including the staff quarters, blacksmith shop, and Anglican church made of wood, and the powder magazine built of stone. In the cemetery, which had been reserved for employees of the Company and their family members, headstones for such individuals as the chief factor, post surgeon, and post chaplain date back to 1802.

Our main reason for taking the train ride along the Abitibi and Moose Rivers and visiting Moose Fort was this: during our paddling of the Ottawa River on this trip, we would be thinking about the 300th anniversary of the 1686 DeTroyes expedition, and their activities on these waterways and at Moose Fort, as well as at most of the other H.B.C. posts that were then in operation. The French felt that their fur trade was being threatened by the English commerce on Hudson's Bay and James Bay, first begun in 1668; they also believed that France had a claim to the region of James Bay. As a result, a force of 106 Frenchmen under the command of Chevalier Pierre DeTroyes, including seventy Canadian militiamen, thirty regular soldiers, and six Canadian officers, was sent northward to this region, departing from Montreal on March 20, 1686. The men spent the first two weeks traveling forty miles up the frozen Ottawa River using dog sleds, hauling their 35 canoes and the supplies that they would need for a round trip voyage of some 2,500 miles. They planned to live primarily on dried corn, supplemented with meat and fish harvested along the way.

When the spring thaw finally cleared the waterways of ice, they paddled up the Ottawa and White Rivers, portaged over the height of land, and then paddled to Lake Abitibi, down the length of the Abitibi River, and along the lower reaches of the Moose River, to reach James Bay on June 20. After capturing the H.B.C. post of Moose Fort on the following day (exactly three hundred years and two months before our family's arrival there), the men proceeded eastward to take Rupert/Charles Fort on July 3, and then westward to capture Albany Fort on July 26. The only other H.B.C. posts at this time were Severn House and York Fort, 400 and 600 miles further to the northwest from Albany Fort, on the coast of Hudson's Bay. Those Frenchmen who did not remain on James Bay to operate the three captured posts left Moose Fort on August 19 bound for Montreal, where they finally arrived in October of 1686. En route home, they paused for a short time at the post on Lake Abitibi that they had built in early June while traveling northward, and also stopped at Ft. Temiscamingue on the upper Ottawa, where they had exchanged their large craft for smaller, lighter versions with native canoe builders in mid May. Only three men were lost during this entire operation of seven arduous months. During our paddling conversations this year, we would often talk of this hardy band of men and their amazing deeds three hundred years ago, as they managed to travel huge distances under horrendous conditions and capture three British forts.

After our train ride back southward, our trip by car took us to the upper Ottawa River, where we visited the site of Ft. Temiscamingue. This post, established by the Compagnie du Nord in 1679, later became a N.W.C. post during the latter 1700s, and a facility of the H.B.C. from 1821 until 1902. All that remains now are two chimneys of mortared stones and two cemeteries.

In the late afternoon, we arrived at L'Auberge des Pionniers, five miles west of the community of Mattawa, where we had come off the water at the end of our Mattawa River trip two years earlier. We had arranged to leave our car there while we paddled eastward over the remaining five miles of the Mattawa, and then about two hundred miles toward the southeast on the much larger Ottawa River. When we would eventually reach the city of Ottawa, or some other point on the lower river, Don and Yvonne, the new owners of L'Auberge, would send Vic, the operator of the riding stables there, to bring our car to us. We enjoyed a restaurant feast at the lodge, followed by a quiet evening, before bedding down in one of the little cabins by the river. Our young voyageurs, Kevin, age 9 11/12, and Ben, 8 2/12, were eager to get on the water and follow the track of the DeTroyes expedition.

We were aware that this year's voyage would provide our first canoeing experiences on a big, majestic river, and because of that, we expected much less variety in the terrain, compared to the smaller scale and very picturesque scenery of the Mattawa and French Rivers. It would also be our first time dealing with huge hydroelectric dams, of which there were four on the stretch of the Ottawa that we intended to cover this year. I hated dams, not only for the way they flooded out many of the natural features of a river, but also because they spooked me considerably. Whether on the upriver or downriver side of a large dam, I was seriously uncomfortable with something as domineering as that. Although we were somewhat prepared psychologically for the massive size of the river and the obstacles of the huge dams, we were not even aware of the challenges that would be presented by the floating log booms that spanned the complete width of the channel at various locations. In addition, unbeknown to us, at about the narrowest location on the entire Ottawa, about ninety miles downriver from the mouth of the Mattawa, a churning, boulder-toothed rapids had drowned five Canadian soldiers traveling in a power boat the previous summer. That set of rapids was now waiting for us, and we would meet in four days.

Day One

We awakened at 5:45 A.M., loaded the canoe in the dim light, and pushed off on the Mattawa River near the cabin at 7:00, with the boys in a stupor and their eyes barely open. Like a silent prowler, grey fog had invaded the river valley so densely that we could barely make out the shoreline passing close beside us. Low in the eastern sky, the sun looked as ghostly as the moon usually does. As the ball of fire rose higher and warmed the air, it soon chased off the thick layer of mist, and offered the promise of a beautiful day.

After about an hour's paddle, we arrived at the Portage de Plain Champ (Flat Field), where the once-frothing rapids now lie vanquished beneath the backwaters of the Hurdman Dam. After making the 320 pace portage on the right shore in ninety minutes, we glided over the unruffled surface for the remaining 21/2 miles of the Mattawa.

At 10:00, we arrived at its junction with the Ottawa River, at the town of Mattawa. When DeTroyes arrived here with his forces on May 12, 1686, en route up the Ottawa toward James Bay, he recorded in his journal: "We went to Mataouan, which signifies in the native language 'Fork of the River,' it effectively being one. The left [the Mattawa River], which is to the south, is the route of the Ottawas [to the upper Great Lakes], and the right, which is north, is consequently my route to Temiscaming...At this place, some natives who lived in a shelter on a point were constructing canoes...While we were erecting a cross at the point of the fork in the river, our interpreter of English cut his leg to the bone with an axe."

The weather was absolutely perfect. With no breeze, the quarter-mile-wide surface of the Ottawa glistened like a mirror, reflecting an exact image of the high, rounded hills clad with pine and hemlock that flanked the valley, and the white-smeared blue dome above. This waterway flows down a giant crack that formed in the Canadian Shield crust in very ancient times, with the north side of the crack thrusting upward and the south side dropping downward. This ancient fault line is still the scene of minor earthquakes at times. After the last of the glaciers had retreated northward and the Great Lakes had been formed from the meltwaters, the eastward outflow of the upper three Great Lakes and Georgian Bay flowed in a mighty, surging torrent down this narrow valley and out to the St. Lawrence. With the post-glacial rebound of the land, this outflow eventually ceased about 4,000 years ago, after which the Ottawa became the outflow for a large watershed stretching to the north, as it still is today. Even before the hydro dams were installed on the Ottawa, its three-hundred-mile section between the mouth of the Mattawa and the junction with the St. Lawrence generally resembled a series of long lakes that were connected by narrow stretches with many rapids. These fast, narrow segments dropped a total of about six hundred feet in elevation. The river now forms the imaginary boundary between the provinces of Quebec on the left shore and Ontario on the right.

As we would often do in the years ahead when paddling on the larger rivers and lakes, we tended to remain relatively close to one of the shorelines of the river, but not so close that we followed the undulations of the shore and added extra miles to our route. This allowed us to readily see our forward progress, by registering the scenery as it passed slowly by, and to enjoy the land, the vegetation, and the wildlife around us. Paddling hour after hour while looking straight ahead toward a distant goal many miles away, all the while keeping far out from shore, can get pretty boring, and sometimes even downright discouraging -- *even for a man as routinized as Tim!* *(Doree)*.

After only 2 1/2 miles on the river, we encountered our first log boom. This was a series of large floating logs that were connected to each other, end to end, with chains. The boom, extending across the entire channel, was anchored securely at each end beside the shoreline. It was used to gather any loose floating logs that might escape from one of the floating loads that were sometimes pulled slowly downriver by a tugboat. The forest industry still had a major presence on the Ottawa River: logs that were cut inland on both the Ontario and Quebec sides were trucked to the shoreline and dumped into the river at various holding areas. Each of these log spillways or rollways was surrounded by a floating boom that kept the logs relatively close to the shore. When enough floating logs had accumulated at a given spot in the river, the boom was dragged entirely around the floating mass of logs, secured into a giant loop, and towed downriver by a tugboat. In this manner, the various sawmills, pulp mills, paper mills, and fiberboard plants that were located downriver on both shores were supplied with logs less expensively than by hauling them the entire distance with trucks.

This first boom on our route was not too problematic, since the weather was very cooperative, with no wind or waves driving the canoe onto the boom or hindering our search for a clear passage around or through it. After paddling along its entire length across the channel, we finally found a small opening that allowed boats to pass through the boom, very near the right shore. We had overcome the first obstacle of the Ottawa.

After we had advanced eleven miles since breakfast, we took a half-hour lunch break on shore at 12:30. A mile later, we paused to study a beaver lodge that stood adjacent to the shoreline. Later in the afternoon, when we passed a log spillway and its encircling boom on the left shore, Kevin asked to be deposited on the floating timbers of the boom, for a little fun and excitement. However, with no logger's spiked boots to give him secure footing, he was only willing to crawl along and sit on the unpredictable boom.

At 7:00, we finally halted for the day, to camp on an island at the now-flooded Rapides Leveiller. To reach high level ground above the river at this site required a strenuous vertical lift-up of about fifteen feet, for all of our gear and the canoe.

Since the boys were still small, this task fell to us parents, but we were fairly small too! Exhausted from twelve hours on the water and more than twenty miles of paddling, with my hands aching, I at first wondered how many women would write themselves into a drama like this, let along live it. Then, not wanting to be a drag on the spirit of my life-partner, I decided I needed to stop that kind of negative thinking! I had hurdled over some fairly large obstacles in my thirty-seven years, I told myself, like graduating summa cum laude from Michigan State and later getting a Master's degree at U. of I. at Chicago, even though no one on either side of my family had ever gone to college. There had been plenty of anxiety and hard work in my life, but there had also been huge rewards as well. Sixteen years earlier, I had willingly thrown my lot in with Tim, at that time a struggling musician with such big dreams and very little money, and we had managed to forge an unusual and wonderful life together. To paraphrase one of the metaphors used by Joseph Campbell: One needs to go out and slay some dragons! So I proceeded, through my fatigue, to help hoist our gear and canoe up the steep 15 foot slope, exceeding previous physical limits. Mission accomplished, I started heating water for dinner, while the boys erected the tent and then sat on a bare rock blowing up the four air mattresses. (Doree)

The voyageurs had either paddled or lined the adjacent Leveiller Rapids, depending on the water level. This particular set of rapids, as well as four more major sets scattered downriver over the next 35 miles, were now all submerged beneath the backwaters of the Des Joachims Dam (pronounced "da swisha" locally, badly garbled from the original French). Since the Ottawa River flows down a deep and narrow fault line in the earth, the water does not usually have room to spread out and form a wide channel in most places behind the dams that have been installed along the river; this only occurs in the area that is relatively close to each dam. In this first case, at the Des Joachims Dam, the water begins widening noticeably about ten miles above it, in three very broad bays separated by narrower sections. By good fortune, during my research leading up to the Ottawa River trip, I had located a book that presented early topographical maps of each section of the river; these charts showed exactly how the channel had originally appeared, before the hydro dams had been installed along it during the 1920s through the 1950s. Thus, I was able to draw the contours of the original channel directly onto our modern topographical maps, so that we could clearly picture the appearance of the original river as we paddled each stage of the now-dammed channel.

To uplift my drooping troops, I reviewed out loud the day's events: between 7 A.M. and 7 P.M., we had traveled 23 miles, spending 2 1/4 hours on land during that time making one portage and taking several breaks. Since we parents were willing to slow down our progress somewhat, we had let the boys paddle much of the day in the bow seat. Kevin had done three miles as the bow paddler, while Ben had managed to do five miles! Kevin also got in an excellent practice session as the *gouvernail*, with his bottom occupying the stern seat and mine perched behind him on the rear tip of the canoe. It was not a very comfortable place for me to sit, with the eyebolt for the painter rope projecting upward and into me, but it was the only place where I could be close by, to offer hands-on guidance to the young paddler. We were asleep by 10:30, much too tired to register the patter of the rain that fell lightly on the tent during the night.

Day Two

We were up at 6:30, and on the water by 8:45. By the looks of the weather, we suspected that a long, arduous, wet day lay ahead (and our suspicions proved to be right). Almost immediately, the rain started falling, and it continued to come down for hours, varying between light and medium, while a strong head wind soon worked the oncoming waves into whitecaps as large as we dared to handle. About a mile from the campsite, we paddled through a narrow area that had once been the Rapides Le Trou (Hole Rapids), which had obliged the voyageurs to make a 300 pace portage of the cargo and then to line the empty canoe. One mile further, we passed over the submerged Rapides des Deux Rivières (Two Rivers), where the crews had made a portage of 820 paces. Downriver a bit, we slowly glided by a delightful little waterfall on the left shore, where Ruisseau (Creek) Hautmesnil flows into the river from the north. After clawing our way forward over seven miles of water in three hours, the waves finally became too hefty to handle; at noon, we were windbound on the left shore. Setting up the tarp shelter beneath a canopy of tall pines, we managed to start a weak, smoky fire with very wet wood and flammable "fire noodles," and devoured a welcome hot meal.

Since I had been exerting too much against the wind and waves to tell stories while paddling, I took advantage of this time relaxing on shore to discuss with the family the early history of the French in America. Jacques Cartier had first explored the Gulf of St. Lawrence in 1534, and again returned to New France the following year, to travel up the St. Lawrence River as far as the Lachine Rapids and the location where Montreal would eventually stand, before spending the winter where Quebec would later be established. His third voyage, in 1541, would again take him as far upriver as the Lachine Rapids, before attempting to establish a colony at Quebec; after wintering there twice, the plans for the settlement were abandoned.

The early 1500s also saw the beginnings of the commerce in furs and hides in North America, involving the European fishing and whaling fleets that annually worked the coastal waters of Newfoundland and the Gulf of St. Lawrence. Encounters between these Europeans and various native groups along the coasts led to informal trading activity; over the years, some of the personnel on the ships began to bring more and more items to exchange for furs and hides. From the early 1580s on, merchants in various coastal French cities sent ships to New France specifically to trade with the native populations. The natives traveled by canoe from many far-flung areas of the interior out to the coastal areas of the Gulf of St. Lawrence and the lower St. Lawrence River, to exchange their peltries for European goods with these ship-based traders. Tadoussac, at the junction of the Saguenay River and the lower St. Lawrence, soon became the site of annual gatherings between widespread native groups and the traders who sailed there from France. This commerce eventually led to the founding of permanent trading centers and settlements along the St. Lawrence, including Tadoussac (established in 1600), Quebec (in 1608), Trois-Rivières (in 1634), and Montreal (in 1642).

During the first five decades of the 1600s, the French inhabitants carried out their trading activities while remaining, for the most part, in these settlements beside the river. Various native populations transported their furs and hides by canoe from the interior regions out to the settlements, and then returned to their homes with their newly-acquired European goods, including linen and woolen fabrics, iron tools, and brass cooking containers. These groups then exchanged a portion of their new merchandise with other native populations who did not have direct contact with the French. This system of inter-native trade was a continuation of a very widespread trade network that had operated for thousands of years before the arrival of the Europeans.

The majority of the very few Frenchmen who lived and worked in the interior regions during the first half of the century functioned as trade ambassadors, rather than as actual traders. Their assigned role was to live with their native hosts, learn their language and customs, develop relationships with them, and encourage them to make the annual voyage out to the French trade fairs that were held each summer at Trois-Rivières and Montreal. During these trade-fests, the Frenchmen from the interior served as translators and cultural liaisons, facilitating both commerce and personal and political relationships. These Frenchmen traveled with the brigades of native canoes when the native traders journeyed back and forth between the St. Lawrence trading centers and their home regions. As a result of their extensive travels, the French ambassadors brought out highly detailed geographical information about the interior areas, thus serving as some of the first European explorers of North America. The earliest of these trade ambassadors and translators was Etienne Brulé, who began his quarter-century of living with the Algonkins and the Hurons in 1610. He was soon followed by such men as Jean Nicollet, Nicolas Marsolet, and our ancestor Olivier LeTardif.

Kevin and Ben were proud to know that a number of our direct ancestors had worked during this period at various occupations in the fur trade. Abraham Martin, arriving within a decade of the founding of Quebec by Champlain in 1608, worked as a ship's pilot, fisherman, and laborer for the trading company of the colony. Olivier LeTardif served as a trade ambassador in the interior, living for about a decade with the Montagnais, the Algonkins, and the Hurons, from about 1618 on. Some time before 1629, he became the official interpreter for the settlement of Quebec, where he later served as a trader and the manager of the colony's trading facility there. From the 1640s to the 1660s, Jean Gagnon, another ancestor, operated a trading and outfitting store with his two brothers in the Lower Town area of Quebec, while Charles Sevestre (yes, he was one of us as well) was employed there during the same period as a clerk of the trading company, running the warehouse. Several of our forebears also participated in the annual trade fairs of the St. Lawrence Valley, which took place each summer at Trois-Rivières and Montreal.

Alexandre Turpin assembled a shipment of merchandise at Quebec in 1678, which he traded to the natives of the Upper Country who gathered at Montreal that summer. After about two decades of trading, he became an investor financing other traders. During the 1670s and 1680s, Pierre Girard transported numerous cargoes of tobacco, brandy, and other trade items in his own pinnace up the St. Lawrence to the fairs, to exchange for furs and hides.

During this period, two principal native groups journeyed from the western interior out to the St. Lawrence Valley to trade each summer, usually traveling by way of the Ottawa River. These were the Algonkins, who inhabited the large watershed region of the Ottawa River, and the Hurons, who resided near the southern end of Georgian Bay. The Ottawas, who lived on the eastern and western shores of Georgian Bay as well as on Manitoulin Island in northern Lake Huron, and also the Nipissings from the area northeast of Georgian Bay and north of Lake Nipissing, were particularly active as traders within the interior regions, as they had been since prehistoric times. These Ottawa and Nipissing traders served as middlemen in a very widespread commerce, redistributing the French merchandise which they acquired from the Algonkins and the Hurons as far west as Lake Michigan and Lake Superior. Beginning in 1641, various of the Iroquois groups who lived south and southeast of Lake Ontario waged intensive warfare against this array of native trading allies of the French. During 1648 and 1649, the Hurons and their adjacent neighbors the Petuns were finally driven from their home countries, as were also the Ottawas. During the following year, the Algonkins of the Ottawa Valley region fled from their homes, while the Nipissings soon retreated from their homeland as well.

In 1653, a number of Frenchmen from the St. Lawrence settlements decided to travel into the interior to locate their native allies (who had scattered throughout the upper Great Lakes region), and to revive the trade with them. This was the first recorded instance of Frenchmen venturing beyond the St. Lawrence specifically to carry out commerce, instead of waiting in the settlements for peltries to be delivered to them by the native populations. After commerce was re-established, large canoe brigades of native traders again traveled from the interior out to the St. Lawrence each year, to transact business at the fairs; when they returned to their home regions, a few French traders traveled with them each time. Some of the earliest such merchants were Mèdard Chouart Des Groseilliers and Pierre-Esprit Radisson. In 1660, only seven years after traders had begun voyaging westward to carry out commerce, a group of seven Frenchmen joined a huge flotilla of some 360 Ottawa and Huron canoes when they returned to their native villages on Chequamegon Bay in western Lake Superior. One of these men was our ancestor Claude David, who was the gunsmith of the group. Three years later, these seven men finally came out to Montreal; after that, increasing numbers of Frenchmen began traveling into the interior to trade each year. In time, trading communities were established in the interior at Sault Ste. Marie, Chequamegon Bay, the foot of Green Bay, and in 1671 at St. Ignace on the Straits of Mackinac. Each of these locales was the scene of a major native village at which a number of Frenchmen lived and worked, mostly voyageur-traders along with one or two missionaries. The traders were very often supported by one or more investors back in the St. Lawrence settlements, who shared in the profits of the commerce in return for the financial backing that provided canoes, equipment, provisions, and merchandise.

Soon after the settlement of St. Ignace was founded, it became the central depot for nearly all of the trade in the interior, serving as the warehouse locale for westbound merchandise and eastbound hides and furs. The native populations who settled at the Straits of Mackinac provided the canoes, long birchbark panels to cover traveling shelters, and provisions for the westbound and eastbound Frenchmen who gathered there each summer. In 1683, due to the considerable importance of this central rendezvous point, a small number of French troops were stationed there, at Ft. de Buade. As various other trading centers were established throughout the Great Lakes region and beyond, and French soldiers were dispatched to live at these places, St. Ignace continued to function as the central depot and resupply center, as well as the primary rendezvous locale, for virtually the entire commerce of the interior.

At 3:00, inspired by these stories of our ancestors and the fur trade, we pushed off from our windbound lunch site. All four of us were wet through to the skin, in spite of the rain gear, and we were cold as well, in spite of the warm meal in our stomachs and the exertion of hard paddling for us parents. With our faces to the wind, we labored against the burly waves for 1 1/4 hours, to forge ahead just two miles. This section of the river had originally been a stretch of fast current that had flowed in a narrow channel between the left shore and a slender island three miles long. When traveling upriver, the voyageurs had often been forced to unload half of the cargo, paddle up the strong current with the remaining half and leave it, and then return downstream to load the other half and paddle it up. As we were slowly advancing against the wind and waves, thankful that the rain had finally stopped, Doree spotted a rather small black bear in the woods that sloped down to the water's edge along the left shore.

At 4:15, we became windbound again, in a quiet little cove on the left shoreline. Doree and the boys were playing checkers atop the high bank, while I was sitting in the stern seat of the tied-up canoe, checking the maps. Hearing a rustling sound on the shore behind me, I turned around. There, just twenty feet away, was the adolescent bear that we had seen about an hour earlier, as we had been progressing slowly against the head wind! He had followed us along the shoreline, and had finally developed enough curiosity to walk down the slope right to us. Startled by my sudden move, the bear whirled and scampered quickly back up the hill and out of sight. I had read that black bears could sprint up to 30 miles per hour for short distances, and I guessed that this one probably attained that speed in his departure!

During the next hour-and-a-quarter, the wind subsided considerably, so we returned to the water at 5:30. A half-hour later, a storm front suddenly swept in from the west, coming at us from behind. As it approached, we could hear the rain striking the surface of the water with an eerie hissing sound. When I glanced back, I saw a solid grey curtain of water advancing quickly toward us, pummeling the surface of the river into a greyish white mass. Immediately after the single black cloud had dumped its heavy rain on us and had moved on, the wind that was pushing that storm cloud arrived. Suddenly, strong gusts were blowing directly at our backs, in the opposite direction of the wind that had been holding us back all day. With a shout of joy, I hoisted our new permanent sailing rig, with the new mast step on the floor and the new perforated thwart, and we streaked forward six miles in one hour. At 7:00, just as we were landing at the campsite that we had chosen, the following wind suddenly picked up even more. At the shoreline, the whitecaps threatened to swamp the canoe before we could get it unloaded. But our efforts prevailed.

While swooshing along under full sail for that hour, we had skimmed over the submerged stretch of about four miles of the Rapides de Rocher Capitaine (Captain Rock Rapids). This place had once required a 3/4 mile portage over hilly and rocky terrain, bypassing the wildest section of this long stretch of white water. This set of rapids had been named after the imposing, mile-long rock that rose high above the water in the middle of the roiling rapids, called the Captain Rock, which is now simply an obscure island surrounded by rather quiet water. Our campsite was located on Maraboo Point, about a mile east of the massive Captain Rock. In the 1600s, the French had used the term *marabout* (pronounced "maraboo") to indicate something standing guard; it was applied to revered objects, including prominent rocks. In fact, DeTroyes referred to this place as Marabout in his 1686 journal. We were fast asleep by 10:00, secure in the feeling that we were being well guarded by Le Rocher Capitaine. We had made fifteen miles today, mostly against strong head winds and relentless waves; but the last six miles had been quickly traveled while using our new permanent sailing rig for the first time.

Day Three

After nine hours of rejuvenating rest, when I crawled out to check the paddling conditions, I found that a moderate wind was blowing toward the southeast, directly downriver. Good news! We were on the water by 10:15, with thick, grey-white cloud cover above us and medium wind and waves heading in our direction of travel. As the square sail happily grabbed the wind, and the wind and the waves grew steadily, we zipped along at a terrific pace. When the hull would sometimes drop down into the bottom of a trough between the three-foot waves, my heart would drop into the pit of my stomach as well. In three hours, we sailed an amazing nineteen miles, with me ruddering with my paddle in the stern as hard as I could to maintain our course, and Doree paddling with fast, short strokes in the bow. As non-working passengers, the boys simply enjoyed the exciting ride and sang. This exhilarating experience (which was rather heart-stopping for me, since I bore the responsibility of ruddering and keeping the craft upright in the heavy seas) ended, as all good things must eventually end, when we reached the Des Joachim Dam. Back about eight miles, a locale on the left shore that we had flashed by had been the site of the Dumoine Post, established by the French at the mouth of the Dumoine River in about 1730. In 1785, during the British era, another post had been built there, by independent Canadian traders.

In the distance, the menacing grey wall of concrete of the Des Joachims Dam stretched for a full half-mile across the channel. At about its midpoint, the tops of the seven floodgates stood a little above the rest of the 180-foot-high wall. Our first challenge was presented by the log boom that curved across the channel, about a tenth of a mile above the dam. The formidable waves and the powerful following wind, which had been so helpful in pushing us here, were now driving the canoe up onto the floating logs of the boom, creating a very disconcerting situation! However, we eventually managed to locate an opening in the obstruction near the right shore, and passed through it safely, to land on the shoreline nearby. While Doree spread out lunch materials, I scouted a portage route through the 3/4 mile stretch of ground that would take us around the dam and back to flowing water in the tailrace. The original carrying route, on the left shore, had been about a mile long, passing over high, rugged hills, and had included a quarter-mile-long lake to paddle across at the midpoint. This procedure had bypassed the two sets of Rapides des Joachims, frothing and boiling in this narrow, two-mile section of the channel.

After lunch, our carrying route took us past the dam itself, first along a trail through the woods and then on an old dirt two-track that was quite overgrown. Eventually, we had to get all of our equipment down from the high rocky area where we found ourselves to the lower level of the land below the dam. Our route passed through an area that had been cleared in 1950, to erect the towers for the high tension lines leading away from the transformer station. However, after several decades, the clearing had become heavily overgrown with tall grasses, raspberry bushes, and low brush, making the rough and uneven rocky terrain even tougher for portaging. Near the end of this area, we had to descend a ten-foot ledge of rock: first I dropped down to the lower level, and then Doree slid the canoe and all of the gear down to me. It took us three hours of considerable effort to finally reach the level area below the dam. Luckily, through all of this, the weather was beautiful.

We then scouted the service road leading to the powerhouse below the dam, as well as the various dirt roads and paths leading off from the road. To our great disappointment, the only possible put-in spot was in the tailrace just below the dam. Here, the fast and very powerful current swept around a bend, making it a very dangerous place for loading and launching. All of the other shoreline areas below the dam, for 11/4 miles down to where the channel broadened, consisted of high, sheer rock cliffs. To top it off, the entire area in which we found ourselves was encircled by a tall chain-link fence garnished with barbed wire at the top, and was closed with a locked gate, offering us no way out!

We looked around for an employee, and yelled to attract attention, but no one responded. I thought, "Canada is certainly a trusting place. Nobody to be seen...Good thing our intentions are not malicious!" Walking to the untended gatehouse at the powerhouse, I noticed an open window, and inside I spotted a red telephone that was within easy reach on a shelf. When I picked up the receiver, the phone automatically connected with a man who spoke French, so I asked, "Est-ce que vous pouvez nous aider?" We wanted someone to take us in a truck out beyond the locked gate and past the steep cliffs of the tailrace. He explained that he was the operator at the Cheneaux Dam, downriver from us, but he would phone the home of the local Des Joachim Dam operator. After a few minutes, we celebrated the arrival of this second man in a company truck. The friendly Frenchman was interested in how we had gotten into the compound, and he chuckled as I explained. He transported us through the locked gate, past the long stretch of tailrace, and two miles further downstream, to the first place where the main road reached the river. We much preferred this safe and friendly landing on Baie Meilleur (Better Bay, very aptly named) to loading in and pushing off in the powerful current of the tailrace. In retrospect, it might have been better to have taken the long, challenging original portage path of the voyageurs on the left shore, bypassing the entire area of the dam, since its long tailrace turned out to be too turbulent for a safe launch. (Doree)

With an impressive rose and gold sunset illuminating the heavens behind us, we glided a mile downriver on the smooth surface, to land on an attractive sand point. Here we set up camp and ate just some gorp for dinner, about which Kevin and Ben had plenty to say! For them, eating a hot meal at the end of a long hard day was an expectation. But Doree and I were simply too exhausted to deal with cooking, cleaning up, and repacking on this particular evening. Since this morning's departure, we had paddled nineteen miles under wild conditions, and then had tackled the extremely challenging portage around the dam, in addition to being transported by truck an additional four miles and then making an easy mile at the end of the day.

After reveling in the clear night sky, with giant stars that looked close enough to touch, we entered the tent at 10:00. While Doree gave the boys massages, I read aloud by flashlight the journal description of a much worse portage adventure that the DeTroyes expedition had experienced, north of here on the White River, on May 30, 1686:

"At a previous portage, the men in one of the last canoes had lit a fire which got out of control. It burned into the woods with great fierceness, pushed along by a very strong wind. The flames did not spread out, but burned a narrow, fiery path along the shore of the lake which we had just passed. The fire caught up with us at a fifteen-hundred-foot portage. We were in great danger because of the confusion in our ranks. Some men were reloading canoes at the top of the portage, others were packing gear over it, while some were returning to the bottom of the portage for fresh loads. There were so many comings and goings that I can think of no better comparison than that of ants bustling around their anthill. When the wind suddenly changed, our destruction appeared inevitable. Whirlwinds of flame swept the length of the portage, making it difficult for me to describe how we protected ourselves. It is equally difficult to describe the grandeur of such a fire, and the speed with which it swept through the bush. Those who were still at the foot of the portage threw themselves, the gunpowder, and other flammable materials into their canoes, and paddled out into the lake. Even there, they were in great danger because the lake was so narrow. They were only saved by covering themselves and their canoes with wet blankets, which protected them from the heat and flames. Lacking such protection, those who were in the middle of the portage had the flames sweep over them many times, and gained the end of the portage only with extreme difficulty, and with the threat of being roasted alive. As for me, I was three-quarters of the way across the portage with Father Silvie when the fire caught up with us. We were obliged to run with all our strength, while the fire pressed so closely that the sleeve of my shirt was burned by the shower of sparks and burning cinders which steadily rained down upon us. Finally, we reached a small clearing at the edge of the water, where we found that those who had managed to cross the portage had done the same as those at the other end; they had taken to the water with their canoes and all the gear and supplies that were indispensable, right down to the sacks of corn, on which the entire detachment lived. We met a group of natives at the clearing who helped us greatly in saving our belongings and other equipment. The clearing was only twenty feet wide, and so soggy that we sank up to our knees in mud. We hurriedly climbed into two canoes which came to pick us up, and moved to the center of the lake, which at that spot was only thirty feet wide. The fire then became so furious that the flames swept like a torrent over our heads, and set fire to the bush on the other side of the lake. It was a very sad thing to see us caught between two such relentless elements in canoes which, being made entirely of birchbark and cedar strips, are extremely flammable. Noting the urgency of getting out of such a tight spot, and thinking that we would be safer in a place that had already been burned over, I moved the men to where the fire had already passed. Two hours later, the men from the foot of the rapids arrived as if nothing had happened. By this time, only a few trees were still burning, the rest being black and stripped of their leaves. Those who are curious as to the cause of the fire should know that the forests of that region are composed entirely of cedar, pine, and birch. These, together with the gum that they secrete in abundance, will burn furiously once they are ignited. In the fire, we lost a canoe, some sacks of corn, and several guns. Some grenades which were in one of the sacks of corn did not explode, although the sack itself was completely burned."

In comparison, we all agreed that the difficulties which the Kent family had experienced while portaging around the Des Joachims Dam this day had been very mild. So we bedded down quite grateful, though a little hungry.

Day Four

After stirring myself at 6:00 to catch up on the diary in the tent, I was out on the shore an hour later. Having no idea that a catastrophe lay in wait less than ten hours ahead, we joyfully shoved off at 9:15, with beautiful sunny weather and a moderate tail wind blowing directly downstream, toward the southeast. This was the Rivière Creuse (Deep River) section of the Ottawa, stretching arrow-straight for some 25 miles downriver from the Des Joachims Rapids. The channel, ranging from 1/4 to 11/4 miles in width, was flanked on the Quebec (left) shore by rocky cliffs that soared to a height of five hundred feet in certain places. With a light assist from the sail, we progressed fifteen miles in four hours.

Ahead, we could see from a considerable distance on the left shore the distinctive headland called Roche à l'Oiseau (Bird Rock) and the adjacent Pointe à l'Oiseau (Bird Point). In 1686, DeTroyes noted here, "One sees on the north shore a high mountain whose rock is straight and very precipitous, the middle a black wall. This rock is named Bird Rock by the natives. Perhaps that is why the natives make their offerings here, shooting arrows over it, to the end of which they attach a little bit of tobacco." The commandant was apparently unaware that one of the cliff faces at this spot was particularly sacred to the native people, bearing ancient pictographs that depicted four canoes with human occupants.

Across the channel and a little upstream from Bird Rock, a beautiful sandy point extended well out from the right shore, like a curved golden claw piercing the blue belly of the river. This was Pointe au Baptême (Baptism Point), a place that had figured significantly in the lives of the voyageurs. This signalled the place where upbound crews traveling toward the interior left the broader channel of the Ottawa and entered its narrower section, on which they would travel some 75 miles to reach the mouth of the Mattawa. Beaching the canoe on the tip of the point at 1:15, we paused for a generous 1 1/4 hour break. This allowed plenty of time for the boys to receive their traditional voyageur baptism, and then swim in the warm shallows beside the long point of sand, under the deep blue, cloudless sky. As was customary, Kevin and Ben each made two vows during the ceremony, promising "to baptize any other voyageur who passed this location for the first time," and also vowing "to never kiss another voyageur's wife...without her consent." Then we enjoyed the customary round of drinks (in our case, just raspberry-flavored koolaid).

Resuming our travels at 2:30, we paddled with a light sail assist over the remaining five miles of the Rivière Creuse section of the river, plus eight miles along the northern end of its Lac des Allumettes section, which broadened to 13/4 miles in certain places. About three miles before we were to branch off from the Lac section toward the east and enter the narrow Chenal de la Culbute, we passed the site on the left shore where the H.B.C. post of Fort William had operated from 1828 to 1869.

The Chenal de la Culbute (Tumbling Channel) was one of two places on the Ottawa River where the voyageurs could make a detour in a side passage, instead of remaining on the main channel. The choice, whether traveling upriver or downriver, depended upon the water level in any given season. The Chenal de la Culbute, aptly named the Tumbling Channel for the multiple rapids and the deep gorge at its western end, was a narrow and rugged passageway that ran nearly straight east. To the south of it, the main channel, called Lac des Allumettes, made a very broad curve that passed first to the southeast and then back north, to meet the outlet of the Chenal de la Culbute. When the water levels were low enough, taking the east-west cutoff route of the Culbute Channel entailed a passage of fifteen miles, compared to 26 miles if traveling on the main channel of Lac des Allumettes. The two routes encircled a rounded triangular island that was called Île des Allumettes. The ancient French name for both the main channel and the island, des Allumettes, stemmed from an incident that was explained by DeTroyes in his journal of the 1686 expedition: "A Jesuit priest who had passed there earlier had forgotten the box of *allumettes* (matches) that he used for starting fires, which is why the voyageurs have given the name to this place." Allumettes were thin splints of wood that had been soaked in a sulphur solution; they were used for transferring to tinder and firewood the sparks of flint and steel that had been caught in a piece of charcloth or other material.

The Chenal de la Culbute route (sometimes termed the Petite Allumettes route) entailed portaging around two rapids, located in the westernmost area of the channel. In comparison, the main channel (sometimes called the Grande Allumettes route) required only a single short portage while traveling upstream, at the Rapides des Algonkins, just west of the bottom of the broad curve of the channel; the carrying path was located on the western shore, beside the passage that ran between the mainland and the present Cotnam Island. Downbound canoes could run the rapids that lay on the opposite side of the channel, between Morrison Island (adjacent to Cotnam Island) and the huge Allumette Island. There may have been a tendency for the voyageurs traveling in the largest and most heavily laden freight canoes to use the main channel, since they could paddle the entire route of 26 miles with just a single short portage. However, when water levels were not too high, and when the canoes were smaller or the amount of cargo was less extensive, the temptation to cut off eleven miles of paddling by taking the Chenal de la Culbute, even with its two portages, sometimes prevailed. For example, Alexander Henry in 1761 referred to making "two short portages" at the Rapides des Allumettes, while John Macdonnel in 1793 noted two Décharges des Allumettes and one Portage des Allumettes; Alexander Mackenzie made two portages here as well, in 1789. In 1821, being unaware of the important issue of seasonal water level variations, Alexander Sherriff commented, "The north channel, called Quelle Butte (sic) Chenal, is always followed by the voyageurs."

When Frenchmen first ascended the Ottawa River in about 1610, they encountered a substantial village of natives called the Algonkins of the Island on Morrison Island, adjacent to Cotnam Island, in the main channel. These people had constructed a barricade across the river here, to halt all canoe brigades of Northern Algonkins and Hurons who traveled up and down the river to trade with the French on the St. Lawrence. After paying a toll to the residents, the travelers were then allowed to proceed. Algonkin scouts stationed on the Chenal de la Culbute caught any canoes that tried to avoid the tolls by taking the northern cutoff route. This custom of collecting tolls here continued until the 1640s, when European diseases and Iroquois raids finally forced the surviving remnants of the Algonkins of the Island to move further north, to the upper reaches of the Ottawa River. It was at their traditional village location on Morisson Island that Champlain was turned back during his first voyage up the Ottawa River in 1613. Upon arriving at their village, Champlain asked the leader Tessouat for four canoes, so that he could continue on upriver to befriend the Nipissings and be taken by them to the Northern Sea (Hudson's Bay). Tessouat refused, explaining that it was a difficult route, and that the Nipissings were sorcerers; however, he secretly wished to maintain the middleman and gate-keeper positions that the Algonkins held, and not let the French bypass them to deal directly with the Nipissings. Thwarted in his plans, Champlain simply gave presents to the leader, erected a cross bearing the arms of France, and departed downriver for the St. Lawrence. However, he was accompanied by Tessouat's son and forty Algonkin canoes loaded with peltries, which they traded on the St. Lawrence below the Lachine Rapids, at the future site of Montreal.

Back to our trip of 1986. When we branched off from Lac des

Allumettes and traveled eastward into the entrance of the Chenal de la Culbute, we encountered a flock of about 75 to 100 mergansers on the water, at the place where the entrance of the Chenal narrowed down considerably, about a mile from the Lac. As we approached, the birds all skittered away to a safe distance, by flapping their wings and their webbed feet, but remaining on the water. It was an extremely unusual sight, seeing them stay on the surface and not fly away. However, at this time of year, they had already shed certain of their crucial wing feathers; until the new ones grew in, the birds could not fly away from danger, only skip along on the surface of the water.

In the narrowed Chenal, by crowding the left shore and remaining behind a long row of islands, we avoided the upper set of the Rapides de la Culbute (Tumbling Rapids) for 3/4 of a mile. When this passage ended, we were forced to make a right turn to the south and then a short lift-over carry of a few yards over a flat rock, which put us on the main channel flowing eastward. At the location of our lift-over, the flat rock had been blasted open in 1854, to create a tailrace for the waterwheel of a sawmill; but the passage was still not navigable for canoes. Almost immediately below the spot where we re-joined the main channel, we entered a deep gorge and encountered an imposing set of rapids. Oddly enough, these obstacles were not indicated on the map here, but were instead depicted nearly a mile further downriver. But we, in fact, were confronting the lower set of Culbute Rapids.

We ferried across the fast current to an eddy on the right shore, so that I could scout the rapids while walking the shoreline. I studied them as far as I could, until there was no more room to walk beside the river, at the point where the cliffs rose directly from the water's edge. Back at the canoe, we held a family conference to consider the situation. I thought there was a 50/50 chance that we could maneuver the course that I had planned through the rapids. It was 7:30 P.M., after an accomplishing day of 29 miles. Even if we capsized, it was time to find a campsite for the night; so we could camp below the rapids, whether we arrived there seated in the canoe or swimming beside it in the water. In the deep, narrow gorge, the daylight was already waning and the heavy evening shadows were closing in. With the steep cliffs extending right down to the water's edge, there was not sufficient room for us to camp there for the night. Since there was no going back, we decided to chance the challenging run. I took down the mast, to protect it from possible damage, and we even tucked our hats into the packs, to avoid losing them if we were to capsize.

Pushing off with high hopes, within thirty seconds Doree and I successfully navigated the obstacles in the white water, just as I had planned the route. With relief, I roared, "We made it!" However, just then we advanced into the area that I could not see when I had examined the rapids from the shore. Suddenly, the canoe was swept around a slight bend to the right and into a series of three or more sets of frothing drops, interspersed with massive wave troughs four to five feet deep. Making instant decisions, we managed to navigate the first ledge and the first of the deep troughs, but then the bow hit a submerged rock head-on. The powerful current instantly swept the stern sideways to the left and overturned the canoe, heaving us into the cold raging water.

Doree immediately grabbed Kevin and her paddle, and held tight to the bow; I did the same with Ben at the stern. In a moment, the roaring rapids twisted the canoe out of my hands, so I started trying to pull Ben toward the right shore. We were both facing downstream, with him on my left in deeper water. I had a secure grip on his life preserver behind his neck, but he was in so much roiling white water that his preserver had become nearly useless. To complicate matters, we were being quickly swept upstream by the back current, back into the turbulence below the drop of the three-foot ledge. I managed to grab a boulder on my right, and got both of us and my paddle up onto the rocky shore.

In the meantime, Kevin and I were able to maintain our hold on the canoe through the enormous troughs and standing waves, as the canoe angled across the channel to the left shore. There, the back current started sucking us back upstream, and it looked like we might soon be swept down even more of the rapids. So we decided to let go of the canoe. "Swim to shore, Kev!" I shouted. The two of us soon crawled out of the water and up onto the rocks of the shoreline. The powerful back current indeed carried the unmanned loaded canoe, wallowing on its side, back upstream near our shore. Then it drifted into the main current and was swept downriver again, through the standing waves below the last ledge drop, and over the final set of rapids a little further downstream. While floating around a slight bend to the right, it angled across the channel again, and finally lodged among many floating logs back on Tim's side of the river. (Doree)

Leaving Ben to make his way slowly forward on the shore with my paddle, I trotted along the boulder-strewn shoreline to catch the canoe before it floated away again. After I had turned it upright, the back current was constantly surging, trying to sweep the canoe and the logs surrounding it back upstream and into the turbulence below the rapids again. The only way I could buffer the canoe from being bashed against the rock ledge of the shore was to stand in the chest-deep water between the canoe and the ledge, holding the craft with one hand. With the other hand, I bailed it out for a half-hour with the thermos jug, since the bailer had been torn from its attachment string and lost in the capsize. After the canoe was emptied, I swam and walked it through the maze of floating logs to the place where Ben had slowly made his way along the shore.

In the meantime, Doree and Kevin had picked their way downstream a quarter-mile along the left shoreline, to the upper end of a former island that was situated to the right of an old abandoned set of steamboat locks. As Ben and I paddled across the river in the near-dark to join the rest of our family, we kept in contact with them by exchanging blasts on our whistles. In between whistle signals, Ben and I sang many verses of *Vent Frais* to keep up our spirits. What a happy family reunion that was, finding ourselves safely together again on solid ground, and with the canoe and all of the gear except the bailer intact!!

By now, it was almost completely dark, and we were getting chilled, since we had been soaking wet for about an hour (I had been in the river up to my chest for half of that time, while bailing). We quickly set up camp on the cobblestone shoreline of the island, amid the many sawn logs that had landed here in previous high-water times, escapees from logging operations. We found that one of the boys' sleeping bags was only moderately wet; so we put both Kevin and Ben in that bag for warmth, one at each end. We were all in bed by 9:30, but Doree and I kept the boys awake and talking for an hour, to listen in the dark for slurred speech and poor concentration, and to note any uncontrolled shivering, some of the obvious symptoms of hypothermia. Had we been up and moving around in a lighted situation, we would have also watched for lack of coordination and a bluish tinge to the lips, further signs of the dangerous and deadly cooling of the body core.

Though quite soggy in our bags, Tim and I were warm, and deliriously grateful that fate had spared each of us injuries or worse. This experience of

119

being out of control left its indelible mark on me. Lying in the tent, I replayed the events over and over into the night, unsure of whether I was awake or dreaming. "We are all O.K." I kept repeating silently to myself. (Doree)

Day Five

After nine hours of much-needed rest, we started our day at 7:30, and slowly began to recover from the previous night's misadventure. We completely dismantled every parcel in each pack, spreading out all of the wet things to dry. Luckily, the day was warm and sunny, which also made the roar of the Rapides de L'Îlet (Island Rapids) beside our island campsite a little less ominous.

Before breakfast, we checked out the old steamboat locks on the left (north) side of the island. This feature had been constructed in 1873 between the island and the left shore, to facilitate steam-powered traffic on the river; it had eventually been abandoned in 1889. On the topo map, this passage was portrayed as open water, which would have eliminated the need to portage around the rapids that flowed along the right side of the island. However, we found that the upper, shallower half of the locks was now dry and choked with sawn logs that had washed in over the years. The lower, deeper half was still clear and filled with water, but it was blocked at its lower end by a log boom. So we would have to portage around the L'Îlet Rapids, on the opposite side of our midstream island, a set of rapids which extended farther downriver than the end of the island.

We kindled a cheery fire, cooked a replenishing feast, and finally reassembled all of the packs. At 2:30, we began the portage procedure. Since there were so many sawn logs projecting out into the fast current, we were not able to line the canoe down either the shoreline of the island or the mainland along the right shore. We first ferried across the fast current of the main channel to the right shore, where we cleared a passageway through the spruce forest, knocking off or bending aside branches. Then we portaged along our cleared pathway to the downstream side of the remains of a wooden barricade, which had been built by lumbermen; it extended at an angle out from the right shore to a tiny island, where it kept floating logs directed down the main rapids instead of becoming hung up on that little island. After reloading, we paddled across a quiet lagoon and down a small rapids in a side channel, then into a placid inlet beside the main channel. Unloading again, we forged a path by breaking branches off many trees, and portaged through the woods a second time, to avoid paddling through the tall standing waves below the L'Îlet Rapids. By 5:15, we were ready to set off downriver, after nearly three hours of portaging. It had taken considerable time and effort, but we were glad to be safe and dry, and to have our gear and canoe in the same condition.

As we continued our progress downstream, we wondered what we would find at the location on the topographical map where the large rapids were depicted; we were amazed to discover that there was not even a riffle there! Obviously, the huge set of rapids where we had capsized were the rapids portrayed on the map; but they were the lower set of the Culbute Rapids, and had been misplaced nearly one mile downstream on the official government map.

We glided smoothly for two miles along the serene Culbute Channel in a half-hour, and by 6:00 had located an excellent camping spot on a point on the left bank, a couple of miles above the community of Chapeau. After setting up camp, a slight drizzle began to fall, so we erected the tarp shelter. The boys joyfully broke up a huge amount of driftwood for the fire, after which we spent a wonderful evening telling stories by the crackling blaze under the shelter, as a light rain pattered onto the brown tarp overhead. Later in the tent, we drifted off into our respective dream worlds by 10:00, having advanced only two miles for the day. However, we had completed the laborious bushwhacking portage around the Rapides de L'Îlet, and, more importantly, we had psychologically healed after the serious capsize.

Some months later, I learned from a friend that he had paddled up the Ottawa River during the early summer of 1986, about eight weeks before we took the Chenal de la Culbute route downstream. To avoid the entire gorge and rapids area in the western portion of the Chenal, where we experienced the capsize and the portages, he made a long overland carry of several miles, skirting the entire area, as suggested by local residents. In the adjacent community of Petawawa, he learned that, during the previous summer, five soldiers from the Canadian Armed Forces Base there had driven a power boat up the Ottawa about twenty miles to the town of Deep River. En route back downstream, they had made a side jaunt into the Chenal de la Culbute, just east of their base, to have a look. Unfortunately, they had been swept down the various rapids, had capsized, and all had drowned!

121

During our family discussions around the fire under the tarp shelter, we noted that the capsize had underscored the importance of inspecting the entire length of major rapids from the shoreline. We had also learned what a heavily loaded open canoe can and cannot handle in roaring white water.

However, we also considered how much less devastating a capsize was for us compared to the voyageurs of old. Our fiberglass canoe had flotation material built into each end, so that the craft floated somewhat even when it was completely filled with water, no matter how heavily loaded or badly damaged it might be. In contrast, a birchbark canoe, made of bark, strips of cedar, lashing roots, and sealant gum, barely floated when it was filled with water while heavily loaded, whether damaged or not. In addition, we were equipped with comfortable life preservers that we wore constantly while paddling, which supported us relatively well when we were in the water, no matter its degree of frothiness or our physical condition; the preservers of the boys were even designed to turn them to a face-up position if they were unconscious. The voyageurs had no such devices to support them in the water after a capsize, whether they were healthy or injured. Finally, much of our gear, made of nylon fabric, plastic, and other synthetic materials, dried quite readily. The clothing, gear, and cargo items of the voyageurs, made of wool, linen, cotton, wood, and various other materials, were often much more difficult to dry.

In spite of our much greater chances of coming through a bad capsize in better condition than the voyageurs, we knew that we were making these journeys in less than complete comfort and safety. These voyages of ours were not intended to be totally safe and comfortable; we were doing them to help us better understand the world in which our French ancestors had lived. We were attempting to find pieces of their stories; but in the process, these ventures were becoming part of our own life stories as well.

Day Six

Arising at 7:00, we stowed the gear in the packs and the packs in the canoe, and left the site which had been our comfortable and secure home for a night. This morning, Mother Nature had provided rather good conditions for paddling: 53 degrees, grey overcast skies, and a medium wind at our backs. Quickly sailing the 21/2 miles to the community of Chapeau, we discovered that there were no rapids just upstream from the bridge, although a small set was indicated at that place on the topo map. Soon, we encountered a huge log boom extending entirely across the channel. However, this particular one had three important differences compared to the previous booms: it was in the form of an immense oval, its interior was nearly filled with floating logs, and there were no openings in the barrier to allow us to travel through. Two men were tending the filled boom, apparently preparing it to be towed downstream by a tugboat. While one of them walked along the floating boom, rearranging the logs inside with a long pike pole, his partner drove a small but powerful motorboat, which he hooked onto the downstream side of the boom and pulled it in various directions to make adjustments. Since there was no opening in the upriver section of the boom for us to pass through, we had to find another solution. First, we paddled hard to drive our bow up onto one of the logs of the boom, after which Kevin and Doree stepped out onto the nearly submerged log and pulled most of our craft over it before getting back in. Then Ben and I did the same procedure in the stern, stepping out onto the boom to slide the canoe over it. After making our way through the maze of floating logs inside, we paddled and climbed over the downriver section of the boom, and were once again in an unhindered forward mode.

With excellent assistance from the sail, by 11:15 we had advanced an extraordinary thirteen miles in 21/4 hours since the morning launch, including the time that was spent sliding over the two sides of the boom! In this span of thirteen miles, we passed through the remainder of the Culbute Channel and then back into the much wider main channel.

At 11:15, we paused for 11/4 hours for a relaxing lunch break, and then sailed the six-mile length of the Lac Coulonge section of the river in an hour, as the strength of the wind and waves increased at a steady rate. At the south end of the lake, the waves finally became too much for us to handle: whenever the canoe dropped into a deep trough between rollers, plenty of water sloshed over the gunwales. Digging in deeply, my life partner and I managed to land safely on the big point that juts out from the right shore at the southern end of Lac Coulonge, to wait for calmer conditions. From 1:30 to 5:00, we all heartily enjoyed our windbound break, singing French songs, telling stories, and toasting our fingers and toes around a cheerful fire, amid the sheltering grove of cedars that had grown on the point. Gesturing toward a place directly across the channel from us, on the north shore, I identified for the family the former location of Ft. Coulonge, a post that had been operated by the French from the 1680s onward, then by independent Montreal traders and later the N.W.C. from the 1760s to 1821, and finally by the H.B.C. from 1821 to 1844.

At 5:00, the waves that were crashing onto the exposed side of the point were still too daunting to handle, so we decided to portage over the point, in order to put in on its lee side. Within a half-hour, we had completed the carry and were sailing again in the heavy surf, over the last half-mile of Lac Coulonge. When the channel turned southward, causing the land mass to block the wind behind us, we paddled on flat water for five miles down the narrower passageway, and then eastward into the entrance of the Chenal du Grand Calumet (Big Pipe Channel). Just as we entered this channel, we passed a white tugboat that was slowly pulling downstream a massive boom filled with logs. A mile down the passage, we set up camp at 7:00, and eagerly dived into a piping hot dinner. An hour after having passed the tugboat, the little vessel slowly chugged by our campsite, with its load following obediently close behind. Evening brought a magnificent sunset, with hues of pinks and fiery reds tinting the high grey clouds, and a bright golden glow spreading just above the jagged tree line off to the west.

This day, under black and grey clouds with occasional rain and a high of 58 degrees, our efforts had enabled us to advance 25 miles between 9 A.M. and 7 P.M., even though a 3 1/2 hour windbound break had consumed nearly the entire afternoon.

Day Seven

Since the air temperature measured only 45 degrees when we emerged at 6:30, sloshing around in the shallows to load and tie in the packs was a chilly operation this morning. Putting our paddles to the water at 8:15, we glided onto the waters of the Grand Calumet Channel. This was the second locale on the Ottawa at which the voyageurs could choose to veer off the wider main channel and take a narrower side route. The two passages here framed the massive Île du Grand Calumet (Big Pipe Island), with the generally wider Chenal du Rocher Fendu (Split Rock Channel) passing along the west side of the island for 16 miles and the narrower Chenal du Grand Calumet (Big Pipe Channel) looping around the east side for 23 miles. The voyageurs normally chose the eastern channel, even though it was seven miles longer, since the drop of sixty feet in elevation was contained in this passage within a single one-mile stretch of rapids, circumvented by one long and very difficult portage. In comparison, the same amount of drop in the western Split Rock Channel was spread out over four separate rapids in a span of about 1½ miles, and these were even more challenging to portage. According to John Macdonnel in 1793, this western channel was passable only for smaller canoes, since they were easier to carry.

Although the air temp was a bit brisk, the weather was gorgeous, with just a few puff ball white clouds decorating the deep blue sky. With a moderate tail wind bulging out the sail, we swept over five miles of dark blue water in the Grand Calumet Channel in 58 minutes, before taking a twenty-minute gorp break on a midstream island. What a pleasure it was to travel on this narrow passage, which varied in width from 1/10 to 2/10 of a mile, after the broad expanses of the main channel! During the next hour, again with considerable help from the wind-filled sail, we whizzed forward another five miles.

At 11:15, after making thirteen miles in three hours, we pulled into the tiny community of Île-du-Grand-Calumet, a single line of buildings running parallel to the riverbank. During our hour-long break, Doree and the boys trekked to the single restaurant in the settlement, happily returning with a feast of hamburgers, fries and cheese curds smothered with gravy, cokes, and ice cream. By now, the temperature had warmed to a sunny 60 degrees.

Now with our furnaces well stoked, by 1:30 we had paddled the last four miles to reach the Calumet Dam. This place had originally been a thundering, mile-long rapids dropping sixty feet in elevation, requiring a grueling carry along the western shore which was called the Portage du Grand Calumet. About 1⅓ miles long, this trail was infamous as the worst carry on the Ottawa, and also the longest portage on the entire mainline route between Montreal and Grand Portage, on the western shore of Lake Superior. The undulating path, passing over a high, steep hill, was challenging and dangerous, and it usually took the entire crew of paddlers to muscle the canoe over its length, double the usual number of carriers. When the DeTroyes expedition arrived here on April 27, 1686, it required two entire days for the party to complete the carry, dealing not only with the very steep slopes, but also with ravines that had turned into boggy areas choked with fallen trees. The rapids, portage, and massive island had all received their name, Big Pipe, from a nearby quarry, where native people had harvested white limestone for many centuries, for carving pipe heads. In 1613, Champlain referred to this locale by its full name, and also described the stone: "the Rapids of Pipestone (*Rapides de Pierre à Calumet*), which is like alabaster."

The massive concrete wall and steel floodgates of the Calumet Dam, running diagonally across the channel for 2/10 of a mile, had been in operation since 1925. Just upriver from the dam, a log boom stretched in a broad arc across the entire width of the river, with no openings in it to offer us passage. We approached a place near the left end of the floating boom, and slowly pushed about fifteen huge sawn logs aside to gradually make our way right up to the obstacle. The boom had been installed to keep logs such as these from floating right up to the floodgates of the dam. We all clambered out of the canoe and stood on one of the flat-sided logs of the boom, sinking it down to water level so that Doree and I could slide the loaded craft over it. Then we advanced to the left end of the dam, which adjoined low land where a long embankment of broken rock six feet high had been installed, to impound the dam's backwater. The steep slope of rock was not an easy place to land and unload. While scouting for a potential portage route around the left end of the dam, we realized that it would be a long, hard carry through the woods below the dam, after which we would have to deal with a stretch of high cliffs to finally make our way down to the water level. In addition, the river just below the dam was filled with floating logs which were impounded by a boom. These logs were being captured after being sent one at a time down a log chute from the boom area above the dam. This upper boom area was the maze of floating logs that we had earlier passed through, to reach the dam and the rock embankment. After walking the length of the dam over to the right shore, I discovered that this shoreline area had thick woods and a similar steep embankment of broken rock leading down to the water, which would make a carry and load-in there rather challenging.

Back again on the left shore, we approached the log chute operator, who agreed to transport us in his truck when he finished his shift at 4:30; but that would not be for 2 1/2 hours. So Doree called the dam operator with the phone that was located at the left end of the dam, and asked him in French "*s'il pouvait nous aider.*" The operator and three of his employees soon arrived in a pickup truck, loaded all of our gear into the back, and transported the cargo, Doree, and the boys to the right end of the dam, by a road that ran some miles away. Meanwhile, another worker and I carried the canoe over the length of the dam. One of the employees then showed us a path that led through the thick woods down to a landing spot on the slope of broken rock, a landing that was rather steeply angled but still welcome. We thanked them all heartily, loaded the canoe, and were on our way at 3:30, two hours after we had first begun to struggle with the boom and its logs above the dam. In retrospect, landing at the right end of the dam and making a short portage along the woods path and down the steep rocky slope below would have been the best route.

Now we were confronted with a very brisk head wind, slowing our pace down to a crawl. After about a mile, we worked our way through a section of strange, swirling fast currents, which were the "tops" of the mostly-flooded Chute de la Montagne (Mountain Falls). This feature, originally a roaring falls that dropped fifteen feet in elevation, had once required a portage of 385 paces over steep hills. Soon, we saw up ahead that a strong current was surging around both sides of a midstream island. Since many more sawn logs were floating down the left channel than the right one, we pulled off to the right, surveyed this nearly flooded Rapides d'Argis, and waited for the persistent head wind to let up a bit. Then I chose a route between batches of floating logs, Doree and I dug in hard, and the canoe swept through the fast swirling currents. At this set of rapids, the voyageurs had carried the cargo for 250 paces and then had lined the empty canoe. DeTroyes explained the name of this place in his travel journal of 1686: "Across from our camp, we saw a cross, at the foot of which is interred one named Dargy [same pronunciation in French as d'Argis], voyageur, who drowned there some time ago in pulling his canoe to the portage above. The portage still bears his name."

The next couple of miles were busy ones for us, as we worked against a solid head wind and large waves, avoided floating sawn logs, and wended our way through the openings in a number of log booms, to finally reach the end of the Chenal du Grand Calumet. Near its mouth, we passed an old log booming grounds that had two offshore shanties built on pilings, one of which was gradually falling down. Loggers had stayed in these shelters while they gathered the loose floating logs that arrived, and then had driven these timbers into holding booms with long pike poles. At the mouth of the channel, we were surprised to find a huge log yard on the point, with mountains of stacked timbers extending all along the shoreline. This, then, was the destination of the innumerable sawn logs that we had encountered at so many places upriver. We breathed a great sigh of relief, since we would face no more challenges from log booms during the rest of our voyage on the Ottawa! (Many years later, we would learn that the procedure of transporting sawn logs down this river to the various mills with booms and tugboats had ended in the early 1990s. Thus, if we had canoed this waterway a decade later, we would have been spared the grief of those challenging booms and hundreds of floating logs!)

Landing at the exit of the Chenal du Grand Calumet, we pitched our camp in an open area of high, lush grass. In the channel here, the Rapides du Sable were now completely submerged. At this place, the voyageurs had done a décharge, hauling the cargo over the path for 135 paces and then lining the empty craft. At dusk, when I ambled down to the water's edge to snap a picture of the massive stacks of logs across the channel, bathed in the rich golden rays of the sunset, a beaver came swimming out of its lodge on the sandy shoreline to the right of our camp. It cruised calmly in the placid water in front of our site, across the little bay, and on beyond the point to our left. Then two more beavers exited from the same lodge, and also started across the same bay. After one of them dived quietly, I decided to purposely make the other one slap its flat, naked black tail on the surface of the water, giving the traditional warning signal. As soon as I snapped a stick, the beaver immediately slapped its tail and dived. What a rare, special treat, seeing these animals going about their usual evening activities at sunset! It always amazes me how beautifully adapted they are to working and traveling underwater, able to remain submerged for up to fifteen minutes at a time. When they dive, a clear membrane covers and protects their eyeballs, so they can remain open; in addition, valves close off their ears and nostrils, and their lips seal off their mouth while leaving their front incisors exposed for carrying branches: truly a well-designed creature!

Thus ended another day on the river. Since this morning's departure, we had put twenty miles beneath our green hull, including the two-hour ordeal of portaging the Calumet Dam and some very challenging paddling below that obstruction. On this year's excursion, we had already covered 140 miles in six traveling days, averaging 23 miles per day, plus the one day that had been virtually lost after the major capsize.

Day Eight

When we crawled out of the tent at 6:00, it was a rather brisk 44 degrees out, with a few scattered clouds marching off toward the east across a pale blue sky. While packing the gear, we were pleased to watch one of the three beavers from the night before calmly swimming back to its lodge in the mist-covered water in front of our camp, after a night of munching bark, green leaves, and water plants.

Within two hours of our put-in at 7:30, we had advanced six miles to arrive at the Cheneaux Dam, beside the little community of Portage du Fort. This dam, built in 1950 at a diagonal across the channel, consisted of a wall running from the left shore to a large midstream island, a second wall connecting this island to its large neighboring island, and finally the domineering row of sixteen floodgates and the power house between the second island and the right shore. Just upriver from the left end of this row of obstructions, we made an easy portage around the end of the wall, which took us through the town park beside the river. After finishing the carry, we enjoyed a relaxing lunch on a flat rock ledge in the warm sun, and were again afloat by 11:00. This portage had certainly been a welcome change from the difficult experiences that we had endured at the two previous dams on the Ottawa! The Rapides du Fort (Fort Rapids), now submerged beneath the backwaters of the dam and the two walls, had originally consisted of a line of three thundering cascades, flowing down the three channels between the shorelines and the two islands, dropping seventeen feet in elevation. In 1686, DeTroyes explained the name of the place where he and his party carried both their cargo and the 35 canoes for 600 paces: "These rapids take their name from the fort which the natives [Algonkins] had constructed in earlier times [during the 1640s] to protect themselves from the raids of the Iroquois." This carrying place was one of the locales at which Champlain measured the latitude with his bronze astrolabe during his first voyage up the Ottawa in 1613. A trading post had been operated by the French at this location from the late 1600s onward.

The bright sun had now warmed the air to 65 degrees, and a light tail wind was pushing us gently forward. Four miles downstream from the dam, I aimed the bow on a straight course directly southeast through the middle of Les Cheneaux Islands, encountering fast and very swirling currents as well as one whirlpool. Les Cheneaux (The Channels) was the name that the voyageurs gave to this stretch of several miles, where swift currents and some rapids flowed in narrow channels between a grouping of about a dozen pine-clad islands. When traveling upriver, the voyageurs crowded the banks and, depending on the water level, paddled hard, poled, or lined the canoe to move forward. Sometimes they had to unload half of the cargo and make two trips up the fastest parts of this section, or instead portage all of the cargo and take the canoe up empty. When Champlain passed through here in 1613, he recorded the name of this section of the river as "Petit Sault," Little Falls.

When our canoe shot out of Les Cheneaux and onto the broad waters of Lac des Chats (Lake of the Raccoons), there was a strong breeze blowing directly at our backs, coming out of the northwest. With the sail tugging the hull forward and our paddles flashing in the sunlight, we zoomed in a rather heavy surf over the fifteen mile length of the glistening blue lake in three hours, to reach the town of Arnprior by 4:00. At this point, we had already advanced twenty-six miles since our morning launch.

At Arnprior, we paddled up the mouth of the Madawaska River to the marina, hoping to arrange to hire a truck that would carry us around the massive Chat Dam, which lay six miles downriver from the town. The marina employees were no help at all, but a local boat owner phoned a truck owner for us; however, the man was not due home for an hour or two. We then traveled a little farther upstream, to the town itself. At 5:00, Doree and the boys hiked into town to buy a hot meal, and hopefully to also line up a truck for the portage trip; they were back in a half-hour, with both! Paddling across the river to a boat dock, we loaded everything into the back of a pickup truck, and happily feasted on chicken dinners while zipping the ten miles by highway around the entire Chat Dam area. This very windy ride in the back of the truck, taking us to the first locale below the dam where the main road met the river, eliminated 8 1/2 miles of river travel (six miles of backwater above the dam plus 2 1/2 miles of channel below it), and spared us from having to make a laborious portage around the combined dam and retaining wall, which stretches for three miles in the form of a huge crooked C facing upriver.

Before the Chat Dam and the long adjacent walls were constructed in 1931 (more than three centuries after our French ancestors had begun paddling this waterway), the stretch of several miles of river above the Sault des Chats (Falls of the Raccoons) offered the voyageurs strong current flowing between a number of islands, which are now submerged. Upbound canoes were often handled by lining, or instead by a demi-décharge, with half of the cargo being unloaded on shore, and the stretch of water being paddled up in two separate loads. In 1821, Nicholas Garry documented the challenges that were faced here: "The passage for two miles is through a winding channel of the most frightful rapids running at least 10 m.p.h. over beds of rock. Here the skill of the voyageurs now shows itself: at one moment using poles, then their paddles, then jumping into the water, now using the tow line, which if it would break would end in certain destruction for all."

Below this area of fast current and islands lay the Chat Falls, which greatly impressed Champlain in 1613: "We proceeded [upriver] on our course to a great falls, nearly three leagues broad, in which the water falls a height of ten or twelve fathoms [fifty or sixty feet] in a slope, making a marvelous noise. It is filled with a vast number of islands, covered with pines and cedars." At this place, a ridge of Canadian Shield granite crossed the entire 2 1/2-mile-wide channel of the river. Seven major passages and numerous smaller ones had been cut through the ridge by the turbulent flow of water over thousands of years; this had produced six major islands plus another nine or ten smaller ones, all standing in a curved line across the channel. This row of large and small waterfalls had created a deafening roar, and had offered a breath-taking scene on the downstream side. On the second major island from the north shore, a difficult portage path led up to quiet water above. The trail was only 275 paces long, but it was steep and uneven, and ascended a high hill; this made carrying the canoes particularly challenging, whether traveling upriver or down.

The massive row of falls and the very long lake above them were both named Chat, translated into English as Raccoon. Most speakers of modern French probably think that this term referred not to raccoons but to wildcats/bobcats. However, in New France, these cats were called *pichou du sud*, while lynx were termed *pichou du nord* or *loup cervier*, and panthers/cougars/pumas/mountain lions (all the very same creature) were called *michipichou* or *tigre*. The translation of the French Canadian name for both the lake and the falls as Raccoon was confirmed by the Anglo John Macdonnel in 1793, when he noted, in English, that these water features were named for the many raccoons that were formerly found in this locale; Nicholas Garry also confirmed this same information in his travel journal of 1821.

Unloading our gear and canoe from the pickup truck at the Quyon Ferry Landing, 2 1/2 miles below the Chat Dam, we were back on the water at 7:00. A supply depot for traders had been established by Joseph Mondion in this area in 1786; fourteen years later, it was purchased by the N.W.C., and the post finally became the H.B.C. facility called Chat House, which operated until 1837. While we glided past the low, reedy shores along this stretch of the river, I explained to the family that we were now leaving the Canadian Shield country on the right (Ontario) shore, while Shield features would continue on the left (Quebec) shore for another eighty miles or so downstream. The bedrock beneath the right shore was a low coastal plain, where an arm of a giant sea had covered this region some 450 million years ago, laying down limestone, sandstone, and shale in the area that extended from the present river for about 75 miles toward the south.

Amid the soft golden hues of sunset, Ben paddled as the *avant* for four miles on the glassy surface of the water. After locating an excellent site on relatively high ground on a large midstream island, we all worked quickly as a team to set up camp in the last rays of light, with Kevin handling the tent almost entirely by himself. As a result, we were all squared away and snug in our sleeping bags within 45 minutes, and fast asleep by 10:00. This day, the thirty miles that we had advanced had set a new record for us, representing the most miles that we had ever covered in a single day of paddling up to this point.

Day Nine

After a sugar-low episode in the night that required a shot of peanut butter, I rose at 7:30, ready to face the challenges of what might possibly be the final day of this voyage, since our campsite lay 25 miles upriver from the city of Ottawa. When we commenced our forward progress on Lac des Chênes (Lake of the Oaks) at 8:45, the conditions were nearly perfect: sunny blue skies, scattered fleecy clouds, 55 degrees, and sparkling flat water. After three hours of fine progress, we took a short break for a snack of gorp while floating in midstream. Then a moderate side wind sprang up, bulging the blue sail a little and offering a welcome assist to our paddle strokes. A little after noon, we halted for a half-hour rest on shore, having covered twelve miles since leaving the campsite. While on land, Kevin practiced his technique of skipping stones across the surface of the water.

Since the side wind and waves increased considerably in strength during our break, we faced a challenging and rather wild sail down the remaining ten miles of the lake, as we dodged numerous sailboats and many windsurfers who ventured far out from the marina and beach at the town of Aylmer. All of this hoopla reminded us that, in the so-called "civilized" world, this was Saturday afternoon of Labor Day weekend.

Arriving at the Rapides des Chênes at the end of Lac des Chênes at 3:00, we took a well-deserved lunch break, and then made the traditional portage of 740 paces over level ground along the left shore, which took us along the edge of a grassy park. In seasons when the water level was not very high, the voyageurs would sometimes line their emptied canoe against the current along this shoreline. When the DeTroyes expedition made the carry around these rapids in 1686, the commandant noted in his journal: "Proceeded to the Portage of the Oaks, thus named because of the quantity of these trees that are found at this place." At one of the houses in the little community where we made the carry, Doree phoned the staff of L'Auberge, to arrange for the shuttle driver to bring our car to us at the end of the day. However, both Vic the driver and Don the proprietor were absent at the moment, due back in about an hour, so no arrangements could be made at that time with the single employee who was on hand.

At 5:15, intent upon covering the final three miles, we pushed off for the last time on this trip. As we approached the Rapides Remic under the Pont Champlain (Champlain Bridge), the canoe ran aground numerous times in the last mile or so, due to the very uneven and rock-laden bottom combined with the shallowness of the water. As a result, I was in the river pushing or pulling during much of that last mile, sometimes stumbling and once turning an ankle as I sought footing amid the thousands of loose broken stones that covered the riverbed. At 6:15, just above the frothing rapids, we landed on the left shore at the north end of Pont Champlain, in Hull/Gatineau, Quebec. Here, we ended our 25 mile day and also our voyage, on the wooded front yard of Amy and Ed Dignan. Directly across the channel lay the high-rise city of Ottawa, capital of Canada and the fourth most populous city in the country, offering great contrasts to the rocky, evergreen-clad wilderness terrain that we had been traveling through for more than a week.

Doree was invited into the Dignan's home to call Vic, to have him bring our car from L'Auberge. During the 4 1/2 hours that it took for him to drive to us, Amy and Ed took very good care of the Kent family, who had been complete strangers until our unannounced intrusion. They drove us to a nearby burger restaurant to pick up a celebration meal, provided coffee and doughnuts, and made us feel very welcome in their warm and friendly home while we waited for our shuttle driver to arrive.

At 11 P.M, we loaded the car with the canoe and all of the gear, said our hearty thank-yous to the Dignans, and headed back to L'Auberge, where we arrived at 3 A.M. Sunday. Since the cottages were all occupied, Vic graciously invited us into his big cabin, where we slept serenely on the floor in our sleeping bags. In the morning, he prepared a huge feast of pancakes and baked beans for us, to begin to replenish some of the weight that we had burned off during the 203 mile, nine-day expedition. We had averaged over 25 miles a day on each of the eight traveling days, not counting the day after the capsize, when we had only made two miles of forward progress.

This voyage had offered several pleasant changes from the two previous trips along the mainline route. Since it took place during my month-long August vacation from the Symphony, I did not have to practice to keep my chops in shape. In addition, the later season brought warmer water temperatures, so we did not have to wear the somewhat confining wet suits, as we had done during both of the June voyages. Finally, there were no blood-sucking insects at all to bother us. In contrast, the two previous jaunts had been made during the shorter June vacation period, when I had been obliged to practice three times a day; in addition, the early season had meant colder water temperatures and large populations of mosquitoes. Another pleasant surprise: by this point, Kevin had grown enough in strength and stature that he insisted on carrying his mother's big and heavy (65 pound) Duluth pack on the portages! On this trip, however, the boys had been afforded fewer opportunities to paddle, since the danger level was often high, with numerous log booms to contend with, as well as long stints of sailing in massive surf and strong winds during many of the days, as the prevailing westerlies remained consistent.

At L'Auberge, outfitted in loaned cowboy hats from Vic, we took an hour's horseback ride along the trails through the woods, before transforming ourselves in the shower. When we finally started the long trek by car toward home, we marveled at what an effortless way this was to travel, compared to paddling a canoe! At North Bay, we stopped for a celebration feast of succulent steaks, potatoes, and salads at a steak house, spent the night at a motel further along the route, and drove throughout all of the following day, to finally arrive home at midnight. What adventures we had experienced since leaving the house two weeks earlier!

VI

Fourth Voyage Lower Ottawa River August 18-21, 1987

Qui ne risque rien, n'a rien.
(literally: He who risks nothing, has nothing.
figuratively: Nothing ventured, nothing gained.)
French proverb

The way to develop self-confidence is to do the thing you fear
And get a record of successful experiences behind you.
William Jennings Bryan

The reward of a thing well done is to have done it.
Ralph Waldo Emerson

After my Chicago Symphony concert at Ravinia Park on Sunday evening, we departed at 9:30 P.M., ready to make the eighteen-hour drive to the city of Ottawa. While we were headed east across lower Michigan in a heavy rainstorm, a jetliner struck the expressway overpass adjacent to the Detroit airport, just after takeoff; all 153 passengers were killed, as were all of the crew members. As we were detoured around the closed section of the highway, this event was certainly food for thought. Although we were headed for a canoe voyage on a major Canadian waterway, we were actually more likely to be killed in a highway accident than in some catastrophe in a secluded location on the river. About 43,000 people die in traffic accidents each year in the U.S., while only a handful of fatalities occur from canoeing accidents in a given year. However, as I surveyed our little family in the darkness of the car, I realized that, although I had carefully planned our activities on the river, and would do all I could to keep us safe during the trip, none of us could know when or how tragedy might befall us. We have to be grateful for every good moment, I mused.

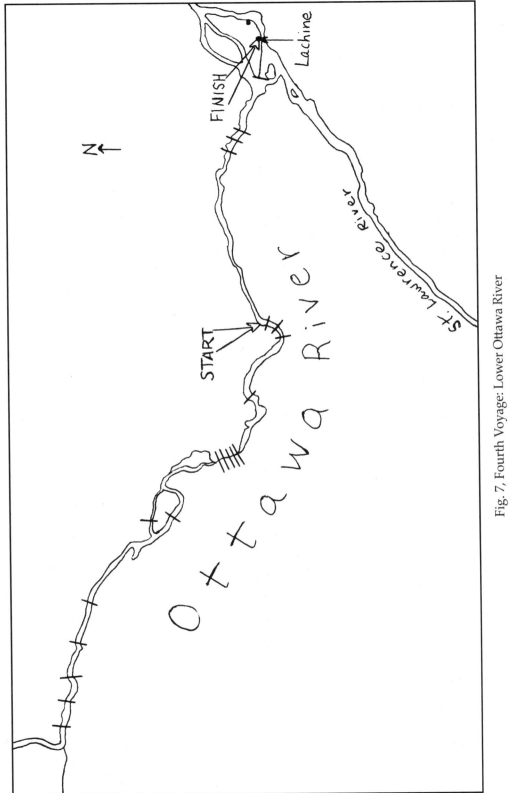

Fig. 7, Fourth Voyage: Lower Ottawa River

Driving through the night and most of the next day, we finally reached Ottawa at 4:30 P.M. Crossing over one of the five bridges to Gatineau/Hull on the Quebec side of the Ottawa River, we first found the planned put-in site, in Jacques Cartier Park below the Pont Alexandra (Alexandra Bridge). Then we assessed by car the shoreline upriver from there, but found no other possible put-in places nearer to the Chaudière Falls for a safe and calm launch. Finally, we drove further upriver to the portage around the Petits Rapides de Chaudière (Little Kettle Rapids) in the riverside community of Val Tetreau, since this feature was located in the 21/2 mile stretch of the river that we would miss, between last year's take-out and this year's paddling route. Walking along the original carrying path of 700 paces that circumvented the Little Kettle Rapids, we ascended the side of a steep hill of nearly barren rock, using a set of steps which the voyageurs had created from thick slabs of stone to ease their labors. Stooping down to Kevin and Ben, I quietly told them that their feet were stepping on exactly the same stones that the moccasin-clad feet of our ancestors had trod. In the adjacent Brébeuf Park, we visited a tall cobblestone pyramid surmounted by a life-size bronze statue of Father Brébeuf. This was a monument to the missionary who had walked this very path in 1615, while en route with Champlain to visit the lands of the Hurons at the southern end of Georgian Bay. Also in the park is a subdued yet moving tribute to the many thousands of French voyageurs who traveled this route, including various of our direct forebears, between 1610 and 1760 during the French regime, as well as over the following century during the British regime. The monument consists of a huge boulder, on one flat side of which is mounted a crossed pair of full size canoe paddles cast in bronze.

Arriving at the home of Amy and Ed Dignan, near the north end of the Champlain Bridge where we had ended the Ottawa River trip the previous year, we were graciously welcomed and treated to dinner. Afterward, we discussed with Ed the details of his shuttle driving duties, and hit the sack early as house guests of the Dignans.

Day One

We roused ourselves early, had breakfast, and were loaded into the canoe and on the water by 10 A.M. Kevin, now age 1011/12, and Ben, 92/12, were both determined to paddle more miles this year than the conditions had allowed during the previous trip on the Ottawa.

Since that voyage, Kevin had finished his three years in Cub Scouts, during which he had earned every award possible, including the Unitarian-Universalist "Love and Help" religious medal; he had recently advanced to Boy Scouts, and had already earned the Mile Swim award. Ben, following the same track of achievements, had completed one year of Cub Scouts. He was particularly intrigued with activities that focused on the ancient ways of native life.

After launching in Jacques Cartier Park, we first paddled a mile upstream, to check out the lower end of the ancient Grand Chaudière Portage on the north shore, which had led around the Chute de Chaudière (Kettle Falls). This magnificent torrent, plummeting forty feet over a ridge of granite that extended across the channel, had worn a deep basin at its foot over the span of thousands of years. Because of the shape of this basin, and the mist that rose from it like steam from a kettle, the natives had named the place Asticou, meaning cauldron; the French termed it Chaudière, in a direct translation of the native word. The original portage of about 200 paces, starting in a small bay at the foot of the rapids below the falls, presented difficulties to the voyageurs in lifting the canoe out of the water and carrying it up a steep hill. After that, the route passed so close to the shoreline that the men were often drenched with spray from the falls when the wind was from the south. When Champlain passed here during his 1613 trip, he described the sacred native ceremony that he witnessed: each person in the party placed a small piece of tobacco on a wooden plate, after which the filled plate was thrown into the cataract, to accompany the prayers of the natives to the powerful spirit of the falls.

Slightly downstream, the imposing Parliament Buildings of Canada, begun in 1860, rose from the high bank on the southern shoreline; beside them lay one end of the Rideau Canal. This water passage, constructed between 1826 and 1832, extended for 125 miles southward to Kingston on Lake Ontario. It offered an alternate water route between Montreal and Kingston, by way of the Ottawa River instead of the St. Lawrence River, for the boats of military convoys. In the minds of Canadian leaders in the early nineteenth century, this was very important, in case war were to ever break out again between Canada and the United States, and the St. Lawrence River were to come under the control of the Americans. A mile downstream from the head of the Rideau Canal, we coasted past the impressive

Sault de Rideau (Curtain Falls), a wall of frothing white water some 35 feet high where the Rideau River falls straight down over a cliff at the very edge of the Ottawa River. In 1613, Champlain noted that "it makes an arch four hundred paces broad. The natives take pleasure in passing under it, not wetting themselves except from the spray which is thrown off." In the stretch of the river for about sixty miles downriver from these falls, the voyageurs had faced only fast current, without any rapids.

It was a bright sunny day, with fat white clouds loafing across a pale blue sky, and the air temp already measured 85 degrees in the shade by 10:30. To top it off, a moderate following wind was filling the sail, causing it to billow forward. Departing from the falls, we covered nine miles in three hours, with a ten minute break en route. Along this stretch, we glided silently on two occasions while watching a solitary great blue heron stalking fish in a reedy area at the river's edge. Here in the lower Ottawa Valley, the rocky hills and low, evergreen-shrouded mountains of the Canadian Shield are still present along the left (Quebec) shore, but they lie back from the water, with a moderately wide flood plain containing rather fertile soil between them and the river. This is in contrast to the upper Ottawa Valley, where the rocky hills and low mountains lie at or very close to the water's edge, with either no flood plain or a narrow one with less fertile soil.

After a 45 minute lunch stop on shore, we were back afloat by 2:15, and advanced another ten miles in three hours. At about the midpoint of this segment of the river, on the north shore at the mouth of the Rivière du Lièvre (Hare River), we passed the site of the Rivière du Lièvre Poste, which the French had established in about 1735, and which Alexander Henry had noted when he passed here in 1761. Nearly a century later, a H.B.C. post had also been operated at this site.

Knowing that we were only a few days away from the St. Lawrence Valley and its sixty or so ancestral communities, our cruising conversation during the afternoon turned to the great numbers of French Canadians in the St. Lawrence settlements who had participated in various aspects of the fur trade. Most of these men and women have gone unnoticed, even among those people who are avidly interested in the history of the commerce in furs and hides. However, these French workers, supplying merchandise, equipment, transport vehicles, and provisions, as well as manpower and many diverse talents, had been absolutely crucial to the success of the business. For instance, seamstresses created shirts and hooded coats, as well as a few other garments and innumerable shipping bags; finger weavers fashioned sashes and garters; pewterers cast buttons; coopers turned out kegs of various sizes; carpenters and joiners assembled rough packing crates and finer chests and trunks; and carvers made stone heads for calumet pipes, as well as canoe paddles. In addition, basket weavers fashioned durable hampers for transporting nested brass kettles; blacksmiths forged axes, hatchets, harpoon heads, and ice chisels; warehouse laborers unpacked, packed, and hauled cargoes; canoe builders fashioned and repaired watercraft; forest workers gathered birchbark, various woods, lashing roots, and sealant pitch for these craft; and farmers raised pigs, peas, corn, wheat, and tobacco to produce provisions. Besides all these individuals working behind the scenes, hundreds of voyageurs, guides, interpreters, and traders from the St. Lawrence communities practiced their occupations on the waterways and in the interior each year. Similarly, large numbers of French, Métis (mixed French and native), and native individuals who lived permanently in the interior produced canoes and equipment, provisions, and trade items, while hundreds of other permanent residents of the interior worked as traders, interpreters, guides, and voyageurs.

Thinking that twenty miles had been sufficient progress for our first day on the water, we decided to check out a potential campsite on one of the long, slender midstream islands. Liking its prospects, we untied the gear from the thwarts and hauled it all up onto the bank. Only after Kevin and I began to get stinging bites on our legs beneath our pants did we notice that the entire area was infested with hundreds (or possibly thousands) of red fire ants! So we hastily loaded everything back in, and paddled another five miles before locating a good campsite at 7:45, away from houses and on land that was neither posted nor inhabited by stinging ants. We had covered 25 miles of the river route today, plus about two miles of paddling at the beginning of the day when we had checked out the Chaudière Falls and the foot of its original portage. For much of the day, first Kevin and then Ben had occupied the bow seat, and each of them had dug in strongly with the paddle.

Before drifting off to sleep, we discussed the tiny red creatures that had discouraged us from camping on their turf fives miles upstream. A colony of fire ants has multiple queens that can produce as many as 1,500 eggs per day for as long as seven years, so the number of ants in a given colony can be immense. These insects sting their prey multiple times, and they also release an attack hormone that calls large numbers of other ants to swarm to the spot and join in the attack. We were glad that we had discovered them at our potential campsite shortly after arrival, rather than in the middle of the night when we had all our gear unpacked and set up!

Day Two

We opened our eyes for the day at 7:30, and were paddling within ninety minute. The weather gods had provided a magnificent sunny day, warming to about 85 degrees by mid-morning, with a moderate wind from directly behind us, making the sail bulge out nicely as we headed due east. By the time we took a lunch break at 11:45, we had covered twelve miles of glimmering blue water. At this stop on Grande Presqu'Île, we were positioned exactly eight miles north of Curran, Ontario, the home area of my most recent Bouchard ancestors. My maternal grandmother Elizabeth Lalonde had moved from the Curran area to Michigan with her parents and siblings in 1884. This area, which eventually became the easternmost tip of Ontario, has been populated by considerable numbers of French settlers since about 1800. Some two miles up the Ottawa from our break spot, near the mouths of the South Nation and Petite Nation Rivers, Fort Français had been established in about 1730; Alexander Henry mentioned this French post in his travel account of 1761. After our rest, we advanced nine miles in two hours with the help of the sail, and took a break at the village of Lefaivre for an hour. A little restaurant in this community was the source of delicious burgers and fries, which Doree and the boys purchased on a foray into town and brought back to the canoe. Afloat again at 3:30, we covered thirteen more miles in three hours, and then located a campsite on an island just upriver from the town of Hawksbury at 6:30.

During this latter stretch of easy cruising, with its relaxed rhythm of constant paddle strokes, we chatted about the career of our ancestor François Brunet dit le Bourbonnais, whose work during the 1670s and 1680s had spanned various early developments in the fur trade. After emigrating from France in 1669 or earlier, he settled in Montreal, and married there in 1672 at the age of 28. During this period, only two decades after the French had begun paddling into the interior to trade, official licensing and contracting of voyageurs had not yet been established. As a result, there is little clear documentation of fur trade activities at this time in notary records. However, LaSalle's own expense accounts indicate that Brunet and his single partner were hired by him to haul freight by canoe between Lachine, seven miles southwest of Montreal, and Fort Frontenac, at the eastern end of Lake Ontario, on four occasions during the period of 1675-1677. The presence of only two paddlers in their craft was not at all unusual at this time: canoes manned by either two or three voyageurs were the norm for about the first seventy years of the French interior commerce, from the early 1650s until about 1720. In 1682, an official system of licenses, as well as notary contracts between voyageurs, traders, outfitters, and investors, was implemented. However, the surviving contracts of voyageur-traders that have been located in the records of notaries in the Montreal region include only one example from 1682, two from 1683, and one from 1684, all representing the hiring of men to travel to the Ottawa Country. This was the term that the French used for the entire upper Great Lakes region, where the commerce was centered at St. Ignace on the Straits of Mackinac. In 1685, two years after the first French soldiers had been sent to establish Ft. DeBuade at the Straits, thirteen men were contracted as voyageur-traders for the Ottawa Country, while one man was sent to Sault Ste. Marie. One of the thirteen traders bound for St. Ignace was our forebear François Brunet, who had moved with his new family from Montreal to Lachine soon after land was granted to him there in 1673; this latter community would be his official residence for the rest of his life.

During the 1670s, two systems of supply and distribution in the interior had been developed, which were continued throughout the rest of the fur trade era. One plan involved *hivernants* or winterers, who remained in the interior while trading for several years at a time. These men were served by *voyageur* colleagues from the St. Lawrence Valley, who transported fresh supplies of merchandise in to them at St. Ignace each summer, and then carried out the *hivernants'* accumulated furs and hides. The other system involved a number of voyageur-trader partners or *voyageur-négociants*. These individuals paddled together into the interior with merchandise during the early summer, traded it over the following twelve to fifteen months, and then transported out the resulting peltries in the autumn. Their downbound journey to Montreal often required additional canoes and sometimes extra paddlers, both supplied from native and French sources in the interior, to handle the outgoing furs and hides, which were often bulkier than the incoming trade goods had been. In some instances, a party of six voyageur-traders paddled two canoes of merchandise into the interior, and returned to the St. Lawrence 11/2 years later in three canoes of peltries. François Brunet, participating in the *voyageur-négociant* system, was hired by investors to trade in the Ottawa Country for a period of eighteen months during 1685-86. At the end of that time, he and his partner, Jean Boursier dit Lavigne, the same one who had hauled freight with him for LaSalle a decade earlier, had 26 extra packs of beaver pelts that would not fit into their single canoe; they left these packs with a trusted friend at St. Ignace, to be retrieved on a voyage the following year.

In all likelihood, these two documented trading trips were not the only commercial voyages that Brunet and his partner made during this period, since hundreds of Frenchmen traveled into and out of the interior as *coureurs de bois*, unlicensed and unregistered "runners of the woods." Family members and friends of these illicit traders often acted as their intermediaries along the St. Lawrence, surreptitiously gathering merchandise and supplies for them from outfitters. These helpers also delivered the furs and hides that the traders gathered illegally to the nearby native villages of Oka or Kahnawake, to be secretly transported two hundred miles southward to Dutch and British merchants at Albany. By 1687, at the age of 42, Brunet had apparently made enough profits on various trips to allow him to remain in the comfort of his own home at Lachine for the remaining fifteen years of his life. As a source of income, he served as an investor, providing financial backing that enabled other voyageur-traders to paddle westward. Contracts from 1688-89 show that he and several of his colleagues at Lachine financed a trader in the Illinois Country during that period.

Brunet's son, François Brunet dit le Bourbonnais, Jr., also our direct ancestor, was born at Lachine in 1682. He carried on in the footsteps of his father, working as a long-term professional voyageur and trader, as was very typical for multiple generations of certain families in the St. Lawrence Valley. François Jr. made a cargo run as a voyageur between Lachine and Fort Frontenac in 1702, at the age of twenty; and from 1705 to at least 1731, he worked as a voyageur-trader based out of both Detroit and the Straits of Mackinac. In 1706, he married Françoise David, the granddaughter of Claude David, our early trader ancestor who had spent 1660-1663 on Chequamegon Bay on Lake Superior. Kevin and Ben were especially tickled to learn that this particular Brunet ancestor operated rather often outside of the official license and registration program. For example, in May of 1713, before François Brunet, Jr. could secretly depart for the interior without a permit, a new six-place canoe and a cargo of trade goods were seized by officials at his home in Lachine. In addition, the following summer, charges were brought against him and four of his colleagues by the commandant at Detroit, for having illegally paddled there with canoe-loads of merchandise to trade but without a license. Seventeen years later, at the time of his 1731 trading voyage to Detroit, François Jr. was already 49 years old; it is not known how many more years he continued in these labors, before his death at Ste. Anne de Bout de l'Île in March of 1740, at the age of 58.

These tales of two of our hardy forebears traveling along these same waters of the Ottawa River were very inspiring to us, and made the miles fly. In two good days of paddling, we had covered exactly half of the 115 miles between Ottawa and Lachine, which was located at the eastern end of the mainline route. Today, our 33 miles of progress broke our old record of thirty miles in one day; and we did not start until late (9 A.M.) and ended early (6:30 P.M.) In addition, we took generous breaks of 45 and 60 minutes for meals, and we encouraged each of the boys to paddle several miles in the bow, even though this slowed our progress somewhat. However, since the following wind helped moderately during the entire day, we still set a new personal record of 33 miles, and we were not even tuckered out at the end of the day! This clearly showed why a helpful sail had been included in the equipment of virtually every fur trade canoe during the French regime.

At the campsite, Ben gathered a generous supply of firewood and built a cozy fire at the water's edge, as we three got the tent and sleeping gear in order. While sitting by the fire for a couple of hours, we watched a thunderstorm with numerous flashes of lightning pass over the area just to the south of us. It was fascinating to observe that powerful weather front only a few miles away, while remaining out of range of its rain, lighting, and winds. (Doree)

Day Three

After nine hours of replenishing sleep that readied us for another day on the water, we were up at 7:30 and in the canoe by 9:00. At this locale, where the Ottawa turns toward the southeast for its final run to join the St. Lawrence, the Laurentian Mountains continue to march off toward the east. This low, evergreen-covered mountain range, which represents the southern edge of the Canadian Shield, lay to the north and within sight of most of the mainline route from here all the way to Grand Portage, on the western shore of Lake Superior. For downbound voyageurs, the parting of the line of low mountains from the Ottawa River here indicated that the men were about sixty miles from the head of the Lachine Portage, and thus only a couple days from the Montreal area and their homes and families.

While we paddled the stretch of river below Hawksbury, we discussed the three sets of long, difficult rapids that had originally been spread out over a span of twelve miles here; they were now submerged beneath the backwater of the Carillon Dam. Collectively called the Long Sault (Long Falls), each of these three rapids had required a portage of both cargo and canoe on the north shore, with the length of the carry depending on the water level; or the loaded or half-loaded canoe was lined along the shore if the water was not too high. After we had progressed three miles in this stretch, which is now just slow current flowing down to the dam, Kevin took over from his Mom in the bow seat; with the assistance of the sail, he then paddled for ten miles! This was quite an accomplishment for a young man who had not yet turned eleven, and who was usually the smallest boy in his school class each year.

Having advanced fifteen miles since our morning departure, at 12:30 we were approaching the Carillon Dam and the set of locks at its left flank. It was fortunate that Doree was again in the bow seat for this stretch of water. During the last mile before reaching the dam, we faced very challenging waves and turbulence, since the rollers had about five miles to build up strength and size while traveling downriver before glancing off the retaining wall of the dam and angling back at us. To increase the stability of the canoe, we dropped the sail for our wild ten-minute ride across this unnerving mixture of wave directions, which finally brought us to the entrance of the locks.

The next thirty minutes in this giant room of still water would be both interesting and rather strange for us as paddlers. Gliding into the open gate of the locks, we found ourselves in a large rectangular chamber about two hundred feet long, bounded on its two long sides by walls of concrete eight feet high, with a massive steel door at each end. Above us stretched a sun-drenched sky of a deep blue color, partially filled with puffs of white clouds. We first waited about twenty minutes, so the operator could see if any other downbound vessels would arrive. Since no others showed up, we would be making the vertical voyage by ourselves. At the sound of the warning buzzer, the surface of the water began to drop very slowly, while we held onto the wooden dock that floated on the surface along the full length of the left wall. During the course of the next ten minutes, we had the distinct impression that the concrete walls around us were rising higher and higher, until they loomed 73 feet above our seemingly tiny canoe.

At 1:00, we paddled out beneath the forward steel door, seventy feet tall, which had slowly risen in front of us, and proceeded down the length of the modern canal for 3/10 of a mile. At its terminus, we explored on the left shore the surviving lower end of the original canal and the remains of its lower set of locks near the end, all of which dated from 1825. The walls and bottom of the canal and locks, made of rectangular blocks of grey stone, were still very solid, while all parts of the wooden doors that had formed the ends of the locks had long since deteriorated, and had been removed. These features had all been constructed by the British in 1825, as part of the alternate water route between Montreal and Kingston that utilized the Ottawa River and the Rideau Canal, instead of the St. Lawrence River. At that time, a canal and set of locks were built beside each of the three major rapids in the twelve-mile stretch of the Long Sault on the Ottawa River. The canal that we were visiting had circumvented the most southerly set of rapids in the series. Since 1965, the one huge set of modern locks that we had passed through has compensated for the entire drop of 65 feet of the three rapids, while the backwater of the dam beside these locks floods all three sets of rapids.

At the southernmost of the three original canals, the one that we were exploring beside the submerged Rapides de Carillon, all but its southern end has been filled in; at the middle canal adjacent to the drowned Chute Blondeau, a segment at each end has been left unfilled, while the rest has been filled in and covered over to create

Parc Carillon. The northernmost of the three canals, running beside the submerged Long Sault and the modern community of Grenville, is still intact along its entire one-mile length. With the completion of these three original canals and locks in 1832, steamboat service was established on a stretch of over one hundred miles of the Ottawa River, extending from Montreal Island up to Chat Falls, with a land road five miles long in the area of the present Gatineau/Hull bypassing the series of falls and rapids between the Chaudière Falls and the Rapides des Chênes.

From 1:30 to 2:45, we took a lunch break at the village of Carillon, beside the remnants of the original canal that we had inspected. After feasting on burgers, hot dogs, and the French Canadian dish called *poutine* (french fries and cheese curds with hot gravy poured on top), we made a pilgrimage to the impressive riverside monument commemorating Adam Dollard des Ormeaux and sixteen other young Frenchmen. In May of 1660, these men from the Montreal area, along with a number of Algonkin and Huron friends, hastily built a stockade on this shoreline beside the Rapides de Carillon. From behind its log walls, they fended off the attacks of two huge Iroquois war parties for several days, before they were finally overrun and massacred. This brave stand by a very small group of Frenchmen and their native allies discouraged the Iroquois, and deterred them from attacking Montreal during that entire summer. When Radisson and Groseilliers passed the site in June of 1660, in a huge brigade of Ottawa and Huron canoes bound for the trade fair at Montreal, they noted remnants of the destroyed stockade on the shore. Some weeks later, when our trader ancestor Claude David paddled past this place with the same Ottawa-Huron brigade, traveling back to their native villages on Chequamegon Bay on western Lake Superior, the grim evidence of the battle was still clearly visible.

When we traveled downstream from the community of Carillon, both shores of the river now lay within the province of Quebec, the right shore no longer being in the province of Ontario. The brightness of this late-summer afternoon was almost blinding. Between 2:45 and 5:30, we advanced twelve miles, entering the blue waters of Lac des Deux Montagnes (Lake of the Two Mountains) after five of those miles. This lake-like section of the Ottawa River varies considerably in width, ranging from as much as 41/2 miles to as little as 3/4 mile. After taking a short rest at 5:30 on Île Robidoux, a tiny island in the middle of the lake, we continued on, passing the native community and Indian Reserve of Oka six miles later, at the narrowest place on the lake. On this point projecting from the north shore, a double native village called Oka or Kahnasatake had been located since 1721; originally, Algonkins and Nipissings had lived on the eastern side, while Hurons and Christianized Iroquois had resided on the western side. Certain of our French ancestors living nearby had attended the mission church of St. Sulpice, which stood between the two native villages and served them both, offering alternating services in the Algonquian and Iroquoian languages. The residents of this double village provided numerous canoes to the French over the span of many decades, as well as many warriors for French military expeditions. The N.W.C. operated the post of Lac des Deux Montagnes here until 1821, after which the H.B.C. ran the trading facility until 1848.

As the day drew to a close, a stunning sunset colored the bottoms of the low white clouds a rich hue of orange-red. At 8:30, we landed at the community of Vaudreuil-sur-le-Lac. The seigneury of Vaudreuil, as well as the adjacent seigneury of Soulanges to the south, had been the home areas of various of our ancestors since they had been first settled in 1702. In the near-dark, we could not locate the short bridge leading from the right shore out to Île Cadieux, since our view of the passage was blocked by a smaller island. We had intended to paddle beneath this bridge and camp a mile beyond it, on Île aux Tourtes (Island of Pies), a rare unoccupied island in the Montreal area, where we figured we would not bother anyone and no one would bother us. However, at this point, our well-laid plans appeared to have been thwarted by darkness. We had wondered how challenging it would be to find places to camp in the greater metropolitan region of Montreal, the second most populous city in Canada (only Toronto has more residents); however, we had not figured on having to search for those camping places in the dark and in areas of manicured lawns and fine houses.

When I approached a home on the shoreline to ask, "Pouvez-vous me dire, ou est le Pont de l'Île Cadieux?" *Madame Lamoreux, the lady of the house, pointed in the direction but, aware of the difficulties we might have in the darkness, graciously offered us her lawn as a tent site for the night! We gladly accepted, and were wrapped in warm sleep within ninety minutes of our landing. (Doree)*

Ben had paddled six miles in the bow this day, in a single long

149

session during the early afternoon. Kevin had likewise served as the *avant* during much of the morning, and again during the late afternoon and the evening, bringing his total distance for the day to twenty miles, in two ten-mile segments! Our dark green canoe had glided over 37 miles of water today, breaking the previous day's record of 33 miles. Although Doree had only paddled eleven miles since this morning's put-in, she had led a number of addition, subtraction, and multiplication sessions in French, and had taken us through various ancient French songs, including her favorite, *A La Claire Fontaine*, which ended each verse with the refrain, *"Il y a longtemps que je t'aime, jamais je ne t'oublierai"* (I've loved you for so long, I'll never forget you). And our French tongues had worked at identifying everything we could see: *le soleil, les nuages, le canot avec les avirons*. In addition, we had answered questions such as *"Qui est dans le canot?" Ou est papa?"* and *"De quel couleur est le ciel, et le bateau?"* We had enjoyed sunny weather throughout the day, with a high of 75 degrees in the shade, and a moderate tail wind had assisted us during almost the entire day.

Day Four

We awakened at 7:00 and I went into the lovely home of the Lamoreux family to phone Ed Dignan in Aylmer, to arrange his delivery of our car to us in Lachine at about 7 or 8 P.M. The boys and I enjoyed toast and jam in the well-equipped kitchen, and I savored a cup of Madame Lamoreux's coffee as we chatted about our long paddling trips. She sympathized! After thanking our hosts for the much-appreciated camping place in their yard, we learned of Monsieur Lamoreux's surprise at finding some vagrants in a tent on his well-manicured lawn. We bid a friendly adieu. (Doree)

For what would probably be the final day of this voyage, we had again been granted warm, sunny weather. While cruising eastward beside Île aux Tourtes, I shared with the family that, from 1704 to 1721, this island had been the home of about half of the Algonkins and Nipissings who had later relocated upriver to Oka, in 1721. The other half of the group had lived a mile or two to the southeast during the same span of seventeen years (across the channel near Ste. Anne), before moving to Oka. The Huron and Christianized Iroquois contingent, who also relocated to Oka in 1721, moved from their village about twenty miles north of Montreal. At the Île aux Tourtes and Ste. Anne locations, and also later at Oka, these native groups had served as guardians of the western flank of the Montreal region, protecting the French settlers from attacks by British forces and their native allies to the south, particularly the Iroquois.

Leaving the Island of Pies behind, we turned southward and paddled right beneath the massive TransCanada Highway, with its huge bridge that joins Île Perrot on the west to Montreal Island on the east. It felt rather daunting to be traveling on the dark-shadowed water beneath such a massive structure! Various of our ancestors had lived on Île Perrot, which had been first settled in 1672, as well as in a string of communities all along the shores of Montreal Island. Thousands of voyageurs, traders, interpreters, and other fur trade personnel had resided in these villages that lay within easy reach of Montreal and Lachine, which were the departure places for westbound brigades. As we were crossing the channel to reach the community of Ste. Anne, at the westernmost tip of Montreal Island, we encountered rather large waves coming from the side; these forced us to take a zigzag course, so that the rollers would be arriving from a direction that we could handle safely. I was glad that Doree was the bow paddler for this traverse. After advancing four miles from our morning launch in 1 1/4 hours, we landed for some well-deserved nourishment at Ste. Anne de Bout de l'Île, Saint Anne of the End of the Island.

This parish, established in 1686 and dedicated to the patron saint of travelers on water, had served as a significant landmark during the fur trade era. At the church here, which was the last stop in settled lands for voyageurs bound for the interior, the men received communion and a blessing from the priest, offered up their own prayer for a safe return, and left a small donation in the collection box. We visited the old church, but we were particularly interested in the convent that stood next door. Its first floor, built of a much darker tan stone than the upper two stories that had been added later, had been the original chapel of Ste. Anne, which the voyageurs had visited long before the present stone church had been constructed. It was customary for westbound brigades to advance the seventeen miles from the Lachine launch site to this chapel, stop to pray here, and then receive a large ration of spirits, which the men often consumed in its entirety at their nearby campsite. Due to the hoopla that often accompanied this bout of drinking, the custom of booze distribution in later years was postponed until the party had progressed another twenty miles, to the head of Lac des Deux Montagnes, well out of sight of "civilization." This move of the distribution spot further to the northwest also decreased the rate of desertion among first-time voyageurs who, after signing a legally binding contract, were having misgivings about the arduous work that they had agreed to perform. The further they traveled from the settlements, the less likely they were to break their contract and sneak back home.

After buying burgers and fries for lunch in the village of Ste. Anne, we were back on the water at noon. We easily shot down the adjacent Rapides de Ste. Anne, which had no obstacles, just fast shallow water flowing down a three-foot decline of elevation. Upbound brigades usually paddled or lined unloaded or half-loaded canoes up this feature, only being forced to portage the canoes when the water level was extremely high. Just below these rapids, the course of the Ottawa River turns eastward and soon joins the St. Lawrence River, forming the broad section of the St. Lawrence that is termed Lac St. Louis. Near here, Champlain took a latitude sighting with his astrolabe in 1613, before commencing his first voyage up the Ottawa. At this western end of Montreal Island, he kept a sharp lookout for "the Iroquois who prowl about these places to surprise their enemies." Some seven decades later, on September 30, 1687, our ancestor Jean de Lalonde and his nine French companions in a work party were massacred by Iroquois warriors two miles to the east of here, near the shoreline of Baie d'Urfé. After their mass grave was discovered 129 years later, in 1866, the remains of the men were entombed beneath the floor of the church at Ste. Anne.

With a stiff following wind and large whitecaps that were coming directly from behind us, we had a heart-racing eastward sail that covered eight miles of Lac St. Louis in 1 1/2 hours, to reach the community of Pointe Claire. While taking a welcome hour-long break in the quiet, sheltered bay beside the church of St. Joachim, our conversation turned to the various ancestors who had lived here since the village and the farms nearby had been first settled in 1713. The ancient stone windmill standing solidly near the church, where the farmers living along the shoreline had brought their grain to be ground into flour, dates from that early era. During our rest stop, gazing out on the sparkling river that is five miles wide at this point, we watched a westbound Great Lakes freighter pass by, traveling along the St. Lawrence Seaway, which has been in operation since 1959. Both the massive waterway and the huge vessel motoring on it made us and our seventeen-foot canoe seem rather tiny in comparison!

Gathering our resolve, we left the placid bay and paddled back onto the exposed waters. Our sail along the ten miles of the eastern half of Lac St. Louis again involved wild wind and waves; but this time, the rollers were coming at us from a side angle behind the craft. Ruddering as hard as I could with my paddle in the stern, with Doree digging in at her maximum strength at the bow, we struggled to maintain a course that kept the waves from sloshing over the gunwales. With the shoreline flashing by at a considerable rate of speed, we sailed to the place where the broad lake, containing the combined waters of both the Ottawa and the St. Lawrence Rivers, narrows down to a width of 3/4 mile and begins to roil down the Sault de St. Louis or St. Louis Falls, also called the Lachine Rapids. This six-mile-long obstacle, dropping a total of 45 feet in elevation, had marked the head of navigation for wooden plank boats heading up the St. Lawrence, ever since Champlain had first arrived here in 1603 with some small boats from his ship of exploration. Since the last 21/2 miles of our route took us along the upper half of the Lachine Rapids, where the water tumbles in the midstream areas, I kept our course relatively near the left shore, as well as I could while dealing with the angle of the big waves. At one point, the official river patrol boat roared out from the left shore to see if we needed rescuing, nearly swamping us in its large wake before we could wave away the offered assistance. When the rescue team departed, they zoomed down a midstream section of the rapids, with their high-powered vessel bouncing on the massive waves and troughs, to show us what we would encounter if we ventured out too far from the shoreline area.

At 4:00, with all of the family singing *"En roulant ma boule roulant,"* we jubilantly cruised onto the smooth, sheltered water of the Baie de Quenneville, at the ancient village of Lachine (now bearing the name of LaSalle). Numerous of our ancestors had resided in this community since it had been first settled by LaSalle and his men in 1667. The village, at the end of this year's canoe trip and the eastern terminus of the mainline canoe route, lay at the head of the seven-mile portage path and cart road that had run between Lachine and Montreal. Here at this little bay had begun and ended virtually every voyage of explorers, traders, missionaries, and military personnel who had traveled to and from *le Pays d'en Haut*, the Upper Country. Due to its location at the western end of the portage, the community here had included myriad warehouses for storing merchandise, supplies, and canoes, as well as various lodgings for travelers. Gliding to a stop near the shoreline, in the small, quiet bay bordered with deciduous trees, bushes, and tall grasses, I hopped from the canoe into the shallows and snapped a picture of an elated Kent family in their places, with raised paddles, broad smiles, and "V-for-Victory" hand signs. Having advanced 21 miles today, we had completed the 115 mile trip in just four days, averaging 29 miles per day. We had now completed, in four journeys, the first five hundred miles of the ancient mainline route that stretched from the Montreal area to northwestern Canada.

After unloading all of the gear, and stacking it beside the overturned canoe in the little park beside the bay, Doree and the boys walked to a restaurant a couple of blocks away, and brought back a celebration meal of burgers and cokes. While we lounged on the grass, eating our joyous meal and basking in the warm rays of the sun, I mentioned that our ancestor Jean Quenneville had been the original owner of this piece of property, beside the narrow bay at the head of the portage path and cart road that had led to Montreal. Three years after his 1674 marriage in Montreal (which was the earliest documentation of his presence in New France after having emigrated from the Old Country), Jean and his wife Denise Marie had been granted this land. In the usual French Canadian fashion, the plot was very narrow in the width that fronted on the river, but extended inland for a considerable distance: in this case, 1/10 of a mile wide by 6/10 of a mile deep. Clearing much of the wooded property, developing a pioneer farm, and raising a family had been the Quenneville couple's work here on this property. A century after Jean and Denise had first acquired the land, British army forces built a sizable military post on their former shoreline. From the 1770s until 1826, this facility served as the departure and arrival point for all voyages to and from the British military posts on all five of the Great Lakes. It was particularly busy during the two wars that were fought against the United States, in 1776-1780 and 1812-1814. By the 1950s, only the stone powder magazine had survived from the array of fourteen wooden and stone military buildings that had comprised the post.

Kevin and Ben were also interested to learn that the pioneer farm of our forebear François Brunet dit le Bourbonnais, Sr. had been located 3/4 mile to the east of the Baie de Quenneville, along this shoreline. Two days earlier, we had discussed the progression of François' fur trade career: first as a voyageur hauling freight between Lachine and Fort Frontenac for LaSalle during the years 1675 through 1677; his later years of trading, including his time at St. Ignace in 1685-87; and finally his role as an investor backing other traders in the Illinois Country during 1688-89.

After our meal, while a local resident watched over our canoe and gear, we walked westward for about two miles along the waterfront area. Along the way, we traversed much of the property where the early residents of Lachine had lived on their long, narrow strips of farmland fronting on the St. Lawrence. At the site of the original core of the village, we visited the place where the first church had stood. During the winter of 1675-76, our ancestor Pierre Gaudin dit Chatillon, a master carpenter, built here the first chapel of the parish of Sainte Ange Gardien (Holy Guardian Angel). Having emigrated from France in 1653, he acquired his farmland at Lachine in 1673, after having spent twenty years living and working in Montreal. His pioneer farm had been located 3/4 mile east of that of François Brunet dit le Bourbonnais, Sr. The wooden chapel that Pierre constructed, in use for 27 years until 1703, was replaced by a larger stone church erected slightly to the west, which was utilized from 1703 until 1865.

While we walked, I also described to the family the infamous Lachine Massacre that had taken place along this very shoreline, on the night of August 4-5, 1689. In the darkness of that night, a massive force of some 1,500 Iroquois warriors quietly surrounded the community, and then attacked by complete surprise. In the grisly fighting, more than fifty French residents were killed on the spot, while another hundred or more were taken prisoner. Of these captives, only about half of them either escaped or were later exchanged; the others were either killed or were adopted into Iroquois families. Thirty homes in the settlement were burned to the ground that night, and nearly all of the livestock at those farms were killed. Among the deceased adults were eight of our direct ancestors, as well as five of their children who were not of our direct lineage. Ironically, one of our forebears who died during this surprise attack was Pierre Barbarin dit Grandmaison, who had come to New France in 1665 as a soldier in the thousand-man Carignan-Salières Regiment. The campaign of these troops, joined by French militia fighters and their native allies, against the Mohawk nation the following year led to a peace treaty with the Iroquois that lasted for thirteen years, until 1680. Twenty-three years after having taken part in the 1666 expedition against the Mohawks, which had brought about a period of peace, Pierre was killed by Iroquois warriors, along with his wife, one of their adult daughters, and her husband. Two other daughters, ages 71/2 years and nine weeks, were captured in the raid, were taken away, and were never heard from again. Their daughter Marie Madeleine, age sixteen, survived the attack, as did her husband of five months, to create the lineage that ultimately led down to me.

At the most distant point of our stroll, we arrived at the head of the Lachine Canal, which extended from the shoreline of the St. Lawrence at this point all the way to Montreal, nearly ten miles to the northeast. I explained that this man-made waterway had been envisioned so that transport of cargo by canoes and wooden bateaux could replace the laborious carrying of cargo by hand and in carts along the path between the two fur trade communities. According to the original plans, the canal was laid out to follow the bed of the Rivière St. Pierre for the eastern third of the route from Montreal, and also include Lac St. Pierre, which lay in the middle section of the proposed route. Before digging was begun in 1701, the owners of the four narrow strips of farmland at the proposed western end of the waterway at Lachine agreed that the canal could cross their property at a diagonal; their approval was recorded in a notary document that they signed on October 30, 1700. Two of these individuals were our ancestors Guillaume Roussel dit Sans Souci (nicknamed "Without Worry") and his wife Nicole Filliatreau. Guillaume had been a soldier in the Troupes de la Marine, the French army that had served in the various overseas colonies. He was among the many hundreds of these troops who were sent to New France during the 1680s and 1690s, to carry out expeditions against the Iroquois and also guard both the St. Lawrence settlements and the interior posts from their attacks. After his term of service was completed, Guillaume remained in Canada, married a widow with five children in April of 1700, and immediately settled at Lachine. Here he worked as a pioneer farmer and a master shoemaker, while fathering seven children in addition to his five informally adopted children.

In 1701, a stretch of canal twelve feet wide and nine feet deep was excavated due east from the St. Lawrence shoreline for 21/10 miles; this giant ditch reached the very slender Lac St. Pierre, which was 8/10 mile long. But then, less than a year after the commencement of the project, the digging was halted, and it was not resumed again until well into the British regime. Between 1821 and 1825, the entire ten-mile canal was finally completed, 28 feet wide and five feet deep, with six sets of locks to offset the 45 foot drop of the Lachine Rapids that it bypassed. The canal was later enlarged several times during the 1840s, and once again in the 1880s, to accommodate steamboat traffic on the St. Lawrence and Ottawa Rivers. Upon the completion of the waterway in 1825, most of the commercial activities of Lachine moved several miles westward along the St. Lawrence shoreline, to the head of the canal; the part of the community that remained in its original location became known as LaSalle.

George Simpson, Governor of the H.B.C. for all of North America, had a home and offices built on the canal near its head at Lachine, and soon made this the headquarters for all Company operations, instead of being based out west at Fort Garry, south of Lake Winnipeg. Some years later, in 1847, a railroad was built between Montreal and Lachine. During both the steamboat era and later after the railway was completed, it was a popular excursion for Montreal residents to ride the ten miles to Lachine on a steamboat or the train, and then enjoy a thrilling ride down the Lachine Rapids in a special wooden boat. Those individuals who had a significant connection with the H.B.C. were able to experience this ride in a large birchbark canoe powered by voyageurs. One such canoe run was immortalized in one of the most famous paintings by Francis Anne Hopkins, whose husband Edward served for two decades as the personal assistant and secretary of Governor Simpson. After Simpson's death, when the H.B.C. headquarters was moved out west to Fort Garry, Mr. Hopkins was employed for ten years as the head of the Lachine/Montreal office, overseeing Company activities as far west as Fort William on western Lake Superior. From 1858 to 1861, the Hopkins family lived beside the canal at Lachine, after which they moved to Montreal for their remaining nine years in Canada. Thus, the scenes of fur trade activities at both ends of the canal were very well known to the artist. On July 25, 1863, the North American Governor of the H.B.C. arrived at Montreal with a high company official from the London office. The two men took the train to Lachine with Edward and Frances Hopkins, after which they all rode down the Lachine Rapids, as passengers in an oversize, ten-place Montreal canoe manned by sixteen voyageurs. Some time later, Frances executed a painting of this scene, which had taken place beside the shoreline where the Kent family was strolling.

After we had returned to the park beside the Baie de Quenneville, I pointed out the native community of Kahnawake, which lay on the opposite shore of the St. Lawrence, a mile to the southwest. This settlement of Christianized Iroquois, occupied since 1676, had served the same functions as did Oka to the northwest on the Ottawa River. It produced considerable numbers of canoes for the French, provided warriors for many French military expeditions, and served as the southern protective guard-post for the entire Montreal region. In addition, both of these native communities were actively involved in secretly transporting the furs and hides that were gathered by illegal French traders southward to Albany, where Dutch and British merchants received them and sent back new merchandise in return. During the winter of 1704, many warriors from the village of Kahnawake were involved in the military expedition that attacked Deerfield, Massachussets, the most remote village in northwestern New England. The details of this raid and its aftermath became one of the most fascinating of our ancestral stories, one that we often discussed during long days of paddling.

In the wee hours of the morning on February 29, 1704, a party of more than two hundred men, including French regular soldiers, civilian militia fighters, and allied native warriors, attacked the stockaded British settlement of Deerfield, as well as the homes of the families living just south of the community. During the raid, fifty residents were killed and 112 others, including twelve-year-old Sarah Allyn, who usually resided with her family just south of the stockade, were captured. No other members of Sarah's family were killed, wounded, or captured in the attack. The captives were taken northward over some three hundred miles of frozen landscape, to live in the French and native communities along the St. Lawrence. Sarah was taken in by a well-to-do merchant in Montreal, joining a family that already had eleven children. Fifteen months after her capture, she was baptized in the Catholic Church, and officially acquired the French name of Marie Madeleine. Five years later, at the age of eighteen, after having become completely assimilated into the French Canadian culture, Sarah/Marie Madeleine married Guillaume

Lalonde, age 26, on April 27, 1710, at Ste. Anne de Bout de l'Île. Having been born and raised at Lachine, Guillaume had lost his father, Jean de Lalonde, when he was killed by an Iroquois war party just east of Ste. Anne at Baie d'Urfé in 1687, when the boy had been only three years old. In the month following her wedding, Sarah/Marie Madeleine was officially naturalized as a citizen of France, along with 82 other persons. Nearly all of these former captives were of English origin, with a few of Irish origin and one from New-Holland.

After Queen Anne's War between England and France ended in 1713, when Sarah/Marie Madeleine was age 21, officials in New England attempted to retrieve from New France all those persons who had been captured during the eleven-year conflict. All captive British children under the age of twelve were forced to return to New England, whether they wanted this or not, while older individuals were allowed to make their own choice; most of them chose to remain in their new country and continue living with their new identity.

The Lalonde couple produced twelve children over the span of 22 years, between 1712 and 1734, while Sarah/Marie Madeleine was ages 20 to 42. Among their seven boys and five girls, only the eldest daughter died young, at the age of nine; all of the other children grew to adulthood and married. In July of 1717, after seven years of marriage, Guillaume hired on to work as a voyageur in the interior for one year, to earn supplemental cash for the family. No other records of his participation in the fur trade have been located; thus, he either was employed in it during only this one period, or he worked illegally as a *coureur de bois* at other times, without official licensing and registration. At various times over the decades, the Lalonde family lived at Ste. Anne, Pointe Claire, Île Perrot, and Longueuil; in 1734, they finally moved west to the seigneury of Soulanges, where they lived out the rest of their lives as pioneer farmers. After 42 years of married life, Guillaume died in August of 1752, when Sarah/Marie Madeleine was sixty years old. She then lived for another twelve years as a widow, finally passing away at Soulanges on December 26, 1764, four years after British forces had vanquished her adopted country. When she died at the age of 72, she had spent more than six decades as a French woman, having been transformed from a girl of English and Scottish ancestry. Whenever we talked about Sarah/Marie Madeleine, we were inspired by the flexibility, courage, and determination that she had needed to meet the many challenges of her lifetime. We were also proud that part of her was now in us.

About 7 P.M., Ed Dignan arrived at Lachine with our car, and left with his daughters who live in Montreal, having provided us with excellent shuttle service. Since we had completed our paddling adventure so quickly, we still had nearly two weeks of vacation time to make pilgrimages to the home locations of various of our ancestors who had lived and died in communities along the St. Lawrence in Quebec Province.

VII

Fifth Voyage
Eastern Minnesota-Ontario Boundary
Waters, August 18-24, 1988

Life is an echo.
What you send out, you get back.
What you give, you get.

Anonymous

Take calculated risks.
That is quite different from being rash.

George S. Patton, Jr.

Success is dependent on effort.

Sophocles

In the long run, we shape our lives, and we shape ourselves.
The process never ends until we die.
And the choices we make are ultimately our own responsibility.

Eleanor Roosevelt

The stunning, poster-size photo mounted on my wall, sporting vivid shades of green for land and blue for water, had been snapped by a satellite camera high above the Montreal area. The view, looking toward the northwest, clearly showed in the foreground and the middle area the portions of the mainline route that we had already paddled: the Ottawa and Mattawa Rivers, Lake Nipissing, the French River, and Georgian Bay. Toward the rear lay the northern shore of Lake Huron, and, fading off into the distance on the gently curved surface of the Earth, stretched the eastern portion of Lake Superior. Gazing at this scene, Doree and I saw that these two huge bodies of water were logically to be next in our canoeing project. However, considering the dangers of such massive lakes, we decided to postpone the Great Lakes section of the route until Kevin and

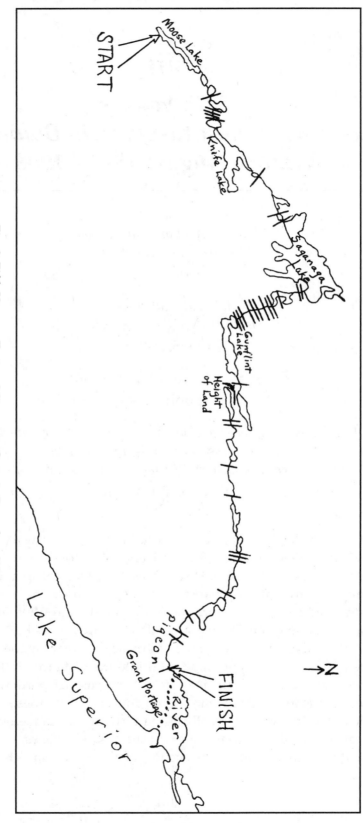

Fig. 8, Fifth Voyage: Eastern Minnesota-Ontario Boundary Waters

Ben had grown up some more. We would continue our westward progression at this time, but from the western shore of Lake Superior. When we would return to Huron and Superior some years later, the boys would be much larger, stronger, and more experienced, better able to do their share of the powerful paddling that would be required on these two vast inland seas.

As I studied period accounts of the canoe route west of Lake Superior, I realized that I had to make a decision about which series of waterways we would paddle. From the western shoreline of Superior, two different passages of interconnected rivers and lakes had been used over the centuries as the main route for traveling toward the west and northwest. These two variants converged at Lac La Croix (Cross Lake), some 140 miles due west of Superior as the crow flies. When the French first arrived to permanently establish the fur trade in this region in 1679, the main native route had long been by way of the Kaministiquia River. Thus, DuLhut and his men built the main post for the northwestern commerce at the mouth of this waterway, where it flows into Lake Superior, and christened it Ft. Kaministiquia. Four years later, this same officer and his forces established Ft. DeBuade at St. Ignace, on the Straits of Mackinac, which was already the central depot locale for the interior trade. In 1684, DuLhut also constructed Ft. La Maune/Ft. Tourette at the northern end of Lake Nipigon, about a hundred miles north of Lake Superior. This post and Ft. Kaministiquia would handle most of the French trade in the region stretching north and west of Superior for nearly half a century.

The Kaministiquia (Kam) River route, in the overall form of an irregular, overturned crescent stretching from east to west, began with the shallow Kam River, which was mighty challenging. Its vertical drop of nearly eight hundred feet over a length of only sixty miles made for a fast current, as well as fifteen sets of rapids that had to be either portaged or décharged, with the canoe partially or fully unloaded. The route then continued along Dog Lake, Dog River, Rivière de la Prairie, Cold Water Lake, Savanne River, Lac des Mille Lacs, Baril Lake, Pickerel River, Brule Lake, Pickerel Lake, Sturgeon River, Sturgeon Lake, and Maligne River, before finally entering the northeastern corner of Lac La Croix. This series of watercourses, 230 miles long, presented 31 obstructions that required either a portage or a décharge. It was the main route that was traveled by native and

French paddlers for the 52 years from 1679 through 1730, and it had been used for many centuries before that as the primary route of native travelers.

In 1731, based on native advice, the French began using the Pigeon River route instead, which flowed into Lake Superior some fifty miles south of the mouth of the Kam River. Overall, this new passage, which meandered slightly along its generally east-west course, was easier to traverse. For starters, it was about eighty miles shorter, measuring some 150 miles in length from Superior to the southeastern corner of Lac La Croix. Although the Pigeon River route required eleven more portages or décharges than the northern route, its rapids were generally shorter and steeper, requiring carries that were shorter than those around the typically long, flat rapids of the Kam passage. In low water seasons, and in certain years in which the water levels were low throughout the entire summer and fall, the rapids and shallows on the Kam route grew to be miles in length, requiring much additional portaging and lining. In contrast, the Pigeon River passage generally retained more consistent depths, even during the drier seasons. One major hurdle of the latter route was the need to portage 8.2 miles around the lowest section of the Pigeon River before it flowed into Lake Superior, to circumvent a 120 foot falls and a series of impassable rapids. This path through the forest, ascending seven hundred feet in altitude as it progressed from east to west, became known as the Grand Portage, the Great Carrying Place. On the entire mainline canoe route, the only longer carry was the La Loche or Methye Portage, thirteen miles long, which connected Lac La Loche to the Clearwater River in the far northwest.

The Pigeon River or Grand Portage route was utilized for a total of 73 years, from 1731 through 1760 during the French regime and from 1761 through 1803 during the following British regime. Then the British merchants were required to move their main facility northward from American soil, to the mouth of the Kam River, where Ft. William operated from 1804 to 1878; during this period, the Kam River route again dominated, for another 75 years. Thus, during the span of two hundred years from 1679 through 1878, the Grand Portage route was the primary passage during the middle 73 years, while the Kam River route served as the main passage for a total of 127 years, divided between the early and late periods of the fur trade (spanning 52 and 75 years, respectively).

After deciding that we would travel along the Grand Portage passage, with its greater likelihood of sufficient water depths, I next chose to travel from west to east, to take advantage of the prevailing westerly winds. These regularly occurring forces of nature had been a great help to us, as following winds, while we had traveled southeast and east during our two voyages on the Ottawa River. In great contrast, however, they had offered nearly daily challenges as strong head winds when we had traveled westward on the French River and Georgian Bay. Thus, we would paddle through the Boundary Waters region from west to east, with the hope of encountering cooperative winds, even though this direction of travel would be upstream for nearly the entire distance.

Considering how to divide into two comfortable trips the 275 water miles from the head of Rainy Lake eastward to the Grand Portage, along the international border between the U.S. and Canada, I checked a road map for access roads in the region. The only route by car to a logical dividing point would take us first to Ely, Minnesota, the canoeing center of the midwest, and then east-northeast to Moose Lake. The shores of this lake would serve as our put-in spot for a 113 mile journey this year, and it would be our take-out place for a voyage of 162 miles the following year. An additional seven miles would be added to each trip while traveling on Moose Lake and Sucker Lake, paddling to and from the actual mainline route that ran along the border.

Before beginning our canoe jaunt, we first spent four days gathering inspiration at a number of important fur trade era sites, in northern Minnesota and in the adjacent region of Ontario. Our stops included the reconstructed fort at Grand Portage, the reconstructed Ft. William on the Kaministiquia River as well as the monument at its original location near Lake Superior, the dramatic 128 foot drop of the Kakabeka Falls on the Kam River, and sites along the Nipigon River and on Lake Nipigon. By the evening of the fourth day, we were ensconced in a motel at Thunder Bay, Ontario, ready to start the paddling expedition the following day.

Day One

We were up at 6:00 and out of the motel within 45 minutes. Arriving at the international border crossing, which is located on the Pigeon River five miles north of Grand Portage, a U.S. customs official searched the front seat area of our car, and then waved us through. At the Grand Portage Lodge five miles to the south, we picked up our shuttle driver, Dwayne, a Swedish-Norwegian-Ojibwa man who worked the desk at the lodge. Departing from the lodge about 7:30, having gained an hour with the time zone change at the Canada-U.S. border, we drove 3 1/4 hours to Moose Lake, east-northeast of Ely. At the public access boat launch on the southeastern shore of the lake, we unloaded the canoe and gear, and saw Dwayne off. In four days, he would deliver our car via a woods road to a site near Partridge Falls on the Pigeon River, 11/2 miles above the head of the Grand Portage. As we loaded the craft and pushed off on our adventure at 11:20, we talked about the time during our very first year of canoeing when we had launched onto Lake One, just 31/2 miles south of here. During the intervening five years, we had certainly gained plenty of experience as long-distance paddlers!

It was a beautiful day, with not a single cloud marring the sun-drenched blue sky, and already the air temperature measured a comfortable 69 degrees in the shade. Against a moderate head wind, we traveled toward the northeast for seven miles on Moose Lake and then Sucker Lake, to reach the international border and the waters of the mainline route. Along the way, a few powerboats of fishermen and canoe shuttlers passed us, oblivious to (or unconcerned about) the noise, stench, and air and water pollution that their engine-powered boats were contributing to the otherwise pristine scene. We smiled to ourselves at the thought of those so-called "canoeists," often laden with unnecessary gear and heavy coolers of beer, who needed a motorized lift from the outfitters' base camps and lodges into the wilderness.

Turning eastward onto Birch Lake and the waters of the mainline fur trade passage, we stopped at 2:10 for a half-hour lunch break on a little island. On this trip, as we paddled along the series of interconnected rivers and lakes that comprise the border, Canadian soil would be along the left shore, much of it in Quetico Provincial Park and the lower reaches of the route in La Vérendrye Provincial Park and Pigeon River Provincial Park. United States territory would extend along the right shore, virtually all of it in the Boundary Waters Canoe Area Wilderness (B.W.C.A.W.), except for the last few miles of the trip, which would be along lands within the Grand Portage Indian Reservation. The B.W.C.A.W., a federally protected region encompassing a million acres, has more visitors annually than any other wilderness area in the U.S., handling more than 160,000 canoeists each year. (In contrast, Quetico Provincial Park receives about 15,000 paddlers annually.) To provide quality wilderness experiences for this immense number of users each year, and to protect the natural resources of the region, a number of regulations have been established: registration and reservations for each party of travelers are required; the number of persons within each group is limited to nine, and the number of watercraft per group is limited to four; the total number of locations at which all parties can begin and end their trips is restricted to 87, and the number of parties that are allowed within the area of each entry point is limited to 280 per night; finally, camping is restricted to the designated campsites that are marked as red dots on official maps. These various regulations help to provide solitude, as well as genuine interactions with nature, to the thousands of paddlers who visit this wilderness each year, seeking a healing antidote to our modern "civilized" ways of life. Since we were registered with the Boundary Waters program of the U.S., we would camp on the right-hand side of the international boundary line each night during this voyage.

After our break on the little island, Kevin paddled in the bow for four miles, against a variable light-to-moderate head wind, to bring us to Portage La Carpe. This year, he was age 11 11/12, and Ben was 10 2/12; both of them were intent upon logging many miles as the *avant* during this voyage, and also carrying more substantial loads on the portage paths. This day, they would have a number of opportunities to fulfill the latter wish, since we had arrived at a stretch of 2 1/4 miles that presented five sets of obstacles.

Hiking the 220 yards of Portage La Carpe (Carp or Sucker Portage) on the right shore (a carry which the voyageurs avoided in high-water seasons by lining) brought us to Carp Lake. After paddling across its half-mile width, a portage of 80 yards on the right took us around a set of rapids to Melon Lake. We proceeded over the 1/4 mile length of this lake to an 80 yard portage on the right, which circumvented a set of rapids flowing out of Seed Lake. Then, traveling the 3/8 mile length of Seed Lake brought us to the outlet rapids of Portage Lake. These rapids looked strong, but they were very narrow; so Doree and I spurned the 80 yard portage path and lined the canoe up the right side of the roiling rapids, wading in the water while the boys stayed in the craft and paddled. After a very short paddle across a widened area of the channel that was too deep to wade, I again waded while lining up the second set of rapids, which were narrow and very strong. At first, with the family in the canoe, I began lining by myself, standing in the strong midstream current and pulling against it; but I could not advance against the force of the water, and was barely able to hold my position. After I managed to get the canoe a little nearer to the right shore and into water that was less deep, Doree joined me on the towing line, and together we were able to pull the craft up through the rapids. The boys, who had been silent during the entire procedure, cheered our success. Our arms and legs were rather wobbly from the exertion, but we were glad to again be moving forward from within the canoe. A 3/8 mile paddle along the full length of Portage Lake brought us to the Grand Portage de Rocher du Couteau (Big Knife-Stone Portage), 410 yards long on the left shore, where we found the path to be quite wet and muddy during the first half of the carry. The name of this portage, and of the adjacent lake, was derived from the upturned, sharp-edged layers of slate that were sometimes found on the portages in this area. After paddling about a mile due east on Lac de Rocher du Couteau (Knife-Stone Lake) or the native-named Mokoman Sakiegan (Knife Lake), we finally landed to camp on a tiny island at 8:00, as darkness was beginning to settle over the land. At our site, the simple pleasures of eating hot noodles with peas and cheese sauce while gazing into a flickering fire warmed our souls.

Since the put-in at 11:20, we had advanced sixteen miles against head winds, including making four portages and lining up a double set of rapids. On each portage, Ben had carried both his and Kevin's pack at the same time, wearing one suspended on his back and placing the second one atop the first, behind his shoulders, in voyageur fashion. For his part, Kevin had carried Doree's bulky Duluth pack, which weighed 65 pounds, using the two shoulder straps as well as the attached tumpline that passed from the pack across his forehead. For years, the boys had been learning about fur trade merchandise and the containers in which these items had been transported by canoe, and they clearly understood how these containers had been carried on land. The boys had heard guides at fur trade sites discuss bales of merchandise as if they were virtually the only containers that were hauled by voyageurs. However, these bundles, consisting of thick outer layers of woolen and linen fabrics or blankets wrapped around smaller articles in the center, with a protective linen wrapper sewn on the exterior with cord, typically made up only about one third of the total number of cargo containers in a given canoe. Wooden crates with cord-lashed lids were used to transport guns, heavy ironwares (including axes, tomahawks, knives, awls, fire steels, hide scrapers, ice chisels, gun worms, and fishhooks), and often miscellaneous items such as gunflints, glass beads, tin plate mirrors, hawk bells, finger rings, candles, and writing paper. In addition to rough crates, various sizes of finer wooden traveling chests or trunks were utilized for carrying especially important items, and sometimes a mixture of personal articles and trade goods. Some of these locked boxes had reinforcement bands of iron, and many were painted or stained, while others were covered with leather. Small wooden kegs were used to carry liquor, pork, beef, grease, fruits, rice, sugar, salt, butter, vinegar, gunpowder, lead shot, and canoe sealant gum, as well as such items as knives, fire steels, glass beads, and vermilion paint pigment. Durable woven lidded baskets or hampers were utilized for transporting nested copper pots and brass kettles of graduated sizes. Finally, strongly sewn bags made of linen fabric were employed to haul personal belongings of the men, their communal provisions of side pork, dried peas, dried corn, biscuits, and flour, and large amounts of lead balls and shot; when carrying this heavy ammunition, the bags were usually doubled, for additional strength. In general, the bales, crates, chests, and bags of cargo each weighed about eighty to ninety pounds, and sometimes up to one hundred pounds, while the lighter kegs and lidded baskets usually weighed from fifty to eighty pounds.

Kevin and Ben liked to use the tumplines for carrying our packs, although they also used the modern-style shoulder straps that were permanently fastened to each of the packs. The tumpline or carrying strap was a traditional native item made of leather or native woven fabric that was adopted by the French for fur trade transport. It consisted of a central band about four inches wide, which passed across the carrier's forehead or head, and two end straps, each about ten feet long, for attachment to the piece of cargo. The versions that were fashioned by the French had a central band made of either leather or heavy linen canvas, and long fastening straps of either leather or cordage. In nearly all cases, each voyageur provided his own *collier à porter* (strap for carrying/tumpline) for a trip, as well as his own paddle. When making a portage, he attached the narrow end straps of the tumpline to one piece of cargo, typically a well-padded bale, which he carried against the low curved area of his back. A second container, usually a crate, chest, bag, keg, or lidded basket, was placed by a colleague atop the first piece, where it nestled in the hollow between the man's shoulder blades and was held in place by one or both of his hands. By leaning slightly forward, much of the weight of the load was supported by the wide center strap across his forehead or head, which utilized his neck muscles, while the rest of the weight was supported by his forward-leaning back. The use of shoulder straps was not usually included in native and French methods of carrying cargo during the fur trade era.

Another of the ancient customs of portaging that we incorporated into our canoe trips involved dividing particularly long or challenging carries into manageable segments, with a *pause* (the French word for rest period, pronounced "pose") built in at intervals. By this method, a portion of the cargo would be carried by the voyageurs over a stage of the trail and laid down; while the men were returning to the starting place for another load, they would be resting. When all of the cargo and the canoe had been transported to the end of that particular stage, the voyageurs would begin hauling it all over the next stage. Traditionally, the length of each segment was based upon the time and effort which were required to pass over the distance; the more difficult and demanding the path, the shorter the distance between rest stops. Thus, the time that was needed to portage between each of the *pauses* was often roughly equal. For the voyageurs, the distance of each stage typically ranged from 1/4 to 1/3 to 1/2 mile, depending on the conditions of the situation. For example, the 8.2 mile length of the Grand Portage path was usually divided into seventeen roughly half-mile segments, offering the voyageurs sixteen rest periods while they walked back to pick up another load.

Today's series of unloadings and reloadings of our canoe at each of the portages had been a good test of the new security straps that I had fashioned, to replace the long and cumbersome single rope that I had previously used to tie all of the packs securely to the thwarts in case of capsize. Each strap, made of three feet of one-inch nylon webbing, was fitted at its ends with a sturdy plastic strap clip. Now, fastening and unfastening each pack individually was a quick task, and any of the packs could be released at any time during the course of the day, in case some of the contents were needed.

At the campsite, it was a delight to quickly start dinner with another new piece of equipment, a tiny, one-burner gas stove; soon we were feasting on beef jerky stew with corn, peas, noodles, and various spices. This stove would be very helpful on our trips, particularly at those times when we would arrive at a campsite late in the evening and find all of the forest wood wet from prolonged rain. Doree would now be able to start dinner almost immediately after arrival, allowing us to do the rest of the camp setup chores while the food cooked nearly untended. The stove would also contribute to our goal of extremely low-impact camping and wilderness traveling. When we departed from most of our campsites, the only evidence that we had been there was the tamped-down grass where we had walked and sat, and where the tent had stood. When we did make a small campfire for some cheerful warmth and light, we burned only dead wood that we could break with our hands. Afterward, we doused the ashes and burned coals with water, and stirred them until they were cool to the touch of a bare hand, to prevent forest fires. Before leaving the site, we would usually bury the remaining charcoal and ashes.

As we savored our well-earned meal in the near-dark, we talked about Dorothy Molter, who for more than fifty years had lived on the island where we were camping. A legend here in canoe country, Dorothy had been the last resident of the B.W.C.A.W., until her death two years earlier, in 1985, at the age of 79. She had dispensed information (on wilderness travel, camping, bears, and fires), first aid (she was a registered nurse), and her own homemade root beer to thousands of grateful paddlers over the course of five decades. In the early period, she had operated a resort here with her husband, and in the later decades after his death, she had stayed on as a volunteer working for the Forest Service.

Day Two

After we roused from our slumbers at 7:30, two female mallards joined us on the sun-warmed grass of Dorothy's former cabin yard for a breakfast of gorp. While we munched, we enjoyed the unusual sight of her flowers in a wilderness setting, including lilacs, tiger lilies, roses, and some lovely yellow blossoms that we could not identify. Part of her old log dock lay submerged offshore, but the National Park Service had dismantled and moved both of her log cabins from the two islands out to Ely, transporting them on the winter ice, to be reassembled there as a museum and an interpretive center. All that remained here at her home site were the flowers that she had tended and nurtured over the years.

When we set out at 9:30, the weather was delightful, with a few scattered white clouds and a temperature of 69 degrees. Against a light head wind, Ben paddled six miles in two hours along the length of Lac de Rocher du Couteau, whose shores were forested with spruce, pines, and scattered birches. Where our route exited the big lake and entered Petit Lac de Rocher du Couteau (Little Knife-Stone Lake), we halted at 11:30 to take a 45 minute lunch break, sprawled out on a massive ledge of bare, sun-baked granite. In low-water times, this narrow passage between the lakes became a short rapids, requiring the first Petite Portage de Rocher du Couteau for the voyageurs. However, since there was sufficient water in this particular season, all I had to do was push the canoe through an area of rocky shallows. Resuming our travels with stoked furnaces, Doree paddled five miles on Little Knife-Stone Lake, before Kevin assumed the duties of the bow position and did the next four miles. At the end of the lake, when confronted with the second Petite Portage de Rocher du Couteau, we décharged: first we carried the gear over the easy 25 yard path immediately beside the rapids on the right shore. Then I dragged the canoe by hand while wading up through the short section of fast current and boulders, to enter Ottertrack (or Cypress) Lake.

Five miles later, we reached Monument Portage, the ancient Portage de la Prairie (Meadow Portage). This carry was a challenging one; although it was only 440 yards long, it had a difficult, steep incline up the first half. Before we tackled it, we took an afternoon snack break, bolstering ourselves with a special treat of chocolate gorp. The voyageurs sometimes called this carry Portage de Marais (Swamp Portage), because its upper end was very swampy and muddy as it reached Lac de Marais (Swamp Lake). Now, a modern dock has been built over the soggy area to help paddlers reach the shoreline of Swamp Lake. The modern name of the carry, Monument Portage, is derived from the three monuments marking the international boundary that are located along the path. A short paddle brought us to Rocher de la Prairie (Meadow Rock), an extremely shallow and narrow passage. To avoid the 25 yard portage, each of us did our part to drag the loaded canoe through the five-foot width of the rock-paved passageway, which brought us to the western end of Lac Saganaga, Lake of Islands in the Algonquian native languages.

A mile to the east, we found a lovely camping spot on a narrow peninsula that projects southward from the north shore, where we could look out toward the northeast onto the main expanse of the lake. We set up camp at 6:00, and enjoyed a repast of fish stew while revelling in the beautiful evening, with perfect reflections of the pine-clad shorelines decorating the tranquil water. After staring into the dancing orange flames of a fire for a couple of hours, telling stories and considering what we had seen and done today, we were snuggled in the tent by 9:30. This day, we had covered seventeen miles in six hours of paddling, had made two portages, and had dragged the loaded canoe through a nearly impassible passageway without having to unload or carry anything.

Day Three

Beginning the day at 7:00, we were off an hour later beneath grey overcast skies dropping scattered light showers. Heading northeast on Lac Saganaga, we surged forward nearly four miles in one hour to reach a tiny islet next to Spruce Island, where we took a half-hour breakfast break. As the morning progressed, the clouds gradually cleared and the sun came out in brilliance, giving us a gorgeous day with a high of 75 degrees in the shade. While Ben paddled six miles in two more hours on the lake, I was lost in my thoughts, semi-hypnotized by the steady rhythm of the paddle strokes and the deep, rich silence. On this year's trip, we were celebrating the tricentennial of the first documented French traders to venture far westward beyond Lake Superior. DuLhut and his men had established Ft. Kaministiquia in 1679, on the Superior shore at the mouth of the Kaministiquia River, and Ft. LaMaune/Ft. Tourette five years later, at the north end of Lake Nipigon, about a hundred miles north of Lake Superior. In 1688, Jacques DeNoyon and his small party of fellow traders traveled westward from Ft. Kam along the Kam River route, passing through Ojibwa territory to reach Rainy Lake. There they built a small post, and spent the winter trading. (DeNoyon was a nephew of our trader ancestor Claude David, who had spent 1660-1663 on western Lake Superior.) The following summer, the men advanced westward down the Rainy River to reach Lake of the Woods, crossing the territory of the Crees and Assiniboines, before returning eastward to Ft. Kam with a rich cargo of peltries. These furs were taken during the same summer of 1689 to St. Ignace, where they were left in the safekeeping of the Jesuit missionaries there. According to a legal agreement which was made at Montreal on September 22 of that year, our ancestor Alexandre Turpin, a trader and investor who backed other traders, was granted ownership of one hundred beaver robes which were stored at St. Ignace. Each beaver robe contained from five to ten tanned pelts, which were sewn together to form a mantle that the natives had used as both a garment and as bedding. These hundred robes were owned by Jean Baptiste Patissier and his five colleagues, who were identified in the transfer as De Noyon, Chicot, Chat, Monbrun, and St. George. It is highly likely that these peltries acquired by our forebear were the very ones that had been collected by the ground-breaking DeNoyon expedition, during their travels to Rainy Lake and Lake of the Woods in 1688-89.

After this expedition, there was no further serious expansion by the French into the region west of Lake Superior for the next four decades. During this period, most of the activities of the French in the Superior region were limited to Ft. Kaministiquia and Ft. LaMaune/ Ft. Tourette/ Nipigon Post. This lack of westward expansion was due to ongoing hostilities between the Ojibwas and the Dakotas to the west, as well as warfare between France and England. After French forces captured the three H.B.C. forts on James Bay in 1686, and the forts of York and Severn on Hudson's Bay a few years later, virtually all of the trade of the entire Hudson's Bay area was in French hands, until the Treaty of Utrecht in 1713. This peace treaty returned control of the Hudson's Bay region to Britain, and relegated the French to their former route to the far northwest, via the mainline passage through the Great Lakes.

Westward expansion beyond Lake Superior was first initiated in 1717, when La Noué traveled west via the Kam River route to establish Ft. Tekamanigan at the western end of Rainy Lake; however, this post was short-lived. True westward movement was begun nine years later, in 1728, when Pierre Gaultier de Varennes, Sieur de La Vérendrye, was placed in command of Ft. Kam and the Nipigon post, thus granting him the trading concessions there. Three years later, he was commissioned to explore the region northwest of Superior, locate a water route to the Pacific, and establish a series of posts which would disrupt the operations of the H.B.C., whose posts were limited to the shores of Hudson's Bay. In return, La Vérendrye was given a monopoly of all of the trade in this vast area beyond Superior, which was inhabited by Ojibwas, Crees, and Assiniboines.

Setting out from the Mackinac Straits in 1731 with a party of some fifty voyageurs, the commandant reached the mouth of the Pigeon River. Here, he faced a mutiny among the men, when they were about to begin traveling up this new route, unfamiliar to the French, which began with a portage that was more than eight miles long. *(Each time Tim related this incident to Kevin and Ben, they were more than a little pleased to hear of such an uprising against an expedition leader, a feat which they pondered on occasion but could not pull off themselves. Doree)* To settle the impasse, La Vérendrye traveled northeastward with half of the men to spend the winter at Ft. Kam, while the cooperative ones traveled westward over the Grand Portage and along the Pigeon River route to reach the western end of Rainy Lake, where they established their first post, Ft. St. Pierre, at the head of the Rainy River.

The following summer, the commandant joined them with the rest of the voyageurs, and they paddled westward down the Rainy River to build Ft. St. Charles, on the west side of Lake of the Woods. Two years later, in 1734, his men descended the Winnipeg River to Lake Winnipeg, and constructed Ft. Maurepas near the mouth of the Red River, just south of the southern end of Lake Winnipeg. This post broke the monopoly that the H.B.C. had held until then on commerce in the huge region stretching to the southwest from Hudson's Bay, where most of the furs had been transported down the Hayes River to Ft. York on the Bay. In 1736, La Vérendrye's forces also built the short-lived Little Vermilion Post, southeast of Rainy Lake at the mouth of the Vermilion River, on or near Crane Lake. Westward expansion continued two years later, when the commandant and his men established Ft. Rouge/Ft. La Fourche, south of Lake Winnipeg at the junction of the Red and Assiniboine Rivers, and also Ft. La Reine, a little further to the west up the Assiniboine River, beside the portage which extended northward from that river to Lake Manitoba. In 1739, some of his men closed the original Ft. Maurepas and rebuilt the post near the mouth of the Winnipeg River. Two years would elapse before the two remaining posts of La Vérendrye were established: Ft. Dauphin, near the water connection between Lake Manitoba and Lake Winnipegosis, west of the midsection of Lake Winnipeg, and Ft. Bourbon, a little west of the mouth of the Saskatchewan River, west of the northern end of Lake Winnipeg. Lieutenant La Vérendrye served as the commandant of all of these "Posts of the Western Sea" until 1744 (he called Lake Winnipeg the Western Sea).

Three additional facilities would be built by the French in the northwest during the 1750s, along the lower reaches of the Saskatchewan River, west of the northern end of Lake Winnipeg. These included Ft. Pascoiac in 1749-50, Ft. La Jonquière further to the west in 1751, and finally Ft. St. Louis/Ft. La Corne in 1753. Thus, the maximum northwestern expansion of the trade during the French regime extended to the Saskatchewan River watershed. This westward reach took over much of the trade that had formerly gone to the H.B.C. at Ft. York.

The extension of the trade west of Lake Superior had begun in 1717, just after the main depot for all of the upper Great Lakes trade had been moved in 1715 from the northern shore of the Straits of Mackinac to the southern shore, from Ft. DeBuade at St. Ignace to Ft. Michilimackinac. The following two decades also saw an increase in the number of paddlers per canoe, and a single increase in the size of the craft as well. Until at least 1710, there had usually been either three or four men per canoe; after 1723, the typical crews contained either four or five men, with some six-man crews. Up to this time, the largest craft had been 29 to 33 feet long. In about 1730, a larger model of eight-place canoe was introduced, measuring 33 to 36 feet in length; this model was usually manned by a crew of seven voyageurs, in some cases eight to ten. The former largest craft, measuring 29 to 33 feet, then became known as the bastard canoe. In spite of the use of considerable numbers of the enlarged craft and their sometimes larger crews, the majority of fur trade canoes were still handled by either five or six men throughout the 1730s, 40s, and 50s. Over the decades, as the crew sizes grew, the number of pieces of cargo in each craft also increased, since more hands were now available for the offshore handling of those pieces.

Back to modern life on the water, as my thoughts returned from the eighteenth century. As we neared the eastern end of Lac Saganaga, we turned southward, and within a half-mile our route took us to the inlet of the lake, at the mouth of the Granite River and the Sault de Saganaga (Saganaga Falls). On the lake near the river's mouth was l'Anse de Sable (Sand Bay), where an early native canoe-building operation had flourished for a long time on a point of land. By 11:30, having covered ten miles in 3 1/2 hours, including a break for breakfast, we were leaving the lake and entering a narrow passageway. The fourteen-mile section of the route that lay ahead, comprised of two short segments now called the Granite River and the Pine River, would present a series of twelve obstructions, about a third of all the obstacles that we would face during this entire trek.

As we approached the small Saganaga Falls, Ben spotted a mink sitting quietly on a log in midstream. We watched in silence as the dark brown animal calmly entered the water and swam to the far shoreline, with its head, tubular body, and tail somewhat visible above the surface. The partially webbed toes of a mink aid in both swimming and diving; this animal can dive to depths of fifteen feet, to catch fish as well as its favorite food, muskrats.

After making the Portage Maraboeuf on the left shore, carrying 200 yards into the Granite River, we enjoyed a lunch break at the end of the path. The right shore, with its thirty-yard portage beside the falls, had been an option. But approaching it from the downstream side (as we were), required a six-foot lift up a cliff at its beginning. Rather tough for us parents, we thought, since the two boys were not yet big enough to help much with such a task. If we had been traveling downstream, we would have simply handed the gear down that cliff, with little effort.

When we put back in at 1:15, Kevin took up the role of the *avant*, to paddle the next five miles in a straight southward course along the Granite River. Having traveled ten miles all morning on the wide expanses of Lac Saganaga, it was a pleasure to be gliding along a narrow channel flanked by high granite hills. Less than a mile from Portage Maraboeuf, at the modern-named Horsetail Rapids, the voyageurs had traditionally made the Décharge Maraboeuf, lining their half-loaded or unloaded cargo canoes. With our smaller craft, Ben and I lined up a shallow and very narrow side channel while fully loaded, passing beneath low-leaning trees that angled drunkenly over the channel, with their feet weakly planted at the water's edge. This particular set of rapids, which can now be circumvented by a 150 yard carry, had caused grief to paddlers on various occasions during the fur trade era. Tangible proof of this was found in the pool just below the rapids, when scuba divers made the first attempt in 1960 to search for fur trade artifacts beneath the waters of the mainline route. As luck would have it, their very first attempt, right here at Horsetail

Rapids, had located an impressive series of seventeen brass kettles of graduated sizes that were all nested together, one inside another! This dramatic find launched a joint U.S.-Canada underwater search program that spanned the next dozen years, examined a great deal of the mainline route, and produced many wonderful discoveries.

Four miles upriver from Horsetail Rapids, an S curve signalled the beginning of a very winding section that headed toward the southeast, five miles on the Granite River and another five miles on the Pine River. This stretch would offer a concentration of ten obstructions before bringing us to Gunflint Lake. A portage of 175 yards, from the upper tip of the S curve to its central bend, was sometimes used to avoid a very narrow passage that presented fast current in high-water seasons. However, we chose to paddle the 11/2 miles around the attractive oxbow bend and dig in with our paddles to ascend the short area of swift water. The lower half of the S-shaped passage, dubbed the Devil's Elbow, was narrow and flanked in some places with high barren cliffs, whose shining granite rose straight up from the water; at one place, a slight riffle roiled the surface at the foot of the cliffs. After paddling through a widened half-mile section of the river called Gneiss Lake, we reached the first of two sets of rapids that the voyageurs had together called the Rapides des Chats (Raccoon Rapids). Doree and I lined up the first set, rather than making the modern-named Gneiss Lake Portage of 140 yards. A 3/4 mile passage brought us to the second Rapides des Chats, a double set of rapids that extended around a sharp curve in the channel. We lined up this pair of rapids as well, which offered a considerable obstacle to us upriver travelers. A very short paddle around a curve to the left brought us to Décharge du Vaseau (Swamp Rapids), which the voyageurs had lined either half-loaded or unloaded. Instead of making the modern-named Granite River Portage here, which offers a 140 yard path on the right, we decided to line the canoe up, in voyageur tradition, but leave it fully loaded. Beforehand, we took a short break on shore, gathering our strength and stoking up our furnaces with chocolate gorp washed down with strawberry-flavored instant breakfast drink.

For good reason, the quiet pond below this low but powerful rapids turned out to be one of the most prolific sites in the underwater search program for fur trade artifacts. Near its top, the channel of the rapids narrows, creating a very powerful surge; below this narrows is a small ledge which drops off, and then a curve. Over the centuries, a number of loaded canoes must have overturned while being lined up or down through this gauntlet, to deposit a flintlock gun, lead balls and shot, gunflints, a gun worm, an axe, and a glass bottle on the bottom. We lined upstream near the left shore, wading deep in the very strong and chilly current, with me pulling the bow line and Doree pushing at the stern. About two-thirds of the way up, at the narrowest place with the strongest flow, we were brought to a complete stop beside a huge boulder. We could barely hold our position, and were about to lose our grip, which would have sent the canoe careening back down the rapids, at the mercy of the current. Then Kevin, sitting in the bow seat, intuitively began lurching his body forward in a slow rhythmic pattern, to urge the canoe forward; Ben soon joined in from his position in the stern seat. Their steady, rhythmic rocking motions produced just enough forward momentum to help us inch forward slowly, and finally make it up through the incline of the rapids. They were extremely proud of their small but crucial contribution toward meeting this challenge.

A half-mile upstream, the channel made an oxbow bend called the Petite Faucille (Little Sickle), which was garnished with three separate sets of rapids. (*I began to think I was in a Kafka novel, with never-ending obstacles! Doree*) In most instances, the voyageurs avoided this troublesome passage by making the Portage du Vaseau (Swamp Portage) across the base of the bend. (However, divers found two flintlock guns, a brass shoe buckle, a lid from a copper pot, and a stem from a clay pipe in the Petite Faucille section, indicating that it had been utilized at least occasionally, sometimes with catastrophic results.) During our third jaunt over the 400 yard length of the Swamp Portage, while I carried the canoe, Doree walked behind me singing French songs, as she had done during each of the previous portages. Her upbeat tunes helped to distract me from the pain that the craft caused, as the portage pads pressed down heavily on the bones of my shoulders. Finally, with relief, I lay the canoe down onto the water. After a 3/4 mile paddle, we lined up a double set of rapids on a curve in the river, spurning the adjacent 260 yard portage path, and entered beautiful Lac des Pins (Pine Lake).

It was now 7 P.M., our favorite time of day on canoe trips, when the muted rays of the sun from low in the west gilded the scene around us, and the mirror-like surface of the water held perfect reflections of the rocky, evergreen-covered shoreline. Traveling a half-mile south on the lake, with all of us scouting for a good campsite, we soon spotted a site, beside the foot of Portage des Gros Pins (Portage of the Big Pines). This carry, which we would make in the morning, would cut off a sharp curve in the river and obviate two shorter portages. As we were silently gliding toward the site where we would spend the night, Doree quietly pointed out an otter that was swimming directly in front of the canoe. For a time, it swam ahead of us, with just the broad, brown wedge of its snout and the top of its flattened head showing. Then it dived, leaving only widening concentric rings on the surface. While we unloaded, we discussed this amazing creature, whose streamlined body, waterproof fur, and webbed toes are so well suited for aquatic life. It spends most of its time in the water, only coming ashore to rest and sleep, and to slide on its belly down banks and shorelines for fun. Since it can dive to depths of fifty feet, it can readily hunt fish, and can also capture frogs and crayfish in the shallows, as well as insects and small mammals on shore.

At the campsite, Doree and I could readily see just how much the boys had grown up since our first wilderness canoe trip here in northern Minnesota five years earlier. Ben went off by himself, returned with a big supply of dry branches for firewood, and kindled a fire, while Kevin set up the tent without assistance. Then Ben blew up three of the air mattresses; after finishing the tent, Kevin joined him to inflate the fourth one. Doree and I stowed all of the gear and the canoe, and cooked a feast of beef jerky stew with rice, plus galette for dessert. After reveling in the warm meal and the blazing fire for a while, we ambled down to the bare rock ledge at the water's edge to admire the brilliant stars above the lake, before finally hitting the sack at 10:00.

Today, between 8 A.M. and 7:15 P.M., we had traveled 23 miles (Kevin six, Ben eight, and Doree nine miles in the bow), including making two portages, lining up five rapids, and paddling up a place of fast current without having to line. After a good night's sleep, we would deal with the four remaining obstacles of this section in the morning.

Day Four

When we headed out at 9:00, the weather was beautiful: sunny, with only a few wispy white clouds streaked across the deep blue heavens. In the heavily sheltered forest, only a slight breeze wafted from the south; we could not know that, a few hours later, after leaving the sheltering woods, we would bear the full brunt of that southerly wind. During the camp-breaking chores, the boys had devised a contest for this trip, to see which of them would paddle the most miles in the role of the *avant*. They would each aim for thirty miles in the bow, which would represent for each of them a quarter of the total voyage; their goal was for their combined mileages to match their mother's distance of sixty miles. (*Of course, I took the hardest miles. Doree*)

We started the morning with the 550 yard Portage des Gros Pins, which offered a challenging incline over a high ridge for most of its first half. At the end of the strenuous carry, I placed our green canoe down onto the waters of the Pine River, which would take us three miles to Gunflint Lake. After a very short paddle, we arrived at Portage de Cheval du Bois (Wooden Horse Portage). The path was only 160 yards long, but it presented very rough terrain over and around truly massive broken boulders; at one point, we barely passed through a narrow space between two huge blocks of stone, before finally arriving at a landing on a wide expanse of barren rock. At the landing spot, Kevin happened to put his pack down onto a nest of yellow jackets that was concealed in the roots of a jack pine. Although he was only stung once on the face, that sting hurt him considerably. On our third trip over the trail, while I was bringing the canoe through the very narrow passage between two huge blocks of stone, I lost my balance and started to fall backward. Doree, following close behind, quickly grabbed the end of the canoe and halted the backward fall of both the craft and me. At the end of the carry, while Ben and I loaded in the packs and secured them to the thwarts, Doree gave Kevin a lesson in using the camera. Afterward, he took her portrait, and then helped her change films.

At 11:15, we left the landing and paddled about a mile to Sault l'Escalier (Stairway Falls), a thundering cascade of roiling whiteness. In the quiet water below this cataract, divers had located considerable numbers of fur trade artifacts, including the barrel of a flintlock gun. We did the seventy yard carry along the left (Canadian) side of the falls, and had lunch at the end of the portage. Then, just around the corner in the river, we lined up an unnamed rapids which had a short portage path on the left shore. When we finished lining at 1:00, we had advanced three miles, had made three portages, and had lined up one rapids, all in the space of four hours, with a lunch break included along the way.

Of the twelve obstructions that we had encountered within a span of fourteen miles yesterday afternoon and this morning, we had lined up six of them, had portaged around five others, and had paddled up a section of fast current in one instance. In each case, the decision of how to handle a given challenge was specific to that given situation. It was based on the water level and the strength of the current at the time, the placement of ledges and boulders and bends in the channel, and our abilities to deal with these various elements, as had always been the case for the voyageurs of old. Just because there was a portage path available, we did not automatically carry around an obstacle; instead, we considered all of the options. While we were lining up these six rapids (as well as various others along the route), we could sometimes hear another canoe party slogging along the path that paralleled the river. I must admit, it was a small delight for us to be confidently lining up the very obstructions that these other parties were portaging around.

As soon as we left the unnamed rapids and glided southward onto the open waters of Magnetic Lake, we had to dig in hard against a rather strong head wind as we crossed the one-mile length. Passing through the narrows at the end of the lake and entering the exposed western end of Lac de Pierre à Fusil (Gunflint Lake), we were immediately buffeted by a powerful southerly wind and big waves. Due to the direction of these oncoming frothing hills of water, we could not head directly eastward along the length of the lake and keep the wave tops from splashing over the gunwales. So we traveled east-southeast, quartering the waves, while gradually crossing to the southern shore of the lake to seek some shelter from the wind and the rollers, which had become serious whitecaps. An hour-and-a-half of considerable effort, and the singing of all the verses of many French songs, finally brought us to the southern shore, at a spot nearly halfway along the eight-mile length of the lake. There we took a well-deserved afternoon break from 2:45 to 3:15. During our rest stop, five mallards happily joined us, to share our snack of gorp. By departure time, the gusting head wind and domineering waves had settled down somewhat, so Ben was able to paddle two miles on the lake before a southeasterly head wind and medium-high waves returned, obliging Doree to return to the bow seat. After another session of hard pulling, we finally reached the sheltered eastern tip of Lac de Pierre à Fusil, which offered placid water and a beautiful stretch of tan sand beach, where we rested for a half-hour. (Nineteen years after our voyage through this area, in May of 2007, a two-week wildfire started from a runaway campfire destroyed 75,000 acres of forest here. The burned-over land, a massive area stretching south and southeast from Lake Saganaga, included the entire area of Granite River, Pine River, and Magnetic Lake, and about two-thirds of the perimeter of Gunflint Lake.)

Leaving Gunflint Lake, Ben again paddled as the *avant* along the 11/2 mile length of the slender Little Gunflint Lake; the first half of it was so choked with thick beds of green reeds that we had only a narrow winding channel to pass through. At the end of the lake, at Décharge des Épingles (Straight Pin Rapids), we avoided the hundred-yard portage path and lined up the narrow fast channel, as the voyageurs had done, which took us into Little North Lake. After traversing its half-mile length and paddling onto the much larger Lac du Hauteur de Terre (Height of Land Lake, now called North Lake), we again encountered strong head winds and moderately high waves coming from the southeast. Since our route would take us due south for 11/4 miles across the exposed western end of the long lake, where we would be pounded by wind and waves all the way, we decided to call it a day at 6:00, and halted in a bay on the northwestern corner of the lake. Near the campsite that we chose, a Forest Service cabin had once stood; the outline of its concrete foundation walls, enclosing a full chimney, was now overgrown with saplings. During nine hours of progress this day, mostly against oncoming winds, we had put fifteen miles under our canoe, made three portages, and lined up two rapids.

Fierce winds lashed us all evening on the exposed south-facing shoreline, as we feasted on beef jerky and mushroom stew and huddled close around the bright fire. During our evening chat, while staring into the flames, we talked about the very ancient habitation site that we had passed in the early afternoon. At the far western tip of Gunflint Lake, where the Cross River flows into the lake, native people had lived over the span of many thousands of years, including the Plano (late Paleo) Period from about 8,000 to 7,000 B.C. and the Early and Middle Archaic Periods from about 7,000 to 3,000 B.C. Excavations at this site had produced projectile points, knives, scrapers, drills, and awls made of chipped stone, as well as various tools fashioned from native copper, in addition to considerable amounts of burned bone from cooking. During the long span of millennia in which the site had been occupied, at least seasonally, the environment had changed dramatically. After the retreat of the glaciers from the region about 8,500 B.C., the environment had gradually evolved from a cool and wet climate with tundra during the Paleo and Plano Periods, to a warmer and drier climate with mixed deciduous hardwood forest during the Archaic Periods. This latter era was followed by a return to a cooler and wetter climate and the growth of a coniferous forest about 500 B.C., which has continued to the present day. As we considered the people who had once lived at the end of Gunflint Lake beside the mouth of the Cross River, we realized that these individuals were known to us only through the slim evidence from archaeological excavations at the Gordon's Site. However, that evidence represented dozens of generations of individuals, people who had had their own personal history, their own abilities and accomplishments, their own traditions and beliefs, and their own codes of conduct to guide their lives. We would never be able to glean these real truths about them from the meager fragments that they had left behind. However, these truths were remembered by the rocks and the water and the wind that sighed in the trees at the site of their former home.

Day Five

Whenever I stirred in the night, the sounds of the tent flapping and the drumming of hard-driven rain against the roof assailed my ears. By morning, the rainfall had stopped, but the sky was still mostly overcast. The wind had reduced to medium force, but it was still coming from the southeast, an unfortunate direction for our travels. Doree, Kevin, and I slipped on our sandy wet socks and soggy shoes and left the tent at 7:30, but Ben chose to languish in his sleeping bag a bit longer. As a result, he received the same traditional treatment as had the *bourgeois* (boss) when traveling with a band of voyageurs: Kevin dismantled the tent right on top of him, while we parents playfully shouted *"Debout! Debout! Debout!"* (French for "Get up!").

Embarking at 8:45, we paddled southward across the western end of Lac de Hauteur du Terre (Height of Land Lake, now called North Lake), toward the long, low mountain ridge that loomed between this body of water and Lac Perche (Perch Lake, now called South Lake). This natural barrier, completely covered with evergreen forest, was located fifty miles as the crow flies west-northwest from the lower end of the Grand Portage and the shores of Lake Superior. Scattered along the longer, winding water route that led from here to Superior, thirteen obstacles lay in the path of paddlers. The ridge of the height of land, reaching nearly a thousand feet above the level of Lake Superior, represented the continental divide between two immense watersheds: waters to the northwest of this land mass flowed to the north into Hudson's Bay, while waters to the southeast of the height flowed eastward into the Great Lakes and the St. Lawrence River, and ultimately into the Atlantic Ocean.

Before portaging over the continental divide, I administered the traditional voyageur baptism to Kevin and Ben, repeating the ceremony which had been carried out here for many centuries, for all travelers making their first trip over this height of land west of Superior. Dipping a bough into the Height of Land Lake, with a serious demeanor I sprinkled each of the boys with water, and made them each solemnly promise to never allow another voyageur to pass this place on his first trip without being baptized, **and** to never kiss another voyageur's wife...without her consent! These were the same two traditional vows that the boys (and the voyageurs of old) had made when they had first passed Pointe au Baptême on the upper Ottawa River. The ceremony at the western height of land, although tongue-in-cheek, underscored the more serious psychological divide that the continental divide had represented in the minds of long-distance canoeists hundreds of years ago. For them, reaching this land mass clearly marked their progress either toward or away from home and loved ones.

The 550 yard carry over the height of land did not actually involve a dramatic ascent and then a comparable descent, since the path was located in a narrow depression that ran through the elevated ridge, with the bottom of the depression lying only fifteen feet above the level of the lake. After we had completed the portage, we resumed our eastward course, paddling the grueling three-mile length of Lac Perche (Perch Lake, now South Lake) against a severe head wind. At the eastern end of the lake, I misread the land in relation to the map. As a result, I thought that I had gotten us off the correct route, and that we were not in the right place to locate the portage. After paddling for about a mile toward the left, searching for the head of the carrying path along the shoreline area, I finally determined where the path had to be, back at the far eastern end of the lake. Before paddling back there, we took a break for lunch, and then returned to the end of the lake. There, at the place where I thought that I had gotten off course, I realized that a low island had hidden from view the actual end of the lake, where the carry was located. I had been right on course originally, and had simply not advanced far enough to see past the little island to the portage landing! While we made the 315 yard Portage des Perches (Perch Portage) on the left shore, Kevin carried the canoe for fully half of the distance. This feat consisted of a 77 pound boy carrying a 69 pound canoe!

During the portage, we sang each of the verses of a strange little ditty that Kevin had just taught us. He and Ben had learned it from our friend Lori, who had cared for the boys while Tim had been on tour with the Symphony throughout Australia during the entire month of February, and I had been traveling with him. This was the new song in our repertoire:

"*Jonathan W. Astor was a master dancing man.*
He danced the day that he was born, his parents thought it grand.
The tango and the samba, he did with great élan,
But most he liked to dance the waltz until the break of dawn.

    (in waltz tempo)
    I like the waltz. It has its faults.
    For there are some dances more fancy.
    I like the waltz simply because
    It makes me feel so dancy.

One day he got an invitation to a ballroom dance.
And he decided to accept for he might get a chance
To dance with lovely ladies with perfume in their hair,
Or even fat and ugly ones, he really didn't care.

But at the ball the same old story made his evening grim.
He was a perfectionist, and none would dance with him.
And so he thought he'd just go home and turn his radio on,
But in the hall he found a girl waltzing all alone.

I like the waltz. It has its faults.
It's not much fun unless danced by two.
I wish I knew somebody who
Would dance with me because I'm so blue.

She was dancing by herself there in a little nook.
He quietly went to where she was to get a better look.
She was a little different than either you or me,
For she did not have two good legs, she had one, two, three.

(Refrain)

Jonathan W. Astor asked her if she'd like to dance,
And she said that she'd be thrilled if she could have the chance.
So they began to dance in a most peculiar way,
For she had three legs, he had two, and those who saw did say:

They like the waltz. They have their faults.
But who's to blame, we can't decide.
Maybe it's him, maybe it's her,
But it is them, that's for darn sure."   (Doree)

After a very short paddle across the tiny Lac la Martre (Marten Lake, now called Rat Lake), we handled the brief twenty-yard Portage la Martre in a very unconventional way: laying down the limb-stripped trunks of a few small fallen trees for use as rollers, we dragged our loaded canoe over these wooden rollers and on the thick moss that covered the ground in various places. Such a technique was certainly not used with birchbark canoes, but our fiberglass craft was unharmed by it. Kevin, now feeling invincible, then paddled for the next five miles, during which a moderate rain fell on and off. While traveling along the full length of Petit Lac Perche (Little Perch Lake), which was 21/2 miles long and only 1/8 mile wide, we passed beneath an impressive high cliff that reminded us of the limestone formation of Starved Rock, which stands tall on a bank of the Illinois River. Then we covered the 21/2 mile length of Lac Roseau (Reed Lake, now called Rose Lake), to arrive at the Grand Portage Neuf (New Great Carrying Place), which was 21/4 miles long.

We were unloaded and advancing along the path by 4:00. As we walked, a moderately heavy rain began to fall, a constant, drumming rain which, unbeknown to us at that point, would not let up during the entire rest of the evening. Using the voyageur technique of dividing long portages into sections, we carried the packs for about a mile, and then went back for the canoe and the few remaining items. On this first stretch of the trail, we were pleased to encounter a red squirrel, eight grouse together in a group, and two beaver dams. The first 1 1/4 miles of the portage trail followed the grade of an old logging railroad, while the last mile, much rougher, passed through a low, boggy forest area along a winding route that led to Rove Lake. By the time we began carrying the packs over the latter 1 1/4 miles of the route, the rainfall had turned the path through the bog into a quagmire of puddles and thick dark mud, which was up to knee-deep on me in some areas. One such place swallowed and kept one of Ben's tennis shoes, when he got deeply mired there up to his thighs. After managing to get all of the packs to the far end of the portage, we started back for the canoe. By now, the path resembled more a muddy stream than a walkway through the woods; in addition, the light was fading quickly. As I carried the canoe over the roughest swampy part of the route, Kevin sang steadily from right behind the canoe, to keep me going. He also occasionally ran around in front of me to support the craft for a time, so I could relieve my shoulders a bit. At the worst section of quagmire, I placed the canoe atop some large fallen logs that lay across the path, to take a short break.

Later, at the place where a huge, three-foot-diameter tree had fallen across the trail, I trotted ahead of Tim, clambered over the log, and held the bow end up, while he lay the stern down on the ground and climbed over the trunk to resume his carrying task. By 7:30 P.M., when it was nearly dark in the thick woods, we finally finished the Grand Portage Neuf, with both boys trying hard to control the chattering of their teeth. We had trudged forward over the path and then back, and then over it again, covering a total of 6 3/4 miles under rather tough conditions. (Doree)

Only after reaching the end of the route did I reveal to the family what Mackenzie had recorded here in 1789, when he noted that this carry was "over very rough ground, which requires the utmost exertions of the men, and frequently lames them." It was clear to us that the word "Grand" in the name Grand Portage Neuf had implied "long," not "excellent!" It should have borne the name Portage de l'Enfer (Portage from Hell).

With the rain falling heavily on us, Doree and I quickly set up the tarp shelter, and piled all of the gear and the tuckered-out boys under it. After filling a kettle with water at the shore, Doree got the fish stew underway on the little stove, while I set up the tent in the rain and inflated the air mattresses inside. Later, with our bellies full of warm food, we stripped off our soaked and filthy clothing, and gratefully crawled into dry sleeping bags at 10:00, exhausted. This was a day we would long remember. Between 8:45 A.M. and 7:30 P.M., we had covered fifteen miles of the route, including making a loaded portage on log rollers and doing three conventional portages (the lattermost one being the long and demanding Grand Portage Neuf, which alone had taken 31/2 hours to complete).

Day Six

Although rain fell during much of the night, by morning it had stopped; however, the sky was still lead-colored and glowering. Well after I had emerged from the tent at 7:00 and coaxed a fire from wet wood, Doree and the boys came out, to dry their clothes at the fire and eventually dress.

We all de-briefed from the previous evening's grueling episode, and transformed our "descent into hell" into a growth experience. Now, we could look back with pride, and also wryly consider the fate of Ben's lost shoe as an offering that had to be made to the Spirit of the Swamp. (Doree)

Before long, to our great delight, the sky cleared and the gleaming sun came out in all its glory!! Did its warmth ever feel good! We took our time to slowly dry out the gear and repack everything, while the sun's bright rays gave us newfound optimism. We could now thoroughly appreciate the new day, including the red squirrel that scolded us from its perch on a high limb, apparently resentful that we had invaded its territory.

My past experiences in facing physical hardships were quite different from Tim's. I hadn't had Boy Scouting, with all of its toughening adventures. When he was eleven, Tim had built a snow shelter in the woods with his brother Mike and cousin Ed, and the trio had camped out in it during an entire January weekend that had reached 27 degrees below zero, with only really skimpy sleeping bags! And I hadn't endured thirty years of a trumpet mouthpiece punishing my face. As a musician, Tim had needed to learn to ignore physical sensations, and to focus only on the music. In addition, I hadn't had a horrible car accident just after my 20th birthday that left me with chronic pain at the base of my spine like Tim had, producing pain which got progressively worse each year. So I didn't develop Tim's attitude that "Life is painful every day; just proceed with it."

What I brought to our paddling adventures was my enduring optimism, a desire to learn and to be adventurous, an athletic body, and an urge to win at such sports like baseball, volleyball, and tennis. By my example, I wanted to teach our boys to have the strength to be courageous and capable, but also to have a cooperative and gentle spirit (which is often ignored by parents). On these trips, I attempted to remake parts of myself: not stopping when my body was laced with pain, delaying gratification by continuing to travel well past my exhaustion before halting our forward movement, and occasionally crawling into the tent for the night without a warm dinner. Most women in our culture, I think, aim to be very comfortable. These canoe trips were the antithesis of that! The trips led me to step way out of the accepted comfort zone, and to get somewhat used to being out there.

On a related theme, my thoughts went back a year, to March of 1987, when I had joined a dozen other folks, including two nuns and two ministers, on a delegation to El Salvador. There, we had embarked on an amazing journey on foot into the war zone of Chalatenango. Some of the villagers who had dared to go back to San Jose las Flores in 1986, returning to their former homes to farm, had met us on the path to their village. We were dehydrated in the 100 degree heat, but walked eight miles carrying supplies to their homes in the war zone, passing at one place a once-lovely hacienda that was smoldering. We hiked past patches of blackened earth, scorched by phosphorous bombs that had been given to the Salvadoran military by our own U.S. government. It was as if I had been in training during my years of canoe trips for what I was facing in the war zone, and also later for mustering the courage to be arrested for protesting to stop the war. In their own way, various of my activities helped me cope on the canoe trips, and in turn, the wilderness trips helped me endure the walk through the war zone. (Doree)

Even though we were rather dirty from the muddy portage at dusk the night before, we did not change our clothes, since the single set of replacement garments that we carried for each of us was reserved for those serious emergency situations when we would need to quickly change into dry clothing to prevent hypothermia. Dirty garments did not warrant a changing, no matter how many days or weeks a particular journey took; the extra clothes were with us only as a safety measure. This morning, when our garments and our bodies were especially dirty from the long, muddy portage that we had made the previous evening, we chuckled about certain of the guidelines that had been issued in recent years to assist in preventing Lyme disease. This disease, carried by a tiny parasitic tick that usually lives on mice, deer, and household pets, was a hot topic in Minnesota and Wisconsin at this time, as well as in the ten other states stretching from Maine down to Maryland where it was prevalent. When a tick carrying the Lyme bacterium bites a human, the site of the bite usually acquires an expanding bull's-eye rash at least two inches in diameter, often accompanied by the flu-like symptoms of muscle pain, headache, and swollen glands, advancing into fever, sore throat, severe fatigue, joint pain, tingling or numbness in the extremities, and changes in vision. However, the infection does not usually occur until the tick has been attached to the body and sucking for thirty-six hours, and the disease is almost always readily cured if diagnosed early and treated with antibiotics.

During our canoe jaunts, we were certainly not able or willing to avoid the thickly wooded and grassy areas where the disease-bearing ticks usually live. However, we did wear hats, long-sleeved shirts, and long pants; and we tucked the bottoms of our pant-legs into the tops of our socks, and applied DEET insect repellent (all of these are also the standard protections against biting mosquitoes and black flies). One of the other effective preventive measures against Lyme disease, doing a full-body check for ticks at the end of a day of outdoor activities, was what made us laugh on this particular morning. After a portage like the one we had just survived, we were usually too dirty and too tired to distinguish any of the hundreds of flecks of mud on our bodies from ticks the size of a pinhead. When we were successful in finding a tick, usually by the movements of its eight little legs tickling our hide, we gently extricated it with our fingers if it had burrowed its head into the surface, avoiding crushing it and forcing its head under our skin. In many cases, we were able to locate a tick by the tickling sensations before it had time to dig in. However, the most practical approach was the wait-and-see one: if by chance a Lyme-bearing tick landed on us, and if by chance that insect managed to burrow its head into our hide, remain there for thirty-six hours, and inject the disease bacterium, the resulting two-inch-wide bull's-eye rash around the site would be obvious, and we could then receive the necessary antibiotics after the voyage, to quash the disease.

We were loaded and underway by 10:30, with Ben poised to work in the bow position for the first five miles. After traveling over the 11/2 mile length of the narrow Lac Entredeux (Lake Between the Two, now called Rove Lake), we arrived at and passed through the very slender passage called Petit Détroit (Little Narrows). This place had sometimes required a ten-yard décharge, involving either a complete unload or a half-unload of the cargo canoes. Then we covered the 11/2 mile length of another narrow body of water, Lac Watap (Lashing Roots Lake), to arrive at the Petit Portage Neuf (New Little Portage). At the far end of this 550 yard carry, we took a lunch break before putting back in at 1:00. While we munched, I explained the two "New" Portages that we had traveled over last evening and today. Originally, the native route between Rose Lake on the west and Mountain Lake on the east had passed by way of Arrow Lake (which was connected to the north side of Rose Lake and extended several miles toward the northeast) and a long, arduous portage that led from Arrow Lake southeast to the midpoint of Mountain Lake. At some point, the traders had switched from this arc-shaped route via Arrow Lake to the more direct passage involving Lac Entredeux (Lake Between the Two) and Watap Lake. This new route had required the New Great Portage, running from Rose Lake eastward to Lake Entredeux, a short eastward water connection, and the New Little Portage, which ran eastward from Watap Lake to the western end of Mountain Lake.

By now, the sky had clouded over again, and a moderate wind blew from the west; grey clouds would march into and out of the scene throughout the afternoon. After lunch, we traveled due east over the eight mile length of Lac de Montagne (Mountain Lake) in two hours, with a rather substantial wind and moderately high waves pushing us directly from behind. During 5 1/2 days on the water, this was the very first helpful following wind that we had encountered! Ben paddled two of the miles on the lake, after which Kevin did six miles, with Mom leading the song-fest. This was the first time that we had allowed the boys to work the bow paddle in a moderately dangerous situation, while being pushed by big waves and a considerable force of wind. At the landing place at the end of the lake, to keep the canoe from being swamped in the heavy surf, Doree jumped in and held the stern directly into the crashing waves while I unloaded in the knee-deep shallows.

With the green-clad Moose Mountain looming over us just to the south, we then surmounted, in quick succession, a series of obstacles. These included the Petit Portage des Cerises (Little Cherries Portage), 500 yards on the right shore; the marshy Fan Lake, a quarter-mile long; the Portage Vaseux (Muddy Portage), 220 yards on the right; Lac Vaseux (Muddy Lake), 1/4 mile in length; and the Grand Portage des Cerises (Big Cherries Portage), 770 yards on the right. The terrain of each of the first two portages appeared to be completely level, with virtually no changes in elevation; the longer third portage was sometimes level and sometimes along a gradual decline, which was so much easier to handle than an incline or rough terrain. Both of the little lakes in the sequence were just small ponds choked with lily pads. My main hindrance on these three portages was the pain in my left foot; I had hurt it earlier in the afternoon while unloading in the crashing surf at the end of Lac de Montagne. (*As stoical as he was at ignoring pain, I knew Tim was really uncomfortable when he mentioned it. Doree*)

After advancing two miles on Lac Orignal (Moose Lake), we landed at a campsite on its southern shore at 6:00. Since 10:30 this morning, we had progressed fourteen miles and had made four portages. A few drops of rain fell as we set up camp, after which we were elated to watch a short segment of a rainbow appear directly across the lake from us. We thoroughly savored our feast of beef jerky cooked with mushrooms, peas, and noodles, and then, pleasantly stuffed, we settled ourselves around the fire to gaze into the dancing, twisting flames. Offshore, three loons patrolled back and forth, occasionally calling to each other with their haunting cries.

At this point, each of the boys had completed 24 miles toward their respective individual goals of thirty miles in the bow seat, and both of them were itching to paddle more. Today, they had traveled the entire fourteen miles in the bow position, except the combined half-mile distance across the two lily-pad-filled pond lakes. Doree had ridden virtually all day as a comfortable passenger, nestled at the very front of the compartment in front of the bow paddler, facing rearward. Along the way, she had happily sung many new French songs to us, reading them from the various sheets of tunes that we had not yet memorized. She also taught us the refrain to some of the songs, to sing at intervals as she belted out their verses.

In the tent, after we had exchanged massages, we all snuggled into our sleeping bags. Although Doree typically drifted off to sleep within about twenty seconds on these exhausting journeys, one or both of the boys invariably wanted to chat. So we continued with our conversation until I could no longer make my brain form words, after which silence fell on the family.

Day Seven

I waked up at 6:30, ahead of the family, so that I could relish in solitude the *lever du soleil* (sunrise) peeking over the edge of the hills on the far side of Lac Orignal (Moose Lake). As I sat taking in the beautiful gold-tinted scene, a red squirrel cautiously advanced to the fire area, and then closely checked me out. In reviewing the wildlife that we had encountered so far on this trip, I noted that we had passed a number of beaver lodges adjacent to the shore, plus two beaver dams beside the Grand Portage Neuf. In addition, various hawks, grouse, gulls, mallards, and a number of mergansers with half-grown broods in tow had communed with us along the route. And amazingly, we had not needed to use insect repellent against mosquitoes or black flies a single time during this trip!

The family emerged from their dream worlds at 7:45, and we departed an hour later. A fast-moving layer of grey clouds filled almost all of the sky, except low on the horizons, while a stiff breeze was blowing down the lake in exactly our southeasterly direction of travel, which would help considerably. We were eighteen miles from the end point of this voyage, but, as was our usual custom, we did not set a goal of completing that distance by the end of the day. Through all of our years of long-distance canoeing, we almost never established a day's end-goal, except in those very rare instances when we needed to arrive at a specific place at a pre-arranged time to rendezvous with a shuttle driver or a float plane pilot. During nearly all of our days on the water, we simply put out our best effort to advance along the route, accepted the challenges as they came our way, appreciated the beauties of the natural world as they unfolded around us, and were pleased with our progress however it played out.

As we glided onto the unsheltered expanse of Lac Orignal, the wind and waves picked up considerably. Sailing fast on the backs of the large waves, we covered the two miles to Portage l'Orignal (Moose Portage) in a half-hour, with Kevin working the bow paddle at full tilt. After unloading, we made the carry of 700 yards on the left shore; the trail, running along the north side of a small stream, was either level or a very gradual decline all the way. However, the footing was quite precarious, over medium-sized broken rocks with water running or standing in the trail over at least half of its length. When we emerged from the wooded path at Lac aux Outardes (Goose Lake, now called Fowl Lake), beams of golden sunlight passed through openings in the thick, grey cloud cover to gleam brightly on the calm surface of the sheltered bay. With Ben as the *avant*, we set out to cover the five mile length of the lake. Shortly, a frisky following wind picked up, and we sailed wildly for an hour, while belting out many verses of *Vent Frais*.

In the middle of the lake, however, we experienced a major slow-down, when I chose to take the narrow channel between the central island and the low island to its right, rather than skirting around the left side of the central island. When we entered that slender channel, we found that it was nearly closed with thick beds of reeds and wild rice. Since Doree was much stronger than Ben and had a much longer reach than him, she took over the bow seat for a time, to help drive our way through the thick vegetation, after which Ben resumed his paddling and our speedy sailing continued. At the end of Lac aux Outardes, beneath the looming Goose Rock Mountain, we unloaded at the head of the portage path, with Doree holding the stern pointed directly into the surf to keep the canoe from being filled by the crashing waves.

Before making the one-mile Portage aux Outardes (Goose Portage) on the left shore, we took a 45 minute lunch break at noon. While we were sprawled out on the portage trail eating our lunch, a snowshoe hare skirted around behind us in the bushes. It was rather unusual to glimpse one of these creatures in the daytime, since they are generally nocturnal, usually coming out in late evening and at night to munch on green plants. I explained to the boys that in the fall, its brown fur with black tips would change to white, and then back again to brown the following spring, triggered by the decreasing or increasing amounts of daylight. With the autumn change of color, it would also grow extra fur on its large hind feet, which would enable it to travel across deep soft snow, thus earning it the name "snowshoe." Just after I mentioned that these creatures could run at speeds of up to thirty miles an hour and leap up to fourteen feet, that same hare bounded fearlessly out of the bushes, leaped over and through the four of us, and scampered up the trail! Between fits of laughter, I suggested that it had possibly nibbled some crazy mushrooms, or was acting on a dare from friends. The boys suspected that I had pre-arranged the whole scene. (*What powers fathers possess in the eyes of their children! Doree*)

The portage began with an extremely steep, rocky hill, after which the path was either level or up a slight incline for the rest of the way. We first carried the packs over the entire length of the trail, passing over and around many trees that had toppled across the path, and also through several boggy, swampy areas. After taking about 35 minutes to reach the far end, we rested during the return walk, in voyageur fashion. On the third trip over with the canoe, to ascend the steep hill at the beginning of the path, all four of us carried the craft in a right-side-up position. Later along the trail, when I was carrying the canoe in the usual upside-down position on my shoulders, we reached a large aspen that had fallen across the path. There, we had to pass the canoe forward hand-over-hand to one another, to snake it through the branches of the tree. It took us 2 1/2 hours of walking and resting to complete the three trips across the mile-long carry.

During all this hiking, I compared notes on the condition of everyone's feet. By this point on the seventh day, after making three trips over each of the twenty portages, we all had feet that felt like they were burning. This was partly caused by wearing wet socks and shoes during every waking minute, and partly by the sand and silt that washed into our socks, which produced friction, abraded the skin, and sometimes raised blisters. The constantly moist conditions, the grime, and the slight wounds all combined to develop mild infections. (Doree)

By 3:30, we were reloaded and again moving forward, traveling down the Rivière aux Tourtes (shortened from Tourterelles, the Pigeon River, called Nantouagan in the Algonquian native languages), which we would follow for the rest of the trip. The weather offered occasional scattered showers, and a high temperature of 65 degrees in the shade.

For the first two or three miles, the Pigeon River was slow-moving, with reedy shorelines. Then it picked up some speed, and its shores became forested with spruce and some pines. As we glided silently along, we could hear in the nearby woods the gradually accelerating rhythm of a male ruffed grouse beating its wings, a pattern that was repeated at least a dozen times -- even though this was not the spring mating season. I could picture the male in the usual position for drumming, standing on a log with his tail feathers fanned out; the distinctive booming sound was produced by his cupped wings moving the air, not by his wings pounding on his chest or on the log beneath him.

During this time of quiet cruising, my thoughts wandered to the fur trade that had been carried out after La Guerre de Sept Ans (the Seven Years' War, which the British called the French and Indian War), and the facilities that had been developed during this latter period at each end of the Grand Portage, where we were headed. Over the course of the 1740s and 1750s, the French developed a small post at the eastern end of The Portage, with a dwelling, a warehouse, and a blacksmith shop. When the French lost control of New France in 1760 and the British took over Canada, a small number of Anglos entered the Montreal-based fur trade, as investors and outfitters, sometimes as traders, and eventually as guides.

Previous to 1760, other than the moderate amount of commerce that was carried out along the shores of Hudson's Bay, British experience in the trade had been limited almost entirely to the small-scale, Albany-based trade. In fact, during the 1750s, of all the furs that were exported from the entirety of North America, only about 20 percent of them were garnered by the British; the remaining 80 percent were collected and shipped out by the French.

I had often emphasized to Kevin and Ben that the St. Lawrence peltries commerce remained very much a French-dominated business for at least the next sixty years, until the 1820s. In the St. Lawrence communities, large numbers of French residents were still employed in a wide variety of occupations related to the fur trade, creating trade merchandise, equipment, canoes, and provisions, as they had done for 150 years during the French period. During the era of British governance, these individuals still worked as seamstresses, finger weavers, pewterers, blacksmiths, carvers, coopers, carpenters, basket weavers, canoe builders, farmers, warehouse laborers, and so forth. In addition, numerous French outfitters and investors continued to operate in the St. Lawrence settlements, while many hundreds of French voyageurs, guides, interpreters, and traders from the St. Lawrence Valley still plied their trade on the waterways and in the west.

Although the primary forts in the interior were commanded by British officers after 1760, and were manned by rather small numbers of British soldiers, only a fraction of the interior commerce was carried out by Anglo traders for a long period of time. The vast bulk of the trade was still done by French and Métis (mixed French and native) individuals. The number of British and Anglo-American investors and outfitters who operated in the St. Lawrence Valley, and the traders of these same nationalities who worked in the west, increased only gradually over the decades following 1760. In 1770, ten years after the British conquest of New France, fully 82 percent of the licenses that were issued for the western trade continued to be issued to Frenchmen. When the famous Beaver Club was established at Montreal in 1785, by a group of the most prominent and wealthy investors and merchant-outfitters at that time, a full quarter-century after the end of French rule, eight of the nineteen founding members, or 42 percent of them, were French Canadian. These eight Frenchmen were joined in founding the Beaver Club by six Scotsmen, three Englishmen, and two Anglo-Americans. After another two decades had passed, in 1804, after a total of 44 years of British rule in Canada, the employment rolls of the Northwest Company reflected the continued dominance of the commerce by the French. Although there were only two Frenchmen remaining among the 45 profit-sharing partners of this firm, which was the most prominent of the Montreal-based fur trade associations, 33 of the 76 traders who actually carried out the commerce for the company at its interior posts were French or Métis, representing 41 percent of the company's traders. In addition, all but two of the 45 interpreters at the firm's posts, a full 96 percent, were likewise French or Métis. Among the guides and voyageurs who wintered at the company's posts in the west, all but sixteen of the guides were French or Métis, while 97 percent of the 657 voyageurs were French, Métis, or native. Even a number of the 22 voyageurs in the interior with Anglo family names may have had French mothers. In addition, the vast majority of the round-trip paddlers who traveled from Montreal to the west each summer were likewise not of Anglo stock.

However, I had often stressed to the boys, a heavily dispro-portionate amount of the modern research and publications concerning the peltries commerce of North America have focused on the activities of the non-French participants in the trade. This decidedly Anglo bias has come about, in part, because the English language records of these individuals have been so readily accessible to English-speaking scholars and history enthusiasts. In addition, since the British won control of the region of Canada in 1760, Anglos have been the ones who, for the most part, have written and controlled the content of the history of the U.S. and Canada, until recent times.

Tim was intimately familiar with the surviving documentation of the French regime and the first several decades of the British regime. He often located, transcribed, and translated (with my help) early French documents from archives in Canada and France that had never before seen the light of day. So he became frustrated seeing the presenters and the exhibits at various reconstructed forts in the Great Lakes region, such as Ft. Michilimackinac, Grand Portage post, and Ft. William, present to the public and emphasize information about only the British era of the fur trade. In these presentations, Anglos were invariably depicted as the ones who did the thinking and made most of the money in the trade, while the French contributions during 250 years of commerce appeared to have been limited to providing thousands of dumb but happy voyageurs, who paddled canoes fearlessly and hauled heavy loads cheerfully for their Anglo bosses. (Doree)

Back to my solitary musings. For years, Kevin and Ben had known, from their many visits to the Straits of Mackinac, that this locale had served as the main center for all of the trade of the upper Great Lakes region, and for the areas that stretched far to the west of the Great Lakes. The Straits posts, first at St. Ignace and after 1715 on the southern shoreline, held this distinction during the entire French era of the fur trade, and during much of the British period as well. It was only when the trade finally expanded further to the northwest beyond the Saskatchewan River watershed, the outer limits of French regime commerce, that the supply line grew excessively long. This made it unsafe for the most distant interior traders to try to paddle from their posts out to Mackinac, exchange their peltries there for new merchandise and supplies with their colleagues from Montreal, and then return to their posts, all before the winter freeze closed the waterways. This distant northwestern commerce, first extending to the Churchill River watershed in 1773, and then over the La Loche or Methye Portage to the Athabasca River watershed five years later, required a summer rendezvous locale that was further to the west than the Straits. So a new gathering place was established for the far western trade, at the eastern end of the Grand Portage.

Beginning in 1778, when a few soldiers were stationed each summer beside Lake Superior at the terminus of The Portage, this became the primary rendezvous place for a meeting of the most distant traders and the outfitters based at Mackinac and Montreal. The following year, Ft. Charlotte was built at the western end of the portage trail, as a storage depot for canoes, merchandise, and provisions. In 1784, the lakeside facility at Grand Portage became the interior headquarters of the Northwest Company. The following year, a detailed summary that was made of the interior commerce compared the furs and hides that were gathered at the three Great Lakes rendezvous centers each year. At Detroit, about 3,000 packs were amassed annually, each pack worth only £10 since they were made up of furs from the warmer, southerly Great Lakes region, totaling £30,000 in value. In contrast, at Mackinac some 5,000 packs were assembled each year, each of which was worth £15, a full 50 percent more than those packs gathered at Detroit, creating a total value of £75,000. Finally, only 700 packs were brought to Grand Portage annually at this stage; each of these packs was worth £40, due to the high quality of the furs from the frigid far north. However, due to the relatively small number of peltries that were gathered at The Portage each year, the total value of these northwestern packs was only £28,000. This was 37 percent of the value of the furs and hides that were assembled annually at the Straits of Mackinac, 22 percent of the total value of all the peltries that were collected each year, and only 8 percent of the total number of packs.

In time, those traders who operated in the most distant Athabasca country, in the far northwest, would be hard-pressed to make the journey from their wintering posts out to Grand Portage and back before the freeze-up of the rivers and lakes. So a secondary, even more westerly rendezvous point was developed in 1788, at the western end of Rainy Lake. Certain resuppliers would paddle to that locale from Grand Portage, to deliver new merchandise and supplies to the Athabascan traders and collect their furs and hides. During the 1790s, the Grand Portage post still received some of the new canoes that were used in the far western trade, as well as some of the provisions for that commerce, from suppliers at the Straits of Mackinac. In addition, the Straits continued to serve as the annual summer gathering place for most of the trade that took place in the upper Great Lakes region. The western rendezvous at Grand Portage flourished until 1803, when the British merchants there moved their operations from U.S territory, northward up the Superior shore to the mouth of the Kaministiquia River, where they built Ft. William on British soil and continued the annual rendezvous there.

Tim was a fanatic about knowing what had happened hundreds and thousands of years ago in whatever place he found himself. He sometimes said he had his own historical movies playing inside his head much of the time. After several decades of being married to the guy, I knew that one of his greatest passions was adding more and more details to those "head movies." His historical interests were especially obvious during these canoe trips, when we would be close together around the clock. I knew whenever he would fall totally silent for a half hour or more that he was off in some previous century or millennium. But on these trips in particular, Tim's hunger for historical details provided the rest of us with lots of welcome entertainment. And this was not just a stream of historical facts. Before each canoe jaunt, he would read biographies and historical novels, taking notes all the while; then he would retell those stories to us during the long hours of steady paddling. Often these would be spread out over multiple days, in serial fashion. Tim's narratives kept us entranced. Strangely, he was not a very talkative guy most of the time. But during the long days of paddling from early morning until evening, we actually hungered for the stories he would tell. And not all of them were about long-ago history.

*Every year, the boys begged Tim to tell one particular drawn-out joke, which eventually grew until it took up the better part of an afternoon. The story line involved three friends, a buzzard, a turtle, and a rabbit, who were hacking out a pioneer farm in the wilderness. The rabbit, who had drawn the short straw, was assigned the task of traveling a great distance to buy fertilizer for the garden. (The challenge of telling the tale is in remembering every detail of his outbound trip, and repeating each of them, in the correct order, during the course of his return trip.) During the rabbit's lonnnnng absence, the other two friends discovered gold on their land, and soon had a fine mansion built to replace their simple cabin. They also hired a cook, a maid, and a French butler to serve them. When the rabbit finally returned and was greeted at the front door by the haughty butler, he asked to see his old friend the buzzard. The proud servant answered, with considerable attitude, "Monsieur Buzzard is in the **yard**." Requesting to see his buddy the turtle, the butler responded, "Monsieur Turtell is at the **well**." At this, the irate rabbit replied, "Well tell them that Monsieur Rabitt is here with the **shit**!" A roar of laughter followed. (Doree)*

After we had advanced about 3 1/2 miles down the Pigeon River, we reached the head of a long stretch of rapids. Its most challenging segment could be avoided by making a 500 yard carry on the right shore at the Décharge Caribou. However, with the water level being quite high from the recent rainstorms, we decided to run the entire stretch, with Kevin wielding the bow paddle. Before commencing the run, I teasingly made the boys slightly nervous by quoting, with as much of a straight face as I could muster, the native saying, "Today is a good day to die!"

We all reveled in the fast, rollicking ride, rounding many curves in the channel. A couple of times, we polished the bottom of the canoe as we grazed over large stones that were lying in wait just beneath the surface. After a calmer but very fast stretch of about a half-mile, we then dashed down another very long series of fast rapids that rounded many bends in the river. The worst of this stretch could be avoided by using the carry at the Décharge Grosse Rocher (Big Rock), which extended for 500 yards along the left shore. The entire span of two sets of rapids plus the intervening half-mile of fast water offered us about two miles of exhilarating action. While we were busy handling the waterway, with the shorelines whisking by, we did not even notice the locations of the upper and lower ends of the two portage paths, where the voyageurs had made two décharges, carrying all or part of their cargo and then lining their empty or half-loaded canoes. Since Kevin had never before had any experience as a bow paddler in moderate rapids, he grew in stature as he paddled ferociously and proudly through the frothing current!

After the river calmed down, Ben took over in the bow, and paddled the remaining five miles of our route. At about the halfway point of this last stretch, we passed on the left shore the expanse of open grassland that the voyageurs had called La Prairie (The Meadow). Here, the crews of entire brigades of canoes had found enough room to assemble and camp together, about five miles above the end of the Grand Portage.

We had pre-arranged to have our shuttle driver leave our car just above the Sault de la Perdrix (Partridge Falls), where the western end of Partridge Falls Road nearly meets the river. When we reached that spot at 6:00, we had covered the nine miles on the Pigeon River in 2½ hours, including relaxing and enjoying the placid narrow channel at both ends and running the fast stretch of rapids in the midsection. While gliding down this waterway, we had scared up at least a hundred ducks along its shorelines.

We were all pleased and proud to have completed this year's challenging voyage -- and with considerable élan! We had paddled 120 miles in seven days, averaging 17 miles a day, while dealing with 34 obstacles. In that array of obstacles, each one a possible portage, we had carried on twenty of them (58 percent), had lined up ten of them, had dragged the loaded canoe over moss and log rollers over one, had paddled up a fast channel once, and had run the only two sets of downstream rapids that were present along the entire route, on the Pigeon River at nearly the end.

From our ending place, we could have continued on by making the nearby 600 yard Portage de la Perdrix (Partridge Portage), followed by a two-mile paddle down the Pigeon River to the Grand Portage, and then a 8.2 mile carry over that trail, which would have yielded a total of 130 miles. However, we were content to halt near Partridge Falls, carry the gear and canoe a quarter-mile from the river to our car at the end of Partridge Falls Road, and then drive five miles on the very rough and rutted road plus five miles on a paved road to reach the Lake Superior shore. We had little interest in hiking the length of the Grand Portage while fully loaded with canoe and gear. (We had previously walked sections of it without loads, as an exercise in historical appreciation.)

Impressing us all greatly, Kevin carried the canoe himself over the quarter-mile distance from the river to our car; this was the first time that he had ever handled the burden of the canoe over an entire portage. As we drove slowly out along the dirt road, a large hawk played with us, flying a short distance ahead of the car and moving from tree to tree beside the roadway for several miles, before it finally bid us adieu.

On this 120 mile trip, Kevin and Ben had each paddled 33 miles in the bow, totaling more than half of the overall distance. This had been a great treat for Doree, giving her plenty of time to sit in the bow passenger's spot and enjoy the passing scenery, as well as the conversation with whichever son was padding in the bow at the time. This voyage represented a major leap forward in the rigorous participation of the boys, compared to all of our previous canoe trips. They were growing up.

Driving to the Grand Portage Lodge, we left the remaining payment for the shuttle driver and picked up the extra set of car keys. Since the facility was fully booked for the night, we traveled twenty miles south to the exotic and unusual Naniboujou Lodge. There, along with an available room, we enjoyed a delicious 9 P.M. feast of baked chicken and barbequed ribs, made up especially for us since the kitchen had already been closed down for the night. While dining in our grubby paddling clothes in the elegant dining room, we were surrounded by brilliant walls and ceiling which had been painted in native motifs and bold primary colors by a Cree man in 1929. Discussing the famous clientele who had once belonged to this exclusive national club of Naniboujou, including Babe Ruth, Jack Dempsey, and Ring Lardner, we could not ignore the stinging and burning sensations of our feet, in our soggy tennies beneath the blue tablecloth. Having been wet during every waking minute for a week, and having slogged three successive times across twenty portages, those dogs were now muttering their protests.

In our rooms, we washed our feet and let the healing begin. After sleeping the night in luxurious beds, in the morning we all donned clean clothes and returned to "civilized" life, which we commenced by walking the cobble stone shoreline of Lake Superior near the lodge, where we communed with the Canada geese there. En route home to Illinois, we spent an entire day taking in the Circus World Museum in Baraboo, Wisconsin, the original 1884 home of the Ringling Brothers Circus.

During our drive back to Oak Park, as we did while returning home after each canoe jaunt, we enjoyed reviewing the many events of the just-completed trip. Then we launched into planning the details of the next year's voyage: the segment to paddle and when to schedule it, the shuttle driver arrangements, any items of gear or clothing that needed repair or replacement, any suggestions for changes in the menu. The distant horizon was bright and enticing, and uncounted adventures beckoned to us.

VIII

Sixth Voyage
Western Minnesota-Ontario Boundary
Waters, May 27-June 4, 1989

I went to the woods because I wished to live deliberately,
to front only the essential facts of life
and see if I could not learn what they had to teach;
And not, when I came to die, discover that I had not lived.
Henry David Thoreau

Growth is the only evidence of life.
John Henry Newman

Growth demands a temporary surrender of security.
Gail Sheehy

Our trip this year would cover the western portion of the wilderness boundary waters between Minnesota and Ontario, in effect, a westward extension of the 1988 trek. Traveling through the same type of Canadian Shield country, we would paddle 170 miles in a meandering course that headed generally east-southeast. As in the previous year, the land along the left shore of the various lakes and rivers would be Canadian soil, much of it within Quetico Provincial Park, while the right shore would lie in the U.S., the first part of the trip in Voyageurs National Park and the following portion in the Boundary Waters Canoe Area Wilderness. We would again travel from west to east, in hopes of receiving some assistance from the prevailing westerly winds, rather than facing them as oncoming head winds. The wind factor would be all the more significant this year because the route, in addition to being nearly fifty percent longer than the previous year, would entail much more travel on open, unsheltered lake waters. Although we would again be paddling against the current in the river sections, the number of obstructions in those sections would be less than a third the number that we had encountered in 1988.

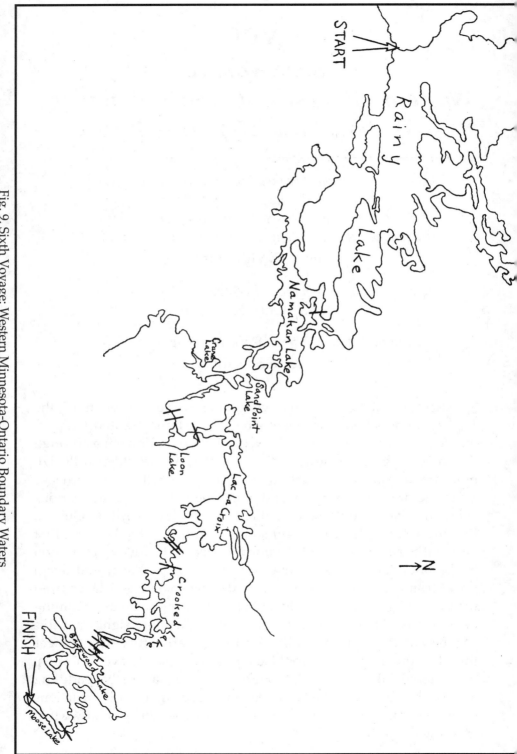

START

Rainy Lake

Namakan Lake

Sand Point Lake

Crane Lake

Loon Lake

Lac La Croix

Crooked Lake

Basswood Lake

Moose Lake

FINISH

N

Fig. 9, Sixth Voyage: Western Minnesota-Ontario Boundary Waters

One of the most significant differences in this year's voyage was the much earlier timing. In 1988, we had traveled in the balmy weather of latter August. However, we were obliged by the Symphony's schedule to make this trip in late May and the very beginning of June, to accommodate the month-long European tour that would commence in latter August. As a result, the early season of paddling would bring us much chillier air temperatures, as well as much more frigid water temperatures.

To arrange for the early release from school of Kevin (age 12 9/12, finishing seventh grade) and Ben (age 10 11/12, finishing fifth grade), I wrote to their respective teachers at the junior high and the elementary school:

"Dear Ms. _____,

Our family is locked into the orchestra's schedule of vacations, which unfortunately does not take into consideration school schedules. This year during our vacation, we will be doing a 170 mile canoe trip, as part of our ongoing family project of paddling the entire length of the ancient mainline fur trade route, from Montreal to northern Alberta in northwestern Canada. After this year's segment, we will have covered about 800 miles of the route westward from Montreal, in six segments.

In preparation for these trips, we dry our own food, order and study the Canadian government topographical maps (onto which we add information about the route gleaned from ancient fur traders' journals and many other sources), ready ourselves to handle any and all medical emergencies, etc. During the trips, we deal as a family with exhaustion and pain, hunger, fear, etc., while enjoying the wilderness and gaining some understanding of history, geography, and the work that many of our French Canadian ancestors did. After the trips, when we are again well rested, well fed, and healed, we enjoy the satisfaction of having overcome lots of tough challenges, and we have a better frame of reference for both coping with the insanities of 20th century urban living and keeping our sanity in it.

This year the orchestra's vacation begins on Saturday, May 20. We have decided that Kevin would miss too much of the end of the school year if we were to begin our canoe trip then, so we will wait until after school on Thursday, May 25 to leave on the expedition. This compromise will allow him to remain in school until nearly the end of the school year, while hopefully allowing us enough time to drive to Canada, manage the 170 miles, and return in time for me to start the Ravinia summer season. Thus, he will miss eight school days, plus the last day on June 7. Would you please send home well in advance any assignments or test preparations he needs to do early, in order to complete all the required work for the school year by Thursday, May 25.

I apologize for any inconvenience this may cause you, and I thank you very much for your cooperation.

Best Wishes,
Tim Kent"

Each year, Doree and I made similar requests for early releases and belated starts of the boys' school days. In each instance, the teachers were very accommodating and encouraging of our projects, especially since the guys did well in school. In addition, a few months earlier Kevin had received the Eagle Award, the highest rank in Boy Scouts, while Ben had recently completed all of the awards in Cub Scouts and had advanced into Boy Scouts. It was clear that the few days that were clipped off the beginning and the end of each school year were definitely not harming their progress, and the learning that they were gaining from the paddling and living-history research trips more than offset the lost school days.

During all of our years of paddling the mainline route from end to end, this would be the earliest trip on the calendar. All other voyages over the span of fifteen summers would be done in latter June, July, or August. Due to the frigid water temperatures of late May, we decided to split among us the two neoprene wet suits that we owned, an ingenious concept that was suggested by Ben. Doree and I would wear the farmer-john bottoms, which were sleeveless and extended from the ankles to the upper chest and snapped closed atop the shoulders, while the boys would wear the long-sleeved tops, which extended from the neck down to snap closed beneath the crotch; in addition, each of us would wear a pair of wet suit boots. If we were to capsize, the suits, although split between us and thus not covering our entire body, would offer at least some degree of protection against hypothermia.

Leaving home in the latter morning on Friday, we drove fourteen hours to Ely, Minnesota, arriving at 12:45 A.M. Adjacent to the parking lot of the Chamber of Commerce, at the eastern edge of town, stood Dorothy Molter's two cabins from the B.W.C.A.W., which had been dismantled, transported out, and reassembled there as a monument in her honor. We had arranged to rendezvous with the shuttle driver at 6:00 the following morning in that parking lot, so we spent the remainder of the night sleeping as best we could in our rather small car. Since we had been enjoying very warm weather in Chicago, we were jolted by the temperature drop that night into the thirties. The waterproof bags inside the packs were already sealed, ready for our launch, with the sleeping bags stowed within the bags. So we spent a very restless four hours in the car, trying to catch a few Zs while wearing only light coats and huddling beneath a couple of skimpy blankets.

Day One

Arising to the clamor of the alarm clock at 5:15, we donned our paddling clothes in the frosty dawn, munched some gorp for breakfast, and awaited the 6:00 arrival of the shuttle driver from Don Beland's outfitting camp on Moose Lake, about twenty miles east of Ely, where our canoe trip would eventually end. During the half-hour that the driver was late, we wondered if he would arrive at all, suspecting that he had either forgotten our arrangements or had overslept. Wondering was about all we could do, since we had no way of reaching him by phone. After his much-appreciated arrival, we drove 2 1/2 hours westward to Ranier, Minnesota, just east of International Falls, where we put in at the public boat landing on Rainy Lake, at the western tip of the lake.

Beneath a pale blue sky, a few cotton ball clouds making their slow rolling journey toward the east, and a beaming golden sun, we launched at 9:45, pleased that the air temperature had warmed to 60 degrees. Elated to be out of the cramped car and paddling on wide-open wilderness waters, with a light westerly breeze directly at our backs, we easily made 7 1/2 miles in 2 1/2 hours. As we advanced eastward along Lac La Pluie (Rainy Lake), we stayed within a mile or so of the southern shoreline, or the many islands that are strewn along that shore, so we could register and enjoy the gradually passing scenery. It would have been discouraging to head directly down the midline of the lake, which ranges from about four to seven miles in width, since we would have been unable to discern our progress in relation to the very distant shores. This body of water extends eastward for some 25 miles to its central narrows, then east-southeastward for another 15 miles. The low, level elevations surrounding the lake are covered with expanses of mostly spruce and fir, with some pines, as are also the myriad large and small islands that crowd much of the lake.

To pass the time during our progress, we discussed the various furs and hides that the native people had exchanged with the French. Two of the most prominent furs were beaver and muskrat, whose microscopically barbed hairs, when shaved from the pelt, could be made into high quality felt for creating broad-brimmed hats. The other members of the rodent family whose furs were traded were black and grey squirrels. Pelts of many of the weasel family were also in demand, including otter, marten, mink, fisher, wolverine, and weasel (which turned from light brown in summer to white in winter, when it was identified as ermine). The fox or dog family was represented in the fur trade by red, black, silver, and cross foxes (all common variants of the very same animal), grey fox, and wolf. Sought-after pelts from the cat family included those of cougar, panther, puma, and mountain lion (four regional names for the very same creature), bobcat, and lynx, while thousands of furs of raccoons (called *chat* by the French) and bears were also exchanged. Besides all of these furs, great numbers of hides from hoofed animals were also avidly acquired by French traders, including deer, elk, moose, woodland caribou (whose original range extended as far south as central Wisconsin and central Minnesota), and bison. The most highly prized among these hides were those that had been de-haired and brain-tanned by native people. Some of the furred animals whose pelts were not included in the commerce included coyote, hare and rabbit, skunk, badger, and opossum. As we chatted, the boys enjoyed mentally picturing each of the various creatures, whose pelts hung on the walls of our finished basement at home.

After taking a half-hour lunch break on Red Pine Island, lounging on a barren granite ledge that angled gradually out of the water, we set out in a rather robust tail wind and foaming whitecaps. An exhilarating, ninety-minute ride beneath a billowing sail, with Doree paddling at full tilt in the bow with short, fast strokes and me ruddering hard in the stern, brought us to the eastern end of Dryweed Island, where we stopped for a mid-afternoon break. While resting for a half-hour, we studied the large-scale, poorly detailed map of Rainy Lake that I had acquired. It was quite a challenge trying to determine on it our exact location, amid the array of evergreen-clad islands and deeply indented shoreline features. Heading southward for a mile, to better align our direction of travel with the following wind and whitecaps for the long stretch that lay ahead, we turned eastward again and rode the wild waves under full sail across the central, wide-open body of Rainy Lake. The voyageurs had termed this portion of the lake the Grande Traverse (Great Crossing).

Partway across this five-mile section, a sudden gust of wind grabbed the map and tossed it overboard. Before we could drop the sail and turn back to retrieve the chart, it had disappeared beneath the waves! Because the map had been made of waterproof parchment, I had simply tucked it beneath one of the straps of the pack in front of me, instead of using the ziplock map holder of thick clear plastic, as I had always previously done when using standard paper maps. With the spiraling of the map into the blue-green depths, the spirit of the expedition leader sank somewhat as well. During seven years of wilderness paddling, I had always felt that I could confidently venture anywhere in the canoe if I had the secure knowledge of where we were at all times on a detailed chart. With a map at hand, I could make judgments about our course, cut off corners, traverse the mouth of bays, and avoid dead-end passages, all the while applying our energy and time to the best advantage. Now entirely lacking a map, I would need to improvise as best I could for the next 25 miles of our route, until the highly detailed series of charts that I had stored in one of the waterproof bags would begin at the distant eastern end of the lake!

In ancient times, both native and French paddlers had known so intimately the network of waterways that they had held extensive, detailed maps in their head. Younger travelers would watch carefully during journeys, and would memorize the landmarks of the myriad routes, under the direction of their elders. The guideposts included land features, rock formations, unusual living and dead trees, bodies of water, and rapids, which were all named to help in identifying and remembering them. Certain of the signposts were man-made, intentionally created at significant places and intersections. The most common of these markers consisted of a blaze on a tree, a light-colored spot that was produced by removing a section of dark bark. The next most common marker was a "lob stick," a tall, somewhat isolated, standing evergreen from which all but the topmost branches had been lopped off, to create an obvious living signal for travelers. We sometimes wondered how many times the guides of canoe parties had become lost or off the course that they had intended to travel, having missed a landmark rock or having failed to notice that a significant tree had been blown down in a storm. Or sometimes the individual who knew the route was separated from the rest of the party, or became extremely ill, or drowned in a capsize, or was killed in a shooting accident. It was sobering for us to consider the amount of specialized knowledge that had been lost each time one of those master guides had perished unexpectedly, before he had fully passed on to a protégé the encyclopedic maps that were stored in his brain. For the Kent family, paddling along a 3,000 mile route that we had never seen before, on waterways which no longer featured blazes on trees or lob stick signposts, having detailed printed maps in hand was an absolute necessity.

Continuing our eastward traverse under a fully-engaged sail, amid the strong wind and moderately large waves, we hailed a passing boat of fishermen. On their detailed series of maps of the lake, they showed me precisely where we were, which helped a bit. A little later, we hailed another boat of folks who were just cruising the lake for fun; they very generously gave us their pocket map of the lake. Although it was even less detailed than the map that I had lost, it was a salvation at this point! Now I could at least guide us on the correct course along the peninsula with five long arms that juts out at an angle from the southern shore, to the place where it nearly meets its counterpart peninsula extending out from the northern shore. The distance between these two land masses, mostly filled by Brule Island, leaves only a quarter-mile-wide passage, which the voyageurs had termed Le Détroit; this was the strait or narrows at the waist of the lake, now called Brule Narrows. While I directed our craft through this pass, we had problems on several occasions with large powerboats driven by inconsiderate or ignorant fishermen. In each instance, as they roared by, the tall wake created by their boat threatened to broadside and capsize our much smaller canoe, requiring that we turn sharply into the wake each time, to cut through the hill of fast-moving water at an angle.

We finally landed for the evening at 5:45, on a little island in Le Détroit that lay just off the southern shore. As we glided toward the rock ledge that would serve as our landing place, a pair of startled mergansers burst up from the near-shore shallows and quickly winged away. In eight hours on the water, we had covered 24 miles, after fourteen hours of driving from home, a short and rough night of fitful sleeping while shivering in the car, and a 2 1/2 hour ride with the shuttle driver to the launch spot.

Shortly after leaving our first rest stop on Red Pine Island at mid-day, we had entered the territory of Voyageurs National Park. From that point forward, the lands along the right shore of our route for the next sixty miles, including 31/2 days of travel along the lengths of Rainy Lake, Namakan Lake, and Sand Point Lake, would lie within this park, which had been established in 1971.

During our evening meal, as the orb of reddish gold eased down beneath the tree line off to the west, a pair of loons cruised on the glassy surface nearby, occasionally calling out their haunting messages. When Doree occasionally imitated their calls, one or the other of the birds usually responded, but with a warbled comment that my wife was hard-pressed to understand. We gobbled down a well-earned feast of beef and noodle stew, and then enjoyed a cheerful fire that Ben had built, on the tip of a very slender granite point that extended out into the water. We had been granted gorgeous weather for our first day out, with a considerable amount of wind assistance as well. It was probably too much to expect that an equally beautiful and cooperative day would follow.

Day Two

During the wee hours of the night, a much less benign weather front moved into the area, and a steady cold rain began to fall. Although I awakened at 6:00, I waited patiently for an hour for the rainfall to either slow or stop, but it only increased. So we finally crawled out of the tent, outfitted with wet suits, clothing, and rain gear, and quietly began to break camp. As we packed the gear and loaded in, the rain gradually reduced to just scattered drops. However, when we shoved off at 9:15, the heavens were pewter-colored and threatening more downpours; the air temperature, a chilly 50 degrees, would not rise at all during the rest of the day.

Cruising out onto the exposed main body of Rainy Lake east of the Brule Narrows, a strong south wind greeted us. Domineering, dark green waves were coming at us directly from the south, not at all conducive to traveling along an easterly course. Then bone-chilling rain started pouring down, driven in gusting sheets. We made a 21/2 mile southward traverse to a group of islands lying off the south shore, advancing slowly and laboriously while singing to ease the effort, and then headed eastward. After passing along the lee side just to the north of two islands, we again had to make a forceful push, crossing against wind and waves for a half-mile to reach the next sheltering island, where eastward progress was again made easier, due to the wind-breaking effect of the island's mass and its tree cover. After making three more traverses in a zigzag course between various islands, seeking respite from the buffeting wind and waves, we headed south into a deep, narrow passageway between two islands, where the boys had spotted a fishing houseboat. In addition to the chill, the driving rain, and the difficult paddling conditions, I was having a terrible time navigating with the small, poorly-detailed map that had been given to us the day before.

Stepping aboard the tied-up houseboat at noon, we first learned from the amicable renters our specific location on the map. Then we relished the warmth of the heated room, the steaming cups of coffee and hot chocolate, and the friendly camaraderie of our hosts, whose temporary floating home we had invaded unannounced. After spending a half-hour amid these creature comforts, it was quite difficult, especially for Doree and the boys, to leave the warmth and shelter of the boat, with its supply of hot drinks, and return to the elements. Certain mutinous thoughts may have even flitted across the minds of my three family members.

On some occasions, Tim is a masterful mind-reader! (Doree)

I had the good sense not to mention to them that life during canoe trips involved being totally immersed in the weather conditions, and often being at the whim of those conditions. Depending on the situation, we could be alternately chilled, warmed, wetted, or blown, sometimes in various combinations and sometimes all within the same day. Except when we were snuggled into our sleeping bags within the shelter of the tent, or occasionally when we were sprawled out beneath the rain shelter when we set it up at a windbound stop or an overnight camp, we were seldom insulated from the elements. Even our high-quality raingear could not keep us dry during a long period of rain. Although the velcro straps on the cuffs of the coat could be closed rather securely around our wrists, some water still ran down our hands and inside the coat sleeves while paddling, and a certain amount of driven rain entered around the entire perimeter of the hood where it framed our face. In addition, a portion of the puddles that accumulated in our lap always managed to find a way inside the knee-length coat and the pants.

During the fur trade era, native and French men and women wore one of three styles of woolen outer garments for protection against cold and rain, while traveling the waterways and living in the interior. These included a waist-length fitted jacket, a knee-length hooded coat called a *capot* or capote, and a long cloak (without a hood for men). Even more effective protection against rain was provided by hooded coats, hooded cloaks, and frocks or coverall shirts which were made of oilcloth. This fabric was a closely-woven linen cloth that was made waterproof by coating it with a mixture of boiled linseed oil and lead oxide. Our own modern raincoats, equipped with velcro-sealing cuff straps and a drawstring hood, were fashioned from Gortex, a synthetic fabric that prevented rain from entering while allowing perspiration moisture from within to pass outward. These garments were much more comfortable than the ancient oilcloth versions, since they were lighter in weight and more flexible, and they also allowed an escape for the moisture that was produced by our body during the exertion of paddling. Even though they were not perfect, we appreciated very much having this modern rain gear.

The standard daily outfit for native and French men working as voyageurs or living in the interior during the French era consisted of native articles from the feet up to the waist, and French items above the waist. If a Frenchman were to dress for canoe travel in the usual European style, with leather shoes, knee-length stockings, and knee-length breeches, these articles would be constantly wet, due to the offshore loading and unloading of the craft, and the regular forays into the water to drag the canoe up rapids and shallows and around obstructions. However, by dressing in native style, with moccasins, tube-like leggings, knee garters, and a breechclout, they could simply remove the footwear and leg coverings and lay them aside, to have dry warm garments to wear at the end of the day of travel. They wore only their breechclout, and in chillier weather the chemise and the hat, cap, or tuque on their head. In comparison, on our modern paddling trips in cool weather, we wore tennis shoes, polypropylene socks and long underwear top and bottom, lightweight nylon pants that dried quickly, a cotton shirt, a cotton neckerchief, a nylon shell windbreaker, and a broad-brimmed, water-resistant hat, with a hooded sweatshirt, raincoat, and rain pants near at hand.

When we reluctantly bid adieu to Mary Beth and Sam and their comfortable houseboat, the rain had slackened somewhat. As we traveled eastward for two miles through the Kempton Channel, the narrow passage between the southern shore of the mainland and Big Island, we were relieved to be out of the battering wind and waves. However, the rain-drenched conifers covering both the mainland and the island still stood dark, brooding, and dripping along the shorelines as we passed. Leaving the channel, we took a half-hour break at 2:00, before paddling eastward for eight miles along the south shore of the open water of Rainy Lake. During the latter afternoon, the rain softened, the wind gradually faded, and the surface of the water flattened. Nearing the end of the lake, I aimed the bow toward the southeast for three miles, and we finally left the broad expanse of Rainy Lake. Passing southward through the slender American Channel, we reached the tumbling whiteness of the Sault de Chaudière (Kettle Falls) by 6:15. We had put in a challenging nine hours to advance sixteen miles, with Doree and her husband paddling while our dispirited young passengers spent most of the day sleeping. But we had finally completed the length of the lake!

For $3.00 we hired the truck-and-trailer portage service, which was usually used for hauling motorboats, to transport our canoe and gear around the falls to the end of the portage, which had originally been a 200 yard carry in ancient times. Cheerfully, we set up camp beside the narrow passage that would lead us to Lac Namakan the following morning. To top off the evening, we were pleased to discover another touch of civilization just a short walk down a path: the Kettle Falls Hotel, which had been built in 1913 to serve passing loggers. In the old dining room, with its gently rolling, warped floor, we merrily treated ourselves to turkey sandwiches, ham sandwiches, potato chips, pumpkin pie, lemon meringue pie, milk, hot chocolate, and coffee. We so deserved that meal, after handling the forty miles of Rainy Lake in two days. By 10:30, we were bedded down in the tent, ready for a very welcome rest.

Day Three, Memorial Day

Rising in well-rested condition at 7:00, we departed two hours later, with the *gouvernail* elated to again be guided by detailed topographical maps. They were safely stowed in the ziplock map holder of thick clear plastic, which was securely attached by its 15 inch clip line to the thwart immediately in front of me. The day was heavily overcast, 50 degrees and holding, with a slight breeze from the south wafting us in the sheltered passageway, only a hundred yards wide at this place. Ben started as the bow paddler, advancing five miles along the slender channel that extended first toward the west through Squirrel Narrows, and then toward the south through Squaw Narrows, before bringing us to the northwestern corner of Lac Namakan (meaning Sturgeon Lake in the Algonquian languages). This body of water, aligned in an east-west direction, measures some twenty miles in length by 11/2 to three miles in width. Our generally eastward route on its waters would cover about ten miles of its length.

When we entered the lake, light rain began to fall, and we encountered a considerable head wind from the south. Doree took over as the *avant*, and we used the lee side of four scattered islands in the western portion of the lake to shelter us somewhat, as we headed southeast for three miles. At 11:45, we took a half-hour lunch break on a tiny rock island just east of Black Point, as the light rain stopped. While we munched on a mixture of peanut butter and honey spread on crackers, I showed on the map how, beginning in the 1770s and 1780s, an alternate route had been sometimes used by paddlers to travel between Rainy Lake and the northwestern area of Namakan Lake. This route joined Namakan at a place three miles northeast of where we were sitting.

From the southern end of the American Channel, we had traveled the standard U-shaped passage along the present international border, first paddling westward and then southward through Squirrel Narrows and Squaw Narrows, and finally toward the southeast on Namakan Lake. As an alternate route, some canoes two centuries ago had headed from the American Channel toward the southeast for a mile. This brought them to the so-called Bear River, which consisted of 13/4 miles of marshy area choked with thick patches of wild rice, followed by a narrow 3/4 mile section of gently moving water that required two portages, with a short paddle separating them. These two carries, dubbed the Portages Nouvelles (New Carrying Places), were 320 and 180 paces long. This alternate route cut some seven miles off the total traveling distance, including the shortened mileage on Namakan Lake. However, voyageurs handling heavily loaded cargo canoes usually preferred the routes with the fewest portages, even if those passages entailed some extra miles of paddling. It was during the carries of cargo and craft that they lost considerable time, and expended plenty of energy; in addition, they were sometimes injured, lamed, or even occasionally killed while making portages. As a result, the customary mainline route here had followed the longer passage, involving waters that were not choked with wild rice and required only one carry of 200 yards, circumventing the Sault de Chaudière (Kettle Falls).

Advancing another mile from our island resting place, we finally reached the open, unobstructed expanse of Lake Namakan, where the strong south wind and the accompanying frothing waves halted our forward progress. Just as we were about to wheel around to the left, and retreat behind a point at the southern tip of the nearby Sixdeer Island, a ranger from the National Park roared up in his powerboat, to see if we needed help. I thought Doree was going to swoon when she got a good look at that handsome ranger in his uniform, presiding over such a sturdy fiberglass boat equipped with not one but two massive outboard engines! I was not particularly elated about his offer of a four-mile ride along our route, to a place where the mainland would block the wind and waves and we could continue on our way. However, it was a matter of either being windbound for hours or days on Sixdeer Island (and maybe having a mutinous crew abandon me there), or accept his offer.

Doree and the boys climbed into the boat and found seats, while I tied our bow line to a fixture at the stern of the boat. As the ranger slowly towed me through the waves for a couple of miles, I kept the canoe from capsizing by ruddering, until we reached the lee side of an island. Then, to hasten our progress, we hauled first the gear and then the canoe into the boat, and he quickly transported us another two miles, to the first of a group of islands that lie scattered west of the Namakan Narrows. During the ride, the ranger reported that the air temperature at the moment was 48 degrees, while the water temperature was 53 degrees; this was not the balmy, sun-drenched summer weather that is depicted in vacation ads! Unloading onto a short, crescent-shaped beach of tan sand at 2:00, we thanked the ranger for his assistance, and saw him off. While I kindled a fire to warm us up a bit before proceeding on our way, Doree did not say much. But I could tell that she regretted having seen her rescuing knight zoom off so soon, on his hundreds-of-horsepower steed.

At certain times, Tim is a rather inaccurate mind-reader. However, I must admit that I didn't mind the boat ride. (Doree)

Reloading and resuming our forward progress at 3:30, we made our way eastward in the rather sheltered passage between various islands and the deeply indented mainland, near the eastern end of Namakan Lake. Then, after completing a mile-long traverse with considerable waves and wind coming from the side, we turned toward the southeast and entered the quiet waters of the Namakan Narrows, a slender, mile-long passageway that leads to Sand Point Lake.

Just inside the entrance of the barren rock Narrows, we passed a small midstream island that presented a dramatic sheer cliff rising straight up from the river channel. We were drawn to an area of brownish red coloring low on the cliff, in a location that was sheltered by a slightly projecting overhang. When we checked it out at close range, we discovered that a considerable portion of the flat rock face at head level had been completely coated in ancient times with red ochre or hematite mixed with grease or oil. Below this area of solid rusty red, a set of pictographs had been created using the same pigment. The painted images consisted of a horizontal line of six large, round dots just above the waterline, above which appeared two figures facing each other. On the left stood a very male human, and on the right an outline of a large horizontal animal, either a cow moose or a bison, with its head lowered. (The original range of the bison in about 1,500 A.D. had extended northeastward to a locale 150 miles southwest of this pictograph.)

Floating silently on the docile water beside these images, we imagined the powerful aura which native people had felt in this spiritual place, hundreds or thousands of years ago, including the shamans who had created the red imagery and the many individuals who had later observed it. It had been customary for people making a pilgrimage to such a site, as well as travelers passing by, to leave a small offering, particularly some tobacco, to the spirits. Many of the Frenchmen working in the early fur trade had also adopted this very ancient custom of native spirituality. As we were quietly pulling away from the site, another park ranger in a powerboat arrived; he was searching for a certain party to deliver an emergency message. After we told him about the pictographs, he recorded the site on his detailed map, examined the painted figures, and indicated that they had never before been reported! We were thrilled to have added a new piece of data to the study of the ancient history of the area.

A half-mile further south in the Namakan Narrows, we easily

spotted another site that had also been considered sacred by the native inhabitants of long ago. This site likewise involved a sheer cliff rising from the water at the edge of a small island. On the flat surface of the rock face, about three feet above the present water level, an elongated, horizontal white creature with a pair of long, slender tails faced toward the left. The image, resembling a leg-less otter about five feet long, with a raised head and neck and two downward-curving tails, had been formed millions of years ago by nature when the landmass of the Canadian Shield had solidified. At that time, a thick forked vein of white quartzite had been set into a matrix of much darker granite. Millions of years later, this dramatic feature certainly must have been perceived by ancient people as a supernatural spirit, to which prayers and offerings were presented. To the left of this naturally-occurring spirit creature, about six feet above the present water level, was a single native-made pictograph. It consisted of a solid human hand print, which had been painted in the usual brownish red medium of red ochre or hematite mixed with grease or oil. As we paused here in the great stillness, I shared with the boys the concept that every thing in the world has a unique story, and every place has many stories. We wished that we could magically know the myriad events that had taken place here over the centuries.

In addition to these two rock painting sites in the Narrows, our paddling route this year was also passing near other locales where ancient shamans had created images with red pigment on cliff faces. Five sites had been located on Rainy Lake, as well as one site near the southeastern end of Lac La Croix. These were all pictographs, involving painting on rock. Native people in ancient times had also created images on rock surfaces by pecking, scratching, grinding, or cutting with stones, producing images that are called petroglyphs. During our travels through this country, we kept an eye out for both of these types of ancient art.

As we exited from the Namakan Narrows and glided onto the glass-like surface of Lac de la Pointe de Sable (Sand Point Lake), the last of the grey cloud cover disappeared from the sky, and the sun finally emerged! This was the first time we had seen its glorious rays since sundown on Day One, having had two entire days since then of somber skies, considerable rain, and unrelenting south winds. Meandering for a mile through the group of small islands that lie scattered across the northern tip of the lake, we located an outstanding campsite, on a small island that summoned us with its sandy beach for our landing. When we came ashore at 6:00, we had advanced twenty miles for the day, some of them against strong wind and serious waves, including the four miles of powerboat assistance from the ranger. Ben had paddled five of the miles, and Kevin just one mile, since Doree's strength had been needed in the bow during the rest of the time.

While smacking our lips over a tomato-beef-and-noodles stew around the evening fire, our conversation turned to the native people who had lived in this area for thousands of years. During the historic era, an Ojibwa fishing village for harvesting sturgeon had stood for a very long time at the easternmost tip of Namakan Lake, on the north shore of the mouth of the Namakan River, 21/2 miles north of our campsite. This massive fish, growing to a length of nearly five feet and covered with rows of spiny plates, must have been very plentiful here, since Algonquian-speaking people had named both the river and the lake at this place Namakan, their word for sturgeon. Some forty miles due east of our camp, an excavated site on the shore of Sturgeon Lake had revealed a series of habitations that had spanned about eight thousand years, encompassing the Paleo, Archaic, Woodland, and historic fur trade periods. Excavations at another site twenty miles further to the northeast, on Pickerel Lake, had shown occupations by native people during that same huge span of time. As we thought about the hundreds of thousands of lives that had been spent in this area, we tried to picture the histories and cultures that had been created by the combined experiences of all these people.

Day Four

When a reveille of birdsongs stirred me from my slumbers, I quietly pulled the camera from the waterproof ammo box in front of my pillow, and snapped a portrait of my three loved ones. Each of them was lying face upward, with sleeping bag pulled snugly around the neck, deep in sleep. I imagined that they were each dreaming of blessedly warm sunshine and vigorously helpful tail winds. At that moment, my heart soared at the thought of how willingly they joined me each year in these long-distance paddling ventures, which were definitely not for the meek of the world! After peeking out the door of the tent, I wakened them gently, reporting that the sky promised considerable sunlight and warmth today. When we rolled out at 7:30, the air temperature was only 45 degrees; but with the first rays gleaming above the eastern tree line a half-hour later, the readings began soaring, finally reaching a magnificent 71 degrees by noon! That sunshine brought us pure bliss!

After the gear had been packed and loaded in, Ben scooped water from the lake with the thermos jug, and added to it powdered milk and instant breakfast drink powder, creating the usual morning accompaniment to our nourishing gorp mixture. During all of our years of wilderness paddling, we nearly always used water that came directly from the lake or river beside us, for both drinking and cooking. (Only when we were a short distance from a city and its outflows did we plan ahead and fill our thermos and collapsible plastic water jug in advance of that place.) In the process of using local water everywhere, we never had a single instance of intestinal illness from giardia lamblia. However, as protection against this water-borne parasite, which is often contained in feces, we could have boiled all of our water for at least a minute; this is the only guaranteed method of destroying this organism. We could also have used a portable water filter or a chemical disinfectant, but only certain of these have been proven to be effective against giardia.

After our bolstering breakfast, we embarked at 9:30, with Kevin eager to test his mettle in the moderate head wind and medium waves that were flowing toward us from the south.

Rather than focusing my attention on the soreness in my shoulders and hands or the chilliness of the morning, from my position behind Kevin, soothed by the rhythm of his paddle strokes, my mind floated back to March 18, ten weeks earlier. On a chilly, overcast Saturday, I had gone to downtown Chicago with my friend Sister Gladys, a nun about sixty years old. We had been working tirelessly for over five years to bring public attention to our government's involvement in the war in El Salvador. This day, walking down Michigan Avenue, as we neared the Tribune Tower, I asked her if she planned to go into the street to block traffic (as an act of civil disobedience and protest). When she said "Yes," it was time for me to decide for myself. Walking a block further in silence, knowing that I wanted to hear Tim's concert that evening, I finally reached my decision. A total of 29 of us, mostly women, sat down across the full width of North Michigan Avenue. Soon, I felt the powerful grasp of two Chicago policemen, picking me up and dragging me forcefully to a paddy wagon. After three hours in the

*Belmont Street lockup, I made my way to Orchestra Hall and took my seat,
just one minute before the 8:00 downbeat. Soon, the ecstatic brass sounds
of Janachek's* Sinfonietta *filled me with joy beyond words. When I opened
my eyes in the middle of a dramatic trumpet chorus, I found myself back
in the canoe. Kevin was singing that playful kid's song* I Love the Waltz.
*I gradually saw that what was required in my efforts to stop this war also
helped prepare me for our long-distance paddling trips: serious planning,
dedication, and courage. (Doree)*

When we halted for a lunch break three hours later, at the southern
end of Lac de la Pointe de Sable, Kevin had helped pull our green
canoe over six miles of water. Two miles back, we had passed Pointe
de Sable (Sand Point), the prominent projection that extends from the
eastern shore deep into the midsection of the lake, the feature that
had long ago given the body of water its name. At the place of our
rest stop, the lake tapered down to a very slender, mile-long passage
called the Little Vermilion Narrows, which would soon take us to
Little Vermilion Lake. This marked the area where we would leave
the territory of Voyageurs National Park and enter the Boundary
Waters Canoe Area Wilderness. In addition, it marked the beginning
of a long rectangular-shaped jog in the mainline route, which would
take us southeastward for ten miles, then northeastward for five
miles, and finally northwestward for five miles. This was also the
transitional area in which we would gradually move from a forest of
mostly fir and red and white spruce, with some pines and scattered
patches of birch and a few poplars, to a forest of generally red, white,
and jack pines.

During our break, we dined on the right shore where a tiny
stream spilled down a flat rock face, forming an attractive miniature
waterfall before flowing into the narrow waterway below. While we
ate, I explained that, 11/2 miles back to the north and west on Sand
Point Lake, a small opening in the southwestern corner of the lake
(which we did not take) had once been a very significant place, the
junction of the mainline route and an important side branch. This
opening, at the northern end of a mile-long passageway called King
William's Narrows, was the outflow of Crane Lake, which connected
with the Vermilion River, Vermilion Lake, the Pike River, and the
St. Louis River to form a water highway extending southward to
the western tip of Lake Superior. As the crow flies, the route would
have measured some 125 miles; however, waterways do not flow

with bird-flight straightness, so the canoe route would have been as much as three times that distance. In 1736, due to the importance of this north-south route, La Vérendrye's men had established the Petit Vermillon Poste (Little Vermilion Post) on or near Crane Lake, near a substantial Ojibwa village. Although the French facility was short-lived, the prominent native community was still located in this area three decades later, and it was again documented there in about 1810.

Beginning his stint in the bow seat at 1:00, Ben had only a gentle oncoming breeze to contend with as he paddled the eight-mile length of Petit Lac Vermillon (Little Vermilion Lake), which is only a half-mile wide at its broadest places. At one point, Doree spotted an otter sunning on the grass along the right shoreline; when the sleek animal finally noticed us, it slid smoothly into the blue-green depths. At the south end of the lake, as we approached the beginning of the Rivière La Croix (River of the Cross, now called Loon River), we flushed up a deer that had been resting in the tall grass by the water's edge. When it bounded away on long, slender legs, with its white tail up and waving, I told the boys that such creatures were terrific athletes, being able to run up to 37 miles an hour and leap as far as thirty feet.

It soon became apparent that the Loon River was very unusual in the northland, having low shorelines of soil, with almost no ledges of Canadian Shield rock showing. In addition, the light green hues of fluttering poplar leaves, contrasting with the background of darker evergreens, was an uncommon sight. On each of the meandering curves, the inside of the turn, where the current was slower and so dropped much of its sand and silt, was shallow and reed-grown; the outside of each turn, bearing the stronger scouring current, was considerably deeper and was cobbled on the bottom with stones. This waterway reminded us of the small rivers in the southern areas of the midwest, and also those much further to the south.

This stretch of very narrow river, with only a mild oncoming current and no wind, offered an excellent opportunity for Kevin to put in a practice session as the stern paddler. During that hour, with his mother providing plenty of forward power from the bow position, he advanced three miles, and gained some skill at both reading the water ahead and steering the craft where he wanted it to glide, much to his delight. Upon reaching Rapids 56, with me again in the *gouvernail* position, we first attempted to paddle up the slender passage, which did not have much drop. However, we were surprised at the considerable strength of the flow, and only made it partway up. After we all quickly disembarked into the frigid water, Doree and I successfully lined the canoe up through the remainder of the strong current, which was the most powerful that we had ever lined. The ancient voyageurs had been obliged to portage at this spot during high-water seasons, when the flow was even stronger.

A half-mile paddle around a right and then a left bend brought us to the Sault La Croix (Cross Falls, now called Loon Falls); this long, boulder-strewn hill of rushing, frothing water dropped a little more than fifty feet in elevation. On the quarter-mile carry along the right shore, which passed over a slight hill, there had been a mechanized rail portage for hauling boats for fishermen since about 1912. Using the phone at the landing, Doree called the operator at the other end, who sent the cable-powered boat trailer down to our end of the railway, into knee-deep water. After floating our loaded canoe onto the submerged trailer, Ben activated it with a push button to emerge from the water and proceed over the very low, gradual hill. As we leisurely walked over the portage path to Loon Lake, Doree commented that this was the easiest carry of our lives, not even involving any unfastening of safety straps and unloading of gear! At the end of the rails, where the canoe floated off the trailer and onto the lake, we paid the $2.50 fee at the operator's house, and also bought some chips, pop, and candy bars. These touches of "civilization," plus the effortless portage, made quite a festive occasion.

Departing at 6:30 in the stillness of early evening, bathed in the copper-colored light of gloaming, we marveled at the perfect reflections of sky, trees, and rock on the tranquil surface of the lake. Soon a beaver slapped its broad, flat tail and dived, creating a pattern of ever-widening concentric ripples near its dome-shaped lodge. As we passed the offshore home, made of saplings and mud, I explained to the boys that beavers sometimes dig into the side of the bank of a lake or a river to create a den, instead of building a free-standing lodge like this one against the bank. In some cases, lodges are built away from the bank, but that is less common.

After a few verses of *A la Claire Fontaine*, we located a campsite at 7:00, on a rounded hill of solid rock near the tip of a very long point. We all agreed that this had been a marvelous day. We had progressed through twenty miles of attractive, sun-washed landscape, and each of the boys had paddled eight miles. At this point, in four days of traveling, we had covered eighty miles, just short of half of the total distance of the trip. Sitting on a shoreline rock ledge that had been scoured smooth and bare by centuries of storms and grinding ice, we salivated over a feast of beef, string beans, and rice, plus galette for dessert, replenishing our empty furnaces. Afterward, the dancing flames of the fire hypnotized us long into the evening, as we listened for the expected calls of loons on Loon Lake. But on this particular night, silence filled our world. Even the loons had taken their distinctive laughter and departed.

Day Five

"Debout! Debout! Debout!" I playfully shouted into the tent of sleepyheads. When we set out at 9:00 under nearly ideal canoeing conditions, with no breeze, a fully clouded sky, and 60 degrees, I had no way of knowing that today's challenges would include some unusual problem-solving, as well as seven miles of extra paddling. From our campsite, we were about three miles by water from the second Portage La Croix (the modern Beatty Portage), an easy hour away. Looking ahead on the map, I saw that I would steer a northeasterly course for 11/2 miles, round a point to go north for a half-mile, travel toward the northwest for a mile, and finally head northward for another half-mile. This gently meandering course would take us to the place where the northern arm of Loon Lake tapers down to a slender tip and ends at the portage path.

As soon as we put paddles to the water, at the boys' insistence, I became engrossed in continuing the ongoing story from the previous day, imagining various details of the life of Sarah Allyn. She was our English-Scottish ancestor who had been captured at Deerfield, Massachusetts in the French-and-native raid of 1704, and had then lived the rest of her life as a citizen of New France. While I was trying to both embellish the story and keep an eye on the map and the landscape, I missed the northward turn, which we should have taken a half-hour after leaving the campsite. Unbeknown to me, we proceeded about 11/2 miles too far toward the northeast, before turning northward by rounding a point. After that, by strange coincidence, the various changes of direction and landscape, the locations of a couple of designated campsites, and even the distances traveled generally matched those of the northern arm of Loon Lake, which I was following by eye on the map. I began to suspect that we might be *dérouté* (off course) when we passed through a narrows that I could not locate on the map; but we continued to proceed happily northward, telling stories and belting out French songs. Paddling to the far northern end of the body of water, we arrived at the landing of a portage. However, I knew that our expected carrying path had a set of rails for hauling powerboats by trailer. Since the path where we had arrived had no such feature, and it also headed off toward the east rather than toward the north, I realized that this could not be our portage. At that moment, not knowing where in the world we were on the map, the bottom of my stomach dropped well toward my feet. How could I have possibly gotten off track on such an easy course? Looking closely at the map, I noted at the far right edge of the sheet a body of water called Little Loon Lake, which paralleled the route that I thought we had taken northward up Loon Lake. However, this particular sheet did not include any water connection between Loon and Little Loon Lakes. That terrain would be depicted on the adjacent sheet, which I had not needed for traveling along the mainline route, and so did not have. Suspecting that there was indeed a connection between the two lakes, and that we had traveled up Little Loon Lake by mistake, I saw where I had probably made the error, missing the correct northward turn three miles back. The two hours that had elapsed since our departure would match rather closely the extra distance traveled, since we generally cruised all day at about three miles per hour, in flat conditions when fully loaded like this for a long expedition.

Doree switched places with Kevin, who had paddled six miles in the bow, and we retraced our route for three miles. Near the end of that hour of paddling, I was very relieved as the connection between the two lakes gradually came into view in front of us. One of the major psychological challenges of getting back on course during a canoe trip is the maddeningly slow pace at which the hoped-for solution unfolds as you advance at arm-powered speed. As we finally advanced northward up the correct waterway, we discussed two of the navigation lessons that I had learned again. First, when you are matching the terrain slowly unfolding in front of you to the details on the map, you must keep track of the elapsed time in at least a general way, in order to estimate and verify the distances traveled. In addition, whenever there appears to be a major discrepancy between the land masses and the features on the chart, you are most likely not where you think you are on that chart. It is crucial during a long-distance wilderness jaunt to know your location rather closely at all times, if you do not wish to waste time and energy while backtracking and relocating the correct route.

Arriving at the second Portage La Croix (Cross Portage, now called Beatty Portage) at 1:30, we effortlessly transported the canoe over the mechanical railway along the right shore. During the simple fifteen-minute operation, we considered the physical exertions that had been made here on this 400 pace carry over the course of several centuries during the fur trade era. While paying the $4.00 fee for the railway service, we learned of an outfitter's lodge that was located on an island three miles to the north in Lac La Croix. With Ben functioning as the *avant*, we eagerly traveled for an hour to the lodge, where we took an hour-long break and feasted on bacon-lettuce-and-tomato sandwiches, chips, and cokes. As we were leaving, the lodge personnel warned us about the "big waters" of the exposed portion of Lac La Croix that lay ahead, beyond the island-filled western half, where the two-mile-wide expanse gives wind and waves space to grow. When we pulled away at 3:45, our ideal goal was to cover the stretch of sixteen miles to and through those "big waters" before nightfall, if possible. Two miles from the lodge, the lake turned due east, forming the east-west "horizontal bar" of the cross-shaped main body of Lac La Croix (Cross Lake). From that point forward, we were able to hoist the sail and take advantage of the moderate westerly breeze along the entire twelve-mile length of the "crossbar" portion of the lake. Ben was absolutely elated; this was the first time that he had ever paddled with the sail raised, and he loved the speed at which our keel swooshed over the water!

As we sped eastward on the backs of the waves, Kevin took a nap behind my seat in the stern, awakening with a start as we sailed past a busy seaplane base located on the north shore. What a rare experience it was to have small but tough pontoon planes both taking off and landing right over us and next to us, as we traveled in the quarter-mile-wide channel between the mainland and the offshore island, directly in front of the mainland base! After passing this unusual attraction, Kevin took over the stern seat and the duties of the *gouvernail*, operating the paddle as a sailing rudder in the stern. This was a moment that Doree and I had long dreamed of: our sons were handling the canoe entirely by themselves, while we relaxed in the midsection area and enjoyed the fast ride!!

Three miles beyond the seaplane base, our course took us past the modern native settlement of Neguaguon Lake (the Algonquian name for the body of water which the French had dubbed Lac La Croix). This community of fifteen homes is located on the north shore of the lake, near the western boundary of the Neguaguon Lake Indian Reserve, which encompasses eleven miles of lakeshore and extends northward from the lake for 11/2 to three miles. The village stands beside the head of the Namakan River, which flows westward in a broad arc to the eastern tip of Namakan Lake. Although the Namakan River route to Namakan Lake is only about 25 miles long, it required seven portages around rapids and falls, compared to 38 miles of paddling on the mainline passage with only two portages, plus one carry or lining at a place of strong current. During the entire French era of the fur trade, and during virtually all of the British period, the longer route was the standard passage, since voyageurs much preferred some extra miles of paddling compared to the dangerous rigors of carrying cargo and craft on land. At the average rate of progress of cargo canoes, the difference of thirteen miles between the mainline route and the Namakan River route only entailed about three hours of additional paddling on the longer mainline passage; however, this longer route required four or five fewer portages, which represented a significant savings of both time and energy. The surveyors of the International Boundary Commission, including David Thompson, traveled both the mainline passage and the Namakan River in 1823. Their assessment of the latter watercourse was reported by John Bigsby: "This stream is a chain of vehement rapids and still waters... This river is unfit for commercial purposes."

The Namakan River was utilized for cargo canoes only during the very last few decades of the fur trade era, after George Simpson, the governor of the Hudson's Bay Company, traveled its waters in 1830 and declared it to be passable. After experiencing only a single trip over the Namakan, this administrator transplanted from London decided that he could judge its traveling qualities far more wisely than the legions of native and French paddlers who had lived in and operated throughout this region during the previous two centuries or more. To be sure, he would not be among those heavily laden, exerting crew members who could be hurt, crippled or even killed on its seven portage paths; his job entailed walking leisurely along these paths, while burdened with only his silver-headed cane, his dapper top hat, and his pocket watch. Physical proof that the voyageurs almost never utilized the Namakan River route was provided by scuba divers in their searches for artifacts from the fur trade era along this passage. In their underwater surveys of the pools below each of the seven obstructions, they discovered a grand total of a single brass kettle, below Squaw Rapids.

After the boys had sailed eastward on Lac La Croix for about five miles, I returned to my usual spot in the stern, while Ben continued in the bow seat. Another five miles with continued assistance from the bulging sail brought us to the narrows near the eastern end of the lake. Here, a broad peninsula jutting down from the north shore and a more slender peninsula extending up from the south shore left a quarter-mile-wide passageway between them. After gliding through these narrows, we turned southward, commencing our trek down the north-south "vertical element" of the cross-shaped Lac La Croix. At the place of our course change, the top portion of the lake continued eastward for another four miles, forming the tapered right arm of the "horizontal crossbar" of the cross. At the eastern tip of this arm, its waters received those of the Maligne River, which represented the terminus of the Kaministiquia River route to and from Lake Superior. Our southern course down Lac La Croix would continue on the Pigeon River or Grand Portage route to and from Superior. This junction of the two water highways, a very significant crossroads, may have also contributed to the French naming this body of water the Lake of the Cross. To mark this important junction, during the fur trade era a lob stick had been created on a slender point that lay 11/2 miles directly east of the narrows, on the land forming the "armpit" below the right arm of the cross. This land feature, called Pointe du Mai (Maypole or Lob Stick Point), had sported a tall living evergreen with just a bushy top, with all of its other limbs lopped off to make a very obvious landmark for travelers. But today, no such signpost marks the place.

In modern times, this locale also represents the western boundary of Quetico Provincial Park. The preserved wilderness lands of this famous Canadian park extend eastward from here for 35 miles, to a boundary line extending northward from the western tip of Lake Saganaga.

As we headed down the lake toward the south, the entire junction area of the cross had the strange appearance of being flooded, since there were no high, rocky shorelines. The trees growing on both the mainland and the various low islands seemed to be rising directly out of the water, without any anchoring land. Since it was nearly dark by this time, at 9 P.M., we settled for the first workable campsite that came into view, a mile south of the lake narrows. Although it was located in a low, swampy area which was loaded with mosquitoes, black flies, and ticks, there did not appear to be any better sites available in the immediate area.

With all of us diving into our respective tasks, we quickly set up camp in the last vestiges of light. When it was time for the boys and the Old Man to hoist the food packs, with a rope thrown over a limb that extended well out from the trunk of a tree, we chose a pine with a diameter of about nine or ten inches, which stood at somewhat of an angle. However, in the dark, we could not see that our choice, although thick enough, was a dead tree. When the heavy packs had been lifted to a height well above my head, the trunk suddenly snapped off at about the five-foot height, and came crashing down with the packs! We each dived for safety, and luckily escaped injuries. This was quite a scare, but when we realized that we were all still intact, we laughed until tears rolled down our cheeks.

While snacking on packaged meat from the outfitter's lodge and our own crackers, lounging around the cheerful fire, we reviewed our fine day. In the flickering firelight, I recorded in my journal: "A long day on the water, from 9 til 9, but a satisfying one for all of us, especially with the sail assist across big Lac La Croix. We covered 23 miles of the trip route, plus 7 miles off course. Kevin paddled 12 miles today, half of them in the stern, and Ben did 20 in the bow! This tied Kevin's personal record for the most miles paddled in one day. Ben is sure elated, and we're proud of both of them! Both boys are really enjoying paddling again this year, hoping to paddle more miles between them than Doree, like they did on last year's trip." After relaxing at the fire until very late, we were finally dreaming in the tent by midnight.

Day Six

Abandoning our sleeping bags at 6:45, we greeted a shimmering day, with the fresh smells of dawn still in the air. The temperature was already 65 degrees (it would rise to 75 degrees in the shade later in the day), and there were just a few shreds of white clouds floating listlessly overhead. As we were packing, a V formation of about sixty to seventy Canada geese flapped and honked directly over our camp, en route to their summer breeding grounds in the north, probably around James Bay and Hudson's Bay. Their fly-over led to an excellent family conversation about perseverance, stamina, and teamwork, since each bird in the wedge contributed to easing the labors of the one following. Flying in a large V formation served two functions. First, it positioned each goose so that it would avoid the stream of turbulent air that swept back from the bird flying just ahead. Second, it allowed each bird to actually save some of the energy that was expended by its colleague immediately in front. As smooth swirling air flowed horizontally backward from the wing tips of each goose, the inside wing of the following bird could ride on the swirl of air that was produced by the outside wing of the bird just ahead. Thus, the inside wing was not obliged to labor as hard, since it was reusing a certain amount of the flight power that was sent rearward by the goose immediately in front of it. During long flights, the birds would rest each of their wings in turn, by switching from one arm of the V formation to the opposite arm.

Heading out at 8:45, Ben occupied the stern seat, while I perched behind him on the triangular tip of the stern; this was not a very comfortable seat for me, but it was the best place from which to offer a little coaching. Reading the land and water and steering accordingly for five miles, Ben reveled in his very first experiences as the *gouvernail*, which made him feel capable and confident. As we slid silently past a point in the early-morning quiet, we enjoyed watching a great blue heron nearby, stepping delicately among the reeds and grasses in the shallows. To pass the time, Kevin led us in interesting discussions of several different subjects. Back at the first rail portage a couple of days earlier, he had found copies of *Psychology Today* and *Readers Digest* in the public outhouse, with a sign urging people to take them, at no charge. Since then, he had been enjoying reading articles from the magazines, and discussing them while we paddled.

At mid-morning, we were approaching a place which the ancient native inhabitants of the region had considered extremely sacred. Only the slightest breeze dimpled the deep blue surface of the glistening water, as we glided quietly toward a locale which I thought of as one of the cathedrals of canoe country. At the western edge of a huge, evergreen-covered island, two imposing cliffs soared straight up from the water, bracketing between them a bay which was a quarter-mile wide and half that distance deep. At the northern cliff, two massive portions of rock near its base had broken loose eons ago and had plunged beneath the surface of the lake; this had created two indented, chamber-like areas on its face, each one sheltered by a broad rock overhang.

The two dominating cliffs flanking the mouth of the bay had been perceived by the native people as a place to worship the spirits who inhabited their world. The lower portions of the vertical face of each of these cliffs were covered with ancient brick-red paintings, forming the largest known group of pictographs in all of North America. The images, created by shamans with hematite or red ochre mixed with grease or oil, included moose, elk, deer, the mythological thunderbird and giant underwater serpent, and an abundance of human hand prints, as well as human stick figures that were either smoking a pipe or carrying a spear. In the world view of ancient native people, the base of cliffs near the waterline represented the junction of the upper and lower worlds. The lower world, located beneath the surface of the water and the land, was inhabited by giant horned serpents and Missipichou, a giant panther; whenever these evil spirits were aroused, they lashed their long tail and created violent waves. The upper world was ruled by giant thunderbirds, whose eyes and mouth emitted lightning and whose beatings wings produced thunder and rain. These benevolent upper spirits waged a constant battle against the malevolent underworld spirits, and in the process they protected humans. Long ago, shamans had painted images on the cliff faces here at the edge of the lake, to appease certain spirits and to request the aid of others. Although hundreds or thousands of years had passed since these paintings had been applied, they were still clearly visible. By good fortune, the minerals that had been absorbed by rain and snowmelt running down the face of each cliff had created a protective coating over the pigment, preserving it through the ages. In the hush that pervaded the place, the cliffs remembered ancient times, and awaited the return of spiritual leaders who would paint further images and worshippers who would present additional heartfelt offerings.

A mile to the south of the sacred cliffs, we passed Warrior Hill, a large dome of solid rock which bore a scattering of pines and a few low shrubs. At this place, ancient tradition relates, Ojibwa warriors dashed repeatedly up and down the tall slope, to develop tremendous strength and endurance. I imagined myself as a young native man in training here centuries ago, preparing myself to serve my people well.

Another mile of paddling toward the southeast brought us to Portage Flacon (Bottle Portage), the place of departure from Lac La Croix, where we ate lunch at 12:30. On the quarter-mile carry across a peninsula to Iron Lake, over the rough and muddy path which Mackenzie had described in 1789 as "very difficult," Kevin insisted on carrying one of the 65-pound Duluth packs! The voyageurs usually made this carry to avoid the two-mile, southward loop in the watercourse that contained several sets of Bottle Rapids; however, scuba divers found evidence that they occasionally took their chances in running these rapids. The pool below one of the drops yielded a well-preserved Northwest trade gun, with its flint still cushioned with a piece of leather between the jaws of the hammer.

After a meandering four-mile jaunt around the various islands that nearly fill Iron Lake, we arrived at Portage Rideau (Curtain Portage), which skirted the thundering Sault du Rideau (Curtain Falls). The modern portage landing, on the right shore, is reached by paddling up the very fast current to a short distance below the falls. The ancient voyageurs had paddled a little further upstream against the strong flow, and then had landed on the steep, rocky shore just below the falls. It was very inspirational for us to walk the series of ancient steps made of flat stones that they had set into the steeply angled slope, to make their unloading and hauling slightly less strenuous. At the steps, the roaring power of the cascade nearly drowned out our voices. Immediately below the smooth, glassy lip at the top of the falls, the blue water was thrashed into a raging sheet of foaming, boiling white, as it raged down an angled slope for about fifty feet. Only a couple of especially brave boulders reared their heads slightly above the surface to disrupt the foaming white sheet, thus inspiring the voyageurs to give the falls its Curtain name. Before leaving this beautiful place, Doree set up the camera for Ben to take his first-ever photo, a portrait of the two expedition leaders standing hand-in-hand beside the cascade.

Above the falls, Kevin paddled four miles in the bow, on the perfectly calm western end of Lac Croches (Crooked Lake). At 7:00, we found a great campsite, a flat grassy area that was located high on a rocky point, at the eastern tip of a mile-long island. Today, we had made nineteen miles plus two portages, and had leisurely enjoyed the pictographs and the falls along the way. We had now covered a total of 130 miles in six days. After replenishing ourselves with a nourishing meal of boiled beef, vegetables, and sliced dried potatoes, we later roasted marshmallows around the fire, and were finally in the tent by 11:00. While drifting off, my brain replayed the sounds of ruffed grouse beating their wings to attract a mate. Ever since we had left the large expanses of Lac La Pluie and Lac Namakan on this trip, and had been paddling on smaller waterways close to the shorelines, we had been regularly hearing grouse drumming out their mating call. Beating their wings against the air while standing on a log, they created the low and apparently alluring sound of "Bum-bum-bum-bum-bum-bum......" In each case, the speed of the beats started slowly, and then increased gradually over a period of about five or six seconds into a veritable drum-roll.

Day Seven

Lac Croche, Crooked Lake, was aptly named by the French for its torturous course, with its upper section running in a generally east-west direction for about twelve miles and the lower section extending north-south for some seven miles, with much twisting and turning of the route. The upper section was filled with projecting peninsulas and islands, so that the mainline passage was almost always narrower than a half-mile; the lower section of the lake was considerably slenderer, more like a winding river. Having covered during the previous evening the first four miles in the northwestern corner of the lake, the area with the most open water, we would travel its narrower passages today.

When my mind surfaced from the dream world at 6:15, a light rain was tapping gently on the tent overlay, so I returned for another ninety minutes of well-deserved sleep. Then, while the family dozed even longer, I brought the journal up to date, writing up the events of the previous evening. When I finally emerged to greet the day at 8:00, the air temperature measured 50 degrees, with solidly overcast skies and a light breeze from the southeast; by departure time two hours later, the air had warmed to a comfortable 65 degrees.

In our usual morning routine, I roll out first to the ring of the alarm clock, dress outside the tent, bring the food packs down from the hanging rope, untie the canoe from its nighttime tree anchor, and organize the packs, which are stored during the night in the exterior vestibule of the tent. Doree and the boys awaken a little after me, and dress inside the tent. Then the boys take care of the sleeping bags, air mattresses, and tent, while Doree and I seal waterproof bags and finish refilling the packs. Whoever has time prepares the instant breakfast drink, which we take down with gorp while loading the canoe and installing the safety straps. Two hours or less from the first clatter of the alarm clock, we are advancing on the water, with all of the gear packed, waterproofed, loaded in, and secured to the thwarts for a day of travel.

With Ben in the bow seat, we forged ahead for ten miles on Lac Croche before our lunch break at 12:30. In this morning stretch, traveling eight miles eastward and then two miles southward, we struggled against strong upriver current in two very narrow places of the lake; one of these locations was just before turning southward, while the second one appeared just at the turn. During our one-hour rest stop on a tiny island, a thunderstorm passed just to the south of us, displaying black clouds and thin grey streaks of falling rain in the distance. While we fueled our furnaces, we discussed the current hot topic of Lyme disease. This year, there had been widespread publicity about this malady, which was spread by tiny ticks the size of "a moving freckle." The week before our trip, the disease had been the subject of the cover story of *Newsweek Magazine*. We laughed grimly at the idea of finding a speck as small as one of those insects on us while we were in the wilderness. When we paddled and portaged twenty miles a day and lived in the woods without bathing, there was very little likelihood that a speck the size of one of those disease-carrying ticks would be obvious enough for us to detect it. In the worst-case scenario, we would contract the disease, easily identify it by its characteristic, red bulls-eye markings, and be medically treated for it after the fact.

After our lunch stop, the sky began to clear, with patches of pleasant powder blue staring through the off-white cloud cover in a few places. Kevin paddled the next five miles in the bow seat, while Doree practiced being the guide from her position in the bow point, reading the map, matching its features to the passing landscape, and determining our course. As we proceeded down the lower portion of Lac Croche, we encountered three areas with moderate to strong river-like current, at each place where the lake became very narrow. In each of these sections, ranging from a quarter-mile to a half-mile in length, we were obliged to paddle hard upstream. In the wider passages, we hoisted the sail and were pushed along rather generously by the north wind. During one of these enjoyable sailing sessions, Ben ruddered for a mile from his position behind me in the stern point.

Paddling for a half-mile against the upstream current in one narrow section, we arrived at the Painted Rocks or Picture Rocks. This impressive formation along the western edge of the channel consisted of a long row of angular, broken cliffs hovering over the water. Along the full length of the undulating granite face, the stone had been stained in hues of red, orange, and white, plus various shades in between, by the natural action of the elements. Under the high overhang of stone, we felt the deep solitude of the place, and heard the whispers of the ancient spirits who resided there. When Alexander Mackenzie paused here in 1789, he noted "a remarkable rock, with a smooth face but split and cracked in different parts, which hang over the water. Into one of its horizontal chasms a great number of arrows have been shot, which is said to have been done by a war party of the Nadowasis or Sieux, who had done much mischief in this country, and left these weapons as a warning to the Ochebois or natives, that, notwithstanding its lakes, rivers, and rocks, it was not inaccessible to their enemies."

After leaving the Painted Rocks, when I hoisted the sail to capture the wind's assistance, the old weathered and cracked mast finally gave out, breaking off with a sudden snap at the gunwale level. Having provided us with five years of faithful service, it had given its all. The wood, old even before beginning its life as our mast, had cracked a little during our first use of the sail on this trip, and I was intending to replace the pole when we returned home. However, we all had hoped that it would survive for the duration of this year's voyage.

A mile further to the south, we reached the end of Crooked Lake and the turn up the Basswood River, with its looping but generally eastward course. There at the southern tip of Pointe du Lac Croche, right at the turn of the course toward the east, we landed on the left shore to make the Portage du Petit Rocher du Lac Croche (Little Rock

Carry of Crooked Lake), circumventing the Sault du Lac Croche (Crooked Lake Falls, now called Lower Basswood Falls). The landing offered a number of convenient, step-like rock ledges to facilitate unloading, and at the end of the easy carry of an eighth of a mile, a sandy beach area made reloading a breeze. If only all portages could be as short and comfortable as this one, which the voyageurs had measured as only eighty paces! In addition, the falls were beautiful, especially the channel that flowed beside us along the left or Canadian side of the midstream island. With sunlight beaming down on the scene, a thirty-foot stretch of seething whiteness roared down a slight decline, just a few feet away from the path.

Especially intriguing was the massive granite boulder which lay in complete isolation several feet offshore, exactly at the lip of the drop. The way the glistening water flowed in patterns of circular ripples around that large rock and over the slight precipice to begin the falls reminded Doree and me of serene formal gardens that we had visited in Japan in 1986. Those quiet gardens consisted of widely spaced boulders that were surrounded by sand or fine gravel, which had been raked into patterns that resembled gentle water currents. The function of such gardens was to ask questions for which there were no answers, and to inspire meditation.

Our easterly route now lay along the short Basswood River, following a double-loop course that would take about five miles of traveling to cover the straight-line distance of three miles to Basswood Lake. Fifteen minutes of paddling brought us to the carry which the French had called Portage de la Pointe du Bois (Wood Point Carry), at the modern Wheelbarrow Falls; here, we walked the easy, eighth-mile path along the left shore. After a two-mile paddle around a loop to the north, we arrived at the first of two rapids which the ancient fur brigades would have lined up when traveling eastward, and would have run down during westbound voyages. The first of these rapids had a very fast, straight flow, with no midstream boulders or standing waves to serve as obstructions. However, in this high-water season, the current was much stronger than Doree and I could possibly line up, so we took the eighth-mile portage along the left shore. Since the path began with a very steep ascent, on the third trip over, all four of us carried the canoe in an upright position up the slope, after which I carried it alone on the level area, in the usual upside-down position on my shoulders.

While reloading after the portage, I explained to the family that the discoveries of scuba divers searching the bottom of the pool below this set of rapids clearly indicated that crews of voyageurs had sometimes run into bad luck when lining up or running down this deceptive drop in the channel. Their finds included a group of 36 axes, a bundle of nineteen ice chisels, and a set of six harpoons, as well as supplies of lead balls and shot, gunflints, knives, whetstones, brass wire, glass beads, vermilion paint pigment, brass thimbles, buttons, brass wire eyelet fasteners, two small buckles, and a pewter pipe. After the various capsize incidents which deposited these items on the bottom, the voyageurs would certainly not have muttered the ancient saying, "`A quelque chose malheur est bon" (From a bad thing can come positive results). It had cost a great deal of energy and sweat to haul the lost articles of cargo westward from Montreal all the way to this place. However, from our rearward historical perspective in the present century, we felt that these accidents had indeed generated positive results. The recovery of this extensive array of artifacts from the fur trade era had brought us a considerable amount of information, and a deeper understanding of the ways of life of the French and their native customers.

A half-mile paddle toward the east brought us to the second set of rapids which the voyageurs had lined up when eastbound and run down when westbound. Again, the flow was too powerful in this season for us to line up. (A crew of five or six tough Frenchmen handling a North canoe could supply considerably more pulling power on the towing line than the Kent family with two young boys.) So we crossed to the right shore, to reach the landing of a one-mile portage. This modern path, now called Horse Portage, skirted a section of the river in which the brigades had first lined up the rapids; then paddled a quarter-mile around a bend toward the left; made a portage of 400 yards over a peninsula (to cut off a northward loop of the river with two sets of rapids); paddled southeastward 3/4 mile to just below the Basswood Falls; and finally made a portage of 150 to 200 yards around the low but wide falls. Their first carry, across the peninsula, was called Portage des Grand Pins (Big Pines Carry), while the one around the falls was named Petit Portage de Bois Blanc (Little Basswood Carry), which ended at Basswood Lake.

Our one-mile trail was not difficult, mostly a level or gently rolling walk through the woods. At one point, we were obliged to climb over the trunk of a tree that had fallen across the path. At another place, the flooded area created behind a *barrage de castor* (beaver dam) required a detour off the usual trail. At the dam itself, we discovered leftovers from the beaver's last meal: tender rushes and poplar branches and bark.

Just as we had begun unloading the canoe to commence this long carry, I had noticed that the winding button on my watch had been pulled out, stopping the mechanism. I assumed that this had probably happened a short time earlier, when I had slipped off the straps of my pack at the end of the previous portage. So I had restarted my watch, which was set at 5:00, and we had begun our usual three-trips-over carrying procedure. As we made each of the three legs, the light became dimmer and dimmer; however, we thought this was simply due to the denseness of the forest. When I finally lay the canoe onto the surface of Basswood Lake at the end of the third trip, to our considerable surprise, it was almost pitch dark! During this final trip over the path, we had assumed that, when we would arrive at the open lake, the residual light of evening would illuminate our way, since we thought it was only 7:00 P.M.

We quickly loaded in and shoved off, beginning to search the shoreline in the dark for any workable campsite. Shortly, we met a canoe with two people who were fishing. When they reported that it was 10:00, three hours later than my watch indicated, we laughed, realizing why dusk had fallen so quickly! They noted that there was a good campsite a half-mile to the south, atop a hill at the end of a long point. In the utter quiet of the inky darkness, we glided across the bay to the point, as several bats swooped around us. After unloading all of the gear and hauling it and the canoe up the hill of nearly barren rock, we quickly set up camp. Each member of the family had learned to do his tasks so well that we could efficiently set up our camp late at night in the dark, nearly as easily as if we had been operating in broad daylight. After ravenously consuming a steaming meal of beef, peas, and noodles, we finally hit the sack at midnight.

This day, we had guided our canoe over 21 miles of water, and had made four portages, one of them a mile long. During the previous evening around the fire, we had decided together that we would enjoy a well-deserved rest day after our progress on this Day Seven, wherever we would find ourselves along the route. As luck would have it, we had made it to a spectacular site high above Basswood

Lake for our day of relaxation. However, we never would have come this far if my watch had not stopped for three hours.

Day Eight

Each of us relished our day of hard-earned rest at this magnificent, wide-open site, on the summit of a high granite hill overlooking the bay adjacent to Sault de Bois Blanc. From our camp, we could hear the roar of the falls a half-mile away toward the north, where we had completed the portage the night before. It was a beautiful sunny day, with some white puffs of clouds sliding slowly across a pale azure sky, and comfortable air temperatures that would reach 70 degrees in the shade by noon. We slept in luxuriously until 9:00, slowly emerged from the tent, made hot chocolate, and then enjoyed a leisurely meal an hour later. Toward midday, we all washed out some of our clothes down at the water's edge, a much-needed task after a week of strenuous travel. Seven days of wearing a wet suit every waking minute had certainly made me smell ripe! After applying toothpaste to our four folding toothbrushes, which were color-coded to designate their respective owners, I laid them in a row on a shoreline boulder for the family.

Back up on the heights, Doree gave the boys a lesson in taking photos, while I updated the journal from the evening before, and added some of my personal thoughts. We had covered 150 miles in the previous seven days, making nine portages (three with trailer assistance) and lining up one rapids along the way. The boys' combined paddling mileage already totaled 83 miles, virtually half of the 170 miles of the entire trip. So they had already met their designated challenge, to match or exceed the number of miles paddled by their mother.

Almost all of the tasks that the boys had assumed on these canoe voyages had previously fallen on me. They now paddled half of the time in the bow seat, portaged one of the big Duluth packs, made the fire, prepared the beds, washed the dishes, etc. As a result, these trips were now immensely easier for me than they had been in the early years when the boys had been very dependent.

Also, now that each of us knew our respective tasks and was doing our share, Tim was so much less the commandant assigning jobs than he had been on the earlier voyages, which was likewise easier on all four of us. Over the past seven years, we three had nudged old Dad to be a much more benevolent leader, even in the worst situations. On the other hand, we had also learned to understand the need for quickly shouted orders in difficult or emergency situations, and to not take them personally. Actually, it was very reassuring for the three of us to have someone as competent and confident as Tim leading these expeditions, and bearing the main responsibilities for the decisions that affected our safety. Someone had to be the definitive leader on trips that were as potentially dangerous as these were. Not all situations in wilderness traveling lend themselves to being decided by committee vote. But we did all have our say in most of the decisions. (Doree)

About 1:00, the boys paddled us in the empty canoe across the bay to Basswood Falls, where we enjoyed a relaxed picnic on a flat granite ledge right beside the thundering cascade. While we ate, we silently watched a cow moose swim across the river below the falls and then clamber up the bank and saunter into the woods. Moving to a quieter location, we napped in the sun like otters, basking in its healing warmth.

After awakening, we discussed the various possibilities of a second watercraft for future family voyages, since the boys were growing larger every year. The possibilities included another canoe (with a snap-down canvas cover to be installed on each of the two canoes), a partially-decked canoe with an additional small, snap-down canvas cover, or a one-man kayak, in addition to our present canoe. Doree and I were concerned about the various problems that would be introduced by splitting the family into two separate craft. These challenges especially involved staying together in dangerous situations, such as open lakes in stormy conditions and long stretches of demanding rapids. We would have to give more thought to the issue.

Near the falls, Ben carved a pine limb into a mythological underwater serpent, while Doree chatted with the wife of a man who was fishing below the falls; Kevin and I rested and played checkers. Occasional black clouds passing overhead dropped light sun showers on us now and then, barely dampening our clothes and not at all our spirits. Around 3:30, we left the falls, with Doree practicing as the *gouvernail* and Ben as the *avant*. After paddling around the sheltered bay for a while, we landed to gather a load of firewood, and finally returned to our camp by 5:30. Then as a team of gourmands we prepared a feast of *pot au feu de boeuf* (boiled dinner with beef), a side dish of *pois aux oignons* (peas with onions), and *galette* (fried cakes), our favorite dessert on these trips.

Later, as we were enjoying marshmallows toasted on green sticks held over the fire, we noted a wedge of Canada geese headed toward the north, flying between our camp and the falls area. Suddenly, the birds were blown out of formation by a powerful gust of wind, which caused them to honk excitedly. Looking toward the west, we saw that glowering black clouds were rushing at us. In less than two minutes, heavy rain began to pelt us in hard sheets, and fierce blasts of wind from the west battered our campsite and the pines nearby. While the family scurried into the tent, I double-checked the ropes that were tethering the canoe to two sturdy trees, and then joined them in the flimsy shelter. After about ten minutes of furiously whipping the tent, the storm front and its flailing wind moved on toward the east, and the rainfall ceased just as quickly as it had begun. Within the confines of the green shelter, I continued my ongoing narrative, a true story from a book about a pioneer boy named Bill Nowlin, who had grown up in Dearborn, Michigan during the 1830s. Finally wrapping up his tale at about 9:00, we all drifted off to sleep within a few minutes. What a pleasurable day of rest and relaxation this had been!

Day Nine

Leaving the tent at 5 A.M., I observed the somber, overcast sky, took a reading of 40 degrees on the mini-thermometer hanging from my neck strap, and noted the moderate wind coming from the northwest. Even without a sail, its push against our backs would be somewhat helpful today on the upper and lower sections of Basswood Lake, where we would travel generally eastward, first for 3 1/2 miles and later for seven miles, and also on the middle section of the lake, where we would head due south for five miles. This Z shaped route was required on a body of water which was so filled with land masses, particularly a huge peninsula jutting upward from the south shore and another one pointing downward from the north shore, that the mainline passage through it was never more than 1 1/2 miles wide. The French had termed this watercourse Lac de Bois Blanc (Basswood Lake), while the Algonquian-speaking native residents had called it Passomenan Sakiegan (Dry Berries Lake). Early travelers noted that the waters along the southern shoreline were very thick with wild rice. Those productive rice beds, thriving in the large, sheltered bays that lined the deeply indented south shore, had provided a reliable source of food each year for the large Ojibwa village that was recorded there in 1768.

When the rest of the Kent family joined me outside the tent, we had a very chilly packing session and breakfast, although the sun did peek through a break in the clouds for a short time to warm us a little, before it was again hidden behind the leaden skies. On our way at 7:00, we traveled the upper leg of the lake by angling against the firm wind that was arriving over our left shoulders and the moderate waves that were coming at us from the left side. When we turned southward for the middle leg of the lake, we were pushed rather strongly from behind for five miles, while I carefully maintained the angle of the craft to the waves. During all of this exertion, I could tell that both my mind and my body, although they had gotten plenty of rest during the course of the full day off, had also lost a bit of their steel in the process.

Just before rounding Pointe au Pins (Pine Point, now called Canadian Point) to take up our eastward course, I pointed out Washington Island, lying just in front of us to the south. This island had been the site of an American Fur Company post. As soon as we made Pointe au Pins and entered the quiet, sheltered waters of the English Channel, between the point and Ottawa Island to the south, we silently glided to a halt, to watch in fascination as a pair of adult bald eagles carried out their activities on the point. One of the birds, perched on a tall pine above the water's edge, was feeding on a large fish that it held in its talons. At regular intervals, its mate made protective flights from its perch on a nearby pine, first circling around the area and then returning to its limb. At one point, the protector flew directly at a smaller bird of prey, which was apparently trying to strafe the feeding eagle and steal its fish. The two birds struck each other in mid-flight directly over our canoe, after which the intruder flapped away to seek an easier source of food. A few minutes later, after the one eagle had finished its meal, the pair cruised in several graceful circles over the area, while whistling to each other, and finally flew off toward the north. What a treat it had been for us to be floating quietly offshore at close range, and take in this drama from ringside seats for about five minutes!

While we took a short gorp break there in the canoe, I noted that Pointe au Pins had been the site of an early trading post. Another trading facility had been located on a point along the north shore about six miles further to the east, where the lake tapered down to a slender narrows. Facilities that had once carried out a brisk business on this lower section of the lake had included the Poste de Bois Blanc, established by the French in about 1750, and the Bois Blanc Post of the Hudson's Bay Company, which had operated from 1823 on.

By this time, the sky had cleared a bit and the air had warmed somewhat, with the temperature rising to about 50 degrees. As we paddled eastward along the lower leg of Lac de Bois Blanc, leaving behind the shelter of the islands beside Pointe au Pins, the unfettered northwest wind caused the waves to grow considerably, and also pushed us along at quite a clip. As we zoomed across Bayley Bay, we passed a very odd sight: it appeared to be a convention of 26 loons, floating together on the water and conversing (in loon-speak, of course)!

Just south of Green Island, we took a short break on the lee side of a tiny island. While resting, I explained that archaeological excavations had recently been carried out on the northern lakeshore near here, at a native site which had been occupied during both the prehistoric Late Woodland period and the historic fur trade era. After we passed through the narrows near the end of the lake, we covered the final 11/4 miles of Inlet Bay to reach the terminus of Basswood Lake waters. When we arrived at Grand Portage de Bois Blanc (Big Basswood Carry, now called Prairie Portage) at 11:30, Doree and I had advanced seventeen miles in 4 1/2 hours, with two short breaks and an amazing eagle-watching session along the way. We had made excellent headway even without the assist of a sail, with the wind simply blowing against our backs.

It was on Basswood Lake near this portage that John Macdonnel, a clerk of the Northwest Company, traveling with his colleagues in a brigade bound for the Assiniboine River in August of 1793, had purchased a birchbark canoe at a native village or canoe-building yard. Seven years later, when Alexander Henry the Younger was headed westward through this region, he encountered natives constructing canoes on one of the islands in the lake; he waited there until a craft of appropriate size had been completed for him. During this same voyage of 1800, Henry also observed native men, women, and children building canoes on Saganaga Lake, to the east of here, as well as on Lac La Croix and Lac Namakan further to the west.

Over the course of a half-hour, we completed the Big Basswood

Portage along the left shore, a carry which had originally been about 300 yards long. The path bypassed the hill of frothing, boulder-laced falls, which was interrupted in midstream by a pine-clad island. During the portage procedure, each of us delighted in knowing that numerous manly fishermen were scrutinizing us as we efficiently did our unloading, hauling, and reloading tasks, as they waited to be ferried out *sans effort* by the powerboats of their outfitters. Each of us did his respective jobs as if by script; after 167 miles of this voyage, we had mastered our family routines very well, and we were proud of it. We were further buoyed by the arrival of pleasant weather: the sky had cleared to scattered billowy clouds in a deep blue dome, and the air had warmed to 58 degrees.

Against a moderate head wind from the south (*La Vieille* would not cooperate and maintain her helpful northwest wind any longer!), Kevin and I paddled a mile toward the southeast, to reach our place of exit from the actual mainline route. Then six miles on a southwesterly course, along the lengths of Sucker Lake, Newfound Lake, and Moose Lake, brought us to Don Beland's outfitting base, just south of the public landing on Moose Lake. En route, while passing through the narrows between the second and third lakes, we paused to watch a mink dive and surface five or six times, as it was fishing.

At the outfitting base, where our car had been waiting for nine days, we loaded the canoe onto the vehicle and the gear inside, and celebrated with a feast of pizza, chips, and cokes. During the meal, we all concurred that this had been an outstanding voyage: hard work but a nourishing and wholesome experience. We had paddled 174 miles, had made ten portages, and had lined up one rapids in 7 1/2 days of traveling, in addition to spending a leisurely rest day near Basswood Falls. The boys had paddled ninety of the miles, more than half of the total distance, and had done a great many of the camp chores, all willingly and cheerfully. Each of us agreed that this had been our very best canoe trip yet. During it, we had all grown in strength, endurance, experience, and bravery, and we had learned more about nature and history along the way. In addition, Kevin and Ben had gained a better understanding of the ways of wind and water, and how to determine and navigate a route.

Driving to Ely, we stopped at the Voyageur Visitor Center, which to our dismay no longer presented any voyageur exhibits; in addition, the projector that normally screened voyageur films was in need of repair! The center now offers displays on the wolf, since it now houses the National Wolf Center. Sigurd Olsen carried out the first wolf research in this region in the 1930s and 1940s, and it has been a major center for such studies ever since. (Isle Royale in Lake Superior is the other major study area for wolf research.) As a result of these studies, as well as many decades of strenuous conservation efforts, wolves in the entire upper midwest area of the U.S. were removed from the list of endangered species in 2007.

We drove to Virginia, Minnesota, where we licked our chops over delicious chicken and fries in a restaurant, overhauled ourselves in a shower adjacent to a gas station, and donned clean clothes. We were back in "civilization." However, during our days on the water, we had gained additional strengths and insights to help us deal with the quirks of our modern culture.

En route home over the next eight days, we enjoyed absorbing history at Bemidji, John Sayer's N.W.C. Post, Fort Folle Avoine, Madeleine Island, Lac du Flambeau, Manistique, St. Ignace, Ft. Michilimackinac, Interlochen, and Sleeping Bear Dunes. At five of these locales, I studied dugout canoes for my ongoing research.

IX
Seventh Voyage
Rainy River and Lake of the Woods
August 13-19, 1990

Life consists not of holding good cards
but in playing those you hold well.

Josh Billings

And the time came when the risk to remain tight in the bud
Was more painful than the risk it took to blossom.

Anaïs Nin

What is harder than rock, or softer than water?
Yet soft water hollows out hard rock.
Persevere.

Ovid

He who dares, wins.

Anonymous

This year's canoe trip would involve two major changes in personnel: it would be the first voyage that we would take without Kevin, and the first one that would include Toby. For a considerable number of years, to accommodate our paddling jaunts and our living-history research adventures, Kevin and Ben had started each school year late and had ended each one early. This year, when Kevin was poised to commence his first experiences at the senior high school, he decided that it was important that he begin the semester on time. So our friend John stayed with him at our house during our month-long absence. Now just a few weeks short of fourteen years of age, Kevin had paddled with us for about a hundred miles during the three journeys of the introductory year; then some twenty miles on an April Fools' Day family trip the following spring down the very frigid St. Joseph River in Michigan; and finally 775 miles during six excursions

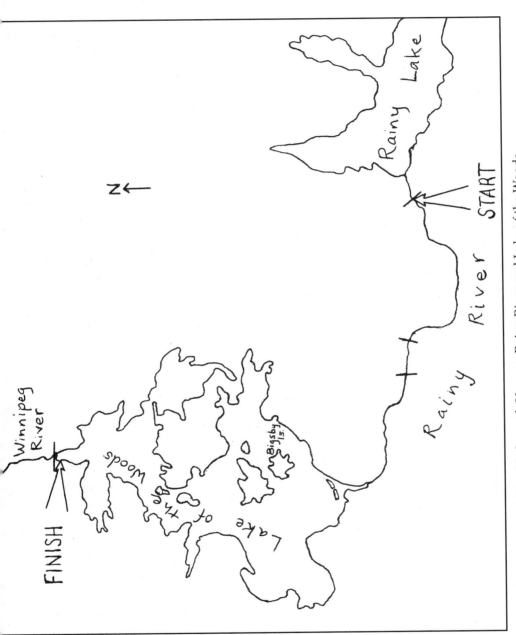

Fig. 10, Seventh Voyage: Rainy River and Lake of the Woods

on the mainline fur trade route. However, from this summer of 1990 on, he would not be traveling with us as we continued to paddle across the *Pays d'en Haut*. His absence left a gap in our manpower, but it obviated the need to expand into a second watercraft for the remaining two thousand miles that lay ahead. Kev chose his own path, to forgo the remaining part of our route and instead focus on other activities.

Toby was the new addition to the Kent family. A loveable, easy-going pup of indeterminate breed (many kids called him a 'Benji dog," since he resembled the long-haired main character in the beloved Walt Disney *Benji* movie), he had joined our family nearly a year earlier. Beginning with this voyage, he would accompany us during nine summers of long-distance canoe tripping. Having a very laid-back temperament, Toby was the perfect mascot for these jaunts, bringing smiles to the faces of his family members under all circumstances (this was his only assigned task on these arduous trips).

Ben, now age 12 2/12, would soon begin seventh grade. He was still rather scrawny, but with each passing year he was growing larger and stronger. With the absence of Kevin, he was now determined to match Doree in the number of miles paddled in the bow position, a challenge that he had formerly divided with his brother.

The voyage this year would first entail eighty miles down the Rainy River, in a winding course that headed generally toward the west-northwest, with Canadian territory on the right shore and U.S. soil on the left. This would be followed by a northerly trek over the length of Lake of the Woods, of which a portion in the southwest belongs to the U.S., and the remainder to Canada. The distance from the mouth of the Rainy River to our take-out place at the north end of the lake measured about 65 to 70 miles. However, depending on the wind conditions, that distance could increase considerably, if we were forced to take a circuitous route around and behind myriad sheltering islands.

Our C.S.O. concert at Ravinia Park concluded on this balmy Sunday evening with Tchaikowsky's rousing *1812 Overture*, complete with live cannons, to which the audience responded with, as I usually said, a "standing ovulation." Afterward I drove the loaded van northward through the night, making it to Duluth in nine hours, after which Doree awakened to drive the remaining three hours to Ft. Frances, Ontario, while I got some sleep.

Day One

After crossing the international bridge over the Rainy River and passing through the Canadian customs check in Ft. Frances, we picked up a take-out burger lunch and made our way to the park on Pithers Point, at the eastern edge of town. This point, marking the western extremity of Rainy Lake and the beginning of the Rainy River, lay directly across the channel from our put-in place the previous year, at the public boat landing of International Falls. The point had been the site of Ft. St. Pierre, built by La Vérendrye's men in 1731 as the first long-term post west of Lake Superior. This facility, used by the French until about 1758, has been reconstructed in the grassy park, although on a reduced scale.

While we savored our lunch in the bright sunlight beside the French stockade wall, I noted for the family the various fur trade posts which had later stood on the northern shoreline of the river, from three to five miles downstream from the point, beginning just below the falls. From about 1761 or 1762 onward, Montreal-based French and Anglo traders had operated Lac La Pluie (Rainy Lake) posts here; these men included members of the N.W.C., as well as members of the X.Y.C. between 1798 and 1804. Their competitors in the H.B.C. also operated Ft. Lac La Pluie here between 1793 and 1797, and again from 1816 until 1902. On the opposite side of the river, Jacques De Noyon and his colleagues, the first French traders to venture far westward from Lake Superior, had wintered in 1688-89, before continuing westward to Lake of the Woods; this had taken place 302 years before the arrival of the Kent family here. In 1717, La Noué had constructed the short-lived Ft. Tekamanigan near the southern riverbank, and the A.F.C. had operated a post there for a decade between 1823 and 1833.

From 1788 onward, this place at the head of the river had served as the site of the rendezvous between the brigades from the far-flung, northwestern Athabasca country and voyageurs from Grand Portage (or Ft. William after 1803), who brought in new merchandise and took out the peltries of the Athabascan traders. This expansion of the transport system far to the northwest of Lake Superior had required the establishment of a canoe production yard at each of the various Rainy Lake posts here, to serve the needs of the very distant brigades. French and native canoe builders were hired to work here in the yards of both the N.W.C. and the X.Y.C., repairing existing craft and constructing new ones. Their French and native colleagues labored in even more extensive canoe yards beside the shores of Lake Superior, first at Grand Portage and later at Ft. William.

In downtown Ft. Frances, we picked up our shuttle driver at North Air Services, and headed west for a couple of miles to the public boat ramp, which is located a mile below the dam. The driver would take our van northward to Kenora at the far end of Lake of the Woods two days later, and leave it in the parking lot of the town police post there.

The backwaters of the hydro dam spanning the border river at Ft. Frances/International Falls, constructed in 1905, had flooded the Sault de Chaudière (Kettle Falls) or Kouchiching in native terminology. The upper falls had originally dropped about ten feet in elevation, while the lower falls had dropped some fifteen feet, with a span of fifty yards of frothing water between the two cascades. The mist that continually rose from the double set of falls had inspired the Chaudière (Kettle) name, while the terms Lac La Pluie and Rivière La Pluie (Rainy Lake and Rainy River) had been derived from the same rain-like mist which hung over the falls at the outlet of the lake and the beginning of the river. This dramatic obstruction in the waterway had required a portage of about 200 yards along the northern shoreline. Each of the various La Pluie posts which were constructed after the French period had been located in the area of the river extending from just below the falls to two miles downstream.

Finally launching at 2:30 P.M., we were grateful for the sunny day with a few puffs of white clouds, and the balmy air temperature of 75 degrees in the shade. The one drawback to the scene was a steady westerly and southwesterly head wind, with moderate waves, which would not calm down until evening. Against this moderately strong wind, we averaged three miles an hour for five hours, during which Ben put in five miles as the bow paddler. Due to our late-in-the-day start, we just grabbed snacks of crackers, jerky, and chocolate gorp as we continually traveled, instead of taking any breaks along the way, either afloat or on shore.

The Rainy River, ranging in width from only about two hundred to four hundred yards, was very impressive to the voyageurs. Reflecting this sentiment, John MacDonnel rhapsodized in 1793, "This is the most beautiful river in the Northwest." Seven years later, Daniel Harmon called it "a beautiful river, pretty free of rapids." In 1823, John Bigsby, traveling with David Thompson and the other surveyors of the International Boundary Commission, gushed that it "took two delightfully placid days, aided by its always sensible and often strong current." It is true that the watercourse offered eighty miles of predictable paddling in a rather narrow passageway, with only two sets of rapids that did not require portages. However, the primary reason for its attractiveness in the eyes of early canoe travelers was that its banks, as well as the surrounding lands, were composed of a thick layer of rich alluvial soil. This soil, and the deciduous trees that grew there, presented a startling contrast to the rough and rocky Canadian Shield terrain, covered mostly with evergreen forests, through which they (and also the Kent family) had traveled westward ever since leaving the lower reaches of the Ottawa River.

The current of the upper river where we traveled this first day was very gentle; in fact, it was virtually unnoticeable except in a few places where a rare section of rocky shoreline or an underwater shelf presented an obstruction to the flow. The right or Canadian shoreline was, in most areas, a high soil bank with a rather steep decline, covered with aspens and other deciduous trees. Along the base of the bank, a narrow flat area extended all along the shoreline; this area was covered with lush grass of a light green hue. The left or American side often had a more gradual slope to the bank, and it was often much lower in height as well. The same trees and grass also clothed this left bank and shoreline. Downriver from Ft. Frances, we passed scattered houses and farms on both sides of the river. Due to the pollution that the pulp and paper mills of both towns pour into the river, we drank water not from the watercourse but instead from our thermos and collapsible plastic jug, which we had filled at a gas station before pushing off; we would not utilize the river water until we were a long distance downstream from the two towns. This was our first Canadian canoe trip in which we had been obliged to carry water for drinking and cooking.

During the course of the afternoon, we encountered several different batches of six to eight ducklings. In each case, the mother decoyed us with a dramatic broken-wing impersonation, to pull us away from her young (or so she thought) as we proceeded downstream. At the junction of the Little Fork River, we silently approached a flock of about twenty white pelicans sunning themselves on a rock ledge in midstream. We had just crossed the easternmost edge of the summer range of these interesting birds; six more of our northward-reaching voyages, all the way to Lake Athabasca, would pass through the upper reaches of their warm-weather domain. When we moved in too close to their midstream gathering place, the pelicans launched themselves clumsily, but were soon gliding along gracefully and efficiently, flapping their wings only occasionally.

We landed to camp on the left shore at 7:30, on a broad bend in the river. The entire area here was open land which was regularly used for either growing crops or pasturing cows, extremely unusual terrain for us in our travels along the mainline fur trade route! This had been Toby's first day ever in a canoe; and after only fifteen miles on the water, he had already become an outstanding tripper. During the first hour or two, he had tried several times to step out onto the surface of the water from the moving canoe. But after those few experiments in his brand new environment, he had perched quietly atop the packs in the midsection area, either watching the scenery pass by slowly or napping.

This was also the first day of paddling for me since I had begun to have serious and constant pain at the base of my spine, sensations which had begun seven months before. The pain had eventually led to injections of cortisone into the spine in May, but they had unfortunately brought no relief. The initial loading in of the heavy packs at the put-in place in the early afternoon had caused moderate pain, but the hours of paddling, involving leaning forward and pulling backward with each stroke, had not hurt much at all. And unloading the gear and setting up the camp had felt just like the end of any other paddling day from previous years. Canoeing was obviously good for all of me! After enjoying the beautiful evening for a bit, we were in the tent by 9:00, and were asleep within a half-hour.

Day Two

When the alarm clock jangled at 6 A.M., we began our day with stretching exercises inside the tent. At first, our backs and necks were very stiff and sore, from the twelve-hour drive through the night plus the first day of paddling; but they soon loosened up. Outside the shelter, mist rose like swirling grey phantoms from the silvery surface of the river. But the rays of sunlight peeking over the tree line soon chased them away, leaving us with gorgeous weather conditions when we set off at 7:20. The air temperature measured 68 degrees, while a beaming sun and a pale blue sky strewn with a few puffball clouds presided over the entire area. For the first half-hour, there was no breeze. Then a light head wind developed which, as is usual during canoe jaunts, kept changing directions so that it was against us no matter what direction the river channel flowed. But a few verses of *Vent Frais* took care of *La Vieille*'s efforts to hold us back and dampen our spirits! Then, from her position in the midsection with Toby across her lap, Doree bellowed the melody, *"Derrière chez nous, y-a-t'un étang,"* after which Ben and I joined in, *"En roulant my boule."* Doree: *"Trois beaux canards s'en vont baignant."* All of us: *"Rouli, roulant, ma boule roulant."*

The current of the river was so slight in this upper section that we regretted that we had not planned this voyage as an upstream one, to travel in the direction of the prevailing westerly winds. However, with Ben plying his paddle in the bow seat, we surged forward ten miles in 2 2/3 hours, passing some farms and scattered houses along the way. At the place where the Big Fork River flows in on the left, in an area that is now preserved as Grand Mound State Park, Alexander Henry had encountered an Ojibwa village of fifty lodges in 1775; here he purchased new canoes from builders residing in the village. A major Ojibwa community had been located in this area for at least three decades before his arrival, and it would remain within a fifteen-mile stretch downriver from here until at least the 1870s. The entire region had originally been the territory of the Cree and Assiniboine nations, with the Ojibwas expanding gradually westward from Lake Superior from the 1720s onward. By the 1760s, they had advanced as far west as the Big Fork River; however, they also shared a village at that time with the Crees at the mouth of the Rainy River, well into Cree territory. When an Ojibwa reservation was established by the U.S. government in this region in 1854, its lands extended eastward from the Big Fork River for about sixty miles to the Vermilion River, and southward from the Rainy River, Rainy Lake, and the international border along the mainline canoe route for some sixty miles.

Continuing on our downstream route, we approached a herd of about thirty young cattle drinking at the water's edge along the right shore; when we came near, they bolted into the trees. A canoe headed toward them in their watering trough was apparently not an everyday occurrence. During the course of the morning, we were pleased to watch the activities of a great blue heron, two bald eagles, and a number of ducks. At one point, five pelicans, flying in a tight, wing tip-to-wing tip formation, glided low over us. When we stopped for an hour-long breakfast break at 10:00, at an abandoned farm near the river which was labeled "Aylsworth, Ont." on the topo map, the dilapidated wooden house, double-room outhouse, chicken house, and barns provided plenty of opportunities for exploring. Although this was farm country that we were traveling through, we rarely glimpsed the farms, since they were almost all located high above the river on the bluffs. However, we did sometimes pass fenced areas where cattle were allowed to graze down to the edge of the water.

Pushing off again, with me now in the bow seat, we made six miles in two hours against a rather strong head wind. To help us move forward under these windy conditions, we sang the light-hearted, nonsensical voyageur song Ah! Si Mon Moine Voulait Danser: *"If my monk doesn't want to dance, I'll give him a hooded cape" (the following verses give him a belt, a rosary, a frock, or a book of psalms). "If he hadn't made vows of poverty, I'd give him a lot of other things. Dance, my monk, dance; you don't hear the dance; you don't hear my windmill; you don't hear my windmill run." Next up, we played mental number games* en français. *The voyageurs of old had been acutely aware of how helpful such distractions were during long stints on the water. (Doree)*

When we stopped at Emo, Ontario to buy a midday meal of baked chicken, fries, rolls, and cokes, we had completed an eight-mile northerly jog in the river's course, and had resumed our generally westward direction. At the little restaurant, we also refilled our water jug and thermos, since the river here was still unfit for either drinking or swimming. Just before departing at 2:00, we found a little shrew dead on the riverbank. Ben wondered if its demise had been caused by the polluted river water.

Three miles of paddling brought us to the Rapides du Manitou (Manitou or Great Spirit Rapids), which the voyageurs had run down when westbound and lined up when eastbound. We all scouted the obstacles from the shoreline, and then, with Ben and Toby cheering us on from the safety of some onshore boulders, Doree and I ran the rapids on the right side. In the process, we avoided the rock-strewn white water and the haystack standing waves that filled the middle passage during its total drop of 2 1/2 feet of elevation. Not all of the fur trade canoes, whether being run down or lined up, had successfully navigated here: in 1800, Daniel Harmon noted that at this place during the previous year, "a canoe was broken and a man drowned." In addition, John Bigsby reported an accident that had befallen the survey party of the International Boundary Commission at this place in 1823: "Our tow-rope broke on our return at the sharpest spot, and the canoe with her men were all but lost."

On the north shore near the rapids, we passed a native community containing about twenty homes, positioned along the southern border of the Manitou Rapids Indian Reserve; this square of reservation land measures about three miles on each side. It was here in this community that Frances Densmore had gathered much of her outstanding historical data about all aspects of traditional Ojibwa culture, during her two decades of research for the Smithsonian Institution between 1905 and 1925. This was also the locale at which a N.W.C. post had operated during the 1790s, and where a competing H.B.C. post was run from 1793 to 1797.

Soon, to our relief, the head wind faded almost completely. After Doree had completed fifteen miles as the *avant*, Ben again took up the paddle. To pass the time, we chatted about the dugout canoe that I had studied north of Tokyo in April, during the Symphony's three-week tour of Japan (which Doree had happily accompanied). That ancient craft, discovered in the 1970s during excavations for a subway line, had been carbon-14 dated to about 2,400 B.C.

Seven miles below the Manitou Rapids, we reached the Long Sault (Long Falls), a stretch of 1 1/2 miles of fast current and riffle rapids in which the water level drops three feet in elevation. This again had been a place where the fur trade canoes had been run downstream and had been lined upstream. While I scouted the route by standing up at intervals in the stern to look ahead, we ran nimbly down this fast section of the river. Finally, we were glad to be traveling downstream, in spite of the prevailing westerly winds that had plagued us during both days on the water. As we zoomed down the last of the riffles, a group of seven pelicans watched us closely from their nearby perch on midstream boulders, as if waiting to see whether we would make it. When we passed by, they flapped away with clumsy dignity. Here at the base of the rapids, a native sturgeon fishery had operated for a very long time during the historic era.

By 8:30, after covering another six miles below the Long Sault, we began looking for a campsite, since we had advanced a satisfying 35 miles during thirteen hours on the water. As we rounded a bend, six deer that had been drinking at the mouth of a stream flowing in on the right shore splashed noisily out of the water and bounded into the woods. Near the mouth of the stream, we landed and cleared a small area for the tent back a short distance from the low grassy bank, in a thicket of old dried saplings that had once flourished there. Having eaten our warm main meal at midday, we just munched on some gorp and crawled into the tent at 9:00, pleased with our progress and the fact that Ben had paddled twenty miles this day!

During the night, we were awakened by the sounds of crackling brush, as a medium-sized animal approached the tent. Toby growled a couple of warnings, and the creature moved on. So our mild-mannered mascot did have some other useful function on these trips besides making us smile!

Day Three

Wrapped in deep sleep, none of us registered the ringing of the alarm clock; I finally awakened at 6:30, very refreshed after eight hours on my air mattress. Outside, the silvery veil of mist rising from the water and coiling skyward was so dense that it completely blocked our view of the river and the trees; but by launch time ninety minutes later, the sun had burned it all away. This was a perfect paddling day: blue sky, scattered tufts of white clouds sailing calmly overhead, 63 degrees already, and no wind. We had no idea that hair-raising challenges would confront us before this day would draw to a close, and we were unaware that fear-quenching songs would play a prominent role in those events.

Ben started as the *avant*, advancing six miles in 1 1/2 hours. Most of this distance involved a northward jog in the course of the river, after which our path again returned to a gently winding westward direction. Then Doree took over in the bow position, and we made another six miles in ninety minutes, before taking a half-hour break on shore to stretch our legs and let Toby run. We had covered twelve miles in three hours of easy cruising. Our usual all-day traveling speed, when the craft was fully loaded with food supplies for a long voyage, and we were traveling on flat water without any helpful or hindering wind, was now about 31/2 to 4 miles per hour. This speed had increased some from the previous years, since Ben had grown a little bigger and stronger (although he was still mighty spindly). After the stop, he assumed the bow duties, and we covered nine miles in

2 1/4 hours, as the beautiful weather continued and the temperature reached a high of 78 degrees. A slight breeze from the west picked up, but it was hardly enough to hinder our progress.

Under these very comfortable conditions, with little need to watch the map closely, I lapsed into automatic paddling, and soon became lost in my thoughts about various of our voyageur ancestors. During the French regime, there had been several different categories of voyageurs. For starters, there were career professionals who worked in the commerce for many years, becoming highly expert at such occupations as canoeman or trader. There were also others, in nearly all instances young single men without much experience in the occupation, who only worked for one or several seasons. The goal of each of these latter men was to earn enough cash to purchase equipment, furnishings, and livestock for his newly-established farm along the St. Lawrence, after which he intended to marry and raise a family on that farm.

For both the long-term professionals and the short-term workers, there were two different types of operations. Certain individuals remained based on the St. Lawrence, working only on summer voyages to transport merchandise to traders in the interior and then haul out peltries, having no permission to supplement their pay by doing some trading on their own. These men were called *mangeurs du lard* (side pork eaters), since they were supplied by their employers with side pork and peas for their meals en route. Other men termed *hivernants* (winterers) traveled into the interior, spent a year or more trading, and then brought out the gathered furs and hides to cash them in. Some of these latter individuals were voyageur-traders, acting as profit-sharing partners with their trader colleagues or with investors in the St. Lawrence settlements who were backing the enterprise. Other winterers were simple voyageurs, receiving a fixed salary to paddle into and out of the interior and to carry out all assigned tasks during the term of their contract. Early in the French commerce, many of these simple voyageurs were also allowed to bring in a certain amount of private merchandise, and trade it to supplement their wages; over time, this custom was phased out. Certain of the employees received a higher salary for special skills, such as translating native languages, keeping accounts, repairing and building birchbark and dugout canoes, or hunting to supply meat for the operation.

After the official system of trading licenses had been established in 1681, a notary contract was drawn up for each voyageur business agreement. These documents spelled out the names of the individuals involved, the place in the interior to which they would travel, the period of time that they would labor there, the items which would be provided to them for their work, and the amount of their financial gain upon completion of the operation. These contracts have supplied us with a gold-mine of information about the fur trade business.

For example, the contract from September 2, 1696, involving our ancestor Jean Baptiste Lalonde dit L'Espérance, indicated that he had been hired in Montreal by Cadillac, to carry out trading for the officer during his last year as the commandant of Ft. De Buade at St. Ignace. According to the agreement, Lalonde was permitted to take in with him to the Straits of Mackinac two pairs of leggings, six shirts, two hooded coats, a blanket, a gun, and twelve pounds of tobacco. At the end of his year of employment there, he would be allowed to trade any and all of these items for his own profit before coming out to Montreal. Cadillac was to supply his provisions and canoe, and pay him two hundred *livres* at the conclusion of his employment as a wintering voyageur-trader. Five years earlier, just one month after his sixteenth birthday, Jean Baptiste had signed a contract to travel to the Straits region and work with a long-term trader and investor there during the spring, summer, and fall. In this informal apprenticeship program, which was arranged with his mother's official consent in front of a notary, the young man was to be paid "according to the time which he will contribute." Such was Jean Baptiste's entry into the world of the fur trade.

Jean Baptiste's son Guillaume Lalonde worked as a professional voyageur on summer runs between Lachine and Ft. Michilimackinac during the 1730s, and apparently earlier as well; this employment continued until he was at least 33 years old. For his journey in the summer of 1736, he earned 213 *livres*, and was issued a breechclout and a pair of leggings before departure. Two years later, his salary for traveling the same route consisted of 200 *livres*, half in currency and half in merchandise at the usual retail price, as well as a clout and a set of leggings.

The third generation of my voyageur ancestors in this Lalonde family, and my last documented forebear who worked in the fur trade, was Guillaume's son Guillaume Lalonde. He was hired in 1758 by the Governor of New France during *La Guerre de Sept Ans* (the Seven Years' War, which Anglos called the French and Indian War), to make a combination governmental-and-commercial summer trip to Ft. Michilimackinac and back. Guillaume's salary for this voyage was 210 *livres*, paid upon completion. At the time, he was age 21 and single, not marrying until three years after the expedition; in addition, no later voyageur contracts for him have been located in the archives. Thus, it appears that Guillaume, Jr. was an example of an individual who had participated in the fur trade on a short-term basis. It was always a moving sensation for me whenever I stood at the grave of my great-grandfather Joseph Lalonde in Black River, Michigan, since his great-grandfather had been this Guillaume Lalonde, the voyageur from the summer of 1758.

After taking a one-hour break for hamburgers in the little town of Rainy River, Ontario, we were off again at 3:00, as the beautiful weather and ideal paddling conditions continued. A mile below the town, we pulled into a very narrow inlet on the left shoreline, to take a close look at four pontoon planes that were parked there. From this point on, the river would widen a bit and curve gradually to the right over the span of about ten miles, until it would flow northward into the open waters of Lake of the Woods. Two miles into the huge curve, Ben had reached a total of seventeen miles for the day as the *avant*, so he traded places with Doree. At 4:15, a mild following wind rose directly from the south, so Ben hoisted the sail, the first time on this trip. From his position in the midsection area, he enjoyed adjusting the angle of the blue nylon sheet to best harness the wind, especially when it grew into a steady assist from over his right shoulder.

While we sailed down the lowest section of the Rainy River, I explained that, during the first decade of the 1800s, a N.W.C. post called Lower House had operated on the left shore in this area. At the same time, the competing staff of the H.B.C. had tried to tempt native customers to trade at their facility, called Asp House, which stood nearby on the opposite shore.

As we neared the mouth of the river, we encountered a succession of large sport-fishing powerboats zipping to and fro. The lack of understanding of the drivers, particularly concerning the challenges that their big wakes caused for us canoeists, was a real pain in the ass! At the mouth of the river on the U.S. shore stood a massive lodge, with a number of associated cabins and rental fishing boats. While passing through that area, we dropped our sail, so that we could watch carefully for crazy boat drivers. At 6:00, we finally reached the mouth of the river, and coasted onto the waters of Lake of the Woods, having covered eleven miles in the previous three hours, and a total of 31 miles during ten hours on the river.

Here at the mouth, a combination Cree-Ojibwa village had stood from the 1760s onward, in Cree territory. A half-century later, the Crees had moved further toward the west, so that the river-mouth community was inhabited entirely by Ojibwas. When Alexander Henry passed through in 1775, he paused at the village, which he described as a summer fishing community containing about a hundred native individuals. From them, he purchased a supply of fish and one hundred bags of wild rice, as provisions for his trading expedition which was headed further into the northwest. The marshes and shallows around the entire lower area of the massive lake were prime areas for harvesting wild rice, while sturgeon were very plentiful throughout its waters; these two sources of food provided the native residents of the region with much of their nourishment. John Macdonnel elaborated on the activities that took place at this river-mouth village when he came through in 1793: he and his colleagues bought new canoes from the native canoe-builders who lived there.

Lac du Bois (Lake of the Woods, or Kaminitik Sakiegan in the Algonquian languages) presented the voyageurs with a stretch of at least seventy miles of challenging and often dangerous travel, from the mouth of the Rainy River north to the outlet of the lake, at the head of the Winnipeg River at the Rat Portage. The route first led northward from the Rainy River mouth for four miles, to a narrow passage between the ends of two long, slender islands called Îles du Sable (Sand Islands, now called Sable Islands). From this place, the paddlers would begin a series of decisions about their route, based on the weather conditions at the time and their assessment of the conditions that could be expected in the hours and days ahead.

A huge landmass called the Aulneau Peninsula extends westward from about the middle of the eastern shoreline, jutting across about three-quarters of the width of the lake. Scattered around all sides of this peninsula lie thousands of islands of all sizes. The standard mainline route, under absolutely ideal weather conditions, headed from the Sable Islands passageway on a course that was slightly west of north, over the Grande Traverse of fourteen miles to reach the huge Grosse Île (Big Island). From there, the route passed along the western side of Big Island, and then in a generally north-northeasterly direction to the end of the Aulneau Peninsula and along its western end, and finally along the same north-northeasterly course to the upper end of the lake. This route entailed a single portage, called the Portage du Bois, at a very narrow and shallow place in the French Portage Narrows; this was the slender passage between the western end of the Aulneau Peninsula and a series of adjacent massive islands. Due to the immense number of islands which had to be negotiated throughout most of the lake, the voyageurs were lost more often while crossing Lac du Bois than on all other sections of the mainline route combined. Since the environment of the lake had again returned the paddlers to rocky Canadian Shield terrain, covered with mostly spruce and pine forest, they found it extremely difficult to distinguish where their route lay amid the thousands of similar, evergreen-clad islands, having no maps of the area except those that were in their heads.

A few fur trade scholars have asserted that a more sheltered course was used as the standard mainline route across Lake of the Woods. According to them, this latter route extended from the Sable Islands passageway on a northeasterly course for about 35 to 40 miles, to the place where the base of the Aulneau Peninsula narrows to a very slender neck of land. After making the Portage de la Tortue (Turtle Carry) across this narrow strip, the voyageurs would continue first toward the northeast for about eight miles, and then travel toward the northwest for a long stretch, to finally reach the upper end of the lake. This course would add at least twenty miles of paddling to the voyage, and it would also increase immensely the number of seemingly identical islands which had to be negotiated around. However, it would take advantage of the landmass of the Aulneau Peninsula, as well as the majority of its surrounding islands, to block the prevailing westerly winds. In addition, the water in these eastern areas of the lake, fed by numerous small rivers, was generally free of the algae that grew in profusion in both the southern and northern sections of the main lake.

However, none of the early accounts reported that this passage along the eastern shore of the lake was utilized as the mainline route. In 1789, Alexander Mackenzie described the route in this way: "The Lake du Bois is, as far as I could learn, nearly round, and the canoe course through the centre of it among a cluster of islands, some of which are so extensive that they may be taken for the main land. The reduced [direct] course would be nearly South and North. But following the navigating course [around Big Island and the western end of the Aulneau Peninsula], I make the distance seventy-five miles, though in a direct line it would fall very short of that length. At about two-thirds of it, there is a small carrying-place, when the water is low." Four years later, John Macdonnel jotted these comments in his journal while traveling over this body of water: "Slept at the Isle au Sable, three leagues from the mouth of the main channel of the [Rainy] River, at the foot of the widest traverse in the Lake of the Woods [out to Big Island]...Made the little portage of Lac des Bois, which is made merely to avoid a circuitous route [around some massive islands] at the most western part of this lake." When John Bigsby traveled here with David Thompson and the other surveyors of the International Boundary Commission in 1823, he recorded the following comments: "We did not pursue the usual commercial route, which runs directly north from the River Lapluie. We were ordered to go round the lake, to discover, if possible, its most northwestern corner, and therefore turned off to the west...Portage des Bois [is] a carrying-place created by the singular meeting of two deep, narrow cul-de-sacs, one on each side of the promontory [the Aulneau Peninsula], which makes the commercial route from the Rainy River to the north end of the Lake only seventy-five or eighty miles."

It is true that native paddlers sometimes traveled from the northwestern arm of Rainy Lake to Lake of the Woods not by way of the Rainy River, but instead along a more direct course, by way of the Rivière du Bois. In these instances, with the paddlers arriving at the southeastern corner of Lake of the Woods, a little south of the base of the Aulneau Peninsula, they would have used the Turtle Portage to cross the peninsula, and then would have proceeded northwestward to the top of Lake of the Woods. This route was documented on maps that were created in 1737 and 1749, using information from La Vérendrye's discoveries. However, the surveyor Henry Hind investigated both the usual Rainy River route and the secondary Rivière du Bois passageway in 1857. Concerning the latter course, he noted: "This...is preferred to the route by the Rainy River, as being more sheltered and free from the long open traverses necessary in crossing to the Rat Portage [at the north end of Lake of the Woods] from the mouth of Rainy River...[But] the results of this exploration established the fact that, however advantageous this route [by way of the Rivière du Bois] may be for Indians, in their small canoes, it is far inferior to that by Rainy River and the Lake of the Woods as a boat [or large canoe] communication."

Since we wished to travel over the length of Lake of the Woods by way of the usual mainline route, we would head north from the mouth of the Rainy River, and would be obliged to deal with the wide traverse that was necessary to proceed from the mouth of the river to the nearest islands. From the outlet of the river at Wheelers Point, we headed due north for four miles across Fourmile Bay, and then glided through the narrow passage between the ends of Île du Sable (Sand Island) and Île des Pins (Pine Island). This pair of very slender, sand dune islands, six and four miles long respectively, lie end-to-end in a northeast-to-southwest direction, and shelter the bay in front of the river mouth from the open lake. Landing on the western end of Sable Island just before 7:00, we took a ten-minute break, to eat the remaining burgers that we had bought earlier in the day at the town of Rainy River.

The vast area of the lake stretched out before us. Ever since I had begun planning this voyage, I had been concerned about what kind of paddling conditions we would encounter when we would reach this very place, and would face the long northward crossing. By good fortune, a mild wind was wafting from the south, creating small northbound waves, while the sun, already low in the west, was warm and bright in a completely clear sky. If we were to camp here for the night, content with the 35 miles that we had already advanced this day, and postpone the long crossing until morning light, the wind and weather could change considerably, and prevent our heading northward across the open water. Since there was very little likelihood of a major change in the weather during the next several hours, we decided to make the big traverse toward the north.

Shoving off at 7 P.M., with our strong Doree in the *avant* seat, we knew that we had less than three hours of fading daylight left. If we had had more hours of light at our disposal, under these ideal paddling conditions, we would have headed directly for Big Island, fourteen miles away on a course that was slightly to the west of north. However, since we would already be completing the crossing in the dark, we decided to travel instead on a course that was slightly east of north, heading for Bigsby Point, the southwestern extremity of Bigsby Island, ten miles away. This large island, lying a mile southeast of Big Island, was the substitute destination of the voyageurs when conditions were less than ideal and it was not possible to head directly for Big Island. When conditions were not very favorable at all, they would travel in a northeasterly direction along the shoreline of Île du Sable for six miles, and then continue in the same direction beside the shore of the mainland for another three miles, to reach Pointe du Vent (Windy Point). From there, a traverse of only 31/2 miles of open water was needed to land at the southernmost tip of Bigsby Island.

Setting out with high hopes, along with a certain degree of trepidation (since this was by far the longest traverse on open water that we had ever made), we raised the sail, and were pleased to see that it provided some excellent assistance. We could make out absolutely no hint of Bigsby Island on the distant horizon to the north. After traveling for a mile, we could just barely make out a slight glimpse of it, as a thin grey smudge slowly emerged at the junction of sky and water. This was going to be a long haul.

As the miles of the lake slowly passed beneath our bow (31/2 m.p.h. does not register as much forward progress when you are traveling many miles from shore), the vibrant red disc of the sun sank lower and lower in the west, spreading hues of red, orange, and bluish violet across the large canvas of sky. From our vantage point far out on the lake, the giant dome of the heavens stretched from horizon to horizon in all directions. Finally, at about 8:30, the last of the red disc disappeared below the waterline, when we were only about halfway across the traverse. Following its departure, we had an additional hour of gradually fading residual light, until the sky was totally dark. Our singing of the ancient voyageur songs became even more important then, keeping our spirits up and our paddle strokes strong. In the inky blackness, the heavens were absolutely crowded with thousands of huge, bright stars, so close that they seemed to be almost within our reach. Marveling at the sight, I thought about the ancient native belief that the Milky Way was the path that the souls of the deceased traveled on their way to the Village of the Dead.

During the nearly three hours that we paddled beneath the billowing sail, the strength of the wind and the size of the waves increased considerably. We were thankful that we were headed in the same direction as they were! As we approached to within a mile or two of the point at the southwestern tip of the island, the following wind and the big waves changed direction a bit, now flowing toward the north-northwest. So I changed our course slightly toward the northwest, to keep the waves from splashing over the gunwales.

Not being able to switch paddling sides very often, due to the angle of the wind from behind, I began to experience numbness in my fingers. So what, I said to myself. Keep singing and keep going. (Doree)

Nearing Bigsby Point, after having covered ten miles, I could hear in the distance the waves crashing against the rocky shoreline. I thought about the damage that those rocks could inflict on both us and our canoe, and decided we could not land anywhere near here. So we passed to the west of the point. We were now coasting along the peninsula that juts southward from the island. Somewhere along its the three-mile length, I hoped to find a landing site that would be sheltered from those strong northbound waves, allowing us to make a safe landfall in quiet waters.

By this point, the sun had been down for about 1 1/2 hours. For the first hour or so of that time, we had navigated by the gradually diminishing residual light in the sky, and finally by starlight alone, since there was no moon visible this week. This was the first time that we had ever seen the Big Dipper and its aligned North Star from aboard the canoe. Our course was taking us exactly toward the immense Dipper, which beckoned us northward reassuringly. This particular scene would be vividly burned into our memories. Since we were comfortable in the balmy night air, and had nearly made it safely across by this time, I could finally see past the danger of the situation, and take in the very special aspects of the setting.

As we approached the northern end of the peninsula, we could clearly hear the powerful waves beating hard against the rocks on shore. In the dim starlight, we could barely make out tall rock ledges all along the shoreline that we were skirting on our right. Above the sound of the surf, I shouted to Ben, "Drop the sail!" This slowed our speed somewhat, and also enabled me to watch for obstructions along with Doree and Ben, instead of only relying on them to call out directions to me behind the raised sail. Just ahead lay the western corner of the island; around it, we hoped to find shelter from the wind and waves. But then an additional concern arose: we could now hear the waves also smashing against offshore reefs and rocky shallows on our left! When I shouted "Now, Doree!" we dug in hard, made a sharp right turn in the surf, and dashed around the corner of the island, all the while hoping that we would miss any submerged rocks on both our right and our left.

When we rounded the point at full speed and reached its lee side, the water was immediately flat and calm. Exhaling in relief, we glided toward the shore, where a rock ledge angled very gradually up from the surface of the water, offering an excellent landing place. We clambered over the gunwales into the water, and staggered to shore with the painter rope from each end of the canoe in hand. Thankful to be safely on solid ground again, we hugged one another. It was 10:15 P.M. A little more than three hours earlier, we had been eating burgers on Île du Sable. Now we were on the other side of the thirteen-mile Grande Traverse, which had worried me throughout the entire planning stage of this trip!

With the aid of the flashlight, we unloaded the canoe in the dark, and soon located a tent site up on the rocky slope, where we would be sheltered somewhat by the trees. It took until 11:30 to set up camp slowly, since we had little energy left. Long after we drifted off to exhausted sleep at midnight, the wind continued to whip our little green tent, even in its partially sheltered location back in the trees. But this did not bother us one bit; we were safely ensconced on solid Canadian Shield rock!

From this day forward, whenever we would sing *A la Claire Fontaine*, I would be reminded of our very memorable traverse beneath the stars, when we had sung not only this song, but also all of the other *chansons* that we knew, during those three long hours of the crossing. The haunting refrain of *Fontaine* repeated over and over in my head as I drifted off to sleep, with the images of my beloved paddling partners imbedded in my mind's eye: *"Il y a longtemps que je t'aime, jamais je ne t'oublierai."*

Day Four

Surfacing at 8:00, we used the morning hours to relax and recover somewhat from the previous day's taxing and perilous adventures. Sitting on the barren rock ledge and gazing at the empty horizon to the south, over the waters that we had traveled the night before, I savored the moment and updated the journal. From 8 A.M. to 10:15 P.M., we had progressed 48 miles, 31 of them on the Rainy River and 17 on Lake of the Woods. About 25 of those miles had been done with some assistance from the sail. This 48 miles was the greatest distance that we had ever covered in one day on the water. During the 2 1/2 days of this voyage, we had already made 98 miles, and had seen a great deal of varied scenery along the way.

While Doree and I packed up in slow motion, Ben picked a batch of lichens from the rocks, to use as bushes for his model railroad layout in the attic back at home. (Yes, he could paddle like a man, but he was still a boy!) He also found considerable amounts of scat on the exposed rock ledges atop the hill behind our camp; we guessed that they had been left by raccoons, since the leavings were full of crayfish remains. A moderately strong wind from the southwest was blowing waves up onto the rock ledge that had served as our quiet landing spot the previous night. So to load the canoe, we carried everything around a corner to a quiet cove with a soft sandy beach. The weather was delightful: 70 degrees in the shade, and sunny skies with a few white clouds drifting slowly overhead. Groups of ten to twenty pelicans cruised by us occasionally, gliding effortlessly in straight-line formations. Their way of flying, seldom flapping their wings, looked so smooth and easy that it was hard for us to remember that these white birds were very large. Since each outstretched wing could measure up to four feet, their total wingspan could reach up to nine feet!

On the beach, we had an early lunch of beef jerky washed down with koolaid, while a red squirrel watched us inquisitively from a safe distance. Setting out at 11:30, we appreciated the help of the moderate wind and waves from the southwest that pushed us, as we traveled northward along the side of Bigsby Island. The waves, approaching the canoe at an angle from our left rear, were not whitecaps; instead, they were broad, deep swells, with troughs about three to four feet deep. After about half an hour, as our craft rose and fell on the rather large swells, Ben, from his position in the midsection, complained of a headache. A few minutes later, he threw up his breakfast over the side, and soon began feeling much better. (As a little guy, Ben had often been car-sick during morning drives while on vacation; so we were accustomed to stopping the car, letting him barf outside, and then resuming our travels, without any fuss.)

The majority of the western shore of Bigsby Island was made up of long stretches of narrow sandy beach, with ranks of tall evergreens standing guard behind. As we coasted past the shoreline, occasional squadrons of forty to fifty pelicans soared by, only about three to four feet above the water; each group flew in a long, single-line formation, with the birds positioned at evenly spaced intervals.

After paddling for ninety minutes, we decided to take a relaxing break on the slender spit of sand at Drennan Point. As we approached the point, Ben threw Toby overboard, and then jumped over the gunwales himself; both boys then swam happily to shore. When we departed from the sand spit, headed northeast up the mile-wide passage between Bigsby Island and Big Island, the wind from the southwest had reduced to a very slight breeze, not enough to fill the sail. At 2:30, Ben exchanged places with his mother in the bow seat, and paddled four miles in ninety minutes, until our break on Painted Rock Island. Shortly before our stop, we observed a group of three loons bobbing together on the water, each one singing out its haunting call. These were the first loons that we had encountered on this trip. Their sudden appearance pleased the lady in the canoe, since loons were one of her favorite birds.

Painted Rock Island had been named for the red stripes that coursed through the light-colored faces of barren granite along its shoreline. Just as we pulled away from our forty-minute break there, Doree spied an inquisitive mink standing on the shoreline rock shelf where we had been sitting just moments before. As we paddled away, it darted under a boulder, and then peeked out the other side so that it could observe our departure.

Our course would now head in a generally northwesterly direction for at least fifteen miles, as we aimed for the western end of the Aulneau Peninsula. Leaving Big Island behind, I mentioned that a Cree village had stood there during the 1760s, at the foot of the large bay that encompasses much of its northern shore. This had also been the site of an active trading post. Now, four major portions of the island form two different reservations belonging to the native people. These had been established in 1873, along with seven other reserves scattered along the Canadian shores of the lake.

As we paddled, I reflected on human life in these regions during previous centuries and millennia, when the survival of the native people had been based upon their deep knowledge of the land, water, and plants, as well as the ways of animals, birds, and fish. This great mass of information had been passed down orally from generation to generation over the centuries, as had also their teachings about their own philosophy, history, and spirituality. Concerning the last subject, I also thought about the pictographs which had been painted on a sheer cliff face on Annie Island in this lake. While creating these powerful, spiritual paintings hundreds or thousands of years ago, shamans had used red pigment to draw an outline of a turtle and a medicine lodge on the flat face of rock.

Ben and I made the eight miles to Rough Island, the last couple of those miles at an angle against a mild head wind, since a new weather front had moved in, bringing with it winds from the northeast. We would have been very discouraged if we had known that this wind, rather light at the moment, would strengthen considerably and persist around the clock for nearly three days straight. As we searched for a campsite along the shoreline of the little island, all we could see was a jumble of broken rock stretching into the distance. But Doree insisted that a good landing spot and a fine place to camp would be found around the very next point. Lo and behold, just beyond the point we came upon a wonderful sandy cove, a much-appreciated feature in Canadian Shield country! A thick wall of spindly birches and poplars with light green leaves crept close to the curved strip of tan sand, while spires of dark green spruce towered over them from behind.

When we landed at 7:30, we had covered nineteen miles in eight hours. I was so tuckered out I could hardly paddle any further. Apparently, my body was still somewhat run down from the 48 mile jaunt of the previous day, which had included the strenuous late-night traverse.

We thoroughly enjoyed cooking our own camping food this evening. This was the first time that we had done so on this trip, having bought hot food in restaurants at little communities along the Rainy River during each of the previous three days. While eating our stew, we reveled in the awesome orange ball of the sun as it slid beneath the distant horizon, deeply reddening the western part of the sky in the process. Although I understood what caused this hue, that knowledge did not detract in any way from my appreciating the stunning beauty of the scene. When late-evening sunlight passes through the atmosphere, it is refracted and scattered. The shorter wave-lengths of blue, green, and yellow scatter the most, leaving the longer reddish wave-lengths to tint the sky. That was the scientific explanation of this spectacular sunset; but its true beauty, and the impact it had on us, could not be fully explained by science.

This was an example of why I sometimes teasingly called my husband Monsieur Je Sais Tout (Mr. I Know Everything). But he didn't usually burden us with his information, and when he did share it, we found it interesting. (Doree)

After gazing for a long time into the dancing flames of the fire, and then massaging one another on our air mattresses spread out on the beach, we crawled into the tent at 10:30. We had reached the 117 mile mark on the map, in just 3 1/2 days of paddling.

Day Five

At 6:15, a major storm swept through the area, with crashing thunder and torrential rainfall that continued for about an hour. We took this as nature's way of telling us to sleep in and heal our much-worked muscles. After finally waking up at 9:30, we relaxed in the tent, looking at the map and discussing what had taken place in this area over the centuries.

In 1732, 258 years before our trip of 1990, La Vérendrye and his men had traveled from the newly constructed Ft. St. Pierre down the Rivière La Pluie (Rainy River) and onto Lac du Bois (Lake of the Woods). Heading northward to the west side of Big Island, they continued along its full length, and then paddled an additional fourteen miles toward the northwest, to land on the southern shore of a long, slender inlet. This waterway, which extended for about five miles toward the west, would later be called the Northwest Angle Inlet. Near the shoreline, they constructed Ft. St. Charles, which would serve as the commandant's headquarters post for his explorations during the following several years, and would be used in the French commerce for a quarter-century, until about 1757. When the dam was constructed at the outlet of the lake in 1898 and the water levels rose three to four feet, the land on which the French fort had stood became an island, which is now called Magnusons Island. It lay seventeen miles northwest of our campsite on Rough Island.

In June of 1736, tragedy struck the personnel who were based at Ft. St. Charles. Three large canoes, manned by nineteen voyageurs and carrying La Vérendrye's son Jean Baptiste and the priest Fr. Aulneau, departed from the post, intending to deliver the accumulated furs and hides to Ft. Michilimackinac, and then bring back new trade merchandise. Three days later, the entire group was massacred by a Dakota war party in 36 canoes, while the Frenchmen were camped on an island in the lake to the south of the fort. This attack was carried out in retaliation for a raid which Cree warriors, armed with weaponry supplied by the French, had made on a Dakota camp. One of the men who was killed, Jean Baptiste Barbary, was a son and brother of our ancestors. The deceased, who had worked for La Vérendrye since 1732, was also a first cousin of Jean Baptiste Lalonde, our voyageur ancestor who had been employed as a trader for Cadillac at St. Ignace in 1696-97. The place of the 1736 massacre of the Frenchmen has long been suggested to have been a small island lying seven miles due west of our campsite. As a result, that island, 11/2 miles east of the international border on the lake, is called Massacre Island.

A swath of territory fifteen to twenty miles wide, extending southward from the western end of the Northwest Angle Inlet down to the bottom of the lake, and westward from the general line of travel of La Vérendrye in 1732, would eventually become the property of the United States. In 1818, according to a treaty between the U.S. and Britain, the international border with Canada was established. It would extend westward along the 49th parallel, from the southwestern arm of Lake of the Woods to the height of land of the Rocky Mountains.

So much for this day's history lessons. Our day began completely overcast, with an air temperature of 67 degrees, and almost no breeze at our campsite on the sheltered lee side of Rough Island. Shortly, however, the grey clouds marched away, leaving an empty sky of light blue, and the temp rose to 76 degrees in the shade. As soon as we departed from our sheltered cove at 11:30, we faced a strong northeast head wind, and medium waves interspersed with a few whitecaps. To seek some relief from the strong gusts, I aimed our bow due north for an hour, until we reached the shoreline of the Aulneau Peninsula, which juts westward through the entire midsection of Lake of the Woods. Then we turned toward the northwest, and were able to use the sail at a considerable angle to travel about four miles along the coast and several adjacent islands. When the route required that I steer a northward course once more, we again had to labor against the head wind and waves, until we entered the southern end of the Tug Channel at 3:00, and took a much-needed lunch break there. This narrow channel ran between the western end of the Aulneau Peninsula on our right and the massive Falcon Island on our left. The shorelines of the passage were mostly high, angled ledges of barren granite, with red and white pines standing tall just back from the edge. At this point, Ben and I had advanced over ten miles of shimmering water in 31/2 hours. At least half of those miles had been hard-won, against tough head winds.

We had now arrived at the junction of the various possible canoe routes that led from the mouth of the Rainy River across the southern half of Lake of the Woods. While preparing for this voyage, I had measured and marked on the maps the shortest route from the mouth of the river to this point, via the west side of Big Island, a distance of 34 miles. By the route that we had traveled, crossing first to Bigsby Island and then paddling around the east side of Big Island, the distance had been twelve miles longer. Thus, unless weather conditions allowed the voyageurs to make the fourteen-mile traverse from the mouth of the Rainy River directly north-northwest to the west side of Big Island, the next shortest route, which we had taken, would be at least a dozen miles longer.

As we were preparing to load in and leave the place of our rest stop, Toby spied a muskrat in a patch of tall cattails next to our beached canoe. We stood in silence for a few minutes watching this contented animal, which had a round, foot-long body and an equally long, rat-like tail. First, it unconcernedly groomed its sleek brown coat, and then it felled one of the standing rushes and proceeded to eat its tender base.

When we set off northward up the Tug Channel at 4:00, with Doree paddling, we immediately encountered a stiff head wind, and large waves sprinkled with some whitecaps. Eventually, our forward progress was reduced to slower than a walking pace, so I tried lining the canoe with the bow rope while wading near the right shore. But before long, I was in water up to my chest, and was struggling to clamber over the many submerged boulders. So we gave up on that method of travel, and Doree and I went back to slow, laborious paddling.

Soon the right shoreline close beside us became a sheer, high wall of rock, with the oncoming waves smacking noisily against its base. Two canoe lengths ahead of us, Ben spotted a mother mallard shepherding her five babies across the passage, trying to stay out of our path. Suddenly, a young bald eagle swooped into view and circled high over the ducklings. The mother duck quacked furiously, trying to discourage the raptor from attacking. Within moments, the eagle soared in low, and slashed its legs into the water as it passed over the intended prey; however, its talons came up empty. Then a second young eagle, with the same dark brown plumage from the top of its head to the bottom of its legs, swooped down. The two large birds called to each other a couple of times, and then both of them landed on the bare limbs of an old dead pine atop the nearby cliff, without making any further attempts at the fleeing duck family. These were apparently a pair of eaglets that had hatched in the same nest at the beginning of the summer. Within three or four months, they grow to adult size, develop all of their blackish-brown feathers, and learn to fly; and beginning at about four months, they leave the nest at intervals to catch their own prey. A minute or two after watching the attempted raid on the ducklings, as we were barely crawling forward beside the rock cliff shoreline, Doree silently pointed directly over our heads. There was a large eagle, perched on a limb of a thick pine, about ten feet above us. This one looked to be about three feet long from the tip of its hooked yellow beak down to the tip of its tail, and it had white feathers on its head and neck, as well as a white tail. With these traits of a mature bald eagle, it was clear that this bird was one of the parents of the two youngsters. It did not stir as we slowly slipped underneath its perch and then continued on our way. I wondered if it had been considering Toby as a possible meal.

Slogging on against the hefty wind, it took us a full two hours to struggle forward just 31/2 miles, to reach the secluded channel where the tiny native settlement of French Portage is located. There, we passed about eight to ten well-kept homes and buildings, two of them flying the Canadian flag, with its red maple leaf standing out boldly against the solid white background. At this point, Ben took over in the bow seat, and we enjoyed traveling through the rather sheltered French Portage Narrows. This slender, rockbound passage, four miles long, contrasted greatly with the wide expanses of water that we had paddled during the previous several days. En route, we noted a number of muskrat lodges, some adjacent to the shoreline and others a little offshore. These mound-like homes, unlike those made by beavers, had been constructed of cattail leaves and other green plants, rather than with saplings and mud.

Halfway through the Narrows, the Portage du Bois or Portage du Lac, the "Portage in the Middle of the Lake," had originally required a carry of about a hundred paces, crossing a grassy swamp. However, the dam that had been built across the outlet of the lake at Kenora in 1898 had raised the water level of the lake three to four feet. As a result, the former portage site was now just a slender passageway that could be paddled through in all canoeing seasons. As soon as we emerged from the French Portage Narrows onto the open waters of the northern half of Lake of the Woods, the head wind was so powerful and the whitecaps so overbearing that we were barely able to claw our way forward across the opening. Soon we found a campsite, in a little sheltered cove on the western shore of the outlet, and called it a day at 8:00.

Since our departure at 11:30 this morning, we had advanced eighteen miles in a day of hard traveling, mostly against head winds and oncoming waves. Ben had done fifteen of those miles, under tough, demanding conditions. Although he was only twelve years old, he had already developed into an excellent canoe tripper!

Loving mother dotes: He was only five feet tall, and weighed only eighty pounds, but Ben was putting out man-sized effort! At the outset of this trip, his face had been completely covered in poison ivy, picked up that week at Boy Scout camp. But his disposition was always so easy-going, and his ivy-tortured face did not obscure his inner beauty. (Doree)

After setting up camp, we replenished our engines with a stew of beef jerky, vegetables, and noodles, and discussed that fact that we had covered 135 miles in just 4 1/2 paddling days. While we enjoyed Ben's fire and traded massages on the air mattresses spread out on the rock ledge adjacent to the water, the blaze crackled, sending sparks dancing in upward spirals. There had been no room for our shelter down near the water by the fire, so we had cleared a space for it on top of the high granite bank, which was thickly overgrown with bushes. Climbing up to the tent at 11:00, we peeled off most of our clothes and faded fast.

During the night, I had a dizzying sugar low, so I had to seek relief with the peanut butter-and-honey bottle, which was hanging high in a tree with the food pack. Afterward, my swollen hands hurt so much that it took a long time for me to return to sleep. On these trips, my neck and bottom ached during the day while paddling, and my swollen hands ached during the night.

Day Six

BRIIIIIIIIIIING! When the alarm clock jarred me awake at

7:00, I could hear the wind whistling through the tops of the pines overhead. The sound reminded me of the second line in the voyageur song *Vent Frais* (Fresh Wind): *"Vent qui souffl' aux sommets des grands pins."* Crawling out to check the conditions on the exposed side of the point, I found the same furious wind and waves from the north that we had struggled against to make it to this campsite. So I settled back in the tent to wait, hoping that the blustery atmosphere might calm down a bit. At 9:45, we finally emerged, and were greeted by beautiful weather: 70 degrees already, a powder blue sky decorated with a just few clouds, and only a light breeze in our well-sheltered cove. We decided to cook our hot meal at this point, so that we could paddle until late evening, if necessary, against the wind. Boiling a stew of beef jerky, vegetables, tomato sauce, and noodles, we were soon lounging against tree trunks and spooning down bowls of nourishing fuel.

As we ate, we heard the cries of eagles near the camp. A brief search led us to two young bald eagles near the top of a tall dead pine, at the side of our cove. They were perched near the nest that had been built by their parents of sticks and twigs, supported by several solid limbs of the long-dead tree. Since the two birds had only dark brown plumage, with no white feathers, they were less than three years old. However, the fact that they were still using the nesting tree as their home base implied that they were actually less than one year old, having not yet struck out on their own; in all likelihood, they had hatched in that nest at the beginning of this summer. Shortly, both birds flew off to the south, to hone their fishing and hunting skills. We wondered what adventures and misadventures they would experience during their lifetime, which could extend for as long as 25 years.

Packing away our gear and hoping for the best, we embarked at 11:50, digging in hard against the head wind as soon as we rounded the sheltering point. For fifteen minutes, although Doree and I put our backs into the task, we barely inched forward, gaining only a quarter-mile to reach the next cove. There, we were *dégradé* (degraded or ashamed in voyageur terminology), windbound. However, we actually enjoyed the enforced relaxation, which allowed us to rest up, and also explore the landscape closely. Near the edge of the water, we found evidence of a beaver's activities, including a freshly-cut poplar sapling with the chips scattered all around its stump. Later,

Ben cleared the brush from a little shaded "camp" area underneath the poplars that stood very near to the water's edge, and built a small fire. There in his private lair, he and Toby napped away the hours in cozy seclusion, cushioned on the bed of moss and grass that covered the rock ledge. Doree and I dozed on a flat ledge at the end of the point of the cove, absorbing the healing warmth of the bright sun.

Later, we chatted about the algae for which this lake has been infamous for centuries, but which we had not experienced to a great extent. The shallow depths of the water, never more than 36 feet, led to rather warm temperatures and an environment that was conducive to the flourishing of algae during the summers. This was particularly true in the southern half of the lake, but it also occurred north of the Aulneau Peninsula as well. In 1823, Joseph Delafield of the Boundary Commission survey team noted that the surface of the water was "frequently with a green scum of vegetable matter." More than three decades later, the surveyor Henry Hind observed the same algae growth in 1857 and reported: "It gave an appearance to the lake like that of a vast expanse of dirty green mud. On lifting up a quantity of water in a tin cup, or on looking closely over the side of the canoe, the water was seen to be clear, yet sustaining an infinite quantity of minute tubular needle-shaped organisms." Although most of these organisms were not poisonous, the lake does produce a certain amount of toxic blue-green algae, called cyanobacteria. During our trip across the lake, we utilized the occasionally green-tinted water for both drinking and cooking, as had thousands of voyageurs before us, and we did not find it objectionable. Our main goal in traveling the ancient waterways was to understand in minute detail what life had been like for our ancestors, even if that meant ingesting algae-laden water.

Our windbound conversations this afternoon also turned to geography. Although we were immersed in Canadian Shield terrain and its coniferous forests, the eastern edge of the prairie lay just thirty miles west of the lake. This nearby expanse of open grassland represented one of the most northeasterly areas of the original range of the bison in the west. This particular section of the prairie had also received its first horses by about 1750, effecting the lives of both the native people and the fur trade personnel in the region.

The brisk wind, which had been blasting us from the north-northeast without letup since the early evening of Day Four, continued unabated as the late-afternoon shadows lengthened. So at 6:00 we decided to set up camp for the night. Back from the shore, we cleared an area in the brush beneath a stand of sheltering red pines, erected the tent, built a fire, treated ourselves to galette (fried cakes with raisins and luscious brown sugar syrup), and told stories until bedtime at 9:30.

Day Seven

I rose to the call of the alarm clock at 5:15, to check on the wind and waves; they were still too hearty to handle. Two hours later, I checked again; this time, I thought the elements would be barely workable, but only if the wind did not develop any more strength. Packing quickly, we were on the water within an hour. Today's weather was again beautiful: 65 degrees in the shade already, and heavens of gentle blue that were strewn with some white puffballs. As we paddled, we breakfasted on the extra galette cakes that Doree had fried the previous evening.

From 8:30 until noon, we bucked against a very stout head wind and rather large waves coming from the north-northeast. During this time, we crawled forward 7 1/2 miles, averaging only two miles per hour. Along the way, we stopped for a few minutes to admire the high vertical cliffs at the south end of Redrock Island, and finally halted for a half-hour lunch break at noon on the lee side of Mouse Island. Then we slowly made our way forward for another four miles, until our afternoon break at 2:45, on a tiny island just south of Whiteout Island. During the course of that 45 minute rest period on land, a minor miracle took place: the often vindictive *La Vieille* became cooperative! The persistent north-northeasterly wind, which had held us back in the latter part of Day Four and all of Day Five, had kept us windbound throughout Day Six, and had suppressed our progress for six hours this day, suddenly changed dramatically. Now, to our great elation, a new weather front arrived, bringing with it a frisky wind from the south-southeast, headed in our general direction of travel!

Hoisting the sail with enthusiasm, we whisked toward the northeast, our stomachs plummeting every time the canoe dropped into the deep wave troughs that were quickly growing. We were tickled and grateful to have the assistance of a following wind, at long last, after laboring against a persistent head wind for several days straight. In my euphoria, when we arrived at the entrance of the French Narrows, where we were to turn toward the northwest, I accidentally made a hard left turn too soon. This caused us to paddle around an island and start heading back toward the southwest, into the big bay that we had just crossed! The voyageurs had referred to this condition as being *dérouté* (off course). Since the land features did not match my map, I immediately stopped, backtracked, and returned to the correct route. Ah, the joys of constantly bearing the responsibilities of the guide and steersman!

Ah, that's my man! Tim was usually so good at choosing our course and the right directions. Since I could not match his ability at reading maps, I remained silent. (Doree)

After a while, Ben relieved his mother in the role of the *avant*. Since we had just passed through the Barrier Islands via the French Narrows, the helpful following wind was now blocked by the islands behind us, and it would not fill out the sail. But the young man was eager to paddle, to catch up to the mileage that Doree had built up while working against the head winds. As we moved steadily forward, I mentioned that a native site dating from about 1600 to 1650 A.D. had been excavated some ten miles to the east of our location, in Rushing River Provincial Park. During that very early historic period, the native people could not have known of the massive changes which would soon be introduced to their lives, with the arrival of a ready supply of French trade goods, and all of the entanglements that would accompany those goods.

When the time neared 5:00, we began to consider the possibility that we might reach Kenora and the end of our voyage before darkness fell. We did not want to approach the narrow channel leading to the town in the near-dark or dark, since it might be difficult to discern the route under those conditions. In addition, this was Sunday evening, and powerboaters out enjoying the lake for the day would be converging on that same narrow passageway as well.

Ben and I paddled in the comfortably flat conditions for about five miles, during which time we enjoyed watching three bald eagles hunting. Soaring on the rising air currents high above the treetops, they scanned the land and water below for prey, using their amazing eyesight. Then Doree felt a subtle breeze ruffling the wide, floppy brim of her blue hat, and raised the sail to capture a slight amount of assistance. This was just helpful enough to encourage father and son to really dig in and attempt to reach Kenora before darkness descended. As we neared the northern channel of Lake of the Woods, appropriately named the Devil's Gap, we encountered a number of powerboats zipping here and there around the area. As we proceeded northward into the slender passage, we had to be very watchful of the wake that was produced by each boat. However, we were able to easily ride over most of those fast-moving waves; a few of the largest ones presented more of a challenge.

The rim of the sun sank below the western tree line at about 8:30. At that point, in the residual light, we still had a couple of miles of narrow channel to cover, and we had many speeding boats to deal with, traveling both north and south. When we were about two canoe lengths away from Devil's Rock, at a turn in the slenderest part of the channel, we saw a powerboat quickly approaching from the north. Suddenly, a huge one also roared up from behind us. We stepped up our pace as much as we could, hoping to pass through the turn before the two craft met us there. We also hoped that the driver of the boat behind us would have the sense to slow down and wait for us. But instead, he roared by, about five feet to our left in the narrow passageway, as the oncoming one arrived at the very same time. The big powerboat traveling in our direction had a very tall wake. As the driver zoomed by us, we tried to turn sharply to the left at just that moment, to cut into his fast-moving hill of water at an angle. However, plenty of that wake splashed over the gunwales, more than from any of the waves that we had encountered during our entire week-long trip. I muttered some expressions that never made their way into the journal.

After passing Devil's Rock, we encountered only a couple more powerboats. The passage soon widened into a bay, and there we arrived at the town of Kenora without further incident, having advanced 27 miles since pushing off from our campsite twelve hours earlier. At 8:45 P.M., I aimed our bow at the very first floating boathouse that we passed at which we could see a person. To our delight, we were given great assistance and a wonderful evening from the owners of the boathouse and cottage, Bob and Olwin Hobday and their son Manning. They lived here in Kenora during the summer, and in Winnipeg during the rest of the year.

Bob delivered Ben and me to the parking lot of the town police station, to retrieve our van. Back at their cottage, we fastened the canoe on top of the vehicle and loaded all of the gear inside. During that process, to our great surprise, Ben hauled the heaviest Duluth pack from the shoreline up the steep set of stairs and the hill to the van! That skinny twelve-year-old had gotten stronger during the course of the trip.

The Hobdays treated us warmly and generously, as if we were members of their immediate family. First, they fixed us a delicious celebration feast of bacon, eggs, toast, bran muffins, and coffee. Then they put us up for the night in their spare cottage, where we welcomed a comforting shower and got ourselves in order. What a fine way to finish a great canoe trip, with their wonderful hospitality!

We had covered the 162 miles of the river and lake route in 5 1/2 traveling days, plus one windbound day, averaging an excellent thirty miles per day on the water. Ben and Doree had each paddled 81 miles, exactly matching each other's distance. Before the trip, I had marked on the maps the route from the mouth of the Rainy River to Kenora by the shortest, most direct route across Lake of the Woods. This course passed around the west side of Big Island and in a very straight line through the maze of northern islands. This shortest passage totaled 64 miles of lake travel. Our route, via the east side of Big Island, plus a long deviation toward the northeast to quarter the northerly wind and waves, had required us to travel 81 miles on the lake. Thus, our trip turned out to be 81 miles on the Rainy River and 81 miles on Lake of the Woods. From our experiences, it was very clear that the mileage that was paddled by the voyageurs on the large lake was heavily affected by weather conditions.

We had not found the algae content in the lake to be a problem, in contrast to the many early accounts that had reported very murky water and a sickening green scum covering the surface. We did see the millions of tiny plants suspended in the water, but it was not distasteful for either drinking or cooking. The Hobdays, lifelong residents on the lake, indicated that this had been the lightest year for algae that they could remember. They also noted that the unrelenting north wind that we had encountered was very unusual for the area of Lake of the Woods.

After the canoe trip, we spent three more weeks in Canada, as I studied seventeen dugout canoes from Winnipeg westward to the coastal range of B.C. Along the way, we also relished a great deal of marvelous scenery and many interesting historic sites. We returned home via Yellowstone Park, Mount Rushmore, Crazy Horse Monument (where I studied another dugout), the Museum of the Fur Trade, and finally a museum in Minden, Nebraska, where I worked with an additional dugout canoe. During this wonderful trip, Doree and I celebrated our twentieth wedding anniversary. For the occasion, we feasted with Ben at an unusual restaurant deep in cattle country on the Canadian plains, where we grilled our own delicious steaks and ears of corn.

During these three additional weeks that we spent traveling in Canada, we often heard detailed coverage on Canadian radio stations concerning the tense armed confrontation and standoff that was taking place on the shores of the lower Ottawa River, at the Mohawk reserve of Kanesatake and the adjacent non-native community of Oka, a little northwest of Lachine. In May, the city fathers of Oka had expropriated a piece of land which for centuries had served as the traditional burial grounds of the native people, intending to use the property to expand their golf course. When the Mohawks declared the land to be their territory, and erected barricades blocking off their reservation as well as the disputed property, provincial police officers and eventually several thousand federal troops, some manning armored tanks, were dispatched to the scene. After heavily armed warriors on both sides had stared each other down at close range for ten weeks, the confrontation finally ended without gunfire on September 26, due to extensive behind-the-scenes negotiations. The Oka Golf Club did not expand, and the disputed portion of sacred land became an official part of the modern Mohawk cemetery.

When we returned home to the U.S. in mid-September, we were amazed to learn that these dramatic events had gone virtually unmentioned in the American media! The story had been intentionally hidden from view.

X
Eighth Voyage
Winnipeg River, August 12-19, 1991

It is not only for what we do that we are held responsible,
But also for what we do not do.
Molière

Too many people are thinking of security instead of opportunity.
James F. Byrnes

Worry is like a rocking chair.
It will give you something to do, but it won't get you anywhere.
Anonymous

The Winnipeg River runs for about 160 miles from the outlet of Lake of the Woods to Lake Winnipeg, through lands which had been originally inhabited by the Assiniboine and the Cree. Its direction of flow is generally toward the northwest, but it makes one very large loop along the way. As a result, we would be sometimes traveling north or south for a considerable distance, rather than on a westerly bearing. Dropping a total of 348 feet in elevation, the river originally alternated between lake-like sections with only a moderate current and narrow channels of racing current which were often interrupted by roiling rapids and thundering falls. These obstructions required a total of 26 portages for the voyageurs. However, seven hydroelectric dams spaced at intervals along the watercourse now harness most of its drop in elevation, and virtually all of the remaining rapids can be run.

By good fortune, a great deal of the scenery, especially that of the upper half of the river, is as wild as it was during the fur trade era. The upper half of the waterway flows through rather flat Canadian Shield country, while the lower half traverses the prairie region, with its deep layers of deposited soils. The upper 55 miles of the river lies within the province of Ontario; the remaining two-thirds is located in the province of Manitoba.

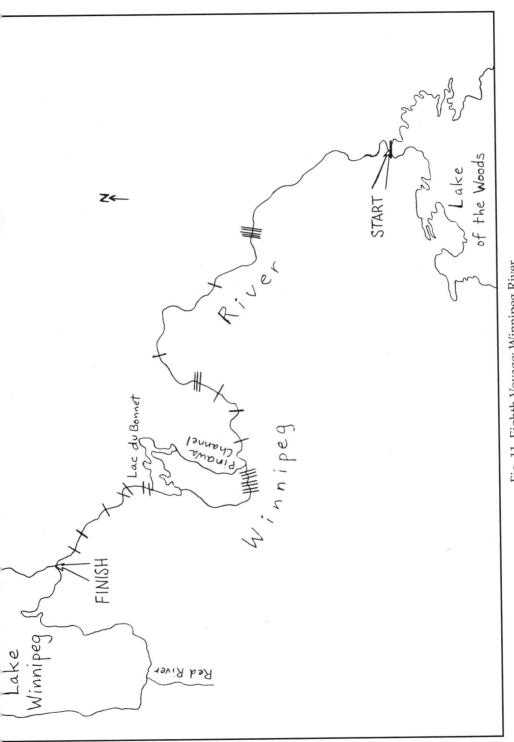

Fig. 11, Eighth Voyage: Winnipeg River

Day One

Fifteen hours of driving through the night and all of the following morning transported us from Ravinia Park, where I had played my closing concert of the summer season, to the town of Kenora, Ontario. Arriving at 12:30 P.M., we stopped at a hamburger restaurant for lunch, and also to buy extra burgers to take out for our evening meal. Then Doree called Bob and Olwin Hobday, at whose boathouse we had ended the previous year's trip, at the north end of Lake of the Woods. We had arranged for them to serve as our shuttle drivers for this voyage, keeping our vehicle until we would phone them from the mouth of the river, in about a week to ten days. When they met us at the restaurant, Olwin said, "When we watched the Grammy Awards show in the spring, we saw that the Chicago Symphony had won the award for the Best Orchestral Performance. Congratulations!" We had recorded Shostakovich's *Symphony Number 1* and *Symphony Number 7* with Leonard Bernstein about two years earlier, during two weeks of concerts that had celebrated the Maestro's seventieth birthday. However, he had not lived to receive the Grammy honors in 1991, having passed away during the previous October. This particular award brought to 58 the total number of Grammy Awards that the C.S.O. had received for our recordings over a span of nineteen years.

Bob led us to a fine put-in place just north of the community of Keewatin, three miles west of Kenora. The little sand beach, at the southern end of the Highway 596 bridge spanning Darlington Bay of the Winnipeg River, lay a quarter-mile east of the head of the ancient portage. That path, the Portage du Rat (Muskrat Carry), had extended for about 150 paces, from a creek mouth on Darlington Bay across the narrow neck of land to Portage Bay on Lake of the Woods.

Putting in at 2:20 P.M. with absolutely beautiful weather conditions, we were elated to exchange our enclosed van for the open-air canoe. Scattered fluffy white clouds hung in place, as if they had been pinned to the light blue background; the air temperature was 85 degrees in the shade, and there was not a hint of a breeze. Everything in the forest seemed to be held in silent, suspended animation, except the gentle current of the gleaming river. For the first couple of miles, much of the solid granite forming the barren shoreline walls was broken into huge squared-off blocks. Red and jack pines stood straight and tall just back from the elevated edge, with the slender spires of spruce trees occasionally lording above them. This was the first time that we had ever canoed within the range of the woodland caribou, a range which stretched from here toward the northwest far beyond our eventual destination of Lake Athabasca. Along our route, we would keep a sharp eye out for these large, stately animals with huge spiked antlers, in the same way that we eagerly watched for all forms of wildlife.

After two miles, we passed the forest-covered Old Fort Island, where the N.W.C. had operated a post from 1790 on; in addition, the H.B.C. Rat Portage Post had done business here from 1836 on. Fifteen years later, the latter facility was moved two miles to the south, onto the shore of Lake of the Woods, after which the community of Kenora grew up around it.

Two hours of relaxed paddling with Doree in the bow seat advanced our canoe five miles. This traveling by arm-powered craft was slow, offering us an abundance of time and opportunities to take in the sights, sounds, and smells, as well as the sensations of heat versus cold, dry versus wet, and heavy exertion versus easy cruising. As we approached a small midstream island for a break, a bald eagle circled overhead a couple of times, and then landed on a limb near the top of a tall dead pine, which stood near the edge of the island. Since a fluffy cloud was positioned in the sky directly behind the tree, the bird stood out in perfect silhouette, a blackish brown eagle against a bright white background. Gliding nearer, we spotted a second eagle near the top of another tall, scraggly dead tree, not far away. Both of them whistled and then flapped away as we landed. At this close range, we were struck by the large size of each bird, with a total wing span measuring about eight feet! At this distance, the splayed feathers at the tip of each outstretched wing looked like five or six long, pointed fingers. During our half-hour break, the eagles again returned to the island; we could hear them exchanging shrill cries back in the stand of red pines, just out of our sight. Meanwhile, as we snacked on jerky and gorp, two large ravens flew very low over us, checking out us and our food. The coal-black birds swooped so low that we could clearly hear the sound of their wings beating the air. All of this avian action took place while we were sitting on the trunk of the largest beaver-felled tree that we had ever seen, about fifteen inches in diameter!

After the break, Ben assumed the duties of the bow paddler, intent on matching his mother's five miles. At this point, he was 13 2/12 years old, about to enter eighth grade. During the previous twelve months, with his appetite seldom assuaged, he had grown three inches in height (to 5 feet 3 inches, a half-inch taller than his mother), and had gained thirteen pounds (to 93 pounds). This added bulk would make him a much stronger paddler than he had been in 1990. In addition to growing in size, he had also just completed all of the requirements for the Eagle Award, the highest rank in Boy Scouts, which he would receive at a ceremony in November.

At mile ten, we slid quietly through Les Petites Dalles (the Little Eaves Troughs), a narrow, quarter-mile-long passageway between the right shore and an adjacent island. At about the middle of the rockbound passage, a double brood of eight adolescent redheaded mergansers scooted away close behind their two mothers, desperate to stay ahead of the ominous green canoe that was bearing down on them.

Doree then took over as the *avant* for the next five miles, soon bringing us to Les Dalles (the Eaves Troughs). This place struck us as being both very special and very spooky. The expanse of the current suddenly narrowed here, being forced to flow between the parallel cliffs of both the left shore and a pair of elongated islands that lay end-to-end. This funneling effect made the current roil and writhe, and also form sinister whirlpools, over the span of half a mile. We coasted down the smooth, downhill stretch in total silence, without paddling, just watching the high walls of rock on each side glide by, and listening to the gurgling, slurping sounds of the several dark whirlpools that we skirted.

Immediately below Les Dalles, two startled cranes flew off in clumsy slow-motion, squawking horribly. At about this location, a short-lived N.W.C. post had been in business during the 1790s, while Les Dalles Post of the H.B.C. had operated here for just a few years starting in 1822. The latter facility had opened in the year following the merger of the two huge competing companies.

We arrived at Cache Point at 8 P.M., having made fifteen miles in 5 2/3 hours, with a relaxing break en route. Not bad after having driven 860 miles through the night and having launched as late as 2:20 P.M.! Even after we landed, the sun continued to beam very warmly; at dusk, the air temperature still measured 75 degrees in the shade. Having eaten burgers twice during the day, we needed no evening hot meal. So we simply set up our camp, enjoyed a fire for a while, and were fast asleep by 10:30.

This night after midnight, the heavens would offer the peak visibility of the annual Perseid meteor shower. We knew that as many as a hundred little fireballs would streak westward each hour, seeming to originate from the Perseus constellation low in the northeastern sky. That massive formation of stars was easy to locate, being K-shaped and about as large as the Big Dipper. However, we were too tuckered out after the long drive and the hours of paddling to stay awake until the wee hours and gaze at the heavens, even though we would have loved to watch this rare celestial action-show, which plays only once a year.

Day Two

The insistent alarm clock roused us from our dreams at 6:45, and we were packed and on the river within eighty minutes. During these exhausting voyages, I found that I would sleep far beyond the optimum eight hours if I did not set the alarm. Rising on time also allowed us to embark in a timely fashion, to take full advantage of the early, non-windy hours of the morning. The gleaming yellow sun in a cloudless blue sky had already warmed the air to 70 degrees at that early hour; in addition, not a hint of breeze was present to disturb the glass-like surface of the river. Ben paddled with me the five miles to the little town of Minaki (the Cree word for blueberry grounds), during the last hour of which a light-to-moderate head wind developed to hinder our progress a bit. Pulling in at a riverside resort, Doree ordered a supply of cheeseburgers, some to eat then and others to take along for later. The proprietor indicated that the predicted high temperature was to be about 90 degrees. After our feast, we were back afloat at 11:10.

Soon I fell into a trance-like state from the steady rhythmic paddling, and my thoughts turned to the hundreds of dried blueberry patties that must have been produced each year at Minaki in ancient times. From the perspective of a three-year-old native girl working alongside the female members of her family and her clan, I pictured the scenes: the expanses of low bushes laden with ripe berries, in the sun-drenched openings between the tall pines; the containers of root-stitched birchbark, filled to the rim with newly-picked blue fruit; the deep wooden mortars and the long slender pestles of wood, which crushed the berries to a thick juicy pulp; and the dark tan mats of woven bulrush leaves, on which the hand-formed patties were laid, to slowly dry and shrink in the heat of the late-summer sun.

An hour later, we took a short break on shore, for a few sips of koolaid and a quick stretching of our legs, and then we began laboring against the strong head wind that had arrived. As an antidote to *La Vieille's* interference with our progress, I chatted with the family about the activities of La Vérendrye and his men on this watercourse. On the map which the commandant created in 1732, after having established Ft. St. Pierre at the head of the Rainy River in 1731 and Ft. St. Charles on Lake of the Woods the following year, he had labeled this as La Fleuve d'Ouest (the River of the West), since it was as yet unexplored and unknown to him. On his chart from five years later, he called it Rivière Ouinipegue (pronounced nearly the same as it is in English, "Winnipeg"). A group of his men, including his son Jean Baptiste and his nephew La Jemmeraye, had paddled down about two-thirds of its length in 1733, and had constructed a trading post which they christened Poste de la Barrière, named after a weir of saplings that Cree fishermen had erected across the narrow width of the river at this place. The trading facility was located just downriver from the outlet of the Falcon River-Whiteshell River route, an alternate canoe passage between Lake of the Woods and the lower Winnipeg River. The Barrier Post was also positioned so that the Frenchmen there could intercept brigades of Cree traders who were accustomed to traveling eastward from the midpoint of the Winnipeg River, up the English River and then down the Albany River, to trade at the H.B.C. post of Albany Fort on the shores of Hudson's Bay. The English River flowed into the Winnipeg River some fifty miles upstream from the Barrier Post. The following summer, in 1734, La Vérendrye's men paddled down the lower Winnipeg River and across the foot of Lake Winnipeg, to establish Ft. Maurepas near the mouth of the Red River.

The location of each of La Vérendrye's trading facilities was chosen for its effectiveness in intercepting Cree brigades that had previously traveled to Hudson's Bay, with the intention of absorbing this commerce which had formerly gone to the British at their Bayside posts. Native brigades had been paddling out to the Bay to trade with Anglos for over sixty years when La Vérendrye first expanded French commerce well to the west of Lake Superior. As the commandant worked his way further toward the northwest each year, he continued to apply the same logic in choosing the sites of his posts. This was reflected in the construction of Ft. Rouge in 1738, at La Fourche (The Fork), the junction of the Red and Assiniboine Rivers, south of Lake Winnipeg; in the building of Ft. La Reine during the same year, a little west of La Fourche on the Assiniboine River, due south of Lake Manitoba; and in the creation of a new Ft. Maurepas in 1739, near the mouth of the Winnipeg River.

These historical discussions of ours certainly made the miles pass quickly. When we halted on shore for a snack break in the middle of the afternoon, we had already pulled the green hull over eleven miles of water since the morning launch. During the break, while munching on peanut butter-smeared crackers and dried apple slices, we were entertained by the activities of two hawks. These birds were particularly interesting to Ben, since his totem animal was the red-tailed hawk. Hitch-hiking on the rising currents of hot air, the two birds cruised in broad circles high over a nearby midstream island, silently hunting for prey far below.

Near 5:00, we rested again for ten minutes, while eating our leftover cheeseburgers from the resort. Then father and son pressed on, first northward and then westward for seven more miles, against a moderate-to-strong head wind, to reach the White Dog Falls Dam. In the process, Ben learned that he could paddle long distances against a stiff oncoming wind nearly as strongly as his mother could.

Five miles before arriving at the dam, we had left the original mainline route, bypassing a winding, seven-mile passage which is no longer accessible for canoes from its upper end. The original river had split into two channels here, flowing along each side of a long east-west island. The dam had been constructed in 1960 at the western end of the southern channel, which had been a long, steep gorge ending in a dramatic waterfall, offering no possibilities to portage. The backwaters of the dam, over which we had traveled, now floods this southern channel. The route which the voyageurs had taken, along the northern channel, is now blocked off at its upper end with broken rock fill, which was installed there at the time of the construction of the dam. This northern passage had originally required three décharges, which had involved unloading all or part of the cargo and running down the canoe, as well as two portages, which had entailed carrying both the cargo and the craft. From east to west, these five obstructions had been called the Grand Décharge, the Portage de la Terre Jaune (Yellow Earth), the Décharge de la

Charrette (Cart), the Portage de la Terre Blanche (White Earth), and the Décharge de la Cave.

We landed on the right shore near the dam at 6:45, to portage around the massive concrete-and-steel obstruction. Within an hour, we had easily completed our three trips over the carry, since the path was downhill over virtually its entire length of 900 paces. On this portage, to his parents' amazement, Ben carried the heaviest Duluth pack, which was a first for him! On the lower reaches of the path, we discovered large moose tracks, as well as moose droppings. At the end of the trail, at a sandy beach in a narrow but deep cove, we decided to call it a day at 7:45 and set up camp there. During twelve hours of traveling, we had progressed twenty miles, mostly against head winds, and had made one portage.

The evening was mild, almost warm. After relaxing in the sandy canyon below the high rock walls for about an hour, we drifted off in the tent by 10:00.

Day Three

When cheerful birdsongs roused us at 6:10, we began our day with stretching exercises, and then broke camp. It was a beautiful morning, 68 degrees, with a blue sky full of billowy clouds. In the sand at the water's edge, Doree found a huge set of tracks from a night visitor, apparently a great blue heron or a crane. The large, three-toed bird tracks measured about six inches in length and about five inches in width.

We headed out at 8:00 under ideal paddling conditions: not too warm, no wind, and beautiful scenery of rocky outcrops and evergreens in every direction. Just around the right turn from our campsite, we ran a fast downhill riffle, which offered no obstructions and only low standing waves at the bottom. Immediately below the riffle, seven stately white pelicans sat in a row on a long boulder in midstream, watching us. Doree teasingly wondered out loud if they were waiting for us to capsize, hoping for a chance to pick our corpses clean afterward. I noted that the elongated beaks of pelicans were designed for scooping up live fish from the water and swallowing them whole. It would be the short curved beaks of eagles, hawks, and ravens that would scavenge our flesh, if we were to ever wind up dead on the shoreline at some point in our journeys.

In 11/2 hours, Ben paddled with me the five miles to the community of White Dog (Wabassimong in the Algonquian languages), on the Islington Indian Reserve. This modern settlement was made up of a row of about fifty houses, strung out along each side of the single road that ran along the high right bank of the river for a mile and a half. Two of the families at the easternmost edge of town had thrown their garbage and old cars down the high rock embankment of the shoreline. We needed to refill our water jug and thermos, so Doree, Ben, and Toby clambered up the bank, while I stayed with the canoe. There was no sign mounted on the general store, but its single gasoline pump out front and its lack of windows (apparently to discourage break-ins) indicated the use of the building. Also, about ten native people and about thirty dogs were all converging there, waiting for the store to open. Among all of these canines in the town of White Dog, all but two were black Labradors. Our Toby, a combination of possibly collie and terrier, seemed to fit the name of the place better, with his light tan coat. Two well-dressed native women approached Doree, smiling warmly, and one asked, "Are you the new teacher?"

At 9:30, the white storekeeper arrived and opened up. He was surly, saying little, watching each person carefully. Every item in the store was very high-priced. Doree bought three pre-made luncheon meat sandwiches, chips, and a two-liter bottle of coke, and filled our two jugs with water.

Proceeding three miles westward in ninety minutes, against a head wind, we arrived at a place where the river bends sharply to the right. There we took a half-hour lunch break, on a beautiful point with a long expanse of pebble beach. It consisted entirely of small, rounded stones in shades of brown and tan, mostly about an inch in diameter. Back in the bushes, we found a wooden sled of the traditional native style, but held together with nails rather than with lashings of cordage or hide thongs. From long exposure to the elements, the wood had been bleached to a light grey hue. If only that ghost-like sled could have whispered some of the adventures that it had seen over the years!

When we returned to the water at noon, the sky had completely cleared, and the temperature had risen to 90 degrees in the shade. A strong west wind arose on the Lac Tetu (Suckling Lake) section of the river. This widened passageway received the waters of the English River, on which native brigades had traveled eastward to reach the Albany River, and eventually Ft. Albany on the shores of Hudson's

Bay. Ben worked a while to complete his ten miles, and then Doree took up the bow paddle. We had a long, slow struggle against wind and waves to reach the northwest corner and outlet of the lake, where Ben paddled a mile from his place in the bow point, to give his mother in the bow seat a little rest. The canoe glided forward about as easily as if we had been paddling a large oak desk.

Just before leaving on this voyage, I had been given a prescription by my dentist for a slight gum infection. When I had asked him about any possible reactions that I might have from the medication while on the canoe trip, he reassured me that it would cause no problems. However, among the various instructions that were printed on the bottle (all of which were rather difficult to follow on a wilderness trip!), one was "Avoid direct sunlight." During the first afternoon and evening on the water, I had encountered no problems from the medication. On the second day, the usual sunburn reactions on my face, neck, and the backs of my hands seemed to be a little more severe that it normally was on paddling jaunts. However, by early on this third day, the redness had become very severe, with stinging and burning sensations. So I immediately stopped taking the pills, and kept wet bandannas tied over my face and the back of both hands throughout the day. With these two changes, the reactions started to diminish, but it took the rest of the trip for my skin to return to its usual degree of English-Irish-German sunburn. (Doree)

After Ms. Kent and I had put in four strenuous hours to advance just eight miles, at 4:00 we reached the ancient Portage de l'Île (Island Carry), at Boundary Falls. At this location, the N.W.C. had established the long-term Portage de l'Île Post in 1789; the H.B.C. had opened a competing facility here four years later. The original carrying route had passed over the midstream island, near its right end. The depth of the path, worn at least a foot below the level of the adjacent forest floor, served as a dramatic testament to the thousands of pairs of moccasins that had trod here over the centuries. In modern times, the channel around the left side of the island had been blasted wide open, making a clear, fast run down, with no standing waves or obstacles except a single huge boulder brooding in the middle of the passageway. Running this left channel with no problems, we took a much-needed food break for 45 minutes, in a cove on the right shore just below the falls. On these trips, I seldom registered hunger; I simply felt run down and lacking in energy whenever my furnace needed refueling.

Following the break, we paddled back upstream to have a closer look at this famous obstacle from the bottom of the right channel. Here, in these deceptive-looking falls, with a sharp drop of three feet of elevation at one spot, a number of voyageur canoes had come to grief over the centuries. In fact, Nicholas Garry of the H.B.C. wrote in 1821: "This is a very dangerous rapid, and so many fatal accidents have attended the [running] of it that it has been interdicted to the servants of both companies [the H.B.C. and the N.W.C., after their amalgamation in that year of 1821].

One of the specific accidents that had taken place here, on August 9, 1800, was graphically described by Alexander Henry the Younger, the N.W.C. trader who was traveling with that particular brigade. All but one of his canoes had been taken over the portage trail, when the four-man crew of the last one decided to run the cataract after partially unloading, to avoid carrying the craft and some of the cargo. Henry wrote: "I perceived the canoe on the N. [right] side coming off to sault the rapids. She had not gone many yards when, by some mismanagement of the foreman, the current bore down her bow full upon the shore, against a rock, upon which the fellow [in the bow], taking the advantage of his situation, jumped, whilst the current whirled the canoe around. The steersman, finding himself within reach of the shore, jumped upon the rock with one of the midmen; the other midman, not being sufficiently active, remained in the canoe, which was instantly carried out and lost to view amongst the high waves. At length she appeared and stood perpendicular for a moment, when she sank down again, and I then perceived the man riding upon a bale of dry goods in the midst of the waves. We made every exertion to get near him, and did not cease calling out to him to take courage and not let go his hold. But alas! he sank under a heavy swell, and when the bale arose the man appeared no more. At this time we were only a few yards from him; but while we were eagerly looking out for him, poor fellow! the whirlpool caught my canoe, and before we could get away she was half full of water. We then made all haste to get to shore, unload, and go in search of the property. The canoe we found flat upon the water, broken in many places. However, we hauled her ashore, and afterward collected as many pieces [of cargo] as we could find. The men had landed a few packages above the rapid [before attempting the run], otherwise our loss would have been still greater. The loss amounted to five bales merchandise, two bales new tobacco, one bale canal tobacco, one bale kettles, one bale balls, one bale shot, one case guns. I was surprised that a keg of sugar drifted down about half a mile below the rapid, as its weight was 87 lbs; it proved to be but little damaged. The kegs of gunpowder also floated a great distance, and did not leak. Whilst we were very busily employed repairing damages, by patching and mending the canoe and drying the property, a few Indians came to us. I employed them to search for the goods, but they could find none."

During the underwater searches for fur trade artifacts which were carried out during the 1960s and 70s, scuba divers discovered more period items in the pool below this rapids than at any of the other rapids that were examined. The finds included an entire wooden case of axes, a bundle of ice chisels, a set of eighteen nested bowls made of solid tin, large amounts of lead balls and shot, two trade guns, myriad glass beads, several knives, a spiked tomahawk, a lead fabric seal, and a piece of twist tobacco.

Departing from the falls at 5:00, Ben and I slogged on with our faces to the west wind through the lower portion of the Eaglenest Lake section of the river. After we had traveled through the faster current of the mid-lake islands and shoals, including passing the 11/2 mile length of Boundary Island, the wind disappeared for the evening as we entered the upper part of the lake. At the boundary line between the provinces of Ontario and Manitoba, Doree took on the role of the *avant* for five miles, until we finally put in for the night at a beautiful sand beach cove, at 7:45.

Since leaving our camp this morning, we had traveled 25 miles in twelve hours, mostly against substantial winds and moderate waves. Having covered fifteen miles on Monday afternoon, twenty miles on Tuesday, and 25 miles today, I had now reached the "paddling machine" stage, able to paddle all day long without feeling it much, except when working against strong head winds; they still drained my energy somewhat. During the course of our travels today, we had observed several bald eagles perched high on dead pines along the edge of the waterway. Projecting limbs of long-dead evergreens were their favorite places to perch, since these limbs had no foliage to interfere with their large wings on takeoffs and landings. (Ben, always sharp, wondered if these skeletal trees were still called "evergreens" even after they had died and had lost all of their green needles.) In addition, we had noted many times today six or seven hawks circling high over an island.

Just before dinner, a potentially dangerous mishap occurred at our camp. I was marking the maps and writing up the end of the day in the journal, while tending the bubbling pot of stew on the tiny stove beside me. When Ben finished inflating by mouth one of the air mattresses, he had a sudden inspiration, which he unfortunately did not think over very carefully. When he playfully lofted the mattress through the air at me, it knocked over both the flaming stove and the steaming pot beside me, spewing stew across the map case and the sand, but luckily not on me! After the initial flurry of excitement, I salvaged for our dinner the half of the stew that had remained on the map case. That was fortunate, since, as the voyageurs used to say, *"On a tous une faim de loup* (we were all as hungry as a wolf)."

After we had eaten, a beautiful quarter-moon rose in the clear eastern sky. The white light from that bright sickle made the surface of the river shimmer, while it also cast long, dim shadows behind every tree and bush. Later, a V formation of about a dozen pelicans cruised silently by our camp, passing directly in front of the silvery crescent. That moment was a quiet but moving benediction to a long day on the ancient canoe trail of our ancestors.

We drifted off to sleep at about 10:00. However, since the evening was so warm, we slept less soundly that usual. At one point, I awakened to the sounds of slow footsteps in the shallow water, very near to the tent. Also, I heard what sounded like water running off the creature's head whenever it dipped its mouth down into the water. Finally, I heard large wings flapping, as a water bird of major proportions took off from the cove. It had most likely been a great blue heron fishing, rather than a crane seeking amphibians.

Day Four

At 6:15, we were off to an early start on another eventful day. As we leisurely took down the tent and packed the gear, I noticed a well-worn game trail coming down the bank from up in the woods. That explained the source of the set of huge moose tracks that Ben had discovered, skirting the water's edge at the north end of our sand beach cove.

When we commenced our forward progress at 8:00, the weather was warm and hazy, 70 degrees already. A strong breeze and medium waves were coming at us from the northeast, making our northward course up Eaglenest Lake slow and difficult. At the northern end of the lake, the channel made a broad 90 degree turn to the west; this was the voyageurs' Grande Équerre (Great Turn). Having forged ahead six miles against the wind and waves in 2 1/2 hours, we paused for a snack break just after the turn, on a small island that was completely surrounded on the fringes of its perimeter with large broken slabs of slate.

Since we had turned due west when rounding La Grande Équerre, the northeasterly wind had fortuitously been transformed into a following wind. So up went the square of blue nylon fabric for a mild assist, helping us advance five miles in the next 1 3/4 hours. Along the way, we encountered a group of about thirty ducklings, with white bodies and black heads and necks. When these young American black ducks noticed our approach, the entire group, still unable to fly, skittered away on the water into a patch of green rushes that flanked the shoreline. As their sixty little wings beat excitedly against the surface of the water, they together made a sound that was amazingly similar to that of a riffle rapids.

When Ben had completed eleven miles for the morning, we took a short break for a snack, after which Doree occupied the bow seat. The sky remained hazy, but the air temp had risen to 78 degrees in the shade, 88 degrees in the sun. Although the breeze from the northeast continued, it had faded some, so that it was no longer vigorous enough to fill the sail. In the silence, the faint sounds of my life preserver flexing with each forward reach and backward pull were very clear to my ears, as were the quiet dip and exit sounds of each of my paddle strokes.

Up to this point in the journey, we had traveled for 75 miles in a winding course that had usually headed either north, northwest, or west. Now we were about to enter the top of a crooked V-shaped jog in the river's course, in which we would travel for about forty miles toward the southwest, and then some thirty miles toward the north.

Immediately after making the change of course, turning to the left, I had anticipated that we would have to make a portage, at Chute à Jacques (Jacques' Falls, now called Lamprey Falls). The voyageurs had made a short carry of sixty paces here along the left shore, to circumvent the original drop of thirteen feet in elevation. However, the backwaters of the dam located five miles downstream, as well as the generous water level during our trip, had transformed this stretch of rapids into just a downhill run of swirling water. The artist Paul

Kane sketched this set of rapids, and recorded the source of its name, when he paddled through here in 1846: "We passed the 'Chute de Jacque,' so called from a man thus named who, being dared by one of his companions to run his canoe over a fall of fifteen or twenty feet, an exploit never attempted before or since, unhesitatingly essayed the bold feat, and pushing off his frail bark, jumped into it, and on rounding a small island darted down the main sheet, his companions meanwhile anxiously watching for his safety from the shore. As might have been expected, he was dashed to pieces and no more seen."

Leaving the Chute, we cruised another five miles to the small town of Pointe du Bois, where a massive dam blocked our passage. The voyageurs had been obliged to make the Portage du Pointe du Bois (Wood Point Carry) here, 285 paces along the right shore, to obviate the ten-foot drop in elevation of the river. We landed on the right shore at 4:00 at the public boat ramp, a little west of the bridge at the mouth of a narrow bay. Just after we had unloaded everything and were ready to start our half-mile portage through the town and around the dam, a powerboat pulled in from the river to the landing. When we asked the driver if there was a grocery store (yes) or a restaurant (no) in the town center, and discussed with him where we ought to put in below the dam, he graciously offered to transport us to a spot below the dam, hauling our canoe and gear on his boat trailer. We gladly accepted his offer! He deposited us at the public park, which was located atop the bluff overlooking the public beach, immediately south of the transformers below the dam. As we rode through the town in his pickup truck, we noted that an earlier possible put-in would have been at the parking lot just below the powerhouse. I sensed that this friendly, middle-aged man would have been just as generous to us if we had encountered each other on the water; I figured he would have been very aware of the challenges that the wake of his craft could present to us.

We took a long-overdue food break on the bluff, then carried everything down to the beach area below, and were off again at 6:15. Immediately, we shot down a slight drop with a fast current, but it offered no obstacles to maneuver around. This spot had required the voyageurs to make the short Portage de la Pointe aux Chênes (Oak Point Carry), about a hundred paces long on the right shore. The Algonquian name for this locale was Kamashawawsing, Two Carrying Places, referring to the two portages in quick succession which were necessary here. Looking back upstream toward the dam, we were struck by the eerie, ugly sight of the former majestic rapids. It was now just a rough decline of dry rocks and boulders below the vertical concrete wall of the dam, with a narrow stream running down its middle bearing the water that was released by the dam's floodgates.

Less than a mile downstream, we paddled through fast water in the narrow channel between the right shore and a small island. This had been the place where the voyageurs had made the Portage du Rocher Brûlé (Burnt Rock Carry) or Portage du Petit Rocher (Little Rock Carry) along the right shoreline for 65 paces. However, the passage, originally dropping eight feet in elevation, had been blasted open in modern times, so that it presented us with only fast current.

Under ideal flat conditions, Ben paddled with me the seven miles to Slave Falls Dam. At this place, the river had originally split around a large island and thundered down more than twenty feet of elevation on each side, in the Chute aux Esclaves (Slave Falls). This magnificent obstacle had required a carry of 660 paces along the right shore. Now a pair of huge dams flank the upriver end of the island, with a portage path that begins in a small bay on the tip of the island, between the two dams. As we approached the landing at 8:00, a beaver swimming in front of us toward the left shore slapped its tail and dived; it did not surface again until it had nearly reached the shoreline. From the right rear corner of the little bay, we followed the trail as it first crossed a set of railway tracks and then became a gravel path flanking the edge of the bluff of the right channel. After a short distance, it joined a cleared and mowed "roadway" running toward the southwest. At the bottom of a small hill, where the mowed roadway continued westward, we took a narrow woods trail that angled off to the right, leading us down to the sandy beach of the shoreline.

We completed our three trips over the portage by 9:00, and set up camp before dark on the tan sand at the end of the path. Another hot day had passed, a very accomplishing one. In twelve hours on the water, we had traveled 28 miles (of which Ben had paddled eighteen), as well as having made our way around two dams. We had also been able to run the Chute à Jacques, which we had expected would require a carry.

This evening was much cooler than the previous one, since the early evening hours had been quite cloudy, with the sunlight blocked.

After trading our usual relaxing massages, we lay down for the night at 10:15, with well-earned weariness.

Day Five

I arose by myself at 6:30, while Doree, Ben, and Toby slept in for an extra hour. The weather was hazy bright, a refreshing 55 degrees. In the early-morning quiet, as I untied the canoe from its anchoring tree back from the beach, I heard rather loud rippling sounds coming from the water's edge. Creeping forward silently to investigate, I came upon thirteen American black ducks slowly working their way upstream, all diving noisily to feed on green plants that grew on the bottom. Thirteen duck tails pointing heavenward in unison made an interesting sight!

The rock formations adjacent to the sandy beach were unusual and fascinating. The main body of the rock was basalt of a jet black color; this matrix was criss-crossed with many slender veins of pink quartzite. Over millions of years, the slightly softer black stone had weathered away some, leaving a spider web of pink veins projecting outward three to four inches from the black surface.

Retracing my steps over the path that we had taken the previous evening, I returned to the upstream end of the island, to visit the head of the channel that was now blocked by the left dam; this concrete barrier was a coffer-dam which had no sluiceway. The narrow channel below the dam was the feature that the voyageurs had called Les Dalles des Morts, the Troughs of the Dead, down which the water from the left-side falls had once roared. After zooming in a straight course for a third of a mile, the frothing water had made a sharp right turn and had then continued straight for the same distance again, before joining the main channel of the river. The name of this channel, the Troughs of the Dead, had apparently reflected the fate that awaited anyone who would attempt to ride down this wild, seething course in a canoe.

After treating ourselves to a relaxed, slow start, we finally put in at 8:45, with excellent conditions for paddling: hazy sunny skies, 72 degrees, and no wind. A half-mile downriver, we watched a great blue heron fishing, as we glided silently by just a short distance away. In the shallows near shore, the long-necked grey bird crouched low on its long bony legs, holding perfectly still. Suddenly, it shot its head downward at a forward angle into the water, and came up with a tiny fish clamped in its long, tapered beak. Later, in the narrows that brought us into Lac Numao, Doree spied a deer standing in the shallows by the right shoreline, drinking from the river. When it saw us, it casually emerged from the water and walked into the woods, without any apparent concern. Shortly before arriving at the sharp right turn in the river that marked the Chute de la Barrière, a V formation of thirteen Canada geese honked directly over us, headed toward the northeast. In less than two hours, we had covered the six miles to the falls, with fine wildlife entertainment along the way.

The Chute de la Barrière (Barrier Falls, now called Sturgeon Falls) was produced by a low ledge of granite bedrock that projected out from the right shore and spanned nearly the entire width of the channel. This obstacle usually obliged the voyageurs to make a portage of 45 paces along the left shoreline. It now bears the distinction of being the only set of rapids on the entire Winnipeg River that is still in its original condition, having never been blasted open, and not being flooded by the backwaters of a dam. Landing on the left bank, we scouted the cataract and decided that we could run down the far left side, where there were no obstructions, just a heavy flow of water in a smooth, glassy tongue. With Ben and Toby on shore beside the rapids photographing our progress, Doree and I raced down the drop; in the process, we did not take in any water from the haystacks below.

At 11:30, we were on our way again. Immediately on the left appeared the mouth of the Whiteshell River, the alternate route for canoes traveling between the northwestern corner of Lake of the Woods and the lower Winnipeg River, which La Vérendrye had documented in 1733. Arrowing over the 21/2 mile length of Nutimik Lake, we noticed that the banks had begun to have much more soil, often in the form of long sand beaches, and less exposed areas of Canadian Shield granite. At the end of the lake was the famous narrows called La Barrière (the Barrier). Here, a large midstream island was connected to the left shore by a narrow neck of land; this blockage crowded the river into a narrow passageway on the right side. It was at this spot in 1733 that La Vérendrye's men encountered a weir of saplings that the native residents had erected across the channel, for harvesting sturgeon with harpoons, and it was near this place that these same Frenchmen established the Poste de la Barrière. When the artist Paul Kane traveled through here in 1846, he recorded in his journal: "We found the black flies and mosquitoes so annoying all night, as to deprive us entirely of sleep." Luckily, we were having little problem with biting insects on this voyage.

While we were traveling the five-mile length of Dorothy Lake, I followed the paddling pace set by Doree (my Dorothy) in the bow position, as was customary. Occasionally during a trip, I would ask her to slow the pace a bit, when I was dealing with a recalcitrant angled breeze or a strong head wind, and needed extra time to complete my J pattern or sweep with each stroke. Otherwise, she set the speed of the strokes, and I simply followed her lead. I had enjoyed watching her paddle in the bow for years now, as she leaned forward at the beginning of each stroke, thrusting the paddle blade deep, and then pulled it back hard while returning her trunk to a vertical position. By working in this way, she used her body weight to add force to the strength of her arms and shoulders. When I dreamily focused on just the shining blade of her paddle, as if it had a life of its own, I saw it cut deep into the water, push the water backward, rise to the surface, swing forward in an outward arc while streaming a cascade of droplets onto the surface of the water, and then smoothly dive again. That golden tan piece of varnished ash seemed to have a spirit of its own, until I noticed the strong arms and hands that were directing its actions.

By this point, Doree had already paddled thirteen miles since this morning's departure, under ideal flat conditions. After completing the length of Dorothy Lake, we took a half-hour break at 1:30, on a small island at the western end of this widened section of the river. This particular place represented the hundred-mile mark of our voyage.

Twenty minutes of cruising beyond the island brought us to the narrows of Grand Rapides, now called Otter Falls. The strong current here, which had originally dropped three feet in elevation, had been run down by westbound voyageurs; eastbound brigades had either lined up it or made a short portage of about 25 paces around it. The backwaters of the modern dam ten miles downstream have now reduced this passageway to an area of fast current, which we easily zipped through. It is highly likely that the name "Grand Rapides" had been applied to this place facetiously by the fur trade personnel, since it had only presented an area of powerful current. However, not all of the voyageurs had taken their canoes through these narrows unscathed. In the area just below the former drop, scuba divers had located an entire wooden case of fur trade articles.

After two more miles of progress, we reached the earthen dam blocking the entrance to the Pinawa Channel on the right shore. This side route, running generally parallel to the main channel, had often been used by the brigades in high water seasons, to avoid the very challenging Rivière Blanche (White River) section of the main channel that lay ahead. The alternate route, about fifteen miles long, extended to the eastern end of Lac du Bonnet. This shallow course, passing through many areas which were thick with wild rice, mosquitoes, and black flies, was only workable for canoe travel during times of high water. Even then, it had presented travelers with a series of rapids that had required eight portages.

A modern river map had indicated that a hundred-pace carry on the right shore would take us around the earthen dam and down to the head of the Pinawa Channel. However, we immediately saw that this would be a dramatic, nearly vertical route down huge pieces of broken rock, descending from the top of the dam to the water far below. This was the steepest route bearing the designation of "portage" that we had ever seen! Checking a snowmobile and cross-country ski trail on the right shore, we found that it looped further away from the Pinawa, never providing an opportunity to get down the steep canyon walls to the river level. The left shore likewise offered only sheer high walls. Another concern of ours was the very low level of the water here at the source of the Pinawa Channel. Since it was already low here, it would certainly not get any better further down. The non-adjustable earthen dam allowed the same amount of water to flow into the side channel at all times, through pipes at its base. Even if we were to manage to get the canoe and all of our gear down to the water level, I imagined that we would be dragging the canoe through shallows during a great deal of this side route. So we decided to use the main channel of the Winnipeg, rather than the Pinawa Channel, which would have only saved us about three miles of travel, and would have probably added a great deal of grief.

While scouting the Pinawa portage, I had twisted my left ankle really badly on a loose rock. I could not have foreseen that this injury would cause me difficulties during the entire remainder of the trip. However, I was thankful that we had been spared one bothersome element on our voyage, one that had plagued Alexander Henry when he had paddled through this place in 1775: "The mosquitoes were here in such clouds as to prevent us from taking aim at the ducks, of which we might else have shot many."

We paddled half a mile to the Sports Club of the town of Pinawa (offering curling, tennis, and golf), where we arrived at 4:45. While Doree was searching for a restaurant, she met a fellow named Barrie on the grounds, working at his hobby of surveying and mapmaking. He arranged for us to have dinner with him in the club restaurant, where we felt a little odd, suddenly emerging from the roughness of the wilderness paddling world into the modern world, where personal appearance is highly emphasized. We feasted on a reuben sandwich, a chicken breast sandwich, and a cheeseburger, while chatting with our new friend. Some years earlier, Barrie had paddled this section of the Winnipeg River, plus the Pinawa Channel, and he was also a local history buff with many interesting stories to relate.

Departing from the Sports Club at 6:45, we were intent upon covering the eight miles to Seven Sisters Dam before dark. We set this goal so that we would not be stuck for the night camping in the huge backwaters area, which was surrounded on both sides for about three miles back from the dam by a tall dike wall made of stones and earth. Ben and I pushed as fast and as hard as we could, without flagging for even a moment. From about three miles away, the huge powerhouse at the dam loomed ominously ahead of us on the mirror-like backwater lake. The sun had been hidden behind dark clouds during most of the two hours that we had been traveling at top speed. However, when we were still about a mile from the dam, the descending fireball finally broke free from the cloud cover and passed into the narrow area of the sky that was clear, just above the western horizon. The beautiful pinkish orange disc cast a shimmering trail of that same hue across the glassy surface of the water, warming our souls in this forsaken place behind the dam. Not long after the rim of the inspirational sun had disappeared below the tree line, we arrived at the dike wall, just to the right of the dam. Since it was then 8:45, we had about an hour of gradually fading light to set up camp for the night.

We quickly unloaded onto the side of the man-made wall of broken stone, which I was pleased to see was gradually angled. From there, it was not too difficult to carry everything up to the top of the dike wall, which lay about twelve to fifteen feet above the waterline.

In addition, at the summit there was plenty of room to pitch our tent, in the area where the wall widened near the powerhouse. So, dealing with the dike had not been nearly as formidable as I had imagined.

Relaxing after all of the work had been completed, we reflected on our day. Under fine conditions, we had put 25 miles of water under our canoe in twelve hours of traveling. In addition, we had checked out the Pinawa Channel, and had spent two hours in pleasant conversation at the club in Pinawa.

Then our family chat turned to the situations that the voyageurs had encountered on the watercourse that we had just covered, in our two-hour push to travel eight miles after leaving the community of Pinawa. Beneath the last five miles of backwaters that we had paddled to reach the dam, the stretch of the Winnipeg River that had originally been called the Rivière Blanche (White River) had once writhed and foamed. This nearly continuous series of white water rapids, covering a span of about five miles, had dropped more than fifty feet in elevation. The obstacles had been divided into seven sets of rapids, each of which had required a short portage. As a group, these were termed the Sept Petits Portages (Seven Little Carries), lying so close together that the entire series could be seen all at the same time from the elevated head of the straight-line sequence. The series of seven portages had only totaled about 500 paces of carrying, but it had involved seven separate unloadings and reloadings, which had cost the men a great deal of time and effort. In modern times, the series of lakes over which we had paddled earlier in the day, actually just widened areas of the river, had been given seven female names. These labels, including Dorothy Lake, had been applied in honor of the seven sets of rapids that had been flooded out by the backwaters of the Seven Sisters dam, which had been constructed in 1931 and enlarged in 1949.

Day Six

I surfaced from my dreams at 6:15, to update the journal and maps from the previous evening, after which the family joined me to begin packing at 7:30. We could not know that a long, hard day lay ahead, one that would hone our skills of patience and perseverance.

Portaging around the right end of the dam, we walked along the gravel service road and then down a rather steep rocky slope, to load our canoe literally in the shadow of the dam. This spot was located about twenty feet downstream from the endmost right floodgate, near the head of the long spillway channel which had been blasted out of solid rock for 3/4 of a mile downriver along the right shoreline. At the moment, all of the heavy outflow of the dam was being released from the far left gates, with only a little water being let out of the right gates. Thus, where we put in, the current was only moderate. We loaded our canoe in the midst of about fifteen people who were fishing at the base of the right floodgate on this Saturday morning (most of whom appeared to be eastern European and Asian immigrants to Canada), and were underway at 8:15. We then enjoyed a very fast ride down the spillway channel for about 3/4 of a mile, zooming past mostly high rock walls. The current was very fast, but without any obstructions. Upon ending this exhilarating ride through the blasted-out channel, we faced the realities of a strident head wind coming from the north and the choppy waves that it was generating.

Immediately after leaving the dam, the river had begun traveling on a new course, one which would first take us generally northward for about thirty miles and then northwestward for some twenty miles, to finally reach Lake Winnipeg. Ben paddled strongly in the bow seat for about four miles, doing excellent work against the persistent wind. I kept our course hugging the right shore, to take advantage of a little shelter from the gusts wherever the river angled slightly toward the northwest. After Doree took over as the *avant*, we faced much larger oncoming waves, as the river proceeded straight north. The miles and the hours crawled slowly by. While passing the Whiteshell nuclear reactor station on the right shore, we clawed our way diagonally across to the left bank, working against three-foot waves. Since the course of the river here angled slightly toward the northeast, we could take advantage of a little shelter from the wind by crowding the left shore. While we made the traverse, we took in some water over the bow from the biggest waves.

Just after the crossing, we disturbed two very young bald eagles that were perched on a small tree beside the left shoreline. These two youngsters, having hatched only three to four months earlier, could barely fly; they simply flapped awkwardly from tree to tree, trying to stay a little ahead of us. Their two parents circled high above, calling out encouragement, and also warning us to stay clear of their offspring! Finally, one of the young ones became either too tired or too frightened to fly any further; it then stayed perched on a large sapling, waiting until we had paddled slowly by.

At 10:45, we took a welcome one-hour break on the western bank, having struggled to push forward seven miles in 21/2 hours under very demanding conditions. However, the warm sun had sometimes broken through the thick grey cloud cover during that time, brightening the scene and making it seem less forlorn. During our break, the air temperature rose to 65 degrees while the sun was out. This period of respite from the grueling labor was very rejuvenating, restoring our energy, allowing our cramped muscles to stretch, and bringing at least temporary relief to our abused butts. Rest periods had also served the voyageurs in the very same way. When the conditions allowed it, the men took breaks that were usually about ten to fifteen minutes long, during which they smoked their pipes. These rest periods were spaced out during the day of travel based on a flexible system of elapsed time and expended energy. The periods of time between them varied considerably, based on the often changing variations in travel conditions. Thus, there was no general rule about the duration of time or distance between these rest stops, which were called *pipes* (pronounced "peeps" in French). However, when the conditions were moderate and the crew could stop generally anywhere they wished, they did tend to take a break after about each hour of paddling. Both the distance and the elapsed time between rest stops, as well as the breaks themselves, were referred to as "pipes." As a result, the length of a certain body of water, or the amount of time that it usually took to paddle it, was often expressed in a certain number of pipes.

Before pushing off, we tried a different arrangement within the canoe, in an attempt to help keep the tall waves from sloshing in over the gunwales at the bow end. Doree traded places with the big black pack, nestling it in the central compartment behind the bow seat; she then took its former place in the stern point behind me. This caused Ben and the bow to ride high over the large oncoming waves; however, it also made steering nearly impossible for me, since the amount of the rearward hull that was in the water had been much reduced. So we switched back to our usual arrangement of having the passenger sit in the central compartment behind the bow paddler.

Beginning at about the Seven Sisters dam, both shores of the river had become high banks of soil, much like those of the Rainy River. This indicated that we had completed the transition from the

Canadian Shield region into the prairie region, with its thick layers of deposited soils. The new environment would continue westward on the mainline canoe route for the remainder of the Winnipeg River, all of Lake Winnipeg, the lower Saskatchewan River, and the route for about forty miles north of the Saskatchewan. This marked the first time in about 1,400 miles, ever since leaving the lower Ottawa River, that westbound voyageurs (and the Kent family) would not be traveling in rocky Canadian Shield country. Although the Rainy River had presented a soil-laden environment, it did not represent an eastern projection of the prairie region; rather, it was simply an accumulation of soil atop Canadian Shield bedrock. Our present environment was truly the eastern edge of the prairie region, even though it was covered with evergreen forest.

We slowly made our way parallel to the left shore against the wind and waves, sometimes receiving a bit of shelter from the shoreline ahead of us, but at other times bucking oncoming three-foot whitecaps. However, through it all we continued to maintain our positive attitude, which was crucial during a canoe trip. Over the course of two hours, we were able to advance five miles to the town of Lac du Bonnet, where we stopped at the marina at 1:45.

My twisted left ankle from the previous day was feeling somewhat better; it seemed to have healed considerably during the night. But it had concerned me when we had made the steep portage down the rocky slope this morning to load in below the dam. The joint hurt only when I turned it or stepped on an uneven surface; but there were plenty of uneven surfaces out here, every time I walked on land!

Doree and Ben, with Toby serving as their guide, found a little restaurant in the town, and brought back a supply of burgers, hot dogs, fries, and cokes to share with me at the canoe. After our repast, while basking in the warm sunlight that occasionally broke through the clouds, we set out at 3:00, and managed to struggle forward for another five miles in two hours, with *Vent Frais* and other songs keeping us going.

When we emerged onto the exposed open waters of Lac du Bonnet (Cap Lake), the brawny north wind that had plagued us for eight hours and eighteen miles was simply too much to handle. Here, the forces of nature had many miles of open water to build up four-foot whitecaps. We managed to land on the point which projects from the western shore at the foot of the lake, where we found two big log homes and a large expanse of mowed grass that covered nearly the entire point. At one of the houses, we explained our predicament to the folks there, who were renting the home for a few days from the owner, their friend. With the kind permission of the renters, we settled into our sleeping bags *en plein air*, beneath a stand of small oaks near the end of the grass-covered point. Here we would wait for a letup of the recalcitrant wind and waves. After a time, we enjoyed the second installment of cheeseburgers, hot dogs, and cokes from the restaurant in the town.

During our meal, we chatted about the strenuous but very satisfying research trip of 6,500 miles that I had made by myself in June, traveling with the van. During that jaunt, I had studied 34 dugout canoes at thirty different locations, on a massive loop that took me through Missouri, Iowa, Kansas, Nebraska, Colorado, Wyoming, Montana, Minnesota, central Ontario, and Michigan. A few weeks later, I had studied another five dugouts in Wisconsin and Minnesota.

After napping off and on until 8 P.M., we finally decided to set up camp beneath the sheltering oak grove, admitting that we were *dégradé*, windbound. This day, while Doree had led us in singing numerous traditional songs to keep us going, in an almost continuous loop of French tunes, Ben had paddled seventeen of the eighteen miles that we had advanced, all against relentless head winds and moderately large waves. Quite a feat for a skinny boy who had just celebrated his thirteenth birthday!

Day Seven

When I emerged from the tent at 4:15 A.M., the weather conditions were benign and welcoming. Bright stars glimmered in the immense black sky, and the formerly boisterous wind and waves had completely calmed during our seven hours of sleep. Dismantling and packing up in the dim starlight, without using a flashlight, we delighted in being so familiar with our gear and procedures that we could easily break camp, put the canoe in the water, load in and secure the packs, and depart, all with only starlight to illuminate the scene.

By the time we put paddles to the water at 5:40, the stars were fading and a dim light was beginning to appear low in the eastern sky; the air temperature was 52 degrees. At the south end of Lac du

Bonnet, the air was clear. However, as we headed northwestward toward the west side of the lake, we entered an area of dense fog. To keep track of our position, we skirted the western shoreline rather closely, catching occasional glimpses of the passing ethereal shore in the dim light and the thick fog. On several occasions, as we glided silently toward a batch of geese or gulls that were sleeping like miniature ghosts on the water, they suddenly exploded from the surface into startled flight.

Gradually, a pale golden light tinged the eastern sky, which slowly turned to a deep pinkish orange, beneath the layer of solid cloud cover hanging low in the heavens. At about 6:30, the rim of the huge orange disc slowly began to emerge above the horizon, but so subdued by the fog that we could peer directly at the fiery ball as it ascended to expose its full size.

We followed the western shoreline for ninety minutes through the mist, passing over the five-mile length of the lake, and then took a break on one of the islands that nearly fill its north end. After a half-hour of rest, we paddled one mile further to the MacArthur Dam, where we landed on the left shore to portage. During that last mile of traveling, I had pointed out that we were gliding over two small sets of rapids which had been flooded out by the backwaters of the dam. These had once required two short carries, first the twenty paces of the Portage du Bonnet (Cap Carry), and then a half-mile later the ninety paces of the Portage du Cap du Bonnet (the Carry of Cap Cape). Near these obstructions at the outlet of the lake, a N.W.C. post had operated for a few years during the 1790s; it was later replaced by a H.B.C. facility after the amalgamation of the two fur trade companies in 1821.

The portage around the MacArthur Dam involved hiking over the embankment above the powerhouse and then down to the long inlet just below the dam. Walking in the lead, I headed directly for the end of the inlet, loaded with my Duluth pack on my back and four smaller items in my hands. Near the end of the carry, as I entered the little woods that bordered the riverbank, my injured left ankle turned, causing me to slide down the small embankment and fall with my load at the bottom. It then took me two trips to get all of my items through the thick growth of saplings along the border of the inlet and to the shore, where there was a landing area which was somewhat cleared. Seeing my hassles from somewhat of a distance,

Doree and Ben were able to hike along a better route to the landing place. However, when Ben was two-thirds of the way down the slope, he fell backwards while loaded with the other heavy Duluth pack; so Doree finished carrying it to the landing for him.

Doree and I finally pushed off at 8:45, and made the five-mile jaunt to the Great Falls Dam in less than two hours, paddling over two now-flooded obstructions en route. The first of these, located three miles below the previous rapids, had obliged the voyageurs to make the mile-long Grand Portage du Bonnet. This long carry had circumvented the highest falls on the entire Winnipeg River, which had dropped about 35 feet in elevation with a deafening roar and a great deal of white froth. Less than half a mile further downstream, they had encountered a rapids that dropped eight feet in elevation. This second obstacle had required the Portage du Petit Rocher (Little Rock Carry), which was sometimes called the Portage du Galet (Gravel Bank Carry), over a trail that was 285 paces long.

For our carry around the Great Falls Dam, we were blessed with warm and sunny weather, beneath robin's egg blue skies that were ornamented with many cottonball clouds. Just to the left of the powerhouse, we unloaded onto the dike wall made of broken stone, and portaged down the hill around the fenced property of the dam. Near the put-in place in the bay just below the dam, my left ankle gave out again, and I fell a second time with my Duluth pack, on the rough stony descent leading to the flat rock ledges at the shoreline. Loading in was a little ticklish here, since the bare ledges that bordered the bay were very slippery wherever they were wet. For a minute or two, I almost forgot that we were having fun.

Shortly after paddling away from the dam site at noon, we pulled up to a wooden dock on the left shore. While I stayed with the canoe, the other members of the family, both human and canine, clambered up the high bank to the town, to look for a restaurant. From the only person who could be found, they learned that the single food source in the entire community (which was virtually a ghost town) was located on the main highway, a half-mile from the river. After walking to the highway, they could locate neither the store nor anyone to give them further directions. So a disappointed crew paddled away from Great Falls, Manitoba at 12:30. As we were leaving, a powerboat pulled up to the dock; its operator, a tattoo artist who commutes regularly from there to the city of Winnipeg to work, explained that the houses had been originally occupied by the construction crews who had been brought in to build the dam. When the project had been completed, all of the residents had departed for greener pastures.

Upon leaving the dam, the course of the river changed to a northwesterly direction, which it would maintain in a gently winding fashion for its final stretch of twenty miles down to Lake Winnipeg. Downstream 1 1/2 miles, we hustled down the fast current in the left channel of the Sault de la Terre Blanche (White Earth Falls), sometimes called the Sault de la Vase Blanche (White Mud Falls), which had been blasted open in modern times to facilitate powerboat traffic. This obstacle, along with its portage of 330 paces over a tall hill on the right shore, had been the subject of a sketch by Paul Kane when he passed through here in 1846; a few years later, the artist produced a painting of the scene. From this point downriver, the voyageurs had been impressed with the low soil banks, which are now mainly farmlands. As we neared the little town of St. George, the low green fields stretching away from the riverbank and the glistening placid river reminded Doree and me of the fields and adjacent canals that we had seen throughout Holland, during the two years in which we had lived in Europe during the 1970s.

Silver Falls, which we had expected to be able to run near either shore, turned out to be just fast water with a surface that was a little choppy in midstream. The backwaters of the Pine Falls dam, six miles downriver, had flooded three obstacles which had confronted the voyageurs in this stretch. These obstructions had obliged the men to make the three Portages des Eaux Qui Remuent (the three Carries of the Troubled Waters or Stirred-Up Waters). The first two portages were located here at the present Silver Falls, where the water had once dropped fifteen feet in elevation down a slope that was two hundred yards long, with six parallel ridges across the channel giving the descent the appearance of a roaring staircase of white water. This impressive obstacle had formerly been circumvented by first a carry of 150 paces, and then a second carry of 285 paces a short distance away. A downstream paddle of 3 1/2 miles had brought the ancient travelers to the third Troubled Waters obstacle, which could sometimes be handled as a décharge, with an unloaded or half-loaded canoe, rather than requiring a full portage of both cargo and craft.

Although the high temperature only reached 68 degrees at the height of this afternoon, the sun beaming down on us felt comfortably warm. As was typical on most long days of paddling, our minds were the main active part of us, with the physical aspects of traveling submerged into semiconscious, automatic activities. In these situations, our conversations, ranging over a very wide variety of topics, kept us well occupied. And sometimes we just day-dreamed in silence.

As the sunlight kissed my closed eyelids, I captured bits and pieces of April of 1990, when Tim and I had flown to Japan with the Symphony. Although his three-week schedule of concerts and recording sessions was heavy, the work load was offset by the special evenings that were hosted by the Japanese, offering extravagant banquets of sushi, sashimi, and tempura. On a day off during the second week, the two of us took a two-hour train ride to Nikko, nestled in the mountains eighty miles north of Tokyo. Dreamy memories of funny little monkeys perched on road signs along the way, the magnificent Toshugo Shrine from the 1600s set in a tranquil forest, and, later in the day, Tim practicing his trumpet at sunset on the hazy shores of Lake Chuzenjiko, at an elevation of 4,000 feet: all of these scenes played out slowly in my mind. The Arais, our Japanese friends from our two years of living in Germany in the mid-1970s, invited us to their home in Kamakura, where we all visited the nearby enormous bronze Great Buddha, more than seven hundred years old. Sakura (cherry blossoms) and peonies were in bloom everywhere; they were particularly profuse in Ueno-Koen Park, where I visited the pandas. All of the Orchestra's concerts were sold out, but in Tokyo I managed to hear Bruchner's Symphony Number Eight *from a dimly lit backstage spot in Suntory Hall. However, the most touching experience of all was traveling by myself to Hiroshima, on Earth Day. The museum there told the horrific story of the massive loss of over 200,000 people, some of them having their skin melted off their bodies from the intense heat, others only leaving shadows of their bodies on the walls of buildings. More amazing, Hiroshima has now completely revived, a thriving port city with a population of one million people...I awakened with a start from my reveries, as drops of water from Tim's paddle landed on the back of my neck. (Doree)*

At 3:45, we arrived at the last dam on the river, Pine Falls Dam, having glided over the final rapids on the river which had once required a carry. Here at the Portage des Pins (Pine Carry), a trail 260 paces long had circumvented a low falls, which now lies silent beneath the backwaters of the dam. Just as we approached the left shore, we surprised a red fox standing in the tall grass on the bank.

The rust-colored animal looked at us for a moment, turned, and casually ambled back into the woods, with its white-tipped bushy tail following close behind. This avid hunter had probably been seeking mice or moles, or even rabbits and hares, in the thick green grass that grew right down to the riverbank at this spot.

We portaged around the dam on the left, hiking over the man-made stone embankment that stood beside the powerhouse, then alongside the bases of the transmission towers, across the highway, and down a tall grassy hill, to a place just below the dam. Dropping our second load onto the ground, we let out shrieks of jubilation. What a great feeling it was to finally have the last of the hydro dams of the Winnipeg River behind us! We had made our way around seven of them during this trip, including three on this day alone.

Avidly harnessing the power of flowing water, Canada produces more hydroelectricity than any other country in the world; in fact, it creates fifteen percent of the total hydro power that is produced on the entire planet. Fully 63 percent of the electricity that is used in Canada comes from hydro dams; however, the people of the U.S. are the main consumers of Canada's energy. Doree and I look forward to the day when we will all conserve electricity better, and also when wind and solar power, as well as underwater hydro turbines driven by underwater currents, will eliminate the need to construct ugly dams, which actually alter the watercourses themselves.

At 5:00, we were afloat again, uplifted by the children's song about selling a few chestnuts for five pennies: *"A cinq sous les petits marons; je vous les donne, je vous les donne."* Shortly, I steered our bow toward the left shore, to land at the little town of Pine Falls, where Doree, Ben, and Toby left to find a phone. They hoped to make arrangements with the Hobdays to meet us at the mouth of the river, about three hours of paddling for us, and about the same amount of driving time from Kenora for them. While the family was gone, I updated the journal, while basking in the sun and the loud country music that floated across the river from a house on the far shore. We were momentarily brushing up against "civilization!"

The family crew soon returned with sandwiches, chips, and cokes, and the news that the Hobdays had suggested an improved shuttle arrangement: they would meet us at noon the following day, bringing both our van and their car. Then, we could head directly for the western U.S., instead of first having to return a shuttle driver to

Kenora. This excellent plan would give us extra time to both proceed to Lake Winnipeg and then spend the night there, before ending the voyage.

For the last eight miles of the river, we coursed over the mirror-like surface, reveling in the perfect weather and the ideal flat paddling conditions, which previous hardships had taught us to appreciate deeply. Just past the pulp mill and its encircling log boom along the left shore at the town of Pine Falls, we rushed down the Mantiou Rapids. This was a half-mile stretch of unaltered fast water and swirling whirlpools, which had not usually required a portage in ancient times. Just below this fun section, I explained that, on the right shore in this area, La Vérendrye's men had constructed a new Ft. Maurepas in 1739, replacing the facility by the same name which they had established five years earlier, near the mouth of the Red River at the foot of Lake Winnipeg.

As we approached the mouth of the waterway after two hours of fast and easy progress, the bright sun was positioned directly in front of us, very low in the western sky. Gleaming brilliantly on the glassy surface of the river, it gave us the surrealistic impression that we were floating on a mirror rather than paddling on water. This was one of those moments which I sometimes referred to as a "Heaven is where you are standing" moment. That particular line from a long-forgotten poem had resonated and stayed with me, and it would come to the surface of my mind each time I would encounter a situation in which everything was just as it should be. Those times were especially obvious during demanding canoe trips, when we would feel the sensations of peace and satisfaction that came when the conditions were just right, for both paddling and reveling in the scenery. This was one of the most valuable rewards that we received from experiencing considerable dosages of discomfort, fear, danger, and exhaustion while paddling. Those negative elements allowed us to know just how bad conditions could get, and to clearly register just how good the conditions were when every element was in order.

As we rounded Bruyère Point on our left at 8:15, marking the final few yards of the river, the broad expanse of Lake Winnipeg opened up before us. The water was absolutely flat, glistening like silver in the early-evening sun. However, as we headed for the left shore to make camp for the night, we immediately received a first-hand taste of some of the traditional features of canoe travel on the southern half of Lake Winnipeg. Shallows with just a few inches of depth extended a great distance out from the shore, and the soft clay bottom sucked and clung thickly to our shoes as we all dragged the canoe, in just a couple inches of water, as close as possible to the shoreline before unloading.

We had finally reached our destination! We landed beside a partially-burned hulk of a huge wooden barge, made of squared beams about fifteen inches thick that had been fastened together with huge spikes, as well as with some bolts and nuts. Bathed in copper-colored light, we set up camp for the last time, and then watched the golden disc sink slowly beneath the horizon beyond Traverse Bay.

Long into the evening, the dancing flames of Ben's driftwood fire mesmerized us. The burning wood crackled and popped, sending orange-red sparks whirling upward into the darkness. Then, as the *coup de grace* of our journey, a fantastic show of northern lights commenced. The rays of the display, in various shades of greenish-white and blue-green, seemed to emanate from an area directly overhead; they covered nearly all of the northern sky, from east to west and from high overhead down to nearly the northern horizon.

This was a profound moment for me, to be sharing the same magical sky that had amazed countless generations of native and French people in the past. (Doree)

This astounding phenomenon, called the aurora borealis, is produced when charged protons and electrons speeding away from the sun (called solar wind) are drawn by the earth's magnetic field toward the magnetic north and south poles. There, the solar wind crashes into atoms of gas in the upper atmosphere, energizing the gas and making it glow. The pastel color of the light depends on both the altitude and the type of gas: greenish-white, green, and red hues are produced by oxygen, pink shades are created by nitrogen, and blue and purple hues are produced by hydrogen and helium. For about 45 minutes, we marveled at the ever-changing patterns and shades of the undulating, swirling curtains of colored light; afterward, sated, we crawled into the tent for a well-deserved rest.

This had been a marathon day. Since 5:40 this morning, we had advanced 32 miles in 14 1/2 hours on the water, without any sail assist, including making three portages around power dams and running one rapids. The total distance from our put-in at Keewatin to this campsite on open Lake Winnipeg had been 163 miles. Young Ben had stretched and strengthened his shoulders while paddling exactly one hundred of those miles in the bow position. We had covered the 163 miles in 6 1/2 days, averaging 25 miles of progress a day, including the portages. In the process, we had circumvented seven dams and had run four rapids.

Day Eight

Opening my eyes to the call of the alarm clock at 7:30, I looked over at Ben, still fast asleep. Now age thirteen, he had come so far since the first trip eight years earlier, testing himself and growing further toward manhood with each voyage, as his French ancestors had done three and four centuries ago. With some regret, I thought of Kevin not being here with the family.

When my two crew members finally surfaced, unlike most of our days on the water, we relaxed and chatted in the tent, as I brought the journal up to date from the evening before. In our conversation, I mentioned that the city of Winnipeg, about 65 miles toward the southwest from our tent, was located at the exact east-west center of Canada. In addition, in our westerly trek over the course of eight voyages, we had now reached the eastern edge of a much drier environment. The region from Montreal to the eastern side of Lake Superior annually receives about thirty to forty inches of precipitation, while the area extending from Lake Superior to the southern end of Lake Winnipeg receives about twenty to thirty inches per year. In contrast, the region through which the mainline canoe route passes from the southern end of Lake Winnipeg to Lake Athabasca is wetted by only about ten to twenty inches of precipitation each year.

Outside the tent, we explored the remains of the old wooden barge beside our camp. In its day, the craft must have been pulled by a steamboat up and down Lake Winnipeg. In honor of our journey's end, Ben created long-snouted, tall-standing effigies of himself, his parents, and his dog, from driftwood branches that he had scavenged along the shoreline. To make the figures look more realistic, he outfitted them with our hats and neck bandannas.

The weather was again ideal: a pale azure sky with a few fat white clouds ambling eastward, a lazy breeze wafting from the south, and 72 degrees in the shade as we broke camp. Looking out on the lake, however, we were dismayed to see that the water level was far lower than it had been the night before. We were now about an eighth of a mile across very gooey mud flats from the shallows! Loading Toby and all of the gear except the two Duluth packs into the canoe, we carried the craft out for a considerable distance, until we had reached a water depth of about two feet. Then Ben stayed with the canoe while Doree and I slogged back for the two large packs. Finally, we had to push the craft out about another eighth of a mile, all the while sinking into the soft muddy bottom, until we reached sufficient water depth for paddling.

While I rode as the lounging passenger in the center section behind Doree, with Toby resting on my lap, Ben gained some experience as the *gouvernail*, working in the stern position to steer us against a troublesome side breeze. It took nearly an hour to travel from the river mouth at Bruyère Point back up the 11/2 miles to the native community of Fort Alexander on the southern shore. Arriving there at 11:30 for our noon rendezvous with the Hobdays, we unloaded for the last time, and portaged everything from the river up to the road which runs from the reservation school down to the riverbank. The Fort Alexander Indian Reserve extends from the mouth of the river upstream for about six miles, to the town of Pine Falls. Walking to the nearby cemetery, we visited its flat-roofed chapel made of field stones, which was apparently no longer used, since it had been vandalized somewhat. We noted that the majority of the names on the headstones were French-Canadian, and that the area of paupers' graves was quite extensive: about twenty to thirty graves had only simple, unmarked wooden crosses.

Near this site, the Poste du Bas de la Rivière (Foot of the River Post) had functioned as a very important facility for the French from the 1740s on, as well as for both French and Anglo traders after 1760. Ft. de La Rivière Ouinipeck (pronounced "Winnipeg") was operated here by independent Montreal traders during the 1760s, and Ft. Bas de la Rivière of the N.W.C. was constructed at this location in 1792, to replace an earlier warehouse of the same company. The H.B.C. facility called Pointe-au-Foutre House did business here during the 1790s, while the X.Y.C. also competed at this place for a time during the same period. After the 1821 amalgamation of the N.W.C. and the H.B.C., this facility just above the river mouth was renamed Ft. Alexander.

For many decades, the posts at this location served as primary pemmican distribution centers, supplying the brigades that traveled along the northwestern portions of the mainline canoe route. From the mouth of the Winnipeg River, it was only about forty miles southwest to an environment of mixed grassland-forest and the original range of the bison, and only another thirty miles further to reach the open prairie grasslands. Buffalo pemmican, produced in these two regions, was transported to the posts here at the river mouth, for distribution as provisions for the brigades which were traveling to and from the far northwest. The same procedure was also carried out at the H.B.C. post of Cumberland House on the lower Saskatchewan River.

In addition, a major canoe yard had been operated at the posts which were located here at the mouth of the Winnipeg, first by the French and later by personnel of the N.W.C. When Alexander Mackenzie of this company traveled through here in 1789, he noted, "Here also the French had their principal inland depot, and got their canoes made." Other than the Cedar Lake section of the lower Saskatchewan River, just west of the upper end of Lake Winnipeg, the mouth of the Winnipeg River was the farthest west on the mainline canoe route at which northern white cedar grew. This wood was by far the most appropriate material for constructing all of the wooden elements of birchbark canoes. In contrast to the limited western availability of white cedar, good supplies of birchbark, as well as spruce roots for stitching the canoes, could be harvested throughout the entire length of the mainline route.

When the Hobday family arrived at Ft. Alexander with both our van and their car, we loaded everything into and onto our vehicle, and then we all drove back to the town of Pine Falls. There we enjoyed a meal of fried chicken, fries, slaw, and cokes, to celebrate that we had now completed 1,100 miles on the mainline fur trade route northwestward from Montreal. Finally, about 4:00, we said our thank-yous and goodbyes to our friends, who had been true Samaritans, willingly helping us out during two different journeys.

Then we began our long trek across the U.S. prairies and plains, commencing a four-week trip in which I would study 34 dugout canoes in the region of Idaho, Washington, Oregon, and California.

Ben's principal at the junior high readily accepted his late arrival, since the canoeing experience had deepened his education in many ways. In addition, after the canoe jaunt, he had also taken in many other educational places. For example, while Tim was poring over dugouts, Ben and I swam in the Snake River at one of the camping places of the Lewis and Clark Expedition; he and I explored the fifty acres of Buchart Gardens near Victoria, B.C., where a limestone quarry has been converted into a landscaped blooming wonder; and we visited Crater Lake in Idaho, the deepest lake in the U.S. at 1,932 feet. In addition, Tim joined us for a weekend of hiking in Redwood National Park, where we admired a redwood tree that is about six hundred years old and is 368 feet tall. Then on to the magnificent Grand Canyon, where we hiked along the southern rim and explored ruins of ancient Anasazi stone houses. Finally, we relished the scenic beauty and the diverse wildlife while hiking in Rocky Mountain National Park, before returning home. (Doree)

XI

Ninth Voyage
Lower Sturgeon Weir River, Namew,
Cross, and Cumberland Lakes,
and Saskatchewan River
August 11-18, 1992

À coeur vaillant rien d'impossible.
(Nothing is impossible for a brave heart.)

French proverb

The tragedy of life
is not so much what men suffer,
But rather what they miss.

Thomas Carlyle

The manner in which
a man chooses to gamble
Indicates his character or lack of it.

William Saroyan

Everybody knows
if you are too careful,
you are so occupied in being careful
that you are sure to stumble over something.

Gertrude Stein

Having previously completed four voyages east of Lake Huron, and then four more trips west of Lake Superior, we would now skip Lake Winnipeg in our westward progression, to return to it in a few years. After we would finish the series of twelve river excursions to the far northwest, finally reaching Ft. Chipewyan on Lake Athabasca, we would then paddle the three massive lakes of

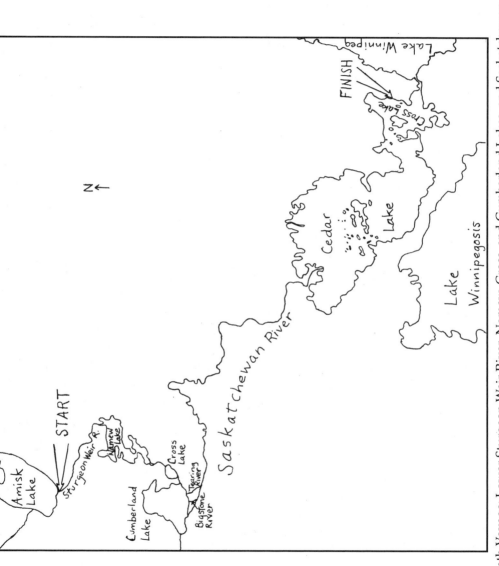

Fig. 12, Ninth Voyage: Lower Sturgeon Weir River, Namew, Cross, and Cumberland Lakes, and Saskatchewan River

Huron, Winnipeg, and Superior, in that order.

This year's voyage, through lands which had been originally inhabited by the Cree nation, would involve two extremely different rivers and the three intervening lakes which lie between them. However, the entire venture would take place within the prairie region. Lying outside of the Canadian Shield environment, the low rock formations which were sometimes exposed along this route were sedimentary limestone, while the forest cover consisted mostly of spruce and larch (tamarack), with some jack pines and scattered birches and poplars interspersed. The first hundred miles of our meandering southeasterly voyage would take place within the province of Saskatchewan, while the latter portion of roughly 170 miles would take place in the province of Manitoba. Since every fifteen degrees of longitude on the globe represents one hour on the clock, we would be traveling in the Mountain Time Zone in Saskatchewan, and in the Central Time Zone in Manitoba. The dividing line between these two zones follows the boundary line between the two provinces.

As was customary, I had spent a great deal of time during the previous winter and spring studying historic travel journals and early maps of the route, and marking on the modern topographical maps the names and locations of the known historic trading posts, native settlements, special land features, and portages. I had also indicated on the charts the obstructions which we would encounter along the route, and the mileages that we would cover on the water. During these months of preparation, I had also repaired or replaced as necessary any items of clothing and gear, working against the running list that I kept of such tasks during the course of each trip. Finally, I had arranged the shuttle driver, and had mapped out the travels that we would undertake after completing the canoe voyage. During the summer, Doree had acquired the various food items, had dried or otherwise prepared them as needed, and had packaged them according to their usages. By August, we were completely prepared, and were raring to go. While paddling this year, we would be celebrating the 350th anniversary of the founding of the fur trade center of Montreal in 1642. The first of our many direct ancestors to live in that settlement had arrived there nine years later, after the population had swelled to 156 persons.

Leaving Ravinia Park on Sunday evening after the closing concert of the summer season, Doree and I traded off the driving duties for the next 22 hours straight. During that period, we stopped only when necessary to refill the gas tank and clear the squashed bugs from the windshield, and one time to consume a chicken dinner after crossing the border into Canada. While the other two humans and Toby slept, Doree mentally replayed the opera excerpts that the C.S.O. had performed on Sunday's program, including arias from Puccini's *Madama Butterfly*, which kept her eyelids from drooping during the long hours on the road. The main advantage of these increasingly longer drives to the put-in place was that Doree and I could each use our non-driving time to doze for many hours, on the elevated sleeping platform that was built into the rear half of the van.

When we finally reached the small community of Grand Rapids, Manitoba at 7:00 on Monday evening, we first visited the mouth of the Saskatchewan River, where it empties into Lake Winnipeg. If the Grand Rapids Dam and Generating Station had not been built two miles upstream in 1965, this grassy area at the junction of river and lake would have been our final destination on this particular paddling trip. The original channel of the river for twelve miles above the mouth, the stretch which the French had called the Rivière Bourbon, had flowed through a limestone gorge in the form of a backward letter S lying in an east-west position. In the lower half of the S, westbound voyageurs had first paddled upriver from the mouth for about three miles to reach the Grand Rapides, which dropped about 45 feet in elevation over the span of three thrashing, frothing miles. Here, they had lined their canoes for nearly two miles against the powerful current, and then had made the mile-long Portage du Grand Rapides along the north shore. In the upper half of the S-shaped passage, they had first paddled upstream for about three miles, then lined up a mile-long rapids (sometimes having to carry over the hundred-yard Portage du Rocher Rouge in that section), paddled another mile, lined up through a set of rapids flowing between a number of islands, traveled an additional mile, and finally lined up the Rapides du Lac Traverse. This had brought them to Lac Traverse (Crossing Lake, now called Cross Bay), the easternmost section of Lac Bourbon (now called Cedar Lake). Eastbound voyageurs had often been able to run down the entire stretch of twelve miles in fully loaded canoes, managing each of its obstacles when the water level was sufficiently high. At the base of the Grand Rapides, native fishermen had harvested large numbers of sturgeon in ancient times, using harpoons to land these huge fish.

When the hydro dam was constructed, the water of the river was redirected straight east through the lower half of the S-shaped passage, by blasting out a new channel. Near the eastern end of this passage, the dam was built, and a straight spillway channel was dug out of the solid limestone, extending due east from the dam to the original channel near the river mouth. Dike walls were constructed westward from the dam for about seven miles along both the north and south shorelines, to confine and funnel the water to the dam, cutting off nearly all of the flow down the original curved route of the lowest portion of the channel. We hiked through the area where the river had once tumbled and raged down the magnificent Grand Rapides. What a strange sensation it was to clamber over and around the rocks and boulders which had once been part of a frightening, teeming rapids, a cataract that had dropped 45 feet in elevation! It is now just a dry, limestone-strewn wasteland, considerably overgrown with low bushes, through which only a small amount of water flows dejectedly down its center. The power dam raised the water levels in the backwaters area by about twelve feet, flooding out the upper half of the S-shaped narrow channel at the end of the Saskatchewan River. This same head pond also converted the section of the river lying just to the west of the original narrow channel, which for many centuries had been a massive widened area of shallow water with surrounding swampy land, called Lac Bourbon (now Cedar Lake), into an even larger shallow, swampy area. Technically, this body of water is now considered to be the tenth largest man-made lake in the world, even though it had already been a sprawling, shallow lake for centuries before the dam was constructed. The massive dam of concrete and steel which has impounded this water produces about one quarter of the electricity that is utilized by the entire province of Manitoba.

Instead of paddling to the ugly flooded area that is surrounded by dike walls behind the dam, we would end our canoe trip by traveling nine miles north of the head of the original twelve-mile channel. Thus, we would remain on the original Lac Traverse section of the lower Saskatchewan, now called Cross Bay, and avoid the entire devastated region of the dam. Our shuttle driver would be Fred Hobbs, the Cree-Irish owner and operator of Hobbs Resort, a fishing camp on the northeastern side of Cross Bay. When we arrived at the lodge, cabins, and campground of his resort at about 9 P.M., we were pleased to learn from Fred that the water level in the main Saskatchewan River, as well as in the Muddy Bay, Cedar Lake, and Cross Bay sections of the widened river near its end, was very high this season. As a result, there would probably be plenty of water in the expanses of reed beds that crowd many parts of these three swampy, lake-like areas in the final section of our voyage, facilitating our paddling. However, this plentiful water depth might also mean that we would encounter flooded shorelines in this same lower region when seeking places to camp at night.

Day One

After six hours of sleep in our van, we awakened to the alarm clock at 4:00 A.M., dressed in our paddling clothes in the pitch dark, and set off an hour later with Fred and his son Corey, age fourteen. We would travel together in our van for 290 miles (all but the last twenty of those miles on paved roads), to the put-in place at the head of the lower Sturgeon Weir River, at the outlet of Lac Amisk (Beaver Lake in Cree). Then Fred would return with our vehicle to his camp, and keep it there until our arrival in about ten days to two weeks.

While driving in the grey light of dawn about ninety miles north of Grand Rapids, I was elated to spot a silver fox, silver-tipped black from nose to tail tip, at the mouth of its den near the road! I interpreted the sighting of this rare creature, which was also my totem animal, as an excellent omen for the voyage that lay ahead. Later, a cow moose trotted across the road ahead of us. When we stopped at Flin Flon for gas, we also bought a good supply of burgers, some to eat then and others to take along for consuming on the river. Near the end of the seven-hour drive, we paused at the community of Denare Beach, near the upper end of Lac Amisk, to arrange our shuttle driver for the 1993 trip. Finally, we arrived at the head of the lower Sturgeon Weir River at noon; our total mileage from Ravinia Park to this launching place had been 1,440 miles.

At 12:45, we shoved off with the lively song *Entendez Vous sur L'Ormeau*, knowing that we would need high spirits to deal with the watercourse that lay ahead. It was no coincidence that the French had called this stretch of 25 miles of water the Rivière Maligne (Spiteful or Malicious River), with its shallow depths, almost continuous rapids filled with rocks and exposed ledges, and fast current due to the drop of 91 feet in elevation. Limestone in hues of light tan and off-white appeared everywhere: along the low rocky shorelines, the exposed midstream boulders and ledges, and the loose, sharp-edged rocks littering the riverbed beneath us. This was a river to be traveled slowly and cautiously.

By good fortune, the weather was cooperative on this day: a light blue sky half-filled with white cloud cover, 70 degrees in the shade, and no wind. As we made our way downstream through the tall evergreen forest, we ran at a leisurely pace each of the rapids that we encountered, scouting the more serious ones from the shore and reading the others from the canoe. From his better vantage point in the bow seat, Ben sometimes shouted out directions to me, to avoid the rocks that he could see suddenly looming under the surface in front of the hull, hidden from my sight. In addition, he applied draw strokes and pry strokes as needed to move the bow around obstructions. In the chilly water, we walked the canoe through the many shallow areas, picking our way around and between the nearly constant obstacles, sometimes stumbling on loose rocks on the bottom even though the water was beautifully clear. Occasionally while we were paddling, the bottom of the craft ground against large rounded boulders, which lay in wait just low enough beneath the glistening sunlit surface so that they did not produce any tell-tale riffles to give us advance warning. If we had been traveling in a birchbark canoe, each of these light scrapes and bumps could have inflicted damage on the bark skin of the craft. At a number of locations, big exposed rocks lay scattered in an irregular row extending almost entirely across the river. At each of these places, we slowly walked the canoe through the narrow spaces between the boulders. Ben and I were in the water nearly as much as we were in the craft, while Doree, as the passenger, was frequently obliged to slosh along in the river, to allow the canoe bottom to float above the threatening rocks. Only Toby, on his perch atop the packs, was allowed to remain dry, an honor that was accorded to our distinguished mascot who kept us smiling with his laid-back demeanor.

At one point, we watched a cow moose and her spring-born twin calves placidly munching water plants in the knee-deep shallows near the right shore, as we slowly waded through the rapids nearby. Amid the babbling and swishing of water tumbling over rocks, we went unnoticed by the three gangly, shoulder-humped animals, which had poor eyesight but sharp hearing. The cow, dark reddish brown in color, eventually clambered up the bank, followed a minute or two later by her light brown calves. The water here was shallow enough for easy wading for the two youngsters, but they had learned to swim at about the age of seven days, and were accustomed to swimming across deep rivers and lakes whenever necessary. Later, on a broad curve in the channel, we startled a gaggle of four Canada geese, who burst into the air with a thundering of wings and excited honking. Not long afterward, this same quartet flapped back upstream over us in a diagonal line, still gabbling loudly. After five miles of tiresome progress, at 2:30 we floated quietly in an eddy for a few minutes, eating our remaining burgers from Flin Flon and resting a bit. The sounds of our chewing were covered by a chipmunk chattering and scolding from the rocky shoreline, as well as a crow cawing raucously from the spire of a nearby spruce.

Ben, now age 14 2/12, was about to commence senior high school after this journey. Since the previous August, he had grown 41/2 inches in height (to 5 feet 71/2 inches, now a half-inch taller than his father) and had gained fifteen pounds in weight (to 108 pounds). This additional bulk, as well as his lanky build with long arms and legs, had made him an even stronger paddler and pack carrier than he had been during the previous trip. Year by year, Doree and I had come to rely more and more on Ben's physical and mental abilities as we took on these demanding wilderness jaunts. This was particularly true in light of the fact that neither of his parents was particularly large. At 5 feet 21/2 inches and 115 pounds, Doree was a half-inch shorter and 37 pounds lighter than the national average for adult women in the U.S., while my height of 5 feet 7 inches and weight of 145 pounds was two inches and 35 pounds less than the national average for adult men.

When we reached the ten-mile mark at 4:30, Doree took over the role of the bow paddler. One mile downstream, we paused for a half-hour break to investigate a trapper's cabin on the high earthen left bank. In addition to the house, a nearby outhouse, storage shed, and dog enclosure were also nestled beneath the stand of tall jack pines and four mature birches. On each of the three log buildings, the cracks between the horizontal timbers had been chinked with slender saplings nailed on the exterior and thick moss jammed into place on the interior. The cozy, low-roofed house was sparsely furnished, with a cast iron stove for heating and cooking, three iron bed frames equipped with mouse-chewed mattresses, and a small table. In addition, several wooden stretcher boards for drying marten and otter hides hung on nails protruding from the walls. On this comfortable summer day, it was not easy for us to imagine the severe hardships that trappers had endured through many lonely winters at this place, where temperatures sometimes sank as low as minus 40 degrees Fahrenheit.

Returning to the river, Doree and I continued to run rapids and wade shallows. However, after only a few minutes, Ben wanted back into the action to further test his new muscles, so Doree obligingly returned to the passenger position. While flashing through one set of rapids, three white pelicans rose awkwardly from a midstream boulder and flapped away in a linear formation. Later, we roused a bald eagle from its perch high atop a dead jack pine. Just a couple of miles further, an otter swimming across a quiet bay in front of us dived silently. Since this sleek brown creature with a long tapered tail was Doree's totem animal, we perceived this quiet sighting as a blessing on our trip. At about 6:00, a line of black clouds rolled in from the west and dropped a gentle rain on us for a half-hour, before continuing its eastward journey. To bring the day to a close at 7:45, we ran a big rapids just above the mouth of the Rivière du Rat (Rat River, now called Goose River), where the voyageurs had nearly always made a portage of 175 yards along the left shoreline. Just below the tossing rapids, Doree located a campsite on a large, open expanse of flat limestone on the left shore, near the end of the ancient portage trail. Here, there had been sufficient room for an entire brigade to overturn their canoes to make the necessary repairs with spruce roots and melted pitch, and to then spend the night beneath the shelter of those overturned craft. While setting up our camp, I imagined the hundreds of times that hearty laughter had echoed off the enclosing forest of spruce and tamarack at this spot. I pictured crews of voyageurs relaxing around their fires, after a long, grueling day of wrestling their bark canoes through the challenges of this difficult waterway.

During our first half-day, we had traveled 21 miles in seven hours on the water, covering more than 80 percent of this troublesome river. We had averaged three miles per hour, even while dealing with all of the obstructions and taking time out for several breaks. Ben had served as the *avant* for twenty miles with no apparent strain, deftly running all of the rapids and easily walking the canoe through shallows and around obstacles, after which he still had plenty of energy left to set up camp. It was very clear to us parents that our son was growing stronger and more capable with each passing year.

We had nearly completed the Rivière Maligne without having to make a single portage, even though this "Malicious River" had indeed been rather recalcitrant. The lack of carries was partly due to the durability of our fiberglass canoe compared to that of a birchbark version, although we were not careless in our treatment of our modern craft. The voyageurs of old had made various portages along this watercourse, and numerous carries were not unusual for modern-day paddlers in state-of-the-art craft, particularly when water levels were low. We may have been blessed with a more generous water level than was usual for late summer; however, the flow certainly seemed quite shallow to us. We were very accustomed to jumping over the gunwales and wading the canoe through shallow areas, as well as through mazes of obstructions in any walkable depths, especially when danger was not a major issue. For us, portaging was always reserved for the very last resort, just as it had been in ancient times.

Lounging on our air mattresses spread out on the expansive limestone ledge, we admired in silence the full moon, hanging fat and white at a low elevation in the southeastern sky. Over the span of thousands of years, millions of people had gazed at that same bright, shadow-casting disc, including our ancestors. I was determined to learn the life stories of as many of those folks as I possibly could.

Day Two

In the chill of early dawn, thick grey mist shrouded the entire river, as a solitary white pelican patrolled the water directly in front of our camp, a ghost-like sentry carrying out his self-appointed duties. Heading directly for the overturned canoe, I used silver-grey duct tape and a short peeled segment of a slender branch to quickly repair the lower cutwater edge at the bow, which had lost a chunk the day before when colliding with a submerged boulder. Ninety minutes later, the restored prow was again slicing through river water, beneath plenty of thin white clouds scattered across a pale blue sky. After a half-hour, the sun burned off the fog hovering over the water, and the air temperature rose to 55 degrees.

The lower reaches of the Sturgeon Weir River were much less formidable, with greater water depths and fewer obstacles. With Ben in the bow seat, we quickly zipped down the last four miles of the waterway, maneuvering around the various obstacles in an almost continuous rapids. At the mouth, where it empties into Lac Namew, we passed the native settlement of Sturgeon Landing, with its few houses strung out over a half-mile along both banks of the river. Flashing through the rapids, we only caught a quick glimpse of this community which anchors the Sturgeon-Weir Indian Reserve, a piece of land measuring 21/2 by 4 miles that nestles between a broad bend in the river and the lakeshore. The Namew Lake Post had been established here at the river mouth in 1778 by Montreal-based traders, while Blondeau's Post, also supplied from Montreal, had operated here for a short time during the 1770s or 1780s.

Three shallow lakes now stood between us and the Rivière Saskatchewan: Lacs Namew, Cross, and Cumberland. These three bodies of water, creating a southwesterly jog of more than thirty miles in the otherwise southeasterly mainline route, had been traditionally difficult to travel, since *La Vieille* easily whipped up considerable wave action in their shallow waters. In addition, the thick reed beds, extending out for a considerable distance from the shoreline on the lowest portion of Namew and all of Cross and Cumberland, made near-shore travel very challenging on these waters.

We would be traveling over the full seventeen-mile length of Lac Namew (Sturgeon Lake in Cree). Although its maximum width is about ten miles, two massive peninsulas jut out at an angle from the east and west shores to nearly meet each other toward the bottom of the lake, creating a narrows which is only 3/10 of a mile wide. As soon as we entered the lake, we faced a moderate head wind and rather large waves from the southwest, exactly against our direction of travel. Setting a course that quartered the waves slightly, I fixed as my goal a prominent headland that protruded from the right shore eight miles straight ahead, and mentally prepared for a long, hard slog.

At this point, with the canoe rocking unsteadily in the waves, I traded places with Ben. While facing forward and holding onto the gunwales in front of the bow seat, he stood up and spread his legs wide, creating a small opening that I could crawl through just above the seat, into the space in front of him. Then, still facing forward and keeping low, he moved backward into the passenger position, all the while maintaining his grip on the gunwales. Ever since the boys had been little, we had regularly changed positions in all directions by this method, with no one ever falling overboard. To help steady the canoe somewhat during these maneuvers, Tim would brace with his paddle, holding it out to the side so that its blade was at an angle in the water.

Having had the luxury of being transported during most of the previous day, I now paid my dues in the role of the avant. *To ease the situation somewhat, I psychologically transformed the persistent oncoming wind and waves into "an opportunity to work off fat." By imagining chunks of fat being carried off by the blasts of wind, I justified the not-so-good sensations of the hard work at hand.*

Facing pain and danger is an integral part of the total package of paddling the immense distances that we cover: nearly 1,400 miles of character-building already behind us, and more than that amount still to go. As a therapist, I often help individuals move beyond denying their sadness or anger, so they can learn from it, transform it, and move on. On these expeditions, I have had to twist my brain in the opposite direction, to actually encourage the blocking of sensations for segments of time. Without developing a positive orientation toward struggle and perseverance, I could never have grown the courage to complete these trips! With each passing year, I have expanded considerably in my tolerance of physical discomfort. Unlike Tim, who has practiced denial of discomfort and pain every day for decades, I am rarely capable of losing myself entirely. But the intense joy of the pristine wilderness that canoeing affords us refocuses my attention. Tim has further helped to disguise our sensations of physical pain during these long, arduous voyages, by telling amazingly involved stories, which he freely embellishes in his delightfully odd and humorous way. (Doree)

By noon, we reached the projecting headland, whose low shoreline of barren limestone ledges we had been watching in the distance, beneath the dark evergreen forest, for most of the crossing. Since the morning launch, we had pressed forward twelve miles in 3 1/2 hours, with the eight miles on the lake having been hard-earned ones against oncoming wind and waves. At the far end of the headland, we took a welcome half-hour lunch break on a long cobble beach. From the water's edge back about ten yards to the tree line of tamarack and spruce, hundreds of lashing storms had kept all but a little sparse grass from taking hold. This swath of land was completely covered with fist-sized stones, an interesting mixture of flat pieces of off-white limestone interspersed with rounded chunks of grey-black basalt and pink granite, both unusual stones in this prairie region dominated by limestone. On this very bumpy "mattress," Ben took a short nap, basking in the comfortable air temperature of 75 degrees beneath mostly cloudy skies. For my part, I daydreamed about the Montreal-based post called White's House which had done business in this area for a few years during the 1790s.

After the break, Doree resumed her work in the bow, as we again labored against the forces of nature for another 2 1/2 hours, advancing six miles to the narrows of Lac Namew. En route through this mile-long passage that led to the Cross Bay section of the lake, both of the shorelines presented low ledges of exposed tan limestone. In this area, Ben spotted a mink at the edge of the water. A short time later, while we were taking a five-minute break at the bottom of the narrows, a strung-out wedge of about 75 Canada geese flapped overhead, looking like a string of dark beads stretched across the grey-white background. We imagined that the moderate honking that was being done within the group kept up their communal spirit, much like the encouraging words that we exchanged in the canoe. Ben then took on the bow paddler's role, in which he continued to buck the head wind and waves to the end of Cross Bay, making just 2 1/2 miles in ninety minutes. Then Doree relieved him in the five-mile stretch of the Whitney Narrows, a slender, reed-grown passageway that was often as narrow as 2/10 of a mile. The Frobisher-Primeau Post, established in 1778, had been operated by these two Montreal-based traders in this area for just a few years.

For our trek across the two-mile diameter of the round Lac la Croix (Cross Lake), Ben again resumed the role of the *avant*. This trading back and forth of the labor between mother and son seemed to work well for my teammates, keeping them both from becoming exhausted and discouraged. To avoid the shallows and the reed-choked waters in both the Whitney Narrows below Lac Namew and in Lac la Croix, I steered our bow for the deepest central areas of these two bodies of water. As a result, we had little problem with either lack of depth or thick vegetation holding us back. As we began our traverse of Lac la Croix, the wind that had plagued us nearly all day faded completely away, leaving a perfectly flat surface for easy traveling. When the sun began to slip down behind the edge of the world, warm golden hues of twilight tinted the entire western sky and the glassy lake.

From the canoe, Doree located a flat limestone ledge at the entrance of Cumberland Lake, which would serve very well for a campsite in this area of mostly muddy, reed-covered shorelines. As we approached the landing place at 9:00, about ten Canada geese and some thirty ducks sprang into the air. Access to the camping spot entailed a short haul of the gear through the deep sticky mud of the lake bottom and a bed of reeds before climbing up onto the low ledge. Toby was overjoyed to have space to frolic on the ledge, since he had spent the entire day lounging atop the packs. Bringing smiles to our tired faces, he barked and rolled onto his back, with his little legs wildly pawing the air. Dried turkey breast and mixed vegetables, along with a handful of rice, were soon bubbling in our single pot, atop the little circle of blue flames of the gas stove. While we munched our nourishing meal, we tallied our hard-earned progress for the day: since 8:20 this morning, we had covered 29 miles, mostly against moderately strong head winds and medium-to large-waves. In the bow position, Doree had worked for eleven miles, while Ben had done eighteen miles in that role.

As we exchanged massages on the air mattresses beside the fire, the hues in both the sky and the bottoms of the clouds gradually shifted, from pale gold to pinkish orange to dark purple, and finally to black. While the bright full moon rose slowly in the southeast, our conversation turned to the significance of where we were in the world. Cumberland House, the very first inland post to be established by the Hudson's Bay Company, had been built in 1774 six miles southwest of our campsite. Before then, H.B.C. traders had operated for more than a century only at widely separated posts along the shoreline of Hudson's Bay and James Bay, supplied by ocean-going ships from the mother country. They had relied on the native customers to haul their furs and hides by canoe out to the coastline, and then return to their home areas with their newly-acquired merchandise. Beginning with La Vérendrye's entry into the region west of Lake Superior in 1731, French traders intercepted a great deal of the commerce which had formerly flowed out to the Bayside posts. This disruptive activity was also continued after 1760 by French and Anglo traders operating out of Montreal. As a result, H.B.C. traders were finally forced to move inland, to deal with the native populations in their own locales, as St. Lawrence-based French traders had been doing ever since 1653, twelve decades earlier.

Departing from York Fort on Hudson's Bay in 1774, Samuel Hearne and six H.B.C. colleagues had traveled southwestward up the Hayes River to the top of Lake Winnipeg. After crossing the top of the lake, they had continued northwestward up the Saskatchewan River to Cumberland Lake. At this place, they had established a post on the southern shore of the lake, two miles west of the mouth of the Tearing River, on the mainline canoe route from Montreal. In subsequent years, the Company would build additional posts further up the Saskatchewan, and eventually throughout all of the far-flung north and northwest, in direct competition with the Montreal-based traders, a number of whom formed the N.W.C. (first informally in 1779, and then formally four years later). As the H.B.C. developed its interior trade, York Fort became the main depot of import and export for that commerce.

In 1776, two years after Cumberland House had been established, the H.B.C. employees there began building birchbark canoes, assisted by native craftworkers. Eventually, this post became the primary canoe-building place for Company posts in the interior, along with its subsidiary facility of Hudson House, about two hundred miles further up the Saskatchewan River. However, the H.B.C. struggled for a half-century to acquire sufficient numbers of canoes that were large enough. This issue was only solved in 1821, with the amalgamation of the H.B.C. and the N.W.C. From then on, the canoes that were built in the interior for the use of the combined companies were provided mostly by the long-established sources of the N.W.C. During its fifty years of dealing with shortages of birchbark canoes, the H.B.C. had actively pursued the use of wooden boats on its transport routes in the interior, wherever such usage was possible. As a result, the Company based on Hudson's Bay was never as deeply focused on canoe transport as the traders who were based on the St. Lawrence.

The H.B.C. made a considerable number of significant improvements in its business practices in 1779, just five years after the Company had first initiated trading in the interior at Cumberland House, and had begun to deal with the transportation of peltries and supplies in the hinterlands. This occurred when the French trader Germain Maugenest abandoned his debts and obligations to his long time Michilimackinac outfitter, and defected to London to work for the H.B.C. His invaluable advice concerning efficient and sensible French methods brought about major operational changes in the Company, which altered considerably the way that the firm carried out business in North America. Thereafter, items of cargo were packed in bales, kegs, and chests that were of convenient sizes for hand carrying, with a weight limit per piece of about ninety pounds; meat was deboned and packed in small kegs, rather than having its bones left in and being packed in large, ungainly barrels; bales of cargo were wrapped in lightweight canvas, for protection against abrasion, dirt, and moisture, and the entire cargo was covered with tarps while en route in watercraft; lidded copper pots were introduced as items of trade; and the point system was introduced for blankets, to identify their various sizes and weights. Maugenest also designed a wooden bateau which was much more efficient for inland travel than those vessels which had been used until then by the Company.

It was also here at Cumberland House, just six miles from the campsite of the Kent family, that the illustrious map-maker David Thompson had first learned the skills of surveying and astronomy. This training, taking place in 1788, was provided by the H.B.C. surveyor Philip Turnor, during the eighteen-year-old Thompson's recovery from a seriously broken right leg. Nine years later, Thompson would switch his allegiances to the N.W.C., and he would ultimately complete his master map of the vast region between Lake Superior and the Pacific in 1814. In 1792, the H.B.C. rebuilt the Cumberland post 11/2 miles further west, a mile down the Bigstone River; the following year, rival N.W.C. traders established their own post nearby. In 1814, Gabriel Franchère observed that, when personnel of the N.W.C. were outbound from their far northwestern posts and were headed for the annual rendezvous at Ft. William, they typically left their native and Métis families at the Cumberland post, until the men returned in late summer.

About a hundred miles southwest of Cumberland was a mixed grassland-forest environment, and the original range of the bison, while open grasslands lay some seventy miles further toward the southwest. In both of these regions, buffalo pemmican was produced, after which it was transported to the two competing Cumberland posts. Each of these facilities operated as a major food depot and distribution center, supplying the brigades as they traveled both eastward and westward along the mainline route.

In about 1875, an accident of nature wrought major changes in the health of Cumberland Lake, which until then had been a body of clear water with bountiful fishing. The Saskatchewan River at that time flowed eastward about three miles south of the lake, while water from the lake flowed into the Saskatchewan via two outlets, the Bigstone River on the west and the Tearing River three miles further toward the east. One spring during the 1870s, massive ice jams blocked the Saskatchewan to the west of Cumberland Lake, causing the river's water to overflow northward for several miles. These raging floodwaters invaded the Torch River and Mossy River, which had always emptied into the western end of Cumberland Lake. As a result, much of the water of the Saskatchewan River thereafter flowed through this newly gouged channel and into the western end of the lake, carrying with it vast amounts of silt, which soon ruined the clarity of the lake and drastically reduced its depth. This invading river water also created a great deal of swampland to the west of the lake, and increased the outflow of the two outlets of the lake, the Bigstone and Tearing Rivers. The silt buildup on the bottom of Cumberland Lake, and the resulting reduction in its depth, continued each and every year, even as we approached the body of water in 1992. Little did we know just how intimately we would experience that phenomenon the very next day.

Day Three

After eight full hours of rejuvenating rest, we surfaced to delightful weather: 74 degrees in the shade, a blue sky with almost no clouds, and virtually no breeze. Ninety minutes later, Doree and I launched westward onto Cumberland Lake and easily made six miles in two hours under ideal paddling conditions. When we arrived at the head of the Tearing River at 11:15, we looked forward to taking a southeasterly course down the fast current of this intimate river for ten miles, and then happily gliding out onto the waters of the Saskatchewan River. However, life does not always deliver the expected.

After traveling just a short distance downstream, we were astounded to encounter a tall dam made of earth and rocks completely blocking the channel of the river! Clambering to the top of the obstruction, we saw that no culverts had been installed at the base of the wall, so virtually no water could seep through to feed the watercourse that we had intended to paddle. The passage behind the new dam, where thousands of canoes had traveled over the span of many centuries, was now just scattered puddles, boulders, and wildflowers growing in muddy soil. What a weird, surrealistic situation this was, an absolute first for us in our years of paddling! All adventures involve some surprises, but this situation was certainly at the outer edge of the range of surprises. Seeking some explanations and some recourse, Ben, Toby, and I hiked three-quarters of a mile on the gravel road that ran westward from the dam. However, we gave up before reaching its end, and returned to Doree at the canoe.

Setting off at 12:15, we headed west on Cumberland Lake, on a course that ran parallel to the southern shoreline. Our intention was to reach the head of the Bigstone River, about 31/2 miles away. This alternate route to the Saskatchewan River, involving the other outlet of Cumberland Lake, would entail a five-mile paddle from the lake down the Bigstone, traveling toward the southwest, plus one portage around a rapids, to finally reach the Saskatchewan. Ben and I worked against a moderate head wind on the lake for ninety minutes, making slow progress. To avoid the thick reed beds standing six feet tall that extended far out from the shoreline, and also to have water that was sufficiently deep to paddle, we were obliged to stay about a quarter-mile out from the shore. As a result, unbeknown to us, we could not discern the very narrow opening in the reeds that marked the head of the Bigstone River. We had already passed that opening when the water depth became too shallow for paddling, only about six to eight inches deep. At that place, the bottom was rather solid, so Ben and Doree traded off pulling the canoe westward with the bow rope for about a half-hour, while I continued to paddle as best I could in the stern. Finally, the position of the radio transmission tower rising high above the community of Cumberland House, about a half-mile inland, indicated that we had indeed missed the river opening and had traveled too far toward the west.

Using his long, slender legs, Ben pulled us nearer to the shoreline. Then we began the slow and very laborious return, all the while searching for the head of the Bigstone River. Here close to the shore, the water was only four or five inches deep, the tall reed beds were quite thick, and the muddy bottom was very soft and irregular, making progress extremely difficult for Ben, even with his long legs and great stamina. Doree and I could barely walk here, since we sank into the gooshy mud up to our knees with each step of our shorter legs. So the task of towing the fully loaded craft, containing two adults and a dog, fell onto the shoulders of our long-limbed, fourteen-year-old son. After more than an hour of this very uncomfortable -- and for Ben exhausting -- situation, baking under a hot Saskatchewan sun with our eyes riveted to the slowly passing shoreline, I finally noted a few vertical saplings that had been inserted into the silty bottom. We fervently hoped that they were an indicator of the obscured river entry! Nearby, Doree spied an opening which was only about as wide as our canoe running through the thick growth of reeds. The slight amount of current flowing toward the south in the opening indicated that this was our long-sought passage! With our hearts singing with relief, Doree and I hugged Ben and thanked him thoroughly for his enormous efforts. He had labored for about 1 3/4 hours while pulling the canoe more than a mile too far toward the west along the lakeshore, and then while backtracking to the river opening.

With all three of us dragging the canoe southward through the shallow, narrow opening, we were soon able to resume paddling. Shortly, the passage flowed into the larger main channel of the Bigstone River, which had many shallow areas and sandbars, tall muddy banks which were very soft, and a thick growth of grasses and reeds four to five feet tall all along the shorelines. After a mile, we heard children laughing and shouting, very welcome sounds to our ears! Soon, we arrived at a place a quarter-mile from the community of Cumberland House, where a road from the town meets the river. Many native children were splashing and swimming in the three-foot-deep water here, flanked by tall muddy banks, in the 80 degree heat beneath a cloudless sky; they were all speaking English with an accent. It had taken us nearly four hours, from 12:15 to 4:00, to cover what we had expected to be an easy five-mile trek, from the head of the blocked Tearing River to the little town of Cumberland House.

Traveling on the upper Bigstone had not been easy, with its shallow depths and numerous sandbars, so we wondered what the paddling conditions would be like on its remaining four miles downstream. Following this line of thought, we began to seriously consider other options. While Doree and Ben walked into the nearby settlement of Cumberland House, Toby remained with me at the canoe. With luck, my teammates would be able to arrange some truck transportation to take us overland for two miles, southward to the ferry crossing area of the Saskatchewan River. They also hoped to get some hot restaurant food, to bolster our depleted furnaces for the long hours of traveling that still lay ahead.

The father of some of the kids who were swimming chatted with me about our canoe trip. He explained that the earthen dam blocking the head of the Tearing River had been constructed by the native residents of Cumberland House three years earlier. It had been installed in an attempt to slow the gradual lowering of the water level in Cumberland Lake, by eliminating one of its two outlets. He also indicated that no motorboats travel from the community up the Bigstone River and into the very shallow lake; they only go down the river, through the set of rapids, and into the Saskatchewan. That is why there are no channel markers at the head of the Bigstone.

At 5:00, Doree and Ben returned with the Métis mayor of Cumberland House, Harold "Butch" Carrière, and his pickup truck. After loading everything into the back, Ben, Toby, and I rode with the gear and canoe while Doree rode in the cab, where she learned about the area. The local population consists of about five hundred reservation Crees (who are well-provided by the federal government), about a thousand non-reservation French-Cree Métis (who struggle on their own to get by), and a few whites. The houses that we saw as we drove through the little non-reservation town were in need of some fresh paint, but a beautiful log church was under construction. Our new friend Butch, a warm and helpful man, would not take any payment for his generous aid in transporting us across town and to the Saskatchewan, to a spot just below the cable ferry crossing, about a mile downriver from the mouth of the Bigstone.

As we were reloading, I realized that this place on the Saskatchewan River was as far northwest as French traders are known to have ventured during the French regime. In addition, only two trading posts were established further west than this location during the French era. Ft. La Jonquière, constructed in 1751, and Ft. St. Louis/Ft. La Corne, built in 1753, were both positioned much further up the Saskatchewan, well to the west. The latter post may have been located as much as 150 miles upstream, near the junction of the North and South branches of the river. The French are not documented as having penetrated further into the northwest beyond the Saskatchewan River system, even though La Vérendrye traveled all the way to the forks of the North and South branches as early as 1739. A decade later, a map based upon the officer's discoveries indicated that he was aware, through native informants, that a route extending away from this river, heading northward via the Sturgeon Weir and then eastward via the Churchill, led to Hudson's Bay. However, planned expansion of the trade by the French beyond the Saskatchewan was interrupted by the Seven Years' War, after which British forces gained control of New France in 1760.

Before pushing off on the Rivière Saskatchewan at 6:30, we savored the scrumptious thick burgers and poutine that Doree had bought at a restaurant in town. Our bellies were jubilant again, and our attitude much revived! During the next three hours, elated to again have deep, unobstructed water, Ben and I pulled our green Canadienne over fourteen miles of river, traveling under ideal conditions as the sun descended gently, bathing the scene with a golden red hue.

This waterway was immensely different from the Rivière Maligne on which we had begun this voyage. We had started on a river with crystal clear water, flowing in a rather fast current over a bed of limestone that ranged in width from a few yards up to occasionally 3/10 of a mile. The Maligne's fast-moving water, constantly murmuring and burbling, flashed beside barren limestone shorelines, beneath a towering evergreen forest. In contrast, the Saskatchewan consists of silt-laden brown water flowing silently in a steady, moderate current, usually ranging in width from about 2/10 to 3/10 of a mile. Having traveled for more than a thousand miles across three prairie provinces, all the way from the foothills of Alberta, this water carries immense amounts of fine sediment, which it constantly deposits: on the bottom as ever-shifting sand bars; in the shallow areas on the inner side of each curve, where the current is slower than on the outer side; and along the shorelines. Beside the water's edge, these deposits have created a flat stretch of thick, sticky mud eight to ten feet wide, sometimes so soft that we would sink in up to our knees when landing. Further back from the water lies an equally wide flat expanse of solid soil, on which grasses and low thickets of stunted willows grow in many areas. Behind the mud flat rises the bank, usually a near-vertical cliff of light-colored fine sediment about ten to fifteen feet high. Atop this crumbling steep bank are found mostly aspen trees, with some spruces further back from the edge. In a great many places, numerous trees have toppled over the edge of the cliff and continue to fall on a regular basis, as the bluff constantly erodes and drops its soil. As a result of this erosion, at the base of the cliff is a slightly downward-sloping area, where the soil has fallen and has then been smoothed level by the action of the river. Myriad animal paths extend from the top of the bluff down to the water, where many creatures come out of the woods to drink. In places where the mud at the water's edge is very soft, the trail for two or three feet from the water is a wide gouge, where animals have dragged their bodies up and out as their legs have sunk deeply into the mud.

The character of each river on this earth is related to the landscape through which it flows, involving the geology, the soil, the climate, and the various types of vegetation that grow in the area. For us, it was fascinating to paddle two such drastically different waterways on the same trip, separated from each other by only a distance of some thirty miles and a series of three shallow lakes.

This was our favorite time of day for paddling, the gloaming of early evening, when the wind calmed, the sun infused the scene with a warm, rose-copper light, and the mirror-like surface of the water offered perfect reflections of land, trees, and sky. As we cruised down the miles of river, passing tall earthen cliffs surmounted with poplars, we encountered three Canada geese that were floating together near the right shore, eight crows that seemed to enjoy flying in formation doing trick maneuvers, and a few ducks gabbling in the shallows. We also passed a beaver that was sunning itself at the water's edge of the left shore, close beside its dinner, a freshly-cut sapling.

At 9:30, we arrived at the first of the two branches of the mouth of the Tearing River on the left shore, just as a beaver glided silently across the Saskatchewan in front of us, undisturbed by our presence. We decided to camp beside this channel mouth, at the place where we could have emerged from the Tearing River had it not been blocked off by the new earthen dam. This locale offered a very rare, appealing campsite on the Saskatchewan, one which was entirely covered with fist-sized cobblestones instead of the usual expanse of gooey mud. These stones had been carried to this place by torrential flows of the Tearing River over thousands of years.

Since the attacking hordes of mosquitoes were so intense, we threw up the tent as quickly as we could, illuminated first by the afterglow of the sunset and then by the bright full moon. Standing outside the shelter, wolfing down the squished remnants of our still-delicious burgers, to the distinctive calling of whip-poor-wills, we soon retreated inside the tent, with its mosquito netting covering the doors and windows.

While trading massages, we reviewed our day, first the bad luck, then the good luck, during the 25 miles of progress in which Doree had done six miles in the bow and Ben had covered nineteen miles there. Now we were able to joke as we replayed the sight of Ben slowly and laborious dragging the canoe above the deep silty bottom, first while we had overshot on Cumberland Lake and then while we had backtracked. At this point, we had covered 75 miles in 2 1/2 days on the water, much of that distance under less than easy conditions.

Day Four

Another hot, cloudless, blue-sky day greeted us, inspiring Toby to roll on his back in the pleasure of a new day. At 8:00, the air temperature was already 72 degrees in the shade, 80 degrees in the sun. In hauling the gear from the campsite to the canoe, Ben put his puny parents to shame, by carrying both of the large Duluth packs at the same time, one on his back and the other one on his front! After settling the hound onto the packs in the midsection, we were underway at 9:30, and quickly covered the three miles to the primary mouth of the Tearing River.

Here, hundreds of eastbound brigades had reached the Saskatchewan River from Cumberland Lake over the centuries. Since the Tearing River is now blocked at its source ten miles upstream, its mouth area is just a broad meadow, completely covered with yellow and pink wildflowers growing to a height of three feet. A trickle of water about eight inches wide flows through the middle of the meadow and into the Saskatchewan, a meager, shriveled remnant of a former pleasant river with a fast current. I stood in wonder, trying to picture canoe brigades paddling up and down a rushing waterway here, where there is now in its place a flowering meadow. In the mud of the shoreline, we noted many distinct tracks of wolves, raccoons, mink, great blue herons, and various smaller birds such as ducks. In the shallows offshore, freshwater mussels had also left their linear tracks on the soft bottom, where they had slowly dragged their paired shells on edge in circular, oval, and long looping patterns.

As we pushed off again, I settled into the bow seat. Dipping my paddle rhythmically into the moderately broad Saskatchewan River, I hummed and sang to myself bits and pieces of Louis Armstrong's trademark song What a Wonderful World:

"I see trees of green, red roses too;
I see them bloom for me and you.
And I think to myself, what a wonderful world!

I see skies of blue and clouds of white
Brightness of the day, darkness of the night.
And I think to myself, what a wonderful day!

Hum, hum, hum..."
I hummed the lines that had not been stored in my memory. Funny how Ben complained when I would forget the words of a line and just hum. In response, I'd say, "My repertoire of songs would be pretty limited if I had to either retrieve all the words or not sing!" and then I'd resume my singing-humming.

With no interfering head wind holding us back, the moderate current helped our forward progress much like a subtle following breeze that barely fills the sail. It allowed the canoe to continue to glide steadily forward during that moment after each stroke when my paddle was out of the water, extending forward for a new stroke.
"What a Wonderful Day..."(Doree)

When a very soft breeze did pick up from behind us, Ben hoisted the sail and we easily advanced five miles, until we ran aground on a barely submerged sand bar. This happened while we were attempting to circumvent a large, exposed midstream sand bar by cutting across the inner side of a curve. To lighten the load, Ben walked in the water along the inside of the bend while Doree and I playfully waded the craft across the head of the sand bar, splashing each other occasionally, and then paddled in the deeper water along the outside of the curve to retrieve our son.

When Ben took over in the bow position, he and I paddled five miles to our 1:00 lunch spot, where we scrambled up to the top of the high bank above a sharp bend in the channel. Since the morning departure, we had progressed twelve miles in 31/2 hours, and had crossed from Saskatchewan into Manitoba just one mile back. The air temperature was 82 degrees in the shade, with not a single cloud to decorate the deep blue sky. So the cool shadows that were cast by the broad green leaves of the poplars on the bluff were very welcome during our rest period. In the dried mud on the sloping cliff face nearby, Doree discovered a trail of huge moose tracks, and also a set of deer tracks.

345

Returning to the water with a well-rested woman in the bow seat, we flashed forward five miles in one hour, without any assistance from the sail. A bald eagle perched near the top of a dead spruce watched us pass by on his river below; later, a small black snake swam in front of our craft, as it made its shimmying way across the sun-drenched brown water. The Saskatchewan River seemed to be constantly meandering, curving, and winding, which made reading the map almost effortless. While traveling around each of the miles-long, gradual bends, it was easy to occasionally glance down and keep track of the matching lazy curve on the detailed map.

In the great stillness of mid-afternoon, since the air was so hot and the water was so warm, all four of us welcomed a delightfully refreshing half-hour swim. During this break, Ben managed to tackle his father and dunk him under the water -- a first. He also bent his mother backward until she too fell in, sputtering. Afterward, he took over as the *avant*, and was pleased to have a mild sailing wind pick up. In the passenger section, Doree and Toby dozed contentedly. During the course of the day, we sighted eight more bald eagles, six of them mature birds with a white head and neck, and two that were less than three years old, still having their original brownish-black head and neck plumage. Each one was keeping an eye out for prey, from a lofty perch in a barren tree.

At the Big Bend, having personally completed 22 miles for the day (with a mild sail assist on about seven of those miles), Ben returned the bow paddle to his mother. At this place, the river makes a huge upside-down U turn, changing direction from the northeasterly course that it had traveled for twenty miles to a southeasterly course, which it would generally maintain for the rest of its length. The outer bank of this entire mighty bend, covering about one mile, consisted of a continuous high cliff of light-colored sediments. In various places, numerous trees had tumbled from the cliff's top into a tangled mass at the base, extending all the way into the water. In this area, Doree spotted an otter lolling in the sun on the far shore. As the shadows lengthened, everything around us seemed to be drowsing in the warm, late-day sunlight.

At 8:30, we decided to call it a day. For some time, we had all been scanning the passing shorelines for a decent campsite. However, the only sites that were available in this entire area were on the flat, first-level terrace just above the river. It would not have been worth the considerable effort to haul everything up the face of the steep bluff rising behind the terrace, to camp on the heights. The site that we chose could only be reached by crossing a stretch of very soft mud, which extended inland for about ten feet from the edge of the water. By experimenting with my paddle blade, I learned that if we were to step onto either the riverbed near the edge or the gooshy mud flat, we would sink down at least eighteen inches into the smelly black ooze. After getting up some speed and ramming the canoe as far up onto the deep shoreline mud as we could, Ben and I climbed out over the bow end and into the thick slime, and then pulled the craft up about five feet, with Doree and Toby still aboard. After they climbed out over the bow, Doree helped us pull the canoe the rest of the way up onto solid ground.

Unfortunately, we had neglected to fill any containers with water while we were afloat. Now, a major hassle to reach open water from the shoreline faced us. Seeking a solution to this oversight, Ben and I threw two seven-foot logs out onto the muck, end to end, to form a makeshift bridge reaching out to the edge of the water. Then I crawled on my knees out to the end of the second log, and from there extended the thermos on the end of a ten-foot limb, to scoop up the brown liquid. Repeatedly passing the partially-filled jug back to Ben, he filled each of the cooking and eating containers, which he had arrayed on the stern of the canoe and on solid ground nearby. I must admit, our stew and koolaid were a tad brown and silty that evening!

This had been a hot and beautiful day; even when we landed at 8:30, it was still 80 degrees in the sun. Although the temperature dropped slightly after the sun sank below the western tree line, it was still a balmy 75 degrees at 10 P.M. In the fading light, amid what seemed like a million swarming mosquitoes, we feasted on a stew of beef jerky, noodles, and green beans. Some of the tastiest meals of our entire lives were those evening suppers at camp after eleven or twelve hours on the water, having had only a cold breakfast, cold lunch, and snacks all day. The enticing smell of the bubbling food wafting from the lidded pot on the miniature stove, spiced with the satisfaction that we felt after a very accomplishing day, made us all the more ravenous for those evening meals.

Beside Ben's campfire, made intentionally smoky with green poplar leaves and limbs to keep the blood-sucking insects at bay, we traded massages and added up the day's progress. From 9:15 A.M.

to 8:30 P.M., we had made 39 miles, with a mild sail assist for only about seven of those miles. Ben had paddled 22 miles, and Doree had covered seventeen. So far, we had averaged more than 32 miles a day for 31/2 days, to advance 114 miles. From inside our insect-proof shelter, Ben noted that the unceasing chorus of mosquitoes outside resembled the hum of traffic on a distant highway.

At about 11:00, we drifted off to the sounds of large fish jumping with reckless abandon in the water flowing quietly beside us, as they fed on insects floating on the glazed surface. As my thoughts unfurled, I imagined myself as a native woman many centuries ago, having set with my daughter our gill net across a portion of the river for the night. Hoping to catch some of the northern pike, walleyes, and goldeyes that live in this waterway, we had launched the canoe in the early evening, had unrolled our seventy-paces-long net made of nettle stalk cordage, and had fastened it at each end to long vertical poles that had previously been driven securely into the silty bottom. The top of the net was supported by a series of foot-long floats made of light wood which were attached to the sturdy top cord of the net, while stone sinkers were tied along the bottom cord to hold the bottom in position. At one corner of the bottom of the net, I had earlier tied a small leather packet of fish medicine, to charm the fish and attract them to the net. In the morning, we would pull the net up over the gunwales of our canoe, extract the fish that had swum headfirst into the mesh and had become entangled at the gills, and roll up the net. Back on shore, we would spread the net out over a long pole rack to dry, as we did each morning, and then we would process our catch. For eating, we would boil the cleaned fish, or instead roast them impaled head upward on a stick thrust into the ground beside the fire. To dry them for later use, we would split the cleaned fish lengthwise, and either lay them on a wooden rack over a slow fire or string them on a cord and hang them in the sun.

Day Five

I had been awakened by a dizzying sugar-low two nights in a row. This had required crawling out of the tent, retrieving my sugar-low kit hanging high in a tree, and consuming some peanut butter mixed with honey. With the multitudes of mosquitoes swarming outside, this procedure had not been much fun. In addition, the L-5 vertebra at the base of my spine had ached very much during each day of this voyage, much more than I had remembered from any previous paddling trip. To compensate for the pain, I had to focus especially clearly on the beauties of the natural world around us, and on the rich history that had taken place here over the centuries, to distract me from the physical sensations.

The incessant croaking of a great blue heron near the tent roused us from our sleep at 7:30. When we were ready to shove off an hour later, the air temperature measured 65 degrees in the shade, the blue sky contained just a few puffy white clouds, and there was not a hint of a breeze. Since a wide swath of sticky mud lay between the canoe and water that was deep enough to float it, we loaded the craft completely while it was still on solid ground, including Toby with his muddy feet. Then we slid it over most of the expanse of mud and partway into the water, after which Doree and I climbed aboard over the landward end. As the youngest member of the crew, Ben was designated as the "pusher," slogging far out in the deep oozing mud to push the craft out into water that was deep enough to allow it to float, before clambering over the gunwales into the bow seat. Just as we pulled away from the site, we passed a place where a moose or elk had come down from the bluff one night at dusk to drink. It had gouged a wide belly-track about six feet long in the shoreline mud when it sank to full-leg depth to reach the water.

Not long after we had departed, a white pelican silently paddling near the far shore greeted us. As we coursed over many miles of smooth brown water, we rousted up occasional ducks, pelicans, and sandpipers. At one point, a large hawk watched us from the top of a dead tree as we approached, and then flapped away slowly. For practice in navigation, Ben read the map from the bow position, while Doree memorized the verses of another French song, using the traveling song sheets that we kept stored in a waterproof bag of clear plastic.

By the time we took a lunch break beside a beaver lodge adjacent to the shoreline, we had made eight miles in 2 1/4 hours. To avoid a messy landing on the muddy shore, we ingested our meal of peanut butter-smeared crackers, dried apple slices, and koolaid while floating offshore for twenty minutes. On these trips, Toby would have nothing to do with his own dog food; he just shared our crackers and apples at lunches, and our stew at the dinner meals.

Beside the mouth of Kapakaneecheewak Creek on the left shore,

Doree first heard the cracking of limbs at the top of the bluff. Scanning the area, she spotted a black bear cub, clinging partway up the trunk of a tall poplar near the edge of the cliff. The mother bear, grunting commands to her offspring, could be heard at the base of the tree. Immediately, the youngster climbed rapidly down, and the two of them crashed off through the brush into the woods, with the mother bear grunting all the while. When we took our paddling trips toward the end of the summer each year, the bear population was usually quite well-fed, having generous supplies of berries, grasses, nuts, roots, insects, and fish available to them. That is probably why we did not have any difficulties with bears seeking our food in camp. However, we always took the time-consuming precaution of hanging the food packs each night on a high limb of a tree, well out from the trunk; and we never left any food items in the tent or scattered around the site while we were sleeping.

The afternoon was very hot and still, 85 degrees in the shade. As soon as I began mulling over the activities of La Vérendrye and his men, fifteen miles and 3 3/4 hours seemed to speed by. En route, we observed at six different locations a solitary great blue heron, standing in the shallows fishing. At 3:00, we arrived at the city of Le Pas (now called The Pas) on the right shore. Here, Ft. Paskoiac had been founded by the French in 1749-50. Two decades later, in 1769, another Ft. Paskoiac had been re-established here by Montreal-based traders. This place had been a traditional location for a Cree village. In 1775, when Alexander Henry and the Frobisher brothers had paddled up the Saskatchewan, they had halted here at the village called Pasquoyah, where they were greeted by thirty native families living in tepees covered with buffalo hides. As a toll for their passage further upriver, the Anglo traders were obliged to hand over three guns, three kegs of gunpowder, four bags of lead balls and shot, a supply of gunflints, a number of knives and other small articles, and three kegs of rum. Now, The Pas Indian Reserve runs along the left shore of the river for five miles westward from the city, extending a half-mile inland, before it arcs northward in a similarly narrow strip for six more miles along the shoreline of Reader Lake.

La Vérendrye and his men had intended to establish a post in this area, if their plans for expansion had been allowed to proceed. They had constructed two posts in 1741, both of them a short distance to the west of Lake Winnipeg. Ft. Bourbon was located on the lowest section of the Saskatchewan River, where it expands into the wide, lake-like body of water called Lac Bourbon (now called Cedar Lake) before narrowing again to flow into Lake Winnipeg. Some fifteen miles south of this post, which had been built on an island, lay the northern end of Lac Winnipegosis, which stretches southward to join Lac Manitoba. On the narrow waterway which connects these two elongated lakes, Ft. Dauphin was also constructed in 1741. Three years later, La Vérendrye had been removed from his position as the commandant of the Western Posts, by the pressure of his creditors and other traders who were resentful of his monopoly of the commerce in the northwest. In 1749, the position of command had been restored to the officer, but he died in December of that year, before he could return to the west. He had intended to further expand his series of posts up the Saskatchewan River, to intercept all the more effectively the brigades of native traders who traveled out to Hudson's Bay to trade with the Anglos at their Bayside posts.

Due to warnings about pollution in the river water downstream from Le Pas, we filled our water jug and thermos at the riverside park where we landed. Then Doree and Ben scouted out a fried chicken restaurant, where they bought a bountiful supply of chicken, fries, and cole slaw, some for eating on the grassy riverbank in the park, and some for enjoying later in the evening.

Shortly after paddling away from the town at 4:30, with Ben in the bow seat, Doree spotted a mink resting on the shoreline rocks. Downstream from the town, the elevated banks of the river became lower, while the forest cover extended down the banks to near the shoreline. Soon we paused near the right shore to examine the largest beaver lodge that we had ever seen. It was actually two massive dome-shaped shelters that had been eventually joined together, by an accumulation of many hundreds of peeled saplings. Due to the lowered water level of late summer, we could see the now-exposed entrance and exit tunnels of the two lodges, which were used during periods of higher water.

A while later, well to the north of the river, we could see a huge mass of black clouds advancing slowly southward, with rain falling in the distance, accompanied by rolling thunder. Within ninety minutes the storm reached us, at about the same time that a following wind from the north came up. Hoisting the sail for some welcome assistance, we also relished the cooling effects of the moderate rain, restoring us after a very sweaty day of paddling. To shelter Toby from the rainfall, Ben covered him with a couple of our nylon jackets. After a half-hour, the storm clouds moved on and the sky cleared completely, leaving us with a beautiful evening.

We passed several bald eagles and hawks, perched on snags of dead spruce trees projecting above the tops of the aspens. In one treetop, a juvenile hawk that was not yet proficient at flying cried out constantly all the while we glided by. However, we did not see any adult hawks in the vicinity. In the quiet calm of early evening, we surged forward fifteen miles during four hours of paddling, including a floating break to eat the remaining fried chicken meals from Le Pas.

At 9:00, we fortunately located a campsite where we could reach solid land on shore without having to cross a gooshy mud flat. This was a place on the left shoreline where a muddy creek about three feet wide and only a few inches deep flowed into the main channel, near the head of a midstream island. Ben climbed out over the bow end and dragged the canoe up the creek mouth about three canoe lengths, where the grass-covered banks of the miniature waterway were much more welcoming than the mucky ones of the big Saskatchewan. After unloading everything, we hauled the canoe up onto the creek bank for the night.

A few moments later, a very special scene was staged on the river directly in front of us. As we had pulled into the site, we had noted some fifty white pelicans sitting on a sand bar that lay halfway across the Saskatchewan from our landing place. Just as the bright white disc of the full moon broke free from the ragged tree line of the far shore, many of the pelicans took flight. This entailed slowly flapping their wings about fifteen to twenty times, with each wing-stroke slapping the surface of the water, as they slowly gained speed for takeoff. When one particular group of five birds had gained enough altitude, they immediately created a V formation and zoomed very low across the river and directly over our camp.

As if choreographed for the second scene in our nature drama, a beaver then swam upstream in front of us, just one canoe length out from shore. While we watched in fascination, it glided silently beside our campsite, went a little beyond it, and then circled back. The apparently calm animal repeated this pattern four times, swimming back and forth in front of our camp, before proceeding slowly back downstream and out of sight. We suspected that the narrow muddy creek beside our camp was its regular route to some place of importance. Maybe it would return and make its way up the little waterway long after we had gone to sleep, when we would pose less of a threat.

In 12 1/2 hours on the water today, we had put 38 miles behind us, with a mild sail assist for about three of those miles; Doree had done fifteen miles with the bow paddle, and Ben 23. Over the course of 4 1/2 days of travel, we had advanced a total of 152 miles, averaging nearly 34 miles a day. As we massaged each other in the tent, hordes of mosquitoes droned outside, while an owl hooted at intervals from the tip of the island next to our campsite.

Day Six

Reveille again consisted of the hoarse croaking call of a heron, this time coming from the upstream end of the adjacent island. After loading the canoe in the narrow creek, Ben pushed us out into the main river at 9:00, where we floated free while downing a breakfast of gorp and chocolate-flavored instant breakfast drink. As the *avant*, Ben did ten miles in two hours, with a moderately bulging sail helping for the first six miles. After a twenty-minute break on the downriver tip of Mistikowun-aketchewan Island, during which we munched on red and black licorice, Doree took up the bow paddle. She then strongly pulled the canoe forward another ten miles in two hours, with a moderate sail assist the entire way.

Smears of white clouds in thin, wide streaks were painted across the entire canvas of sunny blue sky, and the temperature was 80 degrees in the shade. Cruising in a comfortable late-morning trance, I heard soft gurgling sounds beside me as my paddle passed through the water. I was intimately familiar with this carved and varnished piece of golden tan ash, and with this graceful canoe of green fiberglass, and I knew how to direct them to take me and my loved ones safely through a wide array of conditions involving water, wind, land, and rocks.

When some writers describe a canoe trip or the life of a voyageur, they love to multiply their number of paddle strokes per minute by the number of minutes in an hour, and then by the number of traveling hours in a day, and finally by the number of days in the trip, to estimate their total number of paddle strokes in the entire voyage. This is certainly a shallow and non-reflective way of looking at the process of wilderness travel and historical voyages. Neither the amount of time nor the degree of effort that is expended in completing a given task is of any real importance, whether the task is carrying out a canoe trip, or mastering a skill, or creating something. The only goal should be the gradual completion of the task in the manner and quality which was desired and envisioned at the outset, regardless of the time and energy that it requires along the way. The strange concept of figuring the total number of paddle strokes in a given voyage brings to mind the tale of the clock that had a nervous breakdown. One day, it began thinking about how many times it would have to tick during the coming year. Figuring two ticks per second, 120 ticks each minute, 7,200 ticks per hour, 172,800 ticks each day, and 1,209,600 ticks every week, the clock suddenly realized that it would have to tick nearly 63 million times during the next twelve months! The more it thought about this, the more anxious it became. Finally, the clock became so distraught that it suffered a nervous collapse. Confiding in its counselor, the clock complained that it did not have the strength to tick that often. The counselor responded, "How many ticks must you tick at a time?" The clock answered, "Well, just one." "So, just tick one tick at a time, and don't worry about the next one," advised the counselor. That's exactly what the clock did, and it ticked happily ever after. We all need to focus on the simple yet profound concept that even the most massive project is just a gradual accumulation of tiny, manageable increments of effort. Every single paddle stroke, and the resultant forward movement of the canoe from that specific stroke, eventually add up to entire miles, and ultimately to an entire voyage. The number of strokes that were required is entirely immaterial, in the same way that no one cares about the total number of chisel cuts that were needed to complete a marble sculpture.

Since my attention was focused on *avirons* this morning, I thought about the array of paddles that the ancient French canoeists had utilized in various different situations. In nearly all instances, a voyageur provided his own paddle for a trip; only in those rare instances in which the excursion was sponsored and completely outfitted by the government were paddles supplied to the men. Myriad documents from the fur trade era described versions that were fashioned by native and French craftsmen from birch, maple, and sometimes northern white cedar.

Since paddles were designed to efficiently propel and steer the craft, their dimensions were determined by the purpose that each particular paddle would serve. In canoes with only two or three crewmen, which the French utilized for nearly all fur trade expeditions until about 1720, the *gouvernail* sitting at the stern handled the long-range steering and provided a considerable amount of propulsion power. The *avant* at the bow made short-term steering adjustments as necessary to avoid obstacles, but mostly supplied a great deal of power for forward motion, while the third paddler provided only power. In these instances, both of the *bouts* (endmen) required a paddle with considerable width to its blade, for effective steering. As a result, they utilized a moderate stroke speed, to accommodate the heavier weight of these rather wide-bladed paddles. When voyageur crews expanded to four, five, and six men during the 1720s, the *milieux* (middlemen) did not usually participate in steering, mostly providing only forward momentum. Thus, they used lighter paddles with less blade width, to pour their energy into forward power. With these men providing the bulk of the forward movement with their lighter, narrower paddles, the cadence of the strokes was increased considerably. The stern paddler then applied his energy mostly toward ruddering, not having to match the faster strokes of the middlemen. During uneventful cruising, he often sat atop the gunwales and the stern thwart. But to run rapids and navigate fast currents, he stood up to wield his long, wide-bladed paddle, so that he would have both greater power and a better view of the obstacles that lay ahead. The bow paddler utilized a lighter, narrower-bladed paddle while cruising, matching the faster stroke speed of the middlemen. However, in areas of strong current or rapids, he took up a longer paddle with a wider blade and a standing posture, to help with the steering. These standard procedures continued as the crew sizes ultimately increased to seven, and very occasionally to eight, nine, or ten men, after the enlarged *canot du Maître*, ranging from 33 to 36 feet in length, was introduced in 1729.

Various documents from 1632, 1685, and 1738 described paddles for canoes with a small number of crewmen as having blades that were about six inches wide (those that we Kents use have blades measuring 67/8 inches). References from 1826 and 1859 noted the two different size categories that were utilized by the larger crews, including middlemen paddles with blades three or 31/2 inches wide, and bow and stern paddles that were nearly double that in blade width. This custom of carving wider blades on steering paddles was clearly illustrated in a set of four model paddles that were fashioned in New France during the 1740s or 1750s to accompany a canoe model (the craft, paddles, and occupants have all survived intact in France). The *gouvernail* paddle is 38 percent longer overall, and 62 percent wider in the blade, than the three *milieux* paddles. These four early examples also represent a number of different grip styles that were carved at the business end of the shaft during the French era. These grips include straight unflared, flared on only one side, and flared on both sides.

As I glanced down at my varnished but otherwise plain paddle of golden tan hue, my mind wandered to the many different painted designs that had been applied to areas of the blade, shaft, and grip by native and French canoeists during the fur trade era. The typical patterns had included areas of solid color, geometric designs of lines or bars, and dots; these were applied in the colors of brownish red, black, white, and green.

At the junction of a small side stream on the left shore, I steered our bow into the mouth area, and we paused to eat our lunch. A half-mile downriver, the channel split, with the two arms of the river encircling and embracing Kakenoskak Island for three miles before converging again. Shortly below the island, we passed the diminutive Bignell Indian Reserve, consisting of 11/2 miles of river frontage along the right bank, nestled in a curve in the channel. This reservation is rather typical of the tiny disconnected parcels of land which native people in Canada hold, mostly just pinpricks scattered across a map of the country. In the ten provinces, there are a total of 2,370 such reserves, compared to the total of 298 reservations that exist in the U.S. The latter parcels are, on average, 64 times larger than their Canadian counterparts. In fact, a combination of all of the native reserve lands in the ten provinces would not equal half of the Navajo reservation in Arizona. The small size and disconnected nature of the reserve land holdings in Canada have been a major disadvantage for the native people there.

With Ben as the *avant*, we easily sped over ten miles of shimmering brown river water, as the blue square of nylon fabric, bellied out by the following breeze, tugged the canoe steadily along. After Doree traded positions with her son, she and I made eight miles in 2 1/2 hours, sometimes with modest help from the sail and sometimes on flat, unruffled water. Toward the end of this stretch, the south-flowing channel made a sudden bend toward the southwest for 11/2 miles before returning to its former course, a feature of the river that was known as Le Coude (The Elbow).

In the late afternoon, solid white cloud cover rolled in, completely hiding the blue sky and causing the air temperature to drop to 75 degrees. This more somber weather accompanied our entry into the delta region of the Saskatchewan River. Over the span of thousands of years, multiple creeks branching off from the main channel near its end had spread out here in a massive, fan-shaped area more than ten miles wide. Gradually dropping their silt, these secondary branches had caused the swampy lands of the delta to grow slightly longer and wider with each passing year, extending further and further into the waters of Muddy Bay.

At 6:45, we reached mile 190 of the trip, where the map indicated that we were about two miles from the end of solid ground in the delta region. Just ahead lay the area where the river widens out immensely, forming the shallow expanse of Lac Bourbon (with its three sections that are now called Muddy Bay, Cedar Lake, and Cross Bay). I was concerned about finding dry land for a campsite in the sodden, marshy region of the delta, with its extremely low shorelines and thick growth of reeds extending far out from shore. So we decided to take advantage of the *terra firma* that was still at hand, which had now been reduced to just a narrow strip of barely-elevated woods flanking each side of the main channel. Heading for the left shore while gaining considerable momentum, we arrowed through the thick growth of reeds in the shallows, and glided to a stop beside two large beaver-felled trees that were lying just offshore near the water's edge. Using these horizontal tree trunks as convenient steps, we unloaded onto the low but dry bank, and whacked out a clearing in the adjacent brush and undergrowth that was large enough to both set up camp and pull the canoe up onto shore for the night.

As we hungrily took down our stew of beef, peas, and noodles, the sky in the west cleared somewhat. At 8:00 it was still 70 degrees, with a comfortable breeze wafting from the west. We had guided our canoe over 38 miles of water today, from 9 A.M. to 6:45 P.M., with a sail assist on many of those miles. This was our earliest evening camp of the trip, since I did not want the nightmare of being stuck in the dark on swampy ground in the delta area further on, had we continued to press forward until later in the evening. I was also rather concerned about the paddling conditions that we might face in the 25 miles that lay ahead, until we would ultimately reach unobstructed open water beyond the barrier of the Crossing Islands at the beginning of Cedar Lake. The water level of Muddy Bay, the area just ahead of us at the end of the multiple channels of the delta, was unusually high this year. Hopefully, this would allow us to paddle freely through the reedy areas that were seasonally inundated, to reach the open water beyond.

Today, Ben had done twenty miles in the bow, while his mother had covered eighteen. So far, we had averaged almost 35 miles a day for 51/2 days, covering 190 miles. As we relished our galette dessert, satisfied with our excellent progress, a number of wolves howled from the opposite shore of the channel, which was about 2/10 of a mile wide at this location. In this region, moose is the main prey of the wolf population. Since the mosquitoes were horrendous here, we soon took refuge in the sheltering tent, where the fine-mesh window and door screens kept them at bay, and collapsed on our air mattresses, ready to sleep until tomorrow.

Day Seven

When the night's rest ended at 7:00, we were pleased to find a steady wind from the northwest, blowing exactly in our direction of travel. On our shaded side of the tree line, it was 62 degrees beneath a hazy sky. Hastily packing up in seventy minutes, we swallowed our breakfast gorp while underway, between paddle strokes. With moderate assistance from the sail, Ben paddled with me for two hours to cover the gently meandering, ten-mile length of the middle and longest of the several delta channels, which extend like outspread fingers of a hand far out into the waters of Muddy Bay. Along our course down this main channel of the river, I was pleased to encounter no difficulties in following the route. I simply noted the growth of bushes along the nearly submerged banks that ran along each side, following the naturally-marked passageway. As it gradually narrowed from about 2/10 of a mile to less than 1/10 of a mile, the shrubbery moved closer and closer. The slender strip of land and bushes bordering each side of the channel hid from view the shallows and reed beds that stretched away for miles toward both the east and the west.

At 10:15, we took an extended break on Kettle Island, located at the very tip of the main channel in the delta, an island which the map indicated only sometimes stood above water. Looking out over the eight-mile distance across Muddy Bay to our goal of the Crossing Islands, I was extremely elated to see completely open water, rather then a huge expanse of shallows choked with reeds! With Doree in the bow seat, we set off with high spirits and many choruses of *Vent Frais, Vent du Matin*, taking our place within the ranks of waves marching toward the southeast. The steady following wind and the waves, two to three feet high, some with frothy white tops, were pushing us directly from behind. With the sail bulging nicely, we streaked over the eight miles of open water in two hours, and soon pulled into a sheltered place on the southern lee side of the most westerly of the Crossing Islands, for a lunch break at 1:00. By this time, the hazy heavens had cleared to just a few white billows drifting lazily across a deep blue sky, and the temperature had risen to 80 degrees in the shade. Sitting on one of the many driftwood logs that covered the perimeter of the island, we took a long and well-deserved rest, having advanced nineteen miles in five hours.

At this point, we had left behind the poplar-lined shorelines of the Saskatchewan River's main channel, and had returned to a world of evergreen forest, mostly spruce and tamarack, along with some jack pines and scattered birches. (Even though tamaracks lose their soft needles each autumn, they are still considered to be "evergreens.") The group of Crossing Islands that we had just entered separates the Muddy Bay section of Lac Bourbon from the Cedar Lake section of the lake. Kokookuhoo Island, stretching in a southeast-to-northwest alignment for ten miles, is the largest among the group; it is surrounded by numerous other scattered islands of various sizes. Here on one of these islands which delineate the two upper sections of the lake, La Vérendrye had established Ft. Bourbon in 1741. Later, N.W.C. traders had operated the Moose Lake Post on Kokookuhoo Island for a few years, beginning in 1819.

After our restorative break, we threaded our way between various of the islands, and then traveled along the southern shoreline of Kokookuhoo Island. First Ben paddled for five miles, then his mother took over for four miles more. At 5:30, we paused for a quick ten-minute break on a point beside the Kawuwawsik Narrows. This point, projecting southward from Kokookuhoo Island, marked the beginning of the open waters of the Cedar Lake section of the Saskatchewan River, since we had now cleared the array of dividing islands. This wide body of water was so named because it marked the farthest place toward the northwest at which eastern white cedar grows, the wood which was optimum for constructing all of the wooden elements of birchbark canoes. Less than a mile southwest of our craft lay a scattering of five small islands, which together now bear the name Fort Islands. It is not clear whether this name reflects the true location of Ft. Bourbon or not. The southwestern corner of Cedar Lake lies ten miles south of these five little islands, and a strip of land only four miles wide separates that corner of the lake from the top of Lake Winnipegosis, a large body of water which figured very prominently in the activities of La Vérendrye and his men.

At 5:45, the air temperature was still 80 degrees in the shade, there were very few clouds in the sky, and the glorious sun sinking gradually lower in the west seemed to be beaming encouragement at us. In addition, *La Vieille* was continuing to cooperate, graciously providing a moderate wind from the northwest. Since these conditions were so favorable, we decided to make a fifteen-mile traverse on a southeasterly course across open water, instead of following the long route that would skirt various islands toward the east and then follow the eastern shoreline of Lac Bourbon toward the south. When Ben began the crossing in the *avant* position, he could not make out any trace of our destination, Pointe Kakakenowuchewun, on the distant horizon. We could only follow the southeasterly compass heading that Doree determined, to lead us over the sparkling water toward our goal. After an hour of speedy sailing amid moderate waves, Ben was able to make out a thin green line gradually rising along the distant horizon in front of the bow. Thirty minutes later, the following wind completely subsided, causing Doree to release the halyard and lower the sail. At this point, as the waves flattened and the water smoothed out, we were still about ten miles from our goal of the tip of the peninsula, and sundown was only about ninety minutes away. Putting all of our muscle power into each paddle stroke, we forged ahead mile after mile.

At about the midpoint of the crossing, Ben pointed out a rather strange sight: just off to our right, a sea gull was flying in our direction of travel, about ten feet above the water. Directly behind it, flying in its wake, was a pelican, cruising the way pelicans customarily do, in formation! At about 8:15, Doree relieved her son in the bow seat for the last five miles of the traverse. A half-hour later, the rim of the orange-red ball of the sun finally disappeared below the waterline, directly behind us. Drawn like iron to a magnet, we advanced steadily toward the tip of the peninsula, pushing hard in the gradually fading residual light for another hour. When we finally approached land at 9:45, we whooped in relief! We had completed the fifteen-mile traverse in four hours of considerable exertion. During that time, we had enjoyed the help of a moderate wind filling the sail only during the first five miles.

Nearing the end of the narrow peninsula in very dim light, we pulled in near a shoreline that was filled with long driftwood logs floating offshore as far as we could see. These were apparently shoreline trees that had been undermined and eventually felled by storms; their limbs had been removed by being tumbled and ground against the bottom in the shallows. After slowly making our way between and around these barrier logs to reach the shore, it was a real pleasure to finally step out into clear water and onto a bottom consisting of solid sand and broken limestone! This made a major impression on us, after six days of silt-laden brown water, muddy bottoms, and gooshy shorelines. Plunging through bushes four to five feet tall that grew along the shore, I located a clearing just a little inland, a small opening which was surrounded by tall trees. We had found our place of refuge for the night.

With virtually no light, we managed to efficiently unload, carry the cargo and the canoe to the site, and set up camp, all within 45 minutes after reaching land. Each of us had our own tasks to do when we landed at a campsite for the night, which meant no lost time and no duplication of effort. At well-lit sites, we would usually have the tent set up, bedding ready, gear stowed away, supper prepared, and journal updated within an hour of our arrival.

After we had put everything in order, we noticed the bright and nearly full moon beginning to appear through the tall trees off to the east. Being so tightly enclosed by the forest here, we had the unusual experience of observing the huge disc, tinted a very light golden hue, shining at us between the trunks and branches of trees, rather than from a wide-open sky. Since we were so tuckered out after our long day on the water, we went to bed without bothering to cook any hot food, which was especially discouraging for Ben. During the traverse, Doree had assembled peanut butter crackers for our evening meal, and had handed them forward to Ben and backward to me. Then had come chocolate gorp and hard candies. This had been by no means a gastronomic experience, just a refueling exercise.

Trading massages inside the tent, to avoid the droves of blood-thirsty mosquitoes outside, we tallied the events of this long day. In 13½ hours on the water, we had advanced 43 miles, of which Doree had done nineteen as *avant* and Ben had done 24. This excellent progress had brought our total for the trip to 233 miles, having averaged nearly 36 miles a day for 6½ days. We were now 32 miles from our destination. However, as was our usual custom, we did not set a goal of reaching the take-out place by the end of the following day. Nature has a way of foiling such plans and schedules, making fools of script-following travelers.

Day Eight

Stirring myself at 7:00, I spent an hour in the tent updating the journal and map with the previous evening's activities. Finally emerging, I was pleased to note that we had again been blessed with beautiful weather: 75 degrees in the shade, a hazy blue sky without a cloud, and a moderate breeze out of the west, helpful for traveling in an easterly direction. We started our day by picking a nice supply of wild raspberries beneath the spruce and scattered birches that stood behind our campsite. Even Toby relished the juicy red berries as an accompaniment to our usual gorp breakfast. Before long, loaded and ready, the canoe was floating offshore, waiting expectantly for another day of adventures.

After an hour of southeastward traveling, we took a break for fifteen minutes while tethered to a waterlogged tree just off of Pointe du Lièvre (Rabbit Point). Then eight miles of northeasterly paddling, amid moderate waves of glistening water marching in our direction, brought us to Spruce Island. Off the southernmost tip of this landmass, we scared up several hundred terns, small birds that make their living by diving for fish. A short time later, we traveled through a mile-long swarm of tiny green airborne insects, which swarmed around our faces and got into our eyes. We simply pushed on, and after about twenty minutes the swarm receded behind our stern.

During the previous two days on the lake-like expanses of the lower Saskatchewan, we had admired many different water birds: two armadas of twenty to thirty ducks bobbing quietly on the surface; many single pelicans, as well as assemblages of up to eight of them gliding in a straight-line or V formation; a few groups of ten to fifteen American black ducks flying in formation about three feet above the surface of the water; and myriad terns. The latter bird, about fifteen inches long and entirely white and grey except for a cap of jet black on the top of its head, has a long, distinctive tail which is widely forked. Often, we were entertained by watching one of these birds dive straight down into the water from an airborne height of six to eight feet, and come up holding a minnow in its long, red-orange beak. For the voyageurs, the populations of water birds here had been a source of both entertainment and food. When Gabriel Franchère traveled through this stretch in 1814, he noted in his journal that he had prepared a delicious batch of fritters with flour and gull eggs.

Over the course of the morning, the breeze gradually lessened, finally reducing so much that it would no longer fill the sail. Ahead of us lay the northern end of the eight-mile-long peninsula which extends due north and forms the eastern boundary of Cedar Lake. At the base of this feature, the N.W.C. had operated two different Cedar Lake Posts during the 1790s, each of which was in business for less than five years. Some six decades later, personnel of the H.B.C. had also opened a short-term post in this same area, beginning in 1857. At 1:30, arriving at the tip of the peninsula, we halted to eat our lunch, having advanced fifteen miles in four hours since leaving our campsite. During the break, we took a very refreshing swim in the warm water beside the point. We needed to cool down and rinse off some salty sweat, since the temperature had risen to 82 degrees in the shade.

As the beaming sun continued its gradual arc across the sky, Doree took over in the bow seat. Rounding the end of the peninsula, we entered the Lac Traverse (Crossing Lake) section of Lac Bourbon, which is now called Cross Bay. The five-mile-long stretch of water that lay in front of our bow had once been the narrow passage between the Cedar Lake and Cross Bay sections of the lake. Flowing in a southeasterly direction, the channel had originally offered several rapids and a very strong current, requiring at one place the Grand Décharge. Here, upbound canoes had been lined up the passage either empty or with half of the cargo, while the remainder of the cargo had been carried along the shoreline for 230 yards. Now, these features all lay drowned beneath the backwaters of the dam, so that we faced just a flat, unruffled extension of the original lake. Doree and I paddled the five miles in two hours, the last couple of those miles against a moderate head wind. Then we rounded Lookout Point and entered the original area of Cross Bay, where exposed limestone ledges again bordered the shorelines beneath the towering evergreen forest cover. Four miles toward the southeast, now on the bottom of the backwater lake, lay the place where the river had originally returned to its narrow channel, for the final dash of twelve tumultuous miles down to the mouth at Lake Winnipeg. I had intended to change our course toward the northeast after rounding the point. However, due to the waves that were advancing from the east, I was obliged to first steer toward the east for a mile or so, quartering the waves, before finally settling on a northeasterly direction.

With Ben happily ensconced in the role of the *avant* for the final eight miles of our voyage, Doree resumed her private reveries, but started us singing again for the final sprint to the end. We arrived at the Hobbs Resort at about 6:30, where our van had been waiting for seven days. Having progressed 32 miles in nine hours on the water today, we had finally brought to completion the trip of 265 miles. Over the course of 7 1/2 days of traveling, from Tuesday after lunchtime until the following Tuesday after suppertime, we had averaged more than 35 miles per day. Doree had done 95 miles in the role of the bow paddler, while Ben had operated for 170 miles in that position. We had enjoyed beautifully warm and even hot weather every day of the trip, with only two short episodes of rain, one of which had been just a welcome cooling shower. In addition, there had not been too much serious head wind and oncoming waves to contend with, except during the one day on Lac Namew.

As a family, we had worked outstandingly well together, through some very long and demanding days, often laughing and joking. Ben had amazed his parents throughout the trip, with his ability to paddle strongly for hours at a time with no apparent tiring. He also could line the canoe through shallow, marshy-bottomed lakes much more efficiently than we could, with his long legs. Finally, at the end of each grueling day, he still had enough strength left to manage both of the big Duluth packs by himself.

At this point, we were pleased to have completed 1,363 miles on the mainline route, nearly half of its total length. Feeling rather like veterans now, we were ready to face the challenging segments that lay ahead.

After returning home, Ben resumed his life as a ninth grade student, while Tim soon headed out for the Canadian Canoe Museum and various other locales in southwestern Ontario, where he studied 27 dugout canoes. (These were added to the 43 specimens that he had documented earlier in the summer in Michigan, Indiana, Ohio, and West Virginia.) I returned to my therapy work at the psychiatric hospital with a fresh new perspective, while Kevin, just about to turn age sixteen, approached us with an adventure of his own. His refugee friend Adolfo, age eighteen, was departing for Huehuetenango in the far-flung highlands of Guatemala, to return to his Kanobal roots for nearly a year. Kevin proposed skipping his junior year of high school so he could accompany Adolfo. After Tim and I had consulted for about ten minutes, we thought, "This might be the experience of a lifetime for Kevin, so he can see how the majority of people in the world live, in poverty." We are a family that looks for new experiences to mold us into capable, adventurous spirits, so we said, "Go for it, Kev!" (Doree)

XII

Tenth Voyage
Lower Churchill River,
Upper Sturgeon Weir River,
and Amisk Lake, August 17-24, 1993

A great secret of success is to go through life
As a man who never gets used up.
Albert Schweitzer

Mishaps are like knives, that either serve us or cut us, as we grasp
them by the blade or the handle.
James Russell Lowell

Take into account that great love and great achievements
Involve great risks.
Dalai Lama

This year's voyage would take place entirely in Canadian Shield terrain, in a rather flat region that is covered with a mostly evergreen forest of spruce, jack pine, and tamarack (larch). Our meandering southeasterly course of about 190 miles, all within the province of Saskatchewan, would involve three waterways. The roughly seventy miles on the Churchill River, followed by more than a hundred miles on the Sturgeon Weir River, would entail two passages that are each called rivers. However, each of these watercourses is, for the most part, a chain of rather slender lakes, often with a set of rapids or a waterfall at the place where one lake narrows down to spill into the next one. The final leg of our trip would traverse Amisk Lake. The Churchill River traditionally served as the border between the lands of the Algonquian-speaking Crees to the south and the Athapascan-speaking Chipewyans to the north. Thus, our voyage would take us through the original territory of the Cree nation.

Departing from Ravinia Park at 9 P.M. on Sunday evening, after our C.S.O. performance of Mahler's *Symphony Number 1* (one of

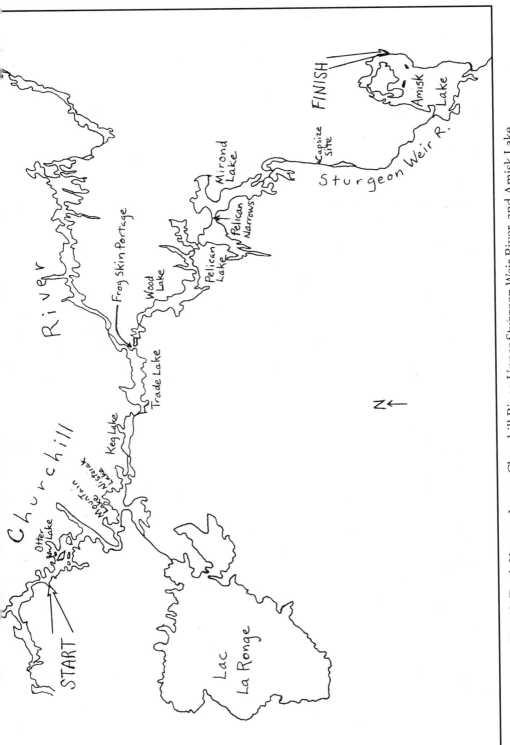

Fig. 13, Tenth Voyage: Lower Churchill River, Upper Sturgeon Weir River, and Amisk Lake

my wife's all-time favorites), Doree and I shared the driving duties throughout the night. At 8:02 A.M., after eleven hours of alternately driving the van and dozing on the sleeping platform at the back, we arrived at Browns Valley, Minnesota, just two minutes late for my appointment. At the home of our congenial hosts Ben and Janet, I studied in detail three dugout canoes that had been found in Lake Traverse, the body of water that forms the border between Minnesota and South Dakota in this area. These three craft would be added to the 39 dugouts that I had studied earlier in the summer in Michigan, Wisconsin, and southern Ontario. In addition, I had spent two exhilarating days during July at a museum in Ohio, documenting every minute feature of a surviving birchbark cargo canoe from the fur trade era, which had been built by Ojibwa craftworkers of the Lake Erie region.

After our welcome interlude out of the van at Browns Valley, another eighteen hours of shared driving brought us to Angell's Resort at Denare Beach, near the north end of Amisk Lake. Here, where our canoe trip would ultimately end, we picked up our shuttle driver. Gordon then rode with us for five hours, as I drove the final 275 miles to the put-in at Missinipe; en route, we stopped to buy a supply of burgers at the town of La Ronge. Finally arriving at the little community of Missinipe, our point of departure on the Churchill River, I first arranged our shuttle driver for the following year at a local canoe outfitter, after which we loaded in at the public boat ramp. Since leaving Ravinia Park a day and a half earlier, we had covered 1,700 miles in the van, to reach this long-anticipated moment.

Day One

With Ben, now age 152/12 and about to enter the tenth grade, in the bow position, we happily pushed off onto the Otter Lake section of the Churchill River at 2:30 P.M. The air temperature was 65 degrees in the shade, the sky was completely overcast with dark grey cloud cover, and a considerable wind was blowing out of the east-northeast. Immediately upon leaving the little inlet and entering the open, unsheltered expanse of Walker Bay, we began our labors against the rather stiff head wind and its accompanying waves, which were moderately large. In addition, a light rain was falling, although it would continue for only about ninety minutes.

As was typical, it only took me about two minutes to fall into the seventeenth century mode and adapt totally to the lifestyle of a wilderness paddling expedition. I was instantly engrossed in assessing and dealing with the wind and the waves, while planning the route on the map and locating that passage amid the undulating shorelines of the mainland and the islands, which were distinguished at a distance only by the various gradations of green of the forest cover. On these trips, I loved the feeling of total exposure to and immersion in the wilderness, with my entire world reduced to my loved ones, the canoe, and the minimal belongings that were necessary for us to move through the natural setting, dealing with whatever challenges we encountered along the way. It was during these voyages that I felt the closest to my French ancestors, since our surroundings looked virtually the same as when my people had traveled these water paths in birchbark canoes centuries ago.

The previous year, our entire paddling route had been located in the limestone country of the prairie region. This year's journey brought us back into the familiar Canadian Shield terrain, whose exposed granite shorelines and evergreen forest were whispering *"Bienvenue, nos amis"* (Welcome back, our friends). The forest cover along the Churchill has a soft, fuzzy appearance, since it consists mostly of spruce trees, along with some jack pines and tamaracks, interspersed with scattered stands of birches and poplars.

However, in spite of the familiar scenes of the Shield terrain, there was a very unusual aspect to our surroundings this year: the water level of the Churchill River was a whopping seven feet below normal for the late-summer season! This dramatically reduced level was the lowest that had ever been recorded during the sixty years that records had been kept, going back to 1934. Although the Churchill basin had received a great deal of snow during the previous winter, this moisture had run off during the spring, and rainfall had been almost non-existent during the entire summer, causing the level of the river to drop precipitously. As we would travel on the excessively low Churchill for four days, seeing its abnormally exposed shorelines and boulder-strewn rapids and falls, I would have serious concerns about the route that lay ahead on the next river. I wondered how much water we might have for paddling after we would cross over the height of land of the Frog Portage, and would face the headwaters of the Sturgeon Weir River. Even at normal levels, this headwaters area often presented a passage that was shallow, meandering, and swampy.

The Crees had called the Churchill River the Missinippi (Big River), and even when it was running at low water levels, its flow was indeed heavy. In the latter 1600s, the waterway had received its Anglo designation, being named after John Churchill, the Duke of Marlborough, who served as the Governor of the Hudson's Bay Company at that time. The first trading facility built at the mouth of the river, where it flows into Hudson's Bay far to the northeast of our location, was also named Churchill Fort, after the same individual, the Big Boss. For about the first forty miles of our journey, the right shore of the river would lie in Lac La Ronge Provincial Park, which extends southward from the watercourse for some fifty miles.

At 4:30, having threaded our way for five miles through the upper portion of the island-studded Lac la Loutre (Otter Lake) in two hours of rather strenuous effort, we paused for a short break. Setting off again with Doree as the strong-pulling *avant*, after about a mile, I realized that the terrain around us did not match where I thought we were on the map. So we backtracked for fifteen minutes to a very slender point, which was the last landmark that I remembered passing at which I had known exactly where we were on the chart. From there, I could see that I had steered our bow from the narrow point southward through a row of three islands, instead of heading toward the southeast to a different group of very similar-looking, evergreen-covered islands. Losing one's place on the map during a wilderness trip, becoming *dérouté* (off course), feels very uncomfortable for two reasons. First, there is the possibility of not finding your way, with its attendant dire consequences. This is augmented by the physical effort that is expended while trying to locate the right track again, while traveling at the slow pace of 3 m.p.h.

Two years after this particular voyage, in 1995, the Global Positioning System (GPS) would be made available to the public. This system, developed by the U.S. military, consists of a hand-held, satellite-based unit which indicates on its miniature screen the exact location of the unit on the globe; it also often provides directions on how to travel to another desired location. However, during our entire fifteen years of paddling the mainline route, we neither owned nor took with us such a device; nor did we carry an emergency signal unit, radio, or cell phone. We wanted to rely completely on our own strengths and resourcefulness to complete these trips, without any backup systems, even though this approach involved considerably greater risks. With the advent of various electronic locational and communications devices, large numbers of people who are entirely unprepared to handle wilderness situations now venture into the wilds every year. Poorly equipped and untrained, they count on their battery-operated devices to keep themselves from getting lost, and when necessary they also rely on these units to contact rescue personnel when they lose their way, or encounter difficulties that they are unable to handle themselves. Every year, considerable numbers of individuals blithely venture into the wilderness, reassured that they will be fine with their GPS unit to keep them on course, and their cell phone handy to contact rescuers when their own resources are not up to the challenges that Nature offers. Unfortunately, in some instances this method produces some very severe consequences.

In ancient times, native and French paddlers had no electronic devices at their disposal. However, they were equipped with many generations worth of experience and knowledge. In addition, there was a considerable amount of canoe traffic on the major waterways at that time, offering fellow travelers who could provide assistance in case of major emergencies. In contrast, the Kent family had never traveled on any portions of the mainline route before, we had no comrades or other canoes with us, and we almost never encountered any other travelers along the way. However, by relying only on ourselves, equipped with appropriate gear, maps, foods, skills, and stamina, we were able to travel the route in relative safety. In the process, we learned a great deal about the hidden depths of the wilderness, and how to both cope with it and thrive in it. We also developed all the more our level of confidence.

For the next two hours, Doree and I struggled with a recalcitrant *La Vieille* and the oncoming waves, to slowly advance another five miles toward the southeast. Ben snoozed, with Toby on the packs behind him providing a pillow. Finally we reached the outlet of Otter Lake, when we arrived at the first set of the Sault de la Montagne (Mountain Falls, this set is now called Robertson Falls). The voyageurs had designated this westernmost of the two Mountain Carries as the Portage Pierreux de la Montagne (Stony Carry of the Mountain). After making the easy portage of eighty yards around the frothing drop, hiking over a ridge on the left shore, we discovered a most welcome sandy beach at the end of the path, recently bared by the extremely low water level. Impressed with this rare feature in Canadian Shield country, we decided to call it a day at 7:00, and set up camp for the night at the front edge of the comfortable beach. While we were erecting the tent and preparing the gear, Toby's antics brought big smiles to our faces, as he sprinted at full speed in broad circles on the open expanse of tan sand. Buried in the recently-exposed beach, I discovered a stave from an ancient oak keg. I wondered whether it was a remnant from a container that had been dropped and shattered on the portage long ago, or if the keg had been broken during a capsize that had taken place somewhere upriver centuries before. Submerged in the soil at the bottom of the cold river, this piece of carefully-shaped hardwood could very well have survived from that period.

Finishing off the remaining burgers from the restaurant stop at La Ronge, we gazed into the leaping orange flames of Ben's fire for a long while. Doree raved about the impressive display of northern lights that she and Ben had witnessed the previous night, while she had been driving and I had been sleeping. However, this evening the heavens offered no such show for our enjoyment. After trading much-needed massages in the tent, we were lulled to sleep by the music of the falls, which rushed and tumbled about a hundred feet from our shelter. This day, after launching at 2:30 P.M., we had covered ten miles in 41/2 challenging hours on the water, and had also made one portage, before deciding to set up camp early. After the very long drive to the put-in and the demanding half-day of paddling, we were in need of a long, refreshing sleep.

Day Two

Returning from the world of dreams at 6:45, we headed out an hour later without eating, beneath skies that had just a few patches of light blue showing here and there through occasional tears in the solid grey cloud cover. A moderate breeze wafted in from the northeast, while the air temperature measured 63 degrees in the shade. After paddling a quarter-mile across a tiny expanse of water, we arrived at the second Portage de la Montagne, which circumvented the cascade that is now called Twin Falls. The carry on the right shore over a narrow peninsula was only four hundred yards long, but it involved a moderate ascent at one end and a steep descent at the other end.

By 8:30, we had reloaded and were traveling down the eleven-mile length of the slender Lac de la Montagne (Mountain Lake). Shortly, we decided to take our breakfast break on one of the many small islands that fill much of the northern half of the lake. On the closest island, to our delight, we came upon a semi-permanent summer fishing camp of a Cree family, which was unoccupied at the time. This particular camp, equipped with landing ramps of lashed saplings for beaching canoes and powerboats, contained five canvas wall tents with exterior frames made of slender lashed poles. Some of these canvas shelters, either white or dark tan in color, were equipped with plank floors, wooden beds, and cast iron heat stoves. In addition, the miniature outpost had a long eating table and flanking benches in the open air, all made from boards mounted across thick posts set into the ground, as well as sapling racks for sun-drying split fish. Nestled into a sheltering row of tall bushes near the eating table stood a conical shelter for cooking and for smoking fish. This structure consisted of a tepee-shaped framework of upright poles, which was covered up to head height on three sides with tarps of dark tan canvas; the top portion had been left open, to allow rising smoke to escape. Inside was a large central fire area, a wall-to-wall drying and smoking rack made of saplings at chest height, and six blackened cooking kettles overturned off to one side. All of these features of the cooking shelter combined to create a scene that looked very much like a setting from several centuries ago. Walking through the camp, we imagined the quiet conversations and the contented laughter that these shelters and table had witnessed over successive generations, as the native people had processed their catch for the following winter's food. A testament to the huge numbers of whitefish and pickerel that could be harvested each year in the lower Churchill River was recorded by Alexander Henry in June of 1776, when he traveled along this waterway. According to his account, there were so many thousands of these fish at the rapids that the voyageurs in his party were able to harvest them simply by striking the fish with their canoe paddles.

As we cruised past various of the other islands near the falls, we counted at least eight additional native fishing camps, all similarly outfitted for rather comfortable long-term living during summers; all of them were unoccupied at the moment. Arrowing down the lake, we observed numerous groups of three or four white pelicans, gliding in straight-line formations only a few feet above the water. Four miles after leaving the falls, as we were working our way between the islands, we were brought to an abrupt and surprising halt at a place where the topo map indicated that there was a narrow passage between two rather large islands. However, with this year's very low water levels, the usually navigable passage was now just a rock-strewn path, with no water at all! So we were obliged to detour toward the north for a mile, to pass around the opposite end of the northern island, after which we glided onto the main open stretch of Lac de la Montagne. In this wide-open expanse, where the wind was no longer blocked by islands, we joyfully raised the sail and were pushed at considerable speed for seven miles, down to the bottom of the lake. At one point during our speedy jaunt, a pair of adult bald eagles stood regally on a barren rock island until we approached quite close, before flapping off toward the east.

Just before reaching the sharp bend toward the left which marked the outlet of Lac de la Montagne, we passed beneath Amuchewaspimewin (Shooting Up Rock, in Cree). At the base of this tall granite cliff, which rose directly from the water and was topped with a thick growth of spruce trees, a native shaman would shoot an arrow from his canoe. If the projectile lodged in the backward-angled cliff, good luck was predicted for the hunting party that was about to depart. However, if the arrow fell back into the water, bad luck was forecast, and the hunters did not go out that day.

Immediately upon rounding the tip of the long, southward-pointing peninsula that created the bend toward the left, we arrived at Stanley Mission, having covered twelve miles in 3 1/4 hours since our breakfast break. Not far from the water's edge on the north shore, on a low, grass-covered rise, stood the Anglican Holy Trinity Church, the oldest surviving building in the province of Saskatchewan. Constructed over a span of six years between 1854 and 1860, the tall steepled church was built of lumber that had been sawn by the Crees. The shingle-roofed building, painted entirely white on the exterior, and white, pale blue, and red ocher on the interior, was fitted with iron hardware and stained glass that had been shipped from England, via the H.B.C. After eating our lunch on the grass behind the church, we picked a generous supply of plump, purplish black saskatoon berries, which we found growing beside the cemetery. Ambling among the well-tended graves, we noted that most of the burials in the older section were each surrounded by a low picket fence, painted either white or light blue. The grave markers in the newest section indicated that a disproportionate number of the deceased in recent decades had been young men in their teens or early twenties.

During the course of the morning, the clouds had cleared away completely, and a radiant sun had warmed the air to a comfortable 80 degrees. When we resumed our travels at 2:15, with Ben as the bow paddler, we opted not to visit the native community of about seventy homes which stands on the opposite side of the channel from the church, on the Stanley Indian Reserve. Since the left turn had changed our course from a southwesterly direction to an easterly heading, the formerly helpful breeze now became a hindering head wind. As a result, it took us 1 1/2 hours to cover the three miles to the Stanley Rapids. Along the way, we observed high water marks on waterside cliffs that were up to nine feet above the present level. At these places, pollen and other minute organic material floating on the surface of the water had adhered to the adjacent cliff face, and had dried there to form a clearly defined record of the water's height at that time. During our laborious paddle of ninety minutes over the glistening water, we gratefully noted what a fine improvement the new inflatable seat pads were for all three of us! Besides making our butts much more comfortable, these air-filled cushions, which attached to the canoe seats with velcro straps, also made the minor imbalances of cargo and people, which sometimes made the canoe lean slightly to one side or the other, almost unnoticeable.

At the Stanley Rapids, where the drop is divided in two by a midstream island, we chose the northern (left) channel, and made our portage on the right shore (along the edge of the island). Our carry took us directly beside the rapids, which now had only a small amount of water flowing amid the jumbled array of massive boulders. Setting out at 4:30, again working against wind and waves, we crossed the three-mile width of Drope Lake. Due to the low water levels, there was no vestige of the usual fast current when we passed through the Goulet de Grenouille (Frog Narrows), which took us from Lac Drope into Lac Nistowiak.

With Doree hard at work in the bow seat, we continued to head into the northeast wind and waves. Seeking a little respite, we made a detour around the lee side of Hall Island, skirting its southern shore, to avoid the brunt of the wind that blasted unhindered across the full width of the lake. As we made our way eastward through Brown's Bay, the end of the lake narrowed and the wind and waves reduced considerably. At 8:15, we arrived at the Portage de la Rivière Rapide (Rapid River Carry, now called Potter Rapids Carry or Drinking Rapids Carry). We circumvented the wild, dramatic rapids by hiking for a hundred yards on the right shore, along a wooden walkway that had been built across the narrow neck of land here to make life easy for fishermen. Since Ben carried at the same time both of the big Duluth packs, weighing together 140 pounds on his back and front, we were able to complete this entire portage in just 45 minutes.

At the end of the path, near the roaring falls, we set up camp for the night. I imagined many brigade leaders over the centuries had announced at this place, *"Nous nous arrêtons ici pour faire la chaudière* (We'll stop here to cook)." Doree rummaged in the food pack to locate the ingredients for a nourishing stew of ground turkey patties, corn, peas, and noodles. While savoring this feast, we also relished a stunning orange sunset as the sun slid behind the tree line off to the west. Since this morning's departure, we had traveled 27 miles, twenty of them against adverse wind and waves, and had made three portages.

Satisfied with our very accomplishing day, we relaxed and chatted about the various posts that had operated in this area. In about 1780, two different Rapid River Posts were established by independent Montreal traders; each of these facilities operated for less than three years. In addition, a N.W.C. post by the same name opened in this area in 1798; it too was very short-lived. Rival traders of the H.B.C. founded a short-term Rapid River House in this general area in about 1796, and later opened another establishment of the same name beginning in 1831, which operated for many years. The rumbling cascade beside our campsite was called Rapid River Falls, yet the mouth of the Rapid River (and its Fisher Rapids) lay three miles west of our camp, on the southern shore of Nistowiak Lake, which was also sometimes called Rapid River Lake. As a result, it was not clear just where these various Rapid River establishments had been located along the shores of the lake.

Day Three

Starting my day at 6:30, with an auspicious clear blue sky above and an air temperature of 55 degrees in the shade, I enjoyed the falls by myself in the early-morning light for fifteen minutes before rousing the family. While staring into the raging white water, I considered the fact that one of Ben's least favorite parts of canoe jaunts was pulling on cold, wet, sandy socks each morning as soon as he left his cozy sleeping bag. To rectify this situation, before this trip, I had provided each of us with a pair of thin polypropylene socks. So now at bedtime each night, Ben would wring out his pair, shake out much of the sand, and put them at the very bottom of his sleeping bag; thus, in the morning, they were not very wet, they were not at all chilly, and he was happy.

Departing at 8:00, we easily ran the set of mild downhill rapids that lay a quarter-mile from our campsite, taking us into Lac de Boire (Drinking Lake). The paddling conditions were absolutely perfect: a cloudless sky, no breeze, and a gleaming water surface that doubled perfectly the exposed rocky shorelines, the stately evergreens that rose above them, and the powder blue sky above. While traveling exactly eastward on the gold-tinted path of the rising sun, we ingested our breakfast of gorp and strawberry-flavored, instant breakfast drink. Ben paddled five miles in 1 1/4 hours, after which Doree took on the duties of the *avant* for two more miles, bringing us to the Sault de L'Île (Island Falls). By 10:15, we had easily made seven miles in 2 1/4 hours, traveling in step with the ancient rhythms of the river and its surrounding woods.

Instead of making the portage that circled around Island Falls, in certain seasons the voyageurs could make a sharp left turn just before the falls and take an alternate route through the Inman Channel, passing between the north shore and Garr Island for 31/2 miles. However, this passage involved two small sets of rapids, which could each require a carry in low water seasons. With the extremely low level of the water during our trip, this alternate route would have been entirely impractical, so we were obliged to deal with Island Falls.

In the middle of the falls stood three low mounds of barren solid bedrock, rounded and smoothed from thousands of years of flowing water and grinding ice. In all seasons except those with extremely low water levels, white water roared in a raging downhill torrent along both sides of these six-foot-tall obstructions. This summer, however, the higher right channel was virtually dry, with all of the flow taking place to the left of the three low islands, which now formed a single unified island.

It took us an hour to first scout the area and then portage all of the gear for a quarter-mile along the right shoreline. Before I began my return trip to bring over the canoe, Ben, with an excited gleam in his eyes, said, "Dad, lets run it!" At first, I was totally against the crazy idea. Along the left side of the island, there was a tremendous flow of dark blue water rushing smoothly down a drop of about ten feet of elevation. At the bottom of the drop, a massive area of roaring white water filled the entire channel, from the midstream island across to the far shore. It was extremely unlikely that the canoe would remain upright through that latter swath of wildness. However, Ben pointed out that there were no boulder obstacles to contend with in the entire distance, just the immense flow followed by lots of turbulence at the bottom. He very much wanted to run down that channel, "for educational purposes." Since the sun was shining beautifully, the temperature was a comfortable 70 degrees, and my fifteen-year-old son was very persistent, I finally agreed to comply with his wishes, against my better judgment. We had no idea just how educational the next hour would be!

At 1:15, father and son embarked, with Doree and Toby poised to photograph our escapade from a nearby vantage point atop the midstream island. I quickly maneuvered the canoe into the central tongue of water, so that we would go over the lip of the low falls at the place with the least drop. The adrenaline was pumping. "Here we go!" Immediately below the smooth, angled drop, as soon as the bow sliced into the frothing white mass of standing waves that loomed up to four feet high across the entire channel, the canoe instantly flipped upside down, hurling us into the maelstrom. After what seemed like a short lifetime, we groped our way to the surface, gasping for air. Each of us was holding our paddle in one hand and grasping the canoe with the other hand, facing one another wide-eyed across the bottom of the upside-down craft. As we were being swept downstream by the tremendously powerful current, we righted the canoe. However, since the craft was entirely filled with water, the gunwales were some six to eight inches below the surface.

About fifteen seconds passed, and we were suddenly swept into a powerful whirlpool. Its deep center sucked most of the canoe three to four feet below the surface, while we both swirled in a circle around its outer edge, held up near the surface by our life preservers. I thought, "We're in trouble, big trouble! We have to have this canoe; it's our only way out of here! You can't have a canoe trip without a canoe!" As the green hull was pulled down, Ben lost his grip on his end, since he was closer to the center of the sucking funnel. Luckily, at my location closer to the outer edge of the whirlpool, my end was not nearly as deeply submerged, so I managed to retain my hold on it. After what seemed like an interminably long time, our beloved craft eventually resurfaced from the swirling vortex. My elation knew no bounds!

We were then swept away from the whirlpool and further downstream, beyond the area of the strongest turbulence, where we were finally able to climb into the canoe, which was still submerged about six inches below the surface. Our arms were too tired at this point to flip the craft and empty it in deep water while swimming, so it took about twenty minutes to slowly paddle the heavy, water-filled canoe near the right shore. When we finally reached a depth that was walkable, about a third of a mile downstream from the place where we had capsized, we hooted in gratefulness. It felt amazingly good to be alive and intact, and to feel solid rock under our feet again! Our upper bodies, now out of the cold water, welcomed the warmth of the benevolent Sun Goddess.

When we reached knee-deep shallows, in one motion we turned the canoe over in the water and emptied it. Then, walking slowly offshore with most of our energy sapped, we pulled it halfway back toward the place where the gear had been stacked at the end of our portage. We were now extremely wary of the tremendous current and the several whirlpools that we would encounter if we were to bring the craft all the way back to the gear, load it there, and try to paddle through that area of heavy turbulence.

After telling Doree the inside story of our *descente à l'enfer* (descent into hell), we carried the gear downstream to the canoe, loaded it in, enjoyed a rejuvenating lunch, and finally departed at 1:00, nearly three hours after having first arrived at the head of the falls. Ben was now a little wiser; he was also delighted to have convinced his safety-conscious Dad to experience those wild and memorable events with him.

Gliding easily over the nine-mile length of Lac de Baril (Keg Lake) in three hours, we reveled in the perfect conditions: pale azure sky with a few fluffy stationary clouds, air temperature of 70 degrees in the shade, and no wind. It almost seemed a shame to let the bow slice through such perfect reflections of sky and clouds. As the miles and the hours slid by, I entertained the family by listing many of the items that French traders had provided to their native customers. In most cases, over 60 percent of the value of each shipment of trade merchandise was represented by fabric, articles for sewing, and finished garments. The fabrics consisted of wool (including blankets), linen, cotton (especially after 1730, when it was first woven in France), and silk. The various sewing and decorating articles included scissors, straight pins, thread (of linen, silk, or cotton), wool yarn, needles, needle cases (made of pasteboard, turned wood, or sheet metal), thimbles, ribbon, binding tape or gartering, and decorative braid and lace. These items were accompanied by a number of accessories, such as buttons (made of brass, pewter, silver, or gold, or of a thread or fabric covering over a core of wood or bone), cuff links, hook-and-eye sets, and buckles. The vast majority of the finished garments that were supplied by the French included stockings, shirts and chemises, *capots* or hooded coats, dress coats, sashes, kerchiefs, hats, caps, and tuques. Less often, they provided leggings, breeches, garters for leggings or breeches, mantles, sets of separate sleeves, and short jackets.

To groom and decorate themselves, native people acquired from the traders combs fashioned of wood, ivory, or horn; various pigments for painting their faces, bodies, and clothing, including vermilion (for red), verdigris (for green or greenish blue), and azure (for blue); and mirrors made of glass or tin plate. Ornamentation also involved finger rings, wrist bands, arm bands, earbobs, various pendants (such as crosses and religious medals), gorgets, and brooches, all of which were made of copper, brass, pewter, or silver; glass beads; brass bells; and numerous items fashioned by the native people themselves from brass or copper wire, as well as from various salvaged metals.

To facilitate hunting and warfare, traders supplied their customers with firearms, gunpowder, bulk lead as well as pre-cast balls and shot, gun worms (charge pullers), gunflints, and sword blades to be hafted as spears, plus the snare-making materials of iron wire, brass or copper wire, and cordage. In addition to their uses in hunting and warfare, steel knives (both fixed-blade and folding-blade styles), axes, hatchets, and tomahawks were also utilized for many other activities. Fishing was aided by iron fish hooks and harpoons, commercially-made cordage (for making hook lines and weaving nets), and ice chisels. Other helpful trade implements for daily life included awls, hide scrapers, fire steels, hoes, and crooked knives. Various recreational items were also acquired from the French, such as jews-harps, brandy, wine, tobacco, tobacco boxes, and pipes made of stone, clay, pewter, sheet brass, sheet copper, or sheet steel.

Within this wide array of trade articles, a great number of them were items that the native people had made since prehistoric times, articles which they had fashioned from the materials that were found in their natural world. However, the European versions were typically created from such materials as fabric, various metals, or glass, which were not found in the natives' environment. In addition, certain of the articles that were provided by the French had had no precedent in the native world, such as firearms, jews-harps, mirrors, and fire steels.

The long conversation about fur trade merchandise certainly made the afternoon fly by. When we reached the outlet at the eastern end of Keg Lake at 4:15, Ben and I flew down the set of fast rapids there, and a quarter-mile later we arrived at Portage de Baril (Keg Carry). This portage skirted the falls of that same name, which dropped six feet in elevation. Although the path was only ninety yards long, it had both a steep ascent and a steep descent, so it took us an hour to complete the carry and reload. Shortly below the portage, we shot down a set of rapids along the left side of a small midstream island. Due to the low water level, all of these rapids were considerably more challenging to run than they would have been in normal levels.

Two miles further, as we neared the rapids in the narrows that would eventually lead us to the Grand Rapides, a line of nine white pelicans watched us from a long, exposed rock in midstream. They finally flapped away at low altitude, in an elongated linear formation. Pulling off on the right (south) shore at 6:00, we assessed the rapids, decided on the best route for lining the canoe, and had a snack of peanut butter crackers to bolster our energy for the task that lay ahead. Then all three of us laboriously lined the craft down the various sets of rapids in the fast current, wading in depths that ranged from our waist up to our chest. One of the biggest challenges was finding solid footing among the sharp, angular, and very irregular rocks that completely covered the bottom in a jumbled mess. It was quite a wild experience, but Ben did a great job of leading us over and around the submerged and exposed rocks, as we were being pushed from behind by the swift current. Another minor achievement had been completed.

A half-mile downstream, we landed at 7:00 on the left shore, to make the Portage des Grand Rapides. This carry bypassed a quarter-mile-long series of low ledges that extend across the entire channel, some of them submerged and others exposed. The path, through a forest of mostly tamarack and poplar trees, was a third of a mile long, with both a steep ascent and a steep descent. Deeply worn into the floor of the woods, this trail clearly remembered when legions of both native and French paddlers had tramped over its length each year, from the spring thaw until the fall freeze-up. During our return trip, unencumbered, we could not resist the huge numbers of ripe blueberries that called to us right beside the path. In an hour, we had transported all of the gear and the canoe over the trail, where we set up camp at its end. After preparing all of the gear for the night, we replenished much of our strength with a stew of ground turkey patties, noodles, tomatoes, onions, and mushrooms. Just like us, the hordes of mosquitoes at the campsite were also ravenous!

Today, in twelve hours on the water, we had covered twenty miles, including making three portages, running three rapids, and lining down another challenging series. In addition, Ben and I had survived the wild run and capsize at Sault de l'Île, which we had run with the canoe empty, knowing that we would almost certainly capsize. By the time we had reached the end of the third portage at 8 P.M., Doree and I were rather exhausted, after a long and satisfying day. To our amazement, Ben still had energy. He had become so strong and energetic on these trips that we could not imagine how we had managed them before he had begun providing so much help!

Day Four

I left the tent at 6:30, but let the rest of the family sleep in plenty of extra time, to allow them to recover after the strenuous activities of the previous day. Beside the portage trail, I picked a good supply of blueberries in my hat, as well as some wintergreen berries that I ate on the spot. With the silence broken only occasionally by a cheerful bird call, it took little imagination for me to visualize a native family collecting berries and medicinal plants in these woods centuries earlier. The wintergreen plant gave its berries, which were eaten by the native people as a stimulant, as well as a remedy for fever and pain. In addition, the berries were also crushed into a poultice that was applied to sore joints, to reduce the pain of rheumatism. Wintergreen leaves, in both fresh and dried forms, were simmered in water to make tea, which was sweetened with maple sugar. The blueberry plant, besides providing little blue fruits, also offered its flowers, which were dried and later placed on hot stones to create medicinal fumes. Breathing in these fumes was considered by the native residents of the forest to be a highly respected remedy for "craziness."

After finishing my berry-harvesting, I clambered up the tall cliff on the point, to get a better view of the final drop of the Grand Rapides, before returning to camp and awakening the rest of the crew. By 8:15 we were afloat, thirsty for another series of adventures.

It was a gorgeous day, with numerous white clouds advancing slowly toward the north, 65 degrees in the shade, and no breeze; the water shimmered in the sun like a huge mirror. As we flashed through the fast current in the narrow passage that led to Lac de la Traite (Trade Lake), six little ducklings skittered away to the base of the rocky cliff along the shoreline, on wings that were not yet ready for flight. When we immediately emerged onto the open waters of the lake, the mother duck swam in front of our bow, leading us further and further away from her babies. Headed east-northeast over the length of Trade Lake, Doree worked the bow paddle for three hours, to forge ahead nine miles.

During this time, with my body on automatic pilot, my mind drifted back to various events in the life of our trader ancestor Mathieu Brunet dit Lestang, who had emigrated from France in 1657, at the age of twenty. The surviving public documentation of his work in the fur trade only commences a quarter-century later, in 1683, when he was already age 46, had been married for sixteen years, and had nine children ranging in age from a newborn up to fifteen years. (Any earlier activities in the trade may have been carried out without official permission.) The earliest surviving document indicates that he made a one-year trading voyage to "the Ottawa Country," as the upper Great Lakes region was often called during that era, a trip which encompassed the years 1683-84. His next adventure in the interior spanned the period from 1685 to 1687, which he spent in the upper Mississippi region of Wisconsin. During that latter interval, he worked as a trading colleague of Nicholas Perrot, who eventually became one of the most famous of the early French traders in the Wisconsin-Minnesota region. Although the resulting furs and hides from this venture were destroyed in a warehouse fire, and with them the profits, Perrot signed a contract in 1688 by which he agreed to reimburse Lestang for the resources that Lestang had contributed to the voyage. However, this repayment would have to be postponed until Perrot would return from his 1688-89 trading trip on the upper Mississippi, when he would have some profits to share. Unfortunately, the 1685-87 venture proved to be one of those rare ones which resulted in a financial loss for all concerned. After that voyage, during the remaining 21 years of Lestang's life, he apparently did not participate in any additional fur trading activities, as either an active participant or as an investor, since no documentary evidence concerning such activities has been found.

As we were approaching the eastern end of Trade Lake, where it begins to narrow a few miles from its terminus, we decided to head for land, to take a lunch break and stretch our legs a bit. While still a considerable distance from the shoreline, without any warning, both Ben and Toby leaped overboard from the passenger section, and happily made the long swim to land. After our usual midday meal of peanut butter crackers and dried apple slices, we returned to the water at noon, with Ben in the bow seat.

Within an hour, we had covered the three miles to Portage de Grenouille (Frog Carry), where we would leave the Churchill River and portage over the low height of land to the Sturgeon Weir River. As we thought back, we were somewhat surprised to note that every lake section of the Churchill River that we had paddled on this trip had been quite green with algae. This phenomenon was probably related to the extremely low water levels that had persisted throughout the hot summer.

If we were to continue further down the Churchill toward the northeast, we would soon encounter the mouth of the Reindeer River flowing in from the left. This alternate route to Lake Athabasca, including the Reindeer River, Reindeer Lake, Blondeau River, Wollaston Lake, and Fond du Lac River, involved more than four hundred miles of traveling to reach the easternmost tip of Lake Athabasca. From there, a long westward journey over the full length of the lake was required to reach Ft. Chipewyan, at the western tip of the lake. David Thompson had been the first recorded European to travel this route, in 1795-96. Although he documented the passage

19. Upper: Preliminary Year. Ben guiding Tim on the first portage between Lac Quatre and Lac Hudson in the B.W.C.A.W.

20. Lower: Preliminary Year. Three tired paddlers arriving at our campsite on Lac Insula in the B.W.C.A.W.

21. Upper: Voyage One. Kevin and Ben at ages seven and five, just after each boy had earned his voyageur sash on the Mattawa River.

22. Lower: Voyage Two. The boys relishing a windbound day on Georgian Bay, enjoying the opportunity to sleep in, relax, and heal.

23. Upper: Voyage Three. During a break on the Ottawa River, Doree demonstrating our homemade sailing rig.

24. Lower: Voyage Five. Taking a lunch break at the outlet of Petit Lac de Rocher du Couteau in the B.W.C.A.W.

25. Upper: Voyage Five. Tim dragging the empty canoe up the second Petits Rapides de Rocher du Couteau, shunning the portage.

26. Lower: Voyage Five. Kevin, 77 pounds, portaging our 69 pound Canadienne, near the western end of the Grand Portage.

27. Upper: Voyage Six. Ben receiving a lesson in the duties of the *gouvernail*, on Lac La Croix in the B.W.C.A.W.

28. Lower: Voyage Six. Father and sons planning the next leg of the route, on Lac Croche in the B.W.C.A.W.

29. Upper: Voyage Six. Doree whipping up a delicious feast at our campsite on Lac de Bois Blanc in the B.W.C.A.W.

30. Lower: Voyage Ten. Tim and Ben in trouble, immediately after they had capsized at the Sault de l'Île on the Churchill River.

31. Upper: Voyage Ten. Traveling in absolute serenity down Lac de Baril after the wild capsize on the Churchill River.

32. Lower: Voyage Eleven. Doree paddling in the rain near dusk on Lac Primeau of the Churchill River, as Ben and Toby nap.

33. Upper: Voyage Twelve. Arriving jubilantly at Ft. Chipewyan on Lac Athabasca, the northwestern terminus of the mainline route.

34. Lower: Voyage Fourteen. Taking a 5 A.M. break at sunrise, after two hours of beautiful starlit paddling on Lac Winnipeg.

on his master map of 1814, this was never the primary fur trade route to and from Ft. Chip. The route along the upper Churchill River, Clearwater River, and Athabasca River would always hold that distinction.

Instead of leaving the Churchill River here at the Frog Portage and traveling down the Sturgeon Weir River, if we were to paddle down the full length of the Churchill to its mouth at Hudson's Bay, we would arrive at the Prince of Wales Fort. This massive, cannon-studded fortress, located some eight hundred miles as the crow flies from the Frog Portage, was constructed of stone by the H.B.C. between 1732 and about 1770.

However, we did intend to make the Portage de Grenouille (Frog Carry), and then travel southward along the Sturgeon Weir. To facilitate the transporting of modern powerboats over the height of land at this location, crossing the stretch of land which lies between the Churchill River and the Saskatchewan River drainage system, a set of rails about 350 yards long had been installed over the low, gradual rise. To carry the heavy boats, a sturdy wooden cart with train-style wheels had been mounted on the rails. Since the cart was at the opposite end of the portage when we arrived at the north end, Ben and I walked to the far end of the rail tracks and pushed the cart back to our end of the portage. As we were approaching the terminus of the tracks on the downhill portion, the vehicle gained more and more speed. Not realizing what might be in store for us, we neglected to curb our enthusiasm, and allowed the cart to roll so fast that, when it reached the end of the rails, the two forward wheels leaped over the low stopping barricade. When our paralyzing laughter had finally subsided and we could stand up again, we three managed to lift the cart back onto the tracks, after which we loaded first the gear and then the overturned canoe on top of the load.

While Ben easily pushed the cart up the gradual slope and then down the gentle decline on the opposite side, Doree, Toby, and I ambled beside him, as I ruminated out loud about the history of this place and the regions that lay to the south and to the north. The year 1775, a full fifteen years after the British had taken control of New France, marked the very first time that traders decided to venture further toward the northwest beyond the Saskatchewan River Valley, which had represented the outer limits of commerce during the French regime. That autumn, Alexander Henry and his four-canoe party, along with the brothers Joseph and Thomas Frobisher and their six-canoe party, decided to pool their resources and manpower for the following year. This was one of the first instances during the British period of purposeful cooperation taking place between a number of independent Montreal-based traders, instead of the fierce competition which had been customary during the previous fifteen years. From this point on, non-competitive arrangements between various traders would increase, helping them to both control expenses and maintain consistent prices. Over the years, there would be numerous informal agreements and temporary companies among various traders, along with their outfitters and investors. Many of these individuals would finally join together in 1783 to establish the Northwest Company (N.W.C.). Two years later, in 1785, the Beaver Club or Coterie du Castor was established at Montreal, by a group of the most prominent and wealthy investors and merchant-outfitters at that time. Eight of the nineteen founding members of this exclusive association were French Canadian; they were joined by six Scotsmen, three Englishmen, and two Americans.

The Henry-Frobisher party of 1775, totaling forty voyageurs plus the three leaders, managed to travel up the lower Sturgeon Weir River as far as Amisk Lake before ice blocked their further progress in November. After the group had wintered on the southwestern shore of the lake, Thomas Frobisher and six men headed northward on foot in April, traveling along the upper Sturgeon Weir to the height-of-land portage which took them to the Churchill River, where they built a small post at the north end of the portage. On June 15, the remainder of the combined party joined them there. Before long, a major convoy of Chipewyans from the Athabasca region arrived, en route down the Churchill to trade with the H.B.C. at the mouth of the river. When the Montreal-based traders convinced the natives to deal with them instead of with the H.B.C., and avoid the long journey down to the Bay, the following day-and-a-half witnessed the exchange of their entire cargo of peltries, which included twelve thousand beavers plus large numbers of otters and martens. Afterward, Thomas Frobisher, bringing along the remaining stock of unsold merchandise, traveled with the native brigade back to their home area on the upper Churchill River, while his colleagues transported out the huge supply of peltries. Due to the huge success of this first trading venture at this locale on the Churchill River, the

French and Anglos thereafter often called it the Portage de la Traite (Trade Carry). Montreal traders would maintain a Poste de la Traite at this location for the next several decades.

However, the Crees had a much different name for this place; they called it Athiquisipichigan Ouinigam, the Portage of the Stretched Frog Skin. Alexander Mackenzie recorded the origins of this name when he passed here in 1789:

"The Kristineaux [Cree], when they first came to this country...either destroyed or drove back the natives [Chipewyans], whom they held in great contempt on many accounts, but particularly for their ignorance in hunting the beaver, as well as in preparing, stretching, and drying the skins of those animals. And as a sign of their derision, they stretched the skin of a frog, and hung it up at the portage."

Due to this incident, the French sometimes termed this place the Portage de Grenouille (Frog Carry).

The exceedingly profitable commerce that Thomas Frobisher and other traders carried out on the upper Churchill in the following year of 1777 inspired a number of independent merchants to expand their operations even further toward the northwest. These individuals combined their stock of merchandise in 1778 to heavily equip Peter Pond with four canoes, for a major venture. It would entail paddling up to the headwaters of the Churchill, making the thirteen-mile carry over the La Loche or Methye Portage, and then traveling down the Clearwater and Athabasca Rivers to expand the commerce into the Athabasca country, by establishing a post on the Athabasca River about forty miles south of Lake Athabasca. This was the first instance in which European traders advanced northward over this very significant height of land, leaving the Churchill River and Nelson River watershed, which flowed eastward to Hudson's Bay, and entering the Athabasca watershed, which flowed northward to the Arctic Ocean. The key to this entire expansion of 1775-1778 had been the 350 yard carry at the Frog Skin Portage, which functioned as the threshold to both the Churchill River and the adjacent Clearwater and Athabasca Rivers.

At 2:30, we were poised to launch onto the Sturgeon Weir River, after an entertaining and nearly effortless rail-assisted carry across the Frog Skin Portage. This was the moment that I had been concerned about ever since we had first discovered that the water level of the Churchill River was an astounding seven feet below normal for this season. In 1789, Alexander Mackenzie had described the headwaters section of the upper Sturgeon Weir River as "an intricate, narrow, winding, and shallow channel for eight miles. The interruptions in this distance are frequent, but depend much on the state of the waters." And those comments had been based not on the drought-level waters that we had encountered on the Churchill, but on more normal levels!

However, to my immense relief, the water level of the headwaters passage in front of us was very adequate; in fact, the waterway was actually stream-like, rather than swamp-like! At the end of our voyage, we would learn from our shuttle driver that the water levels in the Sturgeon Weir River and Amisk Lake were, oddly enough, unusually high during this particular season. This was due to the considerable amount of rainfall that this watershed had received during the course of the summer, in contrast to the almost total lack of rain in the adjacent Churchill River basin during the same period.

As we made our way through the slender, meandering channel of the upper end of Lindstrom Lake, which was the first section of the Sturgeon Weir River, we did find that, in many areas, only a narrow passageway was free of the thick growth of reeds and lily pads that nearly filled the waterway. At several locations, a number of ducks exploded into the air from the placid surface of the water, when we suddenly rounded a bend and startled them into flight. After 3/4 of a mile, we encountered an area where the passage had been dammed by beavers; this required dragging the loaded canoe over the low dam before we could continue. A little further downstream, we also discovered a beaver lodge adjacent to the shoreline, as well as a beaver slide that was currently well-used. The slide, located beneath a tall stand of birches and poplars, extended from the top of the bank down to the water. Here, gliding rodent bellies had completely worn away the grass and reeds, creating a narrow path of smooth, barren earth. Nearby floated some freshly-cut beaver food, consisting of severed sections of birch and poplar saplings.

At 4:00, having advanced four miles in ninety minutes, our green hull finally glided onto the open but island-studded waters of Lindstrom Lake, which ranged in width from about 3/4 of a mile to a mile. In celebration of our great fortune at having a generous water level in this watershed, we decided to take a relaxing half-hour break on a large island. As we approached the landing place that Doree had chosen, a red-tailed hawk circled high overhead. Beneath the dense growth of spruce trees, a thick, spongy layer of moss, mostly light green with some scattered areas of greenish yellow, completely furred the angled bank, offering us a luxurious cushion for lounging.

Back on the water, having now emerged from the close, sheltering forest of the narrow channel, a moderate wind out of the southeast provided us with a head wind and oncoming waves. Bucking against these elements, Doree and I made our way over the remaining two miles of Lindstrom Lake, through a narrow passage, and then across the three-mile width of Pixley Lake. At 6:15, we took a short rest on a point where Pixley Lake flows into Lac de Bois (Wood Lake). At this place stood a cabin and its adjacent outdoor cooking area; at the water's edge was parked a hydrofoil, the type that is often used for swamp travel in the southern U.S. Noting the huge scoop net of fine-mesh material that was attached to the front of the vehicle, we concluded that the residents of the cabin commercially harvested minnows, probably baby pike.

When we departed on the entryway into Lac de Bois, I mentioned that both the N.W.C. and the H.B.C. had operated a short-term post in this general locale during the 1806-1821 period. Each of these facilities had been called Egg Lake Post.

In the distance well to the north of us, we could see and hear a huge thunderstorm in action, as we basked in sunny weather, with a few unmoving white clouds hanging above and a perfect air temperature of 75 degrees. Ahead toward the southeast stretched the thirteen-mile length of Lac de Bois, over which the wind had been blowing unhindered from the southeast for quite some time. Struggling against the stout wind and moderately large waves on the open expanse of water, Ben and I toiled for 45 minutes, until 7:15. By then, the thunderstorm, with its churning black clouds, heavy rain dropping from those clouds, and flashes of lightning, had approached much nearer, rushing at us directly from behind. Toby, who normally perched in a relaxed pose atop the packs, sensed what was coming and burrowed down beneath the bow seat, seeking refuge. When we reached the projecting point on the left shore for which I had been aiming for two miles, we decided to land. By scurrying, we might be able to set up camp before the storm struck. Using a barely-submerged rock ledge that projected out from the shore as our landing area, we quickly unloaded all of the gear and hauled it up the bank to a fine campsite on the point.

While Doree and Ben hastily set up the tent, prepared the bedding, and stowed the gear for the night, I prepared our dinner under the overhanging branches of a big spruce. When the meal was nearly ready, lashing winds and a torrential downpour pummeled the point, but we were ready for the onslaught. I was able to stay nearly dry beneath the broad, sheltering branches of the tree, watching over the dinner, while the rest of the family members completed their tasks inside the tent. After the storm had roared beyond us and was raging southward over the length of the lake, we ate our meal outside, sheltered from the lingering light rain by our rain gear.

This had been one fine day. We had made excellent progress, and had enjoyed a great deal of fun in the process, advancing 23 miles and making one railway cart portage. In addition, our concerns about adequate water levels in the second river of the trip had turned out to be entirely unfounded, for which we were extremely grateful!

Day Five

During the night, another powerful storm rolled through the area, with rumbling thunder and flashing lightning. However, by morning the sky had completely cleared, and the water was entirely placid. Awakening at 6:15 to the haunting calls of loons, we were pleased to be greeted by clear skies and a temperature of 67 degrees in the shade. There was not a breath of breeze to stir the wispy grey mist that hung over the water. Within an hour, we were underway again, with Doree as the *avant*.

As we glided easily over the glass-like surface, our bow paddler softly sang the many verses of *A la Claire Fontaine* (By the Clear Fountain), almost to herself. During the French regime, this *chanson* had been so well-known in New France that it became the unofficial national anthem for the colony. This was particularly true for the French-speaking population after control of the colony was taken over by the British in 1760.

Listening to the ancient melody and words, I was reminded that a great many folk songs of the mother country had been imported to New France during the seventeenth century. These were then passed down, with both their original melodies and texts, from generation to generation. Over time, many of the imported songs acquired a new set of words, ones which reflected the altered ways of life in the new country. In other cases, the old text was retained while the original melody from France was gradually changed, or was completely forgotten and had to be reinvented. As a result, more than nine thousand versions of French-Canadian folk songs, including over five thousand melodies, have been collected in modern times. This wide array often includes multiple variations of certain songs, such as the 130 versions of the story line for the famous song *En Roulant Ma Boule Roulant*.

Songs were sung by the colonists at a variety of festive occasions, both for entertainment and to accompany dancing. In addition, they often complemented rhythmic tasks, such as threshing grain with a flail, spinning yarn, rocking a cradle, and weaving fabric on a loom. Another very prominent application of work songs in New France was the accompaniment of canoe paddling, which was not a task that had been part of traditional life in the mother country. The simplistic themes of the folk songs of New France, including those which were sung by voyageurs, often focused on love, beauty, and marriage; family, parents, domesticity, and home; nature; eating, drinking, and festivities; various occupations; ancient times, places from the past, and death; and nonsense and humor. In addition, some of the songs dealt with religious topics, but others were critical of the Catholic Church, priests, and the strictures that they tried to impose. During extended journeys and at settlements in the interior, the voyageurs and traders were often free from the authority of the government and the Church. This invariably led to the invention of new songs, ones that reflected more the themes of freedom, aggressiveness, vulgarity, bawdiness, and anti-Church sentiments, as well as loneliness. These subjects appeared much less often in the songs of the farmer folk who lived year round in the St. Lawrence settlements, under the watchful gaze of various authority figures. When we sang during our paddling trips, we had no concerns about disapproving ears; there were almost never any other humans around, and we suspected that the animals could not understand either French or English. The birds just chirped louder.

By 11:15, we had covered the remaining eleven miles of Lac de Bois, having taken a ten-minute floating break along the way, and also having made five short pauses to take photos. At the Goulet Herbieux (Grassy Narrows), the outlet of Lac de Bois, we took a relaxing lunch break for 45 minutes. Beside our landing place, the local Crees had constructed a skidway of spruce poles in the tall reed bed on the south shore, to facilitate landing their powerboats during hunting and fishing trips. Directly across the channel from our resting spot lay the Wood Lake Indian Reserve, a piece of land measuring two miles by two miles that stretched along the north shore.

After crossing a tiny lake for a half-mile, we were obliged to drag the canoe through a reedy, overgrown passage in which the open water, less than two feet wide, was only a few inches deep. By taking this shallow route between an island and the southern shore of the mainland, we were able to avoid a mile-long detour around the island. Then Ben paddled with me for five miles to reach the succession of three Galets (Water-worn Stones). These three short drops over ledges, widely separated but all lying within the space of just a half-mile, each required an unload, a short carry, and a reload.

At the first Galet, the portage extended for seventy yards over the small island that divides the rapids in two. The very smooth and flat surface of the nearly barren island, with its gently rounded edges sloping down to the channel of fast-flowing water along each side, apparently inspired the French designation of "Water-worn Stone." Here, modern Cree people of the area had constructed a skidway of poles, with a ramp of poles at each end, for dragging their heavy powerboats and motor-driven cargo canoes over the midstream obstruction.

Just as we were finishing the portage, which we did in the usual manner of carrying everything on our backs, instead of sliding our loaded canoe over the wooden skidway, we met the first of a succession of Cree families who were traveling upriver in their motorboats. Engaging the occupants of the first boat in conversation, we learned from this family of seven that the entire group lived seven miles downriver, at the community of Pelican Narrows, on the Pelican Narrows Indian Reserve. They were headed out on this Saturday afternoon for Lac de Bois, where they would commercially harvest pickerel with gill nets for two days, sleeping overnight and returning home the following evening. They sell these fish, which the French had called *poisson doré* (golden fish) and which Americans now call walleyed pike, to the processing plant in their community, which pays them $1.35 per pound. We also learned from the family that no one is allowed to buy property in these government-owned lands; the few fishing and hunting cabins that we had seen were all on leased property, which costs an annual fee of $100. per cabin site. At this point, we cut our conversation short, since six more boat-loads of native people were waiting patiently at the lower end of the sapling skid ramp, ready to haul their powerboats over the island portage.

A short paddle of only about two hundred yards brought us to the second Galet, which again involved a short carry, this time only thirty yards long, over the midstream island that divides the miniature rapids into two adjacent stretches of flashing white water. On this portage, we met a young Frenchman from Winnipeg, whose family raises 135 sled dogs at a time, both selling and racing them. During the previous year, he had won the gold medal championship for all of Canada in the five mile sprint, in the category of teams containing five dogs or less. When we encountered him on this carry, he was serving as the personal guide for a client on a canoe trip.

At the third Galet, which was about 2/10 of a mile away, we landed on the left shore some fifty yards above the drop, and easily made the sixty-yard portage. Just as we had done at each of the other two Galets, we carried our gear and canoe on our shoulders and backs, rather than utilizing the ramps and skidway of poles to drag our loaded canoe. Heavy powerboats and cargo canoes could endure that kind of rough handling much better than could our fiberglass craft.

A half hour of paddling on serene waters across the width of Lac Muskike brought us to the ancient spiritual place called Medicine Rapids. Here, just above the head of the noisy cascade, a moderately high cliff rose up from the water along both the right and the left shores of the narrow passage. Coasting silently up to the cliff that formed the left shoreline, we discovered two sets of petroglyphs, which had been created in ancient times by shamans using brownish red pigment. The larger of the two sets of artworks had been applied halfway up the side of the sheer face, while the spiritual leader had stood on the low rock ledge that rises about two feet above the water at the base of the cliff. Here he had painted a big-bellied human figure in stick form, with upraised arms and outstretched fingers, standing at the bottom of what appeared to be a large, shoulder-high bowl which measures about three feet across its open top. To the left of this figure and on a lower part of the vertical rock face appeared the second set of images, containing two smaller figures in the same brownish red hue. These included a solid hand or paw print, and a larger unidentified stick figure immediately to the right.

At this sacred place eons ago, native travelers and worshippers had left various offerings, particularly small amounts of tobacco, to both appease and request the aid of the many spirits which inhabited their world. This custom was also adopted by many Frenchmen, both when they were traveling in the company of native people and when they were traveling on their own.

Over the span of thousands of years, innumerable generations of native people in the northern regions had developed their sacred knowledge and rituals, their legends, and a huge store of information on many subjects. These cultural treasures they had passed down orally through time. After the deaths of the last of their holy people and their knowing ones, only remnants such as this and other pictographs, as well as archaeological sites, are left. However, the original significance and meaning of these places have been long forgotten. Archaeologists and ethnologists uncover and preserve considerable amounts of evidence of these past cultures, including some ancient stories that have been handed down to the living native people. These activities shed some light on the ways of the ancient ones, but the vast majority of the information about the people and their lives is lost forever, impossible to reconstruct.

The portage path on the left shore, beginning some twenty yards above the rapids, was about ninety yards long. It circumvented a treacherous drop that had a sinister, side-sweeping action for down-bound craft like ours. However, upbound voyageurs had sometimes been able to make a décharge here in certain seasons when the water level was cooperative, carrying half or all of the cargo on land and lining up the unloaded or partially-loaded canoe.

When we relaunched at 5:30 just below the rapids, we met another set of six native motorboats that were headed upriver to fish. As we traveled over the six-mile length of Lac de Chitique (Pelican Lake) to reach the community of Pelican Narrows, we passed many additional powerboats of native families who were also making their way upstream to fish for the weekend. The young driver of one isolated craft, containing three teenage boys, did not bother to slow down at all as he zoomed by, making no attempt to reduce the wake of his boat as a courtesy to us; we assumed that he and his passengers wanted to capsize us if they could. As they passed us, one of the sitting boys stood up, faced us, and made a "wa-wa-wa-wa" motion with his hand, covering and uncovering his mouth in imitation of the stereotypical Indians who had been represented in Hollywood movies many decades ago. This was apparently his wry commentary on our traveling in a native-style, paddle-powered craft, while they were roaring by, in unmannerly fashion, in a motorized boat of white man style. We did not respond in any way. During all of our trips, we all agreed to not provoke any motorboaters with hand or arm gestures or say anything to them, no matter how badly they behaved. They could make our voyage both miserable and unsafe if they chose to do so.

At various places along the route today, we had seen modern graffiti on rock cliffs, either names or initials, which had been in some cases painted onto the rock and in other instances scraped into its moss covering. At first, we could not imagine who would come all the way out here to this remote place on a canoe trip with a can of paint, a brush, and the intention of defacing the magnificent beauty of nature. However, we finally realized that the graffiti had been applied by certain of the residents of the native settlement of Pelican Narrows, who had ventured out a few miles from their homes in powerboats. We had passed 21 such boats today, as we had approached the small settlement.

At 6:30, we pulled into the community of Pelican Narrows, and tied up at the outermost end of the long wooden dock. While the family departed to hopefully find some hot food, I stayed with the canoe to update the journal. Soon, a float plane roared in, touching down nearby. As the plane bore down on me at considerable speed on the water, the pilot opened his door and motioned wildly for me to get my canoe away from there. With the entire length of the dock to choose from, we had managed to tie up at his personal (but unmarked) parking space! To keep from having our canoe and gear crushed and sunk, I complied.

Before long, Doree and Ben returned from their visit to the Northern Store (the modern version of the H.B.C. post), bringing the only prepared food that was available in the community, some pre-made submarine sandwiches and cheeseburgers, as well as potato chips and cokes. After five days and 102 miles of wilderness travel, these sandwiches had to be mighty bad to taste that lousy to us! These particular ones, purchased by Doree on August 22, were sealed in plastic wrap that bore the inscription "Best if used before September 7." Doree and Toby ended up consuming most of mine.

When the family had started to walk into the settlement to find a food store or a restaurant, they had asked directions from a native man who was somewhat drunk. When he inquired where they were going, Doree told him about our canoe trip to Amisk Lake. He then offered his services as a wilderness guide to that lake, saying that he had been there many times and knew well the country between the settlement and there. When Doree later related the story to me, it reminded me of many historic journal accounts that told of traders hiring a local native guide, only to learn some days out on the route that the hired individual had never traveled that particular route in his entire life! In those cases, it was not unusual to have the so-called guide sneak away in the night, sometimes stealing items from the expedition as he left.

On this sun-drenched Saturday evening, while I waited on the dock for the family to return with food, and later as we sat on the dock and consumed our meal, and again while we paddled away from the town, motorboats buzzed continually on Pelican Lake. As we cruised along the shoreline of the settlement, we thought that it was more than coincidental that the houses that stood along the shore to the west of town, just off of the official reservation land, looked run-down and had junk-strewn yards, compared to the well-kept homes that stood on the reservation land. The parcel of tribal property here, measuring two miles along the shore of the lake, extends for a mile inland. Adjacent to the motel stood the Northern Store, which had no windows and was outfitted with a heavy metal grating that secured the door after hours. We also passed a simple church with a tall steeple, a second church building which was identified by a cross and bell atop its roof, two large buildings that apparently contained the tribal center, and houses organized in neat rows along several streets. A mile beyond the town, as we exited from the eastern end of Pelican Lake, it was such a pleasure to finally escape from the sight, sound, smell, and wakes of powerboats!

Independent Montreal-based traders had established the Pelican Lake Post here in 1779, which operated for only a few years. Later, during the 1806-1821 period, the N.W.C. and the H.B.C. had each set up a short-lived facility at this place; both of these latter posts bore the name of the Frightened Narrows Post.

After the fur trade era had generally subsided during the latter 1800s, followed by the reservation period, most of the scattered native populations in the far-flung north country had congregated at a number of widely dispursed locales, including here at Pelican Narrows. As a result, during the modern era in which we were paddling the mainline fur trade route, there were far fewer people living along most sections of the route than had been present during the previous several thousand years. We very seldom encountered any other two-leggeds as we made our way along the water highway which, in previous centuries, had been a busy and considerably populated thoroughfare. We treasured the isolation, the quietude, and the lack of intrusions of modern culture which the route usually provided, and we were sometimes jarred when we arrived at a town, and especially so at this particular community. One of the reasons that the settlement of Pelican Narrows was irritatingly noisy, with its very plentiful supply of motorboats, was that it had easy access to the contemporary world by motor vehicles. A gravel road extended southward from the town for thirty miles, to connect with one of the east-west paved highways of the region. This probably explained why we had experienced an entirely different mood and lifestyle at this community compared to our stops over the years at various other native settlements along the mainline route.

A quiet paddle through the slender, two-mile passage of the Opawikuschikan Narrows brought us onto the placid waters of Lac Mirond (Heron Lake), a beautiful expanse that extended off toward the southeast for ten miles. The entire surface glimmered, bathed in the waning golden light of evening. After traveling for two miles down the lake, at 9:00 Doree spotted a wonderful campsite on the high western tip of an island. The rocky point offered a perfect place to spend the night. First of all, a ledge jutted out from the bare point, providing a convenient landing place. In addition, just back from the landing spot rose a series of natural ledges, which were arranged like steps to facilitate our carrying the gear up to the top. On the summit, only the central area was crowned with spruce trees. All of the rest of the point was entirely barren, except for some scattered areas that were covered with light green moss, and a few places where grass had taken a tenuous hold in cracks in the bedrock where a little soil had accumulated. The open air helped to keep the site free of biting insects, and it also offered a clear view of both the setting sun on one side of the point and the place where the sun would rise in the morning on the opposite side. At the edge of the stand of spruce trees on the summit, which would shelter us if a strong wind arose, lay a flat, moss-covered area that was perfect for a comfortable tent site. To top it all off, a blueberry patch loaded with ripe fruit grew right in front of the tent area. In other words, this was canoe-camping paradise!

Quickly setting up in a half-hour, while basking in the air temperature which was still a balmy 70 degrees, we then lounged and recounted the events of the day. We had covered a gratifying thirty miles, without any assistance from the sail, in addition to having made four portages. As we chatted, the scene around us, with the copper-colored light fading gradually to pitch black, appeared all the more resplendent from our unobstructed vantage point out in the lake.

Our conversation this evening finally turned to the sensitive subject of residential schools for native children. Between 1892 and 1969, the Canadian government had established a large number of schools away from the reservations. Over this span of three quarters of a century, some 100,000 to 150,000 children, about 20 percent of the entire native population of Canada, had been forced to leave their families and their homes on the reserves at the age of six, and attend these distant schools, which were operated by five Christian denominations. For the ten long years of their tenure, the students were not allowed to speak their native languages nor practice their native spirituality, and they were inculcated with non-native ways of living and thinking. In 1969, this practice was finally halted. Native children are now educated in or near their own communities. Psychological healing has been slowly occurring among the native people, as they recover from the damage that was inflicted by this enforced isolation from their families and their traditional cultures, as well as the physical and sexual abuse that sometimes took place at these schools.

When we settled onto our air mattresses in the tent, many vivid images of the day's events were still swirling in our heads. However, in spite of those mental movies, we fell asleep almost instantly.

Day Six

When my mind returned to the present at 6:00, I could hear waves lapping against our rocky point, coming from the southeast, the direction of our intended travel down Lac Mirond. Crawling out of the tent, I noted that it was already 65 degrees out; high above, a bank of white clouds extended off toward the north, barely moving. The breeze from the southeast that had sprung up during the night was creating moderate waves, which were flowing against our planned direction of travel. Unfortunately, this was not the mirror-like surface that had been so conducive to effortless traveling the previous evening. At 6:50, the rim of the sun peeked above the black wall of the distant tree line at the eastern edge of the lake, tinting the entire sky a pale pinkish orange. The path of deeper orange that the fireball soon cast across the water extended directly to our camp on the point. After Doree had picked a good supply of ripe blueberries in front of the tent, we packed up and were off. This site had been very generous to us, and we left it reluctantly, almost reverently.

Soon, the wind nearly disappeared, as *La Vieille* generously granted us an easy run down the ten-mile length of the lake. In the island-filled narrows at its southern end, Ben spotted big pickerel on three occasions swimming in the clear, green-tinted water five to six feet below our hull. As we were paddling through the river-like narrows that led to Lac Corneille (Crow Lake), an adult bald eagle suddenly swooped down to the surface near us. With seemingly little effort, the bird snatched up a fish in its talons and flapped away for a short distance, to perch on a protruding limb near the top of a dead spruce and then proceed to eat its catch.

This scene reminded me of Tennyson's poem entitled "The Eagle":
He clasps the crag with crooked hands;
Close to the sun in lonely lands,
Ringed with the azure world, he stands.

The wrinkled sea beneath him crawls;
He watches from his mountain walls,
And like a thunderbolt he falls.

Even though I knew that eagles have eyesight that is up to eight times sharper than that of humans, it still impressed me every time I watched one of them flash down to earth and grab a meal. They mostly captured fish and waterfowl, but also mammals and reptiles whenever the opportunity arose.

By 10:50, when we landed on the left shore to make the Portage de la Corneille (Crow Carry), we had advanced eleven miles in just over three hours. In certain seasons, the voyageurs had sometimes been able to run down this set of rapids. However, the extremely high water level during our trip ruled out the possibility of our running the passage; the heavy, turbulent flow was simply too risky for us to handle in a loaded open canoe. As I watched Doree walking ahead of me over the two-hundred-yard path through the woods, leaning forward into the tumpline of her heavy Duluth pack, I smiled to myself. Here was a very youthful and attractive woman; intelligent, highly educated, and well-read; talented at writing, editing, and public speaking; fluent in English, French, and German; very accomplished as a therapist for families and couples and as an adoption counselor; physically fit and adept at tennis and volleyball; big-hearted and broad-minded; talented at drawing and painting; patient, understanding, and deeply emotional; and widely traveled throughout 32 countries on five of the six continents (not yet Africa). Yet in spite of all of her interests and her wonderful attributes, she was still willing to spend her summer vacations doing very demanding wilderness canoe trips with me across the breadth of the fur trade country! When you find a partner like that, you count your blessings often.

At the far end of the carry, we ate our lunch before reloading. Departing when the sun had reached the height of its arc, we easily ran the fast water in the narrows that lay just below the falls. Shooting onto the waters of Lac Corneille, we saw that our route across the north end of the lake would take us on a U-shaped course, first for two miles toward the southeast and then for the same distance toward the northeast. At the bottom of the U, while taking a short break on shore, Ben located a cabin made of horizontal spruce logs, which was apparently used by hunting and fishing parties. A pole framework that served as a summer shelter for cooking, eating, and sleeping stood nearby. Not far away, Doree also discovered a patch of ripe blueberries, some of which begged to be picked and eaten. By 2:00, we had reached the northeastern corner of the lake and its outlet at the Portage de L'Île (Island Carry, now called Dog Carry), an easy fifty-yard portage on the right shore that bypassed the very powerful falls.

Within thirty minutes, we were again afloat, reveling in the beautiful weather with an air temperature of 75 degrees in the shade and much warmer in the brilliant sunlight. Entering the long, narrow Lac du Bouleau (Birch Lake) section of the Sturgeon Weir River, we commenced our trek down the lower portion of the river. The French had referred to this fifty-mile-long section extending down to Lac Amisk, in which the width of the passage usually ranged from 1/10 to 2/10 of a mile, as the Rivière la Pente (Slope River or Incline River).

Laboring against a moderate head wind, it took us four hours to advance slowly but surely over the eleven-mile length of Birch Lake. At one place where the passage narrowed greatly, the fast current of the water became very obvious. About three miles further, we slid past a massive hemisphere of granite bedrock that rose high above the surface in the middle of the lake. Its steeply angled shoreline for about twenty feet above the water was scrubbed bare, while the rest of the greyish pink dome was cloaked in green moss, with scraggly stunted spruce trees rising at widely spaced intervals where pockets of soil had accumulated in crevices in the rock. When we finally reached the Portage de Bouleau (Birch Carry) at 6:40, we set up camp on the left shore beside the head of the path, in a meadow which was filled with wild flowers sporting various shades of pink, yellow and white.

Ingesting our stew of beef, beans, squash, peas, and noodles this evening posed its own set of challenges, since we were obliged to take the food down while wearing our head nets. The swarming clouds of mosquitoes at this place were more voracious than at any other campsite that I could remember. Passing a full spoon up through the drawstring opening in the net, which encircled the base of my neck, and then getting the spoon into my mouth without spilling its contents, all the while keeping the opening in the net as small as possible, was not easy. In spite of my best efforts, a few biting insects managed to enter the drawstring opening with each arrival and departure of the spoon. The one upbeat aspect of the scene was the squadron of about eight iridescent blue dragonflies which constantly dived and zoomed around our faces, greedily gobbling the mosquitoes that we had attracted.

It was not particularly encouraging to know that only female *moustiques* were biting us. During their adult lifespan, which can extend from two weeks to several months, both males and females feed on nectar and juices from plants, mostly from flowers. However, after the female has mated and has produced several hundred eggs, those eggs need to receive nourishing protein from human or animal blood before they are deposited in stagnant water. At this point, the female seeks exhaled carbon dioxide to locate a living blood source, and then further hones in on her prey by detecting body heat, as well as the lactic acid and sweat that are secreted by skin. Individual people and animals are either more or less attractive to the insects, based on their particular breath content, skin temperature, body odors, and sweating rate. Higher skin temperatures, as well as higher humidity levels caused by higher sweating rates, are known to be more attractive to the insects. After the female mosquito has inserted her proboscis through the skin of the prey, she injects saliva which contains an anticoagulant, to keep the blood thin and flowing freely. Most mosquitoes survive through the winter as blood-nourished, autumn-laid eggs, which hatch during the following spring. The main time of day for mosquito feeding is dusk, so during the course of our voyages we tended to be plagued by them only during our evenings on shore, after a long day spent on the open water, and to a much lesser degree during daytime portages.

Brûlots (black flies and their miniscule cousins called no-see-ums in English), were given their "burner" name by the French because of the burning sensations that these insects induce with their bites. These tiny creatures, which were equally as tormenting as mosquitoes for us at certain times, tend to feed during the pre-dusk hours and also during the early morning. We generally avoided their late-day onslaught by continuing our paddling well into the early evening on most days; but we could not avoid their early-morning scourge if we did not push off for the day before dawn. In the world of black flies, it is likewise only the females that drink blood, to nourish their eggs before laying them. However, there are two major differences between these insects and mosquitoes. Instead of depositing their eggs in still water, black flies lay them in clear, moving water. More important from the vantage point of the prey (including us humans), they use scissors-like jaws to snip an open wound in the skin, from which they lap up the flowing blood, instead of sucking it up through a very slender tube. With both mosquitoes and black flies, it is our body's reaction to the insect's saliva that triggers a red welt and an irritating itch.

During our hours outside of the tent, we tried to fend off both of these types of attackers by tucking the cuffs of our long pantlegs into the tops of our socks, and by wearing a long-sleeved shirt with the button areas at the cuffs sewn closed. Our pants and shirts were usually of drab and lighter colors, generally not of darker hues, which tend to absorb bug-attracting heat, and which also resemble more closely the relatively dark fur of the usual prey animals. In the worst of attacking situations, we donned our head nets, which were made of fine mesh fabric. Other helpful defenses included choosing rather dry areas for our campsites, avoiding whenever possible breeding areas of stagnant water, and especially picking elevated places that were wafted by breezes, which tended to drive off the insects. Using little or no soap during a voyage also helped in two ways: first, it avoided the problem of some soaps actually attracting insects. In addition, minimal washing also helped by allowing a layer of dirt and dried sweat to build up on the skin, which tended to mask somewhat its insect-attracting odors. We also tried to maintain a proper attitude about these biting insects, acknowledging that they played their own important role in wilderness life, feeding larger insects, fish, frogs, turtles, bats, and birds.

However, our most effective tool in dealing with mosquitoes, black flies, and no-see-ums, as well as ticks, was DEET. This chemical substance, of which the full name is N,N-diethyl-meta-tulamide, was developed as a repellant for biting insects by the U.S. military and the Department of Agriculture in the latter 1940s; it became commercially available in 1957. No repellant can alter the carbon dioxide content of an individual's breath, or change the skin temperature or sweating rate of a person when they are actively exercising. However, certain repellants can mask the odor of the lactic acid that is secreted by the skin, which is the key to the effectiveness of DEET. By hiding this attractive smell from insects, they are not stimulated to bite even when they land on the skin. Ever since its development in the 1940s, DEET has turned out to be much more effective against more species of biting insects, and resists evaporation and thus retains its effectiveness for nearly twice as long, compared to all other known substances that have been tested up to the present time.

The greater the DEET content in a repellant, the longer it lasts. During our wilderness trips in areas of extreme insect populations, we needed an effective insect repellant from the moment we emerged from the tent in the early morning until we crawled back into that shelter at bedtime, late in the evening. Thus, we used repellants that contained 95 percent DEET, which are good for about ten to thirteen hours without reapplication. In the late 1980s, a rather expensive version of DEET was developed which has an extended duration of release, making a 33 percent concentration effective for up to thirteen hours. However, we simply reapplied a small amount of the 95 percent variety when we arrived at our campsite each evening, which protected us until bedtime.

For health reasons, it is important to use DEET sparingly and infrequently during the course of a given day, and to avoid saturating the skin and clothing. Each morning, we would apply a small amount of the lotion on our face, ears, neck, backs of the hands, and wrists, and to the ankle areas of our socks, avoiding our eyes and mouth. The lotion version, in a small, lightweight plastic bottle, was much more practical for us than the versions in a pump spray or an aerosol spray container, due to the limitations on space and weight in our laden packs.

The use of DEET by adults has very occasionally caused such adverse symptoms as confusion and insomnia, while certain cases of use on children have resulted in more serious neurological problems. These very scattered instances, usually involving liberal and frequent use, especially the saturation of clothing, have led to recommended guidelines for the safe usage of DEET. Repellants containing 30 percent of this active ingredient are typically good for up to six or seven hours of protection for adults. For children, the American Academy of Pediatrics has indicated that DEET concentrations of up to 30 percent are safe for individuals over the age of two months for all-day protection, as reported in the current edition of *Consumer Reports*. All of these recommendations are based on sparing and infrequent applications on only exposed skin, not applied under any clothing, and the avoidance of application to the eyes, the mouth, and any wounded skin, and to the hands of children. Products that contain both DEET and sunscreen are to be avoided, since sunscreen should be slathered on liberally and reapplied often throughout the day, while DEET should be applied sparingly, and reapplied only when the time period needing protection exceeds the effective duration of a single application.

An additional problem, but one that is much less serious, is also related to the use of DEET repellants. This particular chemical acts as a solvent on plastics, such as glasses frames and watch crystals, as well as synthetic fabrics such as acetate, rayon, and spandex. This aspect of our repellant became obvious each time I used a plastic ballpoint pen to update the journal. As the trip progressed, the pen became more and more degraded in those places where my fingers held it to write.

During the fur trade era, native people and voyageurs would have been overjoyed to have had a DEET repellant at their disposal. Instead, they sought protection from biting insects in various ways, when they found themselves in heavily infested areas without a stiff breeze to drive away the critters. Simply allowing a good layer of grease, sweat, and grime to accumulate on their skin was the most common and natural method of protection. Coating their exposed skin with mud, or with bear oil or pig grease, or even butter, was another method which extended back many centuries. Similarly, the building of smudges (smoky fires) using punky wood or green leaves, in the open, or inside a shelter, or even within a metal kettle in a moving canoe, was also a very widespread antidote. From the early 1800s on, certain individuals protected themselves with a netting of gauze or cheesecloth, in the form of a veil, a head net, or a bed screen. However, in many cases, the insect population was so ferocious at a given location that the people were forced to spend the night submerged up to their necks in the lake or river. They would then catch up on their sleep during the following day, while floating offshore in their canoe amid the breezes, when the attacking insects were not present.

At this heavily infested campsite, we felt fortunate to have both DEET repellant and head nets that fit over our wide-brimmed hats and extended down to the base of our necks. After our meal, we discussed our gratifying day, in which we had progressed 27 miles in eleven hours. Thus far, we had advanced 137 miles in 5 1/2 days on the water (including about four miles making detours), averaging 25 miles a day; we had also made fourteen portages in the process.

At 7:30 P.M, the air temperature was still 77 degrees. During this voyage, we had been experiencing unusually even temperatures, with days that were not overly hot and evening that were not at all cool. As soon as we had finished our meal, we dived into the tent, reveling in the protection of its screen windows. The buzz of the hungry hordes outside the mesh-covered openings reminded us of various accounts of voyageurs being haunted by such dense clouds of insects that they could not sleep a wink, even after a grueling, exhausting day of paddling. After we had exchanged massages, I carried out my usual final task before sleeping: killing the mosquitoes and black flies that had made their way into the tent. Since they generally migrated to the peak area of the roof, I hunted them down there with the help of a minimag flashlight, and squashed them against the cloth. Most of their smashed bodies left a red smear of blood on the fabric, blood which they had sucked from us before alighting at the peak of the shelter.

Day Seven

After a very restful eight hours of sleep, I emerged from the shelter at 5:30. Little did I know that the events of this morning would roil and torment my dreams for months to come.

When I stood upright and glanced toward the east, I was startled to see a very bright star, actually a planet, high in the sky. Since this was the only pinpoint of light remaining in the bluish black heavens, it seemed to have a magical quality to it. After packing some of the gear that was outside, I made a silent trip with two packs over the Portage de Bouleau, making my way slowly in the dim, pre-dawn light. Along the four hundred yards of the path, I was very aware of the presence of the spirits of many native and French paddlers who had passed this way over the centuries. As they accompanied me along the route, I felt their affectionate encouragement of our project, as we recreated their travels and sought to understand their ways of life.

When the family left their comfortable air mattresses at 6:00, the air temperature was already 70 degrees in the shade, with thin grey clouds smeared across the eastern sky; not a breath of breeze ruffled the stillness of the meadow and the woods. Within an hour, we had packed up, had made the portage, and were afloat on the mist-shrouded water, well before the sun broke over the eastern tree line. Since the infestation of mosquitoes at the campsite had been so horrible, I registered that it was a pleasure to leave the place behind. Instead, I should have been thankful for the safety and security of the solid ground that it had provided.

For twenty minutes, the canoe glided easily over the smooth, glass-like surface, as the hazy shoreline slipped steadily past us. At the request of my bow paddler, I hummed over and over one of her favorite tunes, the trumpet solo called *Trumpeter's Prayer*, as we slid forward in the utter calm. After rounding a bend to the left, we approached Hanson Lake Road, where a low wooden bridge had been built many years before across this narrow spot in the river. This structure had allowed the gravel road to span the waterway and extend some ten miles further westward, to reach a uranium mine, now closed. The fact that the ancient voyageurs had termed the widened area immediately below the narrows Lac Maligne (Spiteful or Malicious Lake) had not resonated with me.

Staying to the left side of the rocky island that supported the middle of the bridge, we shot down the smooth decline, while Ben, in the passenger section, dipped his tooth brush in the water and casually brushed his teeth. Of the various spaces between the wooden columns of the bridge, only the one in the main current area was open. Each of the other passages had been closed off with long planks that were crossed in the form of an X, installed to show powerboaters where to pass beneath the bridge, in the area of deepest water. As we quickly bore down on the only open passageway, the powerful current that was caused by the high water level (which was two to three feet above normal) swept our craft slightly to the right. The main V of the current was being split by the vertical post that stood at the right flank of the open passage; but I was not concerned, thinking that I still had complete control of our course.

However, to my great surprise, as the persistent flow continued to pull the bow toward the right, the forces of Nature conspired: we rammed head-on into the right piling, as Doree tried at the last moment to deflect the impact with her foot! The bow stopped, and the powerful current immediately swept the stern toward the left and forward. With no way to stop the inevitable, the canoe was flipped over toward the left side, throwing us into the water.

Surfacing and grabbing the overturned, stern-forward canoe, Ben and I were instantly swept through the open passageway to the left of the piling, with Toby close by. Just beyond the bridge, as I looked around to take a count of my family members, I realized that Doree was missing!

"Where's Mom?"

Ben shouted back, "She's caught on the bridge!" Glancing frantically back upstream, all that I could see of her were her lower legs and her tennis shoes, sticking upward amid the timbers. I was convinced that she was trapped head-down in the river, with her feet and part of her legs extending up out of the water! I immediately thought, "Oh, God. This is the setting of a classic canoe drowning, in which the victim is pinned by fast current against either a bridge piling or the limbs of a fallen tree." All the while, we three with the canoe were being swept further and further downstream by the strong flow of the deep water, entirely unable to swim back to Doree's aid.

At the moment of impact with the piling, when the bow stopped, the stern swung around toward the left and then forward, and we were all dumped, I was immediately swept away from the canoe and to the extreme left side of the opening in the bridge. When I ascended from beneath the water, I couldn't see Tim or Ben, as I was pushed hard by the current toward the upstream side of the X planks that were nailed to the left of the open passage. Grabbing one of the boards, I at first wondered what I should do. Could I climb up onto the bridge and eventually reach land?

Holding my head and the upper part of my body out of the water, it was easy enough to "walk" my feet up the planks in the space in front of my trunk, until I got them up to head level and then over the boards. With my body now in the form of a V on the upstream side of the planks, all of me was above water. But now what? While catching my breath, I caught a glimpse of Tim and Ben downriver, swimming in mid-stream; they seemed safe. (But with my lower legs and feet extending above the water, I guess their view of me would have looked like I was trapped in a head-down position.)

With a little time to think and regroup, the water seemed the best way out, rather than trying to climb up the bridge. So, with my arms still holding onto the crossed timbers, I "walked" my legs and feet back down, until they were just barely above the water. "O.K. Time to go." Taking a deep breath, I dropped and lunged forward, going head-first deep into the current with my arms extended. Within seconds, I was swept under the bridge, and on into the safe open water beyond it. Whew! In the distance I could see the heads of my three boys above the surface. (Doree)

At that moment Ben hollered "She's out!," as Doree quickly shot down the fast current. When she arrived at our position well downstream, we were immensely elated to have her back, alive, breathing, and swimming! A short distance away, there was a small and very low island that consisted entirely of barren bedrock. As we continued to be swept downriver, Ben extracted the bow towing rope from its little bag and swam with it to this little place of refuge, while hauling Toby on one of his shoulders. Just as Doree and I and the canoe were being carried past the lower end of the island, he clambered onto the rocky elevation and tugged on the rope, pulling the overturned, waterlogged craft in close. Finally, all four of us, accompanied by our canoe and our gear, had our feet planted safely on solid ground again!

In the shallows beside the miniature island, now overjoyed and lighthearted, we righted the canoe. As we were bailing it out, a man who lived near the bridge came zooming out in his motorboat to offer assistance, which, by good fortune, we did not require, but we thanked him thoroughly. He had heard my shouts to Ben, telling him to swim to the little island with the towing rope. At 8:15, one hour after the capsize, we were again on our way, happily counting our blessings. We had suffered no injuries, and had lost in the melee only the bath kit with tooth brushes, tooth paste, and hair brush.

This capsize experience was an unfamiliar one, since we had not been dunked into the water unintentionally since our previous capsize with a loaded canoe, seven trips earlier in the Chenal de la Culbute on the upper Ottawa River. Since then, we had paddled 1,200 miles without mishap. Among our various misadventures during all of our years of paddling the mainline route, the terrifying ten minutes on this day in 1993, when I was convinced that my dear wife was drowning beneath the wooden bridge, would remain indelibly etched as the worst time of all!

While the capsize and recovery had been taking place, a new weather front had quickly moved in, causing the sky to fill with thick grey clouds and the temperature to drop into the low 60s. One mile downstream, after landing on the left shore just above the Leaf Rapids, we ravenously wolfed down our breakfast, and then made the carry of two hundred yards beside the rapids. They did not offer any major obstructions, but due to the high water level there was a tremendously heavy and turbulent flow, which we did not want to challenge (especially after the major scare that we had just survived). After the portage, Doree and I easily covered the stretch of five miles down the fast and narrow channel to Scoop Rapids. Particularly while traveling along this section, it was easy to see why the voyageurs had referred to the segment of the Sturgeon Weir River between Portage de l'Île and Lac Amisk as the Rivière Pente (Incline River or Slope River). The waterway often appeared to slope in an obvious downstream direction, in addition to having six major drops at widely-spaced rapids over the distance of fifty miles.

At the end of the seventy-yard portage path along the left shore, which circumvented the two ledge drops of Scoop Rapids, we enjoyed watching the behavior of nine white pelicans. When we first arrived, they were all perched in a row on an exposed rock, off to the side of the area of large standing waves. Before long, four of the birds, laboriously flapping their wings and barely becoming airborne, crossed over to the far shore at a very slow speed, hardly clearing the tops of the frothing white haystacks. At the base of the rapids lay a small inlet, which had centuries before given the picturesque falls its name. Here, hungry travelers had been able to easily scoop out a pickerel or two, using a dip net that was always left there for that purpose. After our lunch break beside the inlet, we pushed off again at 11:45. From the pool at the lower end of the portage, we whizzed downstream beside the rocky left shore, traveling first against the upstream-flowing current just below the rapids and then amid the wild haystack waves that were caused by their turbulence.

The brooding weather front that had arrived earlier soon moved on, the sky partially cleared, and the day became very warm, 77 degrees in the shade at noon, and 85 by 3:00. With no hint of a breeze, numerous fluffy white clouds hung in the sky without moving, casting their still shadows on the water. As we traveled the fourteen miles from Scoop Rapids to Rapides du Serpent in 4 1/2 hours, including a floating break of 45 minutes, we sweltered in the heat. During the course of this particular stretch, the shorelines changed from Canadian Shield granite cliffs to low swampy areas. In addition, the forest cover in this section switched from mostly spruce to a much higher percentage of birch and poplar, while many low bushes came down right to the water's edge. Along the way, we passed at least half a dozen beaver lodges, some located offshore and others adjacent to the shore. As we silently rounded one particular curve, we glided quite close to a beaver that was crossing the river. One of the thrills of canoe travel was seeing how close we could noiselessly coast toward wild creatures before we were observed. When the glossy brown animal finally noticed us, it slapped its tail and dived, but surfaced after only a few seconds, looked us over a bit, and then dived a second time. When the same exceedingly curious rodent arose for still another look, it saw that we were still floating nearby, and immediately dived for a third time. We did not observe him again, although we did flush up a number of ducks and geese in the vicinity.

At 4:15, we made the carry of 2/3 of a mile at the Rapides du Serpent, on the right shore through a pine and poplar forest. This path cut across a horseshoe loop in the river that contained two sets of rapids, which were located a half-mile apart. As we sweated beneath our burdens in the hot, close woods, the attacking mosquitoes were horrible. While we were walking back for the second load, Ben ran on ahead, supposedly to escape from the insects. However, he soon surprised us by returning with the canoe on his shoulders! Entirely by himself, he had managed to turn the craft over, raise one end above his head, and then lower it onto his shoulders. This was the first time that Ben had ever portaged the canoe, and he apparently wanted to surprise us with his newly-discovered abilities.

Between 5:20 and 7:00, my energetic son and I advanced seven more miles on the lower reaches of the river, to reach the Portage Pente (Ascent or Slope Carry, now called Spruce Carry), where we landed on the left shore. Along the way, the mosquitoes had been so ferocious, even on the water, that Ben had donned his head net. After carrying over most of the 275 yards of the portage, we decided to spend the night in a large clearing which beckoned to us from beside the path. Completing our evening tasks amid swarms of biting insects was a tough coda to a long day of paddling.

During twelve hours on the water, we had advanced 31 miles, had made five portages (including one that was 2/3 of a mile long), and had survived a rather serious capsize, making it a very eventful and accomplishing day. Over the span of 6 1/2 days of travel, we had covered 168 miles. At this point, we were just four miles on the river and sixteen miles across Lac Amisk from the completion of our voyage. However, we did not set any goal of a projected arrival time, knowing that it was best to let our travel schedule play out according to the whims of Mother Nature.

Darkness soon engulfed our camp. After staring contentedly into the leaping, twisting flames of Ben's fire for a considerable time, we traded massages on the air mattress by the fire, and were finally asleep by 10:00. As I drifted off, I was especially thankful that Doree was lying in the tent beside us, instead of on a slab in a morgue somewhere!

Day Eight

During the night, a major storm with thunder, lightning, and heavy rainfall passed right over our campsite, but we all slept deeply, lulled by the steady drumming of the rain on the tent overlay. Arising to the alarm clock at 6:15, we were packed and afloat within forty minutes. The day offered mild weather conditions, with an air temperature of 58 degrees in the shade, thin white clouds feathered across a powder blue sky, and no breeze. A thick grey *brume* (mist) slowly rose from the water, which was warmer than the night-chilled air. Through the silent, eerie haze, we could barely make out the ghost-like figures of several pelicans cruising up the river, as well as others floating in the pool below the falls.

As we rounded the first curve, the native cemetery of the Amisk Band slowly came into view, located atop a level sand ridge that rose gradually from the left bank. As the mist began to clear, we could discern a dark green background of tall, stately spruce trees, and in the foreground many low white crosses, standing in the short grass atop the ridge. In front of these crosses stood a much larger cross, likewise of wood painted white, as tall as a man. As we drifted past in respectful silence, a nearby beaver slapped its tail on the surface of the water and dived, leaving a pattern of ever-expanding concentric ripples. The Amisk Lake Indian Reserve, a triangular piece of forest-covered land, is demarcated on its south side by the lowest six miles of the Sturgeon Weir River, which runs in a southeasterly direction here. Beginning a mile above where we had camped the previous night, the boundary line extends eastward for four miles, and then southward for an equal distance, ending at the shores of Lac Amisk, at the mouth of the river. The native people have no permanent settlement on this land, but they return here to utilize and care for their ancient burial ground beside the waterway.

Leaving the cemetery behind, as we rounded the next bend, our green hull cruised silently behind two adolescent mallards. When they finally realized that invaders had arrived, the startled pair leaped noisily into the air and flapped wildly off downstream with a great deal of clamor. A few minutes later, we again came up on the same pair; this time, they only paddled casually toward shore, apparently not yet experienced enough to realize the potential dangers that lurked in their world. Near the mouth of the river, a single loon flew high overhead, calling out at intervals as it winged across the sky.

Where the Sturgeon Weir flows out from the forest cover to meet the lake, we gazed southward down the shoreline of Lac Amisk. About a mile to the south lay the place where the forty French Canadians in the ten-canoe party of Alexander Henry and the Frobisher brothers had wintered in 1775-76. They had spent the period from November to May at a spot about a hundred yards back from the shore, on the portage path that had led to nearby Balsam Lake. Remnants of cellar depressions, as well as stone fireplaces two feet high, have been discovered at the site, remnants of the facility which the men had built by constructing five buildings adjacent to each other in the form of a rectangular fortress. The artifacts from excavations at the site are now displayed at the Denare Beach Museum.

During the course of their seven-month stay over the winter and spring, the party had harvested from beneath the ice of Amisk Lake large numbers of lake trout weighing as much as fifty pounds, as well as pickerel, whitefish, and sturgeon, using harpoons, nets, and fishing lines. Thirteen years later, when Alexander Mackenzie and his party paddled across the lake in 1789, he noted in his journal that the lake "abounds with fish common to the country." After another two decades, Robert Hood reported in 1819 that supplies of fish harvested in this lake during the winter were transported southward by dog sled to Cumberland House.

However, the Crees had not named this body of water after its bountiful supply of fish, but instead had called it Amisk, their word for beaver. As a result, the French often referred to it as Lac aux Castors (Beaver Lake). Personnel of the H.B.C. had established a post called Beaver Lake House on the southern shore of the lake in 1776, near its outlet, the head of the Rivière Maligne. This facility had been operated for less than five years.

At 9:00, we commenced our traverse of sixteen miles across the lake, traveling diagonally in a northeasterly direction. Luckily for us, the wind that was beginning to pick up was coming from the southwest, helping our progress across the glistening blue water. After three miles, Doree switched places with Ben, taking over the role of the bow paddler. By the time we reached the midpoint of the lake, the wind had freshened a great deal, and the growing waves were now traveling much faster than the canoe. Although the mast was down, we were still sailing at a good speed, with just our backs catching the strong following wind, as we zoomed up and down the sides of the ever-deepening swells. To quell our fears, and also to free our spirits to savor the magic of the moment, we belted out many verses of various French songs.

After an exhilarating but rather harrowing crossing of twelve miles in three hours, we reached the northeastern arm of Amisk Lake, which is dotted with islands of various sizes. Choosing an attractive one of rather small size, we sped onto quiet waters on the lee side of its eastward-projecting point, and glided to a halt at noon. Clambering into the shallows and then onto the rocky shore, we flopped down on the warm stones and took a well-deserved rest for more than an hour, reveling in the magnificent weather. The sun shone brightly on the barren rocks along the shoreline, and many puffball clouds marched slowly overhead toward the northeast; the air temperature measured a very comfortable 72 degrees in the shade of the adjacent spruce forest. In spite of the balmy weather that surrounded us, in my mind's eye I envisioned the offshore stones anticipating the return of the darkening layer of thick ice that would grow above them in three months time.

Finally, we embarked for the final stretch, with Ben poised to practice his *gouvernail* skills in the stern and Doree ready to pull strongly in the bow. For my part, I was prepared to bask in rare luxury in the passenger's spot behind Doree. Toby sampled the air with his twitching nose, casually took his usual position in the midsection, atop the packs behind the passenger, and promptly drifted off to dreamland. It was pleasing to know that the little community of Denare Beach, our final destination, lay only four miles away, and to note that there was a stiff following wind pushing us toward our goal. At the halfway point, Ben nosed the canoe into a sheltered cove on an island for a short respite. In the process, our green craft drove seven young mergansers who could not yet fly out onto the open water.

At 2:30 P.M. on a Tuesday, we arrived at Denare Beach, having covered twenty miles in 71/2 hours, while taking several generous breaks along the way. This year's voyage had taken us exactly one week to complete, having pushed off onto the waters of the Churchill River at Missinipe on the previous Tuesday at the very same hour of 2:30 P.M. During the trip, we had advanced 188 miles in 71/2 days on the water, averaging 25 miles per day. En route, we had made nineteen portages, had lined down one set of rapids, had run down many small rapids, and had experienced one accidental and one expected capsize. Since adversity and challenges always bring with them opportunities for growth, we had certainly expanded and become more experienced during this voyage!

Upon our arrival, we learned from the shuttle driver (who was very surprised to see us arriving so soon!) that our trip had coincided with a moderate heat wave for the region. During a typical August, the average daily high temperature was about 70 to 72 degrees, while the average nightly low was about 48 to 50 degrees.

Over the course of this adventure, we had passed the time by chatting about such widely diverse subjects as the fur trade, falcons, ferrets, and the historical novel set in Viking times that I had recently read. We had also discussed at length the true story of the French woman named Claude Poumerol, who had triumphed as a gold-medal-winning sprinter at the 1988 Olympics in Tokyo, five years earlier. She had accomplished this feat at the ripe old age of forty, and in spite of having had one of her legs amputated at the knee 24 years earlier, when she was sixteen years old!

Off and on, we also wondered how Kevin was faring in Michigan with the relatives during our trip. This was the fourth voyage that we had made without his strong singing voice encouraging our progress. We had never intended to do these trips as a three-some, but we willingly gave Kev the independence that he wanted, to follow his own course.

During the day-and-a-half of driving that it took us to reach home, we halted to sleep one night in Riding Mountain National Park, where we were pleased to spot in the dusk and dawn hours a deer, a red fox, and a bobcat. We also stopped to take in the fur trade and La Vérendrye exhibits in the historical museum at Portage de la Prairie, west of Winnipeg.

Upon our return to Oak Park, Doree left immediately for France, to guide her mother and sister for two weeks by car around the northern portions of that country, where so many of my ancestors had lived centuries earlier.

XIII
Eleventh Voyage
Upper Churchill River, July 10-20, 1994

When the great scorer comes to write against your name, he marks not that you won or lost, but how you played the game.
Grantland Rice

Experience is a hard teacher.
She gives the test first and the lessons afterward.
Anonymous

If you think about disaster, you will get it. Brood about death and you hasten your demise.
Think positively and masterfully, with confidence and faith, and life becomes more secure, more fraught with action, richer in achievement and experience.
Swami Sivananda

Whether you think you can or whether you think you can't, you're right.
Henry Ford

O ver the winter, as I studied the maps for this year's voyage, I noted that the upper section of the Churchill River, like its lower reaches, is mostly a succession of rather narrow lakes, often with a set of rapids or a falls at the place where one lake flows into the next one. The headwaters of the river includes, from north to south, Lac La Loche (Loach or Burbot Lake, named for the long, slender fish with barbels on the nose and chin, resembling a catfish), Rivière La Loche (now called the Methye River), and Lac du Boeuf (Buffalo Lake, now called Peter Pond Lake). These three bodies of water also constituted the ancient mainline canoe route in this area. Ideally, we would put in at the community of La Loche on the east side of Lac La Loche, paddle southward for five miles to the head of the Rivière La Loche, and then proceed down the forty-mile length of the river. However,

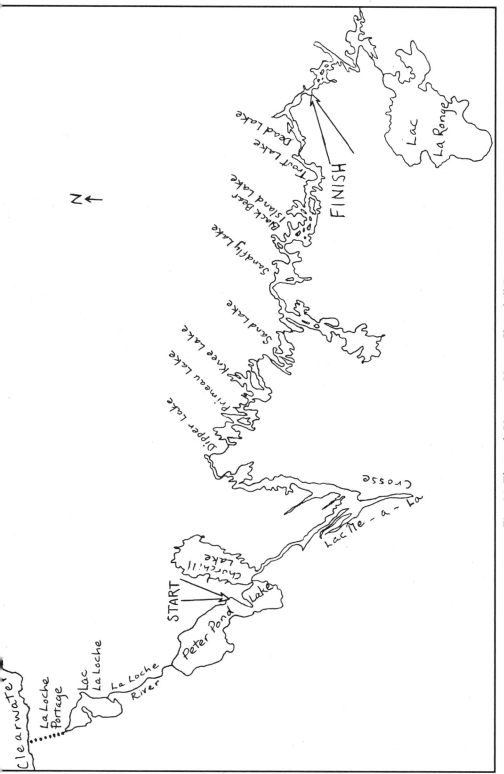

Fig. 14, Eleventh Voyage: Upper Churchill River

this narrow watercourse was famous for its lack of depth and its large number of shallow riffle rapids, as it wound its looping way through reed beds and swampland to reach Lac du Boeuf. This river had usually obliged the voyageurs to do a great deal of dragging, lining, and poling, even in times of average water levels. Alexander Mackenzie commented in 1789: "The River La Loche, in the fall of the year, is very shallow, and navigated with difficulty even by half-laden canoes. Its water is not sufficient to form strong rapids, though from its rocky bottom the canoes are frequently in considerable danger."

During the previous August, while we had paddled the lower Churchill River, we had dealt with a drastically sunken water level, at the all-time recorded low of seven feet below normal for the late-summer season. With that experience clearly etched in my mind, I envisioned forty miles of pure hell for us along the length of the La Loche River, which was excessively shallow even under normal circumstances. I pictured us dragging the canoe through a stone-lined bog, instead of paddling it down a watercourse, if the depressed water levels that had plagued the entire watershed the year before had persisted into 1994. It seemed unlikely that the region had experienced such a tremendous upsurge in its water levels during the previous eleven months that this recalcitrant little river would be manageable.

After deciding to skip this small portion of the mainline route, thus sparing the Kent family from a very unpleasant ordeal, the next step was to locate a place to launch on Lac du Boeuf (Peter Pond Lake). The only paved road in this entire area runs parallel to the east side of the lake, while the detailed topographical map indicates that only one dirt road extends from the highway all the way westward to the lakeshore: Big Buffalo Beach Road. As a result, the northernmost spot on Peter Pond Lake to which we had access for departure was located about 25 miles south of the head of the lake (and the mouth of the La Loche River). This place was also some seventy miles by water south of the community of La Loche on Lac La Loche, where I would have ideally wished to begin our journey.

This year's expedition would cover more than three hundred miles on the Churchill River, as it snaked its way in a generally southeasterly direction across more than half of the width of the province of Saskatchewan. Even though a small portion of the total mileage had been eliminated by skipping the potentially disastrous

Rivière La Loche at its upper end, this year's voyage would still be more than 50 percent longer than that of the previous year. In addition, it would include about forty sets of rapids and falls along the route.

The portion of the mainline route in this area that included Lac La Loche, Rivière La Loche, Lac du Boeuf, and all but the northernmost end of Lac Île-à-la-Crosse was located in the prairie region, while the rest of the Churchill River flowed through Canadian Shield terrain. However, the entire region was mostly covered with an evergreen forest of spruce, jack pine, and tamarack (larch), with some birch and poplar interspersed, particularly in the prairie area. The Churchill River, which the Crees had called the Missinippi (Big River), had served for centuries as the traditional boundary between the Algonquian-speaking Cree nation to the south and the Athapascan-speaking Chipewyan nation to the north. However, the Crees had acquired plenty of expansion room in 1781, when fully 90 percent of the Chipewyan population was snuffed out in a massive, far-reaching smallpox epidemic.

Due to the rotation of personnel on the C.S.O. programs during this particular week, we were able to depart from Ravinia Park at 9:20 P.M. on Friday, after the intermission of the concert. We drove through that night as well as all of the following day and night, making stops only for meals and gas on Saturday at 10 A.M., 1 P.M., and 9 P.M. Ben had turned sixteen just ten days earlier, and was poised to enter the eleventh grade, so he was now fully qualified as a vehicle driver. It was a considerable relief for Doree and me to have our quickly-growing-up son take his turn at the wheel during the long drive to the put-in spot, while we dozed with Toby on the sleeping platform in the rear half of the van.

Day One

After 32 hours on the road, we finally arrived in the early morning light at the little community of Missinipe, where our canoe voyage on the Churchill River would ultimately end in two or three weeks. Parking just outside of town, we grabbed a few ZZZs for 45 minutes, donned our paddling clothes, and left for our 7 A.M. appointment with our shuttle driver, at Horizons Unlimited, Churchill River Canoe Outfitters. A half-hour later, Ric Driediger, the owner of the firm, arrived. He explained that it was then only 6:30 in that locale, since the residents of that region do not observe daylight saving time. So he was happy to note that he had actually arrived quite early for our appointment; we were just excessively early, since our watches were one hour ahead of the local time. Thinking ahead toward the following year's voyage, we discussed the float plane flight that we would need to return from Ft. Chipewyan, after we would paddle down the Clearwater and Athabasca Rivers in 1995. Ric explained various of the details, and indicated that his counterparts in La Loche would easily provide that service for us. Then, after paying the shuttle driver and van storage fees for this year's trip, we departed at 7:30, right on schedule, with our shuttle driver Dale.

During the 270 miles and 5 1/2 hours of additional driving that were required to reach the put-in place on Peter Pond Lake, I handled most of the route, which was on paved roads. However, Dale obligingly took over the wheel on the one stretch of 95 miles that was on a hair-raising gravel road. He was accustomed to dealing with such a soft gravel bed, which required taking a course down the middle, moving over to the right side only in those rare instances when an oncoming vehicle made it necessary. Along the way, one of the loose stones that was hurled up at us by an oncoming logging truck cracked the windshield of the van. (Since this was the third year in a row that our front window had been cracked while en route to or from a canoe trip in the far North, the insurance company thereafter refused to replace our windshield at no cost.)

Seven miles northwest of the community of Buffalo Narrows, at the end of Big Buffalo Beach Road, we finally arrived at the shore of Lac du Boeuf (Buffalo Lake, now called Peter Pond Lake). It had taken us forty hours to travel the 1,930 miles from Ravinia Park (north of Chicago) to the put-in spot, including all of the stops.

To reach the launch site, we carried the canoe and gear from the parking lot of the public beach over the dunes area and down to the water's edge, which was flanked by an expanse of light tan sand for miles in both directions. There, we met Officer Martin, the head of the regional office of the Royal Canadian Mounted Police, and his wife, who is also a Mountie stationed at another nearby post. We discussed the voyage that we were about to begin, as well as the next year's trip, which would start with the thirteen-mile carry across the La Loche or Methye Portage. (The Cree word for the fish that is named loach or burbot in English and *loche* in French is *methye*. Thus, the lengthy portage, the lake, and the river in this area were each sometimes called La Loche and sometimes Methye.) When I mentioned that we intended to hire some men to help us carry our gear and canoe over the long, grueling portage, a project that would include at least one overnight stay en route, the head officer advised that we arrange those helpers through the office of the La Loche Department of Natural Resources, rather that arranging them through the local native band at La Loche.

This was the first year that any Mounties were aware that we were making a canoe trek through their region, and this time it was only due to our accidental meeting with the two officers at the launch site. Each year when we commenced the next segment of our mainline paddling project, we chose not to register at the local office of the Mounties, in contrast to what is highly recommended by them. The registration would include a statement of our proposed route, the length of the trip, and our estimate of how much time would probably be needed to complete those miles. However, if we by chance did not arrive at the finish point within the estimated time span or shortly thereafter, we did not want the authorities to initiate an air and water search for us. If we were to encounter strong head winds or dangerous lightning storms day after day, we could fall as much as a week or more behind schedule, and simply be waiting out the uncooperative weather on shore, not in any danger and certainly not in need of rescue. As a safety measure, when estimating the time that we would probably need to complete a given voyage, and thus the amount of food that we would take on that particular trip, we allowed for an average of only fifteen miles of progress per day, which was much less than our usual rate. In addition, we always included an additional week's worth of food in the packs, as a backup supply. We had no intention of starving to death just because adverse weather was holding us back. Even if we had notified the Mounties each year about our route and our expected date of return, if we happened to suffer major casualties during the early or middle stage of a trip and became stranded, it would be a long time after the accident before the projected return date would pass and the authorities would begin a search. We were willing to take the slim risk that no timely search would be needed. However, we did have an emergency notification plan in place, although an informal one: if we did not return after a considerable amount of time had passed, the shuttle driver who was storing our van at the end of the route would eventually notify the authorities that we had gone missing.

As we prepared the canoe on the sandy shore of Lac du Boeuf, one of the most satisfying moments involved snapping on our brand new, custom-built, red nylon canoe cover. For a number of years, we had anticipated having such a cover, which would shelter us and deflect water when we were paddling in cold, windy rainstorms, as well as while we were running rapids. In the course of discussions with the cover maker about our particular needs, he and I had designed a three-section, end-to-end version, with the bow and stern sections each fitted with a cockpit opening that closed securely around the paddler's waist with a drawstring. Planning the midsection cover had offered more challenges. During these trips on the mainline route with Ben, we always had one passenger traveling in the forward part of the midsection area. However, some day Doree and I would be making voyages as a twosome, and we would then not want a gaping passenger opening in the middle of the cover. In addition, the height of the piled packs in the rear part of the midsection area varied as the food was gradually consumed during a long trip. As a result, we needed a midsection cover which was very adaptable. Ours consisted of two elongated fabric panels that overlapped one another down the long midline of the canoe. These two halves could be fastened to each other in various places with a number of wide velcro straps, allowing the openings for the passenger and the dog to be located anywhere we chose at a given time, and also allowing for various different heights of mounded gear during the course of a voyage. The three separate sections of the nylon cover were fastened to the exterior of the hull with brass snaps that Ben and I had installed along the full length of both walls, just below the gunwale strips. Strategically located small openings in the fabric allowed for attachment to the canoe of the mast, the two mast guylines, the two sail boom lines, the sail halyard, and the projecting eyebolt on the bow and stern decks for the towing lines. In addition, a D ring sewn to the flat area in front of the stern seat provided a secure place to attach the snap clip of the map case.

When we shoved off at 2:40, with Doree leading a song from the *avant* seat, it was 75 degrees in the shade, beneath a nearly solid, white-cloud sky that was decorated with a few patches of deep blue. A light breeze from the east, coming over our left shoulders as we headed southwest, bellied out the angled sail and enabled us to make five miles in the first hour. Our route skirted the shoreline of the Thompson Peninsula, which jutted down from the northeastern shore for seven miles, extending almost completely across the lake. The shore of the peninsula displayed a continuous expanse of sand, backed by poplars along with some birches, as well as scattered evergreens standing much taller than the rest. Moving along at a good speed, we watched several groups of black ducks, some in long V formations and others in single angled lines, flying either high in the sky or so low that their wing tips almost touched the water. I chose this time to explain to the family the name of this particular body of water, Lac du Boeuf. When inbound voyageurs traveling along the mainline route reached the northern end of this lake, they entered for the first time the original range of the buffalo. From here, the remainder of the mainline passage northwest to Ft. Chipewyan lay within the forest habitat of these intriguing, shaggy animals. Their range extended from Lac du Boeuf about six hundred miles toward the north and some five hundred miles toward the west.

As we neared Sandy Point, the tip of the southward-projecting land mass, a moderately strong head wind and waves suddenly confronted us; this was an isolated local weather front that was accompanying a massive black rain cloud. We labored against the wind and waves to advance three miles during the next 45 minutes, and then took a half-hour break at the mile-wide narrows, to rest and eat our remaining burgers, which we had bought at La Ronge during our drive from Missinipe.

During our stop, pelicans in either pairs or small groups glided gracefully overhead, flapping only occasionally. Between bites of burger, I mentioned that N.W.C. traders had established the Lac du Boeuf post on the western shore of the lake in 1790; it had operated for four years. The name Old Fort Point on the topo map, nearly opposite the place where we had put in and six miles north of our resting place, reflected a distant memory of that Montreal-based trading facility, and possibly its original location as well.

Restored and with full bellies, we passed through the narrows at the end of the peninsula and then set off on a traverse of ten miles, which would take us due east across the lower end of Peter Pond Lake. At first, light waves and a head wind conspired against us. But the breeze eventually died out and the waves flattened completely, leaving an unmarred, mirror-like surface to glide across as we traveled beneath a deep blue sky that had partially cleared. During most of the last hour of the three-hour crossing, off to our right along the distant southeastern shore, we marveled at a brilliant rainbow arching between the water and the low-lying white clouds.

Paddling in automatic mode with my mind wandering back centuries, I considered how many hundreds of traverses our ancestor Robert Réaume must have made during his long career as a trader, often under much less benign weather conditions than these. Born at Quebec in 1668 to parents who had each emigrated from France, Robert's earliest surviving fur trade contract dates from May of 1693, when he was 25 years old. However, the responsibilities of this particular task clearly indicate that Robert was by then already a highly experienced and trusted voyageur-trader. He was hired to paddle a canoe with one native colleague to *le Pays des Outaouois* (the Ottawa Country, which was centered at St. Ignace at the Straits of Mackinac), retrieve the peltries and personal effects of the recently deceased Zacharie Jolliet, the younger brother of the prominent traders Adrien and Louis Jolliet, and bring them down that same summer to Zacharie's former business partner in Montreal. Robert's salary of 250 *livres* for this three-month voyage, representing most of a year's pay in normal hiring situations, was another indicator of the respect that he had garnered. Robert accomplished this job ahead of schedule, after which he signed another contract in Montreal on September 10, to return to the same region to trade for investors for more than a year. In June of 1695, he was again hired to carry out commerce in the interior over the following year, this time in the employ of the two commanders of Ft. St. Joseph, which was located near the southern end of Lake Michigan. Immediately following this voyage, at age 28, Robert married Elisabeth Brunet, in September of 1696. Over the next 21 years, the couple would create a family of nine children, first at Montreal and then, from 1702 on, at Lachine.

In 1699, in spite of the closure of nearly all of the interior posts and the western trade, Robert received a permit to trade in the Ottawa Country. His next foray into the interior began in September of 1701, when he, along with two other voyageur-guides and three soldier paddlers, transported to the newly-constructed Ft. Pontchartrain at Detroit the wives and children of the two commanders of the post, Cadillac and Alphonse de Tonty. After wintering there, Réaume and one of his colleagues led the convoy which transported out the very first shipment of furs and hides from that facility. Arriving at Montreal in June, he was immediately engaged for another round trip journey to Detroit, to bring out the second shipment of peltries from the post. After making trading voyages of his own to Ft. Pontchartrain in 1703 and 1705, he later spent the period of 1713-14 there, trading a very large consignment of his own merchandise. The following year, when legal commerce was finally re-established in the west after nearly twenty years of closure, he became the official trade associate of de Lignery, the first commandant of the newly-built Ft. Michilimackinac. This partnership operated during the 1715-16 season, and again in 1718-19. During the intervening two years, he carried out commerce at the same facility, but independent of the commandant and with an employee of his own. When Réaume came down from the Straits to the St. Lawrence during the summer of 1719, at the age of 51, he apparently retired to a more settled life in the Montreal region. There, he spent his remaining 25 years, passing away in March of 1744 at the age of 76; his wife survived him by four years. His very active career as a voyageur-trader, spanning more than 26 years in the interior, had involved the posts on both sides of the Straits of Mackinac, first Ft. de Buade on the north shore and then Ft. Michilimackinac on the south shore.

After Robert Réaume, eight generations of ancestors had continued this particular line of fur trade personnel down to me. The first of these generations was represented by Robert's son Simon Réaume, who also worked as a professional voyageur. His career spanned the quarter-century between 1720 and 1745. According to his hiring contracts, for making summer runs between Montreal and the Straits as well as to Ft. St. Joseph, Simon was designated as being equally qualified as either a stern paddler or a bow paddler.

At about 8:15, with my mind back on the present, we completed our traverse across the lake and entered the Détroit au Boeuf (Buffalo Narrows), the outlet of Lac du Boeuf, a passage which is now sometimes called the Kisis Channel. While traveling through this S-shaped, two-mile-long passage, which is about 1/10 of a mile wide in most places, we passed the native community of Buffalo Narrows, which has a population of about 1,300 residents. Two young women standing on the bridge above us asked where we had started our trip and where it would end. When Ben answered that we were going more than three hundred miles, down to Missinipe, they were impressed: one of them said, "Cool!" I wondered what they thought about our traveling in the paddle-powered vehicle of their ancestors, which their people have generally relinquished for motor-powered cargo canoes and boats.

Exiting from the narrows, we paddled onto Lac Clair (Clear Lake, now called Churchill Lake). It was our favorite time of day, the gloaming period, when golden twilight and beautiful reflections of trees and rocks ornamented the utterly calm surface. As the canoe sped over the southernmost end of the lake, a few white pelicans casually cruising on the water watched us from a short distance away.

At 10:15, we landed for the night on the boulder-strewn shoreline of a point, on the south shore near the outlet of Churchill Lake. A solitary loon, the first one that we had seen on this trip, called out to Doree from its offshore location; she enjoyed answering its call. This peaceful place, illuminated in light pastels by the golden sunset, was also the home of thick swarms of blood-thirsty mosquitoes. Quickly setting up camp, we were thankful to have a shelter with fine mesh netting on its windows, and also to have air mattresses to assist our sleeping on this shoreline, which was completely covered with small boulders. After trading well-deserved massages to the croaking accompaniment of a few frogs, we were fast asleep by 11:30.

In 7 1/2 hours on the water, from our launch at 2:40 until 10:15, we had advanced 23 miles, averaging three miles per hour all day, even including the afternoon break. This had been the best put-in day that we had ever experienced, as far as being well rested and in good condition for paddling. Sharing the forty hours of driving between all three of us had been a blessing, giving each of us sufficient opportunities to catch up on our sleep before reaching the launch site.

Day Two

Awakening at 7:30, I peeked out the front flap of the tent and was greeted by delightful weather: lots of sunshine, a powder blue sky streaked with thin stationary clouds, and an air temp of 65 degrees in the shade. Then commenced the series of tasks that started every paddling day. After doing a few muscle stretchers and then dressing inside the shelter (with my system jolted fully awake by those chilly, wet, sandy socks!), I stepped outside and pulled the packs from the vestibule at the front of the tent, placing on one side the packs that were already set for loading into the canoe and on the other side those that would receive the sleeping bags, tent, and air mattresses. After untying the bow and stern canoe ropes from their overnight anchor, a solid tree trunk, I pulled the tent stakes and removed the vestibule and roof overlay from the shelter. In the meantime, my bustling sounds had awakened Doree, who dressed, roused Ben, deflated the air mattresses, and stuffed the sleeping bags and tossed them outside. Ben was permitted the luxury of cooling it for a few minutes, after which he dismantled the tent and packed it and the air mattresses in the Duluth packs, while Doree and I packed the sleeping bags, first in their red waterproof bags and then in their separate packs. Starting this year, we began smearing petroleum jelly on the top areas of the plasticized nylon waterproof bags, where we folded over the fabric and then pushed the long plastic closure rod over the folded top. This trick, not mentioned by the manufacturer in the accompanying literature, allowed the rod to slide on much easier; it also reduced considerably the wear and tear from the rod on the outer surface of the bag at it closing end. Before these convenient and generally waterproof bags had become available, for years we had used large, heavy-grade plastic bags, which we had twisted closed and sealed in a not-very-effective way with heavy rubber bands.

After Ben and I carried the canoe to the water's edge, all three of us hauled down the packs and the other gear. In the knee-deep shallows, while Doree sat straddled on one end of the canoe to steady it, Ben and I loaded in the packs, after which we all fastened their straps to the thwarts with the seven clip straps. This was followed by arranging the two spare paddles, the ammo box containing the camera, the thermos jug, the bag with daily food and rain gear, and the map case in their respective positions, and finally sealing closed the rear midsection area of the nylon canoe cover. On this particular morning, our usual camp-breaking routine took a little longer than usual, since I also had to practice the trumpet. (To do this paddling jaunt, I had arranged to be scheduled off for several weeks in the middle of the summer season -- with no salary. So, during this entire voyage, I would be obliged to keep my chops in good shape by practicing at least twice each day, since I would still have to play the final two weeks of the Ravinia season as soon as we returned home.)

This morning, rather than quickly downing our breakfast while loading, as we sometimes did, we decided to eat while proceeding on the water. When we embarked at 8:45, my son and I were functioning in unusual roles: he was operating in the stern position, while I was trying to adapt to the role of the bow paddler (not an easy task after eleven years of choosing the route and steering toward it from the stern seat). A moderately strong side wind was coming from the southwest, not very helpful for our travels toward the southeast. While the canoe advanced over the remaining two miles across the foot of Churchill Lake, Doree fed us paddlers, passing a cup of chocolate gorp back to Ben, and reaching forward to pop chunks of the same nourishing food into my mouth. She also scooped up lake water with the thermos, made a supply of strawberry-flavored, instant breakfast drink, and passed the jug around.

Leaving the lake, we entered the relatively straight and narrow stretch of the upper Churchill River that the voyageurs had termed the Rivière Creuse (Deep River, now called the Macbeth Channel). This passage, ranging in width from 3/8 to 1/2 mile, extended toward the southeast for sixteen miles, down to the Aubichon Arm of Lac Île-à-la-Crosse. Along this stretch, I envisioned the first voyageurs who had traveled here, in 1776 and 1777, when the trade had finally expanded over the Frog Portage and into the Churchill River corridor. These had been the very first Frenchmen to have laid eyes on these riverbanks, which had not changed much in the intervening 217 years.

With Ben as the *gouvernail*, we made three miles in an hour; this was his longest and best stint of working as the stern paddler. At one point, an osprey circled very low near us, checked out the intruders who had entered its world, and then flew off. This fish-eating bird looks much like a bald eagle, but it has several obvious differences. First of all, the osprey is considerably smaller, measuring about a foot less in height and about thirty inches less in total wingspan (reaching a maximum span of 51/2 feet overall). Easier to notice are the differences in coloration: the osprey has a white underside and legs, and a wide black stripe extending backward from the eyes, in contrast to the adult eagle, which is brownish black in all places except its head and tail, which are entirely white.

After switching positions with Doree, Ben lounged in the passenger spot while my life partner and I advanced seven miles in 21/2 hours. As we passed close by a single loon floating on the surface,

Doree became engrossed in a long conversation with the bird. Each time it produced its high tremolo call, which has often been likened to the wild laughter of a lunatic, she imitated it closely, which prompted the bird to reply. I could never decide whether her skill at making those loony sounds was the result of her decades of experience as a therapist in a psychiatric hospital, or whether it had come from decades of living with a very unusual husband.

I had been fascinated with these birds for a long time, especially their ability to live almost entirely on the water, only coming on land to nest in early summer, and then in a nest that is located as close to the water's edge as possible. Loon couples, who mate for life and can live from 25 to 35 years, share the egg-sitting duties on the nest for about four weeks during mid-May to mid-July. After the hatching has occurred, they often give the young chicks a ride on their back while they paddle around. These birds are skilled swimmers and divers, eating mostly fish, which they can dive as far as two hundred feet down to catch in their rather long, slender bills. They also consume aquatic insects, crayfish, snails, and frogs. I was particularly impressed with their very distinctive appearance, having a jet black head and long bill, ruby-red eyes, a white-and-black "necklace" around the throat, a white breast, and a black-and-white checkered back.

I was also intrigued by their various calls, which baby loons learn by ear from hearing the calls of mature birds. There is the tremolo call, which is sometimes called the bird's laughter, as well as the haunting wail, most often heard in the evening, which the birds use to keep in touch with each other, sometimes over miles of distance. They also use a hoot call to keep in touch with one another, while males make a yodeling call to defend their nesting territory. These various calls even have different "dialects" in different regions. With their easy-to-spot appearance and their unusual set of calls, which we heard on the water especially in the evenings, these birds always represented to me one of the true hallmarks of our wilderness canoe trips. (Doree)

At 12:15, we landed for a half-hour lunch break. During much of the morning, we had heard thunder rumbling off to the north and west, to our left and behind us, and we had sometimes seen dark clouds dropping rain in the distance to the north. However, our time of avoiding the rain had now ended. During the course of our lunch stop, one passing cloud dropped moderate sun showers on us for about ten minutes. Back on the water again with Ben in the bow position, we were pleased to have a moderate following breeze pick up, filling the sail and pushing us along for about ninety minutes.

By then, roiling black clouds and rainstorms had surrounded us on both sides and also in front. Soon, lightning began to flash nearby and thunder began to crack loudly, forcing us off the water, which we left to avoid an inconvenient electrocution. After fifteen minutes, when much of the storm activity had moved on, Doree took over as the *avant* and we paddled for 45 minutes in light rain, until lightning strikes again forced us to shore. When the rain increased to a moderate downpour, we donned our full rain gear. Sitting on a low boulder a short distance from the water's edge, I used the 1 1/4 hours of enforced time on land to practice. It was an unusual experience having rainwater cascading off my horn while I ran through my usual afternoon routine.

After finishing my practice session, I watched the boisterous show of *son et lumière* (sound and light) in the heavens above us, and remembered some of my weather science lessons from school days. Lightning can flash from cloud to ground (about one-third of all flashes), from cloud to cloud, and even from cloud to open sky. When it zaps through the sky in any direction, lightning instantly super-heats the air along the bolt, causing that air to expand at supersonic speed away from the bolt. The immediate rush of air back into the empty area, where the lightning had just passed and had caused the air to depart, produces the thunder that we hear. When lightning zaps directly down to the ground, it produces a short, decisive clap of thunder, since the sound waves travel unimpeded directly to the listener. However, when the sound from a lightning bolt is absorbed and buffeted by other clouds between the producing cloud and the ground, it becomes the low rumble of rolling thunder. Light travels to our eyes almost instantly, while sound travels to our ears much more slowly, at about a thousand feet per second. As a result, a crack of thunder is heard about five seconds after the lightning bolt is seen, if it flashes about a mile away from the listener. Each additional mile of distance from the listener adds another five seconds or so to the time delay. Thus, a flash-to-bang interval of twenty seconds indicates that the bolt struck about four miles away.

The odds of humans in North America being struck by lightning are roughly 600,000 to 1, and of those individuals who are struck (only about sixty Canadians per year), some 80 to 90 percent survive. Serious burns are not common for lightning strike victims; instead, cardiac arrest is the main cause of death, which can often be rectified by administering CPR. However, survivors may experience loss of vision, loss of hearing, ringing in the ears, memory loss, confusion, and an irregular heartbeat, as well as certain other residual effects.

During our canoe jaunts, when we were exposed to relatively close lightning storms, we tried whenever possible to get off the expanse of open water and onto land. "Close" meant if the strikes were taking place within about six miles of us, measured as roughly thirty seconds from flash to bang. On shore, we put down our paddles and avoided high places and isolated tall trees, all of which might act as a lightning rod, and sought shelter in a low, brush-covered area away from the water's edge. If the strikes are close, there are ways to avoid having the dissipating electricity that flows along the ground also pass through you, and if that does happen, to reduce the physical damage. This involves spreading out at least fifteen feet apart, squatting down on the balls of your feet with your feet together, placing your hands on your knees, lowering your head, and opening your mouth. It is not wise to lie down to wait out a lighting storm, particularly in a tent with frame poles made of aluminum or steel. A silent but fervent appeal to the ancient thunderbird spirits may also be helpful.

When we resumed paddling and sailing in the rain at 5:00, with side-angled waves hitting us from behind, we were pleased to note the effectiveness of the new canoe cover. It sheltered us from both the rain and the wind, and it also kept the waves from splashing over the gunwales into the canoe. In addition, the cover gave Toby the impression that he was avoiding the lightning monster, from his dry vantage point beneath the red fabric shelter, nestled against his buddy Ben.

Shortly, our green bow began slicing through the water of the upper end of the Aubichon Arm of Lac Île-à-la-Crosse. This wider channel, ranging from one to two miles across, stretched off toward the southeast for seventeen miles, to eventually broaden into the main body of the lake. After we had advanced about two miles in the rain, the downpour slowed and finally stopped, and the sky cleared moderately. Doree paddled six miles in two hours, after which Ben did seven miles during the next two hours. It came as no surprise to his parents that Ben had finally become a stronger paddler than his mother, having grown considerably taller and having developed a much longer reach. He and I were now able to paddle faster than the three miles per hour that Doree and I normally covered hour after hour, in flat conditions when the canoe was heavily loaded. When Ben and I dug in moderately, we could cruise for hours at 4 m.p.h., the same speed that the voyageurs of old had averaged in their laden cargo canoes.

Just before 9 o'clock, Doree spotted a narrow sandy beach on the left shore. This unusual and attractive feature lured us to land for the night, since the passing terrain all day had been continuous boulder-strewn shorelines, with low bushes near the water's edge and a poplar-and-birch forest standing behind. After setting up camp on the very slender strip of sand, with the tent just three feet from the water, we spooned down a tasty stew of beef jerky, tomatoes, vegetables, and noodles, as we reviewed our accomplishing day. From 8:45 A.M. to 9 P.M., we had traveled 32 miles, including having spent 1 1/2 hours on shore while avoiding lightning storms. Along the way, we had observed two ospreys, a few great blue herons and loons, and many pelicans, gulls, and ducks. On two occasions, the duck sightings had included a mother tending her brood of five or six ducklings. When it was time to drift off to dreamland at 11:15, we were surprised that there was still considerable light on the water at that late hour.

Day Three

Eight hours of replenishing sleep had readied us for another day on the waterway, a day in which the weather gods would be generous. While we were breaking camp, many ducks winged over our campsite, either singly or in pairs, quacking constantly, as if rumors of outsiders had spread and they were checking out the stories. After I had practiced, we set off at 8:45 with ideal paddling conditions. As we traveled southeastward along the lowest five miles of the Aubichon Arm of Lac Île-à-la-Crosse, it appeared that every one of the pelicans that we had observed during the previous day's rainy afternoon and evening, huddled together in small groups in coves and bays, were now out floating on the open expanse of sparkling water. Some of them were feeding in the shallower areas, dipping their massive pouched bill into the lake, scooping up about three gallons of water along with some small fish, crooking their rather long neck to the side to let the water drain from the pouch, and finally tipping their head back to swallow the captured fish.

Making a ninety-degree turn to the left, we rounded Pointe de

Sable (Sandy Point) and entered the main portion of Lac Île-à-la-Crosse (Lacrosse Island Lake). This right arm of the large V-shaped lake, ranging in width from 11/2 to 31/2 miles, stretched northward for some 33 miles. About five miles southwest of our location lay the Cree settlement of Île-à-la-Crosse, at the tip of a very long point. Independent Montreal traders who later formed the N.W.C. had established a post here in 1777, operating the facility for about fifteen years. Just across the lake to the southeast, N.W.C. personnel had also built a post called Ft. Black, running it for less than five years during the 1790-1805 period. This latter facility had prompted H.B.C. men to open a competing Île-à-la-Crosse post across the lake in 1799, which they operated for some fifteen years. Alexander Mackenzie noted in 1789 that both the lake and the trading settlement had been named after the native game of lacrosse. That same year, Mackenzie also reported that a tragedy had befallen his brigade a short distance from the settlement, as they had been heading northwestward up the lake. One of their canoes apparently capsized during a major storm, since he wrote, "By this unfortunate accident, I lost two men and eleven pieces of goods."

As the morning passed and our own craft progressed without incident, the blue sky cleared of most of its puffy white clouds and the sun beamed gently, without a breath of breeze to stir the air. After Doree had made eight miles in the bow seat in three hours, we reached an impressive sand beach on the left shore, which stretched for half a mile out to the tip of a long point. The forces of nature had clearly left their marks on the terrain here. Driving storm waves had piled up a three-foot hill of sand all along the shore immediately adjacent to the water's edge. In addition, six clearly defined rows of low bushes and reeds, also running parallel to the shoreline, stretched along the full length of the beach. These long, widely spaced rows of vegetation, which included some delicate purple wildflowers being tended by buzzing bees, extended as far as forty feet inland up the very gradual slope, indicating where the water's edge had been located during various recent decades. While we ate our lunch on the warm sand and rested for a half-hour, a squadron of about forty white pelicans soared low over our site. Then, at a much higher altitude, the entire group very slowly glided together in a large circular movement above us for about twenty minutes, presenting a dignified and magical show for our benefit!

Departing at 12:30 with Ben in the bow position, we advanced steadily northward for ten miles. During the last mile or so, a moderate head wind and waves put up some resistance. While passing Little Gravel Point at 3:15, Doree declared, "This'll be a great place for our afternoon break!" On the point, where I measured the high temperature of the day at a comfortable 75 degrees, we discovered a monument to the Blessed Virgin Mary. It had been nailed to a poplar tree at the rear edge of the wide swath of rounded gravel and cobblestones. The little shrine, mounted at head height, was contained within an open-front wooden box that had been painted white on the interior and exterior of all its parts except the roof board, which had been painted black. Inside, someone had placed a statue, a printed picture, and a large oval medallion, all commemorating Mary, while they had also hung a rosary of blue plastic beads from a nail on the back wall. At the front lay a long, slender vial made of clear plastic which, although it was now empty, bore the label "Holy Water from Jerusalem."

After our break of 45 minutes, Doree and I progressed ten miles between 4:00 and 8:00. After about the first mile of this distance, the head wind and waves completely dissipated, to our delight, and the lake became like a huge mirror. At 8:00, we took a short break on a point, to stretch our legs and change bow paddlers, and then continued our progress up the big body of water.

While I passed them peanut butter-smeared crackers, Tim and Ben kept pushing forward, as a moderate wind and waves began to pick up again, this time coming at us from the side. To receive his food, and later a cup of koolaid, Tim extended his paddle forward to me, with its blade in a flat horizontal position like an outstretched hand. To feed Ben, I leaned forward, reached around his neck, and popped the crackers (and later lemon drop candies) into his mouth at just the right time between paddle strokes, so he could continue working without missing a beat. Afterward, I used this same system to hold a cup of koolaid near his mouth; however, to do the actual drinking, he had to stop paddling for a moment, while Tim kept the forward momentum going. (Doree)

At 9:45, as the western shoreline of Lac Île-à-la-Crosse swallowed the sun, the water turned various shades of gold and light bronze. Ben soon located a campsite on the right shore, at the end of a broad point five miles from the northern end of the lake. After setting up camp, all four of us eagerly dived into a stew of jerky, mushrooms, peas, and noodles. This day, we had made 33 miles in thirteen hours on the water, including taking two generous breaks on scenic points (one a sand beach and the other one entirely of gravel and stones). These miles had all been earned exclusively with arm power, since there was no current here to move us along, and we had been granted no opportunities to use the sail.

The evening weather was balmy, with a slight breeze; tiny waves lapped gently onto the pebble beach beside our camp. A thin sickle of white moon hung low above the southeastern horizon, while a single bright star, actually the planet Jupiter, beamed from low in the western sky, which was bathed with residual light until very late in the evening.

As we sat admiring these beauties in silence, it occurred to me that, since Ben has become so helpful on these canoe trips, as a paddler, a story teller, a pack and canoe handler, a tent wrangler, an air mattress blower, and a general helper, the voyages are so much easier than when he was a little boy (and I had so carefully placed him in the canoe so his shoes would not get wet)! (Doree)

Day Four

When the alarm clock jangled at 7:15, we were instantly geared for action, knowing that we had nearly completed the bigger-lakes section of the trip. The narrower, rapids-laced portion of the Churchill River lay waiting for us just a few miles ahead. About fifteen feet offshore from our camp, a pair of pelicans carried out their morning fishing procedures, while a loon wailed its haunting, mournful call at regular intervals from across the lake. By put-in time at 8:40, after I had practiced, the breeze and low waves from the northwest had disappeared, leaving us with perfect paddling conditions: flat water, an air temperature of 69 degrees in the shade, and a light blue sky enhanced with thin wisps of white.

However, within fifteen minutes, a moderate wind and medium waves out of the northeast kicked up, harbingers of an approaching weather front. After two hours and seven miles of northward paddling to the top of the lake, we could see dark skies and falling rain to the north of us, heading at a fast clip in a southeasterly direction. As we began a broad U turn to the right around the end of a peninsula, approaching the narrows that marked the outlet of Lac Île-à-la-Crosse, Doree (in the bow seat) and Ben (in the passenger position) arranged the canoe cover to repel the waves that were smacking them on the left side. Then, occasional peals of thunder and stabs of lightning enlivened the scene beyond the hills just to the east of us.

During the rolling ride across the top of the lake, we rounded with our U turn the tip of the peninsula and the diminutive Wapachewunak Indian Reserve that encompasses it, and then entered the narrows of the lake outlet. This passageway, about 1/10 of a mile wide, curves toward the south for a mile. At about its midpoint lay the Rapides de Shagwenaw, which had no visible obstructions along its length of about 150 yards, just moderately tall standing waves over most of the way and also below the last set of disturbances. As we quickly descended the downhill passage amid the very heavy flow, some of the haystack waves splashed over the gunwales, but the cover deflected them. Judging from the flooded appearance of the shoreline that was flashing by, the water level seemed to be mighty high. Within a short time, we had finished the remainder of the passageway and had zoomed to the landing of the native community of Patuanak, which lies beside the mouth of the narrows and Lac Shagwenaw. Having advanced ten miles in 3 1/3 hours, with about half of that distance against a moderate head wind and waves, we were ready for a noon break.

While I updated the journal at the water's edge in front of the church, the rest of the family wandered off in search of hot food. Shortly, the threatening skies and grumbling thunder moved off toward the southeast, leaving in their wake a nearly cloudless blue sky. Beside our canoe at the landing, two wooden motorboats were pulled up on shore, each one about twenty feet long and bearing a prominent upswept prow that was designed to deflect high waves. Both were painted reddish brown on the exterior and the interior, while one sported bright green gunwales and the other one had gunwale strips painted royal blue. Water travel was apparently still an important aspect of life for some of the people here. This Chipewyan settlement, with a population of about six hundred residents, is located at the terminus of a summer-only gravel road which extends about sixty miles southward to meet a paved east-west highway. Doree, Ben, and Toby soon discovered that the town contains a Northern Store (the modern version of the Hudson's Bay Company store), where they bought delicious take-out meals of chicken, fries, gravy, and Pepsi, as well as plenty more chicken and potato chips for later in the day.

While we were feasting beside the church, a black dog with four puppies wandered up, to investigate the possibility of a handout.

After our refreshing meal, we all took a walk through the town. The houses all looked solid and relatively new, most of them painted white with trim of bright red, blue, or green. The large tribal headquarters building and the Northern Store also seemed to be brand new. The native people with whom we chatted, both on their porches and at the store, were very outgoing and friendly, asking about us and about our canoe trip. The native checkout lady at the Northern Store asked us where we had come from. When Doree answered, "We put in at Buffalo Narrows, a hundred miles away, and are headed for La Ronge," she was incredulous: "By boat??!!"

Departing at 1:15, we easily made the two-mile crossing over the top of Lac de Shagwenaw and then entered, with high spirits, the narrow channel of the river. Ben happily shouted out (in his now-deep voice) the traditional call that commences the Olympics: "Let the games begin!" Over the next 25 miles, the waterway would drop 56 feet in elevation, supplying us with plenty of current, white water, and excitement. However, we could not realize the full measure of the action that we would encounter along the way, since we were still not aware of the unusual water level.

By 4:00, we had covered eight miles of rather narrow, winding channel, and were approaching the first white water. Within earshot of the first set of rapids, we took a fifteen-minute break on the right shore, in preparation for dealing with the many obstacles that lay ahead. As we approached the first drop, with Ben in the bow position, we watched a deer on the shore for a few moments, before it bounded away. Standing up in the stern, I quickly assessed the first stretch. In this especially narrow section of the river, it was obvious that the flow was very powerful, and that the water level was quite high, since the shoreline along the rapids was actually flooded in certain areas. (At the end of the trip, the outfitter who had stored our van provided the explanation, since he had access to the official DNR water data. During the weeks preceding our voyage, a great deal of rain had fallen throughout the entire upper watershed. As a result, although the water of the river was technically at an average level for the previous sixty summers, from 1934 through 1993, it had not been this high during the summer for eight years, not since 1986.) We easily hurled down the first set of rapids, and about four hundred yards downstream approached the second group. Just above the beginning of the drop, while Ben back-paddled furiously to hold our position, I checked them out from a standing position in the stern. Liking what I saw, we shot down without problems.

About four hundred yards away, the Rapides du Tambour (Drum Rapids) lay in wait. This was a rather long and turbulent downhill drop which the voyageurs had often portaged. Well above the rapids on the right shore, Doree spotted the landing of a heavily-worn portage path, whose 300 yard length cut off the entire point, bypassing both the Drum Rapids and an unnamed additional rapids a short distance below it. As we approached the landing, I was rather concerned that we were going to be swept by the very strong current to the rim of the rapids, and then down the seething cascade. So I quickly leaped from the canoe onto some big boulders near the shore. In the process, I caught my ankle on one of the sail boom lines and fell hard, smacking my right ankle on the rocks.

After casing the situation, we decided to portage. However, we shortened the carry by first boulder-hopping right alongside the rapids for two-thirds of its length. When further progress was impossible, we located the heavily overgrown, original portage path through the woods, which we would use for the last section of the carry. On this now-obstructed trail, which is obviously not used anymore, I had a tough time hauling the canoe. Even though Doree had gone through first and had cleared away any loose brush, the seventeen-foot craft on my shoulders often caught on the many saplings that had grown up in the narrow pathway. At one point, when my injured ankle gave way, I fell forward onto my knees. Coming to the rescue, Ben immediately lifted the stern, and in the process caught my hair on the wing nuts that fasten the portage pads to the center thwart. "Let the canoe down, Ben!" I hollered. Then, laughing so hard I could barely speak, I gasped, "Your rescue was worse than the accident!" After that, along the rest of the woods path, Doree walked ahead and bent back as many saplings as she could, while Ben led me and the canoe, as he said, "like a farmer leading a cow."

After completing all three of the legs over the carry, we checked out the rocky shoreline immediately beside the main drop of the rapids. There, a seven-foot wooden cross had been erected, as in ancient voyageur days, to commemorate those who had died while trying to navigate the obstacles here. During the fur trade era, such crosses had stood along the shorelines of many rapids. We thought of the innumerable paddlers who had left their bones along the shores of the entire mainline route over the centuries. In some instances, their bodies were recovered and buried by their fellow travelers or by others who soon passed by; in other cases, the bodies were consumed by the scavenging wild residents of the place.

At the end of the portage trail, we considered how this particular carry had played out. In retrospect, it would have been easier for us to have taken the long but well-used modern path through the birch forest, cutting off the entire point and both of its sets of rapids. However, by doing it our way, we had located the ancient overgrown portage trail, which was historically significant to us, as well as the modern cross that has been erected to honor the memory of voyageurs who had drowned here.

This was the first carry that we had done since adopting our revised portage system, in which a big consolidation pack held the loose smaller items (thermos jug, canoe sponge and bailer, etc.), and a carrying strap bound the four paddles and the entire sailing rig together. We were pleased to note that both of these additions brought significant improvements to our carrying procedures.

As we were reloading below the rapids, to our great surprise, two native men in one of their high-prowed wooden motorboats flashed down the rapids! We then clearly understood the efficiency of this watercraft design, which we had seen at the landing in Patuanak, and earlier on the vessel of a fisherman who had checked us out in the Aubichon Arm of Lac Île-à-la-Crosse. When the water level was this high, that style of upswept bow could handle even deep surging rapids, when guided by a skilled driver.

Underway again at 6:30, we almost immediately encountered a set of rapids which presented mostly high standing waves; these we streaked through after I had scouted the situation from the canoe. Just beyond a half-mile-long, S-shaped turn, we faced the two segments of Rapides de la Feuille (Leaf Rapids), which are separated from each other by about four hundred yards. Feeling confident that the high water would be covering most of the obstacles, I only surveyed from the stern while we raced through both sets. At this point, the river, after its frolicking tumble down seven rapids in quick succession, now rested a bit, flowing evenly and steadily for four miles. We soon pulled off in a shallow side area that was filled with gently nodding reeds, where I practiced in the canoe for fifteen minutes while my mates relaxed in their places. Across from our location on the opposite shore was the mouth of the Mudjatik or Deer River.

With Ben continuing in the bow, we flashed down three miles on the glassy surface of the fast current, traveling around three bends, to reach the Rapides du Chevreuil (Deer Rapids). As we approached the rim of the drop, I stood up, gave the run a quick inspection, and down we raced. Three-quarters of a mile further, in the middle of a bend to the right lay the Rapides de la Pelle (Shovel Rapids), which the voyageurs had sometimes portaged. However, since the main obstacle at this high water level was just a long stretch of large standing waves, we sped down the slope and sliced through the haystacks.

Just before arriving at the latter rapids, we had encountered a couple of outcroppings of Canadian Shield granite, the first that we had seen along the riverbanks on this year's voyage. We had now left the prairie region and had entered Canadian Shield country, although the evidence of this transition would only become gradually visible over the next fifteen to twenty miles.

Below the Shovel Rapids, we pulled ashore at 8:30 and hungrily scarfed down the remaining chicken and chips from Patuanak. Within the span of six miles, we had run seven rapids and had portaged around one substantial set of falls. Ben had handled all of these obstacles excellently in the bow, providing plenty of forward power while I had mostly ruddered, and paddled whenever I could. In addition to running all of these rapids, Ben had also paddled fifteen miles as the *avant* since leaving Patuanak.

At 9 P.M., we returned to our adventures, beneath grey overcast skies and occasional drops of rain, which soon stopped. With Doree pulling strongly in the bow, we hustled down five miles of narrow channel in one hour, on a smooth surface and a strong current. Our traveling for the day finally ended at 10 o'clock, when Ben located a fine campsite on the left shore which was level and somewhat elevated. In thirteen hours of engrossing paddling and scenery viewing, we had put thirty miles under our keel, without any sail assistance. In the process, we had run eight rapids plus a couple of extra riffles, and had made one rather troublesome portage. Thus far, in 3 1/2 days of this journey, we had covered 118 miles.

Even with an overcast sky, we still had plenty of residual light to set up camp. With mosquitoes swarming thickly around us, we were especially appreciative of the efforts of the inventors of DEET a half-century earlier! After crawling inside the tent for a well-deserved rest, we continued to hear the constant drone of ravenous insects outside. Several times during the night, large pike feeding on bugs on the surface of the water near the tent landed with such a loud flopping splash that the sound roused me from my slumber.

Day Five

Again the weather was ideal for unfettered canoe travel: 64 degrees in the shade, a few puffs of clouds in a robin's egg blue sky, and not a whiff of breeze. While we broke camp, birds chirped happily, a woodpecker tapped out a staccato rhythm, and mosquitoes hovered and bit. After I had practiced, we loaded in and were off at 9:00. Two miles down the slender channel, we arrived at the Rapides de la Puise (Dipper Rapids), where the voyageurs had made a 350 yard portage over a gradual rise along the left shore. However, a set of steel-capped wooden rails has now been installed atop the pathway, on which a wooden cart is pushed by hand to haul powerboats around the rapids. After Ben and I had retrieved the rail cart, we loaded it with first the gear and then the overturned canoe, and slowly pushed it along the tracks. Tramway-assisted portages like this one seem to take about as much time as back-and-shoulders carries, but the mechanized ones are much less strenuous.

Soon after the rapids, the channel widened and made a horseshoe bend, and the current slackened considerably, losing its exciting character. Then a succession of about twenty small, bush-covered islands divided the river into myriad channels. We picked our way for three miles through this delta-like section, which was very uncharacteristic for the normally fast-flowing Churchill River. En route through the islands, we stopped to harvest a couple of bulrushes from the muddy bottom. From these, I cut off the tender white basal area, for a delicate, celery-like snack. To pass the time in this less interesting area, Doree taught us two verses of the voyageur song *C'est L'Aviron (It is the Paddle)*, to accompany the chorus that Ben and I already knew:

(verse)
M'en revenant de la jolie Rochelle, (repeat)
J'ai rencontré trois jolies demoiselles.

(chorus)

C'est l'aviron qui nous mène, qui nous mène,
C'est l'aviron qui nous mène en haut.

(verse)

J'ai rencontré trois jolies demoiselles, (repeat)
J'ai point choisi, mais j'ai pris la plus belle.

Leaving the swampy delta area, we glided onto the tranquil surface of Lac Primeau (now called Dipper Lake). There, we were soon buoyed up by the familiar sight of barren Canadian Shield bedrock, on two moderate-sized islands that stood proudly in the middle of this body of water. Immediately to the south of us, a strip of land about two miles long between the river delta and the lake forms the Dipper Lake Indian Reserve, where about a dozen homes are strung out along the lakeshore. After crossing the two-mile width of the lake, we took an hour-long lunch break at 1:30, on a low, bush-covered island of rock at the head of the exit passage. Eleven miles of progress and one portage had earned us a short respite from our labors. During our stop, I mentioned that a H.B.C. facility called Primeau's Post had operated for a few years during the 1774-1789 period on Lac Primeau.

For the next fourteen miles and 3 1/2 hours, Doree worked the bow paddle without a pause. This took us through the entire narrow, looping passageway of the present Primeau Lake, which during the fur trade era was considered to be a continuation of the adjacent Dipper Lake. (At that time, the two bodies of water had together been called Lac Primeau.) The large island which fills the entire center of Primeau Lake now comprises the Primeau Lake Indian Reserve, where about six homes stand along the eastern shoreline. When we were partway through the lake, two young native men who were hunting moose from a motorboat stopped to chat, and to ask whether we had seen any of their prey along the shorelines that we had passed recently. Across the gunwales of the boat, they carried a small canoe turned up on its side. Thus equipped, the pair of hunters could easily travel along the larger lakes as well as up the small streams.

Beginning at about 4:00, ominous black clouds rolled in quickly from the north, filling the entire sky. For the next two hours, wind-driven rain pelted us, first lightly and then in torrential sheets. During the entire rainstorm, with its premature darkness, Ben and Toby remained snug and dry beneath the red nylon canoe cover.

For our part, Doree and I kept the canoe moving steadily forward, sometimes singing and chatting together, sometimes paddling in contented silence, accompanied by the hiss of the rain striking the lake surface, our rain gear, and the canoe cover. This was just one of many instances during this trip in which I marveled at Doree's very cheerful attitude as we traveled for hours in heavy rain. For about an hour during this particular rainstorm, we enjoyed a moderate assist from the sail, when our course down the lake took us in a southeasterly direction and we could harness the south-blowing wind. Luckily, its blusterings faded away during the period of heaviest rainfall, while we were traveling northeastward up the final narrow arm of the lake.

By 6:00, when Ben exchanged places with his mother, the active storm and its rainfall had moved on toward the south, leaving a thick layer of blackish grey clouds to occupy the whole sky above us. Ahead lay a stretch of four miles of slender channel, with a surging current and five sets of rapids.

The voyageurs of old had lumped the first three sets under the single name of Rapides Croches (Crooked Rapids). In the level area just above the first drop, I stood in the stern, surveyed the action ahead, and sent us flying down the easy run. Almost immediately came the second set, with a greater decline and a much faster flow, a small island in midstream to avoid, and plenty of big standing waves to cut through; we whizzed through this group of obstacles while scouting them on the fly. The third set of rapids, a half-mile downstream and around a right turn, offered moderate haystack waves, which I could see while standing in the stern just above the rim; these our bow knifed through with ease. Since Doree was not occupied with paddling during these three fast runs, she was able to note that a large area beside and below the three rapids had been burned by a forest fire within the last few years.

Two miles downstream and around a left bend, we came upon the much more demanding Rapides du Genou (Knee Rapids), which the voyageurs had nearly always portaged. To locate the path around the long stretch of white water, I steered our bow to land on a bare sloping rock shelf on the left shoreline. This spot was about a hundred yards below where the descent of fast water had begun, and just above the beginning of the main rapids. Ben and I thoroughly scoured the entire area, looking for the head of the trail which Alexander Mackenzie had described in 1789 as being "several hundred yards long, and over large stones." Making our way through the thick forest growth, we encountered massive blocks of broken stone, some as big as houses, which lay scattered everywhere, as well as many fallen trees that had criss-crossed each other. We also searched for evidence of a path in the thick stand of young poplar saplings that had grown up some distance back from the shoreline, after a forest fire had cleared the area years earlier. To our dismay, we could not locate a portage trail anywhere! In addition, the terrain was much too difficult for us to bushwhack our way through, especially with the maze of huge blocks of stone that littered the area. There was no other practical recourse for us: we had to paddle down the river.

Walking along the shoreline beside the long stretch of frothing, tumbling water, Ben and I planned our ideal course around and through the many exposed and submerged boulders and ledges. Certain of them remembered the many bottoms of birchbark canoes that they had scraped, gouged, and even ripped open during earlier centuries. The various sets of massive standing waves also looked daunting to us, but the drop of three to four feet near the bottom of the run held the biggest challenge.

A tingling sensation invaded my belly. I knew that, if we did go into the drink, we could all swim, and we all wore life preservers, even Toby. However, most of the danger in a rapids capsize involved the possibility of being slammed between the canoe and a boulder, or of striking our head on rocks. Then, presto! A perfectly-timed break in the solid grey cloud cover opened, allowing some angled shafts of sunlight to beam down. These glowing rays brightened the scene considerably, and made the long swath of white water appear a bit less intimidating. We were going!

When it was time to load in and proceed, Toby, as usual, hunkered down in the woods to hide beneath some bushes when we called him. He had learned that the sounds of roaring white water, followed by a family member depositing him in the canoe, meant wild action ahead -- not his favorite thing. To get the craft into the proper position to begin the run, all three of us lined it while wading back up the hundred yards of fast downhill water. By locating the canoe well above the rim of the drop in this way, we would have a level area and only moderate current to deal with while crossing quickly to the far right side, to get in position for running the upper section of the rapids.

Hoping for the best, we set out on our wild ride down Knee Rapids, with Ben pulling hard and fast in the bow seat, while singing to himself the "Rubber Ducky" song from his Sesame Street-watching days. I suppose this tune had the same calming effect as a voyageur song; it was just a bit less manly.

As we zoomed down the long hill, with both of us paddlers kneeling to lower the center of gravity and make the canoe more stable, the majority of our maneuvers played out just as we had planned them. Due to the high volume of water that was plunging over each major drop, every one of these descents was followed by a section of standing waves that loomed four to five feet tall. Each time the bow sliced through one of these tall haystacks, the wall of water would slam into Ben, knocking his upper body backward for a moment. Then the water would rush down the chest-high spray skirt of his canoe cover cockpit, and back into the river. In the passenger section, Doree held Toby under the canoe cover with one hand, and with the other hand held the two overlapping sheets of the cover securely together in front of her neck, with the fabric positioned like a cape over her shoulders, with just her head protruding. This barrier of nylon cloth over the midsection also helped to deflect the high-rearing water as we descended the liquid roller coaster. At one point, as the hull cut through a set of huge standing waves, I could not keep the bow from slipping considerably toward the left. Seeing our predicament, Ben dug in deeply with several quick, strong draw strokes on the right, to help realign the canoe. Rushing toward the biggest drop near the end of the rapids, which descended three to four feet, I managed to steer the bow into a narrow opening in the ledge that offered a V-shaped tongue of dark water. This reduced somewhat the speed of our drop over the ledge, making it a bit less sudden and a little more gradual. As we flashed down the long stretch of rapids, on two occasions the canoe leaned crazily toward the left; each time, I leaned hard in the opposite direction to offset the movement, and was able to keep the craft upright. At the bottom of the hill, ending our dance with danger amid shouts of joy and relief, we swept into an area of quiet water. There, we caught our breath and let our pulse rate reduce for a few moments, and then rounded a sharp right turn in the channel.

Although the nylon canoe cover had kept the craft from completely filling and capsizing, we had still taken in about four inches of water during the run. This had to be removed before we could tackle any further obstacles, since the weight of the water on the floor made the canoe unstable when it sloshed from side to side (not good for the next set of rapids, which awaited us just a half-mile away). Pulling into a placid area near shore, I bent forward in the stern seat to put the bailer to work in front of my feet. Immediately, I felt a disconcerting sharp pick. Looking down, I noticed that the big diaper pin that I had installed on the torn crotch seam of my pants had opened during the wild action. I shuddered to think of the havoc that this two-inch pin might have wreaked, if it had jabbed me deeply while we were dashing down the rapids!

A half-mile below the turn, we approached the second set of the Knee Rapids, which presented a long stretch of turbulent water flowing through a winding, twisting course. This segment I assessed only by standing in the stern each time we were poised to shoot down another section of the run.

Five minutes later, at 8:40, our green bow arrowed onto Lac du Genou (Knee Lake). We were rather tuckered out after our marathon day, and should have halted near there for the night. However, Ben and I wanted to reach the halfway point of the trip before ending this fifth day. So we pressed forward for another hour, which, by good fortune, turned out to be a very scenic and inspiring hour.

A mile of paddling on docile water brought us across Michikwum Bay, around the tip of a slender peninsula, and to Knox Bay. At the entrance of the bay, as I steered our craft on a course toward the southeast, we were headed directly for the Knee Lake Indian Reserve, a mile away on the opposite shore. This little piece of reservation land, measuring 3/4 mile by 1 mile, encompasses the end of a peninsula, whose tip very gradually reduces in both width and height down to a low, tapered, beak-like form at the water. As we approached this section of ancient native land which is still in native possession, the sinking sun broke free beneath the cloud layer, bathing the entire scene in gold-hued light. From our viewpoint, the illuminated profile of the projecting land mass, with its slopes thickly covered with spruce forest, looked very much like the head and upper body of a dozing green serpent, with its nose pointed southward into the lake.

So that we could record this magical place and moment on film, I reached beneath my stern seat, opened the ammo box, and removed the camera. In the process of handing it forward to Doree in the passenger section, the battery compartment of the camera somehow opened. Luckily, the two tiny batteries simply fell onto the canoe cover in front of me, where I could easily retrieve them and restore them to their compartment. A second blessed moment! Then, as we neared the nose of the sleeping serpent figure, an arc of rainbow appeared over its head in the half-darkened sky, extending from the ragged spruce tops up to the low-hanging grey clouds!

Two miles later, we landed at 9:45 on a small granite island in the middle of the open waters of Lac du Genou. After unloading at the shoreline in the dim light, we faced a tough carry of the canoe and gear up a rather long incline of slippery boulders, to reach the first available piece of level ground. While Ben and I were carrying the canoe, he fell; but neither he nor the craft were damaged, as far as we could tell at the time. Soon afterward, when hauling a couple of the smaller packs, I tumbled into a deep hole between two rocks; again, no injuries resulted. In the subdued residual light and with very few insects bothering us, we set up camp, secured everything for the night, and cooked and downed a well-deserved stew of beef jerky, noodles, and corn.

After the family had bedded down at 11:00, I remained outside to practice and then update the journal by flashlight. Tallying our progress for the day, I noted that, from 9 A.M. until 9:45 P.M., we had progressed 35 miles, most of them without any help from the sail, had made one tramway portage, and had run five sets of rapids. And one of those sets had been the challenging Knee Rapids, which we were supposed to have portaged!

When I finally switched off the light at about midnight, an impressive show of northern lights illuminated the star-filled sky above our site, extending off to the north and west! During each of the previous evenings on this trip, the heavens had been overcast, with no stars visible. Luckily, the clouds this night had moved on during the two hours that we had been on land, clearing in time for my surprise viewing of the *aurora borealis*, with its shimmering ribbons of pastel green light dancing across the sky. Unfortunately, Doree, Ben, and Toby, wrapped in their dreams inside the tent, missed the stunning show.

Day Six

Having traveled 153 miles in 41/2 wearying days, we needed a *jour de congé* (day off), or at least a treat morning with a slow start and a hot meal before departure. We also needed a bit of time in the daylight to reshuffle and balance the contents of the two Duluth packs, to compensate for the consumed food supplies. As we traded massages outside, lying on the air mattresses spread atop the bare granite rock, an osprey landed on the topmost limb of a poplar at the edge of the clearing, and after taking us in flapped off. Lost in my thoughts, I wondered how long this particular ledge of pink granite had waited since the last French or native paddlers of the fur trade era had camped on its sun-warmed flatness.

Mother Nature had gifted us with another magnificent day. At 8:00, there was only a thin layer of hazy clouds floating in the east to decorate an otherwise solid blue sky, the air temperature measured 71 degrees in the shade, a slight breeze was wafting in from the northeast, and, to top it off, there were no hordes of blood-sucking insects around. This site, consisting of bare rock ledges backed by a wide area of tall grasses and surrounded by young poplars and birches, sported many colorful flowers in the grassy area. Some were tall delicate ones of a violet hue, while others had pink, bell-shaped blossoms with yellow rims. Much of the beauty of the natural world is at this small, detailed level -- a single blossom, a moss-covered stone, a mushroom -- rather than in big, majestic expanses. Reveling in the warmth of the healing sun, we stoked up our strength on a stew of jerky, beans, peas, corn, and noodles, and slowly packed up. After I had mixed my trumpet melodies with nature's songs, we made our way with the canoe and gear back over the boulder field and down to the water's edge.

When we finally put paddles to the water at 11:30, having taken two extra luxurious hours to rest, heal, and eat a hot repast, my neck-suspended thermometer registered a comfortable 78 degrees in the shade. Since a huge peninsula projects toward the southwest to nearly fill the midline area of Lac du Genou (Knee Lake), our course would take us northeastward for fourteen miles, along the southern shoreline of that projecting landmass and to the end of the lake. The width of this passage ranges from half a mile to two miles. After advancing five miles in two hours, we decided to take a snack break on a small island. As we approached the shore, Ben launched Toby into the water and then jumped in himself, for an enjoyable swim to land. Resuming our progress, Ben paddled for four miles, after which Doree again took on the duties of the *avant*. Not long afterward, our presence disturbed a great blue heron that had been wading in the shallows near the shoreline; as it flapped slowly away toward the west, the large bird made raucous croaking calls that only another heron would consider attractive.

Arriving at the eastern tip of the lake, we landed at the Pine Settlement Indian Reserve, officially called the Elak Dase Indian Reserve, which includes 11/2 miles of lakeshore and extends inland for half a mile. This quiet fishing community consists of about twenty modest homes and a high-steepled white frame church. The houses seemed to be much less modern and well-tended than those that we had seen in the larger reservation community of Patuanak; several of these in the Pine Settlement were constructed of squared logs. A number of high-prowed motorboats were pulled up on shore; the catch of these fishermen is flown out regularly to wholesale outlets. Doree and Ben scoured the village and church for inhabitants, seeking hot meals to buy, but found no one; all of the residents were probably away at their temporary summer fishing camps. While waiting for my family to return, I watched large pike breaking the surface at intervals, not too far from the shore. The denizens of the deep who live and thrive in the waters of the Churchill River include both northern pike and walleyed pike (which are known in Canada as pickerel). I was also entertained by seventeen contented white pelicans, coasting quietly in a line just offshore. These birds have air sacks under the skin, which give them great buoyancy; as a result, even the slightest waves tip them back and forth like toy boats.

When we pulled away at 5:15, it was 84 degrees in the shade. Headed southward, Ben and I swept almost effortlessly down the fast current of the downhill channel, with its perfectly smooth surface, to make ten miles in two hours. Then we reached the head of the Maskosiwisippi (Grass River). By taking this very narrow passageway, we could reduce the paddling distance to Lac Dreger by two miles, by cutting across the top area of the U-shaped course of the main channel of the Churchill.

The entire four-mile length of the Maskosiwisippi, with its constantly winding hairpin turns, provided us with great entertainment for an hour straight. The slender channel, which varies in width from about thirty to fifty feet, offered plenty of deep water and a moderately swift current. Beds of deep green reeds stood in tight ranks in the near-shore shallows, while low bushes marched right down to the sandy edge of the waterway; close behind, pale-trunked poplars and birches kept silent guard. About halfway down the channel, we rounded a bend and glided up rather close to a beaver cruising in midstream. When the powerful swimmer finally noticed the green monster that was bearing down on him, he slapped his tail and dived deep.

About five minutes later, just as we were rounding another curve, I quietly pointed out a rather large something that was located not far ahead on the left shore. Standing in the lush grass about a yard back from the water's edge, the creature was about three feet tall at the shoulder, high enough so that its coloration was reflected on the glazed surface of the water. Halting our paddles, we noiselessly coasted closer, until the animal stopped munching grass and raised its large head partway up, but did not look in our direction.

Only then did we realize that it was a full-grown bear, but unlike any bear that we had ever seen! Although it had a dark brown head and limbs, the entire upper half of its body, as well as all of its snout except the black tip, was dark tan in color. Having only seen bears of a solid black hue until then, my first impression was that this animal was a grizzly bear, since they vary from black to blond. However, I knew that the modern range of grizzlies does not commence until about forty to fifty miles north of Ft. Chipewyan, well beyond the end of the mainline canoe route, and about a hundred miles west of Ft. Chip. In addition, this particular fellow, standing on all fours, had a rump that was higher than the shoulders, and he also lacked a shoulder hump; these were traits that I knew were in contrast to grizzlies, which have a shoulder hump, as well as a rump that is lower than the shoulders. Although I was very familiar with the standard coloration of black bears, black with a brownish muzzle, I was unaware until this moment that they come in shades ranging from black to brown to cinnamon to blond. And I was totally unprepared for a multi-toned version, especially the odd specimen that was in front of us! Slowly drifting closer, with only the current moving the canoe, we watched the bear in utter silence. When we had finally glided close enough to take a good photo yet not be in danger, Ben backpaddled very gently while I removed the camera from the ammo box. Although I did it as quietly as I could, when I closed the lid of the box the bear suddenly looked up, and noticed us for the first time. As soon as I snapped the picture, it bounded away into the reeds and tall bushes and out of our lives.

As we neared the outlet of the channel and were approaching Lac Dreger, the bushes faded away and the channel twisted and turned in a vast area of bulrushes and reeds, which was heavily populated with red-winged blackbirds. Our one-hour spin down the Maskosiwisippi, from 7:15 to 8:15 P.M., had been a very special adventure. Even the timing had added to the allure, in the quiet cool of evening, with a hazy sky above and the vivid orange ball of the sun sinking down to the black tree line off to the west.

Paddling across two miles of mirror-like surface on Dreger Lake, we rounded a large point and almost immediately located on its flank an attractive campsite, on a tiny projection of bare rock. While we chomped down macaroni and cheese with vegetables, washed down with coffee, about seventy white pelicans floated quietly offshore in a long line, apparently prepared to spend the night with us. In addition, large northern pike occasionally broached the surface nearby while feeding on water insects, re-entering the water with an obvious splash.

As the firelight danced on the surrounding trees, we assessed our excellent day. Since this morning's departure at 11:30, we had covered thirty miles in 91/2 hours. In addition, we had shortened the route by two miles by taking the picturesque Grass River cutoff. Since we had relaxed for two extra hours in the morning before putting in, we were not even beat after thirty miles of progress.

In the earlier years, the boys and I had often pined for kick-back times like those we had enjoyed this morning. However, we had gradually learned to play in our heads Tim's refrain of the old Scandinavian adage, "He who does not sail in fair weather will have to sail in foul." (Doree)

Our meeting with the oddly-colored bruin soon brought the conversation around to the time-tested methods of handling potentially dangerous bear situations. Whenever we encountered black bears, we always kept a safe distance from them, and either departed from the area ourselves or left an escape route for the animals and remained in place until they had departed before we proceeded on our way. Black bears have an innate fear of humans, and if left to their own devices, will normally avoid direct contact. However, if they are surprised they may feel threatened, especially if the situation involves a mother protecting her cubs. In addition, a bear may be aggressive if it is guarding a source of food. A wide detour around the animal, or instead, a quiet retreat by backing away slowly while facing the bear and talking in a soft voice to indicate that you mean no harm, are the best methods of avoiding a serious encounter. It is important not to run, since a human cannot outrun a bear, and running may actually trigger an attack. Climbing a tree might be effective, but the animal may climb up the tree after you. If you remain on the ground, the bear might approach to get a better look at you, or rear up on its hind legs and wave its nose in the air to try to catch your scent.

Signs of aggressive behavior by the bear that might precede an attack could include snapping its jaws together, making a huffing "whoof" sound, or keeping its head down with its ears laid back. However, even a charge is not always a true attack. The bear may bluff its way out of a threatening situation by charging and then veering away at the last second. If it does not break off the attack, it is very important to always aggressively resist the attack of a black bear. This includes yelling, clapping your hands, and waving your arms to intimidate the animal, and fighting back if necessary with any available object, such as rocks or sticks.

On an encouraging note, bears have a sense of smell that is about fifty times better than that of people. This, coupled with the black bear's innate fear of humans, will in most cases result in the animal's departure as soon as its nose senses that people are nearby. In addition, even in the worst-case scenario of a full-fledged attack, very few people die from such an encounter. Black bears kill fewer than one person every three years in the U.S. For each black-bear-caused death, there are about 17 from spider bites, 25 from snake bites, 67 from dog bites, and 180 from bee and wasp stings. In fact, during the year before this book was written, there were approximately three-quarters of a million dog attacks against humans in North America, resulting in more deaths in one year than all of the black-bear-related deaths during the entire twentieth century!

Day Seven

When the alarm clock rang at 6:45, Doree related that she had been awakened during the night by the sound of at least two wolves howling. As she imitated their overlapping calls, rising and falling in pitch, I conjured up the mental image of a pair mated for life, each one having left its original family pack and dispersed, to find a mate and establish a new pack in a new territory. Since they typically leave their pack of origin at about the age of two and can live for as long as fifteen years, some pairs spend a long life together. I pictured two full-grown animals, five to six feet long from the tip of their squared-off snout to the tip of their long bushy tail, with a grizzled coat of grey and brown. In my mind's eye, I could see their coordinated hunting activities, taking down a broad range of prey ranging from moose, deer, and bears down to beavers, hares, birds, and mice, as well as fish, insects, and such immovable targets as berries and grass. I wished that Doree had roused me in the night to hear their howls, and I hoped to hear others later in the trip.

Amid gentle weather conditions (60 degrees, a beaming sun in a hazy sky without clouds, and no breeze), Ben and Tim packed up while birds chirped loudly and Toby munched on grass. After passing the contents of the tent out to them, I wandered off to pick raspberries from the many bushes that had grown out of cracks in the rock ledges adjacent to our camping area. In the placid water beside our point, the bay was wondrously crowded with yellow-blossomed lily pads. A short time later, while steadying the canoe and watching the guys loading in the Duluth packs, I noticed that our sixteen-year-old son was sprouting a beard, after two days of driving and six days of paddling. The hair on the sides of his head was also growing out, since he had for some reason shaved these two areas of his skull just before leaving on the trip. I was taking in the quiet transformation of our younger son -- always so skinny and small -- into a young man. A part of me also thought about Kevin, who was missing out on the closeness that we three were developing on these canoe adventures. (Doree)

On our way at 8:00, we traveled southward for 31/2 miles on Lac Dreger, to reach the elbow turn at the midpoint of this narrow, winding body of water. Just before the sharp turn, the tapering channel was nearly blocked by an island. On its right side lay a set of rapids, while the passageway along the left side, a quarter-mile long, was very shallow and thickly filled with reed beds. I chose the latter route, where, by good fortune, we found a slender opening that extended all the way through, due to the high water level. Near the end of this channel, where the depth reduced to about twelve inches, I walked the canoe through. When we rejoined the main fast-flowing channel, we could hear the splashing turbulent water and see plenty of floating foam from the rapids that we had just circumvented. We then covered the remaining three miles of Lac Dreger, as well as the five-mile width of Lac Croche (Crooked Lake, now called Sandy Lake), which was surrounded by high forest-clad hills, to reach the outlet at its eastern end by noon. In four hours, Doree and I had pulled our canoe over twelve miles of water.

At 12:30, with an air temperature of 75 degrees and a hazy sky above us, we set off on the fast-paced, three-mile run that would take us down to Lac du Serpent. Along the way, the narrow channel would present three sets of Rapides du Serpent (Snake Rapids), in quick succession within the first 11/2 miles. After ten minutes, we reached the first set. Backpaddling hard just above the beginning of the descent, Ben, from his vantage point in the bow seat, declared it to be runnable. My son had a very scientific method for making such decisions. His sphincter muscles served as his gauge concerning the feasibility of attempting a rapids! If he felt the sudden urge to have a bowel movement while surveying a set of rapids, he believed that his built-in meter was indicating that we would probably capsize if we tried to run it. Standing in the stern to get a better look at this particular obstacle, I voiced some doubts about the likelihood of our keeping the canoe upright in the huge standing waves that were rearing their heads at the bottom of the hill; there would be no room or time to avoid them. In response, my son made this comment concerning his father's skills in the assessment of white water: "Dad just looks at the map and he has to crap!"

Atingle with excitement, we plunged down the hill of foaming water. I commanded the canoe to stay in the main heavy flow of the current, and it acquiesced. At the foot of the decline we began hitting the irregular rows of massive, five-foot haystacks. After each breath-catching pass over or through one of these white-topped waves, the bow dived deep into the adjacent trough. Just before the last group of high-rearing waves, the river curved sharply to the left, causing the surging current and the waves along the right side of the channel to smash into the sheer rock cliff at the turn and bounce off at an angle. Unfortunately, our bow dived into a deep trough just as one of those bounce-back waves glanced off the cliff and smacked hard into our right side, instantly overturning the canoe toward the left. Ben and I soon surfaced on the upstream side of the canoe, paddles in hand, gasping. I shouted to him to grab Toby, who was just behind him.

This all happened so suddenly that when the canoe flipped upside-down, my legs were still stretched out in front of me, beneath the bow seat and straddling the base of the mast. In a upside-down position, I managed to extricate my legs, and then got clear of the canoe. I could see Toby's little legs paddling a few feet above me in the churning water, which was white with turbulence, as he swam to the top. There was no time for a panic reaction. With a few kicks and arm strokes, I reached the surface, gasping for breath on the downstream side of the craft. My hat was gone, and the earpiece on one side of my glasses had slipped down below my ear. But the glasses were still held to me securely by the strap that extended from each earpiece around the back of my head.

We were being rapidly swept downstream by the very strong current, and I could hear the roar of the next set of rapids, not far ahead of us. Kicking hard, we tried to edge the heavy overturned canoe toward the left shore. Tim shouted to me to get on the upstream side of the canoe, in case we were swept down those next rapids. Holding onto the gunwales, I made my way to the upstream side and then forward to the bow, where I freed the towing rope from its little storage bag and delivered it to Ben. He was floating on his back beside the canoe, supporting Toby on his chest and kicking strongly. Tim slid onto the broad bottom of the overturned craft and paddled from there, and I kicked as hard as I could while holding onto the gunwales, while Ben and Toby swam with the rope for the shore. Finally, the upstream-direction current that was flowing near the shoreline below the rapids began to slow our relentless downstream movement. Ben made it to land, put Toby on solid ground, and reeled in the rope hand-over-hand, bringing the canoe and his parents into the shallows where we could stand up.

When we rolled the canoe back upright in the waist-deep water, we were elated to see that the mast and the sail had survived intact, even though the mast had pointed straight downward during both the capsize and the downstream drift. We had only lost my hat, but the ziplock seal of the plastic map case had burst open upon impact, and the case was filled with water. The following day, my neck was very stiff and sore, from having been wrenched hard during the flip-over, and I had a nasty-looking bruise three inches wide on my right calf just below the knee, from having banged it on the underside of the bow seat. Over the next three or four days, both my sore neck and the big bruise disappeared. (Doree)

After I had recorded on film the sight of my drenched and bedraggled family, standing in the shallows beside our water-filled, righted canoe, we dumped out the map case, bailed out the craft, and set off again for more adventures.

Our regrouping and moving right on to the next rapids reminded me of a quote from Eleanor Roosevelt: "You gain strength, courage, and confidence by every experience in which you really stop to look fear in the face. You are able to say to yourself, 'I lived through this horror, I can take the next thing that comes along.'" (Doree)

Whisking across the channel to a place near the right shore, we intended to wade the craft through the next set of rapids, which were even bigger and more powerful than the ones that had just trounced us. While Doree and Toby headed for land to lighten the canoe, Ben and I walked in the fast, knee-deep current, not too far from the shoreline. However, we soon discovered that this entailed hiking through a continuous succession of very large submerged boulders. After I caught my left foot between two boulders and twisted my ankle, we decided that we were more likely to break our legs while wading than we were to injure ourselves while paddling down the long hill of rapids. So, after dragging the canoe back upstream to an area of flat water in the midst of the rapids, Doree and Toby climbed back in and we began our fast descent. By steering to the right in the areas of the biggest drops and the tallest standing waves, I was able to guide us through successfully.

A half-mile below this second set, we arrived at the third one, which turned out to be an easy chute with plenty of roiling currents below it. We left behind this last set of Rapides du Serpent, and soon glided onto the shimmering waters of Lac du Serpent (Snake Lake, now called Pinehouse Lake), having spent a total of two hours passing through the three sets of obstacles, including the capsize and the bail-out.

With a brisk wind filling the sail, we sped over the upper five miles of the lake to its *détroit*, passed through those narrows, and advanced two miles in the lower section of the lake, all in two hours. At 4:30, an attractive sand beach on a point summoned us to land for an afternoon break. Along the shoreline in the wet sand, Ben discovered a long series of tracks that had been made by a large bear. The tracks of its front paws had only a short pad area behind the separate group of five toes, while the larger rear-paw prints, about seven inches in length, had an elongated pad area back of the five toes which resembled an excessively wide human footprint. Before landing, off to our right a short distance away, we had been seeing dark falling rain and flashes of lightning, and we had been hearing plenty of rolling thunder; so this was a handy time to leave the water and let the advancing storm sweep over us. After we had rested for half an hour in the light-to-moderate rainfall, serenaded by rumbling thunder, we were preparing to take to the water again. Then the deluge began in real earnest, while the thunder and lightning continued. So we postponed our departure for another half-hour, until the rain had lessened somewhat, and the lightning zaps and thunder crashes had ceased. While resting, I noted to the family that personnel of the N.W.C. had established the Lac du Serpent post near the southern end of the lake in 1786, and had operated it for four years. Concurrently, independent Montreal-based traders had opened a nearby post of the same name in the same year, operating it for a shorter period of time.

Bolstered by an infusion of beef jerky, peanut butter crackers, and koolaid, as well as an entire hour of relaxation, we resumed our progress in the rain, with Ben and Toby napping in the midsection, snug beneath the canoe cover, and Doree and I sheltered beneath our cockpit spray skirts and our rain gear. Traveling due east, we slogged forward for two miles, hindered by a rather strong side wind from the south, all the while looking forward to the place up ahead when we would change our course to the northeast and the wind would become a following one, good for sailing. However, as we made the gradual left turn, the wind completely faded away! We then advanced seven miles up the narrow arm of the lake, which was about a half-mile wide in most places. During this interval, the rain eventually stopped and the sky entirely cleared, leaving behind a beautiful evening, in which several ospreys circled for a long time in the cloud-free sky.

Awakening from his long nap, Ben took the last two miles of the day in the bow seat. At 8:30, Doree found a beautiful elevated site, four miles from the outlet of Lac du Serpent. Located on a point that offered a submerged ledge for a landing place, the site also provided a wonderfully soft, moss-covered area on high ground for the tent, a barren rock area for cooking, and a large ledge down by the water's edge for Ben's evening fire. The large flat top of the point, at one time covered with mature birches and poplars, had been cleared long ago, possibly for regular use as a campsite of an entire brigade; it now had saplings five to six feet high growing over the expanse. There were almost no biting insects at the site, which was a welcome treat. As we unloaded, a large northern pike leaped about fifteen inches out of the water beside the canoe, prompting us to threateningly joke about having it for dinner.

Unpacking our entire array of cargo, to check for any leakage of the waterproof bags that might have taken place during the capsize, we were pleased to find them all perfectly dry. I spread out all of the maps from the map case on nearby rock ledges to dry, anchoring them with small stones, and laid out the rain gear and head nets as well. The sun, a glorious orange ball sinking into the lake, was reflected on the placid surface below the waterside ledge. Our four white plastic bowls sat in a row on that ledge, waiting to be filled with nourishing stew of jerky, noodles, corn, and pea pods. While we ate beside Ben's fire near the water, hundreds of fish flies danced high into the air above us, in the fading pinkish purple dusk. At the same time, a sharply defined half-moon rose in the southern sky, to cast its golden glow over land and water.

Thus ended another day on the river. In 121/2 hours, we had covered 32 miles and had run three rapids, including our capsize adventure on the first set. Relaxing around the fire, we chatted about the fact that whether a given set of rapids is runnable or not is based very much upon the water level at the moment. Our two voyages on the Churchill River clearly bolstered this conclusion. During 1993, when we had paddled the lower section of this waterway, it had been at an extremely low level, seven feet below the summer average for sixty years. As a result, many of the rapids that might have been possible for us to run in normal amounts of water had been absolutely impossible during that trip, since they had presented boulder gardens with minimal water flowing through them. In contrast, during this summer of 1994, traveling on the upper reaches of the same river, the level was at the highest that it had been in eight years. Thus, we were able to easily whisk over and around many obstacles that would have been impassible in a low-water situation. On the other hand, the high water and its very heavy flow also made other normally benign passages into treacherous ones, such as the rapids in which we had capsized this morning. As a result, travelers in different seasons of the same year, and also in different years, can have entirely different experiences on the very same route. This reality concerning the effect of the water level limits considerably the value of river route guidebooks, especially ones that include a designated level of difficulty for each of the rapids. The responsibility for making judgment calls about running obstacles rests entirely on the paddlers themselves.

The same issue of the wide variations facing canoeists also applies when deciding whether to paddle a given body of water based upon the wind conditions at the moment. Traveling on any stretch of water can range from virtually effortless at one extreme to death-defying at the opposite extreme, depending on the presence or lack of wind, especially its strength and direction. Again, sensible judgment calls must balance the risks of the situation against the safety and security of the party. As my old friend Ralph Frese once commented, "Nobody ever drowned on a portage, or while waiting on shore for the wind to calm down."

Later, as I gazed into the flickering flames, I ruminated silently about the old saying "What goes around, comes around." Back in 1986, after our capsize in the rapids of the Chenal de la Culbute on the upper Ottawa River, I had saved eight-year-old Ben from being swept down more rapids when his life preserver was not holding him up in the frothing white water, by grabbing his preserver behind his neck and tossing him to safety on a boulder. Today, eight years later, after our capsize on the upper Churchill, Ben had swum to shore with Toby and the bow line of the canoe, to pull his parents and the craft to safety before it could be swept by the current into another set of rapids. In our modern world, it is rare when parents have the opportunity to physically save their child, and then later the same child has the chance to physically save his parents. Those experiences have certainly contributed to the close bonding between the members of our family!

At about 11:00, as the fire burned down to a bed of glimmering orange coals, a very active show of northern lights played over our heads. At bedtime an hour later, after the dancing pale white and pastel green lights had taken their bows and had disappeared, the gold-hued moon was sinking behind the black horizon in the southwest.

Day Eight

Another splendid day, with a sun-drenched, cloudless sky and an air temperature of 60 degrees (which would rise by fifteen degrees within ninety minutes). As we pulled away from the site at 8:30, with Doree plying the bow paddle, I pictured animals and birds returning to the place, sniffing and inspecting the spot where our tent had stood on the moss, as well as the ledge where we had eaten our evening meal. Working against a moderate head wind from the southeast, we covered two miles of narrow winding channel to reach Lac des Souris (Mice Lake, now called Sandfly Lake). Gliding onto the open water and taking up a southeasterly course, I expected tough going, so immediately sought shelter behind the lee side of the first big island. However, the wind soon died out completely, a generous and much-appreciated gift from *La Vieille*! After advancing seven miles in two hours, we landed on a rock ledge at the northern tip of a mid-lake island, ready for a half-hour snack break. While lounging there, I reminded the family of Alexander Mackenzie's observation about this rather small body of water in 1789: "In this traverse [across the lake] is an island, which is remarkable for a very large stone in the form of a bear, on which the natives have painted the head and snout of a bear; and here they also were formerly accustomed to offer sacrifices." To cross the open expanse of the lake that lay ahead, Ben took over the bow position; he and I then made six miles in 1 1/2 hours. During the traverse, the bright, hazy sky reflecting on the glassy surface of the water made it appear that we were paddling through a thick haze, although the air was actually clear.

At 12:30, we arrived at the slender outlet channel of the lake, and the Rapides des Épingles (Pin Rapids), named for the sharp-pointed layers of stone that are found in the area. Within a half-hour, we had completed the short lift-over portage of forty yards along the left shore, and were afloat again. Three-quarters of a mile of fast current soon brought us to the Rapides du Bouleau (Birch Rapids). Searching the left shore, we could find no trace of the 700 yard portage path. So we pushed off again, inspected the rapids from a floating vantage point just above the rim, and then dashed down the channel on the left side of the midstream island. There were no rock obstructions that required maneuvers, so I just kept our bow off toward the left side of the channel, out of the area of the heaviest flow and the largest of the standing waves. That run quickly took care of a set of rapids that the voyageurs had normally portaged! Ten minutes and one mile later, we arrived at Sault du Canot Tourné (Falls of the Turned-over Canoe, now called Needle Falls), which had gotten its name based upon what would happen to any craft that tried to travel down its challenging decline (as Mackenzie noted, "from the danger to which those are subject who venture to run this rapid"). We were not about to buck tradition here. Finishing the lift-over portage of fifty yards on the right shore in half an hour, we had reloaded by 2:15. But before pushing off, we took a lunch break for 45 minutes, refueling on peanut butter crackers, beef jerky, chocolate gorp, and strawberry koolaid. Since leaving this morning's campsite, we had already put fourteen miles of water and three portages behind us.

We then proceeded northeastward down the five-mile length of Lac Kinosaskaw, at one point causing a great blue heron to abandon its offshore fishing and flap away in slow motion. About two-thirds of the way along this very slender lake, we arrived at a magical place on the right (eastern) shoreline. Over the centuries, portions of the soaring granite cliff had broken off in massive square blocks, which had plummeted down into jumbled piles that extended from the base of the cliff to the water's edge. The crashing fall of these giant rocks, shaking the earth, must have been terrifying to any people or creatures for miles around. The fractures in the rock wall had produced flat faces on both the cliff and on the fallen blocks below. Since these sheer cliffs were reported to bear ancient petroglyphs on many of their flat vertical surfaces, Ben climbed up the stacked blocks and high onto the face of the tallest cliff to investigate. In the process, he discovered that the markings that we saw actually consisted of brownish orange lichens. They had grown into shapes and forms that resembled, when viewed at a distance, the paintings on certain other cliffs, which had been executed centuries ago by native shamans using brownish red pigment.

Ben and I kept the canoe moving forward while Doree and Toby took their afternoon nap. Proceeding through the slender outlet channel of Lac Kinosaskaw for three miles, we landed for a half-hour snack break at 5:30.

Just one mile ahead, the narrows of the Rapides Qui Ne Parle Point (Rapids That Do Not Ever Speak, now called the Silent Rapids) lay expectantly awaiting our arrival. Ever since I had done the historical research for this voyage during the winter, I had dreaded our inevitable meeting with the infamous series of powerful whirlpools that lurk at the foot of this rapids. Various early journal accounts had described them, including Mackenzie in 1789: "There is a very dangerous impediment...which is named Rapid qui ne parle point, or that never speaks, from its silent whirlpool-motion. In some of the whirlpools the suction is so powerful that they are carefully avoided." I had also heard a verbal account of the experiences of two German paddlers at this place in recent years. Unwarned, they had shot directly into the center of the uppermost whirlpool, which had tenaciously held their canoe in its grip for about two days before finally releasing it. In the meantime, the paddlers had jumped overboard and had successfully swum out of the swirling current to the safety of the shore.

Doree was generally very calm on these trips. However, her anxiety about the approaching swirling obstacles was acute enough that I was obliged to steer for shore just before approaching the rapids, so that she could defecate. As for me, although I was on high alert, I was typically more nervous about demanding rapids, roaring falls, and unusual features like these whirlpools while I was researching the route at home, months in advance of the trip. When I later found myself facing the actual challenges, I could focus my energy on reading the elements of the situation, choosing the best course of action, and carrying it out with conviction. Anna Sewell described the phenomenon well when she said, "I am never afraid of what I know."

As we slowly neared the rapids with care, and with our hearts thumping against our ribs, I could see from a standing position in the stern that the slight and gradual downhill run in the narrows had no obstructions to maneuver around. Cautiously paddling down the short decline on the smooth current, I steered our bow to the extreme left in the hundred-foot-wide passage. I wanted to be in the best possible position to suddenly jog to the left side of any swirling water cones as soon as we reached the bottom of the chute. Immediately below the narrows, where the watercourse suddenly widened, a succession of three or four huge whirlpools loomed, each one about thirty feet in diameter. Hugging the left shore as much as we could, Ben and I dug in hard, and quickly zipped by each of the monsters. Then we coasted to a halt well off to the side, to look back upstream at these ominous, living features. The slowly whirling, writhing water made a soft and steady rustling sound, like tiny standing waves. Occasionally, the uppermost whirlpool would suddenly surge louder, and produce slightly taller waves. We were all very relieved to have this infamous but unknown-to-us danger point in our past!

One mile further south, at the next narrows, we came to another slight downhill run, not indicated on the topo map, which had low but very noisy standing waves at the bottom. Doree christened these

Les Rapides Qui Parle de Trop (The Rapids which Speak Too Much), since they made plenty of splashing sounds in relation to their modest, easily-handled waves.

Two miles later, our craft left the slender channel and cruised onto the waters of Lac de L'Île D'Ours (Black Bear Island Lake). Less than a minute after we had entered the lake, Ben spied a large black bear on the left shore, standing on a rock ledge right at the water's edge. As we glided quietly along without paddling, marveling at the coincidence of spotting the big black animal on the shoreline of its namesake lake, it ambled off into the woods. Threading our way for five miles along a tortuous route, we circled around and through several of the islands of various sizes that nearly fill the lake. Finally, on a rocky point at the southernmost tip of Hadley Island, we landed for the night at 9:00. The northern and central routes through the myriad scattered islands pass along either the northern side or the southern side of this huge island.

Pitching our camp on bare rock ledges, we were soon ravenously spooning down a stew of noodles, jerky, and peas. The late evening temperature was very mild, still 75 degrees at 10 P.M.! During our meal, a strong wind suddenly picked up, and we could see black clouds roaring toward us from the southwest. The flames of Ben's fire on the waterside ledge began to dance out of control, so he quickly extinguished the blaze with several scoops of lake water, using the canoe bailer. At about 10:15, as the thunderstorm began to unleash its fury in the distance, we gobbled down the rest of our meal, quickly washed the dishes, and raced to get everything inside the tent, amid the scattered droplets that signalled the advancing storm. Shortly after we had dived into the shelter, the rain began pelting down in heavy sheets. After I had completed my evening practice session, we traded massages, feeling snug and cozy as the rain beat its constant drum roll on the tent roof. We thanked our lucky stars that this heavy storm had held off until we were camped for the night. It seemed that we had been forced off the water for a time during nearly every day of this trip, to wait out periods of severe lightning and thunder, in spite of each of those days having started and ended with beautiful weather.

This had been a gratifying day on the water. Between 8 A.M. and 9 P.M., we had advanced thirty miles, had made two carries, had run one major rapids that the voyageurs had normally portaged, and had run the two little downhill passages in the channel above Black Bear Island Lake (one of which had flaunted its threatening whirlpools). At this point, we had paddled 245 miles in 7 1/2 days, and were about sixty miles from our destination at Missinipe.

Day Nine

I awakened to a silent forest at 6:30, well before the rest of the family, to update the journal entries from the night before and to study the map of the route ahead. I also wanted to check my notes on the life of Alexander Henry, one of the very earliest of the Anglo traders to enter the interior after 1760, as a refresher for the day's storytelling from the stern. It was already 65 degrees in the shade, comfortably warm in spite of the grey, cloud-filled sky and the gentle breeze wafting from the southeast. By our 8:30 departure, the breeze had eased a little, the sky had cleared somewhat, and the temperature had risen to 70 degrees.

Traveling along the north side of Wamninuta Island, with Toby watching the passing scenery from his perch atop one of the Duluth packs, we cruised past an area of impressive vertical cliffs which rose to a considerable height directly from deep water. Each time I passed such an intriguing place, I tried to imagine just how far down in the depths lay the base of those soaring cliffs. Less than a half-mile further toward the southeast along the island shoreline, we were amazed to discover a huge stone in the form of a bear's head, resting on a flat ledge with its snout near the water's edge. The massive rock, measuring about thirty feet in length and six to eight feet in height, lay nestled amid various shades of green: the deep greens of the stately spruce trees that reached skyward above it, as well as the lighter greens of the mosses that blanketed much of the forest floor surrounding it. The ever-changing play of light and shadow on the ground here created a kaleidoscope of enchanting green hues. At this place, as at many locales along the rocky shorelines of the upper Churchill River, the only vegetation to be found growing beneath the trees was a layer of moss covering the stone ledges. I felt certain that this massive rock had been revered by the ancient native people as the residence of powerful spirits, and that it had inspired the name of Black Bear Island Lake. Maybe Mackenzie's 1789 notes about "a very large stone in the form of a bear, on which the natives have painted the head and snout of a bear" had been mistakenly attributed to an island in Sandfly lake, six miles west of here, when he had actually observed the bear-shaped stone that loomed beside us on Wamninuta Island in Black Bear Island Lake.

Reluctantly leaving this serene, sacred place, we rounded a bend to the right and arrived at the central rapids of the lake, in the narrow channel between the island and the northern mainland. This rapids, not indicated on the topo map, offered a fast downhill current that had no boulder obstructions, only low standing waves with lots of swirling currents, which were quite noisy in their splashings. Nearby, we could discern faint pictographs of human figures in reddish brown paint on the rock face; these had been applied eons ago in a sheltered spot beneath an overhanging ledge. Within the span of less than a mile, the northern shoreline of Wamninuta Island had revealed to us four different places which had held spiritual significance for the native residents in ancient times.

Heading due east, we progressed fifteen miles across the island-filled lake in 41/4 hours. Mesmerized by the slowly passing scenery and the glistening water, my thoughts wandered happily over the change of careers that I had experienced during this year. Late in 1993, after a stormy period working with belligerent teens who talked incessantly about drive-by shootings and were filled with anger toward all adults, I had decided to leave the psychiatric hospital where I had worked since the beginning of 1971. In January of 1994, Lutheran Social Services had offered me a position as an adoptions counselor. I relished this new adventure, which was a very refreshing change for me! First of all, the clients with whom I was now working were more motivated and mature people. Besides the international adoption program, in which babies came mainly from China, Russia, and Guatemala, I was also engrossed in the exciting and pioneering concept of open adoptions in the domestic program. Even I needed to get my mind around this new approach, in which birth parents chose the couple who would adopt their baby, and we encouraged a lifelong relationship between them all, in person and forever. (Doree)

As soon as we landed at 12:45 to take a lunch break, the threatening black clouds that had been quickly overtaking us from the west finally reached us, battering our locale with rain, streaks of lightning, and cracks of thunder. Exploring the area, Ben noted that one or more bears had deposited a generous amount of scat here on the rock ledges in recent days. After eating a relaxed lunch for 45 minutes, we were then obliged to wait another two hours for the lightning and thunder to subside, during which time it rained heartily and constantly. To pass the time, we first took a nap. Then, for more than an hour, I related more of the ongoing story of Alexander Henry, as we sat with our backs against the trunk of a spruce tree, whose spreading branches sheltered us from most of the rainfall.

Back on the water at 3:30, Ben and Toby curled up under the canoe cover for a cozy afternoon nap, while Doree and I forged ahead in the rain. When we had covered five miles, and were approaching the outlet of the lake and the Rapides du Hallier (Rapids of the Grove of Leafy Bushes), Ben traded places with his mother, in case we decided to run the cascade. Leaving the canoe at the end of an old overgrown portage path on the right shore, Ben and I examined the entire length of the rapids. Making our way to the falls itself, we waded down to a place near the dramatic drop, which poured with a loud roar over a ledge that extended across the river. Although we decided that we could not run the tumbling white gauntlet, we did locate a portage landing that lay much closer to the drop itself. The first landing that we had encountered, on a much longer trail that was now considerably overgrown, had been used years before, when the water levels had been extremely low. Now, due to the higher water level, we could paddle nearly to the ledge of the drop-off before coming ashore. The three trips over the easy carry of two hundred yards took about an hour, walking along a cleared and level path through the woods. At the slight decline at its far end, while I was carrying the canoe on the third trip over, I slipped on the wet, muddy ground; the canoe fell on top of me, but without any apparent injury to either the carrier or the craft. After loading in, we enjoyed a replenishing snack of chocolate gorp while floating below the falls.

The next rapids, which were located a mile downriver, had a small island in midstream. Staying in the main tongue of water to the right of the island, I assessed the situation while standing up in the stern. Then we streaked down without a problem, slicing through the moderate standing waves. As we were happily coursing down the slope, we disturbed a mother duck and her brood, all of whom frantically scooted off toward the shore. At the bottom, another mother and her big brood floated near the lower end of the midstream island.

Arrowing onto Lac des Morts (Lake of the Dead, now called Trout Lake), Ben and I headed toward the northeast for five miles on this elongated, narrow body of water, until Doree spotted a good campsite at the tip of a slender point. This place provided a very low gravel ledge for a convenient landing spot, as well as a campsite not far above the water which was entirely covered with small rounded stones. Landing at 9:00, we found ourselves 28 miles downriver from this morning's camp, which we had left at 8:30. During the course of that distance, we had made one portage and had run one rapids, in addition to being lightning-bound on shore for two full hours after our lunch break.

As we set up camp for the night amid clouds of blood-seeking mosquitoes, the rays of the golden sunset filtered through the fluffy clouds that hung in the western sky. Later, while we contentedly gobbled our evening stew of jerky, noodles, and corn, washed down with coffee, a line of five white pelicans silently winged southward across the waning sunset. Before we entered the tent for the night, an owl began hooting at regular intervals across the channel from our camp. From our beds within the shelter, we could hear both the haunting calls of the owl and the rather loud and constant hum of thousands of mosquitoes outside.

Day Ten

Since everyone was rather worn down from nine days of strenuous paddling, we had decided the previous evening that we all needed a little extra sleep. So we spun serene dreams until 8:00, when a reveille of bird calls awakened us. The singers announcing the new day included crows, gulls, many songbirds, and a pair of geese flying downriver. While packing, I changed to a new map case, since the old one had torn slightly below each end of the ziplock closure, and had let some rainwater in during the previous day. The sky was completely cloud-covered, the air temperature measured 68 degrees in the shade, and a mild breeze from the northeast caressed our faces.

While checking the canoe, I found two parallel cracks in the hull, in the bilge area of the right wall in the midsection. These had apparently been inflicted when the canoe had been dropped, either by me on a portage, or when Ben had fallen and had lost his hold on one end of the craft, the night that we had to haul everything up a boulder field to reach our campsite. The cracks were not serious, and did not even require any duct tape for now; they would just need to be repaired after our return home.

We were on our way at 9:30, headed northeast down Lac des

Morts (Lake of the Dead). As Doree and I dug in with our first paddle strokes of the day, I commented that Alexander Fraser's House, a N.W.C. post established in this area in 1790, had operated for just a few years. Soon, the head wind from the northeast became moderately strong, making our progress slow as we worked our way down the remaining length of the lake. The map indicated that, upon leaving this body of water, we would be confronted by a series of at least ten sets of rapids within a stretch of eight miles of narrow channel. By 11:20, we had covered five miles on the lake and were approaching the Rapides des Morts (Rapids of the Dead). In 1789, Alexander Mackenzie had recorded the inspiration for the name of both the body of water and the rapids at its outlet: "On the left side [of the lake] is a point covered with human bones, the relics of the small pox [epidemic of 1781], which circumstances gave the portage and the lake this melancholy denomination."

Scouting the outlet rapids from the shore, we found a very constricted channel with a racing downhill torrent of water that was white with fury over its entire length, creating a roar that drowned out our voices; we decided to bypass it with a portage. The carry around the rapids, now bearing the very upbeat name of Trout Portage, consisted of a short walk of 150 yards, along an easy forest trail on the right shore. At about the midpoint of the path, we passed a flat clearing that would have been large enough to accommodate an entire brigade for the night. As I plodded by the edge of the clearing beneath the canoe, I could almost hear the quiet conversation in French from two centuries ago, as one of the seasoned voyageurs shared some tips with a younger man who was out on his first wintering trip.

Finishing the portage at 12:15, a short paddle of about three hundred yards brought us to the next set of rapids. As soon as we had dashed through its frothing water, as well as the big standing waves that reared their heads below, we could already see the next set of obstacles in the distance, just a half-mile away. This latter channel, as narrow as the first portaged one had been, presented a fast downhill stretch of smooth, dark blue water, followed by a sudden drop over a ledge and then a long area of devastating thrashing water. At this heavy volume of water flow, it was unlikely that any canoe could remain upright through that drop and the ensuing melee. Our three trips over the hundred-yard carry, hiking through the woods on the right shore beside the rapids, took 45 minutes. Again, at the middle of this path was a large flat site on which an entire brigade might have camped.

After crossing a mile of open water in a widened area, we made our way through a very slender channel along the right side of several small midstream islands, dealing with fast water and various minor rapids, in the narrow approach to Portage du Galet (Carry of the Water-worn Stone or Pebble, now called Rock Trout Portage). I was uncomfortable having to land for the portage on the right shore so close to the rapids, only about fifteen yards above the beginning of the action. The path, about three hundred yards long, climbed up to the top of a high sheer cliff that overlooked the S-shaped, rapids-filled channel below, and then descended to quiet water below the rapids. Shortly after we began the hike, heavy rain poured down on us, continuing for most of the hour-long portage; then it halted nearly as suddenly as it had started.

By 2:45, we were again afloat. A half-mile downstream, we shot down a small rapids along the right side of an island. Immediately below the descent were a number of very strong whirlpools, which tugged at the canoe as we dug in hard and fast to cross the swirling currents. Entering Lac Mountney, I quartered into the big waves that were being produced by the strong side wind, as we crossed the 1 1/2 mile width of the little lake. Turning southward into its outlet passage, we expected to run a set of minor rapids; but the obstructions were nearly flooded out by the high water level. As the channel immediately began to curve toward the east, we encountered three sets of small rapids that were not indicated on the topo map. After the last of these, we glided along the east-bound passage for a couple hundred yards, to a place where a rapids, supposedly minor in nature, was indicated on the map. However, when I stood up in the stern above the rim of the descent to check out the situation, there in front of me lay a rather demanding run with massive haystack waves at the bottom! As we hurled down this swath of white water, we appreciated once more the wave-deflecting attributes of the canoe cover. Ten minutes later, a half-mile from the end of the eight-mile stretch and its long series of obstructions, we arrived at the Rapides de l'Écorce (Tree Bark Rapids), where the voyageurs had traditionally made a portage of two hundred yards along the left shore. However, due to the high water level, we only faced an easy dash down a smooth flow, while staying well to the right of a pile of submerged boulders! Finally, the last set of rapids at the mouth of the channel, flowing into the lake, was virtually flooded out. After this succession of small adventures, compressed into eight miles and less than five hours, we landed for a break on a point at the mouth of the outlet at 4:00, beside Lac du Diable (Lake of the Devil, now called Nipew Lake).

Although the temperature was 75 degrees, the robust northeast wind made it seem much cooler to us, since no sun was allowed to peek through the heavy cloud cover. At this place where we had landed to rest, we encountered a large camp area where modern fishermen, playing at being woodsmen, obviously stay for rather extended periods on a regular basis. The ground cover at the site was heavily worn, lots of garbage had been left around, and many small living trees had been chopped down for firewood. Toby located an area where fish entrails had been discarded on the ground, and happily rolled in the half-decayed mess! When I smelled him and nearly barfed, I tossed him into the water at the landing area, in an attempt to rinse off the worst of the garbage and reduce somewhat the horrible smell that clung to his fur. We were extremely glad to leave this place and be on our way again! Unfortunately, the stench that Toby carried for the rest of the day continued to remind us of the housekeeping habits of the undisciplined slobs who had repeatedly stayed at that site.

Laboring hard against the head wind and waves, Doree and I slogged forward for two hours, headed northeast down the lake. Then we reached a long series of offshore islands, and were able to find some shelter from the blasting northeast wind behind their lee sides as we continued our progress. Paddling in the narrow channel formed by islands on our right and the mainland on our left, we came upon a mink swimming across the width, creating a delicate V wake with its snout. When we silently approached the slender brown animal in midstream, it dived beneath the surface, and we did not see it again. At 7:30, after a fifteen minute break on the mainland, Ben assumed the duties of the *avant*. Traveling through a number of winding channels between islands for five miles at the eastern end of the lake, we often encountered fast swirling currents in the narrow passageways.

Shortly after we had entered the widened eastern end of Lac

du Diable (Devil's Lake, which is now called Hayman Lake), a float plane buzzed high overhead. Watching it coursing across the sky on a northerly heading, an inspiration suddenly flashed in my head. That would be our solution for handling the thirteen-mile trek over the Portage La Loche, at the beginning of next year's voyage! With our canoe and all of our gear, we would be shuttled over the portage area in a pontoon-equipped aircraft, and then be set down on the Clearwater River, upstream from the carrying path in Athabasca territory. This approach would eliminate an arduous and painful two or three-day hike over the trail, yet we would not have to miss experiencing this famous landmark of the fur trade. While paddling down the Clearwater, we could stop at the northern end of the portage, walk a few of its miles, and absorb some of its history. Doree and Ben were elated with my idea, but Toby was unimpressed; since he would not have been encumbered by heavy packs and a canoe on the carry, he would have gladly walked the thirteen miles of forest path, happily sniffing the odors and wagging his tail.

At 9:00, we landed for the night on a very low rock ledge, beneath a tall stand of stately spruce trees interspersed with some poplars. Ben gathered a good supply of firewood and built a cheerful blaze at the water's edge, where we enjoyed a much-needed feast of jerky, noodles, and mixed veggies. While we ate, with a stunning orange sunset tinting the heavens above us and the water beside us, a wolf howled twice, at not too great a distance. Before we hit the sack, a nearly full disc of yellow moon rose in the southern sky; its reflection glimmered on the utterly calm lake off the tip of our point. That giant orb would be in complete command of the heavens on this night.

This day had been a strenuous and engrossing one. From 9:30 A.M. to 9 P.M., we had advanced 22 miles, many of which had been against a strong head wind and waves. Along the way, we had made three portages, and had run four significant rapids as well as five or six minor sets. At one of the rapids that we had paddled, the voyageurs had customarily made a portage; in lower water levels, we would have also been obliged to make a carry there.

At this point in our voyage, we had paddled 295 miles in 9 1/2 days, and were camped just ten miles from Missinipe. However, even though we were close to our destination, we did not set a goal of arriving there at any certain time. We were fully aware that paddling those last ten miles, and making the three necessary portages en route, could take multiple days if we encountered adverse conditions.

Day Eleven

My dreams were interrupted at 6:30 by the high-pitched squeaks of a chipmunk chirping near the tent, accompanied by the raucous cawing of a crow that was examining our fire area. Emerging from the shelter, I noted that the air temperature was 60 degrees in the shade. At the water, the thin mist, rising ghost-like from the surface, was being slowly burned away by the new sun, while a subtle northwest breeze was producing little waves that lapped softly against the stone ledges. Overhead, only a few puffy white clouds hung in the western area of the pale azure sky. Even this early in the day, I could feel the generous warmth of the sun. Then I realized that this was the first time that we had done a long-distance canoe trip in July; the other voyages had nearly always taken place in August, with a couple of very chilly and rainy ones happening in May and June. On this jaunt, we had noticed how very hot the July sun felt when it shone in full force; likewise, when the July sun was shielded by a cloud, we registered the more gentle warmth that we had become accustomed to during our trips in mid to latter August of most years.

At 7:30, the family stirred and we took on our usual morning chores, preparing to cover the last ten miles with its three moderately long portages. On these trips, each of us knew how to do all of the tasks, so we all simply dived into whatever jobs we saw that needed to be done at a given time, without discussion. After I had practiced, we were on our way at 8:15. A half-hour's paddle brought us to the end of the lake and the Portage du Diable (Devil's Carry), which bypassed a half-mile of roaring Great Devil Rapids. The path along the left shore was generally easy to hike, consisting of twelve hundred yards of forest trail, but its middle section was somewhat muddy. On the third trip over, Ben split the canoe-carrying task with me, which was a great relief for my shoulders, and a first-time novelty as well. Back on the water after nearly two hours of portaging, we did not bother to strap in the gear for the five-minute paddle to the next series of obstacles, Little Devil Rapids, which was a quarter-mile long. At the landing on the left shore, we lounged in the shade for an early lunch break of fifteen minutes. When we set off on the carry of nine hundred yards, the shade of the woods felt very welcome; although it was only 75 degrees out, we had been very warm while paddling beneath the beating sun with virtually no cloud cover.

After traversing the three-mile length of what is now called Devil Lake, we arrived at its outlet and the Portage de la Loutre (Otter Carry). Since the landing on the left shore was located immediately adjacent to the beginning of the first segment of very serious rapids, we waded through the reed beds along the water's edge to guarantee our safe landing. The path, six hundred yards long, had a steep incline at the beginning, as well as a couple of muddy sections along the way. Again, Ben and I traded off carrying the canoe during the third trip over. For this task, we wore our life preservers, so that the pads at the tops of the shoulders helped to buffer our shoulder and collar bones. At the end of the trail, to celebrate our shared toil, Ben and I had a water-wrestling match. First, he knocked me down and pushed my head under water; as he graciously helped me up, I "accidentally" tripped him, so that he went down and under as well. Then Ben went after his mother. The drenching felt great, rinsing off all of the sweat from the three portages that we had put behind us this morning.

Afloat again at 2:15, we made our way southward down the three-mile length of Lac de la Loutre (Otter Lake), gliding over a surface that was as smooth as glass. As we approached the little community of Missinipe, we passed a three-foot-tall wooden cross that had been erected on the western shoreline; it was held upright near the water's edge by several stacked stones. The cross and stones had been recently painted white, and the saplings growing beside the cross had been severed at about waist height. We assumed that this monument commemorated someone who had drowned on Otter Lake near this location. A little south of the cross, seven or eight semi-permanent summer fishing camps of Cree families were spread out along the shoreline, a little back from the water. As we passed the tip of the peninsula at the bottom of the lake and glided around to its backside, to land on the sandy shore beside the outfitter's dock, a float plane zipped by quite near to us during its roaring takeoff.

This brought to a close another segment of the mainline fur trade route. We had completed the voyage of 305 miles in nine full paddling days plus two half-days, from 2:40 P.M. Sunday to 3:00 P.M. Wednesday. Thus, we had averaged thirty miles per day during the ten full days of traveling on the water, with Doree and Ben splitting the bow-paddling duties about evenly. En route, we had encountered some forty sets of rapids; of these, we had portaged eleven, and had run about thirty, including three that the voyageurs had usually portaged. All of the rapids that we had run, with the exception of Knee Rapids, I had assessed only by standing up in the stern as we had approached them; Ben and I had inspected Knee Rapids by walking the upper third of its length.

We had experienced a fantastic trip, our best ever! During this voyage, I had marveled time after time at Doree's very cheerful attitude as she had paddled for hours in heavy rain, sometimes singing or chatting and other times traveling in contented silence. And Ben, who had just turned sixteen, had become a strong, instinctive canoeist, infused with instincts that had been passed down from his voyageur ancestors, and having twelve summers of long-distance paddling already in his bag of experiences. This was the team to whom I very willingly entrusted my life on the wilderness waterways each summer.

Over the course of the eleven long days on the water, these were some of the topics of interesting conversations that we parents had enjoyed with our younger son: his friends; his first job, at a gas station and garage, including his experience with a diabetic wheelchair-pushing lady who gulped down a candy bar that she had grabbed in desperation; cars (classic, modern, repairing, using, abusing); and his future plans, including seeking auto mechanic certification after an early graduation from high school at the end of the third year, beginning thirteen months from now.

As soon as my body registered that we had come ashore long-term, it produced the sensation that appeared at the conclusion of each of our canoe excursions. During the course of a voyage, rolling with the rocking of the craft on the water became second nature. When we landed for a break or for a nighttime camp, I did not register this rolling feeling very much. However, each time we reached our final destination, I definitely could feel it whenever I was standing, during the remainder of the first day back on land. This reaction was similar to that of a sailor who walks onto land after an extended voyage.

After we had all showered at the outfitter's place, we drove to La Reine for a fine restaurant celebration of pike and steak. Then we headed toward Michigan, to join Kevin for a family vacation and a French Canadian family reunion there.

Within a couple hours of leaving the canoe route, I found myself avidly scratching my right ankle. Apparently, I had brushed that area against a small amount of poison ivy on one of the three portages during the morning. As a boy, I had been plagued each summer with massive reactions to this poisionous plant, which had invariably led to a red, oozy rash covering most of my face, neck, and arms. However, this very mild bout of itchy inflamation in 1994, on just one ankle, was the only reaction to poison ivy that I experienced during the entire fifteen years of paddling the mainline route. Some doctors believe that increased contact with the plant may elevate an individual's sensitivity to its poison. Possibly my very heavy exposure to the insidious ivy every summer while I was growing up, in my own front yard and in the surrounding woods, increased my body's reactions to it, while minimal exposure to the plant as an adult may have decreased my sensitivity to it. Not all humans are allergic to poison ivy, but an estimated 90 percent of North Americans are.

Of the three related plants of poison ivy, poison oak, and poison sumac, only the first one was and is present along the mainline canoe route. The sumac version is found only to the southeast of the route, while the oak variety is found only far to the southwest of it. The key ingredient in each of these three plants is a mixture of chemicals called urushiol, which is found within the sap of poison ivy, not on its surface. A strong wind or a brushing pant leg can easily damage the fragile leaves of the plant and release the sap; it can also be released when the plant is burned, since droplets of urushiol cling to smoke particles. This chemical substance is an allergen, which some human bodies identify as dangerous and go to great lengths to fight. After the urushiol has penetrated the surface of the skin, it binds to the membranes of the white blood cells deeper down. Then T-cells of the immune system respond by bringing in a second line of white blood cells, which release toxins that destroy both the membrane-bound urushiol and any other cells in the area, damaging the skin and producing a rash. Fluid oozes from the injured blood vessels and lymph vessels, forming blisters, and the damaged nerves make the area itchy. Contrary to popular belief, blisters that burst do not cause the rash to spread, since they contain only body fluids, not urushiol.

Although poison ivy plants always have three leaflets, it is often difficult to identify and avoid them, since they appear in various forms, including an upright plant, ground cover, climbing vines, and short shrubs. However, if a person realizes that he or she has been exposed to the plant, it is possible to remedy the situation, but only within the first ten to twenty minutes. The treatment involves swabbing the contaminated skin with rubbing alcohol, which dissolves the urushiol, and then washing the area well with cold water, which rinses it away. However, after about twenty minutes of contact without these procedures, the poison penetrates the skin and initiates the immune reaction.

When medical assistance is available, the most common treatment is cortisone, or sometimes prednisone for heavy-duty cases. Other approaches include the use of antihistamines, or the application of calamine lotion, zinc oxide, or baking soda. However, most medical practitioners do not believe that any of these approaches truly lessen the human body's intense immune reaction to urushiol. For the most part, the body's strong response to poison ivy is just something that has to run its course.

After our return to Oak Park, Ben resumed high school, Kevin (now 18) began studying at the local community college, Doree returned to her adoption work at the agency, and I played the remaining two weeks of the Ravinia concert season. Then Doree and I spent four weeks traveling throughout the eastern provinces of Nova Scotia, New Brunswick, Quebec, and Ontario, as I studied dugout canoes. By the end of this latter trip, I had completed my minutely detailed research on 355 dugouts, and only had another 125 or so to examine for my master study, at 75 locales in the Atlantic states ranging from Maine to North Carolina.

In December, Doree and I escaped for a week to Puerto Rico, where we had honeymooned after our wedding in 1970. This trip celebrated the beginning of our 25th year of married life and "canoebial" (connubial) bliss.

XIV
Twelfth Voyage
Clearwater River, Athabasca River, and Lake Athabasca, August 15-23, 1995

The bitterest tears shed over graves are for words left unsaid
And deeds left undone.

Harriet Beecher Stowe

Cowards die many times before their death.
The valiant never taste death but once.

William Shakespeare

The Land Speaks:
I am and you must receive me as I am.
When we meet
Do not come with hope or a faint heart.
Accept each day.
Do your best.
There are no guarantees.

Take care.
Avoid the seething rapids
And sleep soundly on the soft moss,
Dreaming of glorious sunsets
And what the morrow may bring.

George Luste

We were poised to commence our long-awaited paddle to the northwestern end of the mainline route! This year's trip would take us westward down the Clearwater River for more than a hundred miles, dealing with seven sets of falls and rapids along the way, then generally northward down the Athabasca River for nearly two hundred miles, and finally northward for about five miles across the western end of Lake Athabasca. The upper stretch of some thirty

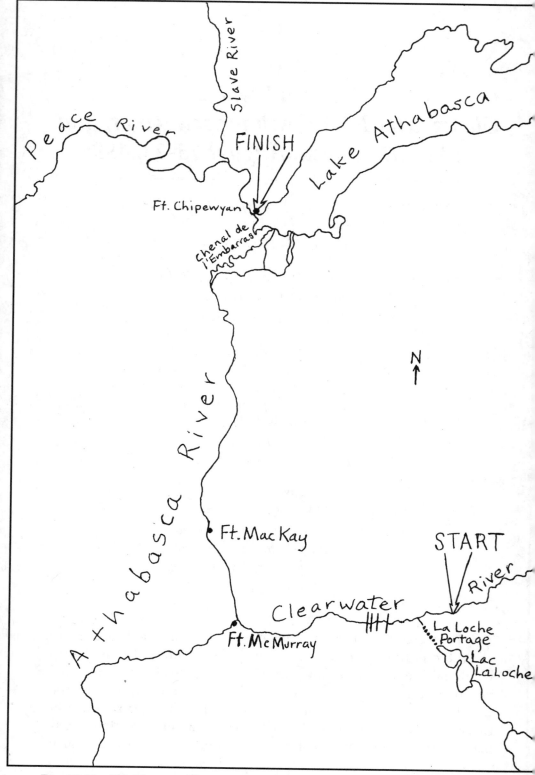

Fig. 15, Twelfth Voyage: Clearwater River, Athabasca River, and Lake Athabasca

miles of the Clearwater would cross Saskatchewan land, while the remainder of the voyage would take place within the province of Alberta.

Since our put-in spot lay immediately west of the edge of Canadian Shield country, we would be traveling in the geological prairie region along both of the rivers, only re-entering Canadian Shield territory when we would begin our crossing of Lake Athabasca. Although the terrain of the region consisted of sedimentary rocks with an overlay of soil, the entire area was mostly covered with an evergreen forest of spruce and jack pine, with deciduous poplar and birch on many of the slopes flanking the rivers, and stands of willow along the water's edge.

Our canoe voyage would take us through the traditional lands of two Athapascan-speaking native groups: first the territory of the Chipewyan nation, on the upper Clearwater River, and then the lands of the Tsattine (Beaver) nation, from about the Alberta border all the way to Ft. Chipewyan on Lake Athabasca.

Leaving Ravinia Park at ten o'clock on Sunday evening, following our C.S.O. performance of Mahler's *Symphony Number 1*, I put in two hours at the wheel before turning the driving duties over to Ben. He then kept us moving northwestward for seven hours throughout the night, a great luxury for Doree and me, sleeping with Toby on the platform at the back of the van! Over the course of 32 hours on the road, we covered the distance of 1,903 miles to La Loche, Saskatchewan, splitting the driving about equally between the three of us. With our destination firmly in mind, we only halted a single time, to refill the gas tank and buy a supply of burgers to keep us going.

The further north we traveled, the more we relished the gradually cooling temperatures. We had just endured the hottest summer on record for the midwest, during which a new all-time high temperature had been recorded for the Chicago region on July 11: a scorching 106 degrees Fahrenheit!

Day One

Arriving at the community of La Loche at 6 A.M. (5:00 local time in the Mountain Time Zone), we slept soundly in the van for two hours, before donning our paddling duds and making our way to La Loche Airways, on the eastern shore of Lac La Loche. Although we were about four hours early for our pre-arranged noon flight, which would deliver us to our put-in site on the Clearwater River, the pilot Gordon Clark had already checked out the float plane and was ready to take us, hours ahead of schedule. Near the far end of the wooden dock, he first roped the canoe in an upside-down position atop one of the two pontoons of the four-seater Beaver aircraft, which was painted silver with red and yellow trim, then helped us load all of our gear into the back of the cabin. After we had each taken our places (with Ben in the honorary co-pilot position) and the engine had roared to life, the little single-propeller plane vibrated from end to end as we taxied to the take-off area out on the lake. Toby hunkered down as low as he could on Doree's lap, terrified at this first-time experience.

However, for us humans, the brief flight of just ten minutes was a fascinating delight! Flying northward at a low altitude over the rather flat lowland which separates Lac La Loche from the Clearwater Valley, we inspected and photographed the gently undulating terrain that stretched out below us, entirely covered with a mottled green of spruce and pine forest. Off to the left in the distance, we could clearly see the northern end of Lac La Loche, and the area where the famous Portage La Loche (also called the Methye Portage) heads northwestward from the lake for nine miles while rising very gradually, to reach the diminutive Rendezvous Lake. From the latter body of water, which is a half-mile across, the path continues toward the northwest for another mile to the rim of the Clearwater Valley, followed by a rather sudden descent over the final 21/4 miles to the river. As the plane glided smoothly over the ridge and into the forest-clad river valley below, Gordon made a ninety-degree turn to the left, aligning the aircraft with a long straight section of water immediately below the Contact or Granite Rapids, which represents the westernmost edge of the Canadian Shield in this region. This mile-long stretch of river offers a reliable landing and take-off area for float planes in all water levels. Touching down gently and coasting to a stop beside the right shore, we unloaded onto the grassy, willow-covered bank, at a place which was located 21 miles upstream from the northern end of the Portage La Loche.

Toby was extremely grateful to be on solid earth again, elated to have the noisy, vibrating "ride from hell" behind him. Little did he know that a much longer flight in the very same aircraft awaited him (and us) at the finish of our canoe trip in a couple of weeks, when we would be retrieved from Ft. Chipewyan and brought back to La

Loche. For our part, we had enjoyed an effortless and interesting plane ride for ten minutes, instead of paddling for twelve miles on the open waters of Lac La Loche, from the town of La Loche to the head of the lake, and then for 1/2 mile up the winding Wallis Creek, followed by an excruciating carry of thirteen miles to the foot of the portage at the Clearwater River. A few hours of paddling 21 miles down the river from our put-in site would bring us to the foot of the path, where we would halt and hike the most dramatic portion of the trail at our leisure. A levitated transport across this daunting, thirteen-mile height of land had been an impossible fantasy for the thousands of native and French travelers who had trudged over it, beneath crushing loads, during the fur trade era. Some two centuries later, we had lived out their fantasy in relaxed comfort, bringing our canoe and cargo across without even breaking a drop of sweat!

Thirty-seven hours after leaving Ravinia Park north of Chicago, at 10 A.M. local time, we launched with a rousing voyageur song onto the waters of the Clearwater River. The heavily overcast sky bore a few scattered patches of blue, the air temperature measured 69 degrees, and the grey-white cloud cover emitted occasional drops of rain. During the flight into the valley, Gordon had mentioned that, due to heavy amounts of rainfall during the previous several weeks, the river level had risen at least two feet during that period. As we glided over the unruffled surface of the water, we could see evidence of this rise in the occasional patches of bulrushes near the shoreline, where the water reached up nearly to their brown heads.

We were now in the fabled Athabasca Country! This was the very first time that we had found ourselves paddling on Arctic-bound waters. By crossing over the height of land of the Portage La Loche, we had passed from the Hudson's Bay watershed into the Arctic watershed, into the region that the fur trade personnel had termed Athabasca. For the remainder of this voyage, we would be traveling on water that flowed to the Arctic Sea, some two thousand miles to the north at the delta of the Mackenzie River.

With the first few paddle strokes on the Clearwater River, which had been sometimes also called the Pelican or Swan River during the fur trade era, I immediately fell into my old familiar rhythm. In most situations, I found the steady, regular activity of paddling to be reassuring, mesmerizing, and soothing, allowing my mind and body to adapt almost instantly to the life of canoe voyaging. Within the first few moments of the first day of each trip, I experienced an immediate and radical change in the things that were of interest and concern to me. This instant adaptation focused my attention on the various elements of wilderness traveling, such as keeping constant tabs on where we were on the waterway, matching the slowly unfolding terrain with the details on the topo map; determining and then locating our route amid such features as islands, shoreline bays, and hidden turns; reading the weather, the wind, and the water conditions, making decisions according to those often-changing elements, and progressing in spite of head winds and uncooperative waves; and keeping the craft on course and relatively empty of water.

This annual reorientation of mental and physical priorities was experienced by the other members of the family as well. Each of us became focused on such issues as reaching the end of long traverses across bays or lakes before darkness settled or before a storm front arrived, and then finding a safe landing spot at the end of those crossings; and locating the beginning of each portage path as well as a high and dry campsite each night. In the process, we altered considerably our expectations about the physical comforts that are a standard part of our usual daily lives back home.

During the trips, we tried to keep our bodies moderately warm, dry, and fueled, for the most efficient and the least uncomfortable traveling. However, in the wilderness we had no control over the elements to which we were exposed, including air temperatures. We generally experienced chilly weather at night and early mornings, and sometimes all day, especially if the weather was heavily overcast or rainy; we added or removed clothing accordingly. But we abandoned our hope of having completely dry clothes. Some days, we dismantled the tent in the early morning in the rain, paddled most or all of the day in the rain, and finally set up camp and cooked dinner in the rain. Although our rain gear was of good quality, it did have its limitations after many hours of constant rainfall. We all understood that the single outfit of spare clothes for each of us that was stored in the packs was reserved for serious emergencies, to help us avoid hypothermia after a bad capsize. On a daily basis, soaking wet tennis shoes, socks, and lower pant legs were accepted as a constant during nearly all of our waking hours.

Another abandoned aspect of modern life involved the expectation of regular meals. On our treks, we paddled whenever the conditions were amenable for traveling, ingesting our meals and snacks on a very flexible schedule that generally kept us from getting too low on fuel, and thus becoming less efficient and less comfortable. We only consumed one hot meal per day, in the latter evening at the end of the long stint of travel, or very occasionally during the day if we had been windbound for a long time or had been forced off the water earlier than we would have customarily ended our day.

We also slept a maximum of eight hours per night (by setting an alarm clock), no matter how long and grueling the days were. I often made do with less sleep, if I hit the sack late after updating the journal by flashlight, or if we wanted to make an especially early start the following morning, or if we were windbound and I had to check on the travel conditions every couple of hours throughout the night, looking for improvements.

In many respects, we adopted the ancient ways and expectations of our ancestors during our voyages, falling back to a mind-set of earlier times, when creature comforts were not as prevalent as they have become in modern times in our First World society. This was one of the purposes of our undertaking these paddling expeditions, to gain a better understanding of the ways and times of the Old Ones.

However, during our trips we most enjoyed focusing on and appreciating deeply the beauties of the natural world through which we were passing, as well as thinking about the history of those uncounted thousands of people, both native and French, who had traveled these routes and lived in these locales long ago. These represented two more of the reasons why we chose to paddle the mainline fur trade route summer after summer for fifteen years.

Seldom during our voyages did our minds alight upon the concerns of our modern life back in "civilization" (or "syphilisation" as Ben jokingly called it); we were almost completely severed from that world. During our jaunts, we did not have the usual background noises and distractions that were often part of our usual daily lives back home. The wilderness was a place of cleansing, of letting go, where we assimilated into ourselves the wild nature of our surroundings, and took up many ancient ways of doing things. On those rare occasions when we paddled by a community, whether it was a tiny settlement or a moderate village or a substantial town, many aspects of that contemporary life seemed rather strange, from our wilderness perspective. To me especially, the life we led while on the expeditions was truly "real life;" my existence during the rest of the year was in many ways unreal, artificial, plastic. After only a short time during each of our trips, when I had become entirely immersed in the ways of life and the challenges of wilderness traveling, it almost seemed like I had always lived that way, that my "other life" had been just a dream, something cooked up in my vivid imagination.

In the moderately fast current of the rain-swollen Clearwater River, we easily advanced five miles in the first hour, with Doree working the bow paddle diligently. Then a moderate head wind kicked up, slowing our progress considerably. The slopes rising on each side of us and flanking the fairly broad Clearwater Valley, having been eroded from the soft limestone and dolomite over the course of thousands of years, ascend to a clearly-defined rim at an elevation of about seven hundred feet above the river. These green-clad hills are thickly covered in many areas with poplar and birch trees, which are so consistent in height that all of the contours of the slopes are clearly indicated at treetop level. Some parts of the valley flanks are covered instead with spruce forest; but in most areas down along the riverbanks, low willows grow nearly to the water's edge. The peaceful, meandering demeanor of the waterway, which is usually about 1/10 of a mile or less in width, has created over the centuries numerous horseshoe bends in its course. On some of the larger bends, we passed beside high, steep sand cliffs, very similar to those that we had seen while paddling on the Saskatchewan River. Since the Clearwater is in the prairie geological region rather than the Canadian Shield region, the shorelines are all sandy, lacking the familiar ledges and boulders of Precambrian granite that are common features along most of the mainline fur trade route. Due to the easily eroded soil of the Clearwater Valley, on many of the undercut riverbanks, the exposed mat of interwoven tree roots, along with its overlying layer of moss, hangs down well below the edge of the precipice, looking much like a person wearing a low cap pulled down to nearly his eyes. Sometimes this thick, dark mat of roots and moss extends all the way down the vertical wall of sand to touch the surface of the water. These various elements caused the passing terrain here to appear much different than the rocky, often barren shores that we had observed during our travels along most of the mainline route.

After making fifteen miles in 3 1/4 hours, we paused for a floating lunch break at 1:15, taking down peanut butter crackers and dried apple slices while continuing to drift slowly downstream with the current. Shortly after resuming our progress, a pair of Canada geese honked and splashed noisily away as we approached them near shore; the two large birds seemed to be intentionally leading us away from what may have been their nesting grounds. Some time later, an adult bald eagle watched us pass directly beneath its perch, on a barren limb projecting above a tall, steep sand cliff. Then it flew off for a short distance, circled back, swooped over us at a low level for an even closer inspection, and finally flapped away down the valley. As the hours and the miles passed steadily, our green hull slid beside a considerable number of bare willow and poplar saplings that were floating on the water. These limbs had been efficiently peeled by the curved, orange front teeth of beavers, who had made a meal of their tasty bark.

At 2:45, we arrived at the upper end of the Portage La Loche, having covered 21 miles of the river in 4 3/4 hours. Along the way, I had kept close tabs of our location on the map, so that I would be certain just where the famous carry was to be found. Landing on the flat, grassy meadow at the foot of the portage, we set out to hike a few miles of its uppermost section, the most dramatic part of the entire trail, to get a feel for this very historic place.

From the shoreline, we followed the path southward for half a mile across a flat area, then for a quarter-mile up a gradual ascent of 130 feet of elevation, first crossing an open meadow near the river and then passing through a forested area of pine and spruce. After fording a very cold creek that was flanked by a swath of foot-deep, slippery mud, we ascended for 11/2 miles a moderately steep slope along the flank of the valley, which was covered with birches, poplars, cedars, and some spruce trees. In this steeply angled stretch of a mile-and-a-half, in which we gained 585 feet of elevation, the trail, about six feet wide, had a deeply rounded cross-section. We tried to imagine how many thousands of pairs of moccasin-clad feet had worn the path down to a depth of about two feet below the adjacent slanted floor of the forest! After hiking for about an hour up this sloping area, we reached the rim of the valley, at an elevation of 715 feet above the river, then advanced another half-mile over slightly descending terrain in the direction of Rendezvous Lake, which lay a mile south of the rim.

Choosing this as an excellent time to take a break, we lounged on the sun-mottled greenery beside the path and discussed the history of this very significant place. Portage La Loche, as well as Lac La Loche and Rivière La Loche to the south of the carry, were all named after one of the most common fish of the area, the loach or burbot, a long slender fish resembling a catfish, with barbels on the nose and chin, which is found in large deep lakes. Since the Cree word for this fish is *methye,* the portage, lake, and river were each sometimes called Methye instead of La Loche. In 1778, Peter Pond and his party of French voyageurs with four canoes were the first Europeans to cross this important height of land. Several independent Montreal-based merchants and traders had combined their stock of trade goods to equip Pond and his men for a voyage up the Churchill River, over the thirteen-mile Portage La Loche, down the Clearwater River, and finally down the Athabasca River, to expand their peltries commerce into the Hudson's Bay watershed. That first year, Pond and his party established a post on the Athabasca River, about forty miles south of Lake Athabasca. During the following two years, they explored downriver to Lake Athabasca, and from the western end of the lake westward up the Peace River for a considerable distance toward the Rockies.

In about 1780, independent Montreal-based traders who would soon form the N.W.C. established a La Loche Post at each end of the height-of-land portage trail; however, these facilities were only operated for a couple of years. In 1819, during the era of intense competition between the N.W.C. and the H.B.C., each of these companies founded a post at the portage; again, these facilities only carried on business for less than three years. Finally, nearly a decade after the amalgamation of the two massive companies in 1821, the H.B.C. established a La Loche Post at each end of the portage in 1830; these were operated for several decades. As a result of these various commercial activities, each end of the carrying path had extensive clearings, and at one time boasted numerous buildings.

During the era of the lattermost H.B.C. facilities, a mid-summer gathering took place each year at Rendezvous Lake. This was the half-mile-wide body of water, bordered with sand beaches, which lay in the track of the portage nine miles northwest of Lac La Loche. At the little lake, brigades bringing merchandise and supplies from the south met with brigades from the far-flung northern posts of the Mackenzie River region, who handed over their bales of peltries and returned northward with new merchandise. In these instances, neither group had to haul their canoes over the portage. Before the remote posts had been established in the Mackenzie Valley, voyageur crews making the entire thirteen-mile carry with their canoes had often paddled across Rendezvous Lake, for a little change of pace in their arduous trek. Alexander Mackenzie documented this custom when he passed through here in 1789: "There is a small round lake whose diameter does not exceed a mile, and which affords a trifling respite to the labor of carrying."

When the Franklin Expedition crossed the portage in 1819, en route toward their explorations in the Arctic, it took a total of six days for the men to make the carry, advancing with their canoes and cargo just two to three miles along the path each day. During this early-July ordeal, the officers recorded in their journals horrible hordes of mosquitoes, horseflies, and no-see-ums, as well as high temperatures of 106 and 110 degrees Fahrenheit in the open beneath the afternoon sun on two consecutive days. (These readings did not quite match the temp of 106 degrees in the shade that we had experienced in the Chicago area a few weeks earlier, on July 11, 1995, but they were nonetheless extreme for the far north country.)

During our hike back down to our canoe, we had hoped to find a place offering a good overview of the Clearwater Valley; but the view in most areas from the rim on down was blocked by tall stands of poplars and birches. So I finally stood atop Ben's shoulders to take a photo, and then sat on his shoulders for a second shot. In contrast to our ascent, the portage area was now absolutely swarming with mosquitoes, causing us to regret that we had not brought our head nets with us. During the descent, Toby oversaw and directed the "parade" of his family members, who were strung out behind him on the path, as he usually did on portages. Stepping out smartly with tail in the air and setting a brisk pace, he glanced back over his shoulder about every twenty seconds or so, to make sure that we were all following close behind. En route down, we admired the many huge mushrooms in hues of red, white, and brown that were growing abundantly in the shaded woods near the path. Back at the meadow near the landing, we harvested and consumed a good amount of blueberries before finally departing at 5:45, having absorbed the geography and history of the La Loche height of land for three hours. We were pleased that the entire region of the Portage La Loche, from the Clearwater River southward to Lac La Loche, as well as the entire Clearwater River Valley from its headwaters area down to the Alberta border, has been permanently preserved as the Clearwater River Provincial Wilderness Park.

To continue our voyage down the river, Ben took over the role of the *avant*. Now 17 2/12 years old, his paddling had become even stronger than the year before. He and I made thirteen miles in the next 2 3/4 hours, passing from Saskatchewan into Alberta after eight of those miles. The canoe slid easily over the placid surface, seemingly as light as a feather floating on a breeze. During this evening period on the water, the sky cleared completely, the lowering golden sun beamed its encouraging rays, and the air temperature became very balmy. On six separate occasions along this stretch of thirteen miles, we encountered a single beaver crossing the waterway in front of us. In each instance, when we glided rather close to the busily swimming animal, it slapped its tail in warning and dived, leaving behind an ever-widening pattern of concentric ripples on the glassy surface.

After all of this quietude, as we approached the Whitemud Falls around 8:30, my anxiety level soared as the dull thundering sounds grew louder and louder. (As Eric Sevareid once wrote, "Canoeing is like war -- placid days interspersed with frantic minutes.") I knew that the river ahead fell in a roaring, twisting course on a quarter-mile rampage through a deep limestone gorge with high cliff walls. If we were to advance over the rim and begin the descent, which drops a total of forty feet in elevation, there would be no way out and very little chance of surviving the ordeal. Ben and I had some high-level maneuvering ahead of us, to land safely on the right shore near the head of the portage path.

In the descending fast water above the first drop of the falls, I steered the bow as close as possible to the six-foot-high bank of the right shore, while Ben back-paddled to retard our forward progress in the strong current. Shortly before the initial drop, we suddenly arrived at the abrupt widening of the channel that I had been seeking, hidden by the bank until that moment. I shouted, "Now, Ben, hard right!" Digging in as deeply as we could, we zoomed around the corner and forward about sixty yards, to enter a narrow channel that flowed behind a small island, and eventually toward the head of the portage. Since the water level was high, my anxiety level was on highest alert: our being swept by the current around either side of the island and then down the huge gorge and its series of falls was too grim to imagine.

Back-paddling hard, we drew up against the steep right bank, opposite the island. From the passenger position, Doree grasped some willow saplings growing from the side of the six-foot-tall embankment, Ben dropped his paddle and grabbed some others growing nearby, and they both held on tightly to keep the canoe snug against the shore. Clambering onto the steep slope, I managed to unload the gear by myself, after which we all dragged the canoe out of the water and up the bank to safety. Whew!

During the previous eleven seasons of paddling the mainline route, I had rarely been as fearful as I was while carrying out this series of maneuvers. In retrospect, having seen the layout in person, I realized that the portage landing just above the first drop was much too dangerous in our high-water situation. Back upstream about 400 yards, we had passed the end of a longer auxiliary portage path, which began above the fast water approaching the falls. I should have taken that much safer route, instead of the trail that began immediately before the brink of the falls! But destiny had brought me to this place at this particular moment in my life, and twelve summers of wilderness paddling had equipped me with the skills to handle this serious challenge.

After setting up camp atop the bank on an excellent site overlooking the upper falls and gorge, we celebrated our safe arrival with a feast: a stew of beef jerky, vegetables, and noodles, washed down with koolaid and topped off with chocolate candies for dessert. All of our activities took place to the accompanying thunderous roar of the nearby falls.

This day, after being flown into the Clearwater, we had advanced 34 miles between 10 A.M. and 8:30 P.M., including having spent three hours at the Portage La Loche. And all of this had followed on the heels of a 1,900 mile drive from Chicago! What a rich, educational, and satisfying day this had been! After trading massages in the tent, we fell into an exhausted sleep at 10:30.

Day Two

Opening my eyes at the end of a sedate and pleasant dream, I was shocked to find myself still embroiled in a demanding and somewhat dangerous canoe trip. When I crawled out of the shelter at 6:45, I was greeted by a blue sky that was half-covered with solid white clouds. Since the air temperature was only 45 degrees, my feet hurt from the cold when I pulled on the wet polyprope socks, but only for a few moments. Making my way to the stream which flowed nearby and into the river, I checked out various animal trails on our side. None of them provided a crossing over the wide mouth area of the stream, to reach the beginning of the portage that circumvented the gorge and its falls. At the mouth itself, across from the island, I located a well-worn path that headed back upriver. This was the end of the 400 yard, auxiliary trail that we should have taken the previous night, which would have eliminated the danger from our landing, by getting us off the water well before the brink of the falls.

While packing up, we ingested our breakfast of chocolate gorp and strawberry-flavored, instant breakfast drink, and then commenced our carry at 8:00, first hauling the gear to the mouth of the stream. At that point, Ben suggested that father and son should paddle the empty canoe from the campsite area past the mouth, to reach the beginning of the portage. As we proceeded slowly, crowding the right shore, all went well at first, except that the craft, lacking its steadying ballast of cargo, felt very tippy to me. When we reached the head of the path and I aimed the bow toward shore, the strong current began to sweep the stern of the light, empty craft around toward the left and down the channel, toward the beginning of the falls. When I instinctively leaned in the opposite direction, toward the shore, the unstable canoe suddenly tipped sharply, and I fell overboard! The stream water was so frigid that I was unable to catch my breath. Ben, ever quick to assess a situation and respond, hopped out into the knee-deep shallows and held his bow end securely. Meanwhile, the stern end, and yours truly gasping beside it in the water, were swept around in an arc and finally came to a stop, thanks to my son's fast anchoring reactions.

We then portaged the gear across the wide stream mouth and to the head of the path nearby. For this knee-deep crossing, Toby rode high and dry on top of Ben's shoulders, while Ben carried one of the Duluth packs. With three more packs, Doree followed close behind, on shorter legs so the water rose partway up her thighs. We were finally in position and ready to hit the trail! While transporting all of the gear to the far end of the 600 yard path, we at one point encountered a squirrel on a tree limb just above our heads. It froze there, hoping that we had not noticed it and would move right on, which we respectfully did. We also met a group of three well-camouflaged ruffed grouse, which were sunning themselves on rocks near the path. The narrow trail through the woods climbed to the top level of the cliffs, and then descended to below the final rapids. On the return trip over, with no burdens, Doree enjoyed harvesting ripe blueberries amid the abundant, heavily-laden patches that we passed.

After completing the third trip over the carry with the canoe, we returned to the high midpoint area of the path, to sit in awe and absorb the sight of the thundering falls far below. During all of our years of paddling the mainline route, these were possibly the most dramatic set of falls that we had seen. In the portion of the spectacular gorge that we could observe, from a vantage point atop a limestone cliff 130 feet high, the roiling white water hurled itself around two large midstream islands, over four or five major ledge drops, and finally down an S-curve in the channel, before the raging flood curved out of sight around a sheer cliff wall. We doubted that even a duck could survive a run down this plunging, rampaging torrent! It reminded me of Lord Byron's quote, "The hell of waters, where they howl and hiss, and boil in endless torture."

Pushing off at 10:30, after fourteen hours of close proximity to roaring waters, the silence seemed deafening. The weather gods were again generous this day, providing a few fluffy clouds decorating a powder blue sky, bright sunshine all around, and a temperature of 65 degrees in the shade.

Within the next eleven miles, six more sets of obstructions still lay in our path. An hour after leaving the portage, after four miles of easy cruising, we arrived at the first of these obstacles, the Rapides du Pas (Step Rapids). When traveling upstream, the voyageurs had made a portage of 130 yards on the left shore, to bypass this riffle extending across the channel. However, in the downstream direction, we were able to easily sweep down the channel that flowed to the right of two small midstream islands. Just a few hundred yards further, we landed at 11:15 on the left shore to make the portage around the Rapides des Pins (Pine Rapids), a stretch of 11/2 miles where the river tumbles and spills over numerous ledges at the bottom of a hundred-foot-deep limestone gorge. This carry, although 1,100 yards (6/10 mile) long, was otherwise ideal, offering a nearly level path in most places, dry humus soil without rocks or mud, somewhat cool air temperatures in the shady poplar forest, and no biting insects. To top it off, the route passed through scenic limestone bluffs and canyons similar to those which overlooked the river gorge that we were bypassing. Along the trail, we flushed up ruffed grouse on three occasions. Completing the carry in an hour-and-a-half, we then enjoyed a leisurely lunch, reloaded, and were on our way again at 1:15.

After skimming down three miles to the Rapides de la Grosse Roche (Big Rock Rapids), we sped down its length after I had checked out the run while standing up in the stern. The high water looked about the same in all parts of the channel, swirling over boulders, and the standing waves below were only two to three feet high. Upstream-bound voyageurs in ancient times had made a portage of 400 yards along the left bank here. A half-mile downriver, we streaked down the Rapides d'Un Coup (One Blow Rapids), which offered a much shorter run and had lower standing waves. Again at this place, when fur trade crews had been traveling against the current, they had made a carry of 200 yards, this time on the right shore.

A half-mile later, we arrived at the Bons Rapides (Good Rapids, now sometimes called Long Rapids). Based on the manuscript version of a Clearwater River paddling guide, I had indicated on our topo map that the portage landing was to be on or near a little point that projected from the right shore. From the canoe, we scoured that shore while approaching the point, and also well below it, finding no path landing in the thick willows that grew all along the shoreline. We then pulled ashore, to avoid approaching too close to the dangerous fast water above the rapids. Ben and I bushwhacked through the cedar and poplar growth inland from the willows, going back upstream as we searched for the elusive portage trail. Near the rapids back upriver which we had run an hour earlier, we found a path for wheeled carts, at the mouth of a stream. So we bushwhacked back to the canoe, paddled back upstream to that trail, unloaded, and burdened ourselves with everything except the canoe. After carrying for fifteen minutes on the cart path, we arrived at the landing and portage trail that we had sought. It was near the beginning of the rapids, much further downstream than I had expected it to be. We then hiked back to the canoe, and flashed downriver to the landing with the empty craft. We had just used three hours of daylight and a great deal of energy getting in position to hike the Bons Rapides Portage!

After bolstering our bodies and our spirits with a snack of beef jerky, crackers, dried apples, and koolaid, we began the 1 1/4 mile carry at 6:00. Along the trail, we passed three large open areas that had only a very few scattered spruce trees, and a thick ground cover of mosses and blueberry bushes loaded with ripe fruit. At one of these openings, Doree picked a few handfuls of berries on the return trip. In two of the open areas, there were numerous hand-sized piles of bear scat, which had inclusions of blueberries. Bruins had been busy here, fattening themselves up for the coming winter. As was often the case on portage paths, I sensed the ghost-like presence and the residual energy of all those human travelers who had preceded us here, over the course of thousands of years. Following the path of least resistance, they too had trod up and down the same ledges and had skirted the same boulders in the trail.

By 7:30, when we had completed the three trips over the portage and had hiked nearly four miles, the sky had completely filled with dark, threatening rain clouds, so we decided to call it a day at the end of the path. There would be just one final portage to make in the morning, at the rapids which lay in the distance within sight of our camp.

Since leaving this morning's campsite, we had only advanced ten miles on the river. However, we had labored diligently all day, completing three long portages, running three sets of rapids, and spending over three hours searching for a portage trail. We were all pretty beat by this time, and welcomed an early halt, although it seemed strange to be setting up camp at only 7:30 P.M., with so many hours of light still left for traveling. We avidly devoured our stew of jerky, vegetables, and noodles, seasoned with fresh garlic and dried tomatoes.

Hopping into the tent at 9:30, just as the sullen skies opened and light rain began to fall, we exchanged well-deserved massages. Soon, my family members were off to dreamland, lulled by the staccato of raindrops spattering on the green shelter. During our journeys, we had discovered that there are few situations more cozy than being warm, dry, and secure in a sleeping bag on a comfortable air mattress inside a tent, with rain tapping on the waterproof fabric overhead. This was especially true when we did not have to soon emerge, pack up the gear, and paddle off in the rain.

For my part, before drifting off to sleep this night, I spent some time thinking about handling rapids, since we had run our very last set on the mainline route this afternoon. During our thirteen summers of wilderness trekking, we had encountered plenty of rapids, and our abilities to both scout them and run them had grown immeasurably over those years. For us, casing a rapids first entailed noting the currents, and locating the V or tongue of smooth, dark, deep water, which indicated the main flow area and often the route with the least obstructions. The worst situations were those in which there was no deep main channel to ride, but instead choppy, thrashing water everywhere, making it difficult to read what lay beneath the surface. We also studied the submerged and exposed obstacles that had to be avoided and maneuvered around, as well as the size and locations of any tall standing waves below the drops, where the energy of the moving water was released. Finally, we looked for any eddies, in case we needed a refuge to rest and regroup partway through the run. All of these elements entered into planning our route.

During this planning stage, my emotional pendulum tended to swing back and forth between fear and confidence. I perceived each run as a fun but potentially dangerous situation, in which we had to make prudent judgment calls about the risks that were involved. Oddly enough, our perceptions of the degree of danger of a given set of obstacles varied considerably based on the weather conditions at the time. The challenges appeared to be much more threatening when it was dreary, cold, and rainy, compared to those times when it was bright and sunny. Since we would be separated from the water during our run by only a thin skin of fiberglass, we could not help but have a close relationship with that water.

We ran every set of rapids that we could safely manage, as the voyageurs had done. In each instance, I thought to myself, "In a very short time, if we're lucky, we'll be looking back on this experience from a safe and comfortable place in the future."

In rapids of any severity, our two paddlers knelt, to lower the center of gravity and thus make the canoe more stable and less likely to capsize. Once we had made our decision to run the stretch and had planned our route, we never hesitated for a moment, but instead stroked with confidence and determination toward the lip of the drop, as a surge of adrenaline kicked in.

As we made the mad dash through the obstacle course, involving a few moments or minutes of furious paddling and instantaneous judgment calls, we ran the gauntlet of churning, leaping, tumbling white water. We maneuvered and negotiated the course that we had planned, making alterations as necessary as we flashed down the route. In each case, as the canoe dipped and leaped, or galloped and bucked like a horse, the roaring sounds of the water heightened our excitement and our exhilaration. The shoreline hurled by in a blur, but only the passengers had the luxury of noticing that; the two paddlers were totally consumed with the constantly oncoming challenges. During each running of the gauntlet, it felt as if our voyageur ancestors were watching over us, guiding the process in their own discreet way.

After the rigors of each fast run, when our booming and skittering hearts had calmed down some, we basked in the feelings of contentment and satisfaction at the bottom, and our tensions and fears evaporated like a morning mist. Fear in dangerous situations is a normal human response. However, the important thing is to meet the challenges in spite of the fear, pushing forward with good judgment.

Although we operated under the considerable disadvantage of having never seen any portion of the mainline route before, we never once asked any local people that we happened to meet for their advice on how to handle an upcoming obstacle. Only canoeists could possibly give us pertinent information, and even if we had spoken to paddlers who had covered the route that lay ahead, their experiences at a particular obstacle may have been at an entirely different water level, and would thus not be very applicable to our journey. If we had questioned motorboaters, they would have minimized distances and strengths of currents, while non-boaters would have overestimated the challenges and the dangers, reflecting their fears and lack of personal experience. We were best off dealing with the obstacles of the route by relying on our own knowledge, abilities, and judgment.

Day Three

Although the alarm clock clattered at 6:00, it was still raining moderately, so I dozed for an additional thirty minutes, during which the rain stopped. The weather felt very balmy, already 60 degrees, with solid grey cloud cover filling the entire sky. Little did we know that, throughout all of this day and the following three days, we would only see a silvery hint of the sun through the solid barrier of galena clouds.

Setting off at 7:45, we arrived within ten minutes at the portage path around the Rapides de la Cascade (Cascade Rapids). These consisted of a number of small ledges extending across the channel, as well as one prominent ledge that passed across the entire distance from bank to bank. The easy carry of 1,400 yards along the right shore, over nearly level, sandy ground, did involve crossing some low wet spots, and at one point wading for thirty yards across a cold stream. A bit beyond the stream, we found two piles of bear scat, each of which was filled with large broken chips of limb bones and hair, apparently from the bear having fed on a moose carcass. From one of the piles, Ben extracted a complete claw of a black bear (which he later fashioned into a pendant). We tried to imagine different scenarios that might have led to the presence of the claw there: maybe the bear had bitten off one of its own claws, after it had been torn loose in an accident and was dangling loose, or it had possibly chomped off the claw of another bear during a serious altercation.

Since this was the very last portage that we would ever encounter on the entire mainline route, Doree and I decided to have a little fun with Ben on it. During our summer of preparatory canoe trips back in 1983, when Ben had just turned age five, Doree had taken a particularly fetching photo of him and me hiking a portage trail in the Boundary Waters Canoe Wilderness Area. In the backside shot of us, we were descending a slight slope toward the water, walking hand in hand. My load consisted of a bulging Duluth pack, plus some loose items in my left hand, while my younger son's burden consisted of a single plastic thermos jug. As an updated spoof of that picture, here on the Cascade Rapids portage thirteen canoe trips later, Doree took another photo of a similar scene, with the two of us again walking hand in hand as we approached the water at the foot of the portage. However, in this case, Ben was loaded with both a Duluth pack and on top of it the large consolidation pack holding various loose items. For my part, I carried just the plastic thermos jug.

After completing the carry in 1 1/2 hours, at the far end of the path we three feasted on gorp and instant breakfast drink, while Toby enjoyed pieces of jerky. This festive celebration marked the fact that we had just completed our very last portage on the mainline route!

The three lake voyages that still loomed in the future, on Lakes Huron, Winnipeg, and Superior, would not entail any official carries, since they would not involve any rapids. I hailed this as a momentous occasion, since I had always perceived portaging in the same way the artist Frederick Remington did, as "torture...as exquisitely perfect in its way as any ever devised."

All of the carries that we had completed, including the fourteen during our preparatory year and the innumerable ones during the twelve river-and-lake voyages along the mainline route, we had done by double-hauling, making three trips over the trail. This was the result of a safety decision that Doree and I had made at the onset, to reduce the likelihood that one of the family members would be injured on a portage by being too heavily loaded. I never carried a pack while portaging the canoe. If I slipped, I was much more likely to regain my footing while bearing only the craft; and if I did fall with just the canoe on my shoulders, I was less likely to damage it and myself in the process.

Our logic concerning double-hauling was also based on another important element. In addition to making each of the loaded trips over the trail less dangerous and grueling, having the luxury of an unburdened walk back in between the two loaded trips allowed us to better absorb and appreciate the sights, sounds, and smells of nature along the way. On our first jaunt over the path, we transported the majority of the packs, plus certain other items such as the ammo box, and at the trail's end I checked the place where I would later wade into the water to unload the canoe onto the surface. Then we enjoyed the restful return trip to the head of the path, taking in the scenery. On the third trip over, I carried the canoe, while the rest of the family brought the remaining miscellaneous gear, the paddles, and the sail rig. As a result, we willingly hiked three miles for every mile of portage length.

While carrying the canoe, my view was mostly of the ground immediately in front of my feet. If I angled the bow end high enough to see into the distance ahead, the stern end of the craft would strike the ground behind me as I walked. Likewise, when hiking down major declines in the trail, or when stepping off a boulder when most of the trail was covered with boulders, the stern often hit the earth in back of me, jarring my neck and shoulders beneath the portage pads. However, there was one positive aspect to carrying the canoe, especially when dealing with very rugged trails. When I was bearing it on my shoulders, especially when hiking on steep inclines or declines and when dealing with a path that was strewn with boulders or fallen trees, I was more likely to retain my balance than when I was burdened with a 75 pound Duluth pack, supported by shoulder straps and the tumpline across my forehead, while carrying miscellaneous items in my hands.

Beneath the canoe on the path, I mostly heard my own heavy breathing, the constant hum of insects hungry for my warm blood, and the thud of my shoes on the ground, plus the occasional scratchings of low-hanging branches scraping the canoe. To give my shoulders an occasional short break, Doree or one of the boys sometimes ran ahead of me and supported the bow end on arms extended above their head, while I rested the stern end on the ground. This way, none of us wasted any energy putting the canoe down on the ground and then picking it up again after the break. En route, one or more of the family members typically walked close behind the canoe while singing, to pleasurably distract my mind. I was not able to join in the songs myself, since I needed to conserve all of my breath and energies for the carrying task. At the trail's end, I waded out into knee-deep shallows and gently rolled the craft off my shoulders and onto the water, in an area where the hull would not strike any submerged rocks.

No matter what burdens we were bearing on portages, the torments of biting insects swarming on our faces and hands and in our mouths, and salty sweat running down our foreheads and burning our eyes, were equally troublesome. For us humans, the very best part of every carry consisted of the light-hearted feeling that swept over us when we glided away from the foot of the path in our reloaded craft. But for Toby, portages were a joy. During his entire life, whenever we observed his nose and feet twitching and his breathing coming fast during deep-sleep dreams, we imagined that he was blissfully dreaming of leading his family along a portage trail, stepping out at a brisk pace and glancing back at regular intervals, to make sure that we were still following him closely.

After loading in at the bottom of a very steep grassy bank between walls of stone, we headed out at 10:10, beneath completely overcast grey skies emitting scattered raindrops, with a comfortable air temperature of 67 degrees. The two sets of minor rapids that lay immediately below the portage were nearly flooded out, due to the high water level. As we proceeded down the meandering course at the bottom of the valley, the undulating, forest-shrouded slopes on its flanks remained generally about the same dimensions, with a span of some 21/2 to three miles across from rim to rim.

On two occasions, we observed swimming beavers, each of which slapped and dived when they noticed our approach. In addition, we twice encountered a group of molting ducks, unable to fly until their new flight feathers would grow in; the birds skittered away desperately on the surface of the water, with their wings rotating like propellers. With Ben acting as the caterer in the passenger spot, we consumed a floating lunch at 12:30, during his mother's run of fifteen miles in three hours on the substantial current. Later, Ben took up the bow paddle, to likewise help pull the craft over the water's surface for fifteen more miles. Rounding a bend, we coasted in silence toward another beaver, which had its head above water. When we neared to about a canoe-length away, he suddenly raised his head about six inches higher, checked us out quickly, and then dived.

Late in the afternoon, much of the solid, slate-hued cloud cover drifted off toward the west, leaving some patches of blue sky (but no sun) exposed between the massive clouds of grey-white fluff. After Doree took over as the *avant*, we forged ahead another fifteen miles. During those three hours of quiet cruising on the flat water, I silently took in my surroundings and contemplated the forces of nature, operating over very long periods of time, which had created the scenes that we paddled through during each of our annual voyages. The earth had its own steady rhythms, including the daily cycle of sunrise, daytime, sunset, and nighttime; the longer cycle of the four seasons; and the much more extended cycles that took years, centuries, and even millennia to complete. During these much longer cycles, various glaciers had advanced, retreated, and ultimately disappeared; the climate had fluctuated between eras of warmth and others of chill; periods of wetness and drought had come and gone; different plant communities and types of forest cover had flourished and then had died out or receded; various populations of animals, birds, and fish had waxed and waned; water levels had vacillated between highs and lows; forest fires had raged through certain areas and new growth had followed. The environment had never been locked into a long-term period of sameness. In addition, over time, many groups of humans had arrived, thrived, and finally had drifted away or had died out. When we traveled through a particular region, we were simply observing its present condition and its current occupants, neither of which would remain the same forever.

Just before we passed the mouth of the Christina River on the left shore, we whizzed through a minor rapids that was nearly flooded out. Below the confluence of this side river, which was much larger than any of the other tributaries that we passed, the Clearwater River (whose water was never all that clear in the first place) lost the rest of its clarity, becoming a very silty brown. For the last five miles of the evening, Ben resumed the bow paddler's role, until Doree spotted a good site on the right shore to spend the night.

This had been an accomplishing day, advancing 51 miles with the aid of the moderate current, and also completing a 3/4 mile portage that had taken 1 1/2 hours. This was the most distance that we had ever paddled in a single day. Over the course of three days on the Clearwater, we had advanced 95 miles, had spent three hours inspecting the Portage La Loche, had made four long portages, and had run three rapids. Our camp lay just six miles from the outskirts of the town of Fort McMurray, and ten miles from the Athabasca River.

The clouds of mosquitoes at the site were very thick, but they hardly bothered us. After eagerly devouring a tasty stew of dried turkey, vegetables, noodles, and Italian sauce, washed down with a chocolate-strawberry hot drink, we were in the tent by 9:15 and asleep within half an hour. As we drifted off, the heavily clouded sky was still emitting a great deal of residual light.

We had not been slumbering very long when a beaver in the river right next to our shelter slapped its tail on the water with a loud smack and then dived, awakening us with a start. She may have come close to check us out, and then had sensed danger; or, she may have been cruising the river and suddenly came upon our camp without warning.

Day Four

At about 5:45, the rain began, at first falling lightly but after a half-hour growing to a moderate downpour. Although the alarm clock went off at 6:00, I lounged in my cozy sleeping bag for another 45 minutes, hoping that the rain would let up, but to no avail. So we got up in the rain, broke camp, and loaded up. We also filled our collapsible plastic water jug and the thermos with water from the Clearwater River, for use on the Athabasca. This would allow us to avoid both the heavy silt content and the pollution from petroleum or any other substances below Fort McMurray and Tar Island. (This supply of untainted water, supplemented with rainwater captured at one of our future campsites, would serve us until the final day of the trip.) When we headed out at 8:00, the air temperature measured 57 degrees in the moderate rain.

Just as we were reaching the outskirts of the town spread out along the left shore, we had our first view of the Athabasca Oil Sands, on a broad bend in the river. The high sand bank along the right shore was covered on its lower half with a black coating of thick, tar-like bitumen. The air also had a slight odor of asphalt to it, from the refineries that separate crude oil from excavated sand beside the open-pit mines at Tar Island, twenty miles down the Athabasca River. According to the Oil Sands Interpretive Center at Fort McMurray, the Athabasca Oil Sands represents the largest single deposit of oil in the world. Pipelines carry crude oil from the refineries at Tar Island to Fort McMurray and then off toward the south, with about three-quarters of the oil flowing to gasoline refineries in the U.S.

Having advanced nine miles in 1 1/2 hours, we passed most of Fort McMurray and reached the far edge of town at 9:30; by then, the rain had reduced to only scattered drops. Doree, Ben, and Toby left me with the canoe on the left riverbank, while they departed to look for a place that sold hot food. As I waited, a woodpecker worked busily for his morning meal, tapping away steadily in some tall trees nearby. Listening aimlessly, my mind drifted back to the men of the N.W.C. who had established the first post here in 1788, naming it the Fort of the Forks. Operating for less than a decade, this facility was later replaced by Ft. Clearwater in 1802, which was in business for less than five years.

After 45 minutes, my family returned from their successful mission, laden with dinners of hot steak sandwiches garnished with onions and gravy, and generous side orders of mashed potatoes and peas, plus three huge cheeseburgers for consuming later in the day. We quickly gobbled the dinners while standing beside the canoe in the rain, which had increased to a full downpour by this time. The rainwater falling onto our plates thinned the mashed potatoes considerably.

Resuming our forward progress at 10:45, we entered the Athabasca or Elk River from the right side fifteen minutes later. Having completed the first segment of our journey, 105 miles in a westerly direction on the Clearwater River, we now turned northward onto the much larger waterway. Doree had learned in town that the Athabasca River was flowing at five feet above its normal seasonal level, due to very heavy rainfall in the entire drainage area during the previous several weeks. The swirling water ranged from dark tan to brown in color, even darker than the hue of the lower Clearwater. Flowing all the way from the Continental Divide in the Rocky Mountains, the Athabasca current had picked up silt all across the wide expanse of plains and prairies. Many of the sandy bank areas, as well as all of the low mud flats along the shorelines, were submerged beneath the flood-stage waters; thus, the shoreline areas did not look as silt-laden as had those on the Saskatchewan River three years earlier.

At the restaurant in Fort McMurray, a colorful old man in overalls had invited Ben and me to join him, since the place was filling up. With eyes widening, he had told us that a young man diving and swimming in the Athabasca River near town the day before had "gone missing." "Heck, he must'a drowned. That current sure makes it hard ta get ta shore." As we paddled into a slight head wind, I kept an eye out for the young man's floating body, which could turn up around any bend. (Doree)

The watercourse, generally ranging from about 1/4 to 1/2 mile in width, was relatively straight, only winding slightly. In many areas in this section, steep sand cliffs rose directly from the water's edge some 250 to 300 feet, along one shore or the other. Often, a long expanse of high, eroding cutbank stood on one side of the river, while the opposite side presented a low sandy shoreline that was bordered with willows. The tall sand cliffs in this first stretch of the Athabasca were nearly solid black, completely soaked with bitumen. In most of the areas that offered high cliffs of sand, tall, slender spruce trees advanced right to the edge of the precipice. Due to the flood-stage water eroding the bank, numerous trees leaned precariously out over the water. Many others had already toppled over the edge and lay pointing downward on the steep embankment, often extending well into the water. In some places, these floating trees, still green, had gathered into tangled masses. Every few miles, a rather large but low island with long tapered ends seemed to float in the river, representing an elevated sandbar that had become solidified with a covering of willow shrubs. Beneath the surface of the water, northern pike and walleyed pike (called pickerel in Canada), as well as whitefish, finned against the strong current, unseen by us, as these same species had also done in the Clearwater River.

Twenty miles below Fort McMurray (*still no sign of the drowned man's body...but I keep looking. Doree*), we passed on the left the oil sand refinery plant of Tar Island, where crude oil is extracted from the sand that is strip-mined nearby. Here, in the area adjacent to the upriver side of the processing plant, the natural high sand cliffs that we had passed upriver had been artificially replicated. These towering formations had been created by massive wheeled machines piling up sand from which the oil had already been removed. In some areas, the processed sand had been mounded up as high as the original natural cliffs, and with about the same angled surfaces. The finished portion of this elongated mound of treated sand, as well as the lower areas of the unfinished end of the mound, had already been replanted with bushes and trees. The top area of the unfinished section bore a number of diagonal roadways on its sides, on which huge vehicles moved to and fro, distributing the cleaned sand. This soil, light tan in color, appeared to be very pure, like sand at a beach. However, this portion of the massive hill that was visible from the river was part of an earthen dam surrounding a tailings pond. Here, the watery toxic remnants from the extraction process had been impounded.

Just downriver from the separation plant loomed another huge mound of sand, nearly as high, which had been excavated from the strip mines nearby; this black, bitumen-laden sand was ready for processing. Three of the largest open-pit mines in the world were located close by, supplying the oil-bearing sand to the refinery. As we paddled past the site, we were very pleased that we could not observe these ugly open mines and the massive toxic tailings ponds from our vantage point. However, we could not miss the riverside extraction plant, with its three very tall pipes that continuously emitted orange and blue plumes of flame as the excess gas from the bitumen was burned off. A second processing plant, with its own open-pit mines and tailings ponds, was located four miles further downstream. Positioned about three miles west of the riverbank, this latter operation, opened in 1976, was fortunately not visible to us.

Alexander Mackenzie had described this source of petroleum at the surface of the earth in 1789: "At about twenty-four miles from the Fork are some bituminous fountains, into which a pole twenty feet long may be inserted without the least resistance. The bitumen is in a fluid state, and when mixed with gum, the resinous substance collected from the spruce fir, serves to gum the canoes. In its heated state it emits a smell like that of sea-coal. The banks of the river, which are there very elevated, [reveal] veins of the same bituminous quality."

A full 160 years later, in 1949, the first attempt was made to commercially mine the oil sand, extract the petroleum, load the product into barrels, and ship it out on river barges. This took place at the locale which was dubbed Bitumount, some twenty miles downriver from Tar Island, which we were passing. Major strip-mining and refining operations had begun at this latter place beside us in 1967.

The vast reservoir of oil that lies near the surface in this region, encompassing an area that roughly equals the size of Florida, is now estimated to be nearly as extensive as that beneath the deserts of Saudi Arabia. By the time of the writing of this book, the extraction of that oil has been stepped up immensely. Major expansions of the operations were commenced in 1996, the year following our Athabasca River voyage, causing the boom-town population of Fort McMurray to swell to 64,000 residents. A four-lane highway now extends northward from the town, where most of the workers live, to the industrial area. The open-pit mines, reaching down as far as two hundred feet, have extended from the riverside sites near Tar Island as much as twenty miles in all directions. There are now six giant extraction plants in operation, drawing vast amounts of water from the river, and sprouting dozens of emissions stacks and flare pipes that spew their deadly byproducts skyward. Twelve toxic tailings ponds surrounded by earthen dams, not lined with plastic and thus susceptible to leaking and seepage, now cover an area of fifty square miles. At some of the sites at which the bitumen-soaked sand is too deep for practical surface mining, steam is injected underground to liquefy the bitumen, which is then pumped to the surface. This is how the situation stands at the current production level. However, the production of petroleum from the Athabasca Oil Sands is expected to quadruple from the current level by the year 2020.

Glad to be leaving this modern industrial area behind, it was a pleasure for us to be soon paddling past high sand banks that contained no bitumen! Ten miles downriver from Tar Island, we were startled to see a brand new highway bridge spanning the river, with four huge concrete pillars supporting a steel roadbed. This surrealistic feature in a wilderness setting was not depicted on our topographical map, but it did appear on the newly printed Alberta highway map. At some point in the future, the bridge would be part of a road to Ft. Chipewyan; however, in the period of our passing through, this road ended abruptly five miles beyond the bridge. (At the time this book is being written, the road extends for a short distance to three open-pit mines which produce oil sand.)

Near the base of the bridge, by the mouth of the Muskeg River, archaeological excavations have revealed a very important site dating as far back as ten thousand years, to the Paleo Period. Ancient native peoples returned to this forested place each summer for thousands of years, to mine and work into implements a chert of very high quality. Items fashioned from this superb, fine-grained material were traded over vast distances throughout much of what is now western Canada. The site has yielded many thousands of artifacts, including spear points, knives, scrapers, flake implements, and microblades. I was grateful that this very significant site, where the Old Ones had lived and worked for uncounted generations, had not been destroyed during the construction of the modern highway bridge.

As we passed the site, I pondered the history of the place, and the thousands of generations of people who had lived here, or who had paddled along this stretch of the river, over the span of a hundred centuries. Along these shores, native people had hunted, fished, gathered plants and roots and berries, prepared foods, tanned hides, mined chert, woven mats and bags, produced stone tools, fashioned bark containers. In the process, these people had loved, worried, thrived, suffered, exalted, died. Although we could never know their names, their personalities, or their individual experiences, each one of them deserves our respect and our admiration.

Pulling into a thick stand of willows nearby, we paused to eat our cheeseburgers from the restaurant in Fort McMurray. This stop, sheltered somewhat from the head wind, also offered me an opportunity to rearrange the maps in the waterproof map case, which was clipped to the canoe cover in front of my seat. Glancing at the next map, I was reminded that the further west we traveled across the continent, the further our compasses became misaligned in a westerly direction from magnetic north. On this voyage, in the area of La Loche, the amount of misalignment had been about 19 degrees, while in the area of the Athabasca River, our compasses were some 23 degrees off. Whenever we took readings with the compass that we each wore suspended from a neck strap, and applied those readings to the topo maps, we had to allow for this westward misalignment. This was not so important when traveling along clearly defined rivers. However, it was a rather significant issue when planning the heading of a lengthy traverse across a major body of water, in determining our eventual landing spot on the distant shore.

After Ben and I resumed paddling, the rain stopped for about ten minutes, the first time that it had ceased in eleven hours (since 5:45 this morning), and the air became very clear. However, the respite was to be extremely short-lived. A very dark, hazy area in the sky, along with thick black clouds so low they seemed to be brushing the tops of the trees, were roaring toward us from the north. As this glowering weather front came at us, the forward edge of its heavy rainfall struck the surface of the river so hard that it sounded like a rapids. When the solid wall of rain finally reached the canoe, it was being driven so hard by the head wind that it hurt my eyeballs. After about ten minutes of this raging, blinding deluge, the storm front moved on, leaving just a light rain to continue.

We soon passed Fort MacKay, on the left shore by the mouth of the MacKay River. In this well-kept little village, four of the houses along the riverbank had large tepees standing in front of them. On the opposite shore lay the Fort MacKay Indian Reserve, running along the shore for 1 1/2 miles and extending inland for a half-mile. No homes stood on this land, since the native population had moved across the river to the little settlement years earlier. The Pierre au Calumet (Pipestone) Post had been established here by N.W.C. personnel in about 1815, operating for less than five years. The competing H.B.C. had founded Berens House here in 1819; it was used only until about the time of the amalgamation of the two firms in 1821. This place is located at about the southern boundary of permafrost; in the regions extending to the north from here, the ground beneath the surface remains frozen solid year round.

Ten miles later, at 7:30, we decided to halt for the night. Since emerging from the tent this morning, we had been deluged with virtually continuous rainfall until 5 P.M., and then again from 7:00

on. Just upriver from the mouth of the rather small Ells River, Doree found a nice cleared spot on the left shore, at the end of a rough access road that was used for putting boats into the Athabasca. This was the terminus of the last dirt road which extends northward down the big river. After setting up, Ben took a short walk, during which he watched in utter silence as two black bears swam across to the far side of the Athabasca, near the mouth of the Ells.

Since we had eaten two meals from a restaurant during the day, and then had snacked at 6:30 in the canoe, we ate nothing more at the campsite. As the rain pattered with a light drumming sound on the roof of the shelter, we exchanged massages and chatted inside until 9:30. Today, we had awakened to rain on the tent, were accompanied by rain during the entire day except between 5 and 7 P.M., and were now preparing to drift off again to the sounds of rain tapping on the roof. During the conversation, Ben, age seventeen with thirteen years of long-distance, wilderness canoe voyages under his belt, announced, "Today, for the first time, I feel like I could make a living doing this, as a canoe trip guide. Tomorrow, I'm going to start mastering the J-stroke!"

This day, we had broken our previous mileage record, having advanced 53 miles from 8 A.M. to 7:30 P.M., with no sail assist but with considerable help from the current. Thus far, we had covered 148 miles in four days, placing us at about the halfway-point of the voyage. On previous trips, Doree and I could paddle 3 m.p.h. on flat water all day, and Ben and I could do up to 4 m.p.h. for hours on end in flat conditions. During this trek on the Clearwater and Athabasca Rivers, with their moderately strong, high-water currents, we could usually make 5 m.p.h., even with a slight head wind holding us back. We did not register the current here until we decided to pull up to the shore; as we paddled in, we could feel the sweep of its strength near the shoreline. The current was accounting for much of this year's unusually generous mileage per day, since we were receiving no assistance at all from the sail.

Day Five

I rolled out at 6 A.M. to the sounds of ...... No Rain!! Outside by myself, I measured the temperature at 59 degrees, and, looking off to the east, reveled at the sight of a very welcome fragment of sun peeking through a minute opening in the solid grey cloud cover.

Little did I know that this would be the only shred of sunlight that would appear this entire day, and that the temperature would not rise a single degree. As I began packing for the day of travel, I could hear a woodpecker searching for breakfast, tapping steadily on a tall dead tree near the tent.

Loading the canoe in the slimy mud at the bank, we were on the river at 7:45. While dealing with occasional bursts of head wind and scattered periods of rain, Doree and I pressed forward for seventeen miles in three hours, during which time we consumed our breakfast and morning snack while paddling. After six of those miles, we passed on the right shore the old oil sand processing plant of Bitumount, dating from the 1949 extraction experiments. It was now just a series of deserted tall buildings with bleak, rusted tin roofs. Ten miles further downriver, our green hull slid past the last of the high sand cliffs of the river. Lower cutbanks and willow-lined mudflats would flank our route for the remainder of the journey.

Remaining relatively close to one or the other shoreline, we were encouraged and entertained by watching the scenery flash by, hour after hour. At one point shortly after our floating lunch break, a startled shore-roving beaver slid down the grass-covered bank and splashed into the river close beside the canoe. At about 3:30, not long after Ben had again switched places with his mother and had resumed paddling, a burly head wind and moderately large waves quickly arrived from the north; soon, serious rain began to fall. Laboring hard with our faces to the unceasing blasts and the uncooperative waves for about twenty minutes, I finally steered the bow to the wind-sheltered, upriver tip of a rather large island. We were *dégradé*, windbound, having advanced 42 miles since this morning's launch, eight hours before.

Ben and I tied the bow and stern lines to a clump of willows that had mostly tumbled into the river, after which we three erected the rain shelter tarp in the thick willow growth on shore. The bright aspect of the situation was this: we now had an opportunity to cook a replenishing hot dinner in the middle of the day! Soon, Doree had assembled a stew of beef jerky and noodles, flavored with Italian sauce and fresh garlic, and had it bubbling and steaming in the stainless steel pot, balanced atop the little ring of blue flames of the gas stove. While it simmered, Ben caught a nap and I brought the journal up to date. What a feast to long remember, savored beneath the cozy shelter, accompanied by strawberry-flavored, hot chocolate drink!

Later, with plenty of time on our hands, we even went so far as to brush our teeth. After five days on the water, this was my first time brushing (during expeditions, I usually preferred to retain the layer of protective patina that accumulated on my face, hands, and teeth), and my family's second time using the tooth brushes. However, none of us went so far as to brush our hair (since we needed to retain that certain look to scare away bears). After two hours at this halting place, the rain ceased and the wind appeared to have died down; so we quickly loaded up and shoved off at 5:45.

However, just as we departed, the wind kicked up strongly. With considerable effort, Ben and I paddled along the 11/2 mile length of the island, in the narrow channel between the island and the left shoreline. As soon as we re-entered the open water of the main channel, we were buffeted by a ferocious head wind and large oncoming waves. The wind whipped the trees and bushes, lashed the reed beds, and piled up row upon row of foam-topped waves. With some of the high waves splashing over the gunwales, I carefully controlled the angle of the craft as we slowly inched our way forward for an arduous half-mile, traveling at a diagonal across the channel, to reach the first midstream island. Near its shoreline, we had to deal with the challenging mixture of a moderately strong downstream current combined with large, upstream-traveling waves. At 6:15, we landed safely on the lee side of the island. Although it consisted of low, soggy ground, not much above the level of the rain-swollen river, we were mighty glad to be back on land of any sort! A short distance inland, we whacked out a tiny clearing in the thick growth of willow saplings, erected the tent, and crawled inside at 7:00, just as a light rain commenced. We had no idea how long the relentless wind would pin us to this little refuge.

This day, we had advanced 42 miles in eight hours, between 7:45 and 3:45. Then we had spent two hours at a windbound stop, struggled forward for two more miles in formidable wind and waves, and finally landed for the day, windbound, at 6:15. We had now reached mile 191 of the route, in five days of travel. After trading massages, and Ben telling stories about his trip to the rain forests of Costa Rica in June, we drifted off to sleep at about 8:15.

During the course of today's hours of traveling and lounging on shore, we had discussed, among other topics, various movies that Ben had seen, Doree's work in international adoptions, and a number of Ben's exceptional teachers and school experiences over the years.

Day Six

When I was aroused by the alarm clock at 5:00, the light rain and strong gusting winds from the north were just as dominant as they had been when we had gone to sleep. Although the tent was somewhat sheltered from the wind amid the thick stand of willow saplings, its upstream end bowed in like a sail most of the time, while the walls often flapped in and out. Toby lay curled up between the sleeping bags of Doree and me, so I cuddled him close and went back to sleep. At 6:00, I used the plastic canoe bailer for a urinal, dumping the contents outside by reaching out of the vestibule of the tent.

Lying in the shelter of green fabric, which was located on dry land at the moment, I was quite concerned that the rain would cause the river to rise and flood us out of our camp. Both the Clearwater and the Athabasca Rivers had already risen considerably during the previous couple of weeks from heavy rainfall, and the waters were continuing to rise with each passing hour of ongoing rain. At our windbound island, there had been only about twenty inches of bank above the water level when we had landed the previous evening. In 1819, the Franklin party, en route to the Arctic, had been flooded out of an island campsite not far upriver from here. Lieutenant Hood had recorded in his journal, "At sunset, we encamped on a small sandy island, but the next morning made a speedy retreat to the canoes, the water having nearly overflowed our encampment." Since there was nothing I could do about our predicament at this point, I lay in my warm sleeping bag and let my thoughts unfurl, contemplating the comfortable shelter and sleeping gear that we had and comparing them to those of the fur trade era.

From the very beginning, voyageurs had adopted the widespread native practice of using the canoe as an instant shelter at campsites. The high ends of the craft provided ample headroom beneath the canoe when it was overturned on one gunwale. When only a few paddlers made up the crew, they could sleep end-to-end under the craft. When it was manned by a larger crew, each paddler slept in a perpendicular direction to the canoe, with only his head and shoulders beneath the craft. As protection against bad weather, a quick native-style shelter was often made, by spreading long sheets of birchbark or a tarp over the canoe, extending over several poles which ran from the raised wall of the craft down to the ground. Such poles were carried by nearly all fur trade canoes, laid on the floor of the craft to support and distribute evenly the weight of the cargo. Setting poles were also often used to support shelters. Sometimes the poles were placed upright instead of lying over the canoe, forming a conical frame over which the birchbark strips or tarps were draped.

The long strips of bark, about three feet wide and up to twenty feet long, were made of several pieces joined together with stitching of spruce or pine roots. The finished strips usually had a slender sapling bound to each end, which facilitated the rolling of the strips for traveling, and also prevented them from splitting. The French called these items *écorce à cabaner*, "bark for making shelters," while the Alongquian-speaking native populations called them *wigwas apakwa*, "birchbark strips or rolls." From one to six of these units were typically issued to each voyaging canoe, based on the size of the craft and its crew.

Tarpaulins were also standard items that were issued to fur trade canoes, for covering the cargo and provisions in the craft while en route and for making shelters while on shore. These oilcloths consisted of a large piece of coarse linen fabric, often tightly-woven sailcloth made of rot-resistant hemp thread, which was painted with vegetable oil treated with red pigment. One of these articles was usually issued for canoes of moderate size, while two were supplied for the larger canoes.

After 1760, during the era of gradual increase of Anglo leadership in the fur trade, birchbark strips for making shelters were gradually phased out of the equipment that was issued to canoes departing from the St. Lawrence for the interior. However, such shelters were presumably used until much later, using bark strips that the men harvested en route or acquired from native suppliers. During the entire British era of the trade, St. Lawrence outfitters continued to supply each of the departing canoes with one or two tarpaulins, for use as both cargo covers and shelters. This was one of the simple yet invaluable tips that the French trader Germain Maugenest suggested to the management of the Hudson's Bay Company in 1781, when he defected to their employment after years of trading via the St. Lawrence Valley. His H.B.C. host reported to his superiors in the

London office, "They have coverings of russia cloth, or raven duck painted, to keep their goods dry in their bateaux or canoes; we have nothing at all."

During both the French era and later, another type of cargo covering besides tarpaulins was also regularly used. Cargoes being shipped out from the interior to the St. Lawrence were often covered with ten to fifteen loose bearskins per canoe. These untanned furs were also used en route as bedding and covers by the voyageurs in camp. In case of loss of the bearskins, such as when gusts of wind blew them out of the canoe, the men were obliged to pay for them, since these pelts were part of the cargo of furs being shipped. Other than these bearskins, throughout the entire fur trade era the voyageurs used only their own personal blankets and hooded woolen coats as bedding in the shelters, with cut tree boughs typically forming a mattress.

Ready-made canvas shelters with a frame of wooden poles were only very occasionally used during the French and British eras of the trade. These tents were reserved almost exclusively for important traders and officials.

On our expeditions, I was thankful to have a modern tent which was made of light-weight nylon fabric, one which had a sewn-in floor, a roof of breathable cloth, and an overlay roof of nylon cloth. In addition, it was fitted with fine-mesh screens over the zipper-closing window and door openings, and it was supported by a framework of light folding poles made of tubular aluminum. This convenient and comfortable shelter took up very little space in the pack, and it weighed little. Not only did it efficiently shed all rainfall, however severely the water was driven by the wind, it was an absolute blessing at campsites that were swarming with attacking insects.

Our bedding was also a godsend, including both the inflatable mattresses made of rubberized fabric and the quallofill sleeping bags, which were very comfortable down to freezing temperatures. Equipped with this bedding, we could sleep in comfort on any ground surface and at any temperature that Nature provided. The voyageurs would have been in seventh heaven to have had this efficient yet inexpensive sleeping equipment at their disposal!

Back to our windbound camp. At 7:45, we all finally awakened, after 11 1/2 hours of delicious sleep. The overbearing wind was still the very same, and the rain was still scattered. Nearby, the wind-lashed surface of the river made constant splashing noises. At 8:30, while still inside the tent, we noted what we hoped were good signs: a bird called out from the far shore, and another large bird flapped noisily over our shelter, calling as it flew. They must have sensed that the unfriendly weather front had passed, or so we hoped! Doree and I emerged to check the paddling situation: the wind was beginning to calm down slightly, but the scene was far from workable. So we assembled a hot meal outside on the tiny stove, standing in the light drizzle. Dining inside the tent, we feasted on a stew of beef jerky, vegetables, noodles, and fresh garlic, accompanied by crackers and instant breakfast drink, and topped off with chocolate candies for dessert. As the light-to-medium rain continued, we passed the time by napping until about 1:00.

A half-hour later, I checked the situation at the shoreline: still, moderately strong head wind and waves, a medium rain that never let up, and an air temp of 55 degrees. I figured it would take about an hour to break camp and be afloat, and then another hour at the end of the day to set up camp again. My two paddling partners were calling to me from inside the tent, urging that we stay at this site for another night, and then get up very early tomorrow and make extra miles. With only half a day of progress possible before dark, involving lots of work and considerable discomfort, I heartily agreed with their proposal. Two of the most important virtues that we acquired from these voyages were patience and the ability to calmly accept the conditions that Nature provided.

Adding water to the leftovers in the pot, I reheated the mixture and soon handed into the tent three steaming bowls of stew, along with three cups of koolaid. For his lunch, Toby scarfed down several pieces of dry beef jerky. After the meal, I cleaned the dishes outside, and then laid out all of our cooking and eating containers on the ground, to gather falling rainwater. There was no sense in running through our supply of untainted water just because we were windbound.

For the next five hours, we passed the time learning new French songs and telling stories. During the course of the afternoon, I settled upon the subject of the one direct ancestor of ours who had been deeply involved in the North American fur trade but, oddly enough, never set foot in the New World himself. François Peron's participation in the commerce was as a businessman, as well as the owner and outfitter of several ships which sailed between his home port of La

Rochelle, on the west coast of France, and New France. Operating from his store on Rue St. Yon in La Rochelle, he dispatched various of his vessels to New France between 1655 and 1663, including *Le Taureau* (The Bull), *Le Petit-François* (The Little Francis), and *l'Aigle Blanc* (The White Eagle). On the outgoing leg of their journeys, the ships transported to the colony much-needed merchandise and supplies, to be sold at François' store in Quebec. They also brought a considerable number of new pioneer settlers, many of whom had been enlisted by François' agents. On their return trip, the vessels carried cargoes of furs and hides gathered in New France and fish harvested off Newfoundland, all of which were destined for markets in Europe.

The first voyage to the colony, in 1655, involved the ship *Le Petit-François*, which transported a substantial cargo of iron in sheets and bars, steel in bars, nails, tin plate, guns, replacement gun barrels, lead, gun balls, gunpowder, axes, drawknives, swords, brandy, wine, tobacco, raisins, cheeses, cooking oil, soap, candles, bulk fabrics, hats, and a stock of miscellaneous smaller items, as well as twenty adult male settlers. Beginning in 1656, François' store at Quebec was operated for six years by a hired representative, and from 1662 on by his son Daniel Perron dit Suire (also our direct ancestor). At the store, which was located on Rue Sous-le-Fort in the Lower Town area, these men were permitted to sell their imported goods, in exchange for furs and hides, to the French residents of the colony (many of whom were involved in the fur trade). However, Peron's storekeepers were not allowed to carry on trade directly with the native populations. Other merchants in New France, as well as the monopoly company of the colony, often paid for space on François' vessels, which imported their merchandise and exported their peltries for them. In 1665, François Peron died in La Rochelle at the age of fifty, after which his son became a farmer-settler along the St. Lawrence.

During our many hours of storytelling in the windbound camp, the rain seldom ceased, but the wind finally died out completely, to our immense relief! At about 7:00, we dozed off to the sound of raindrops tapping a soft rhythm on the tent roof.

Day Seven

When the alarm clock sounded at 4 A.M., a rather strong north wind was again sweeping across our midstream island, so I reset the alarm for 5:30. When it rang for the second time, I awakened but lay still, to eavesdrop on the quiet conversation of my other crew-members. Doree: "Ben, it's stopped blowing, and it's not raining. Let's wake up Dad." Ben: "Let's let him sleep a little longer." I then spoke up: "I'm awake. I just wanted to hear your conversation." As we lay there, a goose flapped overhead at a low altitude; we could clearly hear its powerful wings beating the air. Then an owl hooted from the western shore.

When I crawled out of the tent, the air felt a bit brisk, in the low 50s, but no breeze was blowing. I was elated that we were about to be released from land-locked bondage! While we packed up the gear, Doree sang softly to herself; this was definitely a sign that she was glad to be moving again, too. As we launched at 6:40, a barge slowly passed by us, heading quietly upriver.

Within ten minutes, Doree and I again found ourselves working against a moderate head wind and considerable waves. Shortly below our campsite, we passed the Chipewyan Indian Reserve, which encompasses two miles of the right shoreline and extends inland for the same distance. Under rather tough conditions, we slogged ahead, making seventeen miles in 3 1/2 hours. Along the way, to relieve the tedium, we belted out all of the verses of *Alouetsky*, the "faux Russian" variant of *Alouette*, which Doree and I had learned from a French-speaking folk singer in New Brunswick the previous year. In this version of the song, sung in a minor rather than a major key, the body parts of the skylark are named *la tête-sky, les yeux-avich, les oreilles-avich, le bec-sky, la bouche-sky,* and *le pénis-troika.*

Even with the considerable exertion of paddling, we still felt rather chilly on the water, since the air temperature had dropped. In addition, part of our chill was psychological, since we had not glimpsed the sun for more than four days. At mile sixteen for the day, we passed on the left the southern boundary of Wood Buffalo National Park, a vast preserve which extends northward some 175 miles, nearly to Great Slave Lake. We wondered if a herd of buffalo might cross in front of our canoe. In fact, when the Franklin expedition had passed down this section of the Athabasca River in 1819, en route to their Arctic explorations, Lieutenant Hood had recorded in his journal, "We observed the traces of herds of buffaloes where they had crossed the river, the trees being trodden down and strewed, as if by a whirlwind."

Soon after Ben took on the role of the *avant*, we found ourselves struggling against a more powerful head wind and even more domineering waves, almost unworkable conditions. In some areas, I was able to steer a course that utilized the curving shoreline as a block from the relentless wind. However, I was obliged to stay far enough away from the shore to avoid the great many spruce trees that had toppled in from the bank, yet close enough to the shore to remain out of the large oncoming waves.

Beginning at about 10:30, when the air temperature measured 48 degrees, moderate rain fell for some two hours. My good-natured Doree sang quietly to herself and to Toby, as they snuggled beneath the canoe cover in the dry passenger area. I did not want to break into her reveries, so I chose not ask her to sing louder so I could join in. As I watched Ben in his blue rain gear, digging in with long, deep paddle strokes under these demanding conditions, I thought to myself, "I don't know if having him paddle long-distance canoe trips every summer for thirteen years was a good way to make him into a man. But it sure did turn him into a man! He paddles so strongly, and steadily, and bravely, even when the going is miserable!"

Within a few minutes of each other, three different wedges of honking Canada geese passed overhead, traveling toward the south. These turned out to be harbingers of good fortune. At about 12:30, the rain stopped. Then, lo and behold, the solid pewter sky broke wide open, exposing extensive patches of gentle blue sky and the glorious, golden sun! This was our first view of that magnificent ball of fire in more than four days. After so many days straight of wet, cold, dreary conditions beneath murky skies, it was amazing how much the sun's warmth and light brightened the scene! In a short amount of time, the temperature shot up to a blissful 58 degrees.

At 3:00, having made 41 miles in 81/3 hours, we arrived at the head of the Chenal de l'Embarras (Channel of "Congestion, Hindrance, Encumbrance, or Trouble") branching off from the left shore. Looking ahead 11/2 miles down the main channel of the Athabasca, we had a clear view of a moderately high cutbank on the right shoreline. In the autumn of 1778, on that very bank, Peter Pond and his men had established their famous post, the very first trading facility in North America to be built on waters that flowed to the Arctic. Competing Montreal-based traders had established Ross's Post nearby in 1786, operating it for less than three years. Alexander Mackenzie was sent by the N.W.C. to assist Pond at his post in 1787; the following year, the younger trader succeeded his departing mentor and moved the facility to the south shore of Lake Athabasca, rechristening it Ft. Chipewyan. Our topo map indicated that three small buildings now stood at the place on the riverbank where Pond's Post had once operated, a locale which is still called Old Fort.

The Chenal de l'Embarras (pronounced "lambra" by the locals) marked the beginning of the huge expanse of the Athabasca River delta. This area of lowlands and swamps, fanning out toward the northeast for some forty to fifty miles to reach the shores of Lake Athabasca, includes four primary river channels. On the west, the Chenal de l'Embarras is the first to branch off, taking a meandering northeasterly heading to the lake. Meanwhile, the main channel continues northward for about eight miles, then toward the east for some eighteen miles, before the Fletcher Channel branches off on its northward course to Lake Athabasca. The Main Channel continues eastward for another ten miles before it too heads north toward the lake, splitting into two parallel channels after some ten miles. In the spring and fall, this massive area of wetlands functions as perhaps the largest resting and feeding grounds for migratory birds in all of North America. Within this Athabasca delta and the Peace River delta, which lies immediately to the north and northwest, portions of the four major North American flyways converge. As a result, more than a million waterfowl stop over here to eat and restore their strength each spring and autumn, before continuing their long annual journey toward the north or the south. Many other bird species remain here in vast numbers for the entire summer, nesting in the delta.

We had a major decision to make at this point. If the l'Embarras Channel would be available to us, we would much prefer taking that route. For starters, it would offer a much narrower and more scenic passageway, only about 1/6 to 1/4 of the width of the main Athabasca channel on which we had been traveling. We were also attracted to the shelter which the close-standing forest along the l'Embarras would offer from the gusting wind, which for days had been sweeping southward over the open expanses of the main river channel. After the previous several days of strident head winds from the north, and boisterous waves churned by those winds, sometimes hindering our progress and sometimes locking us on land, any source of respite looked very attractive. Finally, the l'Embarras Channel was the most westerly route to Lake Athabasca. The further toward the west that we would land on the shoreline of the lake, the shorter would be the paddling distance on that body of water, which was often wind-lashed, to reach Ft. Chipewyan.

However, the westernmost passage to Lake Athabasca had not been dubbed the Channel of Congestion, Hindrance, Encumbrance, or Trouble for nothing! Major blockages of downed trees, gathering together in large tangled masses at each end of the route and at various locations along its course, had historically plagued travelers on the channel, necessitating lift-overs or portages at those places. Floating trees, of which we had seen great numbers on our way down the rain-swollen river in the preceding days, would be our main concern if we chose to take this smaller waterway. Lieutenant Hood had noted this important issue in his journal in 1819, while the Franklin expedition was traveling northward down the Athabasca en route to the Arctic: "Whole forests of timber are drifted down the stream, and choke up the channels between the islands [formed by the various delta branches] at its mouth." The slower current and the extremely winding course of the l'Embarras tended to catch and hold driftwood trees much more readily than did the faster current and the straighter course of the larger channels in the delta. As we floated at the head of the Chenal, trying to make our decision, there were no blockages of driftwood logs that we could see in the half-mile portion of the route that was visible to us. So, first taking a vote and then a deep breath, we left the main channel of the Athabasca and dug our paddles firmly into the water of the l'Embarras Channel, hoping for the best.

As we made our way down the moderate current of the slender passageway, which meandered in large loops and bends, we often passed accumulations of drifting tree trunks. The majority of these entire evergreens, extending from the root mass to the tip, had lost most or all of their branches, battered off while descending the Athabasca. But a number of the trees were still entirely intact, having been uprooted from the l'Embarras shorelines in recent days. However, by good fortune, these entangled floating logs had not gathered together in sufficient numbers to entirely block the channel, as they had often done in voyageur days. With each passing mile, we became slightly less concerned about them, although we knew that a major blockage could still appear in front of our bow around any bend.

Just as we had predicted, the narrow channel was much more scenic and entertaining than the wide-open expanses of the main Athabasca channel had been. A thick forest of spruce, with scattered willows near the water, advanced right to the forward edge of the low, eroded banks. In addition, those nearby stands of trees blocked all vestiges of wind, leaving the surface of the unruffled water as smooth as glass.

As dusk approached, we observed swimming beavers on fourteen different occasions. All but one of them first checked us out and then smacked its tail before diving. The one exception, a busy individual who was carrying a willow sapling in his mouth, just dived quietly. One of the beavers slapped, dived, and resurfaced, then repeated the sequence three more times as we glided toward it. At one point, a pair of peregrine falcons soared high overhead, while on another occasion a bald eagle flapped away from its spruce limb perch as we approached. This afternoon-and-evening paddle of nearly six hours was immensely enjoyable and uplifting, as we rejoiced in the benevolent rays of the sun; the attractive clouds, which were spread in thin, filmy swaths across a light blue sky; the cozy channel, which was slender and smooth-surfaced; the scent of fresh willow and spruce wafting in the air; and the many sightings of wildlife.

At 8:40, having advanced 26 miles down the Chenal de l'Embarras in 52/3 hours, we pulled ashore, climbed up the six-foot slippery bank, and located a good campsite in the thick forest. By the time we had set up the tent and had finished our celebratory feast of beef, peas, and noodles, spiced with fresh garlic and washed down with koolaid, darkness had completely engulfed the woods. After trading massages in the tent, we were fast asleep by 10:30, very content with our progress and thankful for our good fortune so far on this channel. Our experiences here had been quite similar to those of the Franklin expedition in 1819, except for one improvement on our part: "At 4 p.m. [July 12], we left the main branch of the Athapescow (sic), entering a small river called the Embarras. It is narrow and muddy, with [spruces] of an enormous size on its banks. Some of them are 200 feet high, and three or four feet in diameter. At 9 p.m., we landed and encamped, but finding ourselves in a nest of mosquitoes, we continued our journey before daybreak."

This day, we had made outstanding progress, spending fourteen hours straight on the water without going ashore, including eating all of our meals while afloat. Luckily, I had on hand the complete set of maps for the l'Embarras route. Until today, I had planned to take the Fletcher Channel through most of the Athabasca delta area, only moving westward to the l'Embarras Channel, via the "Canoe Portage" passageway, for the final eight miles before reaching Lake Athabasca. In fourteen hours of paddling, often against a medium-to-strong head wind and uncooperative waves, but with a moderately helpful current, we had advanced 67 miles. Ben and I had wanted to continue further down the Chenal de l'Embarras, to reach the seventy-mile mark for the day. But Doree, in her wisdom, had insisted on landing while there was still sufficient light in the darkening woods to locate a campsite along the rather high, forested banks. This had been our all-time record distance for a single day of paddling, and we had done it without any sail assist, just with help from the current. En route, we had averaged 4.8 m.p.h. for fourteen hours straight. At this point, we were 32 miles from the mouth of the channel and the shores of Lake Athabasca.

Day Eight

At 5:30, I was awakened gently by a chorus of wildlife sounds, with birds pouring out their songs and a squirrel chirping from a tall spruce. A beautiful orange-gold sunrise reflected on the river, as a thin veil of mist rose in slow motion from the gleaming surface of the water. The air temperature was only 50 degrees, but it felt comfortable, since the air was rather dry. Not far from the tent, we located a tree with the largest diameter that I had ever seen outside of Sequoia National Park. This gigantic spruce had a circumference that was exactly twice the length of my outspread arms, from fingertip to fingertip, totaling 11 1/2 feet.

Pulling away at 7:00, quietly singing *"Il y a longtemps que je t'aime, jamais je ne t'oublierai,"* we glided on the perfectly smooth water as the cool mist licked our faces. After about an hour, the ascending sun had burned off all of the rising mist. As Doree paddled for three hours, then Ben for two, and then Doree again, we made our way steadily down the meandering course of the channel, beneath huge white clouds that hung low without moving in much of the pale azure sky. On two occasions, we slid without a sound beneath a pair of bald eagles that were perched at the tips of adjacent tall spruce trees.

Having consumed the last of our stored water from the Clearwater River, as well as the collected rainwater from our windbound camp, Ben scooped up half a thermos of dark, sediment-filled Athabasca River water, for making instant breakfast drink; this was the only water from this river that we ingested during the entire voyage.

About fifteen to twenty miles from the mouth of the channel, the last of the surrounding spruce forest ended; the shores were then covered with poplars, as well as willows down near the water's edge. Floating or partially submerged entire spruce trees were scattered all along the low sandy banks. Twelve miles from the mouth of the channel, we passed the connector route that extends for 11/2 miles eastward to the Fletcher Channel. This short passageway, oddly enough, is locally called the "Canoe Portage," even though it entails no carrying; perhaps it had formerly involved portaging around a massive driftwood barricade. We were glad that we had taken the pleasant, narrow l'Embarras Channel along its entire length. By good fortune, we had not yet encountered any blockages of tangled driftwood trees along it. Had we traveled the Fletcher Channel for the full distance down to Lake Athabasca, instead of the l'Embarras Channel, our total mileage would still have been the same: the Fletcher, with fewer loops, is four miles shorter down to the lake, but it then requires four additional miles of westward paddling on exposed lake waters to reach the l'Embarras mouth before continuing on to Ft. Chipewyan.

By noon, the beaming sun had elevated the air temperature to a balmy 72 degrees in the shade. About five miles above the mouth, the last possible land for camping ended. From there on down to the lake, there was no earth standing above the surface of the water. Along the swampy, flooded shorelines, the vegetation consisted of grasses and reeds about five to seven feet tall. In one reed-grown area, I was obliged to disembark on a grounded driftwood spruce stump, to defecate before reaching the mouth of the channel. This urge may have been related to my anticipation of driftwood trees impeding the swampy route ahead, in our final run out to the big lake. Dragging the canoe or portaging through the thick reed beds of this swampland would definitely not be a joy!

At about 2:30, we finally arrived at the mouth of the Chenal de l'Embarras, having met no obstructions up to this point. We were about to enter the long-awaited, fabled Lake Athabasca! The sunlight was cheerful, bright, and warm, while a light breeze was wafting in from the northwest. In front of us, the entire delta region of the l'Embarras was scattered with driftwood trees that had been grounded in the shallows. These massive entire spruces, 25 to 30 feet long, usually lacked their branches after their tumbling, battering voyage down the Athabasca. To our immense relief, they were not gathered into large tangled masses that would hinder our progress out onto the open water of the lake!

The terrain surrounding the entire body of water consisted of low, evergreen-covered hills, with a rim that undulated only slightly. During the fur trade era, this watercourse had sometimes been called the Lake of the Hills. Gazing from the mouth of the channel off toward the east, we could see the dark green profile of the forest-clad promontory of Old Fort Point, seventeen miles away. In 1788, a 24-year-old Alexander Mackenzie had moved the Pond Post from the lower Athabasca River to the tip of this point, and had rechristened it Ft. Chipewyan. From the post, he and his men had set off in 1789, seeking a water route to the Pacific Ocean, but had instead discovered that the Mackenzie River flowed northward to the Arctic Sea. Four years later, he and his party had again departed from this facility, still intent upon reaching the Pacific by water. This expedition of 1793, traveling up the Peace River and over the Rockies, was relatively successful, reaching the ocean at the mouth of the Bella Coola River via a combination of water and overland routes. These were the first Europeans to cross North America in the northern latitudes by canoe to reach the Pacific.

We soon learned that the entire mouth area of the l'Embarras Channel, which is the westernmost portion of the overall Athabasca River delta, was extremely shallow. Here, as it did throughout the delta, the river deposited the silt which it had been carrying for hundreds or thousands of miles. These sand-bottomed shallows, offering only about six to twelve inches of water, extended out for about a mile from the terminus of the reed beds, fully one-third of the distance across to the opposite (north) shore of Lake Athabasca. As we slowly made our way toward that far shore of the lake, seeking areas of deeper water, we were grounded three times, in places that had about a six-inch depth. We later learned from Mr. Fraser, a Cree-Scots resident of Ft. Chipewyan, that the water level of the lake had been especially low this summer. The Athabasca River was temporarily high, due to the recent weeks of rainfall. However, this influx did not raise the lake level, since it flows into the 250-mile-long lake very near to the western end of the lake, while the nearby outflow channel at the same end of the lake extracts an equal amount of water.

Having advanced a mile northward on the lake to find workable deep water, we now paddled westward for 1 1/2 hours, against a light head wind and moderate waves, to cover the last four miles to Ft. Chipewyan. As the lake narrowed and the shorelines came gradually closer, they offered a welcome sight: the first Canadian Shield granite that we had observed on this trip. Approaching the end of the lake, we glided past the small but distinctive High Island, a tall rounded formation of solid granite bearing a widely-spaced scattering of spruce trees.

Beyond the island, in the dazzling sunlight we caught our first glimpse of the settlement, in the distance on the low sloping shoreline. Backed by a spruce forest of deep green, that little community was a sweet sight to behold! As we drew nearer, savoring the goal that we had been paddling toward for twelve summers, the most obvious structure that caught our eye was the white frame building of St. Paul's Anglican Church and its tall pointed spire, dating from 1874. It stood at about the midpoint of the row of white-painted frame houses that bordered the shore of the cove, back a considerable distance from the sand beach. Behind this row of homes, which had comprised virtually the entire community until about the 1940s, the rest of the little town had gradually grown toward the northeast for about a mile, expanding on an irregular grid of streets.

Stepping into the knee-deep shallows beside the sandy shoreline at the foot of the bay, we exchanged "high-fives" in tired elation. We had finally arrived at the northwestern terminus of the mainline fur trade canoe route! This was the destination that we had held firmly in our minds while paddling twelve challenging voyages over twelve summers, traveling from Lachine to here.

Ft. Chipewyan is located roughly 700 miles north of the U.S.-Canada border, above the midpoint of Montana's northern line. At the longitude of Juneau, Alaska, it lies ninety miles south of the southern boundary of the Northwest Territories, and about 540 miles south of the Arctic Circle. Located some 575 miles west of the western coast of Hudson's Bay, it is positioned at the very same latitude as Ft. Churchill and Ft. Prince of Wales, which were the most northerly

H.B.C. posts on the Bay. These two facilities, located at the mouth of the Churchill River, were about two-thirds of the way up the south-to-north length of Hudson's Bay.

When we arrived at Ft. Chip at 4:00, we had traveled 37 miles in nine hours since leaving this morning's campsite. During our overall journey, we had covered 296 miles in seven paddling days, averaging 42 miles per day, and had also spent one entire day *dégradé*, windbound on shore.

As soon as we landed, half a dozen young native children from the settlement ran to greet us. We snapped our traditional "victory" photos at the site, including the kids in most of them, after which Doree passed out candies to their eager hands. She and Ben then walked to the Northern Store nearby to purchase a celebration pizza, while Toby and I stayed with the canoe and the children.

After our pizza feast, Tim departed for the public rest rooms at the far end of the beach (which the kids knew were locked). Shortly after he left, one of the little boys, with a gleam in his eye, said to his friends, "Let's go watch Jesus take a leak!" Only then did I realize the impression that had been created in the minds of these children: the unannounced arrival of a dark-skinned, long-haired, bearded man upon the water, apparently from another world, was Jesus! (Doree)

Out on the bay in front of the settlement, Ben practiced his J-stroke as a solo paddler for an hour or two, with Toby as his passenger, while Doree and I took a walk around the little town. The quiet community, which has a population of about 1,200 residents, mostly Chipewyan and Cree, first received electricity in 1959. We were given a personally escorted tour by four nine-year-old girls and an eight-year-old boy: Jennifer Sharfman, Georgette Bruno, Carrie Courtoreille (the French version of the native name Short-Ears), Amy Whiteknife, and Matthew Courtoreille. The French and native surnames of the latter four reflected the fur trade history of this place, and its various populations over the centuries.

We first hiked to the eastern end of the settlement and up Monument Hill, to view the two sites of the famous N.W.C. post. The summit of this moderately tall, rounded hill of pink granite, which is now open, barren rock, is marked with a pyramidal stone cairn; its lower flanks are covered with a short growth of grass and scattered wildflowers. In about 1797, Ft. Chipewyan had been moved from Old Fort Point, 21 miles east of here, to the low land beside the cove immediately west of this hill. (Our arrival in 1995 was only two years short of two centuries after that relocation had taken place.) Six years later, in 1803, the facility had been rebuilt on the higher ground of this hill overlooking the bay, to avoid the perennial dangers of flooding and violent ice action. To the rear of the hill and at its base is now located the town museum, in a 1990 hewn log building which replicates the trading storehouse of the fort.

In the warmth of early evening, the sunlight glinted brightly on the tranquil blue surface of Lake Athabasca below us. On the flank of the hill, while the girls picked a bouquet of colorful wildflowers for me and Matthew picked one for Doree, I gazed out over the water and located in my mind the various competing posts that had once operated at this place. It had been crucial that each company have a facility at this strategic location, since it received all of the peltries from the far northwest region as they were transported southeastward, as well as all of the merchandise and supplies which were redistributed from this depot toward the north and west. A mile-and-a-half to the southwest lay the head of the lake outlet, the Rivière des Rochers (Rocky River). This watercourse flowed northward for 29 miles to join the Peace River and thus form the Slave River, the two main water routes toward the far northwestern fur trade.

Some 3/10 of a mile to the west of us, at the opposite end of the little cove beside the community, the X.Y.C. had operated a facility from 1800 to 1804, until the dissolution of this break-away firm and its reunification with the N.W.C. About 11/2 miles southwest of our location, beside the outlet of the lake, H.B.C. personnel had established Nottingham House on English Island in 1802, running it for four years. Employees of the latter company had again returned nine years later, in 1815, to found Ft. Wedderburn on Coal Island (now called Potato Island), 11/4 miles south-southwest of Ft. Chip.

After the amalgamation of the N.W.C. and the H.B.C. in 1821, personnel of the combined firm permanently occupied the Ft. Chip facility, which was entirely rebuilt at the same location on the hill in the 1870s. These buildings included the trading storehouse, the warehouse, the great house of the factor, the council house, the mess hall, and the blacksmith shop, as well as various other structures, all of which appeared in an aerial photo of the site dating from the 1920s or 30s. None of the log buildings from that period stand on the site today, which is entirely empty and open. However, several of the smaller structures from the 1870s may still exist in the community, having been moved from the fort site and eventually covered over with a layer of clapboard siding. We had walked past one such two-story building, constructed of large squared logs, near the opposite end of the bay.

It was no coincidence that each of the posts had been located in the area of the westernmost tip of the lake, close to its inlet and outlet rivers. The winter ice breaks up earlier at this end of the lake, in late May to early June. This is not only because the depth here is shallower than in the eastern portions of the lake, but also because the Athabasca River channels, thawing in about mid-May, add their warmer flowing waters to the western end of the lake in the spring, helping to dissolve the lake ice. The winter freeze takes place in late October to early November. Generally, the lake and the various rivers of the region freeze over at about the same time, although the largest rivers freeze slightly later, due to their more powerful current.

In about mid-May, southbound brigades heading for the rendezvous at Rainy Lake portaged from Ft. Chip along the western end of the still-frozen Lake Athabasca, to reach the mouth of one of the channels of the recently-thawed Athabasca River. Departing at this time, several weeks before the lake would thaw, usually allowed them sufficient time to reach the summer meeting place, transact their business, depart from there by about August 1, and return to the post and points beyond before the October-November freezing of the waterways in the Athabasca country.

The region of Lake Athabasca was generous in providing food supplies for the fort personnel who resided there, as well as provisions for the brigades that traveled toward the south each summer, and then in October for the personnel who paddled from the fort toward the west and north. The lake, as well as the Slave River immediately to the north, served as an excellent source of whitefish year round; these fish were harvested with gill nets as well as with hooks and lines. In addition, the adjacent delta region of the Peace and Athabasca Rivers attracted huge numbers of wildfowl each spring and fall, to be hunted during these twice-annual migrations.

Southbound brigades from Ft. Chip required more canoes to haul out the shipments of bulky peltries in the summer than were needed to bring back the shipments of supplies and new merchandise in the fall. As a result, employees of both the N.W.C. and the X.Y.C. built many birchbark canoes at the fort and in the surrounding area, as well as on the lower Peace River, using local pine and spruce for the wooden elements. They also rebuilt many canoes that had been originally constructed far to the south with wooden components of cedar, craft which were lighter and thus more useful. The heavier, northern-built canoes, fitted with pine or spruce elements, were the ones that were often left behind in the south when fewer craft were needed for the return voyage to the far northwest. When the Franklin expedition arrived at Ft. Chip in the autumn of 1819, they wintered at the post before departing the following July for the Arctic coast, traveling via the Slave and Mackenzie Rivers, Great Bear Lake, and the Coppermine River. In anticipation of this venture, Franklin had two large canoes built for him at Ft. Chip, one of which measured 321/2 feet in length.

Led by our little troop of youthful guides, Doree and I continued our tour of their community, which appeared to be prospering. At the grass-covered, well-tended cemetery, each grave was surrounded by a low picket fence made of wooden slats painted white. Matthew and Carrie Courtoreille showed us the graves of their two grandfathers, each of whom had been buried that very summer. Matthew suggested that the bouquets of flowers that they had picked for us could be left on some of the graves. So we divided up our two bouquets, and the five children scattered in different directions to place brightly-colored blossoms on the graves of their departed relatives. Jennifer Sharfman led us to the burial place of a cousin, and related the tragic story of this child who had perished at the age of one year. While the baby had been sitting on the floor playing, her father had poured oil around her and then had lit it afire. The following day, the Mounties had found the child's burned bones on the floor. When we asked Jennifer why her uncle had done this, she answered simply, "He was drunk." And the consequences for him? "He was sent away to jail for six years."

At the invitation of the mayor, we pitched our tent beside the cove at the western edge of town, about five feet from the water's edge, near where we had come ashore. This was very close to the place where the men of the X.Y.C. had operated their post from 1800 to 1804. In the gradually fading light of dusk, we could see in clear profile the tip of Old Fort Point, 21 miles to the east across the lake, where the very first Ft. Chipewyan had been constructed by

Alexander Mackenzie and his men in 1788.

After I had finished my diary entries for the day, with Amy Whiteknife sitting on the ground near at hand, she counted the remaining unused pages in the pocket-sized notebook, and contemplated what I might write on them in the next day or so. I then sat with her on the edge of the canoe, and showed her the map of the entire mainline fur trade route that I always carried during our voyages. Pointing out the markings on it which indicated where we had paddled each year to eventually reach her town, I gave a little capsule of those twelve years of canoe trips. Even though she was only nine years old, when I looked into that lovely oval face and those almond-shaped eyes, I understood why many French voyageurs and French and Anglo traders had remained permanently in the interior, establishing Métis families.

Finishing off the last of the pizza, we lounged on the beach beside Ben's fire until 11:15, celebrating the successful completion of this year's canoe venture, which had extended from one Tuesday at 10 A.M. until the following Tuesday at 4 P.M. We had first paddled 105 miles on the Clearwater River, in the process running three rapids and portaging four others, as well as hiking the upper section of the famous Portage La Loche. Then we had covered 186 miles on the Athabasca River, plus five more miles crossing Lake Athabasca. During that entire period of traveling, we had been windbound from 4 P.M. Saturday until 5 A.M. Monday. Thus, we had paddled for seven days, and had spent one entire day on shore without advancing. On both of the rivers, we had averaged 5 m.p.h. whenever we were on the water, due to the moderately helpful current. We had experienced beautiful weather at each end of the trip, and had endured about four days straight of rain, chilly temperatures, and zero sunshine during the entire middle portion of the voyage. Since suffering makes us grow, we had expanded considerably during this trip. Along the way, while encountering a nearly constant series of challenges, we had prevailed in small, undramatic ways.

This had been the first canoe trip since the Mattawa River on which we had not been able to utilize the sail. Not once during this entire voyage had we been blessed with a following tail wind. For 296 miles over the course of eight days, we had either had no breeze or we had been confronted with a contrary head wind. During the twelve to fourteen hours that we had spent on the water each traveling day, we had not once landed to eat a snack or a meal. Instead, the passenger had prepared and handed out food and drink to the two paddlers. During each day, we had only halted at the shoreline for rare emergency defecation stops. These had involved pulling up to a stand of tall willows or a thick bed of reeds, and holding onto them to keep the canoe in a stationary position against the strong pull of the current while the needy traveler went ashore. For other calls of nature, Doree and Ben had used the canoe bailer as a urinal, while I had simply gone over the gunwales at the stern.

When our final evening's fire had dwindled to a bed of glowing orange coals, we were treated to the most spectacular show of northern lights that we had ever seen! To our great delight, huge curtains of light in various shades of pastel green pulsed and rippled across the expanse of clear black sky, overlaying millions of brilliant stars. Sometimes, a giant green curtain folded in on itself, or instead danced up and down. Many years of observations by experts have shown that the latitude of Ft. Chipewyan is the peak zone of activity for the *aurora borealis* in the western hemisphere. The highest frequency of appearance, the most vivid colors, and the greatest amount of activity are observed in the light shows at this latitude. Each of these three elements decreases at a regular rate as the viewer travels toward the north or the south from this latitude. At one point during our dazzling, ninety-minute display, a satellite cruised smoothly overhead, emitting a concentrated white light as it orbited the Earth at a high altitude. Watching the northern lights in awed silence, we all agreed afterward that this magnificent show had been Nature's ceremonial benediction of our family, for having finally reached the northwestern end of the mainline route!

Day Nine

The sound of a lone curious raven landing on our overturned canoe beside the tent stirred us at about 7:00. Since there was no need to rise, pack, and move on per our usual paddling schedule, we relaxed and chatted in the shelter, basking in the warmth of the early-morning sun on the green nylon roof. At 7:30, the air temp outside measured 58 degrees, the sky was nearly cloudless, and a slight breeze caressed our faces. Doree, Toby, and I walked a short distance toward the west to get a closer view of Mission Point and the complex of buildings nearby which had comprised the residential school of the Catholic church. Segregated from the community by a half-mile, this facility for educating the native children of the entire region contained a tall-spired, white frame church, a three-story red dormitory building, and several other lower structures. This complex represented an earlier era, when native kids from a widespread area had been forcibly removed from their families and had been brought here, to live for six years in the residential school, in an attempt to transform them into "white" children.

Nowadays, the majority of the native population of the region resides in the little town of Ft. Chip for most of each year, with only some of them dispersing into the bush to live in more traditional ways, particularly during the warm-weather months. Some individuals commercially harvest whitefish from Lake Athabasca during the summers. The children live in the bosom of their own families, and attend the public school in the middle of town. In effect, the entire community is a reservation, since its official name is the Fort Chipewyan Indian Settlement. An additional nine reserves are located nearby, although only one of them, in the Athabasca River delta, is extensive. It includes the entire area bordered on the west by the Fletcher Channel and on the south and the east by the main channel of the Athabasca River; this area measures roughly twenty miles by thirty miles. Five tiny reserves are scattered just to the east and southeast of this primary piece of land, while three other segments are located at these specific places: along the eastern shore of the Athabasca River for about six miles, just after the l'Embarras Channel branches off; along the north shore of Lake Athabasca for about six miles, a little toward the northeast from the community of Ft. Chip; and a smaller area along the eastern shore of the Rivière des Rochers, to the northwest of the community.

When Ben finally emerged from the tent at 8:30, he and Doree departed for a well-deserved breakfast at the new lodge, built six years before, which overlooks the lake at the eastern end of town. Meanwhile, Toby and I had history to absorb. Standing atop Monument Hill, the elevated site of the 1803 Ft. Chip post, I again enjoyed comparing my topo map to the lay of the land, noting where each of the various posts had been located. I felt like I was part of this place, that I truly belonged here. During the rest of the morning, Doree and I took in the exhibits at the nearby Ft. Chipewyan Visitor Center (which is actually the visitor center for Wood Buffalo National

Park) and the Ft. Chipewyan Museum.

At the museum, I had a long chat about the Clearwater River, the Athabasca River, and Lake Athabasca with Craig, a local Métis trapper, fisherman, and tugboat worker. He explained that the reason that we had enjoyed a substantial current in the l'Embarras Channel was due to the flood stage of the Athabasca River, which was running at five feet above normal level for this season. Under normal circumstances, the l'Embarras would have offered virtually no current, almost slack water. The route that I had originally planned to travel through the delta region of the Athabasca River would indeed have been the customary canoe and motorboat route to and from Lake Athabasca. This route passes southward down the Fletcher Channel of the Athabasca, and, at a point eight miles south of the lake, moves westward to the lower l'Embarras Channel via the short natural waterway that is locally termed the "Canoe Portage," even though no carrying is involved. (There is no channel in the delta that is known as the "Canoe Channel.") Thus, the winding upper section of the l'Embarras Channel is usually avoided, with its additional miles of length. However, the lower portion of this passageway is regularly utilized, to reduce the mileage on the open, exposed waters of the big lake. We had paddled down the entire length of the l'Embarras Channel, and had enjoyed very much its sheltering narrow width, its entertaining winding course, and its helpful flood-stage current.

At the mouth of the l'Embarras Channel, at its entry into Lake Athabasca, no channel is ever dredged through its shallow areas. Motorboat activity keeps one particular passageway sufficiently deep. However, during the week before our arrival, a powerful storm had blown its channel markers well to the west on the lake; normally, those markers indicate where the passage with navigable depth is located across the extensive shallows that span most of the mouth area. Only the navigational channels at the mouth of the main Athabasca River channel are dredged, to facilitate the movement of tugboats and their accompanying long rows of barges. Until about twenty years ago, no channel markers had been required in the delta region; the entire area had been easily accessible for water travel. However, since that time, accelerated sand accumulations have required channel markers at the mouth area of each of the channels.

Nowadays, the channel mouths are normally not blocked by tangled masses of driftwood trees. However, our pilot Gordon had once worked packing fish for one summer at the mouth of the main Athabasca River channel, and had become very familiar with the terrain of the area. He reported that numerous driftwood trees did float from each of the river channels out into the shallow adjacent areas of the lake.

The water levels of Lake Athabasca are not generally affected by the rates of flow of the rivers that discharge into the lake. However, the water levels at various locations on the 250-mile-long lake are altered by strong winds. These winds push the water toward one end of the lake or the other, to such a degree that its fluctuating levels seem to resemble ocean tides.

Spring breakup of the ice in this area takes place, on average, in mid-May on the rivers and mid-June on the big lake. The shallower western end of the lake is usually ice-free for some four months or more, from about mid-June until the freezing of the lake and rivers in late October or early November. However, the eastern end of the lake still has plenty of ice in early July. The western end of the lake is much shallower than its other areas, facilitating its earlier thawing; in addition, the melted rivers also flow into and out of the western end of the lake. In late autumn, the main channels of the Athabasca River remain ice-free for about three to four days longer than the slower and smaller channels, such as the l'Embarras.

After Doree and I had enjoyed the informational exhibits at both the Interpretive Center of Wood Buffalo National Park and the Ft. Chipewyan Museum, we returned to our camp, where we found Ben and Toby relaxing. While the rest of the family departed to acquire more pizza at the Northern Store, I completed my updating of the maps and the journal. Then, after finishing our feast of pizza, chips with dip, and cokes, Ben left at 2:30 for the visitor center, to view the twenty-minute film about the national park; the remaining family members lounged in the tent.

A few minutes later, we heard the drone of a float plane flying very low over the lake in front of our tent. When the plane landed at the government wharf nearby, Doree trotted there to verify that it was indeed our flight out with Gordon. (The day before, I had made arrangements by phone with him for a 3:30 pickup.) For my part, I dismantled the tent and quickly stuffed the last items into the packs, after which we parents portaged most of the gear to the plane. When Ben arrived shortly thereafter, he carried the canoe from the campsite to the wharf. While we loaded in the gear and a disgruntled Toby, Gordon lashed the canoe onto one of the pontoons. In short order, we were gathering speed on the lake and then were airborne; it was 3:30, the time when we had expected the plane to arrive. En route to us, Gordon had experienced such a strong tail wind that his entire trip to Ft. Chip had been made at a speed 30 m.p.h. faster than normal. Thus, it had only taking him a little more than an hour to travel the 170 air miles.

As soon as we lifted off the smooth surface of Lake Athabasca, we eagerly scanned the landscape spreading out below us, keeping a sharp eye out for bison. Wood Buffalo National Park, with the Athabasca River and the l'Embarras Channel forming its southeastern boundary, is the largest park in Canada. Measuring about 175 miles in length and from 100 to 140 miles in width, it extends northward to a line 35 to 45 miles beyond the border of the Northwest Territories. This gigantic preserve contains 17,300 square miles, more land surface than the entire country of Switzerland, and twice that of the Netherlands. The park, consisting of a subarctic wilderness of forests, bogs, meadows, rivers, and shallow lakes, is the home of the world's largest herd of free-roaming bison; it also contains, in its boggy northern portion, the only known nesting grounds of the endangered whooping crane. Ft. Chipewyan, as well as Ft. Smith far to the north, are the two main entry areas for visitors to the park; however, the majority of the buffalo live in the delta area of the Athabasca and Peace Rivers, the area over which we were flying at a low altitude.

The wood bison, the largest land animal in Canada, lives in the park in the areas of open meadow and their forest perimeters. Boat trips with one of the park wardens take visitors from Ft. Chip into the streams and lakes in the Peace-Athabasca delta region, to catch a glimpse of the widely-scattered herd. Sometimes, some of the buffalo wander to the l'Embarras Channel and swim across it, thus entering unprotected Alberta lands; there, they become fair game for local hunters. When this occurs, the wardens attempt to round up the massive animals with a helicopter and drive them back across the channel onto park lands, where they are fully protected.

There are two sub-species of bison, the plains bison and the wood bison. The latter type is taller, darker in color, and woolier, with the bull measuring up to 61/2 feet in height and twelve feet in length, and weighing up to 2,200 pounds; females weigh about half this amount.

The history of the famous Wood Buffalo National Park and its free-roaming herd extends back to 1891, when only some three hundred wood bison were known to exist in all of Canada. They were living in the region which would become the national park thirty years later. In 1922, the preserve was laid aside as a permanent habitat for these last remaining animals, which had already been protected by federal law for three decades.

Simultaneously, events were taking place to the south which would eventually lead to the preservation of the only purebred plains bison in Canada. In 1872, a native man gathered eight orphaned plains bison calves, and raised and interbred them on the Flathead Reservation in northwestern Montana. Twelve years later, in 1884, he sold his small bison herd to two local white ranchers, who continued to maintain and protect this purebred population for more than twenty years. In 1906, all 709 head of their herd were purchased by the Canadian government, and were transported to the newly-established Elk Island National Park, in central Alberta east of Edmonton. Soon, all but about fifty of these animals were transferred to another new national park, near Wainwright, Alberta. There, they were utilized in cross-breeding experiments with cattle, which were carried out by the federal Department of Agriculture. By the 1920s, this herd had not only completely lost its purebred nature, it had also become heavily infected with such cattle diseases as brucellosis and tuberculosis.

It was at this point that the histories of the wood bison and plains bison in Canada became intertwined. In 1925, about 6,600 hybrid plains bison/cattle from the Wainwright park were shipped north to the newly-created Wood Buffalo National Park. This action seriously compromised the future of the only surviving population of wood bison, which had until then maintained both its purebred integrity and its freedom from cattle diseases, in northern isolation. Within twenty years, the park at Wainwright was closed and the remaining hybrid plains bison/cattle there had all been killed off. However, by good fortune, the purebred, disease-free herd of plains bison at Elk Island National Park continued to survive and thrive. To this day, these animals, as well as their relocated offspring, represent the only unadulterated plains bison population in all of Canada.

In Wood Buffalo National Park, gradual but steady cross-breeding in the wild between the original wood bison herd and the introduced hybrid plains bison/cattle seemed to have destroyed the purebred nature of the entire population there. In addition, close associations between these two groups had also introduced cattle diseases to the wood bison herd. Then, in 1957, in an inaccessible corner of the park isolated by about 75 miles of impenetrable muskeg, a pilot passing overhead spotted a herd of some two hundred bison. These turned out to be purebred wood bison, so the sub-species was not extinct after all! When the following winter's freeze of the muskeg allowed park wardens access by land to that area, these animals were captured, relocated, and thereafter kept widely separated from the cattle-inbred and disease-plagued herd in the rest of the park.

For various reasons, the total number of buffalo in the park had plummeted during the decade preceding our visit. In 1985, the overall herd had numbered some 5,000 animals; however, by the time of our visit just ten years later, the total count had dwindled to about 2,500. This massive loss was not only the result of mortality from the widespread cattle diseases. The landscape where the majority of the herd lives, in the southeastern area of the park in the Peace-Athabasca delta region, has been influenced and enriched by spring floods for thousands of years. However, lack of flooding in the years leading up to our visit had caused the delta area to dry out considerably. This had led to woody plants such as willow replacing the rich sedge meadows which are the favorite habitat of bison. Reduction of this high-quality habitat had led to serious reductions within the buffalo population.

In spite of the hybrid nature of most of the bison within the park, which we laypeople could not even discern visually, we avidly examined the landscape as we flew southward over a portion of the preserve. In the maze of forest, meadow, and muskeg that stretched out below us, we looked carefully for any signs of the massive, dignified animals. It was also fascinating to fly just above the very watercourses where we had laboriously pulled our canoe forward during the previous several days. First there was the l'Embarras Channel, with the parallel route of the Fletcher Channel off to the left in the background. Then we passed over the "Canoe Portage," the short connector passage with flows between the l'Embarras and Fletcher Channels.

The powerful south wind that had been so helpful to Gordon during his flight to pick us up at Ft. Chip persisted during our entire return flight, this time as a head wind. As a result, it took a full 127 minutes to make our way through the 170 air miles back to La Loche, a very slow trip which normally takes about ninety minutes. Along the way, Gordon sought out non-turbulent air space, finally locating it at a low altitude. At this very low level, he kept an eye out for the site where a small jet had crashed into the side of a long line of high hills during the previous week, while flying on automatic pilot in bad weather. At one point, we saw in the distance what appeared to be a golden lake several miles in length. This turned out to be a huge, ancient sand dune, which had developed during the wind-swept period after the glaciers had receded from this region. Making our way southward over the evergreen-covered land, we passed over large numbers of pothole lakes which are strewn across the landscape. These shallow bodies of water are fed by underground passages in the limestone bedrock.

Finally touching down on Lac La Loche and gliding to a stop beside the dock, we loaded the van and converted ourselves into land travelers. Flush with elation at having completed our canoe trek safely, we felt like we were from another planet. The speed of our vehicle, causing the scenery to absolutely fly by without any exertion on our part, was mind-boggling! Everything seemed so effortless now, including not having to keep track of the route or the weather, and not having to make constant decisions about where and when to paddle or where to camp.

Our amazement at the rather effortless physical nature of our modern lives continued as we traveled southward to Dinosaur Provincial Park, in southeastern Alberta. This astounding preserve encompasses the richest area of dinosaur fossils in the world, which has supplied many of the specimens for museums across Canada and the U.S., as well as Europe, since the nineteenth century.

Back home in Oak Park, Ben commenced a two-year program of auto mechanic training at the local community college. (In June, he had graduated from high school after three years, by taking a full load each year at the high school as well as Saturday classes at the college.) Kevin had just completed his first six months in the Army, having finished basic training, communications equipment training, and airborne jump school. He was now permanently assigned to the 82nd Airborne Division, and was stationed at Ft. Bragg, North Carolina.

XV
Thirteenth Voyage
Lake Huron
August 4-9, 1996

You don't get to choose how you're going to die, or when.
You can only decide how you're going to live. Now.
Joan Baez

Clear your mind of can't.
Solon

The greatest pleasure in life is doing what people say you cannot do.
Walter Bagehot

Like it or not, it was finally time for us to deal with the three massive lakes that had formed segments of the mainline fur trade route: Lakes Huron, Superior, and Winnipeg. Eleven years earlier, we had paddled 33 miles on the Georgian Bay section of Lake Huron, at the conclusion of the French River voyage; this had taken place during the week before Ben had celebrated his seventh birthday. Three years later, when our two young paddlers were only ten and twelve years old, Doree and I had decided to postpone the excursions on Lake Huron and Lake Superior, as we made our annual westward progression along the mainline route. Instead, we had continued along the waterways that extended toward the northwest from the western shore of Lake Superior. After four voyages, we had skipped over Lake Winnipeg in the sequence, and then had completed the remaining four trips to reach Ft. Chipewyan, at the far northwestern end of the mainline voyageur route.

Now, the only remaining segments to be traveled on the route were the three enormous lakes. During the eleven years and two months since we had paddled the Georgian Bay section of Lake Huron, Ben had transformed himself into a strapping eighteen-year-old and a seasoned paddler. In addition, we had commissioned

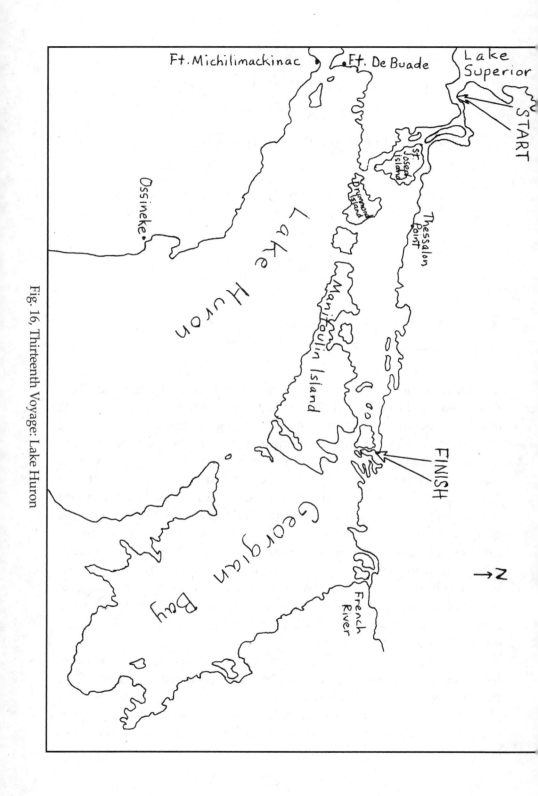

Fig. 16, Thirteenth Voyage: Lake Huron

a snap-on canoe cover made of nylon fabric, and had utilized it very successfully on the two previous journeys. With the growth of Ben and the development of his canoeing skills, along with the protection against wind and waves that was provided by the canoe cover, we were now more properly equipped to face the physical and psychological challenges that would certainly be presented by the three inland seas.

Yes, these lakes are indeed freshwater seas! Based on their surface areas, the ten largest freshwater lakes in the world include the following bodies of water: **1. Lake Superior** (Canada and the U.S., 32,162 square miles); 2. Lake Victoria (Tanzania and Uganda, Africa, 26,988 s.m.); **3. Lake Huron** (Canada and the U.S., 23,089 s.m.); 4. Lake Michigan (U.S., 22,400 s.m.); 5. Lake Tanganyika (Tanzania and Congo, Africa, 13,127 s.m.); 6. Great Bear Lake (N.W.T., Canada, 12,275 s.m.); 7. Lake Baikal (Russia, 12,162 s.m.); 8. Great Slave Lake (N.W.T., Canada, 11,031 s.m.); 9. Lake Erie (Canada and the U.S., 9,930 s.m.); and **10. Lake Winnipeg** (Manitoba, Canada, 9,300 s.m.).

Lake Victoria in Africa is nearly 17 percent larger than Lake Huron, and Lake Superior (the largest freshwater lake in the world) is a whopping 39 percent bigger. However, Lake Huron, which we were poised to paddle, is nonetheless a gigantic body of water! Its surface area is bigger than that of the largest two lakes in Canada, and bigger than the largest lakes in South America (Lake Titicaca), Europe (Lake Lagoda), and Asia (Lake Baikal). In addition, Huron's coastline, measuring 3,830 miles (including all of the islands), is longer than that of each of the other four Great Lakes.

The five Great Lakes, formed when glaciers gouged up bedrock and redistributed loose surface material to create their basins, were originally filled (and continue to be filled) indirectly by flowing watercourses, as well as directly by rain and snow from the atmosphere. Their shapes, their sizes, and the locations of their outlet channels have altered dramatically during the course of the last ten thousand years, since the final northward retreat of the glaciers. These five bodies of water, now covering some 95,000 square miles, presently contain 95 percent of the surface fresh water of the U.S., more than 80 percent of the surface fresh water of North America, and about 20 percent of the surface fresh water of the entire world.

Lake Huron has the largest drainage basin of the five Great Lakes, drawing its flowing waters from a larger expanse of land than each of the other four lakes. Its drainage basin covers a massive 50,700 square miles. However, among the five, it is fourth in its maximum depth and average depth, and third in its volume of water. Surveying from west to east, Lake Superior, with depths up to 1,333 feet, has an average depth of 489 feet and a volume of 2,935 cubic miles of water; Lake Michigan has a maximum depth of 923 feet, an average depth of 279 feet, and a volume of 1,180 cubic miles; Lake Huron has a maximum depth of 750 feet, an average depth of 195 feet, and a volume of 849 cubic miles; Lake Erie has a maximum depth of 210 feet, an average depth of 62 feet, and a volume of 116 cubic miles; and Lake Ontario has a maximum depth of 802 feet, an average depth of 283 feet, and a volume of 393 cubic miles.

Looking at a map of Lake Huron, it was clear to us why its entire northeastern section, now called Georgian Bay, had sometimes been erroneously considered to be a separate body of water. Jutting up from the southeast, the elongated Bruce Peninsula appears to segregate about three-quarters of Georgian Bay from the main lake waters, while Manitoulin Island delineates the western end of the Bay. In fact, the massive continuous ridge of the Niagara Escarpment runs through the length of the Bruce Peninsula, Manitoulin Island, and the entire long string of islands which extends westward to the very end of Lake Huron. This entire ridge consists of limestone, formed from coral reefs and shells of marine animals which lived on the bottom of a shallow ocean that was located here some 430 million years ago.

During our voyage along the north shore of Lake Huron, we would be traveling in a generally easterly direction for some 140 miles, along the so-called "North Channel" of the lake. This is the passageway that is bounded by the long series of islands on the south and the shoreline of the lake on the north, with the width of the passage generally ranging from about ten to fifteen miles. Throughout our journey, we would be paddling through an unusual geological region, passing bedrock of limestone on our right (on the islands) and bedrock of Canadian Shield, Precambrian granite on our left (on the mainland). The overall forest cover on both the mainland and all of the islands except the easternmost one, Manitoulin, would be a mixed deciduous-coniferous woods of maple, birch, pine, hemlock, and fir; Manitoulin Island would offer more of a southern deciduous forest, with more maple, birch, and beech, and less hemlock. During most of the trip, we would be traveling through the traditional lands of the Ojibwa nation, including, from west to east, the clans that had been called Saulteurs (People of the Falls), Mississauga, Nikeekouet (Otter), and Amikwa (Beaver); Manitoulin Island would fall within the original Ottawa territory.

In hopes of garnering the assistance of the prevailing westerly winds, we would be traveling from west to east. However, this would certainly not guarantee that we would be free of the scourge of *La Vieille*'s contrary nature. On the massive expanses of Lake Huron and Lake Superior, the geography tends to create its own local weather patterns. The huge volume of deep water remains rather frigid all summer, while the surrounding land areas, often exposed barren rock, absorb much warmth from the sun during the day. This great contrast of temperatures often leads to the creation of heavy banks of fog in the early mornings, and on many days causes violent air currents to kick up during the late morning or early afternoon. Period accounts from the fur trade era indicate that voyageurs traveling on these massive lakes were quite often windbound by early afternoon. In addition, on about one-third of all days, they were entirely *dégradé*, unable to travel at all. As an antidote to this challenge, they often pushed off in the dark during the wee hours of the morning, to increase the distance that they could cover before the winds typically picked up. However, this approach was sometimes risky, especially on pitch dark nights when the moon was not shining, and wherever the offshore areas presented rocky shallows, reefs, and barely submerged boulders. The account of the Cass Expedition of 1820, written by Henry Schoolcraft, offers examples of the early-morning strategy of voyageurs. As the party ascended the full length of the western shore of Lake Huron in three large canoes, their morning departures ranged from 5:00 to 8:00; then, while traveling westward over the full length of Lake Superior, they set off most mornings between 3:00 and 6:00. During our voyages on Huron, Winnipeg, and Superior, we would adopt a similar approach, to deal with the new challenges that would be presented while traveling on these massive bodies of water.

Leaving Oak Park at 2:30 P.M. on Saturday, we drove for nine hours, taking a meal break for an additional hour en route. Then we halted at the rest stop south of the Mackinac Straits, to sleep for three hours and change into our paddling clothes, before completing the final hour on the road. This trip to our put-in spot at Sault Ste. Marie seemed so very brief; it would be the second shortest drive that we would ever make to begin a canoe trip on the mainline route. The considerable drawback to the brevity of this ten-hour drive, however, was that none of us had a chance to rest well before commencing the paddling voyage.

Day One

At 6 A.M., we crossed the International Bridge over the St. Marys River and the Sault Locks, passed through the border check at Sault Ste. Marie, Ontario, and immediately stopped for breakfast at the West Side Cafe. While there, we also ordered six burgers to take out; these would serve as our paddling meals later in the day. By pre-arrangement, our shuttle driver Michael Turco from the Sault joined us at the modest little restaurant. He would keep our van during our voyage, and then bring it to us upon our arrival at the tip of the La Cloche Peninsula, near the eastern end of Manitoulin Island.

As I headed for the cash register to pay the bill, dressed in my paddling outfit, complete with green neckerchief and broad-brimmed camouflage hat, a middle-aged woman eating at one of the tables muttered "Bushwacker!" I did not respond to her comment, but smiled to myself, since her remark harkened back more than three centuries, to a time when stay-at-home citizens had coined a name for those men who traveled off into the interior country to live among and trade with the native populations. In New France, these individuals were termed *coureurs de bois* (runners of the woods); in exact parallel, in New England they were called "woods runners," and in New Netherlands *busch lopers*. We free-spirited paddlers were apparently still on the outermost fringes of "civilized" society, even after nearly four hundred years!

With Ben, now 181/12 years old, in the bow position, we launched from the shore at RYTAC onto the St. Marys River at 7:45 A.M. This facility, the Rotary-YMCA-Tennis-Athletic Club, also taught sailing lessons from its riverside base immediately west of the city marina. The sky was completely overcast in somber tones of light grey, the air temperature measured 60 degrees, and a gentle breeze from the southeast brushed our faces. While studying the topo maps in advance, I had decided that we would take the channel in U.S. territory which extends for eighteen miles down the west side of Sugar Island (which the French had called Île St. Georges); this passageway is now named Lake Nicolet. This west-side route would serve us better than the passage in Canadian territory which runs along the east side of the island, the watercourse that is now called Lake George, since it curves well to the north and would add an additional ten miles to our trip.

After advancing one mile on the slightly ruffled, grey surface, we had crossed the international border and had just settled into our old familiar rhythms of long-distance paddling. Then, looking ahead, we were confronted with a challenge that we had never before encountered in our thirteen years of canoe tripping. Approaching steadily toward our craft, and heading directly at us, was...a gigantic ocean-going freighter! At this place, alongside Island Number One, the channel is only about 1/10 of a mile wide, due to the many small islands that tightly crowd the river for nearly a mile. We were to share the slender right-of-way with a red-and-white giant of the seas whose name, painted in white letters high across the red bow, we could discern as *L'Orme No. 1* (Elm Number One). At least we were being intimidated by a vessel of the historically appropriate French nationality. While preparing for this trip, I had nervously wondered just what it would be like to meet freighters in various stretches of the St. Marys River, where ship traffic on the St. Lawrence Seaway from around the world funnels down in several narrow passageways. Well, we learned during the next few minutes that the pilots of freighters have very polite and dignified manners, compared to the manners that are exhibited by a great many drivers of motorboats! We barely felt the wake of the giant vessel as it slipped by near us, and the deep thrumming of its engines sounded much more subdued than the obnoxious roar of a motorboat. This was one more lesson to add to our growing range of experiences.

As we paddled southward along the eighteen-mile length of Sugar Island, we passed an intimate little piece of forest-clad land lying just offshore, which sported a sign reading "ISLAND FOR SALE." Not long afterward, we were able to clearly watch a beaver swimming underwater, entirely unconcerned, about four feet from the shoreline and almost underneath our dark green hull. Along the shore of Sugar Island, we passed various prosperous-looking, year-round homes; we wondered whether they had been built with revenues from the casinos which are owned and operated by the Ojibwa nation at the Sault and elsewhere. Some of the houses were equipped with satellite dishes and had powerboats pulled up on shore; however, no arm-powered canoes were in sight anywhere. From at least the 1820s on, Ojibwa villages had thrived along this western side of the island, continuing into the 1870s and beyond. In fact, the entire island had been laid aside as a reservation in 1836, by a treaty with the U.S. government. Immediately to the north of the island, in the vicinity of the mouth of the Garden River, members of this same native nation had also lived in a number of villages from the 1760s until at least the 1870s; this area of land had been ceded to them by the Canadian government as a reserve in the Treaty of 1850, and is still in their possession.

The area of Sault Ste. Marie is the most westerly of the seven concentrations of French speakers who currently live in the province of Ontario. These residents represent the descendants of the French and French-native Métis populations who gathered in this area during and after the fur trade era. Outside of the seven areas of concentration, the majority of the population of Ontario are English speakers. In contrast, 83.1 percent of the residents of Quebec Province speak French, as do 76 percent of the residents of New Brunswick. Overall, 35.8 percent of the population of Canada are Francophones.

In the U.S., the number of individuals who are full or partial speakers of French is much lower. This is mostly due to the widespread abandonment of the French language by the descendants of the early French residents. In the 2000 U.S. census, which enumerated 282 million people, 1.6 million individuals were listed as speaking French at home; these were located particularly in Louisiana and in the New England states. In addition to these people, the estimates of the number of partial speakers in the U.S. ranges from two to five million. Taking a midway figure of 3.5 million for the partial speakers, the total number of Francophones in the country, some five million people, represents only 1.8 percent of the total population. Had the French been victorious in the Seven Years' War (called the French and Indian War by Anglos), the number of French speakers in the U.S. would be immensely greater.

At 10:15, when we reached our nine-mile mark, we passed another north-bound freighter, this time at a place where the overall channel was a generous mile in width. Shortly thereafter, we paused for a fifteen-minute burger stop on a tiny islet. This very peaceful spot, a nesting ground for great blue herons, was thickly covered with white-and-yellow daisies, taller flowers with delicate blossoms of a light purple hue, and knee-high grasses.

When we pushed off again, with yours truly plying the avant *paddle, the sky was still completely overcast. During the entire four weeks preceding this trip, I had been sentenced to purgatory, with my left leg crammed into a knee-high plaster cast. I had torn my ankle tendon during one of my rousing weekly volleyball sessions at the YMCA. Two days before the trip, Dr. Boone Brackett had cut off my heavy cast, and had replaced it with a shorter, removable, ankle-support cast made of lightweight grey plastic. The base of the cast was too bulky to fit into my own tennis shoe, so I had to swallow my pride and wear one of Tim's tennies on my left foot. My ankle still felt stiff and quite vulnerable, not exactly ideal for doing my part during a demanding canoe trek. (Doree)*

Soon, about twenty Canada geese took off in a group from the river, beating the surface of the water with their wings as they gabbled excitedly. A half-hour later, high altitude winds swept away nearly all of the somber cloud cover, leaving a cheerful sky of light blue decorated with scattered billows of white. By 12:45, we had covered fifteen miles in five hours, including the short rest stop. Our excellent progress prompted us to take a relaxing lunch break, while floating in the channel between the southern end of Sugar Island and the northern end of Neebish Island. We had now completed the southward-headed portion of the voyage; our course during the rest of the trip would take us in a generally east-southeasterly direction.

Three miles of eastward paddling brought us across the international border into Canada again, and to the northwestern tip of St. Joseph Island, where we landed at 2:15. By this point, the temp had risen to a very comfortable 74 degrees in the shade. Unfolding a map of the entire mainline fur trade canoe route, I pointed out that the full length of the St. Marys River, flowing between Lake Superior and Lake Huron, was one of only two segments of the overall route which followed the international boundary line. The other segment, much longer, ran along about two-thirds of the northern border of Minnesota, including the eastern and western portions of the Boundary Waters region, the entire length of the Rainy River, and a small area at the southern end of Lake of the Woods. All other segments of the mainline route extended across lands which are now part of Canada.

During our break on the tip of the island, we watched in

amazement as a lightly loaded freighter passed close by, traveling first northward through the Munuscong Channel between St. Joseph and Neebish Islands, and then westward through the Middle Neebish Channel between Sugar and Neebish Islands. In both passageways, the maximum width of the channel, from shore to shore, ranges from about 2/10 to 3/4 of a mile. However, the navigation channel, offering sufficient depth for these massive vessels, runs down just the midline of the passage, in a swath that is only slightly wider than 1/10 of a mile. It was fascinating to observe such a huge ship threading its way quietly and skillfully between these forest-clad islands that nearly fill the St Marys River.

A mile further to the east, we cruised past the attractive red-and-white frame building of the lighthouse at the tip of Shoal Island, marking the western end of the St. Joseph Channel. This passage extends eastward for sixteen miles in a gently winding course between St. Joseph Island and the mainland to the north. Since the channel is nearly blocked at its western extremity by numerous small islands, it has long required the guiding beacon of the lighthouse. As soon as we entered the St. Joseph Channel, we encountered a moderately strong wind and waves coming from the east, directly against our direction of travel. On this sun-washed Sunday afternoon, there were many motorboats and jet skis playing on the water in this channel, which varies in width from 1/2 to 11/2 miles. There was even a float plane repeatedly practicing takeoffs and landings. Ben and I labored against the persistent head wind and waves for 2 1/4 hours to make just five miles.

At 4:45, we landed for a meal and a much-needed break on the mainland shore in Quebec Bay, just east of the St. Joseph Island bridge, which connects the island to the main landmass. At this point, we had reached mile 25 on our route. After snacking on leftover chicken and biscuits from the previous evening's restaurant meal, plus cheese and apples for dessert, we all curled up in the knee-high grass beneath the canopy of maples by the shoreline, and slept deeply for an entire hour. This was a first for us, in all of our years of paddling: taking an afternoon nap when we were not completely windbound. We certainly needed the rest, after our very short night's sleep followed by nine productive hours on the water.

Refreshed after a two-hour break, we again set off at 6:45, to travel through the island-filled middle portion of the St. Joseph Channel.

However, the contrary wind and waves had not calmed at all. Under difficult conditions, Doree and I slogged forward for 2 1/2 miles, slowly passing forested shorelines that presented dramatic cliffs of granite rising some fifty to sixty feet above the water. Then Ben relieved his mother in the bow position for the final three miles of the day, which took us past the northern shoreline of the Île du Campement d'Ours (Bear Camp Island). With such an intriguing name, I was sorry that I did not know its history.

At 9:00, we finally reached mile thirty, having put in an accomplishing 13 1/4 hours of traveling since the morning launch. Our efforts had brought us over virtually all of the St. Marys River portion of the route, with its huge islands called Sugar, Neebish, and St. Joseph. We were now just five miles away from the wide-open waters of the North Channel.

We landed in a shallow cove on the diminutive Belford Island, which sported just a few bushes growing out of cracks in the low lump of solid bedrock. As the sky blackened and filled with brilliant silver stars, the temperature remained a balmy 60 degrees. Unloading in slow motion, we set up camp between two groups of waist-high bushes, spreading out the air mattresses and sleeping bags on the barren rock. We intended to spend the night under the stars without a tent, to make the next morning's departure both faster and simpler. This would be the very first time that we had done this on paddling trips. The cloudless sky did not suggest any rain. However, without the encompassing walls and roof of light green nylon fabric, I felt rather unprotected, as well as not entirely in control of the expedition's gear.

Stretched out comfortably on my bedding, I replayed the events of the day in my mind's eye, then mentally leafed through the pages of prehistory and history of the area through which we had just paddled. *Le Sault* (The Falls) had been a very important place for native populations for thousands of years, serving as an excellent locale for summer villages. Algonquian-speaking groups had called this place *Bawating*, The Gathering Place at the Rapids. The mile-wide channel of shallow white water here, dropping about twenty feet in elevation in a little more than half a mile, provided a reliable and steady source of food from May to November. During this six-month period each year, thousands of whitefish, ranging in weight from about three to ten pounds, could be captured at the foot of the falls, with dip nets wielded from canoes.

At this summer gathering place, widely dispersed native groups had come together for such activities as trading, religious and social ceremonies, seasonal festivals, and sporting events, including lacrosse games and foot races. Long before the first Frenchmen arrived on the scene, Ottawa and Nipissing traders had brought from the Georgian Bay area such trade articles as food items, tobacco, gourd bottles, and woven mats; these were exchanged here for such items as furs, dried meat and fish, and copper.

Etienne Brulé was the first European to visit the place, passing through in 1618. More than two decades later, the Jesuit Fathers Jogues and Raymbault stopped here for a short time in 1641, to preach to the multitudes who had gathered for summer fishing. When French traders began regularly traveling into the interior in 1653, small numbers of them worked at the Sault each year, carrying out their commerce in peltries; Radisson and Groseilliers passed through here in 1659. Nine years later, Fr. Marquette arrived to establish a mission beside the falls, settling, in the customary fashion of the priests, at a place where large numbers of native people already assembled each year during the warm-weather months. It is an oft-repeated fallacy that missionaries established themselves in a certain locale and then native populations gathered around them. Quite the contrary was true: the priests went to where the native people congregated, and then followed them wherever they chose to wander or settle. For example, when large numbers from the Huron, Tionontate, and Ottawa nations moved eastward from Chequamegon Bay (near the western end of Lake Superior) to settle at the Straits of Mackinac in 1671, Fr. Marquette moved with them. (Our trader ancestor Claude David had spent the years 1660-1663 living and working with these three native groups at Chequamegon Bay, before Fr. Allouez spent 1665-1669 there and Fr. Marquette lived there from 1669 to 1671.)

The relocation of these three native nations to St. Ignace at the Straits signalled the decline of the role which Sault Ste. Marie had played until then in the fur trade. It had functioned as the central gathering point for both French traders and the massive brigades of native traders who paddled out to the St. Lawrence Valley each summer to trade. Within a few years, the community of St. Ignace had completely taken over this central role. In 1689, even the mission at the Sault was closed, although the locale continued to serve throughout the French era as the primary gathering place and summer village of the Ojibwa nation. A major part of their catch of whitefish was annually transported southward to the Mackinac Straits, where it was sold to both the native and the French populations assembled there.

Late in the French period, in 1750, Ft. de Repentigny was established as a trading facility on the southern shore of the Sault, beside the half-mile-long portage path; the post was apparently never staffed by any other military personnel than the founder. During the winter and spring each year while the officer was absent in Montreal, the post was operated by Jean Baptiste Cadotte, a French trader who was married to a local Ojibwa woman.

After the British wrested control of North America from the French, the Anglo trader Alexander Henry established a partnership with Cadotte in 1762. Thereafter, independent Montreal-based traders and eventually personnel from the N.W.C. operated posts on the southern shore at Sault Ste. Marie. In 1796, when American laws finally compelled all British military forces to withdraw to areas beyond the international border, and American tax legislation encouraged the N.W.C. personnel to follow those troops, the Montreal-based traders at the Sault moved across to the Canadian side of the falls. By 1798, they had dug a half-mile-long canal parallel to the river, and had fitted this new waterway with a wooden lock 38 feet long at its lower entrance. This allowed fully loaded canoes and boats to be lifted to the level of Lake Superior, and then to be towed along the entire length of the canal by oxen. Travelers on the American shore, in order to circumvent the rapids, continued to use the long-standing traditional procedures. These entailed, when traveling against the current, conveying half-loaded canoes up the rapids and portaging the rest of the cargo over the half-mile path. Downstream travelers were able to run the rapids with fully loaded craft, both canoes and light boats.

When the War of 1812 broke out, a contingent of British-aligned traders from the Lake Superior country, along with British troops from Ft. St. Joseph on St. Joseph Island and some four hundred native allies of the region, carried out a surprise raid on Mackinac Island and captured Ft. Mackinac. Two years later, in retaliation, American forces burned the N.W.C. facilities on the Canadian side of the Sault as well as trader John Johnston's buildings on the U.S. side (for their joint participation in the 1812 expedition against Mackinac), destroyed Ft. St. Joseph, and attempted (without success) to retake Ft. Mackinac. Less than a decade after the end of the war, in 1823, the military post of Ft. Brady was established on the U.S. shoreline at the Sault. That same year, H.B.C. personnel founded a trading post on the opposite side of the falls, which was operated for less than fifteen years. In 1855, the first American canal was opened beside the falls, to facilitate the passage of ships transporting copper and iron ore from mines in the Lake Superior region. Canadians opened their own shipping canal on the opposite side of the channel forty years later, in 1895.

Back to our canoe trip of 1996. Lying on the shore of the little island beneath the star-studded sky, we were fast asleep by 10:00. This had been a long and very productive first day of thirty miles, the last ten of which we had made against a considerable head wind and oncoming waves. Wielding the bow paddle, Doree had done nine of those miles, while Ben had done the remaining 21 miles. Along the route, we had sometimes passed rocky points of islands on which the trunks and branches of evergreen trees were bent dramatically toward the east, clearly showing the effect of many years of domineering westerly winds. I wondered, "Where were those supposedly prevailing winds when we needed them today, to push us along and fill our sail?"

At one point when I stirred during the night, I noted that the half-moon had risen high in the east in the cloudless sky. Its bright light bathed the entire scene in shades of silver, including the waves marching across the water and the barren rock surrounding us. Due to the moonbeams, a short dark shadow extended westward from the base of every bush. The moderately strong breeze coming out of the east continued to huff unabated across our little island.

Day Two

The alarm clock jangled at 4 A.M., summoning me back from my world of pleasant dreams. Opening my eyes, I took in our surroundings. The white-faced half-moon still illuminated the mass of rock that encircled us, as well as the waves that gently lapped the shore near our feet. In the dome of the heavens, the planet Jupiter shone brightly, high above the horizon off to the east-northeast, amid millions of pin-prick stars. The air temperature was still about 60 degrees, nearly as warm as when we had drifted off to sleep in the open air six hours earlier. I thought of myriad native and French paddlers during earlier centuries, awakening well before dawn to similar scenes, but without the aid of a wind-up alarm clock. In those times, it had often been the responsibility of one particular individual in the party to wake up at intervals during the night (guided by an internal clock), add more limbs to the fire, and stir the stew or pea soup that was simmering for the following day's travel rations.

While Toby watched, we three peacefully packed up the sleeping gear in hushed silence, and embarked at 5:00 with barely a sound. After a half-mile, we left the island-studded middle portion of the St. Joseph Channel behind, and paddled out onto open, unsheltered waters. As the canoe rode up and down atop the broad swells that had been created from many hours of constant easterly wind, I noted how such a massive body of water behaved more like an ocean than a lake. Softly singing a number of French songs, we were struck by the magic of the moment, traveling on moonlit waters beneath a gigantic canvas of bright stars. While Doree and I paddled onward, Ben and Toby, cuddled beneath the canoe cover in the passenger section, were soon lulled to sleep by the gentle rocking motion, as the broad swells lifted and lowered the craft.

About 5:45, the sky began to lighten off to the east in front of us, signalling the stars to fade and finally to disappear. At 6:30, the rim of the orange ball of the sun peeked above the jagged black tree line of pines and spruces. Gradually, the wind and waves from the east picked up more and more, making our progress increasingly slower and more difficult. To pass the time, and also to distract ourselves from the heavy labor, Doree and I rattled off sequences of numbers and simple sentences in French, and later sang *Alouetsky*, the "Russian" version of *Alouette*. When Ben awakened, he fed us chocolate gorp for breakfast. After two hours of demanding work and just three miles of forward progress, Doree took a well-deserved break and Ben assumed the role of the bow paddler. The previous hour had been a tough one, with a hefty head wind and large oncoming waves holding back our progress.

Digging in at full strength into the teeth of the wind, father and son clawed our way forward for another two miles. With each passing minute, the seas were becoming more boisterous, and I knew that we could not maintain this degree of effort much longer. As we slowly crawled past the eastern tip of McKay Island and its lighthouse on our left, the frothing whitecaps crashed with showers of white spray against the rocks along the shoreline. Making a sudden left turn just beyond the point, I steered our bow straight toward the north, making a beeline for shore. With the surf splashing over our right gunwale, we poured it on for twenty hair-raising minutes, to cover the demanding mile that delivered us to a safe haven.

Pulling into the sheltered bay just east of the little town of Bruce Mines, we were windbound at 8:00, having advanced only six miles in three hours of considerable work. Directly to the south of us in the distance lay the easternmost tip of St. Joseph Island, while Drummond Island lay some fifteen miles away in the same direction.

To our considerable surprise, on shore in the quiet bay it was a beautiful sunny day, with no clouds, a moderate easterly breeze, and a temperature of 70 degrees in the shade! While the family walked a half-mile to the town, to scout out some restaurant food, I brought the journal up to date beneath a big poplar. During their amblings, Doree and Ben learned that we had landed on the front lawn of the home that had once belonged to the Marquesse of Queensbury. Her husband, the Marquis, had established here at Bruce Mines the first commercial copper mine in North America, in 1842. The two-story, white clapboard house of early Victorian style, replete with a round tower at one corner, dated from that same year. The mines, operated by Cornish workers, had closed after 34 years, in 1876.

Late in the morning, we all took a stroll through the quiet community, which now has a permanent population of about four hundred residents. The high tourist season here is in winter during the snowmobiling season, as well as in the fall during hunting season. In a little restaurant, we enjoyed a tasty lunch of burgers and *poutine*, the delicious French Canadian dish consisting of french fries covered with cheese curds and smothered with brown gravy.

On the way back to our canoe, we met Dr. Peter Beacraft, who was out working in his garden. This intelligent and talented man had cared for the residents of the community of Bruce Mines during his entire career of 44 years. The medical man gave us a tour of his garden, in which he had constructed a stone wall to absorb the sun's heat, which helped to keep his tomato plants warm during the chilly nights in this often uncooperative northern climate. In the house, he showed us some of the 218 paintings that he had created over the years.

One of the most fascinating parts of our conversation concerned his specialization with spinal injuries. Over the span of more than four decades, he had treated a considerable number of local patients who had been amateur hockey players. As a result, he was intimately familiar with the various types of physical damage which accompany that rough-and-tumble sport, and how those conditions gradually progress during an individual's years of maturity and older age. He has given scholarly presentations on his discoveries to various medical organizations over the years. After I had described the considerable pain that I lived with on a daily basis, especially while playing in the orchestra, he carefully felt my spine from top to bottom. Then he had Doree place her index fingers in two specific locations, one at the base of my neck and the other at the base of my back; in each of those places, she could clearly feel an obvious gap! Based on his physical examination of my spine and his long experience with injured hockey players, Dr. Peter was certain that I had sustained these two areas of damage during a severe jarring incident many years earlier. Only then did I realize that, when I had fallen asleep at the wheel during the summer of 1969, at the age of twenty, and had crushed my car around myself, I had not walked away without injuries after all! That roll-over accident had marked the beginning of decades of chronic spinal pain; however, until this moment, I had not linked the gradually increasing levels of pain to the accident.

(At the time of the writing of this book, I am living virtually free of pain, after enduring nearly constant spinal pain in varying degrees for three dozen years, from ages 20 to 56. In 2005, I underwent spinal fusion surgery, in which strips of bone extracted from my right hip were installed along each side of the most damaged vertebrae at the base of my spine. Over the course of six months, the bone masses grew together solidly, fusing the entire area and halting the pinching of nerves which had plagued me for so long. As for the damage at the base of my neck, it eventually healed of its own accord.)

After our walk, Ben and I visited the bar that was attached to the vintage 1842 house, to have a coffee. There, we met a forty-something native woman, who invited herself to our table and bought us drinks (coffee for both Ben and me, then a beer for Ben, then another beer for him). After Ben departed, she talked openly with me about her life as a native woman, having grown up north of here speaking Ojibwa and Cree. She had had five children, and a number of men in her life, which had not been easy. Before she left, she asked whether she could return in the evening and buy us dinner.

Later, while I was talking with the bartender, I made a point of commenting about Europeans having introduced alcohol to the native people. He went into a long diatribe about how whites are not responsible for the behavior of Indians, citing horrible instances among the native people of alcohol abuse, glue sniffing, and kerosene sniffing. When I mentioned our excellent experiences with the Crees and Chipewyans on Lake Athabasca the previous year, as well as with many other native groups at various locations all across Canada, he was not to be subdued. However, he did state that some tribes have tried, with considerable success, to manage the alcohol abuse and the affairs on their own reserves. (Doree)

By early afternoon, with the air temperature measuring 75 degrees in the shade, the sky had completely clouded over, and the east wind had increased in strength, even in the shelter of the bay. While Doree continued to mingle with the folks in the bar, Ben passed the hours reading a book, with Toby curled up at his feet. (Anticipating that we would have entire days of windbound time on our hands during this voyage, we had each brought a couple of books to read, which were protected in ziplock plastic bags.) To while away the time while we were land-locked here, I took a total of four replenishing naps during the afternoon (an all-time record for me!). During my waking periods between those naps, I contemplated the history that had taken place a little to the south of our location.

When the British military forces stationed at Ft. Mackinac had been finally obliged to vacate Mackinac Island in 1796, they had moved northeastward about 33 miles as the crow flies, to the southernmost tip of St. Joseph Island. This event took place exactly two centuries before the Kent family's paddling voyage on Lake Huron; the soldiers' new home was located about seventeen miles southwest of our windbound stopping place at Bruce Mines. British-aligned traders of the N.W.C. also relocated from Mackinac Island to St. Joseph Island at about the same time, establishing a village adjacent to the fort along the shoreline. Daniel Harmon noted when he visited the community in 1800, "The North West Company has a house and store here. In the latter, they construct canoes, for sending [further] into the interior, and down to Montreal." Westbound brigades from Lachine often stopped at the settlement to replenish their food supplies and to replace their canoes as needed, as they had formerly done at Mackinac. Besides its canoe production industry, this locale also served as a major collection depot for provisions for fur trade personnel, such as dried corn and maple sugar, which had formerly been gathered at the Straits. Writing between 1803 and 1808, Thomas Heriot noted: "Near four hundred men ascend [from Lachine] in bark canoes by the Grand River of the Outaouais, in a direct course to Saint Joseph's on Lake Huron, and from thence to the new establishment on Lake Superior called Kamanastiguia [Ft. William]."

Ft. St. Joseph was the most distant military facility of the British in their northwestern holdings. Here, the British Indian Department armed and supplied many native allies in the interior regions, to retain their allegiance and prepare them for any future fighting against American forces and frontier settlements. The distribution of such supplies had formerly been carried out at Ft. Mackinac, Ft. Detroit, and Ft. Niagara; after the 1796 relocations, these activities were continued at the new posts of Ft. St. Joseph, Ft. Malden, and Ft. George.

For sixteen years, military and civilian life continued rather quietly at Ft. St. Joseph, from the move to the island in 1796 until July 17, 1812. On that day, however, things changed considerably. Assembled fighting forces, including British-aligned traders from the Lake Superior region, the 49 soldiers from Ft. St. Joseph, and some four hundred native allies, departed from the island to execute a surprise attack on the American-held Ft. Mackinac, which they captured without firing a shot. Afterward, both the British soldiers and the civilian trading community of St. Joseph returned to live and work on Mackinac Island. Two years later, on July 20, 1814, American forces destroyed the unoccupied British fort and village on St. Joseph Island by fire, after which those same American forces tried (without success) to retake Ft. Mackinac.

After the 1814 Treaty of Ghent stipulated that the combatant countries were to relinquish all conquered territories to their former owners, the British again vacated Mackinac Island, this time on July 18, 1815. Since their former homes on St. Joseph Island had been burned the previous summer, the British soldiers and British-aligned fur trade community moved some thirty miles northeast of the Mackinac Straits. There, they re-established themselves on the southwestern end of Drummond Island, immediately east of Detour Point, the easternmost tip of the Upper Peninsula of Michigan. This place lay some twenty miles south-southwest of the Kent family's windbound location beside the community of Bruce Mines.

The post and adjacent village of Ft. Collier or Ft. Drummond, spread out along the shoreline of Collier's Harbor on the newly-named Drummond Island, functioned as the most northwesterly military facility of the British. Here, as before, allied native groups continued to arrive for the annual distribution of presents by the British Indian Department. Although the direct arming of these allies had ceased in 1815 with the end of the war, the yearly annuity payments continued until 1830. In the early 1820s, the International Boundary Commission determined that Drummond Island lay on the U.S. side of the border. However, British forces continued to occupy their facility there until 1828, when the island was officially turned over to the American government. At that point, to maintain a continued military presence on the upper Great Lakes, and to exercise some control over the native and fur trade populations of the region, the fort and community were relocated to Penetanguishene, at the southeastern end of Georgian Bay. This latter facility operated until 1832.

Closing my historical musings for the moment, I returned to the present to attend a family conference. At 6:30, we decided to leave the outskirts of the little town of Bruce Mines, to find a wilderness setting where we could spend the night without visitors. We set our sights on a small forested island that lay a half-mile to the south, partway out of the bay. As we made our way southward for fifteen minutes, the waves coming from the left side were very troublesome. Upon reaching the island, it was even more challenging to make a landing amid the many rock ledges that lurked in the shallows just offshore. However, we finally arrived safely on its lee side and set up at a cozy site, on a barren flat ledge beside the water.

Seeing Ben reading by the water's edge with Toby curled up beside him, I was reminded of a saying of Groucho Marx: "Outside of a dog, a book is man's best friend. Inside of a dog, it's too dark to read." After a couple hours of swimming and book-reading, and then trading massages in the fading light, we were fast asleep by 9:00. We had advanced just six miles this day, but we had gotten plenty of rest and relaxation.

Day Three

After hours of heavy rainfall during the night, the dawn brought a balmy temp of 69 degrees and fog-filled air. When the alarm clock clamored at 5:15, the sky was mostly filled with lead-colored clouds, with white light from the waning moon peeking through scattered gaps in the grey cover. From our sheltered spot on the west side of the island, the surface of the water was flat as far as we could see. An hour after waking, we departed from the shelter of the bay, jubilant to be once again on the move, after having been pinned to land for 22 hours!

Shoving off into the dense grey mist, I thought of Alexander Macdonnel's experience when he traveled with a brigade over the North Channel in 1793: "We had a thick fog in which we were bewildered for some hours, and [then we] camped." Immediately upon rounding the point and reaching the open lake, broad swells and a moderate easterly breeze greeted us. Before long, this breeze began producing small waves. At 7:30, the golden sun rose in the area below the cloud layer, but within a half-hour the thick pewter skies completely concealed the rising disc. In the bow seat, Doree enthusiastically pulled the canoe over eight miles of water in three hours, sometimes singing *"Entendez-vous sur l'ormeau..."* Upon reaching Poundnet Point at 9:10, we paused for a short break. When Ben took over the *avant* duties, the moderate head wind from the east continued, our third day of such recalcitrant winds. I kept thinking to myself, "When are those prevailing westerlies going to prevail?"

As we paddled eastward on automatic pilot with the miles dropping slowly behind us, we discussed once more my death-defying auto accident in 1969. Perhaps Ben would glean some wisdom from it. Soon the topic moved to the various admirable traits of many small-town residents. Then, at Ben's insistence, I commenced the old familiar story about the turtle, the buzzard, and the rabbit, which I had been telling, with annual expansions and elaborations, for most of his lifetime. However, we soon digressed from the tall animal tale to the subject of the interesting doctor in Bruce Mines, who had shed light on my spinal injuries, had spoken proudly about his son's hockey-playing abilities, and had boasted modestly about his tomatoes. He attributed the success of those plants to the "heat sink effect" of the adjacent stone wall, which he had fashioned of local pudding stones held together with concrete mortar.

Against the moderate head wind and waves, we made a traverse of four miles across the mouth of a large bay, to reach the tip of Pointe du Thessalon. There, a large motorboat with three men aboard coasted to a stop beside our canoe. We half-expected them to challenge us about something, but they simply wanted to ask us where in the world they were!

Thessalon, also sometimes written as Tessalon, Tossalon, or des Tessalons, meant "The Turning Place" in the Algonquian native languages. This very slender, forest-clad point, extending 11/2 miles southward into the lake, marked the most important and the most heavily traveled junction place along the entire mainline fur trade route.

From this spot, canoes which were headed down the major side branch to the Straits of Mackinac broke off toward the southwest. From the Straits, brigades fanned out for the north shore of Lake Michigan, Green Bay, the Fox-Wisconsin Rivers route, and the upper Mississippi; for the east coast of Lake Michigan, the St. Joseph River or the Chicago River, and the Illinois River; and for the west coast of Lake Huron. All of this water-borne traffic commenced its southward departure from the mainline route at Thessalon Point, and later rejoined the mainline route at this same place. The back of my neck tingled when I realized that the vast majority of our ancestors who had participated in the peltries commerce had each in their turn been at this very spot, where our canoe now floated just off the tip of the elongated point. For example, the trader Claude David had continued westward from here in 1660, traveling to Chequamegon Bay on Lake Superior; the trader Mathieu Brunet dit Lestang had turned toward the southwest here in 1685, bound for the upper Mississippi River; and the trader Robert Réaume had likewise traveled southwestward from here in 1695, headed for Ft. St. Joseph on the St. Joseph River, near the south end of Lake Michigan.

Mackinac-bound canoes had headed out from the end of this point on a southwesterly course, over the ten-mile traverse to Île du Thessalon (Crossing Island), which the British had renamed as Drummond Island in 1815. In case a storm arose during this crossing, there was a small island at the 31/2 mile point where the paddlers could take refuge; this diminutive piece of exposed rock is now called Thessalon Island, its name having been transplanted from the original place of Drummond Island. Additional stops during the traverse could be made as needed on two even smaller islands, at miles six and seven of the crossing. Upon reaching the Île du Thessalon, travelers closely followed its western shoreline, or instead made a five-mile traverse across the mouth of Potagannissing Bay to shave off some miles of distance, to finally arrive at the southwestern corner of the large island. From this place, they made the mile-long crossing westward over the Passage Détour, which brought them to Pointe du Détour, the easternmost tip of the Upper Peninsula. Alexander Henry thus described his westerly, Mackinac-bound voyage through this area in 1761: "We proceeded to the Tossalon, and thence across the lake, making one island after another, at intervals of from two to three leagues...The first land which we made on the south shore was that called Point du Détour."

As we proceeded toward the east from Pointe du Thessalon, we entered after two miles the area that we soon dubbed the "Coast of the Whalebacks." Eastward from here for nearly twenty miles, the offshore area along the entire coastline is sprinkled with hundreds of rounded shoals of pink and greyish black granite. Some of them show their bare backs slightly above the surface of the water, while others lie barely submerged. From the viewpoint of a bald eagle cruising high above, the scene would look much like multiple pods of whales breaching the surface all along the shoreline.

At 12:30, we took a break for 45 minutes on one of the miniature whaleback islands, at mile 50 of our voyage. Although my neck-suspended thermometer measured the air temperature at a comfortable 72 degrees in the shade, the sky above was still completely clouded over. In her explorations, Doree located a few stunted blueberry bushes, as well as some miniature pink wildflowers and scattered blades of short grasses. On this slight rise of otherwise barren bedrock, these brave and hardy plants had managed to flourish in the shallow pockets of soil that had accumulated in a number of cracks in the rock. Gazing directly south from our resting place across fifteen miles of open water, I was able to barely make out the eastern edge of Drummond Island and the western edge of Cockburn Island low on the horizon.

Not long after we resumed our trek, the clouds were completely dispersed by high-altitude winds, leaving in their wake gorgeous, sun-drenched weather. Paddling on the sparking blue water in the dazzling sunlight, we wended our way through the quiet passages that extended between the many whaleback islands and the mainland shore. Along the two miles of lakefront of the Thessalon Indian Reserve, which extends inland for two miles, the entire stretch of shoreline consisted of a beautiful beach of tan sand. This feature stood out in sharp contrast to the rocky shores and the cliffs that we had passed all along the Lake Huron route. Back among the tall pines which stood sentinel behind the expanse of beach, a number of trailer houses were scattered. These represented an updated version of the Ojibwa village which has stood at this location since at least the 1820s. At the easternmost end of this long stretch of pristine sand, we halted at 3:30 for a 45 minute break, taking a refreshing swim and a well-deserved rest.

Further east along the coast, we slipped quietly past a group of about two hundred black ducks resting on the water just south of us. Although we ceased paddling and glided along without making a sound, the birds suddenly rose as a unit from the surface, flapping frantically and quacking loudly. Shortly thereafter, to our amazement, the breeze altered its direction, signalling the arrival of a brand new weather front in the area. Having blown persistently from the east for nearly three days, the wind now changed so that it was coming directly from the south! Unfortunately, the string of large islands far off to our right, some fifteen miles away, were too distant to provide any blockage from this new (but somewhat less troublesome) hindrance to our forward progress.

As we pushed on beside the long expanses of rocky, forest-clad coastline, it occurred to me that I had found less historical information concerning the North Channel area than I had typically gathered before each of our previous paddling jaunts on the mainline route. During my study of early travel accounts over the course of the winter, it had become clear that the descriptions of voyages on the large lakes generally contained far fewer details, compared to period descriptions of trips on rivers and smaller lakes, which were interspersed with interesting names and descriptions of rapids and falls, as well as a considerable amount of information about the passing scenery. However, in Henry Schoolcraft's report of the Lewis Cass Expedition of 1820, he explained that native travelers and French voyageurs had indeed given names to virtually every feature along the shorelines of even the largest lakes. But for the most part, these place names had not been recorded and preserved in the same manner as the names of falls, rapids, and interesting locales along rivers and smaller lakes.

When the Cass party was traveling northward in three large canoes up the western shore of Lake Huron, Schoolcraft recorded his observations about this particular issue:

"The view of the lake, which at first pleases by its novelty, soon becomes tiresome by its uniformity, and the eye seeks in vain to relieve itself, by some rock bluff or commanding elevation upon the shore... We have passed several considerable indentations in the shore, and other places which have names known to the voyageurs, or to the Indians. But as most of them are trifling or ludicrous, and I cannot conceive the bare enumeration of the names of unimportant points and places either useful or interesting, I have omitted to record them, a practice which I propose to adhere to during the future progress of the expedition. The Canadian voyageurs have passed the greater part of their lives along these coasts, and in scenes of hardship and danger. These people are continually pointing out to us places where they have formerly encamped, broke their canoes, encountered difficulties with the natives, or met with some other occurrence, either pleasant or disagreeable, which has served to imprint the scene upon their memories. There is perhaps not two miles along the whole southwestern shore of Lake Huron which is not the scene of some such occurrence. It is by no means certain, however, that such points are designated by name in universal use, even among themselves; and in a country where there are no permanent settlements, local appellations are necessarily subject to be changed, or fall into disuse. There are, however, certain prominent points and features in the topography of every savage country which are universally known by established names among themselves, and deserve to be perpetuated in the permanent geography of the country. Such are the names of all rivers, streams, bays, promontories, and mountains, which are proper subjects to enrich our maps, and to employ the pen of the tourist."

The custom of applying names to numerous features along the route happens to be one of the ingrained traits that I have inherited from my voyageur and trader ancestors. For example, along the quarter-mile stretch of the Devil River where I regularly walk our dog, in the woods behind our house, I have applied these labels to various natural features, in their downstream order: Overhanging Cedar, Sucker Bend, Salmon Bend, Presque Île, Slumped Bank,

Driftwood Bend, Stepping Stones Crossing, Gravel Bar, Dead Skunk Passage, Springhole or Hiding Fawn Bend, and Grandfather Pine.

Shortly after passing Bright Point, a needle-like peninsula that projects for three-quarters of a mile into the lake, we decided to halt for the night, at 7:30. With his sharp eyes, Ben soon spotted a fine place to camp, on a gently rounded stretch of pink granite rising from the edge of the shoreline. On the smooth slab of barren bedrock, shaped and polished over thousands of years by grinding ice chunks and storm-lashed waves, we devoured our stew and then exchanged massages. Lounging atop the expanse of pastel pink stone, our muscles relished the warmth that it radiated, having absorbed the energy of the sun's rays throughout the entire afternoon. How many parties of travelers did this swath of barren granite remember warming and soothing over the last hundred centuries?

During the course of this day, we had covered 26 miles between 6:10 A.M. and 7:30 P.M., mostly against a light-to-moderate head wind and oncoming waves. Having reached mile 61 of our trip, we were now directly north of the eastern end of Cockburn Island and the western end of Manitoulin Island, both of which lay some fifteen miles to the south across the North Channel. During the rest of our journey, we would be traveling parallel to the latter island, which measures nearly a hundred miles in length.

Day Four

When the alarm clock went off at 5:15, we awakened to a crescent of white moon, a sky with only occasional breaks in its solid cloud cover, and a moderate wind from the south. To our utter amazement, it was still 70 degrees out; the air had not cooled at all during the night while we slept! After putting in at 6:00, Doree strongly plied the bow paddle as we dealt with the waves and wind that were coming at our right side. Advancing eastward for two miles, we arrived at a two-mile-long stretch of islands, which we hoped to hide behind to gain some shelter from the offshore wind. However, the area of shallows between the islands and the mainland was completely overgrown with thick beds of tall green reeds. So we were obliged to remain on the exposed south side of the islands, riding up and down on the large swells while dealing at the same time with the ever-growing waves that marched at us in even ranks from the right. It was particularly the rising and falling of the swells that made maneuvering around the numerous whaleback islands and barely submerged reefs a considerable challenge. From her vantage point in the forward seat, Doree kept a close watch for underwater obstacles that would suddenly loom in front of the bow. In each of these instances, she called out directions to guide my steering, and also made her own short-term steering adjustments, drawing or prying to quickly move the bow around the object and out of harm's way. At 7:45, we paused for a 45 minute break on the final easternmost whaleback island, having forged ahead just four miles in 1 3/4 hours. This short respite from the unrelenting hard work felt so good that it was difficult for me to tear myself away and continue onward.

With Ben now in the bow seat, we plodded eastward amid the fast-moving rollers which had developed during the previous hour. These waves, now three to four feet high, some with frothy tops, were coming at us from the right, smacking the hull and splashing over the gunwales. The red nylon canoe cover was doing its job well, sending most of that water back over the sides. To rectify the situation somewhat, I altered our course toward the southeast, to quarter the waves and keep them from broadsiding us. However, I could not maintain that heading for too long, or we would find ourselves many miles from shore.

Near De Roberval Point, we began a two-mile traverse toward the southeast, intending to cross the mouth of Mississagi Bay and head for Tonty Island. Busy with the contentious surf, we did not register that a major thunderstorm had swept in without warning from the southwest, behind our backs, literally and figuratively. Suddenly, at about the midpoint of the crossing, lightning flashed on all sides around us, thunder cracked loudly, and heavy rain fell for a few minutes. At this point, we were about equidistant from the island and the mainland, and it would be very risky to attempt a turnaround in the heavy surf and head for the coast. The most logical solution was to press forward, hoping that our upright bodies, the tallest objects above the surface of the water in this area, would not attract a lightning strike before we could reach the safe haven of the island. Knifing through the waves, Ben and I dug in as hard as we could, while Doree loudly belted out voyageur songs to encourage and strengthen her son and husband. Constantly watching the green lump of land off in the distance in front of the bow, I registered that it did not seem to be getting any closer. However, after what seemed like an interminably long time, we finally landed with sighs of relief on the pine-covered island! Glancing at my watch, I saw that it was 10:00. With plenty of exertion, father and son had progressed five miles in ninety minutes while bucking against the big surf.

Our sheltered landing spot on the northern shore was located in a scenic cove, which was lined with thousands of fist-sized cobblestones beside the water's edge, and was surrounded by high exposed cliffs. Like a hound picking up a scent, Doree clambered up the path leading away from the cove and soon located multiple patches of ripe *bleuets* (blueberries). These hardy bushes had sprung up amid the jumbled, lichen-covered rocks, in the sun-warmed openings between the various stands of pine. Responding to her excited call, we all happily joined in the harvest, with even Toby learning to remove the plump berries from the bushes, using his mouth! After eating a considerable amount of the fruit on the spot and also picking nearly a hat-full, we carried our harvest back down to the canoe. On the wide cobble beach beside the water, we enjoyed a special peanut butter-and-crackers lunch, with a few berries placed on top of each mini-sandwich like a dollop of fresh jam. Afterward, the weather conditions were extremely conducive to our taking a short nap, back beneath the shade of the trees, with a hazy-but-bright overcast sky and an air temp of 81 degrees.

At 11:30, after bailing out all of the accumulated rain and wave water from the floor of the canoe, we departed from this wonderful stopping place on the quiet lee side of the island. The only way to determine if we could manage the heavy surf and the relentless south wind was to leave the sheltered side and give the exposed waters on the opposite side a try. After rounding the east end of Tonty Island, Ben and I paddled southward for 1/10 of a mile through the narrow passageway that extends between it and Hennepin Island. As soon as we encountered the exposed waters of the lake, we found ourselves dwarfed by intimidating waves four to five feet high, the tallest waves that we had ever tried to paddle. These green monsters were breaking with loud crashes and plumes of white spray against the boulder-strewn southern shoreline of Hennepin Island, which we had hoped to skirt along its two-mile length. However, if we were to attempt to continue eastward on that course beside the island, we would have no place of refuge along the coast, which was being lashed by row after row of hard-breaking waves. Making an instant survival decision, we spun the canoe around in the tall surf, sprinted back through the narrow channel between the two islands, and returned again to the northern lee side of Tonty Island. As soon as we could locate a suitable spot to land, we would again be *dégradé* (windbound), having made just nine miles of forward progress in six hours since our morning departure.

At noon, we landed at a fantastic sand beach cove on Tonty Island; we had all noticed this unusually picturesque place a half-hour earlier, while we had been headed eastward. The deep cove, outlined by a gently curved swath of tan sand, was framed at each end by high granite ledges. Behind, the island was thickly covered with stands of white pine, maple, and oak, plus some scattered birches and cedars. At about the midpoint of the beach, a path led back through the woods to the opposite side of the long, slender island, which was about 3/4 mile long and 1/10 mile wide. At the far end of the trail, we discovered an even more impressive sand beach, which lay nestled in a deep rectangular bay that was flanked by even higher walls of solid rock. Back at the edge of our landing site, we came upon a pair of oaks that had grown together into a single unit at their bases when they were quite young. At some point, a beaver had chewed through the outer half of each of these trees, on their opposite sides, yet both of them had continued to live and thrive, long after the beaver had abandoned his project! This pair of beaver-chewed trees, plus the two wonderful beach coves on each side of the island, prompted me to dub this location the Twin Site. Ben gathered several armfuls of dry limbs and kindled a fire beside the landing site, while we parents enjoyed the beach on the opposite side of the island.

This was one of the most attractive resting and camping places that we had ever encountered, during all of our years of paddling the mainline route. What an outstanding place to be windbound! Atop one of the high walls that flanked our landing cove, Doree and I discovered several water-rounded rocks that were completely covered with a thick layer of lush green moss. These green-furred stones were arranged within a bed of old fallen pine needles of a reddish tan hue, and were surrounded by little bracken ferns with delicate fronds of a light green shade. The serene, Zen-like composition reminded us of various formal gardens that we had visited in Japan, in which "natural" settings had been intentionally constructed and nurtured, to inspire introspection in both their caretakers and their visitors.

Years before, four large pine logs destined for a sawmill had washed up onto the beach at our site, parallel to and about fifteen feet back from the water's edge. Storm-driven sand had eventually filled the area on the inland side of these logs, creating flat areas that would serve as our benches and a table. On this providence-provided surface, Doree assembled a delicious stew of dried ground turkey patties, broccoli, and rice, which she smothered in cheddar cheese sauce. After our replenishing meal, we explored the island further, swam, and then sprawled out on rock ledges in the sun.

At 1:30, the air temp measured 80 degrees in the shade; the sky had nearly cleared of its clouds, except for a few white fluffs above the northern horizon. While we lounged and chatted, a wary chipmunk dashed in a brown streak across the beach near us and into the edge of the forest, while a less adventurous one chattered at us from high in the trees. Down by the canoe, a killdeer scampered back and forth on long spindly legs just beyond the reach of the gently lapping waves. Other than a few biting horseflies, there were virtually no insects to bother us at this idyllic site. Ben used a small branch of white pine to lazily swat the flies away from himself, as he soaked up the sun's warmth on a bare rock ledge beside the beach.

Late in the afternoon, when I noticed Ben using the Swiss army knife that he carried suspended from his neck cord, my thoughts drifted back over the items of personal equipment that had been brought on canoe voyages by traders, voyageurs, soldiers, and missionaries. Besides his own paddle and tumpline, each individual usually brought along most of these items: a sheath knife, crooked knife, and clasp knife; eating and drinking containers and utensils; a pipe bag containing pipe, tobacco, firesteel, flint, and fire-starting lens; spare clothing and moccasins, capote (hooded coat), hat, and rain gear; sewing needles, thread, and awl; soap, razor, comb, and tinplate mirror; jews harp and playing cards; a gun in its fabric sheath, with powder horn and powder flask, and a shooting bag containing a ball mold, bulk lead, shot pouch or flask, gunflints, gun worm, and gun repair tools. Some of the high-level individuals also carried with them a compass and maps, as well as writing and mapping materials, which included paper, pen, ink, and sealing wax. Each man transported these items in the canoe in a *poche* or *sac* (cloth bag) or a *cassette* (wooden chest or trunk). These private containers were usually limited in weight to either thirty or forty pounds.

At about six o'clock, the wind that had kept us pinned down finally changed directions; it was now coming from the west, we were elated to observe! This was the very first taste of the supposedly prevailing westerlies that we had encountered on this journey, having endured 2 7/8 days of easterly winds and 1 1/8 days of southerly winds. The new version coming from the west soon whipped up whitecaps that smashed against the rocks at the eastern end of the cove. Although the new wind was too powerful for us to handle, it was at least originating from a direction that inspired hope for the future. If *La Vieille* smiled upon us, she would maintain that westerly direction until the following day! After setting up the tent on an open stretch of sand, we drifted off to dreamland about 9:00. Although we had progressed only nine miles today, we had filled our entire afternoon and evening with memorable times at this special windbound site.

Day Five

"Tim! I don't hear any waves!" Soft calls from my dear wife, hungry for miles, as she awakened me at 4:30 A.M., a full half-hour before the alarm clock was set to ring. Folding back the door flap, I was greeted by the largest and brightest Big Dipper that I had ever seen! All of the stars strewn across the heavens looked absolutely huge, due to their brightness, and particularly the planet Jupiter, which was even more brilliant in its place in the eastern sky. With the light of the quarter-moon dimly illuminating the beach, we packed up quickly and were afloat at 5:15, just as the eastern sky was beginning to brighten.

Within fifteen minutes, we had passed through the channel between Tonty Island and Hennepin Island and were gliding onto the open lake, where we had been turned back the previous morning by huge rollers roaring in from the south. Now, the very same area of water was benign, with rows of low waves advancing casually from the west along our direction of travel. Although the westerly breeze was too light to use the sail, we were still thankful for the direction from which it was blowing. At 6:30, the shimmering golden rim of the sun began to emerge above the waterline directly in front of us, tinting both the water and the sky in shades of yellow and gold. It was already a beautiful day, with a few fat clouds in the sky and a temperature of 65 degrees in the shade. Throughout the entire day of clear weather that lay ahead of us, we would be able to see Manitoulin Island low in the distance, off to the south about fifteen miles.

During the first four hours, Ms. Kent's paddle dug in deeply, pulling the canoe forward at a steady rate over twelve miles of water. We were all buoyed up by both our unhampered forward progress and the many voyageur songs that we warbled. After about five miles, we passed the four mouths of the Mississagi River. The documentation of this name extends back to the earliest decades of the 1600s, when Frenchmen first recorded an Ojibwa clan of that name living in this particular region. An Ojibwa village was located in the specific area of the river mouths from some time before 1760 until at least the 1870s; it was the scene of a productive sturgeon fishery during the summer months, as Alexander Henry noted when he passed by here in 1761. The ownership of the land by the Ojibwa nation was made permanent by the Treaty of 1850, which established the Mississagi Indian Reserve. This irregular plot, measuring about three miles in both length and width, extends eastward from the Mississagi River to the Blind River. Personnel of the N.W.C. established the Mississagi Post in this area during the first decade of the 1800s; it was operated for less than five years. Then the H.B.C. opened a post here in 1821, a facility which was run for several decades. Finally, independent traders operated a post in this area into at least the 1870s. Just to the east of this locale along the coastline, other independent Montreal-based traders established a facility in 1827, which was called Mitchell's Post; it was operated for less than fifteen years.

At 9:15, we took a snack break for 45 minutes on one of the tiny Double Islands. Afterward, when Ben traded places with his mother, the west wind finally increased enough to justify hoisting our little square sail of blue nylon cloth. At long last, the prevailing westerlies had prevailed! With a bulging sail, we surged ahead fourteen miles in 31/4 hours, with a brisk following wind and energetic whitecaps urging us along. It felt exhilarating, and also somewhat nerve-racking, to again be utilizing the sail, since we had not been able to use it a single time during last year's voyage down the Clearwater and Athabasca Rivers, nor during the first four days of this trip. An official square sail had been a standard item of equipment on virtually every voyaging canoe during the French regime, and also for many decades during the British period. We intended to use the sailing rig just as the voyageurs of the fur trade era had done for more than two centuries. We wanted to experience wilderness traveling in ways that were very similar to the traveling that they had done. This included sailing a canoe without a keel, lee board, or fixed rudder, which made for slippery, hair-raising times when the surf was up!

Shortly after leaving the Double Islands, we entered the eastern segment of the North Channel, which contained increasing numbers of islands, as well as larger islands, the further eastward that we traveled. This trend would continue for the remainder of our journey. These islands had provided the voyageurs of old with shelter from contrary winds, and also places to land when conditions became unworkable. By good fortune, we had been blessed this day with a following wind, so we would not need to choose our route through the scattered islands with wind-relief in mind.

After about eight miles with the wind at our backs, we began passing the extensive lands of the Serpent River Indian Reserve, which encompasses about fifteen miles of Lake Huron shoreline and extends inland for two to three miles. An Ojibwa village had stood near the mouth of the Serpent River from before 1830 until at least the 1870s, and the large reserve, extending between the river and the lake, had been established by the Treaty of 1850. Offshore to the south of this reservation land lay two long, slender islands, John Island and Aird Island, which were aligned end to end in an east-west position and had a series of smaller islands filling most of the space between them. The rather straight passage between this string of islands on the right and the mainland on the left, about twelve miles in length and ranging from about one to three miles in width, is called the Whalesback Channel.

Not long after commencing our trek along the length of this passageway, we paused at 1:15 to stretch our legs on Nelles Island. Climbing up to the very highest point on this bedrock island, which sported just a few wind-stunted evergreens, we drank in the magnificent view all around us: the expanses of deep-blue water, the myriad islands, and the coastline stretching off for many miles in both directions. Both the mainland shoreline and each of the islands presented two prominent features: a wide swath of barren rock adjacent to the water's edge, which had been scoured bare by the wind-lashed waves of fierce storms, and a thick green forest covering the rest of the landmass. In many areas, the shorelines consisted of tall sheer cliffs that rose directly from the surface of the water, offering no places to seek refuge if a storm suddenly arose.

While we were lounging on the high vantage point of the island, basking in the scenery and the sun's warmth, my thoughts coursed back some three centuries, to survey the life of our voyageur ancestor Pierre Maupetit dit Poitevin. In my mind's eye, I pictured him with his fellow brigade members passing through this very area of the North Channel during the summer of 1718, on his run from Lachine to the interior and then back out to the St. Lawrence. I wondered at which specific locations along these shores the men had camped during that trip. Maybe they had stopped on this very island!

Born at Lachine (west of Montreal) in 1686, Pierre had a father who had emigrated from France and a mother who was first-generation Canadian-born. During the night of August 4-5, 1689, when Pierre was nearly three years old, he and most of his family lived through the Lachine Massacre. However, his father was among the many French residents who were killed that night by the large force of attacking Iroquois warriors. At that time, Pierre's brother Jean was age 41/2, while his sister Marie Clémence was ten months old. Nine years later, their mother remarried, in 1698. In 1702, when Pierre was sixteen years old, he bound himself as a laboring servant to an employer for three years, since, according to the contract of engagement, he had "no other means of subsistence." During his three long years of servitude, he received just room, board, and clothing; upon the completion of his term, at the age of nineteen, he received as compensation a new suit of clothes and a cow.

In March of 1715, when he was 281/2 years old and still single, our ancestor hired on for an expedition to Michilimackinac and beyond. Although Pierre was described as a "voyageur" in this particular employment contract, his terms of service were understood to also tacitly include his participation as a militia fighter in the planned military expedition against the Fox nation. This recalcitrant native group resided southwest of the Mackinac Straits, in the area near the foot of Green Bay. For his services as a voyageur, Pierre was to be paid four hundred *livres*, and to be fed during his period of employment. In addition, as compensation for his supplemental duties as a militiaman, he was permitted to bring in with him a keg containing seventeen *pots* (seven English gallons) of brandy, as well as a parcel containing four *livres* (4.4 English pounds) weight of vermilion paint pigment; these items were intended for trading with the native populations. He was allowed to transport in these trade items, and later to haul out up to two packs of peltries resulting from this commerce, without having to pay any freighting expenses. It was understood, but not explicitly stated in his contract, that the profit-generating trading was to take place in the Straits region after the military activities had been completed.

During this spring of 1715, in order to recruit militia fighters like Pierre for the Fox campaign, trading licenses were unofficially reinstated (having been for the most part unavailable during the previous seventeen years, when most of the interior posts had been closed). In May, the expeditionary forces, including regular soldiers, militia fighters, and native warriors from the St. Lawrence Valley, departed from Lachine. However, they traveled to the Straits not by way of the customary mainline route, but instead by way of the lower Great Lakes and Detroit, so that they could pick up supplies of corn from the Iroquois south of Lake Ontario and from the Miamis at the western end of Lake Erie. The brigade was scheduled to reach the Straits of Mackinac by mid-August, at the very latest, after which they would continue on for five or six more days to reach the theatre of war west of Green Bay by the end of August.

However, for reasons which were never recorded, the fighters did not arrive at the Straits until September, too late to carry out the military expedition that season. It has long been suggested that many of the men did their trading at Detroit in advance of the campaign, rather than waiting until its completion. But in the autumn, all of the hired men were allowed to either remain at Mackinac or disperse from there, to carry out the commerce which had been promised to them, even though their services as militia fighters had not been called upon. According to Pierre's contract, if he and his employer did not return to Montreal that fall, Pierre was to be *libre* (free) at the Straits, not obliged to work for him through the following winter and spring. It was during this autumn of 1715 that Ft. Michilimackinac was constructed on the southern shoreline of the Straits. This facility was needed to provide secure storage space for the merchandise and supplies of the numerous traders, and to provide buildings in which the newly arrived soldiers could live and work, since they were to be permanently stationed at that locality.

The following May, another large force of militiamen-traders departed from Lachine for the Straits, where they were joined by their counterparts from the previous year, along with many additional traders and warriors from various locales in the interior. After carrying out their campaign against the Fox nation, the assembled voyageurs and traders, totaling about six hundred men, all gathered at Michilimackinac in the latter summer. Those who had traveled in during the summer of 1715 (such as Pierre Maupetit) were obliged to return to the St. Lawrence in the fall, while those who had gone up in 1716 were allowed to remain in the interior and trade over the following season.

Two years later, not long before turning age 32, Pierre hired on again as a summer voyageur, for a round trip between Lachine and the Straits of Mackinac. This time, the brigade traveled along the usual mainline route. Immediately afterward, on September 25, 1718, he married Angelique Villeray, who was ten weeks short of age twenty at the time. During the following decades in which they lived on Île Perrot, west of Lachine, the couple had eleven children over the span of 23 years, between 1719 and 1742. Of these children, three died young, while the remaining eight grew to adulthood, married, and created families of their own. Pierre died on Île Perrot in October of 1759, at the age of 73; thus, he did not live to see the complete vanquishment of New France by the British. He was survived by his wife, his adult children, and many grandchildren, including the line leading down to the present author.

After our 45 minutes of resting and mental time-traveling on the summit of Nelles Island, we set off again, with Doree serving as the *avant*. Zooming along amid the large whitecaps, with the burly wind pushing our taut blue sail, we advanced eleven miles in just two hours. While my life partner paddled with swift, short strokes and I ruddered hard, we managed to keep the canoe upright during that entire distance. Whenever a following wind was powerful enough to bring our speed up to 5 or 6 m.p.h., as it did on this day, it also created tall, fast-moving waves that we were obliged to ride. Traveling at that degree of swift speed was thrilling, but dealing with the constant succession of crests and troughs of slippery waves was heart-stopping! It required my constant attention to maintain the proper direction of the canoe as each speeding wave crest swept underneath us. In each instance, it first lifted up the stern and then the bow, and then dropped the entire hull into the following trough. I could not afford to take my eyes off the movements of the water and the craft for even a moment of relaxation.

The foam-topped waves that were marching down the length of

the Whalesback Channel this particular afternoon became even larger at the eastern end of the passage. There, a row of islands nearly fills the channel between the mainland shore and Aird Island. Zipping through the gap in the row between Passage Island and Shanly Island, we sailed for another two miles to reach the Petit Détroit (Little Narrows).

This extremely slender passageway, between the northeastern corner of Aird Island and the tip of a crooked little peninsula protruding down from the mainland, is just thirty yards wide at its narrowest area. When the lake is pushed by a persistent easterly or westerly wind (such as the westerly one that we had been riding for hours), the water rushes through this narrows in a powerful current, flowing in the same direction as the wind. This was not a place to take casually. Kenneth Wells, in his book about cruising the North Channel, made these comments concerning this passage: "Current is the hazard here, current and the chance one must take of meeting in this rock-rimmed gut that certain type of cruising fool who drives his boat like an automobile. With this last-named problem you will have to deal in your own way. I am not even suggesting that you use a rifle, though it is a fact that the head of such a noisesome creature looks its best mounted like a deer's head and slung under the seat in an old-fashioned outhouse." Little did we know that we would encounter not one but two such boat pilots a half-hour after leaving the Petit Détroit. And I would then hold the same sentiments about where the heads of such individuals ought to end up!

Arrowing through the Little Narrows without incident, we immediately took a well-earned break on the end of Aird Island, to rest for fifteen minutes. Shortly after Ben and I resumed our progress at 4:30, large waves struck the hull from the right rear for a time, coming from the south-southwest as we continued on our easterly heading. This temporary alteration of the wind direction was caused as the following wind was deflected around the land mass of the Petit Détroit, which lay right behind us. When the dominant westerly wind returned, I changed our course toward the southeast. This was necessary so that we could clear the next headland of the mainland shore, which lay about three miles in the distance. Riding the boisterous eastbound waves at an angle, we traveled down the midline area of the McBean Channel. This passage, bounded by the lakeshore on the left and a row of islands on the right, varies in width from about 3/4 mile to 11/2 miles. All the while, we struggled to remain upright, as the already-large waves continued to increase in both size and speed. Even worse, as we traveled on our new course toward the southeast, the brisk wind was pushing the sail at an angle from the right rear, unbalancing the canoe.

At this point, two huge cabin cruisers came directly at us, traveling westbound at a considerable speed right down the middle of the passageway. It was immediately apparent that these boats were not piloted by considerate drivers who abided by the standard rules of watercraft operation! As they approached, they did not alter their course in any way to avoid us, nor did they slacken their speed as they headed straight toward our hull. Although we were struggling with the surf in a modest seventeen-foot canoe, powered by paddles and a little square sail, I was the pilot who was forced to move over to the left, toward the lakeshore, to clear the way for these two engine-powered brutes. Their behavior was in complete disregard of the accepted rules of navigation concerning Right of Way:

"1. Power-driven vessels shall keep out of the way of sailing vessels and vessels which are propelled by oars or paddles.

2. Where one of two vessels [the oncoming cruiser in this case] is required by these rules to keep out of the way, the other [our canoe] shall keep her course and speed; but if from any cause the two vessels are so close that collision cannot be avoided, the latter vessel [our canoe] shall take action to avoid collision.

3. Every power-driven vessel that is required by these rules to keep out of the way of another vessel shall, if necessary, on approaching the other vessel, slacken her speed, or stop, or reverse."

It would have required zero effort for the two cruiser pilots to move off to the side a bit in the generously wide channel, and to slow down as well. Unfortunately, with this incident, my exceedingly low opinion of many motorboat drivers was further solidified.

Immediately after the testosterone-fueled boats had passed by at very close range, we managed to slice through the thrashing seas that were created by the tall waves of their wakes mixed with the large, wind-driven whitecaps. However, in the process of changing course to get out of their way, I had lost the proper positioning that I had previously maintained. That former position had allowed us to hold our angled course in relation to the waves, while also keeping on a heading that would clear the approaching mainland.

We sailed on, flashing forward a total of three miles from the Petit Détroit in just a half-hour. We had never sailed at a faster speed than this 6 m.p.h., and never in such a wild surf as this, with gaping troughs three to five feet deep between the whitecaps! Sometimes, the front half of the canoe went entirely airborne when the stern end dropped into a particularly deep trough. On several occasions, we all had to lean far to the right, to keep the craft from being rolled over to the left by the domineering waves that were striking the hull at an angle from the right rear. All the while, I attempted to keep our bow pointed far enough to the right so that we would clear the landmass of the north shore.

At this point, since we had been forced too far to the left by the powerboats, I decided to ease the bow slightly further toward the right, hoping to clear the approaching shoreline. This increase in the hull's angle to the direction of the waves was apparently more than the canoe could handle. Almost immediately, a massive wave hit us hard from the right side, instantly flipping the craft over to the left.

All four of us surfaced quickly, gasping for breath in the shockingly cold water. Ben grabbed his paddle with one hand and Toby with the other hand, to restrain our canine from striking off toward shore by himself, as was his natural inclination. Rolling the canoe back upright, we were elated to see that both the mast and the sail were still in position, undamaged in the course of the flip-over and ready to harness the wind again! Ben tossed Toby up onto the bow seat, and he and Doree swam alongside while holding onto opposite gunwales, to steady the ungainly, water-filled craft and help it move forward. I slid up onto the mostly-submerged stern seat, sat upright, and ruddered in a not-very-effective manner as we sailed the clumsy, submerged canoe for shore, which lay about half a mile away.

At regular intervals, big eastbound waves surged over the sunken hull. As we slowly sailed northeastward toward the shoreline, the powerful waves pushed the craft further and further toward the right, since I had very little rudder control. Shortly after the capsize, we had been headed for a cobblestone beach; but the canoe soon drifted eastward past it, and we found ourselves advancing toward a barely exposed reef. After about twenty minutes of forward progress, having drifted even further toward the right, we were lined up with another cobble beach. However, as the hull continued to be pushed by the surf toward the right, we appeared to be headed for a stretch of tall sheer cliffs, which would probably offer few places to land along the water's edge. Imagining what might lie in store for us if we were to end up at the base of those cliffs, I ruddered as deeply as I could, hoping to keep the canoe aligned with the cobble beach and away from those ominous-looking walls of barren rock.

As the depth gradually reduced, many of the waves around us curled over at their tops and crashed down onto themselves. In this more dangerous area, I wanted to slow our forward speed by lowering the sail. However, since I had to rudder constantly, I could not release the halyard cord normally, by unlashing it from the thwart in front of me. So I swiftly cut the halyard with the folding knife hanging from my neck cord, and the sail came tumbling down.

After a half-hour of submerged sailing and drifting, we finally reached waist-deep shallows and were able to stand upright in the breaking surf. Moving the canoe closer to the cobblestone shore and into knee-deep water, Doree anchored the bow end securely against her body, keeping the stern of the heaving craft pointed into the oncoming waves and holding the bow so it would not grind against the stone-covered bottom. Then Mother Nature laughed at her: although she was trying her best to hold the canoe in position, an especially powerful wave suddenly knocked her backward into the drink. My dear wife recovered with her usual good humor. For our part, Ben and I hastily unloaded the gear and carried it to shore at a half-run. Then my two family members restrained the bucking, water-filled canoe while I bailed it empty. After hauling our faithful craft onto shore, we all slumped down in tired relief beside it on the rock-covered ground. Assessing the situation, we considered ourselves lucky. No damage had been inflicted on either us or the canoe, and we had not lost any gear!

Since it was only 6:00, there were still several hours of bright sunshine and hearty breeze remaining before dark: good conditions for unpacking everything and spreading it out to dry. Although the "waterproof" bags were usually effective for all-day rainy weather and short-term submersions, thirty minutes or more under water was usually beyond their level of protection. As a result, much of the gear would require drying, and it all had to be checked for water seepage. While we all festooned bushes and boulders with our items of cargo, like the voyageurs had done after a mishap, Doree good-naturedly hobbled around the stony, driftwood-strewn area, considerably hindered by her ankle-support cast. Ben spread out all of the wet maps from the ziplock map case on a flat driftwood board, and weighted them down with small stones.

After setting up the tent and bedding in a cozy place that was nestled back beneath tall pines, out of most of the gusting wind, we prepared a feast on a wood fire near the water's edge. Sheltered from the brunt of the offshore wind behind a thick clump of saplings, Doree assembled a stew containing beef jerky, noodles, mushrooms, carrots, string beans, and apples. That feast was so tasty, and so very much needed to replenish our depleted engines!

A few hours later at dusk, after we had repacked all of the now-dried gear, our campsite appeared as if the capsize had never happened. Hunkered down behind the clump of saplings not far from the crashing surf, we gazed into the leaping orange flames of the fire, relaxed, and recovered our strength after one very demanding day. As the last of the skylight faded away in the west, the entire dome of the heavens turned pitch black and filled with brilliant stars. The temperature was still balmy, registering at 62 degrees.

Around the fire, we discussed where we were. Our emergency landing site was located on the Spanish River Indian Reserve, near its western end. This swath of native-owned land stretches for some fourteen miles along the shoreline, and extends inland toward the north for three to four miles. This reservation, and its counterpart the Serpent River Indian Reserve (beginning three miles to the west), represented some of the largest native landholdings that we had encountered along the entire mainline route. Both reserves had been permanently established by the Treaty of 1850. The mouth area of the Spanish or Sagamuk River had been the site of an Ojibwa village from before 1830 until at least the 1870s. During the latter decades of this period, a H.B.C. post was operated in the same general locale.

Reveling in the gyrating flames of the fire and the brilliant constellations above until 11:00, we finally crawled into the tent and gratefully drifted off to sleep. In my last moments of semi-consciousness, my navigator's ears noted that the solid westerly wind and the pounding surf had not settled down at all. This day, we had advanced 41 miles, from our 5:15 launch until the 5:30 capsize. Doree's first twelve miles had been made without a sail assist; then, during the entire rest of the day, we had traveled under full sail, mostly at thumping-pulse speeds in a heavy surf. Having reached mile 112 of this journey, we were now some 28 miles from the endpoint. Depending on *La Vieille*'s cooperation or lack thereof, that distance could take either hours or days to cover.

Day Six

We had stayed up late the previous evening, watching the fire and star-gazing, and we needed extra rest to restore our energy after the wild events of Day Five. So I had set the alarm for eight hours of delicious sleep, finally rolling out of our sacks at 7:00. The sky was nearly cloudless, the air temperature measured a comfortable 62 degrees, and a soft breeze was wafting from the west. This looked like another fine day for paddling on an easterly course.

Embarking at 8:00, Doree and I made seven miles in 2 1/4 hours without the sail, and then four miles in the next hour with a moderate sail assist, after the wind had increased in velocity. Just a few miles from our campsite, our bow glided silently past a very distinctive feature, on the barren granite shoreline of a rather large island on our right. I imagined that Frenchmen had called this perfectly smooth, dome-shaped formation of bedrock *Le Sein* (The Breast), for its great similarity to a breast of a female human lying on her back. From the top of the dome, a wide vein of pink quartzite angled down to its base and then across a gradual slope of bare rock down to the water's edge, about thirty feet away, finally disappearing beneath the lake. The atmosphere felt ancient here. We imagined that many groups of native people over the millennia had considered this unusual formation to be a "Spirit Stone," in which certain of their deities lived. They may have perceived its form as the head of a serpent or a bird, with the dome representing the rear of its skull and the gradually declining slope down to the water representing its elongated snout. This fold of once-molten rock had vivid memories of the passing of thousands of canoes over the course of myriad generations. It remembered the gifts of tobacco and other items which the travelers in those canoes, both native and French, had offered to it.

About five miles after leaving our campsite, the western end of the Montagnes de la Cloche (Mountains of the Bell, now called the La Cloche Mountains) came into view. This chain of rounded, green-clad hills of Canadian Shield granite, extending up to heights of about six hundred feet, runs eastward in a continuous range from here along the full length of the northern shore of Lake Huron and Georgian Bay. At one place along the chain, we slid past a long but rather narrow swath of white quartzite bedrock, which for some reason was nearly barren of the usual covering of evergreen trees. Since this eye-catching feature ascended from the water's edge all the way up the gradual slope to the very crest of the range of hills, we dubbed it the "Queen's Staircase."

At 11:15, we took a half-hour break on the eastern tip of McTavish Island. While we rested and stretched our legs, I mentioned to the family that the N.W.C. had established Fort La Cloche two miles northeast of here on the mainland shore, at the mouth of the Rivière de La Cloche, in 1808. This trading facility had been operated for more than fifty years, first by Nor'westers, and after the amalgamation of the two fur trade companies in 1821, by personnel of the H.B.C.

After our pause on the island, Ben took on the bow paddling duties, since his mother had completed eleven miles during her morning shift in that seat. The wind from the west-northwest had picked up considerably during our time on the island, so that our sail now hurled the canoe forward at about 5 m.p.h. for three miles. Then, the puffing wind finally became too strident for us to handle safely on our present course. We had been traveling more than a mile from shore, racing over the water well to the right of the chain of small islands which parallels the coastline along this stretch. Deciding to travel much closer to the shore, I made a hard left turn and steered our bow through the narrow gap between Hog Island and Channel Island. With the wind and waves coming at us from the left, we pushed forward for 11/2 miles, gliding right up to the base of the La Cloche Mountains, where they rose directly from the water's edge in dramatic fashion.

Having covered five miles in the short span of sixty minutes, we landed at 12:45 for an hour-long break, on a long but slender expanse of beach which was composed of millions of water-worn pebbles. Lounging on my back at this special place, where the glistening blue water met the foot of the green mountain chain, I marveled at the weather that we had been granted: an unblinking dazzling sun, a number of puffy white clouds skating across a pale azure sky, an air temperature of 72 degrees in the shade, and a hefty breeze out of the west-northwest. When it was time to end our break and press on, I had difficulty leaving such a lovely resting place. However, the rest of my family members, finding themselves just a dozen or so miles from the end of the voyage, had begun to salivate and plan the magnificent feast that we would devour when we would eventually come out. Ben went so far as to describe every ingredient of his "super salad;" he even noted how each piece would be cut!

Over the next seven miles, we thoroughly relished traveling at a peaceful rate of speed very near the shoreline, skirting the base of the La Cloche Mountain range. By crowding the shore, I utilized the tall, forest-covered slopes to block most of the wind. In the crystal clear water below us, we could see down to considerable depths along this entire stretch. It was particularly fascinating, and also a little spooky, to observe on the bottom the long decline of cobblestones that extends out for a considerable distance from the water's edge. Each of us was entranced by the above-water and below-water scenery along this segment of the trip.

Peering deeply into the lake, which had a light greenish tint, I considered the great importance of fresh water to all living things throughout the world. Paddling along the surface of this third-largest lake in the world, which contains some 850 cubic miles of fresh water, I was struck by how very blessed the United States and Canada are with natural resources, including this precious liquid. A full 97 percent of the Earth's water is salty, while another 2 percent is held in the polar ice caps. Thus, only 1 percent of the water in the world is drinkable. As the population on the globe burgeons, the demand for fresh water is soaring. At the same time, all over the world, wetlands are shrinking dramatically, and underground aquifers are being pumped out much faster than they are being replenished. The resource of fresh water, and the questions of who owns it and who is entitled to it, will become huge issues in the not-so-distant future.

As I paddled, I mulled over these facts: the world population, now more than 6.7 billion, has increased by a half-billion in just the previous five years. In fact, there has been more human population growth during the last fifty years than during the previous four million years! The world population is now expanding at the rate of about 80 million people per year, while the urban population is now greater than its rural counterpart worldwide. About fifty years from now, the population of the Earth is projected to reach some 9.5 billion people. Then, if we are smart, it will begin to reduce if we all accept worldwide population planning and birth control. The

U.S. population, which has now surpassed 300 million, will likely increase by another 120 million people during the next half-century, before leveling off.

At the present time, about one billion people live in the rich First World countries, representing only 14 percent of the world's population. However, our wealthy lifestyle in these countries produces about a hundred times more stress on the planet than the lifestyles in developing countries. We citizens of the First World countries possess the majority of the world's resources, including fresh water. As a result, a great deal of the responsibility for conserving, wisely using, and sharing those resources must fall on our shoulders. Much of the future of the human race depends upon our actions. Although I find the quiet solitude of wilderness canoe trips very inspirational for thinking about the people and lifeways of the past, I also find it conducive to considering the long-range future of the world as well.

When we arrived at the tip of Pointe Plat (Flat Point), we decided to make a traverse from the base of the mountain range across the mouth of the nine-mile-deep Baie des Îles (Bay of the Islands), to reach Great La Cloche Island. At a location further into the bay, we could have paddled from island to island across its width. However, in a quick conference, we instead chose to cross in a single straight shot, on a course that lay well to the west of the outermost islands. This, however, turned out to be a risky decision!

Shortly after commencing the 21/2 mile traverse, as we traveled on a southeasterly heading, the wind suddenly kicked up boldly as we moved away from the sheltering mountain range. In addition, dark clouds swooped in from the west to cover much of the sky, blocking the sun and making the situation seem ever more threatening. With the blustery wind and the vigorous waves coming at us from behind our right shoulders, Doree and I sped across the expanse of turbulent water in a rather harrowing half-hour. While Ben dozed blissfully with Toby beneath the canoe cover, we parents paddled in silence, except when Doree quietly sang French songs to calm herself. At the end of the strenuous crossing, just off Wells Island, we dived into a quiet cove behind a tiny islet, to catch our breath and let our heart rate subside for a few minutes while floating on the still surface. During this short pause, I contemplated the serene stretch of seven miles that we had relished in peace along the base of the mountain range, followed immediately by this wild passage that we had made with racing hearts across the mouth of the bay. In the process, an old French proverb came to mind: *"Après la pluie, le beau temps"* (literally, "After the rain, the good times;" figuratively, "Good and bad things come one after another"). Wilderness canoe trips are much like life.

Rounding the southern end of Wells Island, we landed on the nearby Grande Île de la Cloche (Big Island of the Bell, now called Great La Cloche Island). At first, Doree and I stretched out on the rolling folds of barren bedrock at the shoreline, letting our tensions unwind and our muscles relax. Then we all climbed up to a higher vantage point, to get an overview of the span of water which we had just traversed. Behind the wave-tossed expanse stood the string of La Cloche Mountains, marching eastward beside the lakeshore, thickly covered with a dark green forest. During our break of 45 minutes on the island, Doree located and picked a good amount of ripe blueberries (as usual), while the wind settled down, the sinister dark clouds moved on, and the sun in the west resumed its reassuring smile.

Surveying the entire scene of water, islands, mainland, and sky, my thoughts drifted off into the distant history of this area. Etienne Brulé had been the first documented Frenchman to travel the entire length of the North Channel of Lake Huron, reaching Lake Superior in 1618. Sixteen years later, in 1634, Jean Nicolet had been the first known European to take this passageway as far as Thessalon Point and then head southwestward to the Straits of Mackinac and on to Green Bay. Beginning in 1653, considerable numbers of French traders had paddled back and forth over the North Channel, to carry out their business transactions at the Sault, the Straits, and many other points toward the northwest, west, and southwest. Our own ancestors, beginning with Claude David, had paddled the full length of the North Channel from 1660 onward. As a result of this considerable amount of canoe traffic, detailed knowledge of the complex route of the Channel, with its myriad islands and indented coastlines, had been committed to paper by the French at an early date. From 1657 on, French maps had reflected a clear understanding of this region, with an amazing degree of accuracy.

A large Ojibwa village had long been located on the eastern shore of Great La Cloche Island, some three miles southeast of our resting place, as Alexander Henry had noted when he passed by here in 1761. The native community had thrived at this particular location until at least the 1830s, its population fed by the corn crops that the people raised on various of the islands in the area.

The name La Cloche (The Bell) prevails in this region, having been applied to the long mountain range that follows the north shore of Lake Huron, the peninsula which juts southward into the lake for nine miles from that shoreline, and the large island and small island which lie just west and south of that peninsula, respectively. Each of these features was named after a very unusual rock that had been located in this area since time immemorial. Although many French travelers had been shown the amazing stone lying near the shoreline, which they had dubbed La Cloche, the Anglo trader Alexander Henry had been the first observer to describe it in writing, in 1761: "There is here a rock, standing on a plain, which, being struck, rings like a bell." Six decades later, when the International Boundary Commissioners were surveying the border between the U.S. and Canada in 1822, John Bigsby provided further details: "It is so called from some of its rocks ringing like a bell on being struck. This particularly applies to one loose basaltic mass lying on the shore, fifteen miles below the Little Sagamuc [Little Serpent River], about three yards square." When Eric Morse was studying and traveling the fur trade canoe routes during the 1950s and 60s, he investigated the situation and later reported, "I had personally been somewhat skeptical of a rock ringing like a bell, and when paddling through was interested to try to track down this curiosity. We were fortunate in finding with no trouble a man who had seen it and knew its location. He took us to a mass of dark basalt, obviously an 'erratic' deposited by a passing glacier, and which when hit with a rock gave out a clear note --- not high-pitched, but a low note reminiscent of a bell-buoy." That magical stone was located in the area where Great La Cloche Island, Little La Cloche Island, and the southern tip of the La Cloche Peninsula all converge.

Immediately south of Great La Cloche Island, seven miles southwest of our lofty resting spot on that landmass, lies Manitoulin Island, across the Little Current Channel. This island, nearly one hundred miles long and containing 1,068 square miles of land, is the largest fresh-water island in the world. Its name, Ekaentout or Île Manitoualin, reflected the ancient belief of the native peoples of the region, who considered it to be the residence of certain of their Manitous, powerful spirits. This offshore landmass was part of the traditional territory of the Ottawa nation, as was also the smaller island lying immediately to the west of it, Little Manitou Island (now called Cockburn Island). In many places on the large island, the soil was sufficiently fertile to grow modest crops of corn. Before 1830, part of the Ojibwa population from the north shore of Lake Huron had joined the long-time Ottawa residents on Manitoulin Island. This was reflected in the Treaty of 1850, in which the entirety of both Manitoulin Island and Cockburn Island were granted to these two native nations. By about 1870, the larger island supported five combined-nation villages as well as one community which was entirely occupied by Ojibwas, while Cockburn Island had a single village which was inhabited by Ottawas. Only one trading post was ever located on Manitoulin Island, at the settlement of Little Current, adjacent to Great La Cloche Island. This facility, opened some time during the first two decades of the 1800s, was operated for less than five years.

Setting off in an easterly direction at 6:00, we reveled in our final, hour-long paddle over placid waters, covering two miles along the northern shoreline of Great La Cloche Island and then two miles across the La Cloche Channel. We finally reached the shoreline of the La Cloche Peninsula, which would mark the finale of this year's canoe trip. Approaching the outermost edge of the little native community of Birch Island at 7:00, we glided past a tiny private lighthouse on a small point of land. The octagonal building, constructed of split stones of a brownish tan color secured with white mortar, had been fitted with a tall, brown-shingled roof in eight segments; a tiny white cupola at the peak housed the beaming light. The diminutive structure looked very much like a *pigeonnier* (dovecote for domesticated pigeons) that one would find at an ancient *manoir* in France!

The tiny settlement called Birch Island, containing some forty homes, is the main settlement on the Whitefish River Indian Reserve. This piece of native-owned land includes the entire nine-mile length of the La Cloche Peninsula, a twisting landmass in the form of a backward S which extends southward from the shoreline of Lake Huron. This projection of land ranges in width from a maximum of about six miles down to 1/2 mile at its slender waist, at the midpoint of the peninsula where the town is located. At its southern tip is located Dreamers Rock, where young men and women sought to connect with their lifelong protector spirit through a vision quest, induced by sleep deprivation, lack of food, and minimal water. Immediately south of the peninsula, about five miles from our halting place at the town of Birch Island, is Little La Cloche Island, separated from the peninsula by the Boat Passage. Westbound canoes on the mainline fur trade route had customarily traveled along this Boat Passage and then northward along the La Cloche Channel (between the La Cloche Peninsula and Great La Cloche Island to the west), to reach the north shore of Lake Huron. The community of Killarney, where we had ended our voyage along the northern shoreline of Georgian Bay eleven years earlier, is located seventeen paddling miles east of Little La Cloche Island.

After unloading our canoe at the public boat landing, just beyond the edge of town, Doree, Ben, and Toby sauntered into the little village, to locate a telephone and call our shuttle driver at Sault Ste. Marie. Staying with our belongings, I brought the journal and map up to date. This day, we had advanced 28 miles in eleven hours on the water, from 8 A.M. to 7 P.M. We had completed the entire excursion of 140 miles in six days, from Sunday morning to Friday evening, having spent two of those days windbound. On those two days when we had been *dégradé*, we had made only six and nine miles, respectively, in the early-morning hours before being forced to shore. Thus, on the four main traveling days, we had covered a total of 125 miles: 30 and 26 miles against contrary winds, and then 41 and 28 miles with helpful winds. Our ratio of windbound days to paddling days, one to three, had matched closely the experiences of the voyageurs of old when they had traveled on the massive lakes.

We had been blessed with outstanding weather on this trip: warm temperatures during both daytimes and nighttimes; mostly bright, sunny days; and starlit and moonlit nights, which had aided considerably with our pre-dawn departures.

When Doree contacted our driver by phone at about 8 P.M., he indicated that he had just settled into his regular Friday night poker game at a friend's house. Ms. Kent said that we would wait patiently, and he indicated that he would head out to retrieve us at the conclusion of his card-fest. However, we had no way of knowing that he would play until 1:00 A.M., and would finally reach us three hours later, after the drive of 160 miles from the Sault!

Several hours into what would eventually be an eight-hour wait for our van to arrive, Doree and I took a leisurely walk toward town. However, at the edge of the community, when we heard the loud shouts of a drunken guy, followed by the violent sounds of glass shattering, we turned back, hoping that we would not have any obnoxious late-night visitors at the boat ramp during our long wait there. When the air temperature dropped below the comfort level, we unpacked the sleeping bags and sacked out on the grass-covered ground. During the several hours that we spent in our cozy cocoons on the exposed surface, I fervently hoped that no rattlesnakes would crawl into our bags seeking warmth. Over the course of the previous several decades, these serpents had been occasionally sighted as far west as Little Current on Manitoulin Island, about nine miles southwest of our location. However, they generally stayed further to the east, close to the mouth of the French River. The prospect of visiting rattlers and drunks did not make for a very restful nap.

Our return home to Oak Park and my return to work signalled my final weeks as a trumpet player. Eight years earlier, I had decided with Doree that I would retire from the orchestra at the earliest feasible time, so that I could devote myself full time to researching, writing, and publishing. I had already gathered enough original historical data to write about a dozen major books, and I was still avidly continuing my research. However, between the orchestra's heavy schedule of rehearsals and concerts and my own practicing schedule, there was simply not enough additional time available to actually bring to completion all of these extensive projects while working the CSO job.

To reach our goals, Doree and I had established an ambitious savings plan, which we had carried out over an eight-year period. First, we paid off our Oak Park house, and then our Michigan retirement house (my boyhood home, which we purchased from my parents, who had lived there since 1948). We then amassed enough savings so that we could live comfortably without any other income for another 121/2 years after my retirement at the age of 471/2, until the orchestra pension would begin at age sixty. The major advantage that we held in reaching our financial goals was that, through our combined salaries, we had a very substantial income compared to our very modest material aspirations. We firmly believed in that old adage, "He who believes he has enough is rich."

The first two weeks of September in 1996 were filled with my last foreign tour, involving various venues in the British Isles, after which I played seven weeks of concerts back home in Orchestra Hall.

Finally, Sunday, November 3 marked my very last day as a trumpet player, which brought a number of sensations, including happiness, relief, lightness, and just a touch of sadness.

My career as a musician was at its end. At the age of 471/2, I had retired even before reaching the peak of my playing abilities, at a time when I knew that I was still improving slightly every single week. I was also at least two decades younger than the typical age for retirement by Chicago Symphony members.

During my younger days, I had wholeheartedly devoted nearly twenty years of effort to preparing myself for a career as a high-level professional player. Then, beginning in January of 1979, I had spent a total of 6,500 days, nearly eighteen years, in the finest symphonic trumpet section in the very best of the major-league orchestras. My biggest dreams had come true, and I had experienced a wonderfully rich and satisfying array of musical adventures.

However, along the way, I had also immersed myself in an entire series of historical activities in which I was doing original and pioneering independent work. This led me down an exciting, enticing, and challenging new career path, one that required my full time attention. Thus, the complete and permanent metamorphosis from musician to historian was very attractive and exciting to me, not in the least bit daunting. During most of my teen and adult years, I had pushed myself beyond the comfort zone and had forged into new and unfamiliar territory. This new chapter of my life was simply a continuation of that pattern.

In January, we prepared our Oak Park house for sale, sold it within two days of putting it on the market, quickly thinned out our belongings, and moved to Michigan on March 30. After a quarter-century of historical research preparation and more than eight years of financial preparation, our next chapter had finally begun.

XVI
Fourteenth Voyage
Lake Winnipeg
June 30-July 12, 1997

May you live all the days of your life.
Jonathan Swift

As a well-spent day brings happy sleep,
So a life well spent brings happy death.
Leonardo Da Vinci

What gives value to travel is fear.
Albert Camus

We were now prepared to paddle over most of the length of Lake Winnipeg, the tenth largest freshwater lake in the world. This body of water, 280 miles long, has 9,300 square miles of surface area, more than that of Lake Ontario and nearly equal to that of Lake Erie. The North Basin of the lake, comprising about two-thirds of its length, has a maximum width of 68 miles, while the South Basin has a maximum width of 25 miles. These two portions are joined at the slender waist of Le Détroit (The Narrows), a passageway which is just two miles wide. Although Lake Winnipeg has a maximum depth of 190 feet at one spot, it is rather shallow in most areas, with only the middle portion of the North Basin extending down more than fifty feet, and virtually all of the South Basin having less than thirty feet of water. Extensive areas throughout the lake have less than eleven feet of depth.

During the entire fur trade era, Lake Winnipeg had the wicked reputation of being the most treacherous lake on the entire mainline canoe route. The convergence of several elements of nature in the area of the lake produced this killer reputation. The first element is the general shallowness of the lake, averaging only forty feet over the entire body of water; this lack of depth allows its surface area

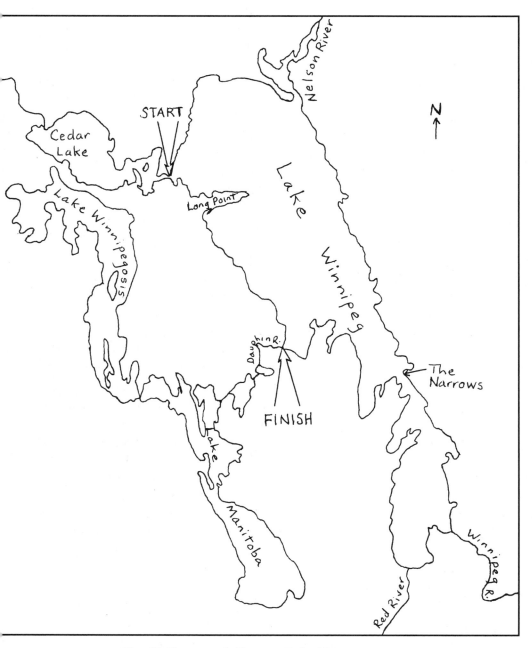

Fig. 17, Fourteenth Voyage: Lake Winnipeg

to be whipped into a frenzy in a very short time. In addition, this long swath of shallow water lies at the eastern edge of the prairie, a vast region of open grassland which offers few obstacles to the powerful winds that huff across it from various westerly directions. Making the situation worse, the entire western shore of the lake is very low and flat, presenting no blockage to these prevailing westerly winds. Localized weather fronts in the area of the lake also create strong winds blowing from many directions, as the relatively cold temperature of the lake water contrasts with that of the surrounding landmass absorbing the heat of the sun each morning. This great contrast of temperatures leads to a regular pattern of furious winds and waves kicking up in the latter morning or the early afternoon on a great many days.

The shallow waters of the lake typically respond to winds from all sources by producing closely-spaced waves with steep fronts, which readily spill over the gunwales of a canoe even when the waves are not excessively tall. The artist Paul Kane noted in 1848 that the waves of this lake, "from the shallowness of this wide expanse of water when set in motion by a heavy wind, are far more abrupt and dangerous for boats [and canoes] than those of the Atlantic."

To this dangerous mix of wind and water was added another element, the considerable distance from shore at which voyageurs were often obliged to travel on this lake, for two reasons. First, the extremely shallow water often extends for a mile or more from the shoreline, causing the waves to break far out from shore. As a result, travelers often sought smoother and easier paddling out beyond the distant breaking waves. In addition, a great deal of the western coastline above The Narrows consists of large points jutting well out into the lake. Traveling along these points and the adjacent bays would entail either intolerably slow progress while skirting the shoreline or instead, the riskier approach of making up to ten potentially dangerous traverses across open water at the mouths of the bays. The shortest of these ten crossings, even when hopping from island to island, involved a distance of four to five miles, which would take an hour or more to paddle. The conditions of wind, weather, and water on this lake could alter drastically in a much shorter interval than an hour.

So, the sudden arrival of strong winds that would very quickly kick up treacherous waves on the shallow body of water, coupled with the canoes very often traveling at a considerable distance from shore, created an extremely dangerous combination. Travel journals of the fur trade era are replete with tales of almost daily frightening experiences on Lake Winnipeg, sometimes including the loss of entire canoes with their paddlers and cargo. For example, when Alexander Henry traveled northward up the lake with his brigade in 1775, he recorded, "We encountered a severe gale, from the dangers of which we escaped by making the island called the Buffalo's Head, but not without the loss of a canoe and four men."

Taking advantage of those rare times when winds were not whipping the lake into a maelstrom often involved night paddling for the brigades. For instance, when the Franklin Expedition was headed northwestward on the lake in three large canoes in 1819, bound for their first exploration of the Arctic region, Lieutenant Hood observed, "A moderate gale raises the waves so high that boats [and canoes] seldom venture from the shore, and are sometimes detained many days with a small stock of provisions. Having a fair breeze, this consideration induced us to run all night." Along the same lines, the H.B.C. trader Robert Ballantyne noted while traveling down the lake in 1845, "We...had a good deal more night traveling than heretofore."

The mainline canoe route over Lake Winnipeg, extending between the mouth of the Saskatchewan River near the north end of the lake and the mouth of the Winnipeg River near its south end, ran along the western shore of the North Basin, across the two-mile-wide Détroit, and along the eastern coast of the South Basin. The eastern coastline of this entire body of water lies adjacent to the edge of the granite Canadian Shield, while the western coast, consisting of limestone, is located within the prairie geological region. The primary forest cover of the overall lake area is made up of spruce and tamarack (larch), with some scattered stands of jack pine, balsam fir, maple, oak, birch, and poplar. The fascinating tamarack tree, a relative of the pines, has soft needles instead of broad, flat deciduous leaves; yet it is technically a deciduous tree, since it sheds its needles each autumn.

Our route down the lake, traveling from north to south in a generally south-southeasterly direction, would pass through the traditional lands of the Cree and Assiniboine nations. In fact, Lake Winnipeg had sometimes been called the Lake of the Crees during the fur trade era. In the latter portion of this period, groups of Ojibwas had moved into the more southerly areas around the lake.

This was to be our first canoe trip on the mainline route since Doree and I had moved from Illinois to Michigan in March of 1997. To join us for the voyage, Ben drove through the night from our former community of Oak Park, arriving in Ossineke at 7:00 on Sunday morning. He had just completed four months of traveling and backpacking in California, the Southwest, and finally Missouri. Within an hour of his arrival, we had packed the van and were on the road toward the northwest. Our drive to the put-in at Grand Rapids, Manitoba took a total of 27 hours, including a half-hour restaurant break in Minnesota at 10 P.M. Along the way, we chose a highway route to Winnipeg that took us by way of Kenora, Ontario, rather than the more customary route via Grand Forks and Fargo, where there had been extensive and far-reaching flood damage along the Red River corridor during the spring thaw. In the early morning light, while I was driving along the east side of Lake of the Woods south of Kenora, I passed on two different occasions a solitary red fox standing beside the road. I interpreted each of these sightings as a clear sign of good luck during the upcoming paddling voyage. (I could not have foreseen that the events of the following two weeks on the water would unfold in a manner which was slightly less rose-colored.)

Day One

Since this was June 30, Ben's nineteenth birthday, we parents cheerfully chirped *Happy Birthday* to him at dawn, when he awakened on the sleeping platform in the rear half of the van. This was to be his fifteenth summer of long-distance wilderness paddling with us. Arriving at the small community of Grand Rapids, we breakfasted at a little restaurant near the mouth of the Saskatchewan River, and ordered a good supply of burgers to take out, for our meals later in the day. We then located the home of Gib and Audrey Hobbs, our shuttle drivers for this trip; they are the parents of Fred Hobbs, who had been our shuttle driver for the Saskatchewan River trip five years earlier. The Hobbs couple would keep our van at their home, and then drive it to us at the end of our voyage. Gib was originally from the grain-farming region of southern Manitoba, while Audrey had been a life-long resident of Grand Rapids. Born and raised on the Cree reservation there, she was descended from both Cree ancestors and a H.B.C. Scots trader named MacKay, who had been posted first at

Cedar Lake on the lower Saskatchewan River and then at the Grand Rapids near the mouth of the river.

As we loaded the canoe in the shallows of Lake Winnipeg, at a diminutive park beside the mouth of the Saskatchewan River, two large Vs of Canada geese flew high overhead, heading northward. The encouraging honking of the lead birds in each wedge, although intended for the geese following behind them, bolstered our spirits as well. Pushing off at 11:30 A.M., under leaden skies emitting a light rain, we had a moderate wind and waves coming from the east and an air temperature of 50 degrees. Traveling toward the south-southeast, the canoe bobbed like a cork amid the unending rows of troughs that came directly at our left side. There was little I could do to alter our direction to the easterly waves and wind, since we did not wish to head out across the lake, but instead to travel down its western coastline. Laboring hard, Doree and I pulled the craft slowly past many areas of shoreline that were covered with pebble beaches. These long expanses of wave-polished stones, having only a very slight rise in elevation, were entirely clear of all vegetation for about twenty feet back from the water's edge. This lack of all growing plants was a clear indicator of the ferocity of the storms that regularly lashed the shores of this lake.

After about an hour, the light rain halted, the pewter-colored sky brightened somewhat, and the air temp rose to 55 degrees. However, during that same hour, the wind from the east had increased considerably in its velocity, now filling the lake with row upon row of whitecaps. Just before reaching Jackpine Point, we landed at 1:30 for a much-needed break, on a broadly curved bay which was edged with a tan-colored beach of pebbles. With a considerable output of effort, we parents had advanced five miles in two hours, amid rows of large waves and deep troughs that were constantly striking and rocking the hull from the side.

To celebrate Ben's *joyeux anniversaire*, the three crew members plus the mascot Toby consumed four of the cheeseburgers from the restaurant, relaxed for a bit in the wan sunlight, and then explored the area. Immediately inland from the lake and its flat pebble beach stood a broad, three-foot-tall ridge of broken pieces of limestone, which had been heaped up by centuries of storm-driven waves and massive, jostling cakes of thick lake ice. Behind this rough ridge stood a narrow screen of willows and poplars, and beyond these stretched a little reed-covered lake, which looked much like a green meadow. In an open pond at the middle of this marshy area, a dome-shaped beaver lodge stood offshore, adjacent to the shoreline. Back at Lake Winnipeg, after hiking along the limestone-strewn coastline to the end of Jackpine Point, we checked out the conditions in the unsheltered waters on the far side of the point; to our dismay, the waves were entirely unworkable! During our return walk, Ben found two piles of beaver scat near the point. Back by the canoe, Doree spotted an impressive fossil in one of the larger slabs of limestone. The remains of this creature from millions of years ago consisted of a ten-inch-long, gradually tapered column of 25 rounded segments, which closely resembled the series of vertebrae of a spinal column.

Later in the afternoon, the sky cleared to a robin's egg blue dome containing scattered thin smears of white. While the strong breeze continued to blow steadily from the east, the air temp rose to 60 degrees. At one point, five white pelicans cruised by quite close to us, in a linear formation barely above the surface of the water. I marveled at their ability to fly at such a low altitude while flapping their wings so infrequently.

After we had napped and read books for hours, we hoped that the unsheltered water beyond the point had calmed enough to continue our travels. However, after putting in at 7:40 and rounding Jackpine Point, we found ourselves in large whitecaps that were crashing onto the rock-strewn shoreline. Dashing for the safety of land, I steered the bow through a narrow passageway between a number of offshore boulders. Unloading the bucking canoe in knee-deep shallows amid the heavy surf, we finally carried the craft onto the shore of broken chunks of limestone, and called it a day at 8:00.

Setting up camp back in the sheltering woods, in a tiny clearing amid a swath of wind-felled trees, we traded massages, read our books further, and finally fell into an exhausted sleep at 10:30. This day, in 81/2 hours between 11:30 A.M. and 8:00 P.M., we had advanced just five miles, and had been windbound twice already.

Day Two

When the alarm clock jolted me from my dreams at 4:45 A.M., I was greeted by a stunning orange-tinted eastern horizon, and a thin sliver of crescent moon hanging low in the west. During the night, the strength of the wind had reduced somewhat, and it had shifted direction; it was now coming from the north-northeast. Under a cloudless sky with an air temperature of 50 degrees, we quickly broke camp, loaded the canoe amid large submerged boulders in moderate waves, swallowed a few bites of gorp, and set out at 5:45. As we commenced a southeasterly traverse from Jackpine Point across the mouth of the adjacent, deeply rounded bay, our green hull passed over the top cable of a suspended gill net. Within ten minutes of leaving the campsite, the wind picked up suddenly, the waves grew menacing, and the situation became too rough to handle. So I aimed the bow southward and we hustled a mile-and-a-half toward shore, to land at the bottom of the bay at 6:30. The beautiful beach of tan sand which greeted us, offering a smooth surface and a very gradual incline, provided an ideal place for a landing, immensely better than the inhospitable, rock-strewn one from which we had just departed. We felt fortunate to have reached this very pleasant place. However, none of us could see into the future to realize just how long the wind would lock us down onto this lovely stretch of beach.

Beside our landing spot, a long string of fresh wolf tracks in the wet sand skirted the water's edge for a considerable distance. The five-inch-long impressions, including four toe pads, four long claws, and a large heel pad, lay in a nearly straight single line, in which the hind paws had landed either near or directly on top of the tracks of the front paws. In my mind, I visualized a massive and wise elderly male, nearing the end of his fifteen-year life, passing along this very coastline just minutes before our arrival. Maybe he had watched us come into the bay before trotting off into the woods.

Exploring inland from our landing site, we discovered a small lake, sheltered from the brunt of the offshore wind by the screen of near-shore trees and bushes. This little body of water sported a sparkling blue surface and a grass-covered shoreline. Back at the narrow strip of Lake Winnipeg beach, while we consumed our breakfast of peanut butter crackers and dried apple slices, a stiff wind kicked up. Its persistent blasts filled the lake as far as we could see with rows of tall whitecaps, which rolled in and crashed onto the beach at our feet.

Pinned to the land at this spot, I was reminded of the reactions of the H.B.C. trader Ballantyne when he traveled down this body of water in the summer of 1845, en route from Norway House (at the north end of Lake Winnipeg) to Montreal: "There is nothing more distressing and annoying than being wind-bound in these wild and uninhabited regions. One has no amusement except reading, or promenading about the shores of the lake. Now, although this may be very delightful to a person of a romantic disposition, it was anything but agreeable to us, as the season was pretty far advanced, and the voyage long; besides, I had no gun [for the diversion of hunting], having parted with mine before leaving Norway House." After two more days of battling the winds and advancing only a short distance, the party was again land-locked on shore for multiple days, to the trader's despair: "We have no amusements except reading a few uninteresting books, eating without appetite, and sleeping inordinately...It is now four days since we pitched our tents on this vile point. How long we may still remain is yet to be seen."

In our case, we were not in any danger of being caught by winter weather far short of our destination, as was the situation with the Ballantyne party. As a result, we could be much more relaxed and philosophical about the delays, taking Ralph Waldo Emerson's approach: "Adopt the pace of nature. Her secret is patience." Since my natural inclination is to seek activity at all times (mental, physical, or both), I had to stretch some and reframe the situation as being good for my development, then accept it and adopt a patient attitude. By nature, Doree tended toward accepting whatever Mother Nature brought and being optimistic. On this particular trip, Ben was somewhere between the two of us in attitude.

As we read books, napped, and absorbed the warmth of the sun, gulls and crows occasionally circled overhead on the wind currents, checking out the intruders. To pass the time further, I gathered various items of gill net fishing gear that had washed up along the beach (Lake Winnipeg has the most extensive commercial fishery in North America for walleyed pike, called pickerel in Canada; the lake also produces large amounts of whitefish and a considerable number of northern pike and sturgeon). My finds along the shoreline included an entire gill net with its attached plastic floats; individual floats (both older wooden ones and modern plastic versions); segments of nylon ropes and cords; an eight-foot-long net marker pole, with several large flat discs of cork encircling the midpoint of the wooden shaft and a lead weight at its bottom end; a rectangular plastic tub for storing and hauling the catch; and a protective forearm sheath for fishermen, made of rubberized fabric with an elastic band at each end. From this mélange of discoveries, letting the material guide my art, I fashioned a rather spooky-and-spunky looking "doll." This involved a series of blue and black plastic floats strung on cords for each of the arms and legs, plus a forearm sheath for the trunk and its sleeveless dress, all topped by a rubber doll's head minus its hair, which had also washed ashore and had inspired my creativity. When Doree chuckled at my artistic product, suspended from the upper end of the net marker pole, I reminded her that, before the era of machine-made, perfectly uniform products, an artisan crafting an item by hand was often not certain exactly how it would turn out until it was completed.

During the afternoon, the wind and waves from the north slackened a bit, and the white froth atop the waves disappeared. However, the size of the waves and their adjacent troughs did not reduce enough to allow us to travel safely. Soon, the wind refreshened itself and the whitecaps returned, so it was just as well that we had not ventured out.

While wandering by myself along the shoreline, I was elated to discover an ancient gunflint from a flintlock firearm, back a few feet from the water's edge! Made in the blade style, it measured 13/16 inches in length by 7/8 inch in width, a medium size that would have been used in the type of smoothbore shoulder gun that was termed a fowler. Fashioned of dark grey flint with off-white inclusions, the gunflint had quite possibly been manufactured from local stone by a native individual; it was considerably worn at the working end of the blade from a great deal of usage in a gun. To magically know the many incidents in which that gunflint had been involved over its lifetime would be quite a gift!

This fortunate find set my thoughts adrift over the long history of the fur trade in the area of northern Lake Winnipeg and the region stretching beyond it toward the east. Some 68 miles to the northeast of our launch site at the mouth of the Saskatchewan River, across the top of the lake, lies the head of the Nelson River. This solitary outlet of Lake Winnipeg, flowing generally northeastward to Hudson's Bay, carries a tremendous volume of water, since the massive watershed of the lake stretches from the spine of the Rocky Mountains eastward to nearly the shores of Lake Superior, receiving the waters of the entire Winnipeg, Red, and Saskatchewan river systems. This voluminous amount of water, raging for more than four hundred miles down the tortuous channel of the Nelson River across the Canadian Shield, was usually too powerful and turbulent for safe travel in canoes and York boats. Luckily, a more manageable waterway, the Hayes River, flows roughly parallel to the Nelson, and empties into Hudson's Bay very close to the mouth of the Nelson. This smaller river served as the primary water passage between Lake Winnipeg and Hudson's Bay during the entire fur trade era. From the outlet of the lake, travelers on the route down to the Bay followed the upper fifty miles of the Nelson River, then about forty miles on the connecting Etchimanish River, and finally some 330 miles on the Hayes River, including its broadened sections called Oxford Lake and Knee Lake.

The various trading facilities which were established at or near the estuary of the Hayes and Nelson River mouths from 1682 onward represented a fierce competition between French and British personnel. Control of this locale was of considerable importance, since it offered both a port for ocean-going ships from Europe and a major river route that extended deep into the interior. In 1682, Groseilliers established Ft. Philipeaux for the French a short distance up the Hayes River (which the French had christened La Rivière Ste. Thérèse), while the British personnel of the H.B.C. constructed Fort Nelson the same year on the Nelson River near its mouth. The following year, Radisson's nephew Chouart built a post about five miles up the Hayes, while the British established a new Fort Nelson on the opposite bank of the Nelson River. In 1684, La Martinière built a post a short distance up the Hayes from its mouth, directly across the river from the brand new facility of York Fort, which was begun in that year by H.B.C. men. A decade later, in 1694, French naval vessels captured York Fort; it was briefly retaken by the British two years later, but then it was captured again by the French and renamed Ft. Bourbon. It remained in French hands until the 1713 Treaty of Utrecht finally gave the H.B.C. complete control of the entire Hudson's Bay region. However, York Fort was again captured in 1782 by French naval forces, who burned it to the ground; the facility was then rebuilt by H.B.C. personnel the following year.

Beginning in 1774, the H.B.C. was finally forced by its Montreal-based competitors to establish interior posts, beginning with Cumberland House on the lower Saskatchewan River. From that time on, the route from York Fort to the west, via the Hayes-Etchimanish-Nelson Rivers, the top of Lake Winnipeg, and the Saskatchewan River, became the primary passage for the interior operations of the Company, as it gradually expanded throughout most of the interior regions. At its lower terminus, York Fort became the main H.B.C. center for the administration of business, the transshipment of materiel in and peltries out, and the manufacture of trade goods for all of central and western Canada, operating until 1957.

Over the decades of H.B.C. use of this major water trail, a number of trading facilities were established by the Company between York Fort and Lake Winnipeg. These included, in upstream order from Hudson's Bay: Rock House, established in 1794; Swampy Lake House or Logan's Depot, built some time between 1816 and 1819; Oxford House, begun in 1798; Windy Lake House, initiated in 1824; and Sea River Post, established some time between 1794 and 1802. Near the outlet of Lake Winnipeg, a few miles down the Nelson River, Jack River House was built in 1801, operating until 1817; in the meantime, Norway House was established directly at the head of the outlet in 1814; when it burned a decade later, in 1824, it was rebuilt a few miles downstream, at the former location of Jack River House, where it has operated ever since. The facility of Norway House, in its crucial location at the junction of Lake Winnipeg and the main river route between Hudson's Bay and the western posts, played a key role in the transport system of the H.B.C. Operating as an important depot for storing inbound merchandise and supplies and outbound peltries, it also became the administrative center of the entire Northern Department of the Company when the firm merged with the N.W.C. in 1821.

Since we were firmly pinned to shore by the wind, we passed the day by contemplating this wide-ranging history, exploring nature, reading books, and dozing, occasionally breaking the relaxed routine to snack on beef jerky, chocolate gorp, dried apple slices, and koolaid. By good fortune, the weather was very pleasant, with a beaming sun, a clear sky, and a high temperature of 70 degrees in the shade.

At 7:30 P.M., realizing that we were not going to advance any further this day, we erected the tent on the narrow beach, with its back wall pressed against the adjacent screen of trees and bushes. After exchanging massages, we chatted until 9:00. Even at that advanced stage of the evening, there was still no abatement of the wind and waves, with whitecaps continuing to roll in constantly from the north-northeast. This day, we had covered only two miles, and had been windbound from 6:30 A.M. onward.

Day Three

When the call of the clock awakened me at 4 A.M., the sounds of howling wind and crashing surf were very evident from inside the tent. Crawling outside, I immediately registered that yesterday's wind from the north-northeast, rather than calming during the night, had increased to gale strength. The lake was now filled with long ranks of huge whitecaps marching to the shore. These rollers, up to four feet tall, created a constant deep roar as they broke and foamed in the shallows offshore. Some of the biggest waves rushed up onto the gently sloping beach to within three feet of our tent, their arrival adding a hissing sound at regular intervals above the general roar. The closeness of those waves to our shelter reminded me of the experiences of the trader Daniel Harmon when he passed over this lake in 1800: "Last night, the wind blew so high that it drove the water of the lake to such a distance up the beach, that we were under the necessity of removing our baggage further into the woods at three different times."

In the wee hours of this particular morning, the shoreline of Lake Winnipeg looked much like the coast of a wind-lashed ocean! It seemed highly unlikely that we would be able to move from this site today.

Our little green tent, nestled into an indentation in the coastline at the bottom of the bay, standing at the very edge of the shoreline bushes and trees, was sheltered from much of the wind's fury. Also by good fortune, the weather for this windbound day was beautiful, already 65 degrees by early morning light, with a pale blue sky streaked with a few gauzy stripes of clouds. To top it off, with so much wind gusting through the area, there was not a single biting insect around to bother us!

We passed the hours of this bright, sunny day by reading, chatting, swimming, and exploring. In addition, I thoroughly inspected and carried out a few repairs on our gear. When I checked the waterproof bag which usually held Ben's sleeping bag, the spare maps, the replacement films for the camera, and our extra reading books, I found that it had taken in a considerable amount of water from the bottom of the canoe, water which had been carried in by our feet and legs during the departure in the surf the previous morning. The maps were somewhat wet, so I spread them out to dry, after which I pulled the waterproof plastic liner out of the exterior covering of plasticized nylon fabric. Discovering small holes in the liner in four or five places, I sealed them with duct tape from the repair kit. With the same tape, I also repaired a number of little holes in the tent fabric, three in the walls and two in the window screens. Although these openings in the shelter were tiny, they could still have allowed the entry of blood-sucking insects in the future.

Meanwhile, Ben frolicked on an air mattress in the thrashing surf. At midday, we kindled a wood fire back in the screen of poplars and willow bushes that stood behind the beach, offering a partial shelter from the wind. There Doree assembled a delicious stew of beef jerky, noodles, parsley flakes, and parmesan cheese, which we washed down with koolaid and followed with gummy bears for dessert. She made a full pot of this stew, leaving half of it on the warm ashes for our evening meal. As we relished our tasty lunch, a sobering thought seeped into the back of my mind. We had advanced only seven miles over the course of three days, representing our slowest rate of progress in fifteen years of wilderness paddling. At this rate, there was a very distinct possibility that we could run out of food before reaching the end of our voyage, some 340 miles off to the south at the mouth of the Winnipeg River!

After we had finished our repast, a squadron of four white pelicans glided low over our site in a close formation. When my gaze shifted from their graceful, disciplined flight pattern to the sky above, I realized that, during long windbound days such as these on the shores of massive lakes, my attention centered quite often on the *nuages* (clouds). As I remained stationary for long periods beneath these wide-open vistas of the heavens, my mind focused for longer periods and more intently on the cloud formations, compared to when we were paddling. During those times while we were on the move, I paid less attention to these features in the sky, since my attention was often distracted by the tasks of navigating, map reading, and pulling the canoe forward over the water's surface.

As I stared into the huge blue dome of the heavens above, I resurrected some of my science lessons from school days. Water vapor rising from lakes, rivers, and seas, as well as from damp earth, floats invisibly in the atmosphere. It is only when this moisture-bearing air rises to higher altitudes and cools that the vapor condenses into water droplets, forming on the surface of dust or other minute particles that are floating there. Thus are born clouds, masses of condensed water droplets floating in the sky on currents of air. When the conditions are right, the droplets grow by colliding with other droplets until they become too heavy to float, after which they fall as rain (or as snow in winter).

The thin smeared wisps of clouds that were present on this particular day represented cirrus clouds, thin white strands or patches which float at higher altitudes in fair weather. These clouds are sometimes blown by the wind into long streamers or rippled veils that fill a wide area of the sky. Stratus clouds consist of thick or thin sheets or layers, featureless and generally grey, which are often widely spread out and drifting slowly. These low-altitude clouds, which sometimes cover the entire sky, creating an "overcast" day, can produce drizzle or light rain. The third primary type, called cumulus, is represented by puffy white clouds that are dense, sharply outlined, flat-bottomed, and detached from one another. These fair-weather, ascending billows of brilliant white often float lazily across the sky. However, they sometimes develop into massive, powerful storm clouds called cumulonimbus, swelling upward at their tops to altitudes of as much as ten miles or more, forming a flat anvil top, developing an ominous dark underside, and releasing heavy rains that are often associated with thunder and lightning, hailstones, and high winds.

About 6 P.M., as we chatted at the edge of the water, Doree glanced down the beach and noted what appeared to be numerous long, slender plumes of black smoke, rising straight up above the treetops for about fifty to sixty feet. These odd features extended down the coastline as far as two miles, all the way back to Jackpine Point. Upon closer investigation, we learned that each swirling plume was made up of thousands of black insects that looked like large, fat mosquitoes. We had earlier noted these creatures lining the underside of many of the leaves of the bushes and poplars along the shoreline. In the meantime, they had formed into these swirling columns which extended upward from the tops of the trees. Back in 1822, when John Bigsby had participated in the International Boundary Commission survey of Lake Huron, he had observed a similar phenomenon: "In the evening, many of the trees were enveloped and surmounted by myriads of flies, in a spiral pyramidal wreath, constantly rising and falling. At a distance, they looked like a thin smoke."

The good news: the insects seemed disinterested in us. At 7:45, we finally hit the sack, after a full day of entertaining and relaxing activities on shore. During the three windbound days that we had just experienced, I had read much of the book Recessional *by James Michener, which centers around the issues of older folks needing additional care in their later years but wanting to retain their independence. This reading led to a number of interesting discussions between the three of us, concerning our aging parents' lives as well as our own twilight years that lie ahead. I joked with Ben, "Imagine your Dad in forty or fifty years. You'll be taking his hand gently as you go for walks in nature, and he'll be repeating the stories of our trips over and over." However, it was rather sobering to think of my wiry adventuresome mate as an ancient geezer. Who would leave first, and when? Finally I dozed off, marveling at the many adventures we've had together during almost three decades of marriage. (Doree)*

Day Four

Up to the reveille of the alarm clock at 4 A.M., we were highly primed to do some serious paddling, having made only a meager seven miles in the previous three days. To our utter delight, the weather conditions looked very conducive for advancing on the water! The wind had completely calmed, and there were only light residual swells disturbing the otherwise smooth surface. With a beautiful yellow-tinted horizon off to the east and an air temp of 50 degrees, we were on the water by 4:45. Our hearts soared like hawks to be finally released from land, 46 hours after we had been forced ashore!

Just beyond Aministikooskok Point, we glided noiselessly past a pair of adult bald eagles who had constructed their nest high in a poplar tree near the water's edge. Building a large, snug nest such as this one of sticks and twigs, a mated pair of eagles often returns to utilize the same treetop construction year after year, sometimes for as long as two decades. As we glided by, I wondered, How many years has this particular pair of birds reared their young at this nest?

After about five miles, Doree and I began a southeastward traverse across a bay to reach the base of Longue Pointe. This massive peninsula was an obstacle on the mainline route that I had not been looking forward to meeting. The long arm of swampy, forest-covered land, extending due east from the mainland out into the lake for 25 miles, tapers gradually from a width of ten miles at its base to a pointed tip. This famous obstacle in the lives of the voyageurs, which they had often dubbed Le Détour or La Pointe Maligne (The Spiteful or Malicious Point), would usually take them a full twelve hours to pass in good conditions, six hours out to the end and another six hours back. Since the land of the peninsula was so low, swampy, and thickly covered with tangled forest growth, the men never attempted to portage over it, at either the base or partway out toward the tip. The only practical approach to handling this feature entailed paddling around it for at least twelve hours, hoping for good weather all the while.

Soon after commencing our traverse to reach the base of Longue Pointe, a moderate breeze from the south picked up, forcing me to turn the bow southward to quarter the oncoming side waves. After two miles, when we had come within a mile of the shoreline, I was able to turn eastward again. When the wind switched to a southwesterly direction, Ben hoisted the sail, which provided a light assist as we advanced five miles to reach the base of the half-mile-long Sturgeon Skin Point. There, Doree and Ben cleared some stones from the very short and shallow channel that extends across the base of the needle-like point. Their efforts allowed us the fun of floating over its base, instead of skirting around the tip. Immediately after traveling through this entertaining little passageway, we took a morning break at 8:45, having covered fifteen miles in four hours. During this hour-long break, three separate wedges of black ducks flapped overhead, each group winging toward the north.

After our replenishing rest we returned to the water, determined to travel around the entire length of Longue Pointe, which commences at about this place. We fervently hoped that *La Vieille* would remain in a good mood for the next twelve to thirteen hours, while we plied the paddles. With a light sail assist, we immediately made a traverse of five miles across the mouth of a deeply rounded bay; this maneuver cut three miles from the route, but it took also us 21/2 miles away from shore. At the tip of the point which marked the end of this crossing, we quietly cruised by an eagles nest high in a poplar. The two new offspring of the resident family, covered in all-black plumage, perched at the edge of the nest of sticks, while the parents kept a close watch from the tops of two nearby spruce trees.

With the following wind lightly filling the sail, we thoroughly enjoyed cruising about a half-mile or less from the shoreline, as the hours and the miles dropped gradually behind us. At one point, as I glanced down at the Clément brand paddle in my hands, my mind wandered over all of the myriad individuals who had been involved in its creation in Quebec Province, as well as all those who had played a role in it ultimately ending up in my hands. I thought of the woodsmen who had harvested the ash tree in the forest; the various people who had been involved in transporting the log to the canoe paddle factory; the craftworkers who had fashioned and smoothed the blond wood into a 62 inch paddle, and those who had varnished it to a durable, glistening sheen; the many individuals who had played a role in all facets of its marketing and its international shipment from Quebec to Illinois; and finally the staff members at Ralph Frese's Chicagoland Canoe Base, who had sung its praises and had sold it to me, along with three other identical ones. When I considered the faithful service that these four paddles had provided to our family during fifteen years of wilderness jaunts (and each of them was still continuing to serve us very well), I was reminded of all of the people who had played a role in their previous existence, before they had become part of the Kent family's gear. These thoughts then led me to the subject of the interconnected web of life on this planet, in which all of the members of the human race and all the members of the natural world reside together and interact with each other.

As we headed gradually toward the distant tip of Longue Pointe, platoons of three or four pelicans occasionally glided by us in tight formation, almost skimming the surface of the water. Peering straight down into the depths below us, through water which was tinted a light olive hue, we could easily see huge boulders resting on the bottom. Long stretches of the slowly passing coastline were made up of millions of small pebbles in shades of white and tan, while other segments consisted of lengthy expanses of tan sand. These shoreline areas, swept bare of all vegetation by repeated slashing storms, were backed with mostly poplars and spruces. In 3 3/4 hours, Doree covered twelve miles in the bow seat, until we halted at 1:30 for a lunch break. We were enticed to shore at this place by a rare sight, a grove of gnarled cedars which had grown up at the mouth of a little brook. When we departed an hour later, the mild wind had faded completely, leaving us with ideal paddling conditions: completely calm water, a light blue sky with a few stationary white clouds, and a temp of 72 degrees in the shade. "It d'unt git better'n 'is!"

Exchanging positions with his mother, Ben joined me with the bow paddle to advance nine miles in 2 1/4 hours, reaching the very tip of Longue Pointe at 4:40. It had taken us six hours of paddling, plus an additional hour for a break, to reach the far end of the peninsula. On a scattering of exposed offshore rocks near the tip, hundreds of gulls squawked their disapproval of our intrusion. The memory of that moment at the tip of the point has remained clearly imprinted on my brain, including the eerie sensation of being in a very vulnerable place, out 25 miles from the main western shoreline, only a few miles from the midpoint of the North Basin of the lake.

After only a brief floating pause, we began the long haul back to the mainland shore of the lake. Immediately upon rounding the sheltering point, we faced moderate swells from the southwest for about an hour, as we skirted many troublesome boulder fields that lurked just below the surface in the extensive shallows. After an hour, the wind and waves again mellowed to almost perfect conditions, with the water sparkling in the late-day sun. Doree then took up the role of the *avant* to make six miles in two hours, after which Ben put in another 2 3/4 hours, to finally finish the day at the base of the peninsula.

We had pushed hard to return to the base of Longue Pointe, driven by a single thought: if rough conditions should arise the following day, we preferred being back on the mainland shore, rather than on the long, exposed, battered point jutting out into the open waters of the North Basin. At 9:45 P.M., we landed with exhausted relief, after seventeen hours on the move. This day, we had embarked at 4:45 A.M. and had advanced 55 miles, with about twenty of those miles involving a mild to moderate assist from the sail. During that span of 55 miles, we had observed ten bald eagles: two pairs of nesting adults, two youngsters at the nest, and four adults that were hunting for fish, exhibiting their outstretched total wingspan of nearly eight feet.

Establishing our camp on a gravel beach, we cooked a restorative stew of beef and turkey jerky, noodles, corn, mushrooms, zucchini, carrots, and peas. Then, to make the next morning's departure both quicker and easier, we simply spread out our air mattresses and sleeping bags on the gravel beside the beached but loaded canoe, with our nylon tarp close at hand in case of rain. As protection against the voracious mosquitoes that populated this site, we applied DEET repellant, donned our head nets, and removed only our shoes for sleeping.

While preparing to spend the night on the ground in the open air, Doree commented that the ancient voyageurs had not been equipped with such wonderful luxuries as air mattresses, sleeping bags, DEET, and head nets! In fact, during some nights while traveling on Lake Winnipeg, the men had gotten no sleep at all due to the hordes of attacking insects. Such was the case with the brigade of Gabriel Franchère, a trader for Astor's American Fur Company, when they passed through here in 1814, outbound for Montreal: "We camped at the bottom of a little bay, where the mosquitoes did not suffer us to close our eyes all night. We were rejoiced when dawn appeared, and eager to embark to free ourselves from these inconvenient guests."

When we bedded down at 11:00, the air temp still measured a rather comfortable 60 degrees. At this point, Toby became rather confused, since the "zipper house" of green fabric that normally sheltered him and his family each night was missing! At first, he crawled into Doree's sleeping bag, then into mine, seeking some shelter.

At one point during the night, when a single cloud passing overhead dropped some drizzle on our site, I got up, spread the tarp over Doree and me, and told Ben that it was available if he wanted to join us. However, the solitary cloud moved on and no more rain came down, so he needed no additional covering. During the course of the night hours, I awakened a couple of times to the beautiful sight of *la nuit étoilée* (the starry night), with millions of bright stars decorating a perfectly clear sky. In the process, I observed that the heavens had not turned totally black, having instead retained a dark greyish hue.

Day Five

RIIIIIIIIIIIIING. At 3:30 A.M., the alarm clock went off, jarring us awake. Apparently, our most diligent gouvernail had decided that 41/2 hours of sleep was sufficient recovery time after the seventeen hours of traveling and 55 miles of progress of the previous day. A considerable wind and accompanying waves had kicked up during the night, so Tim decided to give the conditions additional time to either improve or worsen. Ahh, sweet sleep! I resumed my dream...I was back in Guatemala again, on a visit to Antigua -- volcanos, the colorful woven huipils, *the celebration of Good Friday before Easter with brilliant paintings made of dyed sawdust spread out artistically on the ground. When the alarm rang a second time at 4:45, the wind had reduced somewhat; Tim optimistically interpreted this as a sign of workable conditions for advancing down the coast. Packing the sleeping gear quietly in the dim light, we pushed off at 5:45, with nary a word and without even a bite of gorp, since we had eaten our dinner the previous evening at 10:30. (Doree)*

As we traveled on a southwesterly course, we very soon found ourselves dealing with a relentless head wind and moderately large waves that were coming directly at us, from the southwest. For more than two hours, Doree and I labored to claw our way forward just three miles, until we decided to land for a break. Our chosen resting spot was at the base of the three-mile-long peninsula that flanks the eastern side of Gull Bay. This slender spit of sand and gravel, in all places less than a tenth of a mile wide, separates the northern half of the Bay from the open lake. Approaching its shoreline at 8:00, we saw that the area was already occupied by about fifty white pelicans, and a squadron of twelve more was gliding in low to make a landing very close to us.

After taking a well-earned breakfast break of thirty minutes, we resumed our labors. However, while traveling along the peninsula against the strident wind, we quickly found that we could barely make any progress with the paddles. So we climbed over the gunwales and lined, dragged, and pushed the canoe in the near-shore shallows, to advance just two miles in 11/2 hours of hard slogging. Along the way, we passed a total of eight unoccupied summer fishing camps of native families, who had constructed little huts of boards near the shorelines of gravel and sand. One of these camps was even equipped with a wooden swing set for children. Finally, about a mile from the outer tip of the peninsula, we halted at 10:00, conceding that we were once again *dégradé*.

When we beached the canoe and walked out to nearly the tip of the peninsula, we disturbed hundreds of white pelicans. These birds, so dignified in flight, have a mighty awkward-looking takeoff! First there is an ungainly forward waddle, then a spreading of wings, and finally a slow-speed liftoff into the air. We also scared up hundreds of terns, which flapped off in one massed group. At the outermost tip of the peninsula in the distance, there appeared to be a huge black item on the ground, which we could not identify. As we approached it, legions of black ducks suddenly burst into the air with a thundering of wings. At the same time, zillions of terns swooped in large circles above our heads, and platoons of pelicans cruised by in synchronized line and wedge formations. We had never before seen such a heavy concentration of water birds on a single spit of land!

Back in the low dunes area directly behind our landing spot, Ben discovered a pelican nest made of dried grass, which contained three chicken-size eggs, brownish-grey with black splotches. The many other nests of similar construction that we found in the same general area were all empty, except for one that contained a pair of eggs of the same brown-grey-black pattern. A short distance offshore, two newly-hatched, gawky pelicans bobbed happily on the surface, glad to have exited from their crowded eggshell enclosures. We had stumbled (literally and figuratively) onto an extensive nesting ground of white pelicans!

After napping for a couple of hours (nearly completing our previous night's sleep), we cooked a fine stew of beef jerky, fresh garlic, noodles, corn, and shallots. As the hours of the afternoon and early evening passed, the wind remained solid from the southwest, never letting up enough to permit us to make the long traverse that lay immediately ahead. That crossing stretched southward for eight miles, from the tip of the peninsula to the mainland shore. At 7:30 P.M., we finally ceased our reading and waiting for the weather to change, and set up the tent for the night on the exposed spit of land. Our timing could not have been better! Just as soon as we had erected the tent, a ferocious wind and black rain clouds sped in from the west, battering the green nylon shelter into which we had just dived.

This day, from 5:45 A.M. to 10 A.M., we had progressed just five miles in 41/4 hours of heavy effort, after which we had found ourselves windbound again. At this point, five days into the voyage, we had arrived at mile 67, having made all but twelve of those miles in a single traveling session.

Day Six

Throughout the night, the wildly flapping tent seemed to be in imminent danger of collapse from the pounding of the fierce wind, which howled for a number of hours from the west, and then from the north. We waited until 8:30 to see if it would die down and allow us to move forward, but to no avail. So, after securing all of the items of loose gear, to keep them from being whisked away by the wind in our absence, we all hiked out to the end of the peninsula, to inspect the traverse that lay ahead. Domineering waves coming from the northeast kept us from making that southerly crossing.

The weather was comfortable, ranging between 55 and 60 degrees, depending upon whether the sun was fully exposed or was hidden behind one of the many fluffy white clouds that were charging toward the south across the powder blue sky. We spent the morning napping, reading, and watching terns dive head-long into the lake for little fish, zooming wildly down from heights of twenty to fifty feet. Toward midday, I noticed that the weather front had moved off to the south; as a result, the waves from the northeast had reduced considerably.

At noon, we bolstered our strength for the trek that lay ahead, with a hearty stew of turkey jerky, shell noodles, tomatoes, shallots, fresh garlic, and apples. While we ate, an orderly line of about twenty pelicans cruised very low right over us; they seemed to be actively encouraging us to travel southward, to follow their lead. The gliding birds reminded me of miniature pterodactyls, ancient flying reptiles that had been equipped with a wide flap of skin extending from their torso to each of their outstretched limbs.

Loading in and gathering our courage, we put paddles to the water at 12:50, ready to take on the southward traverse of eight miles. Our distant goal was Pointe Maligne (Spiteful or Malicious Point, now called Wicked Point). From the beginning, we were confronted with rather large swells from the north-northeast, the residue of the persistent winds that had been blowing from that direction. However, when the canoe was well clear of the peninsula, we were also buffeted by rather strong gusts and waves from the north-northwest, from which we had been sheltered while we were near the promontory. The combination of the two angled elements coming from behind created some very unusual steering challenges for me, as the craft rocked and pitched amid the roiled seas! From the passenger spot, Doree constantly sang out French songs, to encourage the two hardy paddlers.

About halfway across the demanding traverse, three native gill net fishermen approached us from the north, coming up from behind in their twenty-foot boat with high upswept ends. When they generously offered their assistance, I asked them if they might follow us until we were safely across. Patiently accompanying us for about fifteen minutes, they remained until we were out of the worst of the danger and had advanced to about three miles from land, at which point we waved our thanks and goodbye. We appreciated their support, since their help would have been valuable if we had capsized. Our presence on the lake may have given them food for thought, prompting them to think about how their ancestors had traveled on these home waters before the introduction of strong boats equipped with powerful motors.

The forest-covered land was drawing closer with each paddle stroke. During the crossing, I attempted to steer a course that would let us pass beyond the approaching Wicked Point. However, due to the angle of the powerful waves that swept us along, we were forced to land two miles short of this projecting landmass. Ben and I had paddled the eight miles of the traverse in 1 3/4 hours, traveling at the considerable speed of 5 m.p.h. We had appreciated the assistance of the wind blowing against our backs, but we had chosen not to increase its push by raising the sail, which would have complicated the slippery situation even further.

After landing in a rather heavy surf on an open sand beach, we celebrated our safe arrival with peanut butter crackers and chocolate candies. This feast was followed by hours of relaxing and reading books, sheltered behind a screen of poplar saplings near the shoreline. Later, Doree and I ambled southeastward for a quarter-mile, along a ridge which marked a higher shoreline of the lake in ancient times. As we approached a small cove, an adult bald eagle flapped from the bank into the edge of the water. There, he stood with his wings half spread, with some of the feathers drooping down into the lake. When we froze, he watched us for a minute or two, then walked awkwardly out of the water and inland to some poplar saplings, waddling with his wings half extended and slumping. He appeared to be dying, or at least to be very sick. It was shocking and saddening to see such a majestic creature in this condition. With wrenched hearts, we softly offered him our best wishes, backed away respectfully, and left him to face his future in peace.

By 7 P.M., the waves had reduced only moderately, eliminating the possibility of our making any further progress and pinning us to the land for the night. Surveying our activities of the day, I noted that we had been windbound all morning, had advanced across a wild traverse of eight miles, and then had been windbound for the remainder of the day. We had now reached mile 75 in six days of traveling, with 55 of those miles having been covered on a single day.

After trading massages in the tent, we were deep in dreamland by 8:00.

Day Seven

When the alarm clock shocked us awake at 2 A.M., we discerned a novel sound -- utter silence, with no pounding of waves! The clear sky glimmered with bright stars, while the planet Jupiter shone even more brilliantly from low in the southeastern sky. Off to the east, the heavens were tinged a very pale orange-white. After happily packing in the dim light, Doree and I launched at 3:00, with a brisk air temperature of 40 degrees and a mild wind from the southeast. As the canoe arrowed effortlessly over the barely ruffled surface of the water, illuminated only by starlight, it felt like we were having a mystical experience! After about 45 minutes, while rounding Wicked Point, we could barely make out a number of ghostly white forms at very low altitude in the distance. We thought they might be white boats at anchor. When we drew close, gliding in silence, we finally identified these apparitions: they were pelicans, fast asleep on exposed offshore rocks! As we glided by, dipping our paddles as quietly as possible, only some of these large birds awakened and flapped away, along with a few black ducks.

At 4 A.M., we took a brief floating break, entertained by the songs of various birds warbling in the near-darkness; an hour later, we landed for fifteen minutes to stretch our legs. By that time, the gentle breeze had disappeared, the stars had faded away, and the eastern sky contained a deep orange area at water level and a lighter yellow-orange area extending well above the horizon. Just as we resumed our paddling, the orange rim of the sun broke free of the waterline, tinting the placid surface of the lake all the way to the shore beside us.

Under these ideal conditions, we cruised along easily, some fifty yards out from a shoreline that often consisted of a pebble beach in the foreground and a thick spruce forest standing behind. In a few areas, sheer walls of limestone rose behind a block-strewn shore, while at other places only a narrow strip of sand lay between the water's edge and the tall spruces. In those latter areas, many of the trees closest to the water had been undermined by violent storms, had toppled into the lake, and had been driven ashore and pummeled by waves until they were bare skeletons. Having covered twelve miles in three hours of paddling, we halted at 7:15 for a half-hour break. It was now 50 degrees out, and the canvas of pale blue sky above had only a couple of thin white smears off in the east.

During the next three hours, Ben and I advanced steadily for nine miles. As we skirted Kitching Point, a young bald eagle perched in the top of a poplar squawked at us, launched into the air, and circled once before returning to its perch. All the while, the youngster's protective mother glided in circles high overhead, carefully watching this new experience of her offspring. Doree spotted the family's nest at the top of another poplar tree, adjacent to the water's edge.

At about this point, we noticed that the lake had acquired a milky tan color, in contrast to the nearly clear, lightly green-hued waters that we had noted on previous days. This new appearance, reflecting the increased amount of fine silt that was suspended in the water, would continue for the entire remainder of the lake to its south end. This feature had inspired the Crees to apply the name *Winnipeg*, meaning "dirty water" or "muddy water," to this lake in ancient times.

At 11:15, when we paused for fifteen minutes on land, the temperature had risen to 66 degrees in the shade. Many puffy white clouds with black undersides had drifted in to cover much of the sky, and an erratic wind from the southeast had arrived. With Doree carrying out the bow duties, we dealt with a modest head wind at times, but encountered waves of only medium size. After two hours, Ben took over as the *avant*.

During a three-mile traverse across the mouth of a relatively small bay, cruising about 3/4 mile from the shoreline, we were all peacefully chatting, without a care in the world. Then, to our utter surprise, a hefty head wind and large waves from the southeast kicked up within just a couple of minutes. Father and son had to dig in very hard for about twenty minutes to gradually angle toward land for a mile, while maintaining control in the gusting wind and the three-foot waves. When we finally reached the shallows near the pebble beach shoreline, Ben leaped into the waves and securely held the canoe pointed into the surf, while Doree, Toby, and I clambered over the gunwales. We then dragged the loaded craft sideways up the incline of the beach, out of the worst of the waves, hastily unloaded the two heavy Duluth packs, and finally hauled the lightened canoe up to safety. At 2:00, having progressed 26 miles in eleven hours, we again found ourselves windbound! We had just been given a personal demonstration of how quickly violent winds and waves could appear out of nowhere on this treacherous lake.

We passed the rest of the day exploring, reading, and finally setting up camp when the blustery wind showed no signs of lessening. While hiking along the edge of the extensive marsh that lay inland from our site, Doree discovered numerous stands of purple irises in resplendent bloom. Back on the beach near our landing spot, I found a small, spiral-shaped fossil cephalopod set in a backing of limestone, beautifully polished by wave action over thousands of years. In the same area, I also located a two-inch-long, brown stone which had been shaped and smoothed by the forces of nature into the distinct form of a canoe.

Our evening feast consisted of a stew of beef jerky, shell noodles, green tomatoes, fresh garlic, peas, and apple slices. Hitting the air mattresses to trade massages at 6:30, we were fast asleep a half-hour later. After our long and productive day, we slumbered like logs without stirring for ten restful hours.

Day Eight

Arising at 5:15, we emerged from the tent to a gorgeous morning. A golden sun was just peeping over the eastern horizon, the air temp measured 50 degrees, and a slight breeze from the southeast was rustling the tops of the poplars. When Ben and I plied our paddles at 6:05, I aimed our bow on a southeasterly course, against a moderate head wind and waves coming from the south-southeast. After making five miles in 1 1/2 hours, we had nearly reached Dancing Point.

Looking ahead, I warned my grown-up son that we were about to face tough conditions, as soon as we would round that projection of land and bear the brunt of the weather. As we started around the point, I first saw major whitecaps out in the unsheltered water ahead. That unsettling sight reminded me of a comment by the artist Paul Kane, when he traveled over this lake with a H.B.C. brigade in 1845: "We left in the morning with a strong breeze, which changed into a perfect gale, making many of our [hired paddler] Indians seasick." Advancing a little further, we suddenly found ourselves amid very big swells and waves that had been able to develop, entirely unobstructed, across some sixty miles of open lake. At that moment, with water sloshing over the gunwales, I knew that these seas were more riled than we and our heavily loaded canoe could handle!

Having been forewarned of trouble ahead, Ben reacted instantly when I shouted, "Turn us around to the right, Ben!" He dug in hard and deep with repeated draw strokes on the right side of the bow, while I applied equally hard sweep strokes on the left at the stern, causing the hull to rotate quickly in the dangerous surf. Lickety-split, we ducked behind the sheltering landmass of Dancing Point, and soon glided into a beautiful and tranquil cove near its base. Upon our arrival there at 8:00, six pelicans vacated the area, swimming slowly away without concern, while a group of ducks, in complete contrast, flapped away in utter panic. Unbeknown to us, this place would serve as our most lengthy *campement dégradé* (windbound campsite) on the entire mainline route. Luckily, it was a very attractive and comfortable location, and offered a considerable variety of natural features for us to explore and learn about over the following days.

Most of the cove, very gradually curved, was edged with a narrow swath of pebbles near the water's edge, backed by a fifteen-foot-wide beach of tan sand exhibiting a very slight rise; behind the beach stood a rather thick poplar forest. Exploring the immediate area, Ben located a long set of moose tracks, which indicated where the large animal had wandered along the coastline, ambling into and out of the shallows. Inland, he also discovered several piles of marble-sized, dark brown moose droppings beneath the trees.

From the little bay, we hiked eastward along the coast, intent upon reaching the point and proceeding around it. The weather conditions were absolutely super for a windbound stop: the sun beamed happily, the air temp measured 72 degrees in the shade, and only a couple of white smears extended across the eastern part of an otherwise deep blue sky. Near the point and extending around it, thick slabs of limestone in various sizes had been mounded up by storm waves and lake ice cakes along the coastline, extending inland from the water's edge as much as thirty feet. Atop this broad, continuous pile of broken rock, light tan in color, pockets of soil had accumulated and mature poplar trees had grown. Behind this linear pile lay an extensive swamp, containing standing water, tall grasses, and bushes. The water from this marshland flowed into the lake in various places, sometimes filtering through the pile of broken limestone pieces, and sometimes running over the edges of the limestone bedrock in those places where it had been left intact in its original location at the shoreline. At these latter areas, the water cascaded gently down step-like formations in miniature waterfalls two to three feet tall, near the edge of the lake.

At the tip of the point, along a swath about two hundred feet long and stretching some forty feet inland, every one of the trees and bushes had been twisted and snapped at knee-to-chest height; in each case, their upper broken portions had been toppled away from the water. This violent action against the resident plants, including numerous trees with diameters up to fifteen inches, looked like a track where a giant monster had thrashed through the area. However, this wrenching damage, along with the considerable amounts of broken limestone slabs that had been heaped up on the land, revealed the tremendous power of the jostling cakes of lake ice as they had been tumbled about by storm waves during each spring thaw. Some fifty feet back from the water's edge, an unoccupied eagles nest made of sticks was perched securely in the forked crotch of a poplar tree, about fifteen feet above the ground. On the far edge of the point, along its unsheltered side, we waded out among the wave-flooded bushes that stood along the southeastern corner of the landmass. There, we could observe the wild surf advancing in unending rows of tall whitecaps across the lake, lashed by the southeast wind.

While Doree and I relaxed in the sun on the point, Ben and Toby searched for fossils within the limestone slabs that were scattered nearby. The human seeker of the pair soon located an excellent snail-shaped cephalopod, about two inches in diameter, which had been set into a matrix of limestone millions of years before. Then, a large power boat appeared, cut its engine, and coasted to a halt some distance offshore from the point. One of the men on board hailed us to ask if we needed any help. Working out of the community of Dauphin River, fifty miles to the south, these gill net fishermen very seldom encountered canoe paddlers on this not-very-hospitable lake.

I replied that we were O.K., just windbound, and then inquired about any recent weather predictions. One of the men replied that the winds on the lake had been predicted to exceed 30 m.p.h. during the rest of this day, as well as all of the following day. That was how we learned that we would not be moving forward anytime soon.

Another of the men indicated that they would be anchoring their headquarters boat in the deeper waters out from this bay throughout the night and much of the next day. Then they would empty their gill nets in the area and return home with their catch of pickerel. When I asked if they might sell us some of those fish, one of them answered, "We'll bring you out to the boat and give you some!" (Doree)

The four members of the Kent family walked down the beach to a place opposite the deep-water anchorage of the thirty-foot headquarters boat. Then Norman Halchuck came in to shore with their smaller work boat to pick us up, driving the bow right up onto the pebble beach. This hardy, custom-built aluminum boat, fifteen feet long, had been designed with a considerable height, and with a high rocker and sheer at the bow end. This upswept configuration of the bow allowed the craft to slice efficiently through tall waves, and also to slide up onto the shore when landing. Powered by a 155 horsepower outboard motor, it was used by the men to place and empty their gill nets. We later learned that this specialized craft and its massive motor, crucial for doing their work in safety, had required an outlay of $30,000. Climbing over its high walls, we were ferried out to the grey-painted headquarters boat, where we met Norman's son Andrew, age 13, Norman's younger brother Lawrence, as well as John Szklaruk. The three adults regularly work out of the lakeside settlement of Dauphin River, and live in the nearby communities of Gypsumville and St. Martin. They have a mixed ancestry of Ukranian, English, and Scottish forebears. We guessed that the Scots lineage was reflected in the red hair of Norman and his son Andrew. Norman's wife was a local Cree woman from Dauphin River, while Lawrence was engaged to another local Cree woman.

Chatting on the deck of the sturdy boat in the bright sunlight, we learned much about these amiable young men and their work. To become licensed commercial fishermen, they had been required to first work as helpers for other fishermen for a period of two years, before going into business for themselves. The government licensing office sets quota limits on the poundage of pickerel (called walleyed pike in the U.S.), whitefish, and sauger that may be harvested from the lake; however, there is no limit imposed on the poundage of northern pike that may be taken. The men sell their catch to an agent at the community of Dauphin River, who trucks the fish to Winnipeg for filleting and freezing. From there, the frozen fish are distributed far and wide.

Lawrence and John had attended some years of high school,

while Norman had not gone beyond elementary school. Norman's son Andrew would soon begin high school at the town of Ashern, which would require a round trip of 100 miles each day on a school bus, from his home in Gypsumville. During our conversation, we learned that the high winds and gales of this particular mid-summer had been unusual; the customary July weather on the lake is beautiful and generally calm (at least from their perspective in high-walled boats equipped with very powerful engines). In addition, the water level of the lake this year was about two feet above normal. As we floated in the sheltered cove beside Dancing Point, we could see the tall whitecaps sweeping from the southeast across the open portion of the lake. The men indicated that the big storms that had whipped the lake this summer had made the catches in the gill nets very poor.

Just before our arrival, John had cooked a breakfast of bacon, eggs, and toast for the crew. Since we had eaten shortly before, we declined their offer of a meal, but joined them in their six-foot-tall cabin, to chat further while they ate. Two sets of bunks lined the walls, along with a bottled gas range, a storage cupboard, and an ice cooler at the far end of the oblong room. On the opposite side of the central dividing wall of the cabin was the ice room, where the catch was kept chilled. Andrew had just iced down a newly-harvested tubful of pickerel plus a three-foot-long northern pike. Usually, the men made one-day runs; however, since fishing had been so poor this summer in their usual areas of operation closer to home, they had ventured further north for this two-day trip. On such occasions, they set their nets on the first day and gathered the catch on the following day. Their nylon gill nets have a square mesh that measures 2 1/8 inches on each side, allowing smaller fish to pass through the openings.

While Toby licked clean the plates of the crew, we enjoyed a few pieces of their delicious applesauce cake. The generous guys also gave us a big slab of the cake to take back to camp, along with a pair of twenty-inch pickerel or walleyed pike (which acquired this latter name from the milky color of its eyes). In addition, Norman presented Doree with a special item, a stone from inside a sunfish, which they call a "pearl of the lake."

During much of the afternoon at the campsite, we read books. Since the air temp measured 75 degrees in the shade, a bit warm for long stretches of sitting in the sun, I lounged in the shallows offshore to read, with my lower half cooled by the water. About 4:00, Ben kindled a wood fire while I filleted and skinned the two pickerel, after which Ben fried the fish steaks in oil. These were accompanied by noodles garnished with reconstituted tomatoes and mushrooms, and were followed with the gift cake from our new friends. During fifteen years of wilderness canoe trips, Doree had often fantasized about having freshly-caught fish for dinner. Finally, her wish had been fulfilled, by a friendly party of commercial fishermen!

During the meal, our conversation turned to the traveling foods, beverages, and condiments that had been common during the French regime. The main foods which were transported into the interior from the St. Lawrence settlements on fur trade and military voyages consisted of bread, peas, corn, and pork. The flour was nearly always ground from wheat, since that was the primary grain that was grown in the Valley; very little rye and barley were raised. Both white flour and whole-grain or brown flour were provided to travelers. In addition to flour, a great many expeditions also carried both fresh bread and *biscuit* or *galette*, which were forms of hard flat cakes or thick pancakes (In English, this unleavened traveling bread is called hardtack or sea biscuit). The *biscuit* for interior travel was made in several varieties: of white flour, of whole-wheat flour, and aniseed-flavored versions of the two biscuits.

Dried peas, both green and white varieties, as well as dried corn were commonly carried on canoe voyages. Both of these items were grown in considerable amounts along the St. Lawrence. Rice, imported to New France, was occasionally listed among the provisions in the records of military and trading voyages. In contrast, oats were grown on the St. Lawrence farms for animal fodder, rather than for human consumption. However, oats sometimes replaced wheat in times of shortage, in both the settlements and at the interior posts; during the British era, oatmeal was more commonly used for provisions at facilities in the interior.

Pork and grease were staple foods on canoe expeditions; in some instances, both of these items were carried. These foods were produced by local farmers along the St. Lawrence. Pork fat meat, with or without streaks of muscle meat, was called *lard* or sometimes *porc* by the French. This fat meat from the side of a pig was salted or smoked; in English, it is called bacon, side meat, side pork, or salt pork. The French term *lard* is not to be confused with *graisse*, rendered (melted) pork fat, which is called "lard" in English. Lean pork, which was salted or smoked, is also occasionally found on invoices of provisions as well. It is listed as *jambon* in French and ham in English. Beef was not often consumed during canoe voyages of the French era; it was only occasionally utilized by military officers in the forms of beef, veal, and beef tongues. During the British period, the amount of beef which was supplied to expeditions increased somewhat, as both provisions for paddlers and as merchandise for the interior. Beef for canoe provisions was produced in the St. Lawrence Valley by local farmers.

Rendered (melted) lard or grease, termed *graisse*, was often issued as canoe food, to be added to corn or pea soup and to fry *galette* flour cakes. The grease was sometimes composed of straight pig fat, and sometimes of a mixture of fats. In 1785, one recipe for the "grease" which was transported into the interior as traveling food included 1/3 tallow from beef or sheep and 2/3 pig lard.

Imported raisins and prunes were also sometimes carried on voyages by French traders, and were present at the interior posts.

Brandy and wine were the two common beverages that were consumed during canoe journeys. During the French era, *eau-de-vie* (brandy, distilled from wine) was by far the most common traveling beverage; however, brandy was sometimes accompanied by wine within the same set of provisions. A number of invoices from the French period list "wine" or "Spanish wine" among the provisions. During the French era, both red and white wines were shipped into the interior. French traders sometimes mixed wine and brandy together, both for use during voyages and at the posts. Invoices and other documents of the British and American eras show that rum often replaced brandy during that later period of the trade, while several varieties of wine were also added. Alcoholic beverages provided considerable lift to voyageurs and soldiers during long journeys. Certain French military campaigns carried a ration of four *pots* (totaling 61/2 English quarts) per month for each soldier and native warrior on the expedition. This ration of brandy per month would yield a little less than 1/2 pint per day. Voyageurs also received rather regular treats of spirits while en route.

Coffee and chocolate were carried into the interior during the French era of the trade, for use by both military officers and traders. Chocolate had been introduced into France during the 1640s, and coffee in the 1660s. Both of these drinks were usually prepared with water, although milk was sometimes used as the base for both beverages. Hot chocolate was sometimes whipped to produce a foam, after the addition of one egg yolk per cup. The foam of French *chocolat a l'Angloise* (English style chocolate) was made by adding egg whites instead of yolks. Chocolate drinks were flavored with sugar and sometimes cinnamon. Coffee was brewed with very finely powdered grounds in the pot, in the style of Turkish coffee. The grounds were then allowed to settle at the bottom of the pot before the beverage was poured.

A number of condiments were imported into New France and carried into the interior beginning in the 1600s. These included salt, pepper, white sugar, brown sugar, cloves, nutmeg, olive oil, and vinegar. Salt is the only one of these items that was found often in canoe provisions of the French era; pepper and nutmeg were used less often en route, and the other condiments were rarely used while on voyages. However, each of these condiments was utilized at the distant posts. French invoices reveal that pepper was carried into the interior both as whole corns and in ground form.

Provisions for the return voyages of St. Lawrence-based expeditions, as well as for journeys within the interior, were often gathered at central depots. During the French era, large amounts of provisions were gathered at Michilimackinac and Detroit. The native foodstuffs which were produced for Michilimackinac included corn, dried meat and fish, deer and moose grease, berries, and maple sugar. Peas were also raised there by the French. At Detroit, both native and French farmers raised large crops of corn, beans, peas, and some French wheat, as well as considerable amounts of grease, for travel provisions. In the regions further toward the north and northwest, wild rice and pemmican (pounded dried buffalo meat mixed with melted fat and sometimes dried berries) became important foods for canoe journeys. Provisions depots were established at the posts of Bas de la Rivière and Ft. Garry near the southern end of Lake Winnipeg. These posts received the buffalo products from the prairie region of the Assiniboine and Red Rivers. Cumberland House, on the Saskatchewan River northwest of Lake Winnipeg, also became a provisions depot, the gathering point for the buffalo that were harvested on the prairies and plains of the Saskatchewan River region.

At our windbound site, it was a beautiful sunny day and, due to the high winds in the area, there were virtually no mosquitoes; however, there were considerable numbers of biting horseflies that tried to gnaw holes in us throughout the day. We each read our books at separate locations: in the warm sun, in the water, and in the shade of the screen of poplars that lined the edge of the beach. On several occasions, iridescent black dragonflies alighted on each of us humans (but not on Toby), for some reason always landing on our left shoulder. In each instance, the broad-winged insect sat unconcernedly for a considerable time on its shoulder perch, before finally zipping away in helicopter-style flight. Taking a break from reading, Ben inflated one of the air mattresses and enjoyed floating out in the cove. At one point, I removed a lead weight from a gill net that had washed up on the beach, and fashioned it into a miniature dugout canoe for Doree. Toward the end of the day, as I sat beneath the screen of poplars, I finished the final page of the thought-provoking book *Black Elk Speaks*. Laying it aside, I heard rustling sounds in the leaves close beside me. Less than three feet away, a little red squirrel sat perched on a small log on the ground. After casually chewing a seed, she eventually skittered off and scampered up and around the trunk of a nearby tree, showing little fear.

In the evening, we stared into the leaping flames of our fire on the beach until late, knowing that, on the following day, the winds from the southeast would again be formidable, keeping us pinned to the land. As we sat quietly in the fading light, a mother duck shepherded her five offspring across our little bay, urging them to practice swimming in a long line in front of her. We smiled as we watched one frisky duckling repeatedly veer away from his orderly siblings. The scene brought to mind the antics that were represented in the 1960s recordings by "Alvin and the Singing Chipmunks." "Alvin, Alvin, Aaaalvin!"

When we finally drifted off to sleep at about 11:00, it felt very strange to already know for certain that *La Vieille* would be keeping us windbound at this site the next day. Our fur trade ancestors had not been equipped with long-range, radar-guided weather predictions (which we had received from the fishermen), although they had been very adept at reading approaching weather. For example, they knew that, if high altitude cirrus clouds remained thin, fair weather would continue; if they thickened and spread, rain would probably arrive within the next 48 hours or so. Another indicator of approaching rain showers was the rapid upward growth of cumulus clouds on a summer afternoon; the faster the tops climbed, the more likely that it would rain. Likewise, a very tall cumulonimbus cloud with a flat anvil top and a very dark bottom signalled the imminent arrival of a heavy rain storm. These people, deeply attuned to the weather conditions that affected their lives, could read weather signs in nature as easily as we can read printed text in books.

Day Nine

After a delicious sleep of eight hours, we awakened at 7:00, then lounged in the tent and chatted relaxedly for another hour before emerging. At this point, it was already a balmy 70 degrees in the shade, and the sky was completely filled with billowy white clouds. In our well-sheltered cove, the southeast wind was very mild. However, from the incessant rows of whitecaps that were advancing across the water out on the distant open lake, it was clear that the wind was already strong on the other side of Dancing Point, and it would increase to nearly gale proportions as the day progressed.

Our fishermen friends had just emptied their very long gill net in the bay, and had discovered that the entire net had contained only two pickerel. Doree asked if she could buy them, and she also offered to pay for the two others that we had so enjoyed the previous day. Although one of the men suggested a total fee of $5.00 Canadian, Ms. Kent gave them $7.00 U.S. (worth about $9.00 Canadian at that time), and she was elated at the transaction. They were heading home, having had little success during this two-day jaunt: their catch had totaled only five tubs of fish, compared to their usual haul of twenty or more tubs on a good day.

From the morning's radio broadcast, John had good news and bad news to pass on to us. In the former category, he reported that new evidence had been collected on Mars indicating that this distant planet, now a desert, had once contained much water. As to the bad news, he reported the weather forecast: the high winds from the southeast on this day would be followed by gale force winds from the same direction during the next day; small craft warnings had been issued for both days. To this last item of news, Norman added, "And this big fishing boat is considered a small craft, **not** your canoe!" So our residency at this site would now be even more extensive than we had expected.

Years earlier, we had learned that Nature is impartial and impersonal when it dispenses its benevolence or malevolence on the inhabitants of a given region. It is usually just a matter of luck or happenstance as to who is blessed and who is beleaguered by its forces. Winds and water and storms do not lash at us out of hate or spite or anger; nor do they have a kindly side. They are simply there, immense and strong, and indifferent to us as we travel through their domain. We are insignificant in their realm, as are all people, which was one of the most valuable lessons that we learned during our wilderness journeys.

When we lived in and traveled through the wilderness, without the technologies that insulate us from the forces of the elements in our usual daily lives, it was not appropriate for us to think of conquering or dominating Nature; this was utterly impossible. In the wilds, we were reminded of our great vulnerability, as well as the absolute necessity of accepting and working with whatever situations the natural world offered. This approach entailed enduring and operating within, rather than battling fiercely against, such elements as winds, rain, water currents, tough landings, and challenging portages. These features were not at all within our control. You take whatever the water, the sky, and the land give you. This approach involved thinking of the conditions of a given situation not as elements that had to be vanquished, but rather as factors to be weighed, judged, and sensibly dealt with in a harmonious manner, like any of the other challenges in our lives (both the obvious external ones and the hidden internal ones).

Ours was the ancient native approach to the natural world, immersing ourselves in it, becoming attuned to it, fitting into it, passing through it, and absorbing it, while attempting to find a balance with its rhythms. We simply became more of the tiny pieces in the total picture, joining the other creatures who had been present on the scene before we arrived there. When the conditions were conducive to forward progress, we paddled. When they were not appropriate for traveling, when excessively strong winds, high waves, or lightning prevailed, we waited patiently on shore. In those cases, we made the best of the enforced halt by examining in detail the natural features and the wild inhabitants of the place, contemplating the prehistory and history of the region, reading, and chatting among ourselves.

This approach was an exercise in patience and steadiness,

accepting with a considerable degree of serenity the conditions as they presented themselves. We burnished our patience during the days of slow progress against head winds, and even more so during the entire days and nights of no forward progress while we were pinned to shore. Actually, this approach of advancing in steady but sometimes small increments, while living in the moment, allowed us to appreciate more deeply the various aspects of the present, enjoying the gradual accumulation of forward progress with little thought of the more distant goals along the route. It also cleared our minds for considering and fully appreciating the past history of the area.

We did not **do** the Churchill River, or Lake of the Woods, or Lake Winnipeg, or any other waterway, as paddlers are so accustomed to expressing it. We traveled over the surface of these bodies of water when Mother Nature cooperated and allowed us to do so, sometimes providing us with helpful elements and sometimes offering us challenging features. For example, during our journey on Lake of the Woods, a following south wind was a considerable help to us during our night-time traverse across thirteen miles of open water to reach Bigsby Island. This crossing, done with the benign cooperation of *La Vieille*, was immediately followed by three straight days of unrelenting head winds from the north, which held us back as we slowly and laboriously made our way down the lake.

Even when progress was slow and strenuous, we achieved satisfaction from having made that progress with our own bodies and minds. We had to use our good sense along the way, such as adjusting our course to angle across waves, and seeking some shelter from powerful winds on the lee shore of points and the lee side of islands.

During each of our canoe voyages, we were obliged to entrust ourselves to Nature. In the process, our minds functioned much like they had been originally intended, having been developed over millions of years to assess challenges and dangers and keep alive. On these trips, life was simple and straight-forward; we had few needs and wishes. Some of our wishes included finding workable conditions for forward progress and for fully appreciating our surroundings, having enough food in the packs to fuel us and sufficient clothing and rain gear to protect us, and locating campsites that provided decent landing places and a sufficiently cleared and level area for cooking and sleeping.

However, when all of these wished-for conditions did not materialize, we still persisted in our advancement, with an upbeat attitude. We knew that all adventures provide surprises, and they also offer no guarantees concerning either our safety or the eventual outcome. As the mental and physical challenges of each voyage unfolded over time, they actually energized us rather than wearing us down. By sharing and living through these challenging times, including the very real dangers, we acquired satisfaction and a sense of accomplishment, as well as a great deal of knowledge, experience, and quiet confidence.

All morning, we read and relaxed in our sheltered little bay, as the whitecaps reared their frothy heads in the distance out on the open water. About noon, threatening black clouds rolled in from the southeast, and the air chilled considerably. However, no rain fell, and the menacing clouds were soon blown away by high-altitude winds. When Doree announced that it was time to prepare the day's pickerel, she gathered an armful of wood and stacked the twigs to start the fire. I looked appreciatively into the eyes of the fine fish before proceeding to behead, gut, fillet, and skin them. Then Ben buried the refuse in a shallow hole in the shoreline gravel and covered it with a limestone slab, to keep Toby from excavating it. Our son again enjoyed frying the fillets, while Doree prepared a great-tasting pot of noodles, tomatoes, peas, and sweet pea pods, which we ate with gusto. Considering the many windbound days that we had already experienced during most of this Lake Winnipeg trip, Ben commented during our meal, only half-facetiously, "Now this is what I call a family summer vacation!" For his part, Toby wolfed down his share of the golden-fried fish, and also scoured the frying pan afterward with his very thorough tongue.

During my afternoon wanderings, I discovered a considerable pile of moose pellets not far from our camp, in the screen of poplars that edged the shore. It appeared that these spindly-legged giants visited this bay rather regularly. I also located several snail-shaped cephalopod fossils in the limestone slabs which lined the cove. Using the canoe as a back rest, surrounded by delicate wildflowers which presented white petals with yellow centers, we lounged on the sand beneath the shade-casting trees to read. Around the attractive blossoms, two different types of bees flitted from one yellow center to the next, gathering pollen. At one point during the afternoon, while Doree was washing her hair in the shallows, a large black-and-yellow butterfly flapped by me on an erratic zigzag course. After a hot afternoon of reading, I committed an act which was unique in our fifteen years of long-distance paddling trips: I took a bath and laundered my inner and outer shirts! During the following couple of hours, as we snacked and read, I stood to let the sun and the breeze dry my pants and boxer shorts which I left on, while my two shirts dried on some splayed limbs of a shoreline bush.

With the daylight waning, we crawled into the tent for massages and sleep. It had been an extremely relaxing and peaceful day in our sheltered cove, hidden from the wind and waves that were beating incessantly against the other side of the nearby point.

Day Ten

During the night, it rained a little, with the droplets tapping lightly on the tent roof. We slept in until 7:30, knowing that gale force winds from the southeast would stop us if we bothered to pack up and tried to advance a little. (At bedtime the previous evening, there had still been a hearty wind and heavy waves beyond the point.) The sky was overcast with a layer of whitish-grey clouds, so dense that we could gaze directly at the sun without having to squint, while the air temp measured 68 degrees. Stout winds from the southeast whipped the top halves of the trees that flanked our sheltered little bay, even on the protected lee side of the appropriately-named Dancing Point. At one point, three white ducks with black heads paddled silently to our shoreline to check us out, then cruised away just as quietly. In audio contrast, the swampy area that lay behind our camp was alive with a diversity of bird calls.

My inner and outer shirts, having dried on their bush support during the night, represented an unheard-of phenomenon on a canoe trip: clean, non-sweaty shirts on the tenth day! Only an extended series of windbound days could produce such a luxury.

After we had all taken an extended walk along the bay, Doree and Ben decided to further hone their specialized paddling skills on the sheltered surface of our cove. At the bow, Doree worked on drawing, prying, turning on a dime, back-ferrying, and braking. Ben, ensconced at the stern, practiced each of these maneuvers as well, plus steering the course. We three humans had a great time during this session (which I relished in the exceedingly rare role as lounge-lizard passenger). However, all the while we were offshore in the canoe,

Toby ran back and forth along the coastline, barking loudly. Trying to read his thoughts, I imagined that he was encouraging his family to keep safe; but maybe he was urging that family not to forget him! After the practice session, Ben floated for a while offshore, lounging on two air mattresses. Toby curled up beside Doree's feet while she and I read our books.

By noon, although the wind still raged from the south and southeast, the sky had replaced its pewter-hued canvas with white wisps of clouds against a gentle blue background. On a wood fire, Ben whipped up a tall stack of buttermilk-and-blueberry pancakes, while Doree created drop dumplings to accompany a stew of noodles, peas, and beef jerky. As the day continued to heat up, we quietly consumed our meal in the shade.

By 4:00, when we dined on leftover stew and pancakes, the air temperature had soared to a scorching 90 degrees in the shade! Three hours later, black and grey clouds drifted in to fill the sky, but the temp only reduced to 75 degrees. Since the wind had now lessened considerably, we hoped that we would be able to move forward on the following day. This voyage had been an extremely unusual one for us: of the ten days thus far, nine of them had been either partially or completely windbound. We had advanced a total of 107 miles, but we had made 81 of those miles in just two days of traveling (covering 55 and 26 miles). However, during this odd trip we were enjoying some new and enriching canoe-trip experiences; these included a great deal of onshore exploration and plenty of reading. Already, I had finished three books: *Black Elk Speaks*, Moore's *Black Robe*, and Michener's *Journey*. We entered the tent at 8:00, exchanged massages, and were fast asleep within a half-hour.

Day Eleven

We awakened at 3 A.M. to the clamor of the alarm clock. Far to the north of us, a thunderstorm raged, with lightning flashing brightly every few seconds, illuminating the dark clouds that covered most of the sky. At a distance, this activity presented the appearance of artillery fire in a war zone, and it sounded much like that as well. Toby, fearful of the flashing and booming monsters, cowered in a corner of the tent. We returned to sleep, to wait out the storm for a couple of hours. At 5:00, while the rest of the family continued to slumber, I hiked out to the end of the point, to check out the paddling situation. There was already a heavy surf, advancing at a fast pace from the east. While walking back along the bay, I found a pile of moderately large scat, possibly from a wolf, lying just off the critter path that skirted the shoreline amid the young poplar saplings. Back to sleep until 8:30.

When we all emerged from the tent, it was already 83 degrees out, under a blue-grey hazy sky. After a breakfast of gorp and peanut butter crackers, we embarked with the canoe empty, to paddle around Dancing Point and check out the conditions; there, we discovered that the surf was much too rough for us to handle. Back in the cove, we lounged and read in the shade, while Toby actively pursued the innumerable horseflies, trying to capture them between his snapping jaws. As protection against these hard-biting insects, Doree and Ben had extra-long pantlegs that nicely covered their ankles. Since my pants cuffs were a bit shorter, and thus less effective in repelling the flies, I tucked them beneath the tops of my socks. In addition, I used a leafy limb to swat those flies that attempted to bite me through my socks, in the narrow area between the tops of my tennis shoes and the tucked-in cuffs. Nearby, a solitary duck slept on a rock, while another one sunned itself on the sandy beach. Wandering along the water's edge, I came upon a slab of limestone measuring about twelve by eighteen inches which, by itself, was not at all exceptional. However, this stone was balanced so perfectly atop the similar slabs beneath it that it rocked back and forth with the gentle ebb and flow of each wave! Such are the little surprises that are offered by Mother Nature when we slow down our pace and observe the world closely.

At noon, it was 85 degrees in the shade, beneath a hazy blue sky; from our sheltered spot, the winds and waves in the distance seemed to be abating somewhat. With an optimistic outlook, we devoured a feast to bolster our strength, broke camp, and packed the canoe. We were unaware of the conditions that reigned on the opposite side of the point, but we were eager to simply move forward. Underway at 1:30, we began to round the land mass, but immediately encountered boisterous whitecaps advancing from the south-southeast. Although we managed to plow forward for a half-mile around the point, keeping the canoe upright but not empty of water, we were then forced to make a dash for a safe haven on shore. Flashing through an obstacle course of exposed and submerged granite boulders, we landed on a narrow sand beach area, a short ten minutes after having departed from the previous campsite. At least from this new location, we could see the route that lay ahead down the coast. Whenever the weather would finally settle down, we would know when the conditions were amenable for traveling.

To entertain himself, Ben sat atop one of the barely-exposed, offshore granite boulders which had been transported here by glaciers thousands of years before, and let the waves smash hard against his body up to his chest. From the beach, as I gazed off toward the south, I could see two long, low promontories: Driftwood Point three miles away, and far off in the distance Morass Point, twenty miles away. None of us could predict when the weather would finally quiet and allow us to paddle by those landmarks.

We spent much of the remainder of the day reading. Doree, having already finished Michener's huge book *Recessional*, had now completed his *Journey*. Ben had already read *Black Elk Speaks* plus Edward Abbey's books *Desert Solitude* and *The Monkey Wrench Gang*. What a literary canoe trip this had turned out to be!

I was deeply immersed in reading at the water's edge, with the waves hurling themselves onto the beach literally at my feet. Suddenly, I heard rather loud quacking sounds, coming from the other side of the bush beside me. When I peeked around the greenery, I saw a mother duck with one baby close beside her, bobbing offshore in the surf. Five or six more of her ducklings were walking awkwardly on land, at the very edge of the water. Then a large wave rammed against the shore, driving the entire family into the rocks and bushes and out of my sight. I hoped that they would be able to remain together under these demanding conditions; but these youngsters had probably been through numerous similar situations ever since their hatching.

Examining the gravel along the shoreline, I found a water-smoothed chunk of brownish-red granite, which was laced with considerable amounts of silver-colored mica. It reminded me of the many barrels of glittering mineral "treasures" which Jacques Cartier's party had gathered along the St. Lawrence during the 1530s and had excitedly transported back to the mother country, only to learn that their finds were worthless.

Later in the afternoon, we witnessed a fascinating migration of dragonflies. Over the span of five or six minutes, about a hundred of these large insects zoomed to shore at about the height of my head, riding on the swift, warm air currents that blew from the south-

southeast. During the evening, many dragonflies cavorted offshore, as we enjoyed our second view of the moon on this trip, a narrow slice in the eastern sky (we had last seen a slender crescent of *la lune* upon awakening before dawn on Day Two of the voyage).

By 9:00, the waves had reduced considerably, but not enough to permit safe traveling. So we quickly set up the tent and sleeping gear back in the shelter of the trees, to grab a few hours of rest.

Day Twelve

When I checked the conditions at the shoreline at 3 A.M., there was still a brisk wind with moderately large waves coming from the south-southeast. When I awakened again to the alarm clock an hour later, my second walk to the water revealed that a very heavy thunderstorm with plenty of lightning was racing in from the west. During the tremendous downpour that soon followed, one particular lightning bolt struck with an immense POW! that was so near the tent that it made me jump with a start in my sleeping bag. By 5:30, the storm clouds had migrated out of the region, although an occasional grumble of thunder could still be heard off to the west. In the aftermath of the storm, the wind died out completely and the light rain soon ended. The birds began fluting happily in the woods all around us, and out on the water, there were only residual swells from the south-southeast, the aftermath of the severe winds that had whipped the region for four days straight.

At long last, it was finally time for us to move on! Hastily packing up, we were on our way at 6:20. It was sheer joy to be paddling forward on workable water, after having been *dégradé* in the area of Dancing Point for four complete days and nights! However, this long stay, which had far exceeded our previous record for length of time pinned to land by weather, had turned out to be a very interesting and broadening experience for each of us.

With a few paddle strokes, our course was set southward. Immediately, Doree and I began a three-mile traverse across Driftwood Bay, headed straight for Driftwood Point. When lightning flashed not far to the west of us, we hurried across the open water as quickly as possible, while angling against the moderate waves from the south-southeast that had developed. After an hour of hard exertion, when we reached the point with relief, Ben stretched his legs a bit on land. All along the shoreline here, the point was covered with storm-beaten driftwood trees stacked up to a height of about two feet, thus giving the promontory its name. For the next 2 1/3 hours, Ben and I cruised over eight miles of water, staying very close to the shore for safety, as occasional *tonnerre* rolled in the distance and *éclair* flashed twice. Most of the low coastline that we passed had been newly eroded, as evidenced by the many steeply tilted or fallen spruce trees near the water's edge, joining great numbers of entire spruces that had been long ago toppled and washed ashore. At one spot, we cruised past many similar evergreens that had been snapped off at knee height by storm-driven lake ice. Others just behind them had been bent down to ground level by the same relentless forces, and their bark had been skinned off to a height of fifteen feet or more. However, most of these more fortunate and less battered trees, although bearing major ice-gnashed scars, had eventually returned to a nearly upright position.

Right after passing the mouth of the Warpath River, we landed on an inviting gravel beach at 9:40, for a half-hour break. From the mouth of the river, a long sand bar extended far out into the lake. This watercourse had once represented the traditional boundary between the lands of the Cree nation to the north and those of the Ojibwa nation to the south. Not far inland, Doree located a patch of pink-blossomed wild roses which were flourishing in the short summer season.

Upon our departure, as distant thunder rolled off to the southeast, a light rain commenced. While storm clouds advanced over us on a straight course from west to east, the rain fell for about half an hour. Then we enjoyed a few minutes of a following north wind, during which time we received a slight bit of assistance from the sail. Eventually, when the various inconsistent forces of nature became organized, we faced a moderate head wind from the southeast.

At 1:30, just after passing Morass Point, we took a pause for fifteen minutes, pleased to have advanced 21 miles in seven hours since leaving the campsite. With ominous grey clouds filling much of the sky, the temperature had risen to 72 degrees. As the oncoming wind gradually faded away, Ben and I surged forward seven more miles in 2 1/2 hours. To pass the time while Doree and Toby were taking their restorative afternoon nap, my son posed complicated riddles for me to solve.

Just before reaching Carscallen Point, we glided past a long row of impressive shoreline cliffs composed of limestone, whose thick green forest cover on the top marched right to the edge of the precipice. The form and height of these rock features reminded us of the Canadian Shield country that we had observed along much of the mainline route, although that Shield terrain consisted of granite. Gazing at these craggy limestone cliffs, the words spoken by Chief Seattle in 1853 immediately came to mind: "Even the rocks, which seem to be dumb and dead as they swelter in the sun along the silent shore, thrill with memories." I was fascinated by the immense number of specific events that these rock walls had witnessed during the last ten thousand years. Paddling by within sight of this place, thousands of individuals, both native and French, had encountered widely differing situations here. Sometimes the water had been entirely calm and easily traveled; at other times, the same water had been a raging sea with giant waves that had delivered damage and death. In those dangerous instances, native paddlers had thrown offerings overboard to propitiate their gods, offerings in the form of tobacco or other items, or sometimes a living dog with its legs quickly trussed together. These cliffs had witnessed canoes laden with native warriors who were outbound for a surprise attack on a village of their traditional enemies; later, these same individuals had passed by on their return voyage, sometimes flush with victory and thrilling tales, other times defeated and grieving for the dead colleagues they were bringing home, men who had been their beloved relatives and friends. In many instances, the names that were applied to natural features commemorated certain events that had taken place there. Did any living individual know the story behind the name of Dancing Point, where we had just spent four days windbound? Over the millennia, each of the natural features along a given route had borne a great succession of different names, reflecting the myriad events that had transpired at that specific place in different eras. Virtually all of that human history had disappeared without a trace, lost without any chance of recovery. This particular set of limestone cliffs did not even have a known name anymore, but it still retained its innumerable memories.

When we arrived at Carscallen Point, we took a break on land, while a hundred or more dragonflies circled and hovered quietly offshore. In the placid water to the west of our resting spot, the series of St. Martin's Islands stood in a five-mile-long row, parallel to and several miles from the mainland shore.

Between 4:45 and 8:30, Doree and I covered eleven miles on an unruffled, mirror-like surface. With each stroke of her paddle, the blade flashed in the hazy sunlight, creating a mesmerizing gleam, gleam, gleam. On the water north of Caribou Island, we received a pleasant surprise, a chance meeting with our fishermen friends from the cove beside Dancing Point! Partway through our five-mile traverse across a deep bay to reach Clarks Point, threatening waves from the south-southwest kicked up suddenly out of the blue. While Ben sang to bolster us, my life partner and I dug in hard against the oncoming waves for the last three miles of the crossing. The high limestone cliff formations at the tip of the slender, two-mile-long promontory of Clarks Point were an impressive sight. Unfortunately, I was very busy dealing with the troublesome waves during our passing, and could not safely reach beneath my seat and remove the camera from its ammo box to record the scene. Since we were pretty whipped when we finally rounded the point at 8:30, we took a half-hour break on land, stoking up on strawberry-flavored, instant breakfast drink and beef jerky. Then Ben and I paddled for another hour, to advance three miles and reach mile 150 of the trip, where we decided to halt for the night.

After landing at ten o'clock, we gazed eastward in the twilight over the pink-tinted waters which constitute the immense mouth of Sturgeon Bay. In front of us stretched the first huge expanse that south-bound voyageurs had faced on this lake. Weighing various factors, they had decided at this place to either traverse for thirteen miles in an easterly direction across the mouth of the bay, or instead to skirt along its entire, deeply concave coastline, adding 25 miles to their route. Off to the east in the rapidly diminishing light, we could glimpse a series of low islands which appeared as smudges on the horizon, five miles in the distance. For the voyageurs, the crossing of Sturgeon Bay had consisted of five miles of open water out to those islands, then four miles of short traverses within the island group (from Round Island to Dahls Island to Inner Sturgeon Island), and finally four more miles of open water, to eventually reach the huge mid-lake peninsula that juts upward from the south.

We reveled in the absolutely flat surface of the lake, which had been an extreme rarity for us during most of the previous twelve days. It looked like a giant watercolor painting, with various shades of light blue and pink reflecting on it from the sunset, the sky, and the clouds.

The only drawback to this magnificent scene was the population of voracious mosquitoes that lived at this site; they were horrendous! In just a half-hour, we quickly secured the gear and set up camp, then traded well-deserved massages in the insect-proof shelter, to the repeated calling of a nearby whip-poor-will.

After tallying the events of the day, I announced that, having put in more than fifteen hours on the move, we had advanced 43 miles between 6:40 A.M. and 10 P.M., with just a few minutes of sail assistance during that entire time. At this point, after twelve days on the water, we had covered 150 miles, some 23 miles short of half of the projected length of 345 miles of the voyage. During two travel days, we had made 98 of those miles (55 and 43 miles, respectively, representing 2/3 of our total progress), while the other ten days had been either partially or completely windbound. During seven of those latter ten days, we had advanced 5, 2, 5, 8, 26, 5, or 1/2 miles, respectively, before being driven to shore by powerful winds; on the other three days, we had not made any forward progress at all.

In the tent, blessedly sheltered from the humming swarms of mosquitoes, we held a serious family conference. The uncooperative wind conditions of ten of the last twelve days could very well continue as we would make our way down the southern half of the lake. If that were to be the case, we would in all likelihood run out of food before reaching the mouth of the Winnipeg River, about 195 miles distant. Our present location was a crucial place for making a decision about whether to continue onward or to call a halt to our journey. Up until now, we had been excessively windbound while traveling along a moderately indented shoreline. Looking ahead to the next 95 miles of the route, between here and The Narrows (where the mainline route crosses over to the east side of the lake), the passage would include traverses across the much wider expanses of Sturgeon Bay, Lynx Bay, Kinwow Bay, and Fisher Bay. Unfortunately, these major crossings could hold us back for days at a time if the contrary winds were to persist.

In addition, we had just paddled the much more attractive and inviting northern half of Lake Winnipeg. There was no doubt that, in comparison, the southern half would be a major disappointment. To the south of The Narrows, we were well aware that the depths of the heavily silted waters are much reduced, with the shallows often extending out a great distance from shore, sometimes up to a mile. In general, the soil of the bottom and the shorelines consists of sticky, fine clay silt. To avoid the innumerable boulders which are strewn in this muck amid the shallows, it would be wise to limit paddling to only the daylight hours, thus eliminating the possibility of night traveling, when the winds would be generally reduced. Another drawback to the southern waters was the considerable amounts of toxic blue-green algae called cyanobacteria which thrive there, feeding on an overabundance of the nutrients nitrogen and phosphorus. At the end of our Winnipeg River voyage six years earlier, when we had arrived near the southern end of this lake, we had received a good dosage of the shallow depths that extend far out from shore, and the clinging, gooey muck that covers the bottom and the coastlines and sucks at feet and legs. From that experience, we were abundantly aware that it was no picnic traveling on the southern part of Lake Winnipeg.

Finally, our very reasons for paddling the length of the mainline canoe route were to obtain knowledge and understanding of the ways of our ancestors during the fur trade era, to relive many of the experiences of their travels during that period, and to gain a first-hand knowledge of the routes that they had covered. This was what our trips were all about, rather than paddling every single mile of the mainline route. We were focusing much more on the journey than on the ultimate destination. Over the course of the previous twelve days on Lake Winnipeg, during both our traveling days and our more numerous windbound days, we had fulfilled that mission, experiencing deeply what canoe travel on this body of water involved, and also learning a great deal about its lands, its plants, and its wild inhabitants. We had approached our traveling on the lake in much the same way that the voyageurs of old had done. On six of the potential traveling days, we had awakened between 2:00 and 4:00 A.M., on another day at 4:45, and on two days at 5:15, in an attempt to utilize the early-morning hours for paddling, before the brawny winds picked up. However, *La Vieille* had generally been uncooperative, as she had also been in 1845 when the brigade of the H.B.C. trader Ballantyne had needed a full fifteen days to travel the length of this lake.

We carried out our canoe trips as an entirely private educational and enrichment project, not as a public stunt or an epic journey. In fact, we had not intended to write a book or otherwise publicize our experiences.

Carefully considering all of the various facets of our present situation, we made a decision. The next day, we would make our way seven miles to the south, to the lakeside native community of Dauphin River, and at that place we would end our Lake Winnipeg adventure. A road from the outside world leads to this settlement; so our shuttle drivers could deliver our van to us there. A deeply experienced 157 miles on this lake was sufficient for our purposes, and we felt no shame in halting at Dauphin River, rather than paddling the full distance to the Winnipeg River mouth, as we had originally intended. In this regard, we took consolation in the knowledge that the famous Canadian paddler and researcher Eric Morse, during his many decades of outstanding groundwork for his classic book *Fur Trade Canoe Routes of Canada/Then and Now*, had not, in fact, paddled a number of very important segments of the mainline fur trade route. In just the western half of the route alone, these untraveled sections had included all of the Athabasca River and Lake Athabasca, all of the Saskatchewan River, and the lower portion of the Winnipeg River.

By 11:15, content with our group decision, we were each submerged in our respective dream-worlds.

Day Thirteen

Boom! Boom! In the middle of the night, we were suddenly awakened by two loud rifle shots that rang out in quick succession, apparently coming from the water just offshore from our camp! Quickly unzipping the tent flap, having no idea what to expect, I stuck my head out and peered into the dim moonlit night. From a small boat floating in our little cove came the shouts of two adult males. Judging from the excited tone of the shouts, as well as the splashing sounds of one of the men running through the shallows from the boat to the shore, I discerned that these were hunters who had felled a moose, which had wandered down to the water's edge to drink.

After this abrupt and violent awakening, it took a while for us to drift back to sleep. When the alarm clock rang at 5:15 A.M., a thick grey fog obliterated the junction of the sky and the water to the south of us. Shortly, the first arc of the orange-red ball of the sun emerged above the lake to the east, tinting the sky and shedding a path of pastel colors across the docile water, along the exact route of the traverse across the mouth of Sturgeon Bay. Within minutes, the entire

A Modern-Day Voyageur Family*

eastern heaven was painted solidly in several shades of orange. It was already 72 degrees, the same balmy temperature as when we had hit the sack. Off to the south, thunder rolled like tympani almost constantly, and lightning flashed twice as a dark storm front rushed across the region from west to east, soon completely filling the sky and obliterating the sun.

At 6:00, after we had loaded and were about to depart, lightning cracked loudly and sharply very near to our location, and rain began to fall. Suiting up in our full rain gear, we prepared to wait out the thunderstorm. With intermittent lightning bolts striking nearby and lots of thunder rolling loudly, we stood at a distance from the lake in a heavy downpour for 2 1/2 long hours. Removing the closed-cell-foam pad from the passenger spot on the bottom of the canoe, Doree covered Toby with it on shore, to keep him somewhat dry. She also patted him reassuringly, since his fears of thunder and lightning had set him to trembling all over. Whenever we became chilled during our extensive wait, we jogged up and down the shoreline or moved around actively on the beach, to get our circulation flowing.

To pass the time, I let my imagination wander over the extensive history of the fur trade era around Lake Winnipeg and the region immediately to the west. Aligned in an end-to-end, north-south position, Lake Manitoba and Lake Winnipegosis lie some thirty to fifty miles west of Lake Winnipeg; taken together, their combined length is nearly the same as that of Lake Winnipeg, and runs parallel to it. The Dauphin River serves as the single outlet of the two smaller lakes, flowing eastward from the upper area of Lake Manitoba into Lake Winnipeg, just seven miles to the south of where we were standing.

These three bodies of water constituted La Vérendrye's region of the "Western Sea." His expansion of posts into this area between 1734 and 1741 broke the monopoly that the H.B.C. had held until then on the peltries commerce in the huge region stretching southwest from Hudson's Bay. Before the establishment of La Vérendrye's forts, most of the furs and hides from this vast area had been transported by Cree and Assiniboine traders down the Hayes River to York Fort on Hudson's Bay. After the arrival of the French, much of this trade was diverted up the Winnipeg River and eastward to Montreal.

La Vérendrye's facilities in this region included Ft. Maurepas, established in 1734 near the mouth of the Red River, just south of the southern end of Lake Winnipeg; Ft. La Reine, constructed in 1738 a little to the west, on the Assiniboine River beside the portage that extended northward from the river to the southern end of Lake Manitoba (the commandant christened this carry as Portage la Prairie, and the lake as Lac de la Prairie); a new Ft. Maurepas, established in 1739 by the mouth of the Winnipeg River, near the southern end of Lake Winnipeg; Ft. Dauphin, built in 1741 near the water connection between Lake Manitoba and Lake Winnipegosis; and Ft. Bourbon, established in the same year of 1741 on the Cedar Lake section of the lower Saskatchewan River, just across a very narrow neck of land from the northern end of Lake Winnipegosis. The operation of these various facilities, which comprised the most westerly posts of the French regime until 1749, involved a great deal of canoe traffic along the lengths of Lakes Winnipeg, Manitoba, and Winnipegosis, as well as on the connecting watercourse of the Dauphin River.

During the later British era of the trade, numerous posts were constructed throughout this region as well. David Thompson explored the area of Lakes Manitoba, Winnipegosis, and Winnipeg, as well as the connecting Dauphin River, during the period of 1797-1798; this was immediately after he had switched allegiances from the H.B.C. to the N.W.C. in 1797. Many pairs of adjacent posts were established in the area by the fiercely competitive N.W.C. and H.B.C., before the amalgamation of the two firms in 1821. For example, for a few years during the period of 1790-1805, personnel from each of these companies operated two separate trading facilities at the mouth of the Dauphin River: Latour's House for the Montreal-based N.W.C., and Ft. Suspense for the London-based H.B.C. Both of these posts closed within less than five years.

After we had stood in the pouring chilly rain for 21/2 hours, waiting to depart, the sky finally lightened in color and the rain eased up somewhat. So we decided to shove off at 8:30, but we hugged the coastline closely, with the hope of avoiding a lightning strike. Remaining near the shore required our vigilance to avoid snagging the canoe, since much of this coast has submerged boulder gardens that extend well offshore. After an hour, the rain ceased and a few blue tears began to appear in the thick grey cloud cover; occasionally, the sun splashed its cheerful beams of hope through these holes. At the same time, a moderate wind from the northeast arose, which was helpful for traveling due south. Hoisting the sail, Doree and

I covered seven miles to reach the community of Dauphin River in two hours. As we neared the shore at the settlement, the wind freshened considerably, forming whitecaps and pushing the sail hard -- alarmingly hard. This was no place to have a mishap, in the last few minutes of our entire voyage. We poured it on, zooming toward the coastline. At last, on our thirteenth day of the trip, we landed for the final time at 10:30 A.M., having traveled 157 miles on the changeable and formidable body of water that is called Lake Winnipeg.

As soon as we had unloaded everything onto the shore, Doree, Ben, and Toby departed on foot, to find a phone in the native settlement of Dauphin River and notify our shuttle drivers in Grand Rapids, 2 1/2 hours away by road. While I was updating the journal at the canoe, Clifford Summer, a native resident of the community, stopped by to visit with me. Born and raised here in Dauphin River, he had gill-netted on Lake Winnipeg in his younger days. He noted that a total of 25 men from this locale currently fish on the lake. Especially in the fall, whitefish are taken in Sturgeon Bay directly out from the settlement. Two of his sons had been the hunters in the boat near our tent the night before, who had shot the moose in our cove. That particular animal had been a young bull, two years old. The native people, he explained, are allowed to hunt moose year round, without any limits. They usually seek these animals after dark by boat, when they come down to the shoreline to drink and to enter the water for some relief from the biting insects.

The Dauphin River Indian Reserve, stretching along the lakeshore for two miles and extending inland for about a mile on both sides of the river, is home to some ninety individuals. The road from the community out to Route 6 had been constructed in the mid-1960s. Previously, the roadway had been a muddy dirt track suitable only for horse-drawn vehicles; as a result, most of the transport of people and goods had been carried out with watercraft on the Dauphin River. This waterway, flowing into Lake Winnipeg here, is the outlet of Lake Manitoba and Lake Winnipegosis, lying some 35 miles to the southwest as the crow flies.

Another visitor of mine at the canoe was Emery Stagg, the chief of the Dauphin River Band. After chatting for a bit, he departed, and soon returned with a gift for me: the book entitled *Paddle to the Arctic* by the famous Winnipeg adventurer Don Starkell.

Ben and I followed a narrow road, not knowing exactly what we might find. There were scattered one-story houses of wood, mostly small and needing some paint. Noticing that someone was sitting on the open-air porch of a bigger house up a pathway, we made our way there and introduced ourselves to a native woman. Before long, several other family members came out to say hello, most of them somewhat reticent. We were invited to have some toast and a cup of much-appreciated steaming coffee. We looked into the curious eyes of hospitable strangers, who quietly listened to our tale of paddling from Grand Rapids, in our canoe which was just down the path at the edge of the water.

Leading us from the new friends we'd met, Shannon, a young European-looking-but-native woman with blonde hair, showed Ben and me the way to the only restaurant in the community. A small CLOSED sign on the door dashed our hopes of procuring a few big burgers! We learned that the owner had departed that morning to pick up supplies in the nearest town, almost an hour's drive away.

Shannon then directed us to the solitary general store, where I plaintively asked the proprietor if she knew of someone we could hire to cook a meal for us, since we had just come off the water. A thirtyish native woman who was in the store at the time, asked, "Are you the Kents?" This was certainly a "Doctor Livingston, I presume?" moment! Ben and I were quite taken aback, not imagining how someone in this little native community, where we had landed only minutes before, would know our name! As it turned out, Audrey Letandre was engaged to Lawrence Halchuk, one of the friendly and generous fishermen whom we had met on the lake beside Dancing Point about a week earlier.

Leading us to her home, Audrey prepared for us an excellent feast of moose roast, "cooked in milk to eliminate the wild flavor," she explained. In case we didn't care for moose meat, she added six massive grilled burgers and a mound of grilled potato and onion slices to the menu. The smells wafting from the grill tickled our attentive nostrils. Audrey eagerly shared stories with us, including an explanation of a glamour photo of herself that was displayed on the refrigerator. Her cozy abode and her welcoming demeanor warmed both our hearts and our chilled bodies. After enjoying our portions of the feast at Audrey's house, Ben and I felt ready to nap. But remembering old Dad at the canoe landing, we headed out to deliver Tim's share to him, along with a celebratory beer. That extraordinarily delicious meal, especially the succulent moose roast, along with the hospitality of the Good Samaritan who made it for us, created a series of vivid images that we have always remembered!

We were soon joined once again by Audrey's niece Shannon Letandre, who had been raised here on the reserve; she was now a university student in Winnipeg, enrolled in the Native Studies program. She plans to eventually record for posterity the oral traditions of her people. While we waited for the Hobbs couple to arrive from Grand Rapids with our van, Audrey and Shannon gave us a special tour of the reserve by car, and related lots of information about both its history and the activities of its current residents. (Doree)

After expressing our appreciation to all those who had helped us in various ways, we began our homeward trek, stopping in Ashern for a restaurant celebration and a free shower, and then driving on through the night. On Sunday morning, we arrived at Kakabeka Falls on the Kaministiquia River, where we relished its impressive, mist-shrouded setting and contemplated the arduous portage that this massive obstacle, dropping 128 feet in elevation, had required. Then we moved on to Ft. William, where we were pleasantly surprised to find the annual rendezvous in progress: musicians performed period music in the central square, staff reenactors gave presentations and demonstrations inside the buildings, and weekend voyageurs camped outside the fort walls. That night, we slept in our van beside the Lake Superior shoreline.

On Monday, thinking ahead toward our Lake Superior journey the following year, we gathered data and maps at the travel information station at Schrieber. Then we drove along the northern shoreline highway to Sault Ste. Marie, checking out the lake and arranging a food cache drop at the community of Michipicoten, in case we decided to take that approach in 1997. En route, we were highly inspired by our visit to Agawa Rock, a soaring cliff wall at the shoreline which bears impressive ancient pictographs.

Throughout our day and night on the road, the surface of the lake was like a huge mirror. We thought, if only we could be blessed with such cooperative conditions during our paddle along this coastline next year! During most of this day of driving along the flank of the massive body of water, we noted that thick fog banks would probably be a major challenge during the following year's journey.

XVII
Fifteenth Voyage
Lake Superior, July 2-10, 1998

Who does not grow, declines.
Rabbi Hillel

Men fear death, as children fear to go in the dark.
And as that natural fear in children is increased with tales,
so is the other.
Sir Francis Bacon

You've got to jump off the cliff all the time
And build your wings on the way down.
Ray Bradbury

All things are ready
If your mind be so.
William Shakespeare

We were about to paddle an immense expanse of water: Lake Superior, the largest freshwater lake in the world, which has a whopping 32,162 square miles of surface area. The deepest and coldest of the five Great Lakes, Superior extends down to depths of 1,333 feet, while it has an average depth of 489 feet. The lake contains about three quadrillion (that is a 3 followed by a row of fifteen zeros) gallons of water, more than the contents of the other four Great Lakes combined. That liquid, fully 10 percent of the supply of fresh water on the surface of the entire globe, is enough to cover all of Canada, the U.S., Mexico, Central America, and South America with a foot of water. This massive lake, actually a huge inland sea, measures 160 miles in maximum width by 383 miles in length, measured down the midline of its vast arc. It has a coastline totaling 2,730 miles, counting the shorelines of its islands.

Glancing at a map, it was very clear to us why the native people had dubbed this body of water Gitchi Gumi or Missi Sakiegan (The

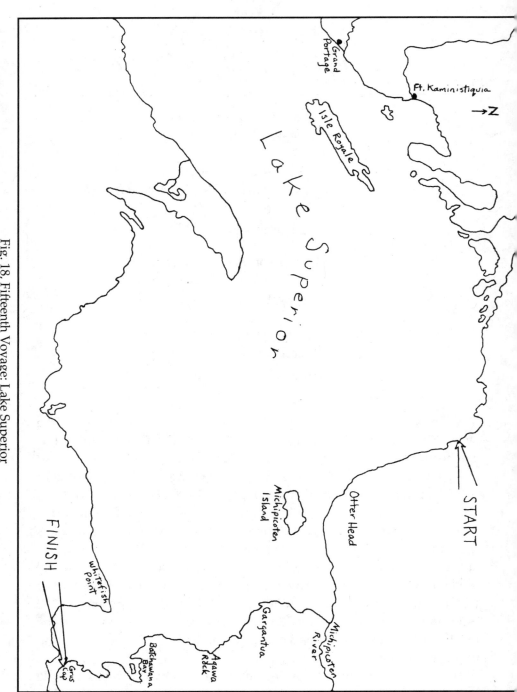

Fig. 18, Fifteenth Voyage: Lake Superior

Supreme Lake, The Big Lake), and why the French had christened it Lac Supérieur (or sometimes Lac de Tracy, Lac de Bourbon, or Lac de Condé, when the cartographer wished to ingratiate himself with important personages at Versailles).

During our previous two voyages, we had been windbound for about one-third of the time while paddling Lake Huron, and about three-quarters of the time during our storm-plagued trek down Lake Winnipeg. In preparation for this Lake Superior journey, with those two previous trips clearly in mind, I had thoroughly studied the mainline route which extended for about 450 miles along the northern shore of the lake, from the head of the St. Marys River to Ft. Kaministiquia and Grand Portage. After much consideration, I came to a decision: we would paddle the most scenic and wild portion of the coast, which was also the most exposed and storm-battered section. Our route would extend from about the northeastern corner of the lake, along a generally southeasterly course, down to the St. Marys River. By traveling this passage, we could gain a deep understanding of the challenges of long-distance canoe travel that the voyageurs of old had faced on this body of water, while reliving many of their experiences; and we could also immerse ourselves in the wildest natural environment of the lake.

This stretch of some 270 miles of coastline, representing about 60 percent of the Lake Superior mainline route, would include Pukaskwa National Park, Lake Superior Provincial Park, and many other sections of land which are still in equally pristine condition, having no road access to within many miles of the shoreline. We would omit from our journey the stretch of some 55 miles along the northern coast of Lake Superior, with its coastal highway and string of little settlements, as well as the swath of about 125 miles that extends in a southwesterly direction along a row of islands and peninsula tips from Copper Island to nearly Grand Portage. Our journey would take us along the exposed eastern shore of the lake, which bears the forces of the prevailing westerly winds and the massive waves that are thrown up by those winds, having as much as 90 to 250 miles of unbroken water in which to build. In addition, we would pass many long sections of the coast which present sheer cliffs rising directly from the water, areas in which there would often be no landing places for as much as four or five miles at a time. Since we wished to truly experience the dangers and challenges of the fur trade route along the northern coastline of Superior, and to see as much unspoiled and outstanding scenery as possible, this was definitely the portion of the route to encounter these elements.

From our experiences on Lakes Huron and Winnipeg, we knew that the prevailing westerlies and other long-distance winds, as well as the violent local weather fronts for which Lake Superior is especially famous, might provide considerable drama. The formation of this local weather takes place in a rather expected pattern. Each morning, the rays of the sun gradually heat the masses of granite rock which surround the lake. Then cool air drifting across the surface of the frigid water passes over these rock areas, the air is heated, and it rises to form cumulous clouds. This powerful rising action typically creates strong air currents, which kick up the surface of the lake from latter morning or early afternoon until early evening.

The surface of the water, due to its great depth in most areas and its very long stretches of open, unbroken expanses, responds to turbulent air currents by forming large broad-based waves and swells. In this respect, Superior behaves more like an ocean than a lake. This is in contrast to the reactions of smaller, shallower bodies of water, which typically work up narrow-based, steep-fronted waves.

Whenever possible during this trip, we would use the strategy of the voyageurs, by rising at or before dawn to take advantage of the calm conditions before the lake began to kick up, and then returning to the water again if it settled down during the evening. Some period travel accounts indicated that the brigades typically departed between 5 and 8 A.M. while traveling on Lake Huron, and between 3 and 6 A.M. while paddling on Lake Superior. Even with our early-morning-launch approach, we still expected that we could be windbound about one day out of three, a ratio that was recorded in many fur trade journals.

Also in typical voyageur fashion, we would attempt to remain relatively close to the shoreline, so that the sprinting distance to a place of refuge would not be too great when a squall swept in. In 1720, the Jesuit Fr. Charlevoix described this procedure while he was traveling on Lake Superior: "When you are least thinking of it, the lake becomes all on fire, the ocean in its greatest rage is not more tossed, in which case you must take care to be near shelter, to save yourself." George Heriot, writing between 1792 and 1816, noted, "Lake Superior...is subjected to frequent storms, and a swell similar to that of the tides of the ocean rolls in upon its coasts. The navigation is here dangerous when the wind blows with strength, and travelers for this reason keep near the north shore." When Henry Schoolcraft traveled over the length of this body of water with the Cass expedition in 1820, he noted, "We generally kept within a mile of the shore, and often much nearer so that it was constantly in plain sight."

However, that safety rule was not as simple to carry out as it sounds, both for the ancient voyageurs and for the Kent family. The coastline is studded with bays of various sizes, including the large Michipicoten Bay, Batchawana Bay, and Goulais Bay; closely following their deeply indented shorelines at all times would add innumerable miles to the total journey. As a result, judgment calls had to be made on a regular basis, deciding if the weather looked auspicious for making an extensive traverse across the mouth of a bay, which could reduce the mileage considerably. We hoped that *La Vieille* would be cooperative during our trip, allowing us to cut across some of the smaller bays, and possibly even the large ones as well, reducing the length of our voyage.

Whether we would be obliged to paddle every one of the 270 miles of our route along the coastline, or whether we would be blessed with cooperative conditions for making a few or many traverses across bays, was not of vital importance. However, it was crucial to our survival that we not capsize during this particular journey. The water temperature of Lake Superior averages 39 degrees throughout the year, warming only a little during midsummer. At those low temperatures, if we went into the drink, we would not last for too long while trying to reach shore and seek some warmth. Within a relatively short time in the water, hypothermia would take away the use of our arms and legs, and reduce our core body temperature to fatal levels. When John Bigsby traveled over Superior with the International Boundary Commission survey team in 1823, he recorded one such incident: "Everything looked innocent and pretty...Any thought of danger seemed absurd; and yet it was here that two well-manned canoes of the North-west Company were cast ashore about the year 1815, and nine persons drowned...We must suppose that the disaster commenced some distance from land, and that the winds drove the canoes upon this strand." We fully absorbed the message.

We Kents carried out our annual trips on the mainline route to seek understanding of the old ways and to deeply appreciate nature. However, we did not intend to pay for that knowledge and appreciation with either our health or our lives. Yet we understood that virtually all canoeing is situation-specific. This monster lake could be accommodating, and it could also be murderous. If we were lucky, we would be exposed to equal doses of both extremes of its mood swings. However, I was not particularly encouraged when, shortly before we commenced our Lake Superior jaunt, I received the following message in a Chinese fortune cookie: "A thrilling time is in your immediate future."

En route to our put-in, we spent a day time-traveling at the Straits of Mackinac, visiting Ft. Michilimackinac and various places in and around St. Ignace, where many of our fur trade ancestors had lived and worked during the French regime. Toward evening, making our way some sixty miles north to Sault Ste. Marie, we crossed the International Bridge into Canada at about 8 P.M., and then stopped for a snack of pie and ice cream at the West Side Cafe, near the international customs office. Since we were ahead of our pre-arranged schedule, we had some time to kill before our ten o'clock appointment with our shuttle driver, Michael Turco, who had served us in the same capacity two years earlier, when we had paddled Lake Huron.

When he arrived at the restaurant, right on time, we departed for the drive of 250 miles along the northeast shore of Lake Superior, to reach our put-in spot. This was to be at the mouth of the Pic River, the northern boundary of Pukaskwa (locally pronounced "puckasaw") National Park. About two hours into the trip, a moose trotted across the pavement in front of the van; later, we observed a red fox and then a silver fox standing beside the roadway. During the entire drive, the night was brightly illuminated by the half-moon and millions of stars in a cloudless sky. Wherever we passed within sight of the Superior shoreline, we could see that the water was smooth and placid. We hoped that these very amenable conditions would continue in the hours and days that lay ahead! At Wawa, we took a break for 45 minutes at a restaurant/gas station, having a snack of blueberry pie and coffee.

Day One

At 3:15 A.M., with eyes like slits, we approached our destination, having traveled 410 miles from our home in 71/2 hours of driving, plus numerous stops. This was by far our shortest trip to the put-in spot during fifteen years of paddling the mainline route. Unfortunately, the brevity of this particular drive did not provide us with many opportunities to sleep.

As the dirt road neared the mouth area of the Pic River, it petered out into soft sand. Since Michael Turco was driving at this point, I suggested that he stop at this place; we could haul our canoe and gear by hand over the remaining distance, to reach the water's edge on the north side of the river. Not even slowing down, he insisted that he could drive much closer to the river. Within moments, the van was mired in the very soft sand. As he spun the wheels, the vehicle quickly dug itself deeper and deeper; soon, the muffler and gas tank were touching the surface of the ground.

A part of me wanted to whack the driver over the head -- just a fleeting message from my amygdala, the primitive area of the brain which responds without thinking when we are under duress. (Doree)

Ben, ever the problem-solver (blessed with lots of prefrontal cortex in his brain), excavated the jack in the jam-packed back of the van and raised the right rear tire (the source of drive power of the vehicle), after which I shoveled out the sand from the area around and beneath the tire. Then Ben located a few driftwood boards, jammed them into the hole beneath the tire, and Doree gently drove forward a short distance, without spinning the wheels. After nearly an hour of effort, we were glad to be out of that uncomfortable predicament! Our shuttle driver remained quiet, and never apologized.

Following another hour of unloading, hauling everything across the dunes area down to the water's edge, and loading the canoe, we were ready to launch. During the course of this procedure, the sky had begun to lighten off to the east and the stars had commenced to fade, starting at about 4:30.

Under a clear sky with an air temperature of 50 degrees, we were afloat at 5:15. Thick grey mist rose from the Pic River water, in both its channel and where it flowed into Lake Superior a short distance away. This surreal phenomenon was caused by the warmer air making contact with the surface of the frigid lake water. And the water was indeed cold here; just three miles out from this spot, the depth of Gitchi Gumi measured 540 feet. Based on numerous accounts of the fur trade era, we expected to face varying degrees of navigational hindrance from thick fog on about a third of the mornings; we also anticipated being windbound on roughly an equal number of days.

In ancient times, native people had dubbed this waterway the Pic (or Pijitik) Sippi (Mud River), since its greyish water, laden with clay silt, clouded the clear water of the lake at its mouth for a mile or more. However, on this particular morning, the fog hid any such staining of the lake from our sight. As soon as our green bow nosed from the mouth of the moderate-sized river onto the surface of the open lake, the canoe began rising and falling with the moderate swells that were flowing from the south-southwest. With a combination of much eagerness and some trepidation, we began our long-anticipated adventures on the monster lake!

About two minutes later, after we had fallen into our familiar rhythm of all-day paddling, an onshore wind from the east picked up. As a result, during our traverse across the deep cove called Playter Harbor, we dealt with a mixture of swells and wind which were arriving at a considerable angle to each other. After advancing 31/2 miles during the first hour, we paused for a fifteen minute break on Picture Island, where raging storms had kept the bedrock shoreline nearly barren of vegetation for up to sixty feet from the water's edge. As we would do many times during this trip when landing for a break on a shoreline of bare rock, we used a couple of driftwood tree limbs or small logs as rollers, to bring the bow far enough onto land to secure it. While we munched our cheeseburgers from the cafe at the Sault, the rim of the golden sun peeped over the ragged top of the dark evergreen forest off to the east.

Looking off to the horizon lying to the west, southwest, and south of us, we could see nothing but wide-open expanses of water. The nearest landmasses in each of those directions lay 90, 110, and 140 miles away, respectively. Nature this massive and powerful, even when it was in a tranquil mood, made us feel tiny and somewhat insignificant. It was abundantly clear just who was truly in charge during our journey over this body of water, and it was definitely not we puny humans!

From the put-in spot, we had been traveling in the northernmost end of Pukaskwa National Park, which stretches southward along the coastline for some fifty miles. This huge preserve of wilderness, extending as much as thirty miles inland, had been established only fifteen years earlier, in 1983. It felt wonderful to be once again immersed in the old familiar Canadian Shield country, in which we had not traveled for two years, since our Lake Huron trip! The scenery during last year's trek on Lake Winnipeg, in limestone country with mostly low shorelines and surrounding land, had been much less inspiring than this. Our entire voyage on Lake Superior would take place in the rugged granite bedrock environment of the Precambrian Shield.

At the end of the final Ice Age, some 10,000 years ago, the glaciers had retreated northward from the Lake Superior basin. The massive gouged-out depression then filled with glacial meltwater, up to a level which was much higher than the modern water levels. As the liquid gradually receded, extensive cobblestone beaches were left exposed, some of them several hundred feet higher than today's water levels. Over time, the lake developed large populations of northern pike, walleyed pike, whitefish, lake trout, and sturgeon, which abound to this day. Superior is now home to a total of 78 species of fish, including the only sustainable spawning lake trout population in the five Great Lakes.

During our journey through the region, we would be passing through two different forest areas, with Michipicoten Bay marking the general dividing line between them. To the north of this huge bay, the land would be covered with a mostly coniferous forest of spruce, fir, and some tamarack (larch), with poplar and birch found in patches; along the bay and to the south of it, the hills and valleys would be clothed in a mixed coniferous-deciduous forest of pine, hemlock, fir, maple, and birch. These two forest regions also demarcated the traditional lands of the resident native populations, with the Cree nation inhabiting the area as far south as Michipicoten Bay, and the Ojibwa nation inhabiting the land from the bay southward to the St. Marys River. However, the Ojibwa population had later expanded further northward during the fur trade era. A place with an annual temperature swing of as much as 120 degrees is inhabited by tough and resilient plants, animals, and people.

Besides supporting deer and moose, the region where we had commenced our trip also represents the southernmost breeding grounds for woodland caribou in Canada. Pukaskwa National Park supports the southernmost herd, numbering some forty animals. Just west of the Pic River mouth, the Coldwell Peninsula and Pic Island each shelter a small herd, while some thirteen miles further to the west, Slate Islands Provincial Park is home to the densest population of woodland caribou in all of North America, with a herd that fluctuates between about one hundred and six hundred animals.

When using our compasses during this trip, we would need to allow for a discrepancy of 3 to 5 degrees east of true magnetic north when figuring our readings. This was because the directional line running through Lake Superior to true magnetic north extends through the western end of Isle Royale. In comparison, during our trek down the Athabasca River, we had to allow for a discrepancy of 23 degrees west of true magnetic north.

As we relaxed on Picture Island and the rays of the sun played on my face, my thoughts wandered back over the early history of the Pic River mouth area. From at least the 1760s, it had been the site of an Ojibwa village, and had remained so from then on. By the Treaty of 1850, the Canadian government had established the Pic River Indian Reserve on the north side of the river, commencing one mile above the mouth and extending upriver for 21/2 miles and westward for one mile. The native community here now contains about fifty homes. The mouth of the river had also been the site of a series of trading posts, beginning with the Pic River post that was established by independent Montreal-based traders in 1779 and was operated for about two decades. Then, in 1803, two competing facilities were built beside the mouth, one by personnel of the N.W.C. and the other by men from the break-away firm called the X.Y.C. The lattermost post was run for only a couple of years, while the N.W.C. post was operated for more than fifty years, first by men of that company, and after 1821 by personnel of the combined H.B.C. and N.W.C. firms. In 1823, John Bigsby described this facility as "a picketed square, formed by the superintendant's house, other dwellings, and storehouses."

From the 1670s onward, native and French traders had utilized three canoe routes to travel between Lake Superior and Hudson's Bay. One consisted of the Pic, Kenogami, and Albany Rivers, while further to the west, a second route involved the Nipigon River, Lake Nipigon, and the Ombabika, Kapikotongwa, Ogoki, and Albany Rivers. The third route lay to the east, utilizing the Michipicoten River and several northward-flowing rivers.

At our island stopping place, the huge slanted panels of storm-cleared bedrock that lined the shoreline were criss-crossed with countless narrow cracks. Within some of these slender fissures, tiny pockets of soil had been gradually deposited by wind and water; in these places, scattered blades of grass, as well as little flowers with delicate, bell-shaped purple blossoms, had managed to take hold. Offshore, two loons floated peacefully nearby, curious about the new visitors in their domain.

Shortly after our departure from the island, a moderately strong head wind and waves from the south-southwest picked up. We labored against them for a half-hour, moving forward 1 1/2 miles, until the ever-growing elements finally became too hearty for us to handle. Making a sharp left, we dived for shelter up the mouth of the rather wide Rivière Blanche (White River). The waves, running hard for a considerable distance up the mouth area, crashed onto the rocky shorelines. Traveling about 2/10 of a mile upriver from the open lake to find a placid haven, we landed in an area that was flanked by high broken formations of pink granite laced with thick veins of white quartzite. These masses of bedrock, rounded and smoothed by thousands of years of ice and water action, were covered at the top with evergreen forest and in many lower areas with a thick carpet of light green moss and numerous stands of blueberry bushes.

After just five miles of progress on the very first morning, we were already windbound, at 7:30 A.M.! All four of us curled up to rest in various shaded hollows among the rock ledges, where we slept deeply for three hours, only occasionally disturbed by the tickle of ants scampering over us. When I finally awakened, I immediately thought of Etienne Brulé, the first Frenchman to have seen the massive expanses of Lake Superior 380 years earlier, in 1618. I also considered the adventures of our trader ancestor Claude David, who had spent the period of 1660 to 1663 on the shores of this immense body of water at Chequamegon Bay, just seven years after the first Frenchmen had entered the interior regions specifically to trade, in 1653.

At 11:30, we lunched on chicken sandwiches that we had brought from St. Ignace. It was certainly a beautiful day to be pinned to the land, with an air temperature of 72 degrees in the shade, a cloudless blue sky above, and a stiff breeze coming from the south-southwest. Back from the water, Doree located a lovely grouping of purple irises amid tall grasses, while Ben found a large northern white cedar unlike any that we had ever seen before. All of the limbs of this venerable tree, up to five or six inches in thickness, curved boldly upward, looking very much like a series of bark-covered mammoth tusks.

After about an hour of exploring, including clambering up to the very top of the cliffs, we paddled across to the opposite side of the river. We wanted to spend some time at a broad, inviting grassy area that had beckoned to us; it was located beside an extensive "bone yard" of battered and bleached driftwood logs that had been cast up onto the shore. Picking our way over and through this stretch of storm-tossed logs, and then through a long expanse of boulders of various sizes, we hiked downriver to reach the high walls of pink granite at the junction of river and lake. Near the mouth, Doree found a piece of ancient wreckage from a wooden ship, heavily worn from untold years of wave action and bleached by the sun to a light grey hue. It consisted of a foot-long section of a thick sawn plank, into which three iron elements had been installed. Near each end, a long hand-forged nail had been driven from the top down into the edge of the plank; in addition, a fifteen-inch rod with a round cross-section had been inserted at a diagonal through the plank, again into its edge. This artifact, of indeterminate age, brought to mind the solitary sailing vessel that had plied Lake Superior during the French period. This ship was the twenty-ton pinnace of the Sieur de La Ronde, measuring some 50 to 55 feet in length, which had been constructed near the head of the St. Marys River at Pointe aux Pins in 1734, and was sailed on the lake until some time in the 1740s.

On our return trip, we expanded our search inland from the river, closely examining a broad expanse of water-assembled cobblestones which ranged in diameter from about six to fifteen inches. This jumbled area, devoid of all plants except the ancient dried lichens that encrusted the stones, stretched from the river's edge all the way back to the woods. In it, we located a number of "pukaskwa pits" that had been created in the thick layer of stones; these pits were each some four to five feet across and about two feet deep. Similar ancient, native-made hollows in cobble beaches have been occasionally found all along the northern coastline of Lake Superior, as well as along the north shore of Lake Huron and Georgian Bay, on Lake Nipissing, and along the Ottawa River. They usually range from about three to ten feet in diameter by two to four feet in depth, without any encircling wall of stones around their perimeter; however, some of them do occasionally have such a raised wall. One particularly distinctive pit which was discovered some years ago measured five feet in diameter and three feet in depth, and was surrounded by a three-foot-tall wall of piled stones. The pits often date from the Middle Archaic and Late Archaic periods, between 5,000 and 1,000 B.C., while some date from the more recent Woodland periods. These enigmatic shelters, originally fitted with a roof structure of wood and hides, may have been utilized by the native populations for a variety of purposes, including as hunting blinds, lookout guard posts, meat and fish-smoking huts, food caches, and meditation or vision-quest huts. As we examined each of the pits flanking the White River, we imagined some of the scenes that may have taken place here over many thousands of years.

Back at the grass-covered site, we napped, read books, and explored further inland. We also chatted about Tim's two-volume set Birchbark Canoes of the Fur Trade, *which had come out six months earlier, as well as his latest work called* Tahquamenon Tales, *about our living-history reenactments, which he had sent off to the printing plant the day before we had departed on this trip. Since he had not yet learned to type at this point, I had typed into our home computer every one of the 905 pages of text of these three volumes, many of which Tim had read to me out loud from his scrawled handwritten sheets. During this laborious process, I had frequently asked, "Honey, do you think anyone is really interested in all this detail?" We both laughed about this initial lack of regard on my part. When hundreds of folks had soon placed orders, I had developed a more appreciative attitude about his work. At one point in our conversation, a friendly and inquisitive chipmunk visited us, hoping for a handout. I complied with a few bits of gorp, but Toby did not acknowledge the little fellow with more than a passing glance. (Doree)*

Throughout the remainder of the day, the clear weather continued, with the sun smiling down warmly on us and the air temperature reaching a very comfortable high of 79 degrees in the shade. Since the stout gusting wind and the rows of oncoming whitecaps did not let up at all, we finally decided in the early evening that we were definitely windbound. Since we would not be proceeding any further this day, we set up the tent in the grassy area to spend the night. On our first day, we had advanced only five miles before being forced to land. Hopefully, this would not become a regular occurrence, as it had during the previous trip on Lake Winnipeg.

Day Two

When I drifted off to sleep, I had no idea just how long and interrupted my night would be. I first awakened to the alarm clock at 1 A.M., and stumbled through the boulder field in the dim light down toward the mouth area, to check for any changes in the paddling conditions; the situation was still too rough. At 2:15, on my second trek to the mouth, I noted that the wind had begun to lessen some. However, even if we were to embark, there was no light on the lake to guide us, since clouds had moved in to fill the entire sky, blocking all moonbeams and starlight. At my 4:30 check, a new blustery wind from the northeast and remnant swells from the south-southwest still made the water unworkable; a few sprinkles of rain had begun to fall. Finally, when the clock aroused me for the fourth time at 7:00, I found that the lake had calmed, with only moderate swells coming from the north-northeast, while the wind from the same direction had reduced to a gentle breeze. This scene was very conducive to traveling on a southward course!

When we happily pushed off at 7:45 amid a light rain, the moderate swells were coming from behind my left shoulder, raising and lowering the canoe in a steady rhythm. The leaden sky was completely overcast, and the air temperature measured 65 degrees. While Ben and I advanced southward for eleven miles in 3 1/2 hours, we all ingested our breakfast and later a morning snack while afloat. After four of those miles, I mentioned to the family that the water just a mile out from shore was 560 feet deep. Some five miles later, we passed the area in which John Bigsby had made this observation in 1823: "The Smaller Written Rocks are in a sandy cove defended by islets, fourteen miles southeast from the Peek (Pic) River. They are smooth and coated with tripe de roche and other lichens. Various names and figures of animals have been traced on them, both long ago and recently." During the same voyage, he also noted a larger set of Written Rocks well to the northwest of here, on a series of small near-shore islands six miles east of Copper Island. Unfortunately, we did not find the lichen-covered, engraved cliff faces of the Smaller Written Rocks as we passed by the area. The voyageurs had referred to both of the widely-separated sets of engraved cliffs as Les Petits Ecrits (The Little Writings).

In some sections of the coastline cliffs and hills that we glided beside, the pink granite was laced with wide vertical veins of black basalt. Over millions of years, this softer black material had broken and eroded away at a faster rate than the durable surrounding stone.

This had created strange, deeply indented, black "stairways" that extended from the water's edge up the full height of the cliff faces, right up to the evergreen forest at the top. One particular granite formation adjacent to the water consisted of a long, horizontal elevated area that was surrounded on all sides by a lower flat area. This barren acre of rose-colored bedrock resembled the ruins of an ancient fortress on a bare island; it must have been given many interesting names by local residents and travelers over the millennia.

At 11:15, pleased with our progress of eleven miles, we landed for a half-hour break just before reaching Baie de l'Oiseau (Bird Bay). We were enticed to shore by an impressive huge cove, which was rimmed with a slightly inclined beach of sand and cobblestones, and was flanked at each end by tall exposed cliffs. About seventy feet back from the water, the beach was littered with hundreds of battered driftwood trees for a space of about fifteen feet, extending all the way back to the forest. By this time, some blue areas were visible in the sky and the air temp had risen to a very comfortable 72 degrees in the shade, while the light breeze continued from the north-northeast.

After returning to the water, Doree wielded the bow paddle for two hours, covering seven miles, even though she had felt queasy at the campsite this morning and had thrown up there. At 2:00, we took a break for fifteen minutes on a barely submerged, storm-scoured rock ledge near shore. Since the underwater ledges in this lake receive a good scrubbing from storms on a regular basis, they do not accumulate a slippery green growth over them, making our landings and departures on them more secure.

By now, the grey clouds had bid adieu, leaving behind a light blue sky decorated with a few puffy white clouds. During this rest stop, Ben made his way to the barren shoreline, carrying Toby on his shoulders. Standing in the knee-deep shallows, I prepared the camera to capture the extraordinary scene of the softly rounded hills of barren pink stone. Once on land, when Ben realized that his mother was taking his portrait at a distance, he suddenly turned his back to me and dropped his drawers, thus creating the rare sighting of the moon at midday. The nerve of some people's children! (Doree)

Afloat again under ideal traveling conditions, we glided over eighteen miles of sparkling blue water between 2:15 and 7:15, with Doree occasionally refueling us all while Ben and I kept the canoe surging steadily forward. With each stroke, his paddle created curls in the water that spun backward. Most of the cliffs that we passed bore at least some trees, bushes, and grasses on their upper areas. However, one particularly tall example, having been broken into myriad blocks and columns by tremendous forces of nature, did not have a single shred of vegetation on it, from the water's edge up to the summit. Inland seven miles from this stretch of coast stands Tip Top Mountain, rising more than 1,500 feet above the lake; at an elevation of 2,120 feet above sea level (the lake's surface is about 600 feet above sea level), this peak represents the highest point in the province of Ontario.

Mesmerized by the steady cadence of the paddle strokes and the shimmering water, I easily imagined myself as a native man of the Archaic Period, paddling a birchbark or dugout canoe along this same shoreline four or five thousand years ago, hauling a cargo of chunks of copper stowed in hide bags. My fellow villagers and I had laboriously extracted this pure ore in shallow pit mines on what would later be called Isle Royale, in the western part of the lake. As we transported the precious red metal toward our main village hundreds of miles to the southeast, I pictured in my mind's eye the various implements (including lance points and awls) and ornaments (including pendants and tubular beads) that we would fashion by cold-hammering and grinding the magical red rock, using stone hammers, anvils, and grinders.

Upon reaching the mouth of the Rivière de la Cascade (Cascade River), I returned from my reveries and we paused for half an hour to enjoy two beautiful features. First of all, the cove had an attractive sand-and-cobble beach that was very similar to our resting place from eight hours earlier, including its hundreds of accumulated driftwood logs at the rear. In addition, at the north end of the little bay, the twin chutes of the Cascade Falls, separated from each other by a ninety-foot-wide swath of high rock, dropped precipitously over a cliff some thirty feet tall. At the base of each narrow channel, with a dramatic flair, the frothing white water fell directly into the lake. In the woods that stood sentinel behind the beach, Ben discovered an old rundown log cabin. He dreamed of coming back to this place some day, repairing the roof of the little building, and then spending a summer in seclusion. (Little did he know that just five years later, he would become a professional builder of log homes, constructing impressive ones for both himself and his clients.)

After this well-deserved rest stop, even though we were pretty tuckered out, Ben and I pushed ahead on the serene surface of the lake for another 21/2 hours, covering eight more miles in the mellow, copper-colored light. After three of those miles, we passed the end of the promontory called Tête de la Loutre (Otter's Head), a two-mile-long peninsula whose forest-clad tip angles gradually down to the water. This famous landmark, containing an isolated, upright pillar of rock about thirty feet tall, was usually considered by the voyageurs as the halfway point of the journey between Sault Ste. Marie and Ft. Kaministiquia/Ft. William.

At 10:10, as a beautiful sunset tinted both the sky behind us and the water around us in vibrant shades of orange, pink, and purple, we landed for the night on a very extensive beach of sand and cobblestones. After setting up camp on the second terrace of cobbles, we ravenously consumed a delicious stew of noodles, beef jerky, peas, and corn. During our meal, we also drank in the stunning scenery, as the vivid colors gradually faded over the Otter's Head peninsula, four miles to the west of us, and night folded in around us. The entire area of our site was brightly lit by the half moon, which hung low in the nearly cloudless southeastern sky. Crawling into the tent at 11:30, we fell into an exhausted sleep a half-hour later. This day, during 14 1/2 hours on the water between 7:45 A.M. and 10:10 P.M., we had covered a satisfying forty miles.

Day Three

When the alarm clock ended our dream-time at 5:00, after a quick five hours of sleep, we hastily packed up and were paddling on the quiet water an hour later, beneath a clear sky. The temperature was already a balmy 68 degrees, with a subtle breeze from the east. As we glided out of the large sheltered bay and entered the exposed open water, we encountered a moderate head wind and waves coming from the southeast. Working against these elements, it took us two hours to laboriously advance five miles on a southeasterly course, finally reaching the mouth of the Pukaskwa River at 8:00. There, at the southern boundary of the national park, we took a twenty-minute break on a long sandy beach. Resuming our progress, Doree continued to work in the bow until 10:30, during which time we ate while paddling. She covered a total of twelve miles in 4 1/2 hours, including the twenty-minute beach break, often toiling against a persistent head wind.

After trading seats with his mother while afloat, Ben took over as the *avant*. Passing occasional loons and ducks floating calmly on the water, we eventually paused at 11:15 for a fifteen-minute rest on a small cobble beach. The air temp was 70 degrees, beneath fat white clouds pinned against a deep blue canvas. Following the coastline, we finished turning southeast and then headed directly toward the east, on a course that we would maintain for the next forty miles or so, to the bottom of Michipicoten Bay. Soon, the moderate wind from the southeast that had been beating against our right side miraculously changed, becoming a following wind from the west! So we happily raised the sail and enjoyed a slight assist as we advanced eight miles in two hours. At 2:10, we took a break for 45 minutes on some massive rocks that had been piled onto the shoreline by heaving cakes of lake ice. Some eleven miles off to the south, I could clearly see the eastern end of Michipicoten Island, which had been called Île Maurepas during most of the fur trade era. We had been traveled parallel to this seventeen-mile-long mass of bedrock since pushing off this morning.

At 3:00 we were off again, with the wind and waves continuing to arrive from directly behind us. Sailing briskly for an hour, we sped over four miles of shimmering water, as both wind and waves increased. Finally, they both became dangerously boisterous, with whitecaps flashing their frothy crests all around us as they sped beneath our hull, making for a slippery ride. In the distance, the only place of refuge that we could see along the rockbound shoreline was a stone-lined bay with a cobble beach covering part of it. I suddenly ruddered the hull at an angle toward the left, and we whisked across the wild surf toward the bay. Near the shoreline, Ben dropped the sail and Doree and I paddled hard to cut across the breaking waves and into the quiet cove at the lee end of the bay.

We were windbound at 4:00, after ten hours on the water and 24 miles of excellent progress. In the distance, about seven miles ahead, lay the rounded silhouette of the high rock hills that we would travel beside when we would eventually be allowed to advance. The tallest of these was Bare Summit, rising about 1,250 feet above the level of the lake. From the map, I knew that these hills stood behind a long, continuous row of very tall cliffs. These sheer rock walls lined a four-mile stretch of the coast in which there were absolutely no landing places for canoes. Since the planning stages of this trip, I had been concerned about the paddling conditions that we would have when we would round Pointe Isacor and face that particularly daunting section of Superior.

After tethering the canoe offshore across the narrow tip of the cove, with the bow and stern lines tied to trees on opposite shores, we relaxed in the area of large rounded boulders that filled its shoreline. Nearby, a few brilliant orange tiger lilies grew on the rocky banks of a small stream that flowed into the lake beside the cove. Bedding down to absorb the sun's warmth during our late-afternoon nap, we each pulled our neck bandana up over most of our face and tugged our hat brim down, as protection against the biting flies and black flies. Uneasy about the stretch of dangerous coastline that lay ahead, I did not drift off.

Within a short time, a dark shadow streaked across my barely exposed, closed lids. Opening my eyes, I was greeted by the sight of an adult great blue heron gliding in very close on its six-foot wingspan, with its neck held in the form of an S and its long legs trailing straight out behind. The large bird, feathered in hues of grey, blue, and white, landed at its platform nest, which it had built at the top of a tall tree standing beside the stream. Near this nest was also a second one in an adjacent tree, which was soon visited by another adult heron. After feeding their offspring in the nests, the two birds flew off, returning a few minutes later. With each new arrival of the adults, the youngsters in the two nests chuckled and squawked excitedly, anticipating the supply of food that would be delivered, consisting of small fish, frogs, or insects. This pattern of activity continued during the entire time that we remained at the cove, with the birds apparently undisturbed by our presence.

After 41/2 hours of waiting and resting, the whitecaps had finally subsided, so we departed at 8:30 P.M. Ben took the bow paddle, in case we would encounter heavily demanding conditions in the dangerous section of coastline cliffs that lay six miles ahead. At first, a moderate following wind continued to blow from the west, assisting our progress for a while until it gradually faded away. In two hours, we made our way over six miles of smooth surface, reaching Pointe Isacor at 10:30. The last of the sun had dipped from sight beneath the tree line about thirty minutes earlier. However, the half moon, hanging low in the southeastern sky off to our right, had gradually brightened, lighting our way. After six months of apprehension, I was immensely pleased to see that we would have excellent conditions for paddling the section that lay ahead! I had been warned about the dangers of this specific area by a ranger of Pukaskwa National Park thirteen years earlier, and by Verlen Kruger himself, probably the boldest living paddler, just the previous year.

After rounding the point, father and son dug in hard and deep, cruising at a fast pace over the placid surface. In the dim light of the moon, which was reflected on the perfectly calm water, we glided silently beside the long stretch of continuous sheer cliffs, which soared dramatically from the surface of the water to a height of 600 feet. Looking ahead, I could see that there were only three areas where boulders lay exposed in the water offshore; otherwise, our route appeared to be clear of obstructions. This was a magical Zen moment, made all the more so by the ease of our progress, after half a year of dreading tough and dangerous conditions at this place. Along the entire stretch of four miles, it was obvious that there were no safe landing sites at the base of the intimidating cliffs that towered over us. A few small, gravel-covered areas were to be found; however, these places stood barely above the surface of the water. They would be quickly inundated by waves of any substantial size, trapping anyone who might land there.

At 11:30 P.M., we finally passed the last of the long procession of cliff faces, and turned left into the first alcove that we encountered, called Baie du Mélèze (Tamarack Bay). Almost immediately, Doree spotted a workable campsite on a very narrow cobble beach that angled up from the water's edge. At 11:45, we began unloading in the moonlight, amid a large offshore boulder garden. Within a half-hour, we had unloaded everything, had hauled the canoe ashore and tethered it to a tree, had erected the tent and stowed the gear, and were inside the shelter, ready to trade massages. After another half-hour, we were deep in dreamland.

What a day! From 6 A.M. to 11:30 P.M., over a span of 17 1/2 hours, we had advanced 34 miles, including spending the period from 4:00 to 8:30 P.M. on land windbound. In addition, we had safely passed one of the most dangerous rockbound sections of the entire northern coastline.

Day Four

We were activated at 6:30 by the piercing calls of an entire colony of gulls, perched on a barely-exposed rock ledge in our bay. Quickly breaking camp, we set off at 7:50 on mirror-like water with outstanding weather conditions: an air temp of 70 degrees as the sun pushed up from the tree line, thin streaks of white clouds in a pale blue sky, and absolutely no wind. At this point, the tone of the journey changed slightly for me. We had successfully traveled past the infamous series of cliffs that offered no escape; now, that particular burden had been lifted from the shoulders of the *gouvernail*.

Although the voyageurs had often utilized *chansons* to deal with boredom, fear, or exhaustion, this moment of departure felt perfect for a few celebratory verses of *Entendez-vous Sur L'Ormeau!* By midmorning, Doree and I had made six miles in two hours, arriving at the mouth of the Rivière du Chien (Dog River, now sometimes called the University River), where we ingested our breakfast while afloat. If we had hiked upriver from the mouth for a mile-and-a-half, we could have viewed the hundred-foot drop of Denison Falls; however we decided to continue on down the coast, rather than taking time out to make this inland detour. After another three miles of progress, Doree switched places with her son while we remained afloat.

After Ben and I had cruised for eleven miles, remaining within a safe mile or less from the shore, we neared Pointe Perquaquia. A considerable west wind had picked up during the previous hour, but the weather conditions appeared to be otherwise benign, so we decided to make a southeasterly traverse across the bottom area of Michipicoten Bay. Although this maneuver would take us out 31/2 miles from the coastline, the frisky wind was blowing from the right direction to help us along, and we could see no evidence of any storm brewing. With the following wind bulging out the little blue square sail at a 45 degree angle, we skimmed across the stretch of four miles in less than an hour, cutting six miles off our total voyage. During the traverse, the canoe seemed to become a living thing, coursing over the water.

Completing the crossing at 2:50, we landed in a sheltered, gravel-lined cove near Pointe Enfumé (Smoky Point), beneath a high spruce-covered cliff. We would have to wait here for the growing wind to slacken before we could continue. In seven hours since leaving the campsite, we had covered 24 miles, twenty of them while skirting the shoreline and four more while traversing the bottom of the large bay. It was a very comfortable 79 degrees in the shade, with a few puffball clouds dragging their patches of dark shadow across the water and the land. After we had relaxed, traded massages, and explored the immediate area, we finally prepared a mouth-watering stew of turkey jerky, noodles, peas, and apples, all cooked together.

While we munched our dinner, I related some of the history of the area at the bottom of Michipicoten Bay, at the mouth of the Michipicoten River. The French had established Ft. Michipicoten there in 1726, and had run the facility until the end of the French regime. Then, a series of independent Montreal-based traders, beginning with Alexander Henry in 1767, operated a Michipicoten Post there for more than a half-century; it was eventually run by men of the N.W.C. Competing personnel of the H.B.C. established a nearby post in 1796, which lasted for less than five years; they again opened a facility there in 1816, which was operated for many decades. An Ojibwa village had been located near the mouth of the river by at least the 1760s; it continued to thrive in that same area from then on. In the Treaty of 1850, the Gros Cap Indian Reserve, about four miles square, was established for these villagers at a nearby location, on the north side of Michipicoten Bay.

Two canoe routes extended from the bottom of Michipicoten Bay to Hudson's Bay. With this fact in mind, the French had built Ft. Michipicoten at the mouth of the river of that name, to attract Ojibwa and Cree traders who resided north of Lake Superior, hoping that they would not travel down to Hudson's Bay and do business with the British traders of the H.B.C. The most heavily utilized and the most direct canoe route, covering some five hundred miles, involved the Michipicoten, Missinaibi, and Moose Rivers. Various chroniclers mentioned this passageway, including Jonathan Carver, who labeled on his 1769 map the river flowing into Michipicoten Bay as the "Michipicoten River, leading to James Bay [the foot of Hudson's Bay]." George Heriot, writing between 1792 and 1816, noted, "The River Michipicoten communicates with the territory of the Hudson's Bay Company." In 1823, John Bigsby described "the Michipicoton River, which is large and long, and is the nearest way from hence [the Michipicoten Post] to Moose Fort, in Hudson's Bay."

Another route to the latter northern bay entailed the Magpie River, which flows into the Michipicoten River a mile above its mouth. From the headwaters of the Magpie, travelers used the Kenogami and Albany Rivers to reach Hudson's Bay. In fact, the French operated Ft. Des Français at the junction of the Kenogami and the Albany between

1685 and 1687, and later ran an outpost of Ft. Michipicoten at that same locale, for a few years beginning in 1741, all with the goal of siphoning off trade that would otherwise flow to the H.B.C.'s Albany Fort.

After we had spent four hours windbound in the little cove, the wind had mellowed sufficiently for us to continue safely, so we resumed our southward trek at 6:15. Immediately, our hull crossed over the northern boundary of Lake Superior Provincial Park, which extends more than sixty miles to the south along the coast and as much as 23 miles toward the east. As the *avant*, Doree made four miles in 1 1/4 hours; then Ben covered five more miles in a similar period, during which we rounded Cap Maurepas. Right after crossing the mouth of the deep cove called Brulé Harbor, Ben spotted an excellent campsite, where we landed for the night at 8:45. Two miles to the northeast of us, the forested summit of Brulé Hill stood 1,070 feet above the surface of the lake, while less than a half-mile offshore, the water extended down to a depth of 408 feet. (In fact, more than 80 percent of the entire area of Lake Superior is deeper than 300 feet.)

During our several hours of evening paddling, the wind had died out completely and the lake had become absolutely calm, providing ideal conditions for traveling well into the night. However, to my disappointment, the sky had also clouded over entirely, blocking any potential moonlight that would have allowed us to continue into the late-night hours. Our situation reminded me of Schoolcraft's comments while traveling with the Cass expedition in 1820, after the party in three large canoes had been windbound for six hours: "At five o'clock in the evening the wind abated, and we left Presque Isle with the design of continuing in our canoes all night, but at eleven o'clock the wind had freshened to such a degree, and the night had become so dark, that we were compelled to encamp, after having gone about twenty miles."

This day, we had traveled 33 miles in thirteen hours, between 7:50 A.M. and 8:45 P.M., including a four-hour break during the afternoon for wind reduction, rest, and cooking. What a treat that had been, enjoying a long rest and a piping hot meal during the middle of the day, while waiting for the wind to dissipate! This was truly a great rarity during our sixteen years of wilderness journeys on the water. During three days of paddling so far, our efforts had brought us over 107 miles, plus the first day in which we had made only five miles before being *dégradé*. These last two days had each included a long afternoon break, while we had waited on land for heavy winds to reduce to workable levels.

After setting up camp, we relaxed at the fire for about an hour, staring into the twisting flames and watching the orange-red sparks spiral heavenward. Occasionally, a puff of breeze caused the fire to flare up, casting flashes of light on the trees looming around and over our campsite. Eventually, our conversation turned to the subject of human longevity, and how it has increased over the centuries. Presently, the average age at death in the U.S. is 75 years for men and 81 years for women, averaging 78 years. However, if an individual lives beyond the age of 65, he or she will likely live to an average age of 83.4 years. In Canada, both men and women live, on average, two to three years longer than residents of the U.S. In the St. Lawrence settlements of New France, up to the end of the French regime in 1760, the average age at death for men was 61.9 years, and for women 61.6 years.

At 11:00, although we parents did not feel very elderly, we finally hit the sack, leaving young Ben to linger at the fire a while longer before crawling into the tent.

Day Five

During the wee hours of the morning, I was awakened at one point by the sounds of raindrops drumming lightly on the tent roof. When the alarm clock clattered at 6 A.M., we were greeted by perfect paddling conditions: flat water, no wind or fog, and a solid cloud-covered sky. The air temperature registered 69 degrees, but the air was so humid from the rain that it felt unusually balmy. To our surprise, both Doree and I had a lower lip that was considerably swollen; this was apparently a reaction of our sunburned lips to the spice mixture that we had used when drying the turkey jerky, which we had eaten in the stew the previous afternoon.

Pulling away from the shore at 7:10, Doree sang out, "And I say to myself, what a wonderful day," from Louis Armstrong's famous tune. She and I were soon served a breakfast of chocolate gorp and strawberry-flavored, instant breakfast drink by our passenger son. My lovely wife of 28 years worked in the bow seat for 41/2 hours, steadily pulling the canoe over sixteen miles of water, about half of which were covered with the assistance of a slightly filled sail. Shortly after leaving the campsite, we headed straight across the mile-wide mouth of Baie de la Vieille (Old Woman Bay), cutting 11/2 miles off our total voyage, as the water swirled past the hull at a good clip. Along much of this morning's stretch of sixteen miles, we passed close beside the bases of numerous formidable cliffs rising 500 to 600 feet above the lake. It was a bit spooky peering into the depths of the very clear, green-tinted water, and imagining just how far down the bases of these stone walls extended below the surface. In many cases, the area beneath the surface immediately in front of a cliff contained massive blocks of stone, which had broken loose from the wall and had plunged into the lake. On the face of one high, evergreen-capped cliff, a miniature cave had been formed immediately above the surface of the water, by the erosive energy of millions upon millions of wind-lashed waves.

Just before we rounded Cap Chaillon, a group of five otters surfaced in front of our canoe and swam with us for a few minutes, remaining a short distance ahead of the craft. When they halted and we glided silently nearer, each of the sleek brown animals stretched its neck and upper body out of the water to get a better look at us, and repeatedly made rather loud snuffing sounds through their noses. This body-extending action was a typical one for otters, who often survey their surroundings by raising their head high while treading water. As we continued on our way, the quintet of friendly and curious otters continued to commune with us for about ten minutes, until we had traveled around the cape; then they doubled back.

From Cap Chaillon, we headed due south across the mouth of a large bay. This five-mile traverse, which took us nearly two miles out from the shoreline, cut two miles from our total mileage. At the end of the crossing, we paused at 11:25 for a half-hour break, landing on Squaw Island to stretch our legs. After leaving the little island, Ben and I labored for two miles against a moderate head wind and waves from the south-southwest, until we reached the outer end of Cap Gargantua. Then the wind, blocked by the half-mile-long Hursley Island, quieted considerably for our visit to the exotic rock formations which had made this place famous many centuries ago.

Gargantua (referring to a *Gros Mangeur* or Big Eater) was the second most prominent character in the 1532 novel by the French writer Rabelais entitled *Horribles et Epouvantables Faits et Prouesses du Trés Renommé Pantagruel* (The Horrible and Dreadful Deeds and

Prowesses of the Very Renowned Pantagruel), and the primary character in the 1534 sequel called *Vie Inestimable du Grand Gargantua, Père de Pantagruel* (The Invaluable Life of the Great Gargantua, Father of Pantagruel). In the ancient French legends which had inspired these two books, the father of the gigantically-proportioned Gargantua was named Grandgousier. With these various legendary figures as their inspiration, the ancient voyageurs had christened several of the natural features at and near this cape on Lake Superior. Immediately south of Cap Gargantua lies Baie du Pantagruel, while Baie du Gargantua is located three miles further toward the southeast. Between these two bays and inland 1/10 of a mile stands Coteau du Gargantua (Gargantua Hill), while the prominent Coteau du Grandgousier looms 1,030 feet above the lake level two miles further inland. However, it was the shape of the two-mile-long, outermost end of the cape, with a lake-side profile that matches perfectly a certain human male appendage, that earned it the name of the giant Gargantua.

This mysterious place had been considered the home of powerful spirits by the native populations for thousands of years. Near the center of the shoreline of the cape, three massive adjacent rock slabs stand at the very edge of the water at an almost vertical angle, rising eerily out of the lake. In addition, two vertical formations are located a few hundred yards offshore, forming two miniature, heavily eroded islands. One of these offshore masses of bedrock, with the profile of a squashed pyramid more than thirty feet high, has a six-foot-tall, elongated oval opening just above the water level at its very center, which runs entirely through the rock. It was this cave-like feature that had prompted the bawdy voyageurs to dub this landmass the Île du Gargantua, noting its similarity to a particular area of the female anatomy. In 1823, when John Bigsby visited the place, he commented: "Small detached pointed rocks and solitary ridges rise out of the water naked. One of these, a few hundred years from the point, is a rude pyramid from fifty to sixty feet high. Its strange shape, dark color, and the surrounding gloom, have induced the Indians to worship it as an idol. It has given to the place the name of Gargantua."

Close by, the elevated portion of the second tiny island has the appearance of a deep saddle, with the two tall side projections, each about twenty feet high, flanking a deeply concave central area. The voyageurs named this feature La Chaise du Diable (The Devil's Seat).

The barren, flat base surrounding both of these tiny elevated islands, rising just barely above the water on calm days, consists of a crumbly brown rock that contains many small quartzite crystals, as well as rounded cavities in which such crystals had grown millions of years ago when the molten material had cooled and solidified. At the moment, we were sheltered from the wind and waves by the nearby Hursley Island. However, it was easy to see that even waves of moderate size would crash over this base rock surrounding each of the diminutive islands. As a result, the only bit of vegetation on them was the grouping of three green bushes that had taken a precarious hold near the elevated tip of Île du Gargantua. This very unusual place, with its two Spirit Stones, had inspired fear and respect in the minds of native people long ago.

After a half-hour of absorbing the eerie magic of this special locale, we departed at 1:50. The powder blue sky had nearly cleared, now containing only a few thin vestiges of white clouds, and, according to my neck-strap thermometer, the air temperature had risen to 76 degrees in the shade. After one mile, we rounded the cape and left the shelter of Hursley Island and the adjacent chain of four tiny islets. Then we were immediately confronted by swells of alarming size and tall whitecaps on the open lake, which were advancing from the south-southwest. Turning on a dime in the surf, we dashed back a half-mile, to seek refuge at the last cobblestone beach that we had passed. After just fifteen minutes, we had been driven ashore, forced to wait for calmer conditions.

However, this was a fantastic location to be pinned to land! The wild rock formations, which were similar to those of Gargantua Island, offered plenty of opportunities for interesting exploration. In addition, the deep-blue waves bashing against the convoluted volcanic shoreline reminded me of beautiful photos of Hawaii. Late in the afternoon, Doree cooked a feast of tomatoes, parsley, macaroni, beef jerky, parmesan cheese, and spices, to celebrate our progress of twenty miles already this day, as well as the fact that we had now passed the halfway point of the voyage, in just 3 1/2 paddling days. After the meal, we all napped for two hours, to make up for each of the short nights that we had experienced since the trip had begun.

After four hours of waiting, the wind had reduced considerably, so we packed up and set out again at 7:00. Before long, the wind from the south-southwest disappeared, but not so for the large, broad swells that were flowing from that same direction. While dealing with these features, the largest that we had ever paddled, I was reminded of Schoolcraft's comment while traveling on this body of water in 1820: "The sea-like swells of the lake broke furiously upon the shore long after the wind had entirely ceased." Daniel Harmon had also reported similar water conditions facing his brigade in 1800: "Although the swells in the Lake are very high, we have made good progress during the whole day." As we rode the broad hills of rising and falling water for 1 1/2 hours, we advanced five miles, passing at about the halfway point Devil's Warehouse Island. The entire northern end of this half-mile-long island presented a vertical cliff face of great height, an impressive sight. At 8:30, we decided to halt for the night, landing on a mile-long stretch of cobble beach at the southern end of Gargantua Bay. The stone-covered shoreline brought to mind an expression that I had read somewhere, which referred to "the loose change dropped from the pockets of a retreating glacier 10,000 years ago."

An hour later, it was still a very balmy 70 degrees out. The mosquitoes were voracious at this site; however, by good fortune, this was the first time during the five days of this journey so far that we had needed to apply insect repellent. The thirst for blood of this particular population of mosquitoes brought to mind the words of John Bigsby while he was traveling on this lake in 1823: "We were sorely mosquito-bitten at Pine Point. The whole party heard the shout of 'Alerte!,' our usual morning reveillez, with vast content." Three days earlier, he had noted the complete lack of biting insects, due to frigid temperatures: "At 5 A.M., June 8, the thermometer stood at 30 degrees Fahr., so that we had no fear of mosquitoes."

While setting up camp, we relished the stunning *coucher du soleil*: as the orb of the sun sank slowly beneath the lake, the thin wisps of clouds and the blue sky above were gradually painted a wide array of golds and yellows. Afterward, we relaxed at the fire and exchanged massages, as the hushhhhhhhh, hushhhhhhhh, hushhhhhhhh of remnant swells gently lapped the cobblestone shoreline. We were bedded down by 11:00, to replenish ourselves while the sun illuminated the other side of the world.

This day, between 7:10 A.M. and 8:30 P.M., we had put 25 miles behind us. Our traveling day had included an afternoon break of five hours, while we had waited for the wind to reduce in strength. Again, we had enjoyed the rare treat of a long break and a hot feast during the daytime, coupled with taking advantage of the good traveling conditions at both ends of the day. At this point, in four paddling days plus one windbound day, we had reached mile 137 of the voyage, and had already cut off a number of miles by making traverses across bays.

Day Six

At 4:30 A.M., I rose to the call of the clock, but found an uncooperative wind blowing from the southeast, which induced me to reset the alarm. By 6:15, when it rang again, the wind had eased back to just a soft breeze, definitely amenable to our traveling on a southeasterly course. The air temp was 67 degrees, and only a very few white clouds were smeared across the blue sky. While we broke camp, a chipmunk chattered at us from a nearby log, while a single loon cruised back and forth in front of our cobble beach, just as it had done the previous evening at sunset.

With Doree wielding the bow paddle, we took to the water at 7:10. Nearly all of this day's route lay within view, stretched out far ahead of us. Five hours later, having advanced seventeen miles with just one hour of light sail assist along the way, we headed toward the shore to take a half-hour break. The place that attracted us was a long, beautiful sand beach that featured, at its far right end, a creek flowing into the lake. As we approached the beach, Ben, in the passenger spot, suddenly threw Toby overboard and then jumped over the gunwales himself, to happily swim to shore. In this shallow area near shore, warmed by the brilliant sun, the glistening water was not very chilly, especially for a dog and an exuberant young man with excellent circulation. Nearly all of the clouds had departed from the pale azure sky, the air temp had risen to 75 degrees in the shade, and the light breeze continued to waft from the south.

After our break, eager to reach one of the major highlights of the trip, Ben and I established a rather brisk pace with the paddles, covering three miles in 45 minutes. To our delight, the canoe glided over the barely-ruffled surface as if we were immune to gravity. A half-mile from our long-anticipated destination, the sacred painted cliff of Agawa Rock, our green bow slid past what is now called Sinclair Island. During previous centuries and millennia, this barely-exposed mass of bedrock had certainly borne many other titles, names which had reflected its spiritual significance. Like the pictograph-covered cliff face that lay ahead, the native people had also considered this place to be inhabited by powerful spirits. At one shoreline spot on the undulating, rounded surface of the little island, which rose just above the waterline, the granite had eroded at a faster rate than the curved veins of quartzite which coursed through it. This had created the appearance of a large spider-like creature, fashioned from white quartzite, crawling across the pink surface of the island. According to native beliefs, quartzite veins represented places where lightning bolts, produced by giant thunderbirds in the heavens, had struck the earth. As a result, these veins of white stone were considered to be imbued with power. Near the fantastic spider-like figure, a deep opening in the bedrock at water level produced deep croaking sounds each time a wave flowed into it, adding to the mysterious aura of the place. Not only did this mass of rock have a spooky, mystical appearance, it also had a matching sound!

Around the next point, Agawa Rock loomed into view. I was struck by the glorious scene. Gliding up to the base of the imposing cliff in reverent silence, I nosed the bow into a tiny cove which lay off to the left side. There, Ben tethered the canoe to one of the huge blocks of stone that lay in a jumbled pile beside the water's edge, blocks which at some point had broken from the cliff and had crashed down with a massive roar. Eons before, shamans had stood numerous times on the eight-foot-wide, downward-angled ledge which projects out from the base of the cliff face, just above the level of the lake. On the stone wall, these spiritual leaders had created pictographs using red ocher pigment mixed with a medium of water or grease. Over the centuries, these images had gradually accumulated until they totaled more than 117 figures, covering much of the lower surface of the cliff in the area from about four feet to ten feet above the ledge.

During our paddle of twenty miles this morning, we had perceived our mission as a pilgrimage to Agawa Rock. En route to this ancient site, which had served as one of the most important sacred places for native people of the entire Superior region, we had discussed various figures of ancient native spirituality, including Missipichou, the giant Underwater Serpents, and the giant Thunderbirds. And there they all were, along with an entire array of other images, painted ages before onto the greyish pink face of the cliff!

In ancient times, the people had talked to their gods at this place, painting pictures of those spirits as part of the communication. The most prominent images included three Missipichou figures, the giant underwater panther that had two large horns, one on each side of its head, as well as a row of dragon-like spines along the full length of its back and tail. Other paintings represented giant Underwater Serpents, which lived beneath the lake with Missipichou. These various underwater spirits, when angered, could lash their tails and create huge waves and turbulent waters. The images also included giant Thunderbirds, who lived in the sky and could create powerful winds and rainstorms with their outstretched wings, and who could emit bolts of lightning with their eyes. In addition to various other mythological creatures, the images painted on the stone wall also included caribou, moose, a horse and rider (or a shaman transforming himself into a horse or a moose), bears, beavers, fish, turtles, eagles, cranes, sand pipers, and a louse. Other of the brownish red pictographs included canoes with human occupants (occasionally using paddles), standing humans playing tambourine-like drums, and abstract symbols such as straight lines in horizontal and vertical alignments, triangles, circles, and spheres.

Thousands of years of accumulated experiences, knowledge, and understanding of both the natural world and the supernatural world had gone into the creation of these images. In various instances, the shamans had for some reason painted new images atop earlier, faded ones. In addition to the 117 figures that have already been identified on the cliff, there are also numerous others that are now very faint and unclear, and have so far defied identification. In ancient times, the entire cliff face was gradually covered with a protective coating of minerals, which were dissolved in rain water and ran down the rock face over the span of many centuries. This clear to whitish calcite layer eventually sealed the paintings from direct exposure to the elements, preserving them long after the death of the last individual who had remembered the songs and rituals that had been associated with the images.

We spent more than an hour on the low projecting ledge, absorbing the paintings and discussing in quiet tones their possible meanings. It would have been a sacrilege to speak in a full voice at this place. We also admired the impressively high and absolutely vertical cliff with its bare flat face, which had served as the canvas for these spiritual paintings long ago. When it was time for us to leave, Ben dived into the shining, blue-green water, swam along the base of the cliff to the tethered canoe, and brought it to his parents waiting on the ledge.

Hoping that our gift of tobacco had appeased the underwater and sky spirits, who had been very kind to us during this voyage, we departed from the sacred site. Sailing at a fast clip before a strong tail wind from the west, we leaped forward five miles in an hour. Surfing over the large waves that were at about our limit of workability, we arrived at a very long and wide beach on Agawa Bay, and landed with considerable relief at 3:30. Until the brawny wind would abate somewhat, we would be windbound here.

By good fortune, we had been forced ashore at a beautiful place, which offered a long crescent of sand beach that was backed by a forest of tall, stately pines. Relaxing on the warm tan sand, it was easy to picture hundreds or even thousands of native people gathering here during prehistoric times, on this picturesque bay beside the mouth of the Agawa River, not far from their sacred cliff. Such gatherings would have been much like those that people had held in France, when they had visited their cathedral and its environs on certain spiritual holidays.

Hiking a mile-and-a-half toward the northwest, we arrived at the mouth of the Agawa River, where a native village had thrived for centuries during both the prehistoric and historic eras. During summers, large numbers of people had gathered here, to fish in the river and the lake, hunt, and gather plant foods and medicines, as well as to find marriage partners, participate in religious and social ceremonies, and trade. In the late fall, they had broken into small family groups and had dispersed into the interior, to fish, hunt, and trap over the winter, and to harvest maple sugar and syrup in the spring, before returning again to their main summer village. Late in the fur trade era, in about 1828, a small H.B.C. outpost had been established here at the river mouth; this facility had operated until at least 1879.

While I returned to the canoe, Doree, Ben, and Toby made their way to the nearby roadway, the Trans-Canada Highway, to check out the possibility of buying burgers somewhere, but without any luck. Later, Ben discovered a wooden cooking spoon on the beach, and carved it into a miniature canoe paddle to wear in his hat band. During her explorations, Doree located a patch of ripe blueberries to harvest, as well as wild roses in hues of red, pink, and white that were growing together in an extensive patch.

For my part, serenaded by the sighing of the wind in the canopy of pines overhead, my thoughts wandered back to the ancient native spirituality that had been practiced in this region, along the north shore of Lake Superior. In addition to the "wilderness cathedral" of Agawa Rock, native people believed that their benevolent and malevolent spirits also resided at various other locales in the region, some of which were documented during the fur trade period. For example, in 1767, Alexander Henry wrote: "Naniboujou...was represented to me as the founder, and indeed creator, of the Indian nations of North America...Sacrifices are offered on the island which is called his grave or tumulus by all who pass by. I landed there, and found on the projecting rocks a quantity of tobacco, rotting in the rain, together with kettles, [intentionally] broken guns, and a variety of other articles. His spirit is supposed to make this its constant residence, and here to preside over the lake, and over the Indians in their navigation and fishing." A decade later, when John Long traveled the north shore in 1777, he noted: "At the entrance of this lake is a high rock, somewhat in the shape of a man, which the Chippeway Indians call 'Kitchee Manitoo,' or the Master of Life. Here they all stop to make their offerings, which they do by throwing tobacco, and other things, into the water; by this they intend to make an acknowledgement to the rock, as the representative of the Supreme Being, for the blessings they enjoy, cheerfully sacrificing to him their ornaments and those things which they hold most dear." John Johnston, describing incidents that took place on the lake in 1792, wrote, "The Indians have many superstitions with respect to this mountain which, with every remarkable or dangerous place on the borders of the lake or interior country, has its Genii, to whom they never fail to make a speech, accompanied with a present of tobacco and sometimes their silver ornaments, whenever they pass." During his voyage along the north shore in 1800, Daniel Harmon recorded: "We are encamped near a large rock, on which the Natives, as they pass this way, leave an arrow or two, or some other article of little value to appease the Devil, or Muchamunatoo, as they call him, and prevent him from doing them harm."

However, it was not only the native people who left such offerings during their voyages. In many instances, this custom was adopted by the French as well. For example, in 1623-24, Brother Gabriel Sagard recorded that his French interpreter, possibly Etienne Brulé, followed the practice of native travelers in making an offering of tobacco to a man-shaped rock that lay alongside a river.

Whether the French participants in the fur trade knew it or not, native spiritual beliefs were even reflected in the canoes in which the French traveled. At the canoe building yards in both the St. Lawrence Valley and at various interior locales, the vast majority of the people who constructed and decorated these craft were either native or Métis (mixed native-and-French) individuals. Since prehistoric times, it had been a standard custom to depict on the raised ends of canoes images which represented the protective spirits of the builders or users. These painted or engraved figures served as invocations to the gods, asking them to provide safe conditions for the inhabitants of the canoe during its travels. When the craft were constructed for the use of the French, these symbols continued to be applied by the native builders. During his 1694-97 tenure as the commandant of Ft. De Buade at St. Ignace, at the Straits of Mackinac, Cadillac described this native custom: "Their canoes are painted various colors, and are ornamented on the prow with figures or with the arms of the leader; you see on them the war mat, the crow, the bear, or some other animal such as I have already mentioned --- the guardian spirit which is to guide the enterprise."

At this point, my wandering thoughts returned to my family and our journey along Lake Superior. After we had feasted on a stew of beef jerky, noodles, tomatoes, mushrooms, and spices, the wind and waves died down somewhat. This had been another enjoyable afternoon break with a hot meal, during a wind-imposed period of nearly three hours.

Resuming our travels at 6:15, we paddled under ideal weather conditions along the remainder of the beach-lined bay, then along a stretch of high cliffs. After about five miles, we left the lands of Lake Superior Provincial Park. By the time we reached the mouth of the Montreal River, 21/2 hours and eight miles after setting out, the wind and waves had faded entirely away. It was absolutely calm: no sighing of wind, no lapping of waves, no calling of birds. Pulling into the harbor at the mouth of the river, we found that there was no restaurant in the tiny community of Montreal River Harbor, which contains about fifteen houses. So Doree and Ben bought hamburger and buns at the local bottle store, and convinced a traveler who was vacationing nearby in his motor camper to grill them for us. Hungrily gobbling down five of the burgers in the fading light, we saved the remaining three for the following morning. This would be the only settlement that we would encounter during our Lake Superior venture.

At 10 P.M., bathed in the hues of a magnificent orange-red sunset, we crossed the very fast and powerful current at the mouth of the river, paddled around the corner from the little village, and set up camp. Accompanied by the occasional sounds of trucks whizzing by on the nearby Trans-Canada Highway, we dozed off around 11:00.

We had experienced another excellent day on the water. According to the map, we had covered 33 miles between 7:15 A.M. and 8:45 P.M., including a 2 1/2 hour windbound stop during the afternoon. At this point, we had advanced 170 miles over the course of five paddling days.

Day Seven

We arose to the sound of the alarm at five o'clock, just in time to see the yellow-tinted disk of the moon being swallowed by the lake on the western horizon. Ten minutes later, the last vestige of *la lune* disappeared for the day. The water looked very cooperative, with only slight swells arriving from the west. The air temperature was balmy, already 65 degrees, so we did not have to wear our jackets while packing up; in the heavens, there were only a few thin, wispy lines of white clouds off to the north.

Just as we departed, a vivid purplish-red crescent of sun emerged above the tree line, setting the lake on fire and coloring the filmy strands of clouds that hung above it. A short time later, as we traversed the mouth of a deep bay, we watched a pair of coyotes ambling along the shoreline for about ten minutes. These long-legged animals, orange-tan with black highlights, were apparently headed somewhere to bed down after their night of searching for food. Since they are omnivores, their most recent menu could have included the entire gamut of small mammals, reptiles, amphibians, birds, bird eggs, insects, and fruit. I imagined that these two individuals were a mated pair just beginning their adult lives together, which could extend to the ripe old age of ten years.

After Doree had made five miles in the bow seat, all the while savoring the passing scenery at a comfortable paddling pace, Ben traded places with her. Immediately, he and I headed directly across the three-mile-wide mouth of Alona Bay, which took us out 1 1/2 miles from shore but cut two miles off the total voyage. By the time we had reached our destination, Pointe aux Mines (Point of the Mines), a moderate following wind had picked up, yet there were no signs of any approaching storms. These conditions inspired us to set off on a traverse of eight miles, which would cut off a series of broad bays and a long curving stretch of shoreline. Although this route would take us out two miles from shore, it would eliminate three miles from the total distance. Digging in deeply, with a considerable push from the sail helping us along, we completed the crossing in 1 3/4 hours.

While we were cruising along, Ben told us about some of his experiences and observations in El Salvador, where he had spent three months during the previous winter. Three days a week for a month, he had worked on a water project at the village of Agua Blanca, which had been built in a very dry locale. He had traveled to and from the little community by Land Rover, making the ninety-minute trip each way from his home-base village of Perquin. Many of the homes in Agua Blanca had been built in the traditional style of vertical poles set into the ground with a thatched palm roof; some of the more prosperous ones had been constructed of concrete blocks with a roof of ceramic tiles. A typical house for a family of five measured 12 by 20 feet, about the size of a two-car garage in America. There was no electricity in the settlement.

About thirty families had been involved in the water project. It entailed installing long expanses of underground pipes, which transport the water by pump from a distant spring to the holding basin of each family, as well as digging proper latrines that would not pollute the water. Martin, an engineer from Ireland, was planning and overseeing this self-assistance project.

While working on the water project, Ben once saw a young mother, age 22, diligently digging a latrine for her family's home. Laboring with a pickaxe in the stifling heat, which was over 90 degrees, the woman had dug a square pit that measured three feet on each side and ten feet in depth. While doing this task, she had propped her baby atop a pile of dirt nearby, beneath the shade of some banana trees.

Ben's descriptions of life to the south segued into a rather complicated discussion of poverty, and different kinds of poverty. People in Central America very often have access to food from the trees and from small garden plots, and their living quarters are rather inexpensive to build. Ben's view is that some of the NGO projects are bringing things to the villages that contaminate their lives. Certain projects provide the peasants with work, for example, but they also bring in much garbage and pollution. According to his assessment, the peasants would often be better off if they were not exposed to the materialism that is rampant in our western culture. Working just to buy more and more things, which sustains capitalism, may capture these people in its web. Who can say that having Salvadorans produce items for the residents of First World countries is going to lead to a better quality of life for them?

When our focus returned to our canoe trip on Lake Superior, I mentioned that the coast along the first ten miles that we had covered this morning, between the mouth of the Montreal River and Pointe aux Mines, had been of considerable interest to French entrepreneurs during the French regime, for its potential as a mining locale for copper and silver. However, serious mining efforts had only begun with Alexander Henry during the period of 1768 to 1774, and had continued during later decades and well into the following century. These latter mining operations had eventually led to a native uprising and armed attacks by native warriors, who were deeply upset about sacred materials being removed from the earth and taken away by Europeans.

At 10:45, we landed at Pointe Mamainse, which was surrounded by a huge array of reefs and low barren islets made of chocolate-brown volcanic rock. *Mamainse* was the term in the Algonkian languages that denoted a collection or an assemblage. In this case, the "assemblage" consisted of thousands of barely-exposed rock surfaces of various sizes, which extended all along the shoreline and out into the blue-green water for fifty feet or more. In the bright sunlight, the innumerable rounded bumps of brown stone had the appearance of a vast number of large amphibians that had dragged themselves into the shallows or up onto the shore, to expose their creased backs to the warm rays. While exploring the coastline, Ben located a deep crevice that cut straight inland from the water's edge for at least a hundred feet. Whenever the lake would be whipped into a fury, raging storm waves would bore into this ten-foot-wide passageway, to claw away at the high earthen bank with its evergreen forest covering at the far end. About a mile offshore from this eerie place, the depth of the cold water had been measured at 594 feet.

After our break of 45 minutes, we were again on our way. While Doree and Toby took a midday nap, Ben and I advanced five miles to round Coppermine Point. It was a blissfully sunny and calm day. In the huge, embracing silence, the sound of my own relaxed breathing was very obvious. Gazing off over the vast expanse of the western horizon, where the nearest land mass lies some 150 miles away, I mentioned that, twelve miles directly west from our location, the wreck of the freighter *Edmund Fitzgerald* lies on the bottom. It rests beneath 530 feet of water, where it sank on November 10, 1975. Although the glimmering surface of the lake was absolutely serene at this particular moment while we were looking westward, I still shuddered when my mind conjured up the sixty-foot waves that had disabled that massive ship, 729 feet long, and had sent it to the bottom, along with its crew of 29 men, just 23 years earlier.

As we headed southeast, a following wind from the northwest picked up, inducing our now wide-awake Doree to hoist the sail from her position in the passenger spot. Zooming over five miles of water in the ever-growing surf, we were finally forced to seek refuge from the unruly whitecaps when the wind began tearing off their tops. Turning left to round Pointe de la Galette (Pancake Point), we traveled a mile into the deeply indented Baie de la Galette, and coasted to a stop at a several-miles-long crescent of sandy beach at 2:45. Having advanced thirty miles already this day, we would now be pinned to the shore for who knew how long, until the wind and waves would lessen.

It was a feeling-good sunny afternoon, perfect for a respite from canoe travel: 78 degrees in the shade, with almost no clouds in a blue sky, and a stiff breeze coming from the northwest. Propelled by the warmth of the day, we strode clothed into the lake for a brief refreshing swim, then collapsed on the hot sand. When hunger moved me, I cooked a feast of beef jerky, noodles, corn, peas, carrots, and spices....on top of a wooden picnic table! We were experiencing a culture shock at this place, having momentarily left a rather demanding and potentially dangerous wilderness trip and landed on the public beach at Pancake Bay Provincial Park. We were suddenly amidst lots of kids swimming and playing in the sand, sun bathers worshipping the sun's rays, and many huge camper trailers. We were quite struck by the considerable attention that these 20th century people paid to the various aspects of their personal appearance, including their hair, makeup, and clothes. In complete contrast, we were involved in a challenging voyage that placed essentially no value at all on appearance. We had not changed our clothes for a week, and during that time I was the only family member who had used a hair brush.

As it turned out, the picnic site where we had set up our cooking stove had been reserved by Suzanne, a woman from Toronto who was vacationing here with her three-year-old daughter Marta. But when they arrived, Suzanne was amenable to my finishing cooking our meal at their table, while the two of them went swimming. Afterward, I had a long conversation with Suzanne, who works with refugees and had adopted Marta, a friendly and chubby little girl, from Guatemala. We two adults shared our experiences, including my adoption work and Suzanne's experiences in navigating the rituals that had been required for Marta's adoption, including making two trips to Guatemala. We also discussed Adolfo and William (Kevin and Ben's refugee friends from Guatemala), my long time connection with the sanctuary movement, and Ben's recent experiences in Central America. Tugging on her mom's arm, Marta indicated that she was eager to eat and play with her mom. And Tim wanted to depart, to continue our canoe trip, so I bid adieu to my new friend and her daughter. (Doree)

After 3½ hours in "civilization," hoping that the wind had let up enough out on the exposed open water, we embarked at 6:15, and immediately raised the sail to capture the force of the following breeze. As soon as our craft had cleared the sheltering shoreline behind us, it became obvious that the wind was still in an overbearing mood. Sailing at a fast pace across the bay, swept along by the slippery, intimidating surf, we again found ourselves seeking the security of solid ground. After covering 2 1/2 miles in a quick thirty minutes, we landed on another sand beach. Until the conditions would ease up considerably, we would again be windbound.

After resting and reading for 2½ hours, we set off once more at 9:20. The burly wind had dropped, but the resultant swells were still massive. Shortly, the orange ball of the sun slipped below the waterline in the west, while the bright disc of the full moon rose above the trees off to the southeast. Riding the ascending and descending hills of water in the quickly-fading light, wending our way around numerous large boulders, we had covered only two miles in a half-hour when I decided that these conditions were simply too dangerous. However, deciding to call it a day and actually reaching dry land to spend the night were two entirely different things! In an area of extensive shallows, we dived for the safety of a sand and cobble beach. Dashing through an obstacle course of exposed and barely submerged flat ledges and boulders, with the swells smashing against them with plumes of spray, we finally landed at 9:55. During this sixteen-hour day, which had included not one but two windbound sessions totaling six hours on shore, we had put 34 miles under our hull.

Quickly determining that the mosquitoes were horrendous at this site, we pitched our camp as speedily as possible, and were happily snoring in the insect-proof shelter an hour after landing.

Day Eight: The Day of the Hair-Raising Traverse

Arising at 7:15, we found an air temperature of 65 degrees in the shade, with hazy clouds filling the entire sky and no breeze. Broad swells from the west-northwest, the residue of the previous day's persistent wind, were still tumbling onto the array of flat ledges and boulders in front of our site, where we had safely maneuvered and landed the night before. After loading the canoe, we gobbled a couple handfuls of chocolate-almond gorp, washed them down with a few swallows of instant breakfast drink, and were off at 8:30, with Doree plying the bow paddle. We had no idea of the dangerous situation that we would confront just seven miles ahead.

In an hour, we made the three miles to Pointe de la Corbeille (Basket Point), with the moderately large swells arriving from the right. Along the way, with Doree calling out directions from her vantage point in the bow seat, I managed to steer through the labyrinth of submerged ledges that extend far out from the shoreline. At the location of each broad ledge, where the water was shallower, the swells became especially tall and the troughs between them became especially deep. Immediately after rounding the point, we coasted and munched a snack in the cathedral-quiet shelter of the lee shore, glad for the temporary respite from the interminable rising and falling of the swells. On the map, I noticed that a half-mile-long triangle of land covering the very tip of the peninsula, along with a half-mile stretch of nearby coast on the western shore of the peninsula, comprised the Obadjiwan Indian Reserve.

We had now reached another potentially troublesome section of the Superior route, one that had been lingering in the back of my mind for many months. Baie de Bachouanan (now called Batchawana Bay) is a long rounded indentation that extends eastward from the coastline of the lake for nearly thirteen miles. Closely skirting the full length of its undulating shore would involve thirty miles of paddling. However, under ideal weather conditions, a south-southeasterly traverse of 51/2 miles across its mouth would obviate this extensive and tiresome detour. When the situation offered less than ideal conditions, an alternate route across the mouth could be traveled. This entailed a southeasterly traverse of four miles out to the southern end of the large Île de Bachouanan, which fills a considerable portion of the center of the bay, followed by a southerly crossing of three miles from the island to the southern headland of the bay, on the coast of the lake. We decided that we would travel along this second route, first paddling out to the island and then from the island southward to the mainland.

At 9:50, Doree and I began the traverse out to Batchawana Island. Not long after our departure, a moderate wind and waves from the west-southwest picked up. So Ben raised the sail, it caught the breeze, and we sailed comfortably across the expanse of four miles in 65 minutes, aiming for the southern coast of the island. During the crossing, I mentioned that the N.W.C. had established a post on this bay in 1819, which was operated for many decades. Along the entire coastline of the large island, a broad boulder garden extends well out from the water's edge. However, we picked our way through the many scattered obstacles and landed on the island without mishap at 11:00, having advanced seven miles in the previous 2 1/2 hours since leaving the campsite.

Shortly after our landing on the island, the formerly moderate wind freshened considerably, producing row upon row of tall whitecaps sweeping in an east-northeasterly direction across the lake as far as we could see. At this point in the voyage, just 35 miles from the head of the St. Marys River, we actually welcomed the windbound rest break. Having pressed forward steadily, we had covered 200 miles in six paddling days, plus the one windbound day with its five miles and this morning's progress of seven miles. We would remain here on the island however long it took for the conditions to smooth out, before making the southward crossing of three miles to the mainland.

The weather was hazy and overcast, 74 degrees in the shade, with a solid wind blowing from the west-southwest. Along a narrow swath of sand on the gravel beach, just a few steps from where we had landed, Ben discovered clear tracks of both a moose and a wolf near the water's edge, where they had each recently come to drink.

During the course of our windbound time on the island, which we spent relaxing, chatting, and exploring, I mentioned that, about a hundred miles directly to the west of us, soundings had located the very deepest trench of Lake Superior, measuring an astounding 1,333 feet beneath the surface of the water.

After about three hours, a volatile storm front roared in from the west, darkening the sky and pelting us with heavy rain for 45 minutes. Then the atmosphere became very still, as the sky brightened somewhat. Immediately after the storm had passed, the water on the route of our three-mile traverse to the mainland at Rudderhead Point looked very flat, as if the rain had beaten it level. Doree suggested that we take this window of opportunity and go for it, with the husband-and-wife team operating the paddles.

Setting out at 2:45, we entered the waters between the island and the southern mainland. Soon, large swells from the west-southwest, the residue of the former wind, resumed in force. In addition, to complicate matters further, a moderately heavy wind and waves from the northeast kicked up. With hills of rising and falling sea flowing at us from the right side, plus vigorous waves and wind coming from behind my left shoulder, it became a very hair-raising challenge to control the direction of the canoe and keep it on course! By maintaining the angle of the craft to the waves, I hoped to keep most of them from splashing over the gunwales. To help me continually register how the conflicting swells, wind, and waves were pushing and rocking the canoe, so I could respond quickly with steering alterations, I pressed my knees firmly against each of the hull walls beside me. My legs then acted as sensors, letting my body actually feel how the craft was rolling or sliding at each moment.

During much of this crossing, while I stared at the green-clad heights of the far shore, that headland seemed to remain the same distance away, not coming any closer. I fully understood that if we were to capsize, the wind and waves could carry us across the width of cold Superior for thirty miles, probably depositing us in the area of Whitefish Point in Michigan. Concerned about hypothermia defeating us in the frigid waters of the lake if I lost my grip, I was determined to keep the canoe upright and the Kent family safely in it! As my life partner and I dug in and pulled as hard as we could to cross the span of three miles to Rudderhead Point, we poured all of our fear-induced energy into the paddles, and willed the canoe onward.

For all three of us, this was the most unsettling experience of the entire Superior journey, as the craft bucked, rolled, and pitched amid the ridges of dark water. At times like this during our canoe trips, the responsibility for the safety of the family weighed particularly heavily on my shoulders.

Eventually, the generalized green forest ahead began to take on the look of individual trees, clearly indicating that we were drawing closer and closer to the safety of the point. After 45 minutes of flat-out exertion, we giddily arrived and stepped over the gunwales into the chill of the shallows, as the breaking waves pounded and kneaded the shoreline nearby. The sensation of solid earth beneath our feet was absolutely heavenly! With sighs of relief, we rejoiced that the traverses to and from Batchawana Island were now behind us. By making this pair of crossings, we had eliminated 23 miles from the coastline route. However, the second traverse, the arduous one, had sorely challenged both our physical and our mental stamina! Relaxing in the shelter of the thick cedar forest, I updated the journal while Doree recovered her strength and studied our sheets of additional voyageur songs. Nearby, Ben rested his overextended right shoulder, since this was his day to allow it to heal from the demands of the previous several days. A short distance away, Toby dug enthusiastically into chipmunk holes in the forest floor, entirely oblivious to the tense situation that had just passed.

After resting and letting the northeasterly wind and waves reduce for 11/2 hours, Doree and I again took up our paddles at 5:00. After we had rounded Rudderhead Point, Ben hoisted the sail and we commenced a double traverse toward the south, across the mouths of both Bluewater Bay and Sand Bay. With the sail providing a considerable amount of pull, we flashed over this stretch of eight miles in 1 1/2 hours, passing close by Île aux Erables (Maple Island) along the way. Then, out of the blue, a moderately robust northwest wind and rather large waves sprang up quickly, forcing us to head for shore much earlier than we had intended. Sprinting through a maze of shallow reefs, we landed in the crashing surf on a cobblestone beach at 7:00. Our landing place was located in an unoccupied wooded area, just north of the very last of the cottages that line this stretch of the coast. Three friendly men from various of the nearby cottages came to check on us, and warmly welcomed us for a night's sleep in their neighborhood.

At 8 P.M. it was still a very comfortable 71 degrees, beneath a blue sky dappled with billowy white clouds. After feasting on a well-earned stew of rice, turkey jerky, corn, peas, shallots, mushrooms, and spices, we enjoyed cups of strawberry-chocolate milk for dessert. On the narrow flat terrace of cobbles above the incline of the beach, there was just enough room to pitch the tent in front of the woods. These rocks beneath our feet had been rounded and smoothed from thousands of years of tumbling action in the water.

As we arranged the shelter and the bedding, we watched the brilliant orange orb of the sun ease down slowly beneath the lake on the western horizon, north of Whitefish Point in Michigan. In front of us, driven forward by the relentless wind, an unending succession of waves hurled themselves onto the shallow rock ledges that extended far out from the water's edge. We had spent much time and effort this day in avoiding similar submerged ledges and boulders that stretched well offshore. This was a far cry from our experiences during the northern and central portions of this voyage, in the region of high impressive cliffs, which had presented hardly any submerged obstructions along the coastline.

Reviewing our day, I noted that, between 8:30 A.M. and 7 P.M., we had traveled eighteen miles, nearly all of that distance in three traverses. These crossings were to and from Batchawana Island, and then across a pair of large adjacent bays of the shoreline. We had also waited out two windbound periods totaling 51/2 hours, and had been finally forced to shore early in the evening, *dégradé* once again. Having progressed 222 miles in seven paddling days and one windbound day, we were now only about twenty miles from the head of the St. Marys River. After this accomplishing and sometimes terrifying day, as the gentle light of the moon bathed our camp, we drifted off into our respective dream worlds around 10:30.

Day Nine

At 4:30, we awakened to the reveille of the alarm clock, but chatted casually for fifteen minutes before beginning our day. While rubbing Doree's sore neck, I let her know that, for a woman just five foot two and weighing 115 pounds, she had dug in during that treacherous crossing from Batchawana Island like an old sailor keeping his boat afloat come hell or high water.

Crawling out of the tent, I greeted the new day and a navigable lake that looked amenable to traveling on a southerly course, having only small residual swells coming from the northwest. The air temperature measured 59 degrees, a little fog was rising from the water off to the north of us, and a few long wisps of flowing white clouds were brushed across the northern portion of the sky. The fading full moon, pale white in color, hovered directly over Île Parisienne, seven miles away toward the southwest.

As we sloshed in the cool, knee-deep water to load and strap in the gear, bathed in dim moonlight, the cobwebs in our heads from the short night mostly cleared. Soon, off in the east, the orange and pink shades of the rising sun tinted much of the sky and cast a narrow streamer across the water, brightening us even more.

We were underway at 5:45. The vault of the sky was now painted light blue, while the placid surface of the water contained hues of blue, purple, and magenta. As we headed out, a mother loon and her seven babies skittered away from the shoreline area ahead of us. As was customary on most mornings during these trips when Ben was considerably short on sleep, he broke our contemplative mood and sang his paraphrase of the 1960s song by The Righteous Brothers called *Lovin' Feeling*: "I've got that pukey feeling, and it's strong, strong, strong."

By 7:15, Doree and I had advanced four miles to reach Goulais Point, which was covered with long, early-morning shadows. During much of the distance, there had been a veil of fog, what the voyageurs had called *brouillard de l'aube* (fog of the dawn), rising from the water near the land masses; by the time we arrived at the point, it had been burned off by the heat of the sun. To our great surprise, this particular mist was the only instance of foggy conditions that we had encountered since our put-in morning! The year before, after we had paddled Lake Winnipeg, we had driven along the north shore of Lake Superior, to catch a few glimpses of the huge body of water in advance of our 1998 trip. During those two days of travel by van, we had observed thick fog blanketing the entire shoreline, as well as the adjacent offshore area, during both nights and mornings; these fog banks had lurked until midday. We had expected to encounter a similar fog-bound lake in 1998, since this was typical; but such had not been the case.

Goulais Point, where we paused to stretch our legs, had been called Pointe aux Chênes (Oak Point) during the fur trade era, while the adjacent Goulais Bay had been called Anse à la Pêche (Fishing Cove). These two geographical elements acquired their Goulais labels some time before 1850. An Ojibwa village had stood near the tip of Goulais Point since before 1830, where it had continued to thrive from then on. The Treaties of 1850, 1859, and 1879 had declared the entire seven-mile-long peninsula to be the Goulais Bay Indian Reserve; now, however, the reservation consists of a mere three miles of coastline along the east side of the peninsula, extending inland for a mile.

Anse à la Pêche (Fishing Cove, now called Goulais Bay) extends inland from the coast of the lake toward the northeast for nearly nine miles. To paddle around its entire coastline would entail a jaunt of 21 miles. Thus, when the conditions allowed, it was customary for the voyageurs to make a five-mile traverse across its mouth, thereby cutting sixteen miles from the shoreline route.

Ben, his shoulder now mostly recovered, occupied the bow seat for this crossing over the mouth of the bay. Soon after beginning the traverse, a breeze picked up from the east, our left side, mixing with the light swells that were coming from the right. However, the breeze soon faded away, and we again had ideal conditions for the crossing, riding easily on the low swells. After completing four of the five miles of the traverse, it seemed unlikely that adverse wind or waves would be arising anytime soon. So instead of finishing the crossing, I altered our course toward the southwest, to parallel the coastline, taking us on a direct route toward the base of North Gros Cap, five miles distant. Along the way, we spotted several crows in flight, as we had also noted on a couple of occasions during the previous day. Covering the entire stretch of nine miles in 2 1/4 hours, we stopped to stretch our legs and take in a fix of gorp.

An upbound freighter crept slowly by, five miles away. Off to the west in the haze, across the twenty-mile width of Whitefish Bay, we could see the elevated, forest-covered Michigan shoreline, but the mouth of the Tahquamenon River was not visible. Overhead, the sun moved gradually in its grand arc toward the west.

After our short break, Doree again assumed the role of the *avant* for the last segment of the voyage. As we cruised on automatic pilot, my mind wandered happily over all of the hours, days, and weeks of paddling during the previous sixteen years when I had gazed at her strong back, encased in that bright yellow life preserver. The widely varying weather conditions had induced her to wear beneath her preserver a nylon jacket, or a long-sleeved shirt, or a little black bare-midriff top, or nearly nothing on really warm days.

After four miles, we completed our paddle around the looming bedrock headland of Gros Cap (Large Cape), which marks the lower end of Lake Superior and the head of the St. Marys River. At this place, the river is 31/2 miles wide, extending from Gros Cap across to Pointe aux Iroquois. Two huge upbound freighters passed slowly by, 11/2 miles from us, in the shipping lanes that run down the midline of the channel.

During the previous hour, a stiff breeze and waves from the northwest had kicked up. Considering the size of the quickly-growing whitecaps that were lathering the lake and the river, we figured that we would likely become windbound during the stretch of nine miles down the river if we tried to reach Leigh Bay, just west of Sault Ste. Marie, where we had originally intended to end our trip. So Doree and I decided to complete our journey here at this quiet, scenic spot, well removed from the heavy freighter traffic that we would encounter in the narrowing river ahead.

At 11:00, we approached the little shoreline community that is also called Gros Cap. The weather was perfect, with an air temp of 68 degrees in the shade, and just a couple of fat white clouds drifting lazily across the sun-drenched blue sky. Since Ben had been dozing with Toby in the passenger spot, I awakened him at this point, so that we could all savor together this very special moment. Singing a couple verses of *Vent Frais*, we glided into the shallows, coasted to a stop, and stepped into the cool water. At that very moment, our fifteen-year project of paddling the mainline route of the fur trade from end to end, from Montreal to Ft. Chipewyan, drew to a close.

Hailing a local woman who was hiking up Gros Cap with her three kids to pick blueberries, we asked her to snap our portrait with our camera, so that all four of us could be in the photo with our faithful green craft. Before unloading for the last time, we clasped hands across the canoe, in celebration of the safe completion of our long series of journeys. I lamented that our older son Kevin was not here at this festive moment; he had participated in the preliminary year of paddling, as well as the first six years of traveling along the mainline route. In 1990, he had begun to seek other avenues of interest, and Toby had joined our family and our canoe expeditions.

Ambling to the little restaurant that was located nearby, Doree and Ben bought a victory feast, and phoned our shuttle driver at the Sault, to request that he bring the van to us. While we savored our chicken and fries beside the canoe and relaxed in the sun, we assessed this Superior trip, as well as the entire mainline project.

Two hours into the very first morning, after just five miles of progress, we had been *dégradé*, pinned to the land for the remainder of the day. Then, we had covered the remaining distance of 235 miles between Friday morning and the following Friday morning. The cooperative conditions on the lake had allowed us to move forward very well on each of those days. Thus, we had averaged 31 miles per day for seven days straight, the same rate of progress that we had achieved during our Lake Huron jaunt. And today, we had covered the remaining eighteen miles during the morning of the final day, bringing the total actual distance of our journey to 240 miles. By making a considerable number of traverses across bays, we had reduced the total coastal distance by at least 65 miles.

In spite of our excellent progress each day, we had been windbound at least once each afternoon of the trip, except on Day Two, as the wind and waves had regularly increased to unmanageable levels during the afternoon hours. This was a typical weather phenomenon, one that we had fully expected. The wind turbulence each afternoon, pinning us down on the land for spans of three to six hours, had led us to enjoy a leisurely repast: we had pulled the Duluth pack marked "A" to an upright position, removed the stove from its top, and grabbed one plasticized dinner-for-four. In no time, the aroma of bubbling broth was teasing our nostrils. Having the main meal at this time of day had allowed us to paddle until late in the evening, eliminating the need to cook at the campsite late in the day when the mosquitoes were ravenous.

We had utilized the early-morning-launch strategy of the voyageurs when possible, even though we had often paddled until late the previous evening. On various of the mornings, I had set the alarm clock to ring at 1:00, 2:15, 4:30 (three mornings), 5:00 (two mornings), 6:00, 6:15, 6:30, 7:00, or 7:15.

We had been blessed with beautiful weather during the entire nine days, except the 45 minutes of heavy rain that had fallen while we were stopped on Batchawana Island during Day Eight. The very comfortable morning temperatures had made camp breakups and departures especially easy. Since we had been windbound for several hours every afternoon except one, we had enjoyed many opportunities each day to wander on shore, exploring and absorbing the scenery. Yet we had also been able to make excellent forward progress every day, seldom encountering head winds. This had been one fantastic trip!

Our overall project, paddling the mainline fur trade route from end to end, had been an extremely enriching experience that had spanned fifteen summers, after our first summer of introductory trips. During that preliminary year, Ben had been four years old, going on five; he had not yet turned six when we had started paddling the mainline route. The entire project had served as a great impetus for growth for him and Kevin, both physically and psychologically. Kevin had joined us for the introductory year as well as the first six years on the mainline route, from ages six to twelve.

While we were contentedly reminiscing about our adventures during all of these sixteen summers on the water, the eight jets of the crack flying team of the Canadian Air Force suddenly swooped low over us, in a tight formation. On subsequent passes that covered a span of about fifteen minutes, the ace pilots formed their planes into various arrangements overhead. Finally, two of the aircraft drew a huge heart in the sky above us, with their decorative white exhaust. We had not realized just how closely the Canadian people, along with their government and Air Force, had been following our progress and adventures. What an honor they had bestowed upon us, immediately after we had completed the fifteen-summer project that focused on our shared history! (We were later told by our shuttle driver that this air show had been offered for all of the people of the Sault area, as part of a national holiday celebration that was observed by all Canadians on July 10 each year. However, our belief that it had been presented entirely in our honor never diminished one iota.)

While waiting for our van to be delivered, we lounged, napped, and soaked up the gentle warmth of the sun's rays. Fading in and out of dreamland, my mind drifted back over various events in the history of New France, events whose dates related to the present year of 1998. Quebec, the first permanent settlement in the St. Lawrence Valley, had been established in 1608, exactly 390 years before. Within about a decade of its founding, various of our ancestors who had been employed in the fur trade had arrived from the mother country, and had commenced their activities as citizens of the New World. In 1688, Jacques De Noyon and his trader colleagues had been the first Frenchmen to venture well to the west of Lake Superior, traveling as far as Lake of the Woods 310 years before our Lake Superior venture. One decade later, in 1698, nearly all of the posts in the interior had been closed. Only the facilities of Ft. Frontenac, the Chicago post, Ft. St. Louis in the Illinois Country, and Ft. La Tourette/La Maune at the north end of Lake Nipigon (north of Lake Superior), had been permitted to remain open. Finally, our last documented ancestor who had worked in the fur trade, Guillaume Lalonde, had made a trip as a voyageur between Lachine and Ft. Michilimackinac during the summer of 1758, 240 years before.

Lounging with my back against our canoe, I also pictured the details of certain events that had happened during the summer of 1662, on the opposite shore of this St. Marys River, just 31/2 miles southwest of here. At the place which would thereafter be called Pointe aux Iroquois, a party of Ottawa, Ojibwa, and Nipissing warriors, all residents of the Lake Superior region, had valiantly attacked and defeated a major Iroquois war party. This incident marked the last time that Iroquois forces ever invaded the Lake Superior region.

My mind also wandered to a locale some seven miles southeast of our location, which had been christened Pointe aux Pins (Pine Point). Here, various of the early ships which had plied the waters of Superior had been built. The succession of vessels had begun with the pinnace of the Sieur de La Ronde in 1734, which was followed by the lake barge and the sloop of Alexander Henry in 1771, the schooner *Athabasca* of the N.W.C. during the 1780s, and the larger schooner of the N.W.C. called *The Otter*, which had been constructed at this Pine Point shipyard in 1793.

After we had spent a relaxing afternoon dozing in the sun, time-traveling, and chatting, our driver finally arrived with the van at 5 P.M. Loading in the gear and lashing the canoe on top, we traveled through Sault Ste. Marie and St. Ignace, crossed the Mackinac Bridge, and arrived at our home in Ossineke in less than four hours.

The next morning, we gathered at the wall map for our annual "red pen ceremony" for the last time. With a flourish of a red marker, I colored in the fifteenth and final segment on the map, as I had done after each of the previous fourteen expeditions that we had completed along the mainline route.

Later that afternoon, my gaze happened to fall onto the large, poster-size satellite photo that is still displayed on my wall. The northwesterly view, revealing the gentle curvature of the earth's surface, encompasses the region from near Montreal to the entire stretch of Lake Superior coastline that we had just paddled. Photographed at high altitude, the various waterways, all a beautiful shade of deep blue, look as if they could be paddled with ease. However, our experiences on those watercourses had given us a realistic view of just what is entailed in navigating them, and had also fostered in us a great deal of respect for our fur trade ancestors and the thousands of other individuals who had traveled those same routes, centuries before.

XVIII
Musings of the Kent Family

Life can only be understood backwards.
But it must be lived forwards.

Soren Kierkegaard

To be able to look back upon one's life in satisfaction
Is to live twice.

Kahlil Gibran

Not to know what happened before one's birth
Is always to remain as a child.

Marcus Tullius Cicero

A few weeks after completing our Lake Superior voyage, I spent three days and nights traveling with my friends, the Saginaw Voyageurs. This adventure entailed paddling along the western shoreline of Lake Huron, in a fiberglass reproduction of a 34 foot expedition canoe that had been constructed by my dear octogenarian friend, the master designer and builder Ralph Frese. This broadening experience, plying a paddle in a craft that measured exactly twice the length of the Kent family canoe, provided a fascinating peek into how the massive fur trade canoes had behaved on the big lakes.

For nearly four decades, I have gone to great lengths to understand the lifeways of our French ancestors who were involved in the fur trade, as well as the ways of their native counterparts, and to immerse myself in the natural world in which they lived, worked, and died. These efforts, which also involved my beloved family members Doree, Kevin, and Ben, have focused on life as it was carried out in both the St. Lawrence Valley and in the interior regions far to the northwest, west, and southwest of the St. Lawrence.

One aspect of this quest has involved delving deeply into the original documentation of the period, often locating, transcribing, and translating previously unknown records. (*Let him get his hands on some French documents that haven't seen the light of day for three or four hundred years, and he's in hog heaven! Doree)*

In addition, our family activities have focused on living-history research, recreating in minute detail the ways of the 1600s, as well as paddling the ancient mainline canoe route from end to end. These reenactment activities, carried out with seventeenth century gear and canoe, and the long-distance paddling, done with twentieth century gear and canoe, have helped to shed light on a vast number of the smaller details of daily life which were not recorded on paper during earlier centuries. By filling in many of the gaps and hollows that are present in the archival record and the archaeological record, these pursuits have been invaluable in our attempts to fully comprehend the times of our ancestors in New France. Damon Keith once described this approach very well: "Tell me, and I'll forget. Show me, and I'll remember. Involve me, and I'll understand."

We were highly motivated to paddle the mainline fur trade route from end to end for several related reasons: we wanted to see what our forebears had seen, we longed to experience what they had experienced, and we hoped to be capable of enduring what they had endured. Through this canoeing project, we intended to gain many insights into the physical, mental, and emotional lives of the French and native men and women who had participated in the fur trade.

My insatiable curiosity, as well as my unbridled passion for acquiring an insider's view of life during previous centuries, propelled us into this challenging fifteen-year effort. (*You can't imagine what being married to this highly-driven guy for nearly forty years has been like! Doree*) By physically experiencing on a daily basis much of what these people had experienced, and in the very same landscapes in which they had operated, we hoped to form links with them personally. Then, we would not only carry part of them in our genetic material, in our blood, we would also have a considerable understanding of what their lives had entailed.

We all know that the present is what the past has made. Looking backward helps to explain who we are and how we got here in this condition. My zeal for the tiniest details of times past, seeking to gather the scattered pieces of the stories of those who came before us, cannot be satisfied by most popular history, which compresses the past into a number of iconic figures and a few simplified images. I am determined to assemble not a simplistic overview but a vast, highly detailed picture of earlier times. The richness, the variety, and the stability of the ancient culture of New France have provided us descendants with a lasting heritage. However, ever since the military and political victory of Anglo forces over French forces at the close of the Seven Years' War in 1763, the heritage of the French in North America has been very much minimized, downplayed, and under-celebrated. My life's work is dedicated to offsetting this unbalanced bias, which has been firmly in place in the U.S. and Canada for two and a half centuries.

One idea resonated especially strongly with me as we sought to emulate the ancient ways of our fur trade ancestors. It was generally the braver and hardier individuals who were willing to leave the known life of the St. Lawrence Valley for the dangers and uncertainties of the interior. Some of these people departed on one or many May-to-October trips into *le Pays d'en Haut* (the Upper Country) as *mangeurs du lard* (pork eaters, St. Lawrence-based voyageurs). Others opted for a fifteen-month stint, or multiple years, or even decades, of employment in the interior as *hivernants* (wintering voyageurs or traders). In both the short-term and the long-term cases, their willingness to accept the rigors of this chosen lifestyle, with its arduous and often dangerous daily routines, separated these individuals from the general population of New France and elevated them to a special status. It was with these stand-out people in particular that we forged links, when we carried out our living-history reenactments and our long-distance paddling jaunts, and in the process learned firsthand the realities and inside workings of their lives.

Through these activities, we sought to both comprehend and honor the lifeways and traditions of our French ancestors, as well as the native people with whom they had lived and worked. We were well aware that their era was not one of utopian harmony, goodness, and ease. Likewise, we understood that the basic needs and desires of humanity were much the same then as they are today; the general nature of human behavior has not altered greatly. However, by knowing what it was like to live during their era, we sought to fathom what they had been required to do in order to survive, thrive, and ensure their own future and that of their descendants.

In addition to seeking insights into the lives of the French and native populations during the fur trade era, we also paddled the mainline route each summer for fifteen years to gain a richer knowledge of the natural world, and to develop a deeper appreciation for that world.

The scenic beauty of the wilderness, along with its relative silence, its solitude, and its virtually complete isolation from people, brought to us a renewal of spirit, and equipped us to better handle the challenges of modern "civilization" (which is often much less civilized than life in the woods and on the waterways). Our total immersion in the wilds during our annual trips helped us maintain a balanced perspective on our priorities, our values, and our interests. In the process, we acquired a deeper understanding of the crucial healing role that wilderness plays for people today. These voyages underscored for us the great importance of preserving wild places, keeping them free from developments such as homes, resorts, dams, water diversions, logging operations, and mining projects. People from all walks of life and from all economic levels benefit from spending time in wilderness settings, helping them to get back on track and keep on track. One of the more prominent and powerful of the rejuvenating wilderness immersion programs is the Outward Bound program (which Ben jokingly calls "Hoods in the Woods"). Our own travels burnished our reverence for the treasures of unspoiled nature, and deepened our sense of kinship with the natural world.

Each year, our canoe trip represented a major exercise in imagining dreams and establishing goals, and then in persevering to reach those goals and fulfill those dreams. On the water, it required a combination of determination and optimism, looking far beyond such elements as fear, discomfort, and exhaustion. If during the voyage we happened to become lost, we were obliged to regain our place on the route through our own problem-solving. Or if we were to break or lose some piece of gear, we had to either mend it ourselves or do without it for the remainder of the trip. These unforeseen elements reminded us that nothing in this life is guaranteed to proceed as planned, and that the journey itself is often what is most important.

During each winter and spring, as I prepared for the upcoming segment of the mainline route, I studied numerous period reports and accounts, and acquired the topographical maps pertaining to that specific section. The portion that we would paddle each year was based partly on the locations of modern roads intersecting with the mainline water route; these roads would provide access for our van and lead us to the shuttle driver for that particular voyage. On the topo maps, I marked such features as the rapids and falls, the portage paths, the distances along the course in five-mile increments, and plenty of historical information, including the locations of ancient posts, forts, and native villages.

During the many months of planning, my adrenalin was already pumping in anticipation and enthusiasm. At these times in particular, there was a strong temptation to schedule much longer segments of the route each year. However, we had commenced the entire mainline project when the boys were only five and seven years old, and Doree and I were by no means seasoned paddlers at that time. It was important that we gain momentum year by year with successful, encouraging experiences, and gradually increase the length of the trips. When we were well into the project, our drive to the put-in place would take up to forty hours; then the water journey of up to three hundred miles would take as long as two weeks, entailing strenuous days of twelve to fifteen hours on the move. In each case, we were satisfied that these trips were extensive enough for our family vacations, and not so strenuous that our enthusiasm would diminish.

Along with my eager anticipation of the upcoming journey each year, there were usually a couple of elements that I gleaned from my studies which did not particularly generate enthusiasm. These infamous features along the route, including portage landings that lay very close to the brink of massive sets of falls, long stretches of rockbound coastline where there were no places for emergency landfalls, and massive sucking whirlpools lurking at the base of rapids, were somewhat worrisome. However, I did not let these things play too heavily on my mind, as the old Swedish proverb admonishes: "Worry gives a small thing a big shadow."

In this respect, we were somewhat blessed by the fact that we had never personally traveled any segment of the mainline route. Every single mile of each section of the route was brand new territory for the Kent family. Although I had read early accounts describing certain dangerous features, we fortunately had no clear mental images of those challenges that we would ourselves face in due time. Mark Twain's wry comment was applicable to our situation each year: "To succeed in life, you need two things: ignorance and confidence." During the course of the fifteen years in which we paddled the mainline route from end to end, our blend of experience, confidence, and enthusiasm changed gradually. With each passing year, we acquired more and more experience and confidence, yet our level of enthusiasm did not wane at all. In fact, quite the contrary was true: each year, we became more and more enthralled with the long-term project.

It could be said that we prepared for these strenuous summer journeys each and every day, all year long. Trying to lead healthy, sensible, and disciplined lives, we ingested a proper diet, exercised moderately every day, maintained an appropriate body weight, enjoyed a full measure of quality sleep each night, and used no tobacco or drugs and seldom alcohol. In addition, we worked successfully in satisfying occupations, sought a balance between our labors and our recreations, and burnished healthy personal relationships both within and outside of the family. Each of these ingredients contributed to our overall physical and mental stability, and increased our abilities to cope and thrive during the canoe jaunts.

I found the utter simplicity of wilderness canoe tripping to be extremely attractive and comforting. During our voyages, we had with us just the watercraft, a minimal amount of necessary clothing and gear, and a moderate supply of food. Traveling in this manner, life was stripped down to its bare essentials: forward progress, safety, food, clothing, and shelter at night. Drinking water was constantly available just beneath the gunwales, while daytime warmth and dryness became secondary luxuries that were not to be expected. Within our tiny circle of loved ones, we were all working together toward a common goal in a healthy physical activity, while chatting hour after hour all day long, about subjects that ranged from the deeply serious to the delightfully frivolous.

As we proceeded, we made it a point to maintain an upbeat attitude, traveling together in a peaceful mood. This serene mentality, aided by the steady, mesmerizing cadence of our paddle strokes and our deep breathing, was heightened by the realization that, along each segment of the mainline route, it was highly likely that we would never pass this way again. This one time through would probably be our only opportunity to take it all in, to absorb its numerous and varied aspects. As we traveled, we interacted with, rather than fought against, the natural world. However, we also understood that the sheer physical effort that was required to reach and travel through the richly historic and scenic places along the route made the experiences immensely deeper than if we had driven to those places in our van, stepped out of the comfort of the vehicle, and instantly observed the attractions. Along the way, the many physical and mental challenges that we encountered honed our optimism and our stamina, rather than wearing us down. That old saying, "Wherever you go, there you are," certainly applies to canoe trips. Each individual carries along his outlook, personality, attitudes, talents, and weaknesses wherever he goes. We did our best to keep our outlook bright and appreciative.

We were able to maintain a relaxed and optimistic attitude throughout each trek partly because of the solid preparations and the precautions that preceded and accompanied each voyage. These sensible safety elements took much of the concern out of traveling on our own through remote wilderness areas. For example, we always clipped into place the webbing straps that secured each of the packs to the thwarts, since it was not possible to predict when a sudden squall would kick up, or when some other emergency might arise. (Many paddlers only fasten down their gear before pushing off to run a rapids.) In addition, we constantly wore our life preservers, from before the morning loading until after the evening unloading. By taking these simple precautions, there was never a need for us to suddenly scurry to grab floatation devices and secure the cargo when a serious situation arose. Even at landing spots that presented a sudden steep drop-off beyond a submerged ledge, or rocks that were slippery with a covering of moss, lichens, or algae, there was no problem when we fell into the drink when loading or unloading. By being fully prepared, we could focus all of our attention on the jobs and the challenges at hand, and on the rich wilderness surrounding us. On shore at night, we always fastened the bow and stern ropes of the canoe to solid trees, tied the life preservers and paddles to a tree (with the paddle grips pointed upward, so that salt-hungry animals would not gnaw on those sweaty treats), and left the bailer, sponge, and sail attached to the craft. Thus, even after a heavy windstorm during the night, we would find our vehicle and equipment available and ready for action, without having to mount a search for them. These preventative activities did not indicate that we were beset with worries; quite the contrary was true. By working out these precautions in advance, we were freed from concern about unforeseen events that could imperil our safety. As a result, we could fully appreciate the adventures as they unfolded, knowing that we had prepared as well as was reasonably possible for whatever might emerge.

Every aspect of our wilderness living and traveling, even if it had at first seemed somewhat strange or demanding, soon became a standard feature of daily life. By quickly turning all of our activities into regular routines, the tasks soon became second nature, with each of us knowing how to do them. While in the canoe, my jobs as the *gouvernail* included examining the terrain up ahead and the map in front of me, choosing the most appropriate route, steering our course, and providing a considerable part of the propulsion power. In the *avant* position, Doree, Kevin, or Ben contributed heavily to the forward power, set the paddle pace, and watched for close-range obstacles, which they both called out to me and helped steer around with draw or pry strokes. I tended to make most of the decisions about when to take rest stops and when to halt for the night, but the threat of an ornery crew tempered my decisions and I often accepted their influence. (Although I tended to lobby for fewer breaks and for extended paddling into the evening, when we did pause on land during strenuous sections, I found it especially difficult to tear myself away from the repose and resume our labors.) In our later years, we took many of our breaks while afloat. At campsites, we shared and rotated the various tasks over time, based on individual preferences.

For better or for worse, I bore the greatest amount of the responsibility for our safety and our successful completion of each trip, as the navigator, constant paddler in the stern, and maker of many of the final decisions. I suppose this was appropriate, since I had acquired the canoe and gear, planned each voyage, ordered and studied the maps, arranged the shuttle driver, studied the history of the route, and served as the main instigator and promoter of the project. For her part, Doree took responsibility for the healthy food and drinks plus pleasure foods, as well as her crucial role as family therapist and mediator, French coach, and song leader. Although I handled the majority of the annual preparations, Doree, Kevin, and Ben were very willing participants each year, and they were nearly always good-natured about the heavy demands of each voyage. For my part, I did not particularly relish bearing so much responsibility on my shoulders, especially in dangerous situations. It was not a very comfortable sensation knowing that my family's safety and well-being rested squarely on my decisions and on my successful performance. Through it all, with each annual journey, we came to share deep bonds, as we faced and handled as a unit the myriad physical and mental challenges that came our way.

During these demanding trips, we fully depended on one another, for the performance of needed tasks, for companionship and friendship during this period of total isolation from all other humans, and for reassurance, cooperation, and clear thinking in times of danger and potential disaster. Long-distance canoeing entails working and living together around the clock in very close proximity: in the craft, at the campsite, and in the tent. To achieve the best results, this requires close relationships, many conversations, numerous jokes, and a great deal of cooperation. I would not undertake such trips with anyone other than my own loved ones, since we know one another so intimately. Within our family on the trips, there was little jockeying for authority, no showing off of one's knowledge, strength, or experience, and only seldom friction or strain during a voyage. We understood each other thoroughly, and we trusted one other explicitly with our lives. Particularly during the second half of the fifteen-year project, as Ben grew in size, power, and experience, we came to rely heavily on his excellent judgment and bravery in emergency situations. We could all talk freely as we proceeded, and thus avoid the buildup of hostilities. Likewise, there was no concealing of weaknesses, doubts, or fears from one another. In contrast to our little family unit, the members of a voyageur party would have tended to hide their anxieties from each another. They would have presented an air of strength, confidence, nonchalance, and lack of worry to their colleagues, which in turn would have encouraged such attitudes among the entire party. It was no coincidence that several of our ancestors had borne the nickname of *Sans Peur* (Without Fear) or *Sans Souci* (Without Worry).

Our expeditions expanded, deepened, and strengthened our family bonds, by allowing us to experience together so many incidents that would not have presented themselves in our usual daily lives. For me personally, fulfilling my dream of traveling the mainline route from end to end was not the only reward; the adventures that we encountered along the way became all the more valuable and treasured because we had shared and endured them together.

Each journey presented nearly as many mental challenges as physical demands. First was the sheer drive that was required to travel the route, mostly ignoring the sensations of our bodies. In addition, we were obliged to make serious judgment calls on a regular basis, weighing and assessing the risk factors of a given situation against our abilities, and estimating the likelihood of our success as well as the extent of the damage if we were to fail. The myriad decisions that were required along the way involved various situations, including choosing the specific traveling route based on the conditions; scouting a set of rapids and determining whether to portage or to run it, and if attempting the run, deciding just how to handle the obstacles; choosing where to portage when the path could not be found or it had long since disappeared; determining whether to make a traverse or not, based on the distance involved and the potential for an adverse wind or a storm arising; and choosing the time to leave the water and the time to return to it when a lightning storm was active in the area.

Other than two spare paddles and one spare map case, we did not carry any extra equipment, and we had only one set of backup clothing per person, reserved for serious mishaps that threatened hypothermia. Our party did not include any extra canoes or additional paddlers, which would have engendered a sense of security (real or imagined), and there were no sources of outside assistance to call upon in case of emergencies. (There was no camera crew, either.) We were obliged to rely on each other and to look inward for strength, fortitude, and perseverance, to help us find solutions to challenges and carry out our decisions in unfamiliar territory. Other than our own confidence and abilities, the standard reassurances that we could give ourselves included knowing that each of the family members was in good health, that the canoe and all of the gear were with us and were intact, and that we were certain exactly where our present location was positioned on the map.

With each passing year, we became more adept and skilled at all of the requirements of long-distance tripping, and in every instance we were pleased to discover that we possessed greater capabilities than we had imagined. One of the most important elements in our success each year was having the will, the deep commitment, to meet the challenges and to grow and learn in the process. Our commitment and enthusiasm allowed us to deal with each of the adversities as they arose, and to keep our spirits up all the while.

On any canoe trip, there will always be a certain tension between wanting to travel slowly and casually, halting for numerous recreational stops along the way (the natural inclination of Doree, Kevin, and Ben), versus making steady forward progress along the route (my natural inclination). In our case, we were engrossed in a

703

long-distance voyage each year, in which we had to successfully reach the distant end point; we were not making casual round-trip jaunts from a stationary base camp. This was the reality that determined our strategy and our overall pace. Over time, my family members came to realize the wisdom of the old Scandanavian adage, "He who does not sail in fair weather will have to sail in foul." For my part, by laboring so heavily as the full time stern paddler and navigator, I soon learned to treasure any time spent on land without a paddle in my hand. As a result, we struck a comfortable balance: we did not push furiously ahead, but we did try to make progress whenever the conditions allowed, taking a reasonable number of breaks en route as needed. For us, what was most salient was our common desire to fully take in the scenery and the wildlife of these historic places, to absorb the flavor and solitude of wilderness paddling, and to derive satisfaction from meeting the physical and psychological demands. At the conclusion of each trip, we seldom had the sensation that we wished we had lingered somewhere for a longer time. In this regard, it was helpful to know that, during the following summer, we would again be immersed in the next section of northern wilderness, deep in fur trade country.

One subject about which we all agreed from the very beginning was our deep respect for Mother Nature. As a result, we sought to practice non-impact traveling at all times. This meant cooking our meals on a tiny, one-burner gas stove; utilizing only dead wood for our small recreational fires, and burying the charcoal remnants when we departed from a campsite; using biodegradable soap for washing dishes and hands; burying all food remnants and bodily waste materials; and transporting out all of our trash, as well as any other trash of portable size that we found along the way. We usually left only footprints and temporarily tramped-down vegetation, but we took away a great deal: inspiration, appreciation, serenity, and a deep sense of history, nature's forces, and timelessness. We made every effort to not interfere with the elements of nature that we passed through and beside.

Along each of the wilderness sections of the mainline route, the terrain and scenery that we traveled through and absorbed were mostly unchanged compared to preceding centuries and millennia. To be sure, during that long expanse of time, the type of forest cover had varied over the thousands of years, as the climate had segued back and forth from warmer and drier periods to cooler and moister periods, in interminably long swings of climatic cycles. In addition, the destruction of forest fires and the stages of regrowth that had followed had caused short-term changes in the appearance of the woods. However, the surrounding hills and valleys, the rocky shorelines, the various color shades and surface textures of the water, and the dome of the sky, with its sun, clouds, and stars, had been the very same throughout all of the prehistoric and historic eras. Besides seeing the same sights that the French and native residents and travelers had seen in their day, we also heard the very same sounds that they had heard: paddles dipping, water moving, trees and bushes sighing in the wind, birds singing and cawing and honking, wolves howling, frogs harrumphing, fish breaching the surface with a splash, squirrels scolding, mosquitoes droning. These sounds were truly echoes from the past in the wilderness world of the present.

The one significant difference in the environment of the mainline route between our modern era and previous times is the virtual lack of people on most portions of the route now, either as residents or as travelers. During major segments of each of our trips, we did not encounter any other two-legged mammals. Because of this widespread lack of humans in the wilds, due to their concentration in a few scattered communities, a great deal of the route is actually more pristine in appearance than it was when native and fur trade personnel populated and traversed the area in considerable numbers.

Compared to the fur trade era, our canoe was built of different materials, and some of our items of gear and clothing were different. However, the natural world through which we traveled was virtually identical to that of earlier centuries, and our activities and experiences while paddling the route were generally the very same as those of our predecessors. Days and nights on the water were still long, laborious, sometimes dangerous, and satisfying, while windbound times on shore were still spent resting, healing, repairing gear, and fending off attacking insects.

Sadly, the mindset today concerning nature and its value is often much less respectful than in previous times. In our era, we are equipped with a scientific explanation for a great many phenomena of the natural world. As a result, we are less awestruck and fearful of Mother Earth's powers than were earlier generations. Because of this, we tend to treat her soils, minerals, waters, air, plants, and animals with less care and respect than they deserve. We would all do well to return to the thinking that is reflected in an ancient native proverb: "Treat the earth well; it was not given to you by your parents, it was loaned to you by your children. We do not inherit the Earth from our ancestors; we borrow it from our children."

During the course of our journeys over the ancient water highways, lots of friendly and relaxed talk passed between us, both reminiscing about the past and making plans for our respective futures. These countless hours of conversation, taking place while we paddled, and during mealtimes, and around the fire at night, varied widely in their subject matter. In addition to discussing fur trade history, our ancestry, and native life, we also talked about the many adventures and mishaps that the boys had experienced at school and in Boy Scouts, books that we had read, and movies that we had enjoyed, with some of these stories stretching out over several days, in serial fashion. We also practiced mental math and spelling and basic conversations with the boys, all in French, and learned new voyageur songs as well as additional verses to songs that we had mastered previously.

Along the way, we reviewed many of the tales that had been recorded over the centuries about events that had taken place in the distant past, both in the interior regions through which we were traveling and back in the St. Lawrence Valley. We also imagined the wide array of other incidents that had not been recorded on paper, oral histories that had been lost with the death of the last person who had known the stories. Our thoughts extended to both those few individuals who had become well known, as well as the countless others who had been long forgotten. We tried to envision the human dramas that had played out hundreds of years ago, involving joy, grief, loneliness, hunger, pain, birth, and death, the stories involving uncounted generations of native people as well as many generations of French individuals. We also talked about my work with the documentary record of New France, reconstructing the life stories of many of our ancestors and their neighbors. While traveling along the mainline passage, we clearly felt the direct links with both our forebears and all of the others who had paddled these very same waters, those individuals who had passed by the same terrain, had portaged over the same paths while hearing the same roaring falls, had experienced similar weather, and had been bitten by the ancestors of the insects who now sucked our blood, three to four centuries later.

During each of our extended gab-fests, I tried to keep at least part of my brain focused on the map in front of me and on the passing terrain, to maintain our course. Very occasionally, I would become especially engrossed in some particular topic and either take a wrong passage or miss a turn, making us *dérouté*. Then I would have to pay the piper: an uncomfortable period would vex me until I had gotten us back on track, and could again match the features of the land and water to the features on the chart.

Sometimes when I wove long tales for the family, I imagined an old retired trader or voyageur sitting before his fireplace in one of the settlements along the St. Lawrence, or a native elder sitting beside the fire in his bark-covered lodge in the interior. In each case, the younger generations encircling the old man gazed into the flames while listening to the tales of his younger days. By sessions such as these, information was passed down through the ages, including the knowledge and wisdom that was gained from both the successes that were achieved and the mistakes that were made.

Through our story-telling sessions, Doree and I tried to convey to our sons a profound respect for those individuals who have been through this life before us. Population experts have estimated that more than 80 billion people have lived on this planet, of which about 6.7 billion are currently living here. Some 90 percent of these individuals from the past lived in hunting-gathering cultures, about 6 percent in agricultural cultures, and 4 percent in industrial cultures. These billions of people experienced an immeasurable amount of happiness and sorrow, joy and pain, and satisfaction and grief. It is vitally important that we, as well as the rest of the people living today, understand that there have been many other eras, and many other ways of doing things and thinking about things. No period of prehistory or history can be considered to have been the best time to have lived; each era has its better features and its worse features. Living in today's world, with its fast transportation of people and material goods, instant communications, high-level technologies, advanced medicine, and mass education, it is tempting to believe that our time is by far the finest time to have ever lived. To put this issue into perspective (even if only to better appreciate the innumerable advances), we must know about the different environments and cultures in which other populations have lived over the millennia, and the different ways of doing and thinking that they have applied. Americans, by constantly receiving printed and broadcast information that has been extensively manipulated and filtered, tend to perceive the United States as the "center of the universe" during this present era. However, it is eye-opening to study history and learn that there have been numerous other important centers of civilization over the millennia, many of which are now considered to be rather insignificant areas of the world. We would all do well to deeply consider the myriad contributions that present and previous generations throughout the globe have made to the ways of life that we now enjoy, and give them appropriate credit and appreciation. Heavy sacrifices and heavy prices have been paid for the comforts and the conveniences that we so often take for granted.

Learning about the past and remembering are crucial to our future as humans. A great percentage of the younger people today tend to grow up in and live in a permanent and perpetual present, with very little understanding of even the not-so-distant past. The age-old process of learning stories that explain our past and our present condition, and help guide us toward the future, is fast fading from our overall culture. Knowledge of our own history and that of other people around the world, and interest in that history, is not widespread today. This lack of understanding and interest is, in large measure, a result of our extreme focus upon materialism. Acquiring things, rather than gaining knowledge, understanding, and mastery, is now at the forefront of most people's lives in our first-world society.

From our own paddling and living-history reenacting experiences, we each gained a considerable number of benefits. In addition to a sense of accomplishment and achievement, one of the most significant benefits was the knowledge that we very rarely ever reach our physical or mental limits. We have immensely greater stores of stamina and endurance than we can imagine; if the situation demands it, we can nearly always press ourselves harder and farther than we thought possible.

We also experienced a major surge in our self-reliance. In our modern society, there are few opportunities for us to accomplish a particular task entirely by ourselves. Most of us pay for others to provide our food, clothing, housing, heating, transportation, and entertainment. However, during a long-distance paddling trip, when we looked at the route map at the end of a long, eventful day or a week, and saw the progress that we had made by our own efforts, it was immensely satisfying, knowing all of the challenges that those miles had presented. The journeys also offered many opportunities for smaller doses of satisfaction during each day. The completion of each task, such as finding the head of a portage path, or locating a place to camp, or gathering an armload of firewood, was rewarding. The completion of even simple jobs brought a pleasure that was both direct and immediate. For example, producing a fire to cook a meal and cheer the evening involved gathering tinder and various sizes of firewood, clearing the fire site of all burnable materials down to the bare earth, arranging the fire materials, and finally igniting them. The completion of each small step in the process of creating the fire provided its own reward, even before the blaze had been lit. In contrast, in our modern, generally indoor life, we simply activate the stove and a source of perfectly even cooking heat is immediately at our disposal. For warmth, we simply adjust the furnace thermostat on the wall, and then take for granted the steady maintenance of a comfortable room temperature. We pay for these conveniences just as indirectly, with funds that we earn by doing an occupation that is unrelated to cooking heat or home heating.

We all see things differently over time, sometimes after only a day or two or a week, based on our intake of information and our experiences. Each time we emerged from a mainline voyage, we returned to our contemporary world with a somewhat changed perspective on our lives. Having endured the demands and the physical hardships of wilderness traveling for up to three hundred miles, we could now more fully appreciate the relative comfort and safety of our existence during the rest of the year. With the memories of the tough trips firmly tucked away in our bag of experiences, we could reframe various situations in our daily lives. For instance, while I walked home from the train in a driving rain in the chilly darkness after a concert, I was not nearly so uncomfortable when I rearranged the scene in my mind. I was safely on land, I knew exactly where I was located, I was entirely familiar with the route home, I was not being attacked by hordes of blood-sucking insects, and I was walking toward our own plot of land. That land would offer a heated shelter, dry clothes, cooking equipment, refrigerated food supplies, dry toilet paper on a handy dispenser, and comfortable sleeping equipment, all of which were already in place, requiring no unpacking and preparation for the night!

Even the challenging conditions during one portion of a canoe trip allowed us to appreciate more fully the benign conditions with which we were blessed during other times on the water. Bone-chilling wetness, relentless head winds, and daunting waves allowed us to better cherish warmth and dryness, calm conditions, and a helpful following wind. In addition, being sometimes off track or injured allowed us to prize knowing just where our present position was located on the map and that everyone was in good health. Finally, serious threatening dangers, while making a long traverse amid intimidating waves or while capsizing in turbulent rapids, gave us a renewed appreciation for the wonderful sensations of standing safely on the shore with all family members, canoe, and gear intact.

However, the extensive knowledge and the many benefits that we derived from paddling the mainline route did not come without costs. As the Roman satirist Juvenal once noted, "All wish to possess knowledge, but few, comparatively speaking, are willing the pay the price." Nearly everything in this life costs something. Discoveries and wisdom do not come easily, and there are always prices to be paid for every forward stride, every achievement, every pleasure.

Our canoe trips required leaving the creature comforts, the relative security, and the known elements of our usual daily lives, and accepting and embracing the discomforts, the insecurities, and the myriad unknown elements of a journey in unfamiliar territory. With every adventure come certain risks, and absolutely no guarantees. However, the more difficult it is to accomplish something or to obtain something, the more we value and appreciate it. As practical, responsible people, we carried with us certain fears and apprehensions about each of the trips. However, we anticipated the potential problems as best we could, prepared for them in a reasonable manner, and did not let our misgivings limit us and keep us from fulfilling our dreams.

During the voyages, we trusted ourselves and each other, and took reasonable, responsible risks. While striving toward our goals, we set clear objectives and then applied persistence and patience to reach those aims. Henry Ford once said, "Obstacles are those frightening things you see when you take your eyes off your goal." Our massive paddling project, when taken one step at a time, was not overly daunting. There were indeed a great number of challenges that arose every single day along the way. But when we faced each demand as it arose, each one in its turn became manageable. We chose to make these voyages of our own free will. Although they involved relinquishing our usual sense of relative security and protection from harm, they enabled us to acquire a certain kind of wealth, the most important kind.

We heartily encourage other families and canoe enthusiasts to paddle the mainline route from end to end, or at least certain portions of it. However, we wish to be very clear in our statement that each and every segment of the route holds many demands and dangers in store. Such a project ought to be undertaken only with appropriate and complete gear, and only after sufficient education, training, and physical conditioning have been completed. We entered into this project in excellent physical shape, reasonably well educated, and with a responsible and independent attitude. We then trained ourselves year by year as we proceeded, starting with modest and manageable goals and expectations, and gradually working our way up to the more demanding segments. This we did in an entirely independent manner, not expecting to be rescued by others if we tackled challenges that exceeded our abilities.

These words of caution are actually offered as encouragement, not discouragement. We all need to expand our horizons, stretch and test ourselves, and make life more adventuresome. A major ingredient in all human endeavors is ignorance of events that are coming in the future. In a great many instances, this ignorance is a major blessing. Few of us would undertake new, challenging activities if we knew their eventual outcome in advance. We simply need to keep moving forward, armed with equal amounts of preparation, determination, optimism, and hope for the best.

Our fifteen summers of traveling the mainline route as a family constituted an immense voyage of discovery. Viewing the wilderness route from the vantage point of a canoe, at the gradual, steady pace of a pair of flashing paddles, helped us to see the ancient world through the eyes of our fur trade ancestors and their native colleagues. However, our private fifteen-year pilgrimage, which we carried out to both experience and celebrate the places and the heritage of our forbears, also taught us a great deal about ourselves and each other. These lessons, and the confidence and satisfaction that they wrought, will serve us well in the decades ahead. In addition, the priceless memories of the myriad adventures that we shared and endured together will function as flint and steel to ignite our imaginations for the rest of our lives.

The many rivers that we paddled represent metaphors for the constantly flowing stream of the remainder of our days. There will be long sections virtually clear of obstructions, and others fraught with hindrances; gradual and sharp curves; fast and sluggish currents; turbulent rapids and smooth, placid sections; silt-laden and beautifully clear waters; and foggy and clear air, which will either inhibit or enable the view of the terrain that lies ahead. In each instance, we will read the conditions, assess the situation, determine our course, and dig in with self-assurance and high hopes.

Pensées d'Une Femme Sage
(Thoughts of a Wise Woman)
Dorothy J. Kent

Now looking back on the fifteen years of paddling the fur trade route, I wonder how in God's name I managed to do it! Leisurely it wasn't. Comfortable it wasn't. Real dangers lurked, and wild capsizes became part of the experience. I occasionally flit back in my memory to seeing life from underneath the capsized canoe: watching in slow motion our dog Toby above me, using his natural swimming skills, and finally, peering into the light turquoise water, extricating my legs from under the thwart and thinking, "I'd better get up to the surface." When everyone turned out to be O.K., we moved on. Pride stirred for a short while, but humility in the face of nature was a wiser companion.

During the years of paddling, my life also consisted of many other challenges; my work with adolescents who were in a psych hospital was one of those. Teenagers seem to be able to smell fear, so all the practice with canoeing helped me to hold my own with angry and often destructive kids. Being able to soothe myself, calm my breathing, and think a few steps ahead were all helpful at work (and also while paddling). Finding a way to overcome fear also helped in 1987 while I was in El Salvador, walking into the war zone to deliver food. And the lessons of the canoe trips helped in raising our two boys.

Years after the canoe trips had ended, I picked up a book, *The Four Agreements* by Don Miguel Ruiz, which I've shared with many clients. The part about making agreements and not breaking them ("Be impeccable with your word") was an idea that worked well on the paddling jaunts. Were there thoughts of mutiny? To be sure. When the weather turned frigid and it started raining, part of me wanted to abandon ship, but I didn't. In addition, I managed to not hurl insults or disparage my mates.

Another of the agreements, "Don't take anything personally," helped us to cope with the many challenges. In the middle of a terrorizing or calamatous moment, I might be tempted to let loose with: "What the hell did you get us into? I can think of a lot of trips that are more kick-back than this!" Tim, too, would have his moments of shouting a command in an emergency, and I would need to tell myself, "Don't take this as an insult...he's just under duress at the moment."

The third agreement is about not making assumptions. For example, "He obviously hates us and wants us to drown" would be one of those faulty assumptions that would derail both a relationship and a trip. No, I didn't say that to our *gouvernail*. I did say, "Tim, you must be out of your mind to think we can go to bed on just gorp, instead of a hot meal!" Generally, we began to negotiate these decisions. The kids and I soon learned to be better at dealing with both the challenges and the negotiations.

The fourth agreement, which we had in our repertoire even before Ruiz' book came out, is "Do Your Best." It became a standard joke between my husband and me when I'd say, "I'm doing the best I can!" And Tim would say solemnly, "That's what I was afraid of." Then we'd burst into laughter.

As a therapist, I often recommend Ruiz' *The Four Agreements* to people who have relationship problems (no paddlers have come to me for counsel yet). It reinforces four really important and vital rules. I've begun using "paddling in a canoe through rough waters" as a favorite metaphor in sessions. I ask couples if they have prepared themselves for their "canoe trip" (marriage). What preparation and planning preceded their trip? Do they have some essential strategies that will get them through the next major rapids? How will they recover if there is a capsize? Some couples will put in the time on skill building and practice. Many won't. Similarly, few people will be willing to take on a 3,000 mile wilderness route in a canoe. But those who follow the rivers less traveled are likely to survive and thrive, and that will make all the difference.

In our own marriage, when a conversation gets heated, we might ask the other, "Is this a riffle or a fifty-foot drop?" Then we might stop to collaborate, take a few deep breaths, even laugh, and then listen to each other. "The portage path might be a better option," one of us might suggest, "but we'd better chuck some of our baggage."

On a final note, I offer this quote from T.S. Eliot's *Quintets*:

"We shall not cease from exploration,
And the end of all our exploring
Will be to arrive where we started,
And know the place for the first time."

And what a voyage it was, our fifteen years of paddling the mainline route!

My Thoughts
Kevin S. Kent

It was 1984, I was seven years old, and Ben was five. We had driven such a long, long distance from Chicago. I remember being on an endless highway, crammed into the back seat of our Chevy Malibu with Ben, two sleeping pillows, and some of the gear. The paddles were poking into me, and it was crowded and difficult to nap comfortably. We stopped at the border of Canada and a man in uniform looked us over thoroughly. Dad got questioned a lot because he fit the "wolf man" profile, and for the next several years it was always the same at the border. When you grow up with your Dad, you don't really think he looks "strange." It would take about three more years for me to understand what Black people and Hispanic people go through all the time. Once Dad was walking Ben and me to Longfellow School and a woman drove up and asked, "Boys, is that man bothering you?" I thought it was pretty funny until Dad nudged me and said, "Tell her, boys, I'm your Dad!" Over the years on the canoe trips, we had a great time with that story!

The night before that first trip on the mainline route, on the Mattawa River, we stayed in a cabin. In the middle of a dream, Dad gently shook me awake, saying *Debout! Debout! Debout!* But it was still pitch dark, and I wasn't ready to be awake; my eyes were so heavy. But Mom helped me and Ben get dressed. We put on our nylon jackets, our life preservers, and our lanyards with a Swiss Army knife and a waterproof matches case. Ben and I each carried our sleeping bag in our own pack, our seat board, and our own paddle. In a trance, we watched Mom and Dad carry the canoe to the big river and place the gear into different compartments. Mom, on this trip and many others, lifted us from the shore into the middle of the canoe, to keep our feet dry and warm. She usually looked out for our comfort. Dad called it "coddling" us. What I called it is reassuring.

We each sat on our little seat board, and boy, our little skinny rumps began to hurt after a few hours. We were the passengers a lot of the time on this trip, but occasionally we dipped our little paddles in the water and helped out. Dad had a paper with notes written on it about a book he'd read. He started telling us the story, but before long, with the sunshine in our eyes, we couldn't stay awake for the conclusion. Later, he saw we were awake and caught us up on the story.

We were in and out of sleep, watching the shoreline passing. When the wind got to be too much, Mom and Dad had us all sing *Vent Frais* in a round: Mom first, then Ben and me, and then Dad.

Finally, I got my turn in the bow seat, using a full length paddle. Mom's singing gave me the rhythm, so I would paddle in sync with Dad. Pretty soon, I had two miles under my belt!

The second day, arriving at a portage called Portage Pin de Musique, Dad realized that the tie down rope was missing. I had forgotten it back at the campsite! So he and I paddled the empty canoe back a half-mile to get the rope. He let me sit in the *gouvernail* (his) position, where I learned how to make the canoe go straight -- sort of -- after going in circles. But I learned fast. I felt proud when Ben and I earned our voyageur sashes two days later, after showing how we could paddle up the river, turn around, and return to a landing, all without any help from our parents.

At each campsite, I was always glad to run around, pick berries, and go off with Ben looking for small twigs and bigger limbs to start a fire. Later, I'd blow up my own air mattress. After a couple of years of having mostly a free ride, Mom and Dad upped the ante: by the time I was eight or nine, my jobs included setting up the tent by myself and blowing up two air mattresses. Dad often had to practice the trumpet, which seemed a lot easier than blowing up the mattresses! By the time I was done blowing, I joined Mom at the fire. I couldn't keep from moving burning sticks around, and I always wanted a huge fire, which my parents vetoed -- over and over again. Huddled around the crackling fire, we talked about the day, and old Dad would tell us about geography and history, before I even knew the words!

On the second trip when I was eight, at Little Pine Rapids, Dad told me to take the bow rope and walk along the shore, holding on. He held onto the rope at the stern, and the canoe was out in the water. Dad said we were doing what our voyageur ancestors had done, lining the canoe down the rapids. I began to feel something (I would later identify it as pride). Mom told me she was proud of me, and put her arm around my shoulders. We ran several more rapids, and things seemed to be humming along. Then, before we knew it, water was sloshing over the sides of the canoe, into our laps! Then, amazing to me, the canoe rolled us right out into the frothing cold water! It seemed like we were really doomed: suddenly, big hailstones were coming down on us, as we gasped for breath and held tight onto the canoe. Dad yelled, "Kick hard!" and we put everything into it, to get the canoe to shore. For a kid like me who liked to test the limits, I suddenly was at odds with my own nature, wishing we were safe. My teeth were chattering, but the shore was getting nearer, and I knew deep down that my parents would take charge and take care of us. We climbed up on a ledge and stood there shivering in the rain. Then Dad was handing Mom some dry clothes for Ben and me, and the rain had stopped! Going through all this on our first capsize, and then getting back into the canoe to continue made us a little giddy.

The seven years I was on the canoe trips made me a lot less fearful and pushed me to be courageous at times, like the first time I ever ran a rapids while paddling in the bow, on the French River. Dad's remark when we were about to run each rapids was: "Today is a good day to die!" He said it was a native American saying. It made us laugh, even when there was a really challenging section ahead. Like during the third year on the mainline route, on the Ottwa River, when I was almost ten. We'd had such a sunny day, heard more great stories from Dad, and sang a bawdy drinking song of the voyageurs. The sun was setting, which told me we would soon be settling into a campsite to stretch our legs, eat, and have fun. I remember staying in the canoe with Mom while Dad scouted the frothy river that was in front of us, with boulders blocking a clear route toward calmer waters. Dad actually had a "conference" with us, and said, "It's possible we'll capsize, but it's time to make camp. We can camp below the rapids, whether we get there sitting in the canoe or swimming beside it in the water." I seemed to think that was a reasonable statement. To go back the way we came wasn't a real possibility.

So Dad lowered the mast and we shot down the rapids. Dad yelled, "We made it!" But then we began to really go down deep into white water and then bounce up high. This water was a lot more powerful than the year before when we had capsized on the French River. Before I knew it, the canoe overturned in really wild water. I was near Mom and we held onto the canoe, but Dad and Ben were no longer near us. Mom kept looking at me and said, "We're O.K., Kevin, just hold on." I did. We got very near shore and she said we were going to let go and swim for shore, since the canoe was going to swirl and go down more rapids. "O.K., let go." We swam to shore and watched our canoe take a second trip down more rapids. We were soaked and starting to get cold. As we walked along the rocky shore, I finally spotted Dad and Ben on the opposite shore, where the canoe had gone to their side. They bailed it out and came across to us at a good camping site. We spread out our gear, ate gorp, and Ben and I got into the one dry sleeping bag. That night, I had some rough dreams of being in the water. The thoughts were with me for the next few days, even though we were safe.

The next several years, Ben and I competed to see if we could match Mom's total miles. It was great to be paddling in the bow, especially under a full sail, racing the waves. Sometimes they caught up with us and slid under the canoe. What a strange sensation!

When I was two weeks away from my twelfth birthday, I amazed my other family members. When we finished the canoe trip near Grand Portage, I let Dad know that I wanted to carry the canoe all the way to the car, which was a quarter-mile away down a dirt path. Along the way, Mom checked me out occasionally, not wanting the 69 pound canoe to squash my 77 pound body. Never having carried the canoe herself, she was astounded at my strength. On that same trip, I sometimes carried her big 60 pound Duluth pack on portages.

On that same trip, there were days when Mom and I faced each other for hours in the bow while I paddled or she paddled. She tormented me (lovingly of course) by having me add, subtract, multiply, and divide in French. Then we moved on to more interesting topics, like Freud's concepts of the id, ego, and superego (I had picked up a *Psychology Today* magazine in an outhouse a couple days back). I was intrigued with the idea of the superego, which was where the feeling of guilt emerges. I didn't have a lot of that. Mom said it was because I had been raised as a Unitarian Universalist.

Many memories are packed away in my head about the long and arduous canoe trips. All the time we spent being squished into the canoe helped our sharing and bonding. I must have heard the story of Mom's pregnancy and my birth several times. And Dad shared lots of information about our ancestors in the fur trade. I learned a lot about geography, about history, about paddling, and about myself. Looking back, I can't really imagine that just before I turned thirteen I decided to stop paddling with my family.

In 1992, maybe because of what I had learned along the canoe route, I left in August and flew to Guatemala City to join Adolpho (a refugee friend of mine since fourth grade) for a year in his homeland. In the remote Province of Huehuetenango, I learned to survive on little food and to navigate the cultural waters, which were very different from the canoe route, but they were filled with difficulties and excitement as well.

My Reflections
Benjamin T. Kent

Looking back over the years of our canoe trips, I see these adventures as major contributions to my developing into the man I have become. Every summer, we left the urban world of Chicago, where people are stacked on top of each other like firewood, and entered the land of wilderness and open spaces. In these settings, my imagination could run wild and be free to dream, to dream about the past and the future. Looking around me at the grandeur of the rock formations that had been created billions of years ago, I could imagine how that rock had once bubbled and flowed. The smooth contours and broken, jagged designs gave me a long perspective on time, one that the human brain can hardly grasp. I also pictured glaciers slowly moving forward and backward over the land, leaving their marks on what now exists. These places helped form me.

Some of my earliest memories consist of riding in our canoe, hour after hour, looking out at the world unfolding in front of me, wondering what might be around the next bend. Some memories are of hot summer days on still lakes, with only my thoughts to fill my brain. Others are of moments of fear, with events happening at such a fast pace that only my automatic responses carried me through. I learned to deal with situations of exhaustion where quitting was not an option, where my endurance was tested and the parameters of comfort were stretched. This was a different world, where I had to make choices for myself about what could be endured and what could be considered fun and enjoyable. It is all a matter of our perceptions. Every trip, I stretched my boundaries of physical endurance, strength, and comfort, until situations that many people would find very unpleasant became everyday and comfortable.

After extended periods of time in the wilderness, coming back to urban living became a struggle for me. This lifestyle, with worries about keeping my clothes clean and my appearances up, focusing my energies on pursuits other than enjoying and working with the natural world, became trivial and not very enjoyable. I needed to be in wild and natural places, roaming and exploring, to feel complete and to be part of the natural world, not just a visitor in it. I began traveling more, searching the world around me, seeing the ways other people live and looking for the place where I would fit in. Traveling to El

Salvador and living for months in a community in the mountains also gave me insights into what it felt like to be a member of a community in a wild and beautiful place.

I needed to be in the North Country, in Canadian Shield terrain, and to be near a big lake. Along our canoe route, I remembered finding old log cabins, tucked away in the forest and looking like wonderful places to live. I dreamed of eventually living in one myself, and started my search for a place to call home. I eventually found a good spot in beautiful country near Lake Superior, with like-minded people. Now I live in one of those log cabins in the woods. This dream was turned into reality by working hard alongside good friends and my dear companion Emily. This happened one piece of effort at a time, just like on the canoe trips, which played out one paddle stroke at a time. When progress seems to advance at a snail's pace, we just keep on going forward until we reach our goal, then continue on to the next challenge. Living this lifestyle in the woods is not the easiest path, but doing things "out of the box" never is. Every struggle has made us stronger and prepared us more for what lies ahead.

Now my daughter Amaya is growing up surrounded by trees and water. As a family, we go on canoe trips, do back-country skiing, take long hikes, tend our garden, and acquire food from our surroundings. Amaya has a natural drive to overcome obstacles and succeed when put to the test. She climbs trees fearlessly, swims happily in the frigid Yellow Dog River near the cabin, and has no qualms about trying new things. I look forward to seeing her grow up in the woods, experiencing all of the wonders of nature and living in harmony with the environment. Our adventures continue, as we learn new skills and live our lives one day at a time in the beauty of the natural world.

I owe much of this lifestyle to having been raised as a wilderness paddler, every summer from the time I was five years old. Even when I was a boy, I sensed how valuable these experiences were, and this came out sometimes in my school work. When I was eleven, with seven summers of paddling already behind me, we were studying about the ancient Egyptians and were assigned to make an art project about them. On a thin brass sheet, I embossed a scene showing two Egyptians standing and paddling a canoe. On the mounting paper beneath the metal sheet, I wrote in big letters with gold ink, IN MY AFTERLIFE I WOULD LIKE TO GO CANOEING.

Appendix

Our survival, safety, and relative comfort during our journeys depended, to a considerable degree, on our canoe and its related equipment, our clothing, and the gear, maps, and foods. Our outstanding voyaging craft, the practical, durable, and relatively light-weight garments and gear, the accurate maps, and the energizing and tasty foods and beverages that we carried were indispensable to our success, while we traveled through the wilderness as a self-propelled and self-contained family. The articles which are presented and discussed in this Appendix are not in any manner linked to commercial endorsements; they are simply offered here to indicate the various items that served us extremely well, under hard and demanding usage.

Canoe and Related Equipment

Old Town canoe, Canadienne model, designed by Ralph Frese of the Chicagoland Canoe Base. This hull design is now produced and sold as the Penobscot 17 model, Old Town's top-of-the-line cruising canoe, and is billed as "the fastest canoe on the market." Length 17'1", width 35", weight 69 pounds, total carrying capacity 1,100 pounds, with removable portage pads on the center thwart.

Canoe cover, custom-made by Dan Cooke Enterprises (7290 Stagecoach Trail, Lino Lakes, MN, 55014-1988, (612) 784-8777), full length, in three sections, held in place with rows of snaps installed through the hull beneath the gunwales, with two spray skirt cockpits at the seats and an expandable passenger-and-gear-storage area in the midsection that is fitted with a variable overlapping closure system.

Bow and stern painter ropes, nylon, each one 25 feet long, tied to the large eyebolt installed through the deck, stored in a small nylon drawstring bag that is also tied to the eyebolt.

Sailing rig, homemade, described on pages 61-62 and 94, with a permanent, widened and perforated thwart behind the bow seat, and a permanent mast step fastened to the floor below.

Inflatable seat pads, attached to both canoe seats with wide velcro straps.

Seat board (homemade) on the canoe floor, inflatable seat pad on the board, and closed-cell-foam sleeping pad as a backrest against the thwart, for the passenger in the midsection behind the bow seat. Seat board 7 x 15 inches, with two 1 x 1 wood strips screwed across the full width of the underside near each end as feet, a 3 inch oval perforation for carrying, and an 18 inch cord with a clip at its end for attachment to the thwart.

Bailer, homemade from large chlorox bleach bottle, with a lightweight string with a clip at the end, for attachment to a loop of nylon cord encircling the thwart in front of the rear seat.

Five clip straps, for attaching packs to thwarts, homemade of 11/2 inch nylon webbing straps fitted with strap clips at each end which fasten to each other.

Four paddles, Clément brand, two 54 inch for the bow and two 62 inch for the stern, the two backup paddles each having a fabric sheath over its grip, to protect it from abrasion.

Garments

For each person:
One pair of tennis shoes

One pair of socks, of polypropylene fabric for quick drying.

One pair of underwear, boxer style, of silk or polypropylene for quick drying (the bottom leg seams of the standard cut wreak havoc on the wearer's bottom when pressed against the canoe seat for twelve hours a day).

One pair of pants, with long cuff areas, of lightweight nylon fabric for quick drying.

One shirt, of cotton, long-sleeved and long-tailed, with cuff openings sewn shut against biting insects.

One bandana, of cotton fabric, for the neck.

One hat, with wide brim against sun and rain.

One hooded sweatshirt.

One nylon shell jacket, without lining for quick drying.

Four wrist and ankle elastic cuffs (homemade) or rubber bands, against biting insects.

One rain suit, Campmor thigh-length coat of gortex with hood tightening cord and vecro wrist closures, pants of PVC rubber (without cotton lining for quick drying), plus two rubber bands to hold these garments in two compact rolls when not in use.

Emergency backup clothing: one pair of tennis shoes or wetsuit boots, one pair of socks, one pair of underwear, one pair of pants, and one shirt.

One full neoprene wetsuit for both Tim and Doree, Body Glove brand, including farmer-john over-the-shoulder bottoms, long-sleeved top, and boots with side zippers, for capsize safety during cold-weather voyages.

One short-sleeved undershirt, cotton, for sleeping in warm weather.

One set of long underwear, top and bottom, of polypropylene fabric for quick drying, for sleeping in cold weather.

One head net, against biting insects.

Two glasses straps, for Doree only.

Gear

One neck lanyard for each person, with the bare essentials for survival: **Swiss army knife, waterproof match case with matches and striker strip, metal whistle**, and **compass**, plus **one thermometer** for Tim's journal records of weather conditions.

One life preserver (PFD Type III) for each person, Extrasport brand, and also **one canine version for Toby** (with back handle for assisting him during capsizes).

One tent, regular Eureka Timberline four-person model, with supplemental front vestibule, shock-corded aluminum poles, and metal stakes. Since we did not own the Outfitter Timberline model, which has heavy duty door zippers, our standard door zippers failed and were replaced with larger and more robust versions at no charge on two occasions during the sixteen years of the project. The additional vestibule at the front was excellent for storing the wet packs and footwear at night, sheltered from the elements and animals yet not in our sleeping area.

One rain shelter tarp, nylon, 10 by 12, with long nylon cords and plastic stakes.

One small hatchet with sheath, for stake driving and emergency chopping.

One rubberized air mattress per person, rather weighty, especially when wet, but a luxurious item after an exhausting day of paddling.

One sleeping bag per person with stuff sack, North Face Cat's Meow model in regular size, three-season bag rated down to 15 degrees Fahrenheit.

One pillow sack per person, homemade of cotton fabric with velcro fasteners, to hold pants, shirt, and jacket during the night as a pillow.

One alarm clock, traveling windup style.

One sugar-low kit, plastic bottle containing mixture of peanut butter and honey, stored with plastic knife in small nylon sack fitted with long rope, for suspending from a handy nearby tree during the night.

One multi-fuel stove, Coleman Peak 1, for either white gas or kerosene, with padded case. Full tank is sufficient for cooking about ten to twelve evening meals. Excellent for low-impact camping, as well as for wet weather, for after-dark-arrival campsites, and for short-term windbound sites during the day.

One steel fuel bottle, quart size, filled.

Lighter fluid, one small can.

One collapsible plastic water jug, half-gallon size.

One thermos jug, plastic, with attached carrying handle, quart size.

Stainless steel nested cooking kit, containing two pots with lids, one combination pot lid-and-small frying pan, and pliers-style pot-lifting handle.

One plastic bowl per person, plus **one for Toby**.

One small plastic cup per person.

One soup-size spoon per person, of very durable plastic.

One peanut butter-honey mixture dispenser stick, a salvaged plastic handle from a kitchen spatula.

One metal pot scrubber.

One small bottle of biodegradable liquid soap.

One small plastic shaker of salt-pepper mixture.

(No eating forks or knives, cooking spoon, cooking flipper, large frying pan, or folding fire grate included.)

One nylon drawstring bag for holding cooking items: stove (protected against rought handling inside nested cooking kit with one of the plastic eating bowls over the top instead of pot lids), bowls, cups, spoons, pot scrubber, soap, and salt-and-pepper shaker.

Two ropes for hoisting food packs at night, nylon, each 25 feet long.

One large ziplock plastic bag for storing maps in pack.

Multiple spare camera films, in two separate ziplock plastic bags.

Spare camera with lens and batteries, padded with bubble wrap.

One digging tool, durable plastic yard-and-garden trowel.

One spare map case with attachment cord and clip, multiple spare ziplock bags, multiple spare large plastic bags.

Multiple rolls of toilet paper, stored individually in ziplock bags.

One pair of spare eyeglasses in a hard case and one spare glasses strap, for Doree only.

One large plastic bag with rubber band for closure, for storing all spare clothing.

One large plastic bag with rubber band for closure, for storing all spare footwear.

One toilet kit, in ziplock bag, containing: sun screen, insect repellant, tooth brushes, tooth paste, dental floss, small bottle of biodegradable soap, hair brush, steel mirror, spare bottle of ibuprofen.

One repair kit, containing: various needles and threads, buttons, safety pins, tent repair kit, rubber air mattress repair kit, wire, screws and nails, nuts and bolts, glue, duct tape, plastic tape, sandpaper, fishing line-sinkers-swivels-and-hooks, small knife sharpening stone, and spare whistle.

One first aid kit, containing: burrows solution for ear infections, alcaine anesthetic for eye injuries, antibiotic for eye injuries, oil of cloves and cavitt for tooth pain from lost fillings, bacitracin ointment, alcohol, peroxide, ibuprofen, diahrrea tablets, antihistamine for insect bite allergic reaction, aloe vera creme for insect bite itch and sunburn, Dial soap, two dozen bandaids, one dozen large and one dozen small butterfly closures, six 4 x 4 inch gauze pads, twelve telfa pads of various sizes, roll of 1 inch dermicel tape, roll of 2 inch gauze bandage, 3 inch ace bandage, six large safety pins, tweezers, single-edge razor blade in a sheath, waterproof matches, small pencil and notepad, thermometer in case, Q-tips, scissors, needles, curved needles and sutures, needle case, hemostat, dental floss, and extractor for snake bites. (We did not include laxative, antacid tablets, or vitamin C.) We also carried with us the outstanding book *Wilderness Medicine, Beyond First Aid,* by William Forgey, M.D., which is aimed specifically at back country travelers who have no access to timely professional medical assistance. During my winter preparations each year, I read portions of this book; however, I could only handle reading a few pages at a time, since the contents often made my stomach churn. The text presents the worst-case scenario of virtually all possible mecical emergencies, and describes in detail how a lay person is to handle each of them. Although we were modestly prepared to handle whatever medical situations might confront us, by good fortune, we were never obliged to carry out any major medical treatments on each other. As part of our preparations for trekking in the remote wilderness, it was crucial that each of us had received a tetanus shot five years or less before the end date of each given trip.

One waterproof steel ammo box, with its clip strap, containing: camera, spare camera batteries, spare films in a ziplock plastic bag, sunscreen, sunscreen lip creme, dental floss, ibuprofen, insect repellant, diary notebook, two or three ball point pens, notes for stories to tell stored in a ziplock plastic bag, sheets of new French songs in a ziplock plastic bag, two mini-mag flashlights with spare bulbs and multiple sets of spare batteries, two filled lighters with spare flints, water purification tablets, spare plugs for air mattresses, spare wrist watch, spare small ziplock plastic bags, spare rubber bands, check book, small nylon pouch with wallet, cash, credit card, telephone card, contact information for shuttle driver and others, and set of car keys. (Our passports for crossing the U.S.-Canada border, the certificates proving that Toby had received an updated rabies vaccination and a Lyme disease booster vaccination, and a Canadian auto insurance card, which was obligatory whenever our travels included more than one province, we kept in the van during our journey, instead of with us on the water.)

Two Duluth packs, Model Number Four, heavy canvas.

One large black duffle bag, 13 x 33 inches, heavy nylon.

One medium blue duffle bag, 10 x 20 inches, heavy nylon.

One medium red duffle bag, 10 x 20 inches, heavy nylon.

One small red duffle bag (daily bag), 9 x 15 inches, heavy nylon.

One large black duffle bag (consolidation pack), 18 x 42 inches, heavy nylon.

Four waterproof storage bags, Voyageur's Expedition Camp Pak, 22 x 54 inches, plasticized nylon outer bag and heavy plastic inner bag, with plastic slider rods.

One small jar of petroleum jelly, to lubricate bags for slider rods.

Two short bungie cords, for bundling together the four paddles and the sailing rig for portaging.

Organization

Keeping all of our articles of clothing and gear organized and in their respective places at all times during our wilderness jaunts helped us avoid the frustration of searching for misplaced items. It also added a sense of security and regularity during a period in which life could often appear to be insecure and irregular. For starters, our individual neck lanyards held the bare survival essentials. In addition, every other item of our clothing and gear belonged in a certain location in the canoe or in a specific pack, and each pack had its own place in the craft, easily accessible by unclipping a particular fastening strap. The most often-needed articles, such as outer garments, rain gear, sun screen, insect repellant, foods and beverages for lunches and snacks, were always close at hand, and the two spare paddles were within easy reach, between the walls of the craft and the packs.

In Duluth Pack marked A
In a waterproof bag: half of the stored foods and beverage powders in ziplock plastic bags, half of the stored toilet paper in ziplock plastic bags, stove in nested cooking pots, fuels for stove and lighter, first aid kit, repair kit, spare map case, and spare large plastic bags.

In pack loose: cooking kit, dining shelter tarp with stakes, spare footwear in a large plastic bag, toilet kit, and empty collabsible plastic water jug.

In Duluth Pack marked B
In a waterproof bag: half of the stored foods and beverage powders in ziplock plastic bags, half of the stored toilet paper in ziplock plastic bags, spare clothes in a large plastic bag, and spare camera.

In pack loose: tent bag, tent poles bag, hatchet, digging tool, air mattresses, and two food pack ropes.

In Black Pack
In waterproof bag: two sleeping bags, pillow sacks, sleeping shirts, alarm clock, polypropylene long underwear outfits, petroleum jelly for waterproof bag slider rods, consolidation pack, two bungie cords, part of spare gorp supply in ziplock plastic bags, and part of spare peanut butter-and-honey supply in plastic bottles within ziplock plastic bags.

In Blue Pack
In waterproof bag: one sleeping bag, spare maps, spare films, and spare eyeglasses for Doree.

In Red Pack (close-at-hand items)
Sweatshirts in individual ziplock plastic bags, rain gear, head nets, part of spare gorp supply in ziplock plastic bags, and part of spare

peanut butter-and-honey supply in plastic bottles within ziplock plastic bags.

In Daily Bag (foods, beverages, and close-at-hand items)
One plastic cup, peanut butter-honey mixture dispenser stick, gorp in ziplock plastic bag, snack items in ziplock plastic bag, peanut butter-and-honey mixture in plastic bottle, Ritz crackers in ziplock plastic bag, dried apple slices in ziplock plastic bag, jerky in ziplock plastic bag, sealed packets of koolaid and instant breakfast drink mix and powdered milk in ziplock plastic bag, and windbound reading books in individual ziplock plastic bags.

In Consolidation Pack on Portages
Five clip straps, passenger's seat board and inflatable seat pad and closed cell foam pad, bailer, waterproof map case, canoe cover center section, thermos jug, Daily Bag, and Blue Pack.

On portages, the two canoe cover end sections, the two painter ropes in their small nylon bags, and the two seat pads remained attached to the craft. The four paddles and the sailing rig were bound together into a single unit with the two bungie cords.

During our first trip over the trail, Ben carried Duluth Pack B plus the Consolidation Pack on top of it, Doree carried the Red Pack and the Ammo Box, and I carried Duluth Pack A. On the second carrying trip over, while I was burdened with the canoe, Ben carried the Black Pack and Doree carried the combined bundle of the paddles and the sailing rig. They were both lightly loaded so that they could quickly drop their loads whenever necessary, to assist me with obstacles hindering me along the way, and also take the craft from me at intervals, to either allow me to rest or to give me some relief in portaging the canoe.

During a journey in which we carried sufficient food supplies for three adults and a dog for twenty days, plus extra backup food supplies, the weight of the various items of cargo and the four mammals in the canoe totaled about 650 pounds. To this amount was added the weight of the canoe cover, the sailing rig, and the two painter ropes. Since the Canadienne was designed to carry up to 1,100 pounds of contents safely, our total amount represented a relatively modest cargo, roughly two-thirds of the safe maximum amount.

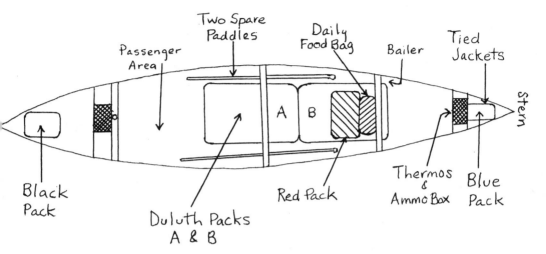

Two Spare Paddles

Passenger Area

Daily Food Bag

Bailer

Tied Jackets

Stern

A B

Black Pack

Duluth Packs A & B

Red Pack

Thermos & Ammo Box

Blue Pack

As shown in the diagram, the bow half of the craft contained about 330 pounds of weight: Black Pack (13 pounds), Doree (115 pounds), Ben (140 pounds), Toby (20 pounds), half of Duluth Pack A (30 pounds), plus the weight of about 12 pounds of the clothing, shoes, and nylon jackets worn by Doree and Ben, the three life preservers, and two paddles. The stern half contained about 320 pounds: half of Duluth Pack A (30 pounds), Duluth Pack B (75 pounds), Red Pack (26 pounds), Daily Food Bag (9 pounds), Tim (145 pounds), Ammo Box (14 pounds), filled thermos jug (4 pounds), Blue Pack (9 pounds), plus the weight of about 8 pounds of the clothing, shoes, and nylon jacket worn by Tim, his life preserver, and two paddles. Since Toby often perched for much of the day atop the packs in the stern section, his weight of 20 pounds often moved to the stern half. A great part of the weight and space within the two Duluth packs and the red pack were represented by the food supplies. As a result, as the voyage progressed and food and beverages were consumed and toilet paper was used, these three packs became gradually lower and lighter.

Selected Catalog Sources for Clothing and Gear

Campmor
P.O. Box 680
Mahwah, New Jersey 07430-0680
1-800-525-4784
www.campmor.com

Piragis North Woods Company
105 North Central Avenue
Ely, Minnesota 55731
1-800-223-6565
www.piragis.com

Duluth Pack Company
1610 West Superior Street
Duluth, Minnesota 55806
1-800-777-4439
Retail store:
365 Canal Park Drive
Duluth, Minnesota 55802
1-800-849-4489
www.duluthpack.com

It is important to bear in mind that there is no single method or piece of equipment that is the perfect one for any given task on a long-distance canoe trip. Different paddlers devise or use their own preferred methods and articles to handle each task.

Maps

During each of our journeys, we carried the series of detailed topographical maps that pertained to our particular route, as well as an overview map which showed the entire journey on a single map. For the latter chart, I usually cut the appropriate portion from a provincial highway map, since it indicated the roads or communities in the region, to which we might travel for assistance in case of major emergencies. While studying the topo maps and marking them before each journey, I cut off most of the superfluous portions that did not relate to our paddling route, and I often taped together certain of the trimmed sections that we would be using.

During the trip, in a waterproof ziplock plastic map case in front of me in the stern seat, I kept the individual topo map that was in use at the time, the next topo map in the sequence, and the overview chart. This map case, to which I had attached a 15 inch cord with a clip at its end, was safely clipped to a D ring that was affixed to the canoe cover in front of the stern seat.

The large-scale topographical maps which we utilized are produced by Natural Resources Canada. Created at a scale of 1:50,000, in which a mile is represented as 1.27 inches, these polychrome charts offer great detail and excellent legibility, as well as 25 foot contour intervals. (U.S. topo maps of the same general detail are produced at a scale of 1:62,500, in which a mile is represented as 1 inch.) The Canadian charts are available at the Canada Map Office, 615 Booth Street, Ottawa, Ontario, K1A 0E9, (613) 952-7000, or via its website at www.cits.rncan.gc.ca.

For additional information concerning canoe trips, one should contact the appropriate department of each province:

Department of Tourism, Fish, and Game
150 St. Cyrille Street East, 10th floor
Quebec City, Quebec

Department of Natural Resources
Queen's Park
Toronto, Ontario

Tourism, Recreation, and Cultural Affairs
200 Vaughn Street
Winnipeg, Manitoba R3C 1T5

Department of Lands and Forests
Natural Resources Building
109th Street and 99th Avenue
Edmonton, Alberta T5K 2E1

Foods, Beverages, and Their Preparation
(Doree)

This was the general outline of the content of our meals and snacks during our paddling trips:

<u>Breakfast</u>
Gorp
Instant breakfast drink mixed with powdered milk

<u>Lunch</u>
Peanut butter-and-honey mixture
Crackers
Jerky
Dried fruit
Koolaid

<u>Dinner</u>
Stew containing jerky, vegetables, noodles or macaroni,
*   spices, and vegetable oil*
Koolaid
Coffee, tea, or hot chocolate
Hard candies
Sometimes dessert of galette, pancakes, instant pudding,
*   or hot cereal*

<u>Snacks during the day</u>
Gorp
Nuts
Jerky
Graham crackers
Hard candies
Koolaid

*Gorp (from the 1950s slang expression **G**ood **O**ld **R**aisins and **P**eanuts) is a hearty travel mix that is excellent for paddling trips, both as a nourishing breakfast to start the morning and as a high-energy snack throughout the day on the water. Over the years, I came up with different varieties, but the version with lots of chocolate chips was the all-time favorite of the entire family. No matter whether the weather conditions were comfortable or*

734

miserable, when we labored hard all day keeping the canoe moving forward, gorp provided us with an energetic start in the morning and boosted our energy levels between meals throughout the day and into the evening.

For my gorp recipe, I combine as Part A: 4 cups of oatmeal, 1/2 cup of wheat germ, 1/2 cup of seeds (sunflower, sesame, etc.), and 1 cup of sweetened coconut. Add a generous amount of cashews, almonds, walnuts, or peanuts, to your taste. In a warm saucepan, mix together Part B: 1 pound of brown sugar and some honey according to your taste, 1 cup of vegetable oil, plus vanilla flavoring if you wish. Mix Parts A and B in a large bowl, then, if you choose, add any variety of dried fruits to your taste, such as raisins, dates, cherries, or cranberries. Heat oven to 375 degrees, spread the mixture on cookie sheets to a thickness of about an inch, bake for 15 to 20 minutes to a golden brown, turn with a spoon or flipper, and brown the second side for about 15 to 20 minutes more. Cool the baked product in large metal bowls. If you wish, add chocolate chips to the no-fruit version when it has cooled to a warm temperature. (If the chips are added while the mixture is still hot, it will be pretty messy.) When the product has completely cooled, spoon it into doubled ziplock plastic bags.

We used several flavors of Carnation Instant Breakfast mix, including vanilla, chocolate, and strawberry, which we added to powdered milk and water to create an energy-rich drink for the morning start.

For quick and convenient lunches, which were sometimes assembled by the passenger and served to the paddlers while they were hard at work in the bow and stern, I found that a combination of peanut butter and honey spread on Ritz crackers was nutritious and not very messy. At home in advance, I mixed natural chunky peanut butter and honey together in a large bowl, then spooned the thick mixture into quart-size plastic camping bottles with screw-off lids. Ritz crackers seemed to be the most durable for paddling, especially when the packs were jostled around a lot during loading and unloading and on portages. We kept the crackers in their lightweight cardboard boxes in the food storage packs, to reduce the crushing effects of rough handling of the packs.

Over the years, we made jerky from lean beef, turkey, and whitefish, but found only beef to be really palatable after a long, challenging day on the water. I discuss the drying of meats, fruits, and vegetables below. The best dried fruit for us on the trips was apple, cut into quarter-inch-thick slices and dried, as well as commmercially-made raisins. Pre-sweetened koolaid, although it contains aspartame, was more convenient than hauling and measuring sugar to mix with unsweetened koolaid.

For vegetables in our dinner stews, we dried corn, tomatoes, green beans, green peppers, zuchini, onions, and peas. To spice the stews, I used various combinations of beef bouillon, chicken bouillon, instant soup mix, parsley flakes, seasoned salt, onion flakes, salt, and pepper. We transported the vegetable oil in quart-size plastic camping bottles with screw-off lids, and placed each bottle in its own ziplock plastic bag to guard against leakage. For our after-dinner drinks, we used instant coffee, tea bags, and instant hot chocolate mix.

My pre-mixed dry ingredients for the fried treat of galette included, for one family unit, one cup of flour, 1/2 teaspoon of baking powder, and a pinch of salt. Before frying the small patties in oil, I added 1/2 cup of water and some cinnamon. After the patties had browned on both sides, I added additional oil, brown sugar, and raisins to make a syrup. With great relish, we spooned the delicious product directly from the communal frying pan into our mouths. We used these same syrup ingredients to accompany pancakes made from commercial bisquick mix.

For the preliminary year and the first year on the mainline route, we used commercially-produced, freeze-dried foods for only the main course of our one hot meal per day. Since we found these ready-made dishes to be far too light on protein and far too heavy in sodium, we decided to dry our own meats and vegetables, as well as fruits, from then on. For the first year of these drying efforts, we used our home oven as the drying chamber, with its vent blocked off with a sponge and a trouble light as the source of low heat.

Since this procedure was both cumbersome and slow, we soon purchased an inexpensive, forced-air food dehydrator. We were very pleased with the products that came out of our Harvest Maid dryer (manufactured by American Harvest, P.O. Box 159, 4064 Peavey Road, Chaska, Minnesota, 55318, (612) 448-4400) Since the electric appliance supplied both heat and forced air currents, the drying process was much faster and more efficient than when using only heat.

For making beef jerky, I used about one pound of very lean, ground trimmed London broil per family dinner, which dried down to about four ounces of weight. Since illnesses such as salmonella and E. coli sometimes arise from homemade jerky that is stored long-term in an unrefrigerated situation, the USDA recommends that the meat be first heated to 160 degrees before the dehydrating process. Then, a temperature of 130 to 145 degrees is maintained during the drying of the very thin patties. After the patties had been thoroughly dried, we broke them into inch-square pieces, and packaged them in family-meal-size portions. We first placed each portion in a tiny brown paper bag, then the bag was inserted into a ziplock plastic bag. The paper of the bag absorbed much of the remaining traces of fat that had not been trimmed from the meat, and kept the sharply pointed edges of the dried product from puncturing the plastic bag. After each trip, we stored any leftover dried meat, vegetables, and fruits in the refrigerator until the following year.

Meats and fish require the highest drying temperatures, ranging from 130 to 145 degrees. Fruits and vegetables require less heat, around 135 degrees, while nuts and seeds need about 105 degrees, and herbs and spices only around 95 degrees.

When we halted for the evening, or when we were pinned to land by the wind during the day, it was easy to open the top of Duluth Pack A and remove a pre-packaged dinner plus the gas stove and cooking kit. When we used both the stove and a wood fire, we sometimes simultaneously cooked the stew in one pot, heated the hot water for tea, coffee, or hot chocolate in the second pot, and fried the galette dessert in the tiny frying pan. Then, spreading these three pans out on a rock ledge beside the row of empty waiting bowls and the cups of koolaid, we were ready to feast.

Each evening at the campsite, I selected from one of the food storage packs the supplies that we would need for the following day's breakfast, lunch, and snacks, and transferred these items to the daily food bag, where they would be near at hand during our travels.

Index

The following listings do not include the names of most of the rapids, falls, islands, bays, channels, points, peninsulas, portages, narrows, native reservations, or smaller posts that are mentioned in the text.

The Author

Timothy Kent is an independent scholar and lecturer living in Ossineke, Michigan. He and his family, including his wife Doree, their sons Kevin and Ben, and their dog Toby, paddled from end to end the 3,000 mile mainline fur trade canoe route across the U.S. and Canada, from Montreal to Ft. Chipewyan, in a series of annual segments. In addition, the author spent two decades researching and replicating the main articles of native daily life and the primary French trade goods, and then utilized a decade of vacations with his family living with only those articles; this program of living-history research resulted in the entertaining volume *Tahquamenon Tales, Experiences of an Early French Trader and his Native Family*.

His other works to date include the book *Paddling Across the Peninsula, An Important Cross-Michigan Canoe Route During the French Regime,* as well as three monumental double-volume sets. These works are entitled *Birchbark Canoes of the Fur Trade; Ft. Pontchartrain at Detroit, A Guide to the Daily Lives of Fur Trade and Military Personnel, Settlers, and Missionaries at French Posts;* and *Rendezvous at the Straits, Fur Trade and Military Activities at Fort De Buade and Fort Michilimackinac 1669-1781.* For the latter two sets of volumes, Tim twice received the prestigious State History Award from the Historical Society of Michigan. He has also nearly completed a highly detailed study of some five hundred dugout canoes across the U.S. and Canada, ranging from the southern tip of Texas to Nova Scotia to the Yukon, which will result in a major publication on these craft.

Of the 725 direct French and French Canadian ancestors whom Tim has researched (originating from over 120 communities in France), many were involved in the fur trade of North America, from about 1618 to at least 1758. They were engaged in the occupations of fur trade company manager, clerk, trader, interpreter, guide, voyageur, merchant/outfitter/fur buyer, investor, laborer, tradesman (cutler, gunsmith, post carpenter, etc.), birchbark canoe builder, and trans-Atlantic shipping merchant. In addition, other ancestors served as soldiers in Canada, in the Carignan-Salières Regiment during the 1660s and the Troupes de la Marine in the 1680s and 1690s. Biographies of these various fur trade individuals are in preparation for publication, along with works on the very early protohistoric period of the fur trade and the traditional birchbark canoes of the native populations of the midwest.

He is pictured authentically dressed and equipped as a French trader of the 1600s, on East Moran Bay at St. Ignace, Michigan, at the Straits of Mackinac. Along this shoreline, his direct ancestor François Brunet dit Le Bourbonnais landed in the summer of 1685, having traveled here from Montreal to trade over the following fall, winter, and spring. Another direct ancestor, Jean-Baptiste Lalonde dit L'Espérance, arrived here from Montreal in the autumn of 1696, hired to carry out trading for Cadillac, the commandant of Ft. De Buade at St. Ignace.

In the photograph, the author is armed with an original wheellock pistol dating from about 1615 to 1640, which is accompanied by an original gunpowder flask which also dates from the seventeenth century. From the waist down, he is dressed in native fashion, with moccasins, leggings, knee garters, and a breechclout, along with a *sac à feu* or belt bag which was fashioned from a complete skunk pelt. From the waist up, he is wearing a mixture of native and French articles, including a linen chemise, a shooting bag and sheathed tomahawk, a shoulder-suspended pistol holster, a knife in its neck sheath, a necklace of fox leg bones and black bear canines, a conch shell moon ornament, and a nose ring and ear ring made of copper rod. His black felt hat is decorated around its crown with a string of whitefish vertebrae, and on its upturned brim with a wing of a male mallard and two deer dew claws. This admixture of cultures was very typical for Frenchmen living in the interior regions of North America during the fur trade era.

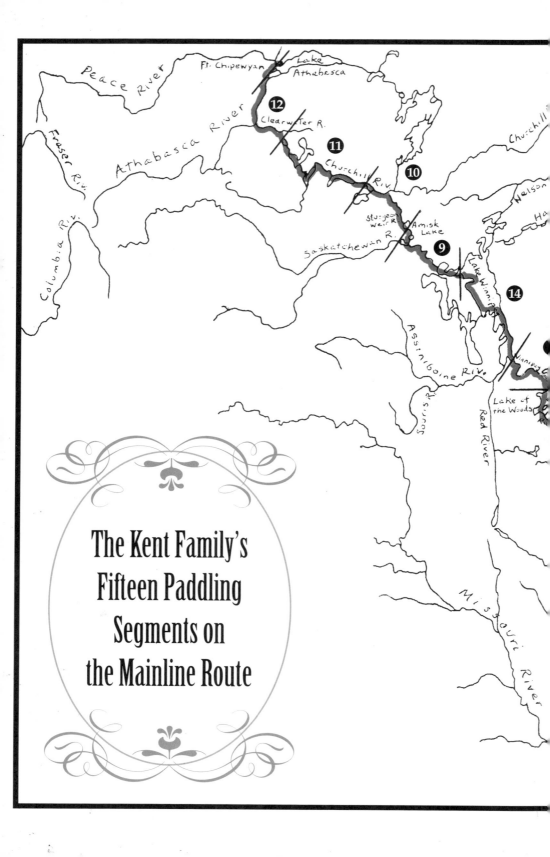

The Kent Family's
Fifteen Paddling
Segments on
the Mainline Route